# RWANDA'S GENOCIDE HERITAGE

DELIA DUONG BA WENDEL

# RWANDA'S GENOCIDE HERITAGE

## BETWEEN JUSTICE & SOVEREIGNTY

Duke University Press *Durham and London* 2025

Printed in the United States of America on acid-free paper ∞
Project Editor: Lisa Lawley
Designed by Courtney Leigh Baker
Typeset in Garamond Premier Pro and Proxima Nova by Copperline Book Services

Library of Congress Cataloging-in-Publication Data
Names: Wendel, Delia Duong Ba, author.
Title: Rwanda's genocide heritage : between justice and sovereignty / Delia Duong Ba Wendel.
Description: Durham : Duke University Press, 2025. | Includes bibliographical references and index.
Identifiers: LCCN 2025009904 (print)
LCCN 2025009905 (ebook)
ISBN 9781478032472 (paperback)
ISBN 9781478029106 (hardcover)
ISBN 9781478061311 (ebook)
ISBN 9781478094418 (ebook other)
Subjects: LCSH: Rwandan Genocide, Rwanda, 1994. | Collective memory—Political aspects—Rwanda. | Collective memory—Social aspects—Rwanda. | War and society. | Transitional justice—Rwanda. | Rwanda—Politics and government—1994–
Classification: LCC DT450.44 .W463 2025 (print) | LCC DT450.44 (ebook)
LC record available at https://lccn.loc.gov/2025009904
LC ebook record available at https://lccn.loc.gov/2025009905

Cover art: Conservationists clean and dry the bones of genocide victims in a field near Murambi, Rwanda, 1996. Photo by Mario Ibarra, Ibarra archive, Chile.

The open access edition of this work was made possible by generous funding from the MIT Libraries. Thank you to MIT Libraries for providing funding to make this book open access.

FOR LINH, SAFWAN, LIAM, AND LIOR:

the future of our past.

## CONTENTS

# ABBREVIATIONS

CLADHO
Collectif des Ligues et Associations de Défense des Droits de l'Homme (Collective of Leagues and Organizations for the Defense of Human Rights in Rwanda)

CNLG
Commission Nationale de Lutte contre le Génocide (National Commission for the Fight Against Genocide)

CONADEP
Argentinian National Commission on the Disappearance of Persons

ECOSOC
Economic and Social Council (United Nations)

FAFG
Forensic Anthropology Foundation of Guatemala

FAR
Forces Armées Rwandaises (Rwandan Armed Forces)

FPH
Fondation Charles Léopold Mayer pour le Progrès de l'Homme (Charles Léopold Mayer Foundation for the Progress of Man)

GOR
Government of Rwanda

HRFOR
Human Rights Field Operation in Rwanda (United Nations)

ICTR
International Criminal Tribunal for Rwanda (United Nations)

IITC
International Indian Treaty Council

IMIC
International Monitor Institute Collection, David M. Rubenstein Rare Book & Manuscript Library, Duke University

KGM
Kigali Genocide Memorial

MIJESPOC
Ministère de La Jeunesse, des Sports et de La Culture (Ministry of Youth, Sport, and Culture)

MINESUPRES
Ministère de l'Enseignement Superieur, de la Recherche, et Culture (Ministry of Higher Education, Scientific Research, and Culture)

MINIREISO
Ministère de Réinsertion et de l'Intégration Sociale (Ministry of Rehabilitation and Social Integration)

MINITRASO
Ministère du Travail et des Affaires Sociales (Ministry of Labor and Social Affairs)

MINUBUMWE
Ministry of National Unity and Civic Engagement

NGO
nongovernmental organization

*OFFICIAL GAZETTE*
*Official Gazette of the Republic of Rwanda*

OHCHR
Office of the High Commissioner of Human Rights (United Nations)

PHR
Physicians for Human Rights

PRIMATUR
Office of the Prime Minister, Government of Rwanda

RPA
Rwandan Patriotic Army, the former armed branch of the RPF

RPF
Rwandan Patriotic Front, a political party

RWF
Rwandan franc, the national currency

SIU
Special Investigations Unit (OHCHR and ICTR, United Nations)

UN
United Nations

UNAMIR
United Nations Assistance Mission for Rwanda

UNDP
United Nations Development Program

UNHCR
United Nations High Commissioner for Refugees

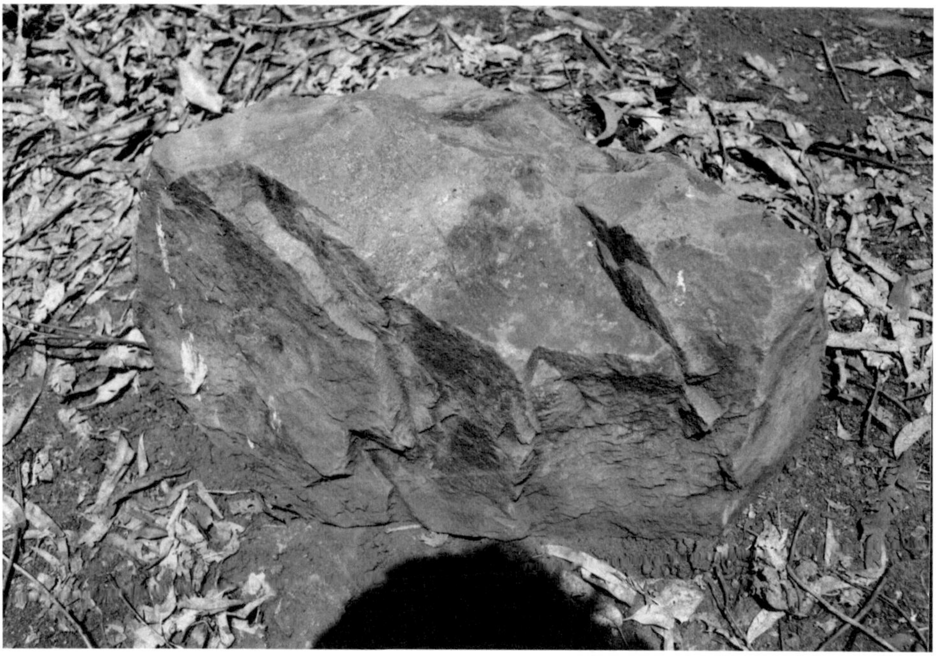

The former director of Rwanda's Genocide Memorial Commission included this 1995 photograph of a rock in his memoir as a poignant representation of the genocide. His caption: "Gros plan de la pierre sur laquelle les têtes d'enfants de moins de cinq ans étaient fracassées avant de les jeter dans les puits perdus à côté" (Close-up of the rock on which the heads of children under the age of five were smashed before being thrown into the nearby pit). Kanamugire, "Témoignages recueillis" (2013), 107.

# PROLOGUE A ROCK AMONG MANY

A vegetal enclosure encircles a former septic pit where forty-seven young children were found dead in 1994. When I visited in 2018, the plant leaves were dense, and I did not attempt to peer beyond them (figure P.1). The planted cluster is a spare but meaningful marker of Rwanda's genocide heritage. Immediately after the genocide, in place of the *imihati* (corn plants), an *ibuye* (a single rock) marked this mass grave. The *ibuye* was more than a landmark. It was used in the brutal killings. In multiple photographs taken over several years, Louis Kanamugire and Mario Ibarra—who together piloted the state's approach to genocide memorialization—documented the *ibuye* obsessively.[1] Their images and words have etched this site into my memory, a powerful metonym for the brutal inhumanity of the genocide. And yet the *ibuye* is not included in—or really even legible to—official genocide histories.

My search for the *ibuye* began with its absence from the national *Genocide Sites Map*. Jean-Damascene Gasanabo, the director of the National Research and Documentation Center at the now-dissolved National Commission for the Fight Against Genocide (CNLG), suggested that I speak to Paul Rutayisire, a historian at the National University.[2] Rutayisire was from Rwamagana District and wrote extensively about genocide histories in eastern Rwanda.[3] He was familiar with the *ibuye* and the genocide crimes committed there. Rutayisire connected me to the local representative for Ibuka, a genocide survivors' association, who met me at the site.

The Ibuka representative told me that the local genocide organizer to whom the land had belonged had died. His house was destroyed, leaving the makeshift memorial to stand on an empty lot bordered by village houses on either side. The *ibuye* was also no longer there. It was, perhaps, relocated to the side of the lot, where many rocks were piled (figure P.2). Despite its absence, both in place and in

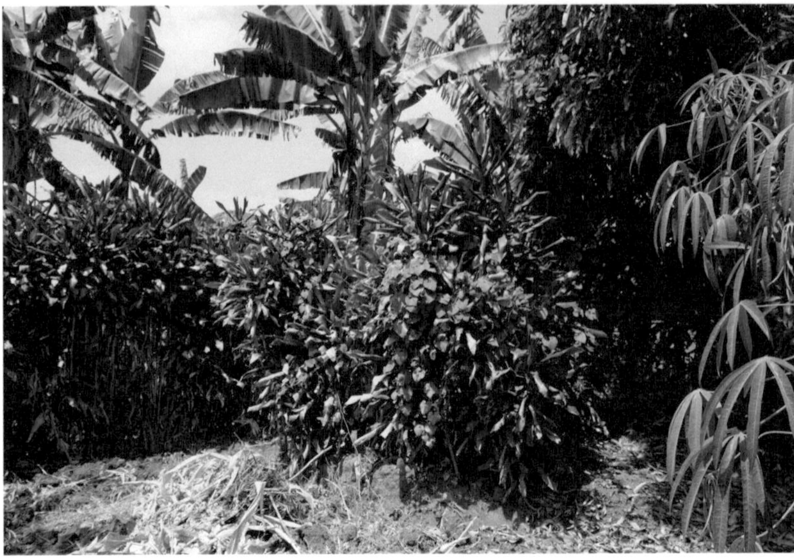

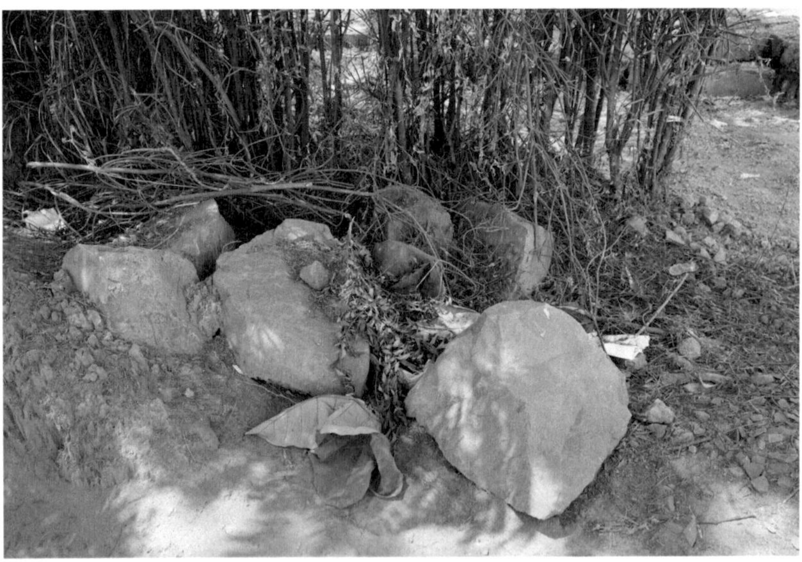

FIGURE P.1. *Imihati* plants encircle the site where the bodies of forty-seven children were found, 2018. Photo by Delia Duong Ba Wendel.

FIGURE P.2. The original *ibuye* (rock) has been displaced to a pile of rocks at the massacre site, 2018. Photo by Delia Duong Ba Wendel.

national registries, the *ibuye* is not forgotten in local memory. It is also not the only memorialized rock in the area. In the course of my visit, the Ibuka representative took me to the "other" rock nearby. There, a thin eucalyptus tree had been planted to remember a family killed in the genocide, marking a rock where attackers sharpened their weapons. I began to more fully recognize the *amabuye* (rocks, plural) all around. Each *ibuye* registers multiple individual engagements with its history of violence. They are also part of a constellation of underrecognized sites like them.

By contrast, the country's official state memorials are well-known and marked sites. They are typically located in everyday places—churches, schools, government offices—transformed by the massacres of Tutsi that they once held. Viewing the dead in a site of killing is central to the state-authorized approach to genocide memorialization. I call this *Rwanda's genocide heritage aesthetic*. Most government-managed memorials display the bones of victims in buildings conserved to maintain damages incurred during the massacres. Many sites also contain belowground crypts where extensive stores of victims' remains are kept in coffins or on shelves. The memorials are "authorized" in the sense that they are representative of state histories; are funded, maintained, and curated by government institutions; and are officially sanctioned sites of public education and commemoration.[4] On the whole, state genocide memorials and narratives are afforded more space, visibility, and power than other sites of memory in the country.

During the past thirty years, Rwanda has put memorials and annual commemorations at the center of initiatives that promote national and international recognition of the genocide. The government attaches corrective social and political functions to authorized genocide memorials, claiming that acknowledgment and remembrance are critical to forms of justice and reconciliation. Genocide memorials contribute to this effort primarily as places of memory and witness. At the same time, genocide memorials and history have been closely controlled by the national government, with significant impacts on free speech. The involvement of genocide memorials within larger state strategies of social regulation has been consistent since 1994 even if, as this book shows, the sites' origins and early development began with a wider and more disparate range of actors and motivations.

That national genocide memorials are among the most visible and accessible sites of memory in Rwanda is the result of an iterative, and at times inconsistent, three-decade government process of ordering the country's memory landscape. Since 1996 the list of national-level sites has expanded and contracted based on sites' ease of access, valuation (as representative of genocide), and funding. The government has also progressively expanded its control of genocide memorials, including the controversial relocation of local memorials, and the victims buried there, to regional sites.[5] The work of organizing genocide memory was institutionalized in October 1995 with the formation of the state Genocide Memorial Commission. In 2003 the government partnered with the Holocaust memory organization Aegis Trust to fund and shape its genocide memorial program. The organization's initial involvement in the development of a new national genocide memorial and archive in Kigali in anticipation of the tenth anniversary soon expanded to consultations at several memorial sites.

Rwanda's authorized genocide memorials are situated within a diverse memory landscape. Like the *ibuye*, scores of local genocide memorials remain underrecognized as sites of memory. Most were sites of killing. The memories of those acts, and their victims, are maintained discreetly through traditional religious practices, Christian crosses, or commemorative plantings by local genocide survivor organizations and the communities living near them.[6] There are also countless massacre sites that bear no marking at all, including hidden graves where the dead were disposed. Other sites anchor memories that are unauthorized, such as those of Hutu survivors whose Tutsi spouses or children were killed.[7] There, victims and the violence they endured are commemorated, but surviving relatives remain unacknowledged. Yet others, often the most difficult for outsiders to locate, are sites of prohibited memories. Those places include the unmarked sites of attacks on Hutu communities during and after the genocide by the Rwandan Patriotic Army (RPA) and the government led by the Rwandan Patriotic Front (RPF).[8] Thus, sites of memory that are not authorized by the state are, to varying degrees, marginalized, silenced, or erased from view.

This book contends with the realities of the RPF regime's social and political control while also grappling, often paradoxically, with the complexities and dilemmas negotiated by the people who shaped Rwanda's genocide memorials and live near them. This prologue provides context for that exploration. It locates the book's research methodology and contributions within a wealth of scholarship on genocide memorialization, which has amply demonstrated the relationships among a memorial aesthetic, state sovereignty, and the shaping of everyday life in the country. In the following chapters, I retrieve a less understood set of justice and human rights objectives that the preservation of Rwanda's genocide heritage originally set out to enact, and the dilemmas encountered therein. To do so, I draw from interviews with Rwandan residents, original memorial workers, and authorities to explore the social and political effects of the display of the dead. My research tempers views on both ends of the political ideological spectrum in which Rwanda's genocide memorials are situated. On the one hand, it contests views that memorials are exclusively antidemocratic and dehumanizing. On the other, my recognition of the sites' ethical and political tensions does not support the theory that a double genocide occurred in Rwanda.[9] Instead, my research explores the ethical stakes and afterlives of genocide memory. It also puts Rwanda's genocide heritage in dialogue with other efforts to represent the erasure of a people in public spheres both inside and outside Rwanda. In doing so, I explore the political co-optations of those efforts head-on as well as the repercussions for groups still struggling for recognition.

---

THE 2007 REORGANIZATION of the Genocide Memorial Commission within the newly formed CNLG was pivotal, along with a series of new laws in 2008, to ratifying existing state practices of genocide remembrance and speech regulation. One of the most impactful of those laws established the government's reach to punish genocide denial, which criminalized a wide-ranging set of speech and behaviors along with the expression of genocide ideology.[10] Another law placed all genocide memorials and burial sites within the public domain (under state control) to relay an authorized history of the genocide.[11] It effectively reorganized Rwanda's authorized genocide memory landscape, establishing a primary memorial in the capital (the Kigali Genocide Memorial), below which thirty district sites are situated. It also designated aesthetic and historiographical standards for state genocide memorials, mandating that conserved evidence of the genocide, including victims' remains and weapons used in the killings, be displayed.[12]

Accordingly, genocide memorials are not merely historical sites. They are central to the state's larger postgenocide sociopolitical objectives, including its "strategy to fight genocide, crimes against humanity, genocide ideology, and denial."[13] This statement was included in the government's 2012 UNESCO application to acknowledge four genocide memorials as world heritage sites (an inscription achieved in 2023). The sites' roles in "fighting genocide"—as a reassertion of moral values contrary to the genocide, as a matter of ideology, and as a representation of state (RPF) intervention to end the violence—have been a part of the sites' mission from their inception. State stewardship changed the status of genocide history from one that was largely dismissed as internecine civil war to an internationally recognized occurrence of targeted mass violence. Today the genocide is foundational to how the government narrates Rwanda's history and future.

Genocide memorials are also government-regulated public spaces that locate commemorative ceremonies. Across the country, memorials host genocide commemorations every year, either during the week of national mourning (beginning on April 7) or on dates when attacks occurred at the sites. Local commemoration ceremonies mandate the attendance of area residents, especially in rural areas. This is not so much a requirement of law as of citizenship.[14] Over the years, through legislation governing comportment during the commemoration period, public speech, criminal activities, and the education of children, among other initiatives, citizens' rights and inclusion have been increasingly regulated through residents' acknowledgment of genocide memory.[15]

Not surprisingly, state interests have most affected the public form and experience of genocide heritage today. On the one hand, government control of genocide memory seeks to guarantee that this period of inhumanity will not be forgotten. State institutions, annual commemorative rituals, educational programs, and places of memorialization do this work. On the other hand, as historian René Lemarchand notes, the same government control reveals certain blind spots or omissions in official memory.[16] This speaks to conditions of unequal remembrance in the country, where the recognition and empowerment attained through genocide heritage are not widely available to all. The unevenness in terms of how certain memories gain wider visibility and collective recognition reflects the vastly different levels of power that individuals and groups possess to make their memories public and take steps toward repair. It is a politics of memory that is echoed in a network of power differentials felt in citizenship, economic opportunity, symbolic representation, and psychological and physical health.

---

MOST PRECEDENT RESEARCH on genocide memorialization has been concerned with tensions between state and individual forms of remembrance and the relationships between social inequality and public representation. That scholarship has been guided by the following primary questions: Who is included and excluded from authorized genocide memory? How do differences in social position or power affect whose narratives are supported in state-authorized histories? How do those differences, in turn, affect who receives government assistance and benefits? The display of victims' remains at memorial sites amplifies the stakes of these questions. Memorials that conserve massacres and display victims are emotionally and physically jarring places; they were especially so in the immediate aftermath and for survivors living nearby. Compelling people to see bodies and bones, to commemorate the genocide through government-organized ceremonies at memorials, to replicate omissions from state-authorized genocide historical narratives or withhold complexities to comply with them, and to forgo private burials for genocide victims, regardless of survivors' and families' preferences, uneasily reproduces forms of autocratic governance. Memorial sites are also fodder for voyeuristic and reductive coverage of the genocide by journalists. Viewing the aftermath, then, animates a range of tensions and inequalities between Rwandan residents, between citizens and the state, between those with privilege and those with lesser status, and between foreigners and local residents.

Much of the scholarship critical of state-led memorialization was based on research undertaken from 1994 to 2004. This first decade after the genocide was a period of significant instability. Residents navigated profound grief and fear while displaced by violence. The new governing regime fixated on security and control amid humanitarian crisis. Despite the difficulty of living alongside the sites, a range of experts posited that memorialization could have positive effects on reconciliation and conflict prevention. Six years after the genocide, anthropologist Susan Cook summarized those aspirational links based on interviews with representatives of the government, foreign aid agencies, and nongovernmental organizations.[17] Those sociopolitical impacts are what sociologist Claudine Vidal sought to evaluate, drawing from interviews and observations of the first six genocide commemorations (from 1995–2000). In addition to clarifying important historical details of those ceremonies, Vidal has written incisive analyses of what she called the government's selective curation of official genocide memory, and the ways that the presence of victims' skeletal remains restricts the possibility of reconciliation.[18] The long-term research engagements of anthropologist Jennie Burnet and political scientist Timothy Longman have built on these threads, illustrating Rwandans' diverse views of government memorialization and commemoration, including those of genocide survivors, women, individuals from multiethnic backgrounds, and government critics. Both Burnet and Longman highlight views on the display of bones and bodies (especially the state's insensitivity to survivors' emotional needs and desires for burial rituals and mourning) and the dominance of political interests in deciding what is remembered and how.[19] Political scientist Susanne Buckley-Zistel's research, undertaken outside Kigali from 2003–4, expands on the social divisions underlying and fueled by authorized genocide remembrance, and forgetting, in the country.[20] Very little of the early historiography on genocide memorialization and its reception was written by Rwandans.[21] A notable exception is an essay by Célestin Kanimba Misago, whose writing is significant as he was both a state official (the inaugural director of the CNLG) and an archaeologist involved in the first conservation practices at and near the Murambi massacre site.[22] His analysis represents a rare recounting of key ambivalences associated with the memorials' reception and intent: the ways in which they simultaneously provoked trauma, provided some measure of commemorative healing, and seeded nascent forms of national unity.

Considering that research together with the *ibuye*, the reflections of Louis and Mario, and their images and reports has prompted me to carve more space for irresolution in my historiography. The first four years of Rwanda's genocide heritage development (1994–98), on which this book focuses, present a prehistory of its more overt politicization: During those years the first experiments in the preservation and conservation of killing sites and victims' remains took place, shaping Rwanda's genocide heritage aesthetic. I do not downplay the existence of political motives in this early period. Instead, I suggest that state objectives evolved paradoxically alongside other ethical demands, including those oriented toward human rights and justice. A sole reading of genocide heritage today as the calculated and sensationalized display of the dead exists in tension with the context in which that aesthetic developed. Instead, when understood as a paradox, the politics that force viewers to see genocide heritage are co-located with the ethics of viewership that those sites demand.

In subsequent decades, research has elaborated three related inquiries. Many scholars have been keen to compare Rwanda to other states' memorialization of atrocity to illustrate the globalization of violent memory representation and performance. A key conclusion of those analyses claims that Rwanda's genocide memorials exemplify dark tourism and thereby perpetuate and encourage sensationalized and reductive narratives of violence.[23] Others have noted the predominance of international influences and funding—including from foreign aid agencies, UNESCO, and Holocaust memory organizations—in Rwanda's curatorial approaches and emphases.[24] I explore both of these conclusions in the following chapters, specifying the nature of international influences in the immediate aftermath when the approach to genocide memorialization initially developed. In doing so, I do not undermine the central roles of Holocaust memory, foreign aid agencies, and (much later) UNESCO in Rwanda's genocide heritage. Instead, I argue that those influences were most prominent *after* the first decade of the memorials' existence.

A second line of inquiry has explored the Rwandan state's approach to genocide memory curation as a process that is historically differentiated and evolving. This scholarship argues that the state is not a monolith, even in the context of autocratic governance; it comprises diverse actors navigating local situations, national directives, and global influences in discrete historical periods. As a result, we gain a finer-grained understanding of the interface of society and state, including the governing regime's increasing reliance on genocide memorialization and commemoration, laws, and education to effect social and political control today.[25] We also gain a sense of that memory work's progressive institutionalization and the expertise (from Rwandan academics and experts, especially) from which it drew.[26] This book contributes to this line of inquiry by exploring the origins of the state's approach, including the first experiments in preservation and conservation and the relationships among nascent memorialization, exhumation, and reburial practices.

In doing so, it illustrates the often-competing ideologies, diverse local initiatives, and global influences that shaped Rwanda's genocide heritage.

A third line of inquiry has extended precedent studies on the intentions and reception of state memorials by drawing from sources other than state representations. A significant subset of that literature draws from feminist research methodologies and attention to gender-differentiated perspectives on genocide memory maintenance.[27] Another key aspect of that research draws from oral histories and interviews with Rwandans from diverse positionalities, including memorial workers, exhumers, convicted perpetrators, genocide survivors, returnees, and youth to explore how those groups understand their identity and possibilities for peace in relation to state representations of them and the nation.[28] We learn much from that work about the private and public spheres in which relations of self and society are articulated, which provides a better sense of the lived experience of belonging and conflict in Rwanda. We also learn more about the communal "work" that memory maintenance does alongside the political aims of the governing regime, and the affective registers of genocide history preservation.[29] Another key contribution of this research highlights the silences in government narratives and the presence of a subaltern memory landscape that remains outside state management.[30]

My approach to research privileged the views of those who did genocide memory work and the dilemmas they faced. This became possible only with newly available information—including archival photographs and videos of the first memory conservation, exhumation, and reburial practices and interviews with the individuals who did that work. Those sources draw context and affect into conversation with the politics of memory. They allow me to directly contend with the controversies that preserving scenes and evidence of violence provoked. At the same time, the following chapters take heed of the ways in which the present shapes the past in Rwanda. Much of the research conducted for this book took place more than twenty years after the first preservation practices began. That research surfaced both the original motivations behind genocide memorialization and the forms of social and political control reproduced through those sites today. The origins and the legacies of these sites are both germane to understanding the social and political work that memorials do. Toward the end of this book, I discuss unauthorized and prohibited memories that persist in the country. Understanding genocide heritage in that larger landscape of memory in Rwanda uncovers the perspectives regulated away by the governing regime's control of genocide remembrance. It situates memory representation as undeniably central to projects of state sovereignty but equally enduring in activism for justice.

The stakes could not be clearer in Rwanda. But the subaltern struggle to be seen, to gain social recognition and political rights, is global. Philosopher Judith

Butler reminds us, "The public sphere is constituted in part by what can appear, and the regulation of the sphere of appearance is one way to establish what will count as reality, and what will not. It is also a way of establishing whose lives can be marked as lives, and whose deaths will count as deaths. Our capacity to feel and apprehend hangs in the balance."[31] Butler argues that whom—whose lives and deaths—we represent in the public sphere reflects a society's values: who and what it considers valuable.[32] Those public representations, they note, build our capacity for knowing the world around us. Butler warns that our capacity to not only apprehend reality but also to *feel* is contingent on radically inclusive public representations. By extension, understanding the politics of who and what is remembered is as important to constituting one's civic responsibility as the feelings and social relations enacted through remembrance. Reinvigorating the latter requires contending with the presence of and absences in memory representation—recognizing the *ibuye* among the rocks. That work in Rwanda holds important lessons for feeling and apprehending the world around us.

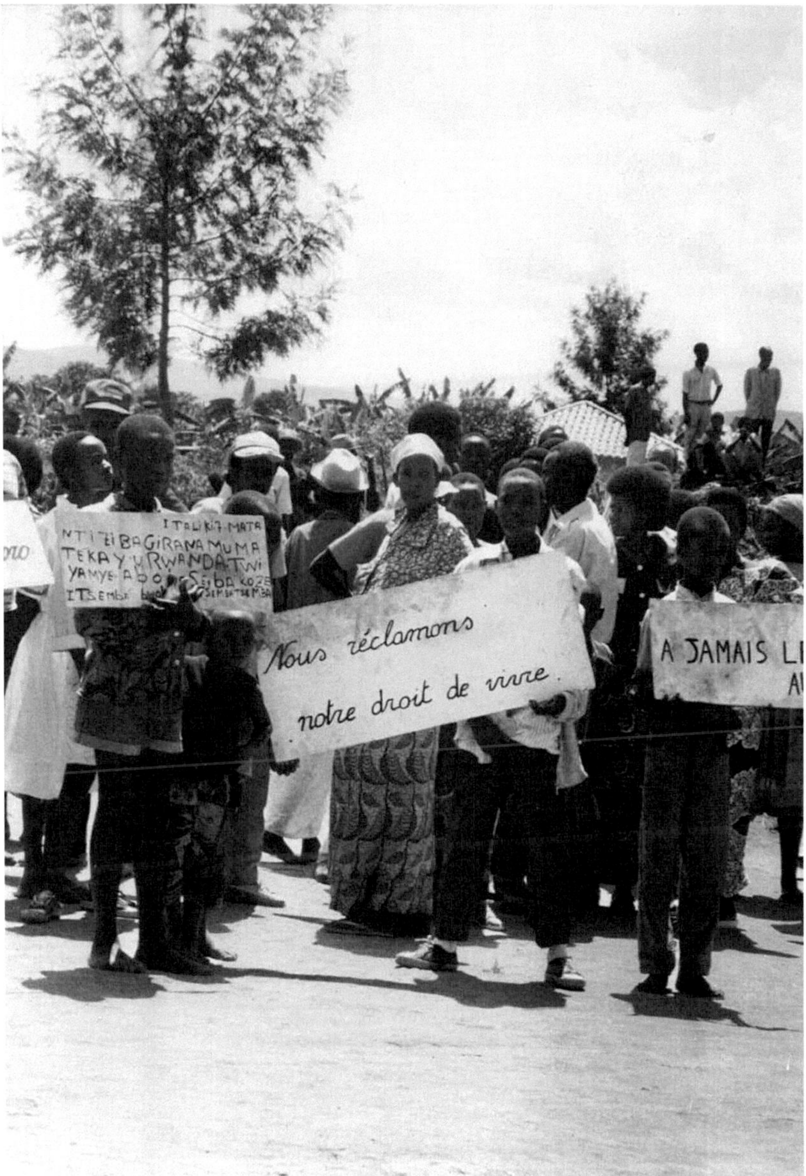


A crowd gathers for a genocide commemoration in 1995. Children were given signs that declare (in Kinyarwanda, *left*, dated April 7) "They will not be forgotten to Rwandan history. We hate the people who committed genocide" (*itsembabwoko n'itsembatsemba*) and (in French, *center*) "We reclaim our right to live" (*Nous reclamóns notre droit de vivre*). Photo by Mario Ibarra, Ibarra archive, Chile.

# INTRODUCTION TRAUMA HERITAGE AS REPAIR

Louis Kanamugire shifted uncomfortably in his seat. "The work was necessary to make history known, so that it would not be erased."[1] He paused and looked away. Louis was explaining why he and his team conserved killing sites and victims' remains after the 1994 genocide in Rwanda. A former high school teacher who had worked for UNESCO's local Rwanda office, he was tapped in 1995 to lead the government's newly created Genocide Memorial Commission.

Louis cleared his throat, continuing, "People didn't understand. We didn't understand either, at least not before we started. We thought it was just something that people were saying. But once we went there and saw the . . . the corpses . . . everywhere . . . that's when we understood the significance of . . . of what happened."[2] Louis expanded, returning to the different reactions that people had to the sites' conservation, "There were people who were against it, who didn't want [the killings] to become public knowledge. And survivors themselves were against it because they didn't want their people to be exposed. They said that respecting victims meant burying them, not displaying their bones. And there was the Church too—they didn't want people to keep saying that they had participated in the genocide. There was opposition from all sides. Even in the government—only a few people understood."[3]

We were sitting in an outdoor café in the Rwandan capital, Kigali. It was mid-July, and the sun was peeking through the clouds, which were on the verge of rejecting the dry season. Louis was speaking about his early work to develop genocide memorials. We had been stitching together that history through multiple conversations over the years, always at the same café. Every time, Louis recounted the circumstances of that work slightly differently. I couldn't tell if the gaps in narration were a result of my questions seeming obvious and not worth addressing. I frequently asked, *Who decided . . . ?* Or perhaps the origins of genocide memorialization were too politically sensitive, rendering Louis somewhat hesitant to disclose details. The issue of various publics' responses to the display of victims' bodies and bones in genocide sites was an uneasy and controversial subject—so much so that Louis was not willing to engage the topic directly until 2018, six years after our first meeting.

Within a week of the first killings in April 1994, genocide organizers affiliated with ethnic Hutu political extremists began executing ethnic Tutsi en masse, along with Hutu and Twa political moderates.[4] Genocidal massacres largely took place in churches, government offices, school complexes, and other public buildings where large numbers of people sought refuge. In the months that followed, massacre sites and victims' bodies began to be maintained in place to display evidence of the genocide for public viewing. That phenomenon developed into what I call *Rwanda's genocide heritage*, which aimed, as Louis had put it, to make the recent history of the genocide known, incontrovertibly and in public space, as a form of justice. Rwanda's genocide heritage was made possible by preservation and conservation practices along with related photographic, video, and cartographic documentation. It was further supported by two tandem efforts that also attempted to order the country's aftermath landscape: reburial and exhumation. Reburials served as a counterpart to display, returning victims to some measure of dignity in consecrated mass burial sites and through communal rites. The practices of preservation and reburial were not entirely at odds, however, as most ceremonies that accompanied early reburials included the temporary display of genocide victims. Those ceremonies prefigured the national commemorations that have become public performances of genocide remembrance today. By contrast, the first exhumations were efforts in unearthing. Those practices entailed locating victims and removing their remains from hasty mass graves to investigate their identities, their manner of death, and those responsible. Exhumations were largely undertaken within genocide investigations. But the individuals who conducted them were also preserving massacre sites and organizing reburial ceremonies. Exhumations constituted part of the backstage work that facilitated both the mass reburial of victims and their display.

This repertoire of approaches to ordering the aftermath first developed from 1994, after the killings occurred, to 1998, when foreign governments and the United Nations finally recognized the violence as a genocide. It was ultimately steered by Louis, the first director of the Genocide Memorial Commission, along with higher-level authorities in the new governing regime. But efforts to preserve and conserve victims' remains and killing sites occurred before the commission was established and, in many cases, were led by nonstate actors, including local residents, recent returnees, and foreigners. Rwanda's genocide heritage was thus initially the result of ad hoc efforts that incorporated diverse local initiatives and experiments to prevent the decay of victims, their belongings, and weapons and scenes of killing. Over the past thirty years, that memory work has been progressively institutionalized and managed by the government. Today genocide heritage forms part of a state legal-memory apparatus that manages national remembrance and regulates speech and citizenship, with significant restrictions on civil liberties. The early history of genocide heritage preservation, exhumations, and reburials reveals how and why publicly viewing the aftermath became so central to national genocide memory. It also opens to view conflicts between the state-controlled future of the past and other, unauthorized views on genocide heritage that endure today.

Rwanda's genocide heritage originated in four massacre sites—the locations of the first preservation and conservation experiments—that have since become nationally recognized memorials.[5] Preservation—whereby gruesome evidence of the killings was protected from removal and frozen in time—comprised the earliest initiatives, which began before the sites were formalized as memorials and a full year before the Genocide Memorial Commission was created (figure I.1). The first preservation efforts took place at the Nyarubuye and Ntarama Churches, rendering them places of witness that rendered the genocide viewable long after its occurrence. Louis's involvement in the new agency converted the first preservation experiments into a government-led *conservation* program. Conservation entailed further intervention, beyond protecting sites as they were found (figure I.2). It involved treatments to stabilize the progressive deterioration of victims' remains, belongings, massacre sites, and weapons used in the killings. The first conservation efforts, at the Murambi Technical School and Nyamata Church, attempted to restore genocide evidence to killing sites that had been emptied of victims by the perpetrators. As the decay and deterioration of genocide sites countrywide made preservation untenable, however, all memorialization efforts shifted to the conservation of genocide evidence and the restoration of killing sites. This involved cleaning up the massacres and the bodies and bones of victims so that they could be placed back in sites of killing. Preservation and conservation were urgent practices in the context of ongoing violence, attempts by perpetrators to destroy evidence of crimes, and massacre sites' deterioration in the rain and sun. After the genocide, moreover, residents experienced a significant scarcity of resources, which meant that much had to be done with little means, using simple approaches with tools and supplies at hand. It was emotionally and physically grueling work.

Displaying scenes and evidence of homicidal and sexual violence in public spaces was also, from the beginning, rife with controversy. Most major massacre sites were located in living communities and surrounded by homes. As Louis al-

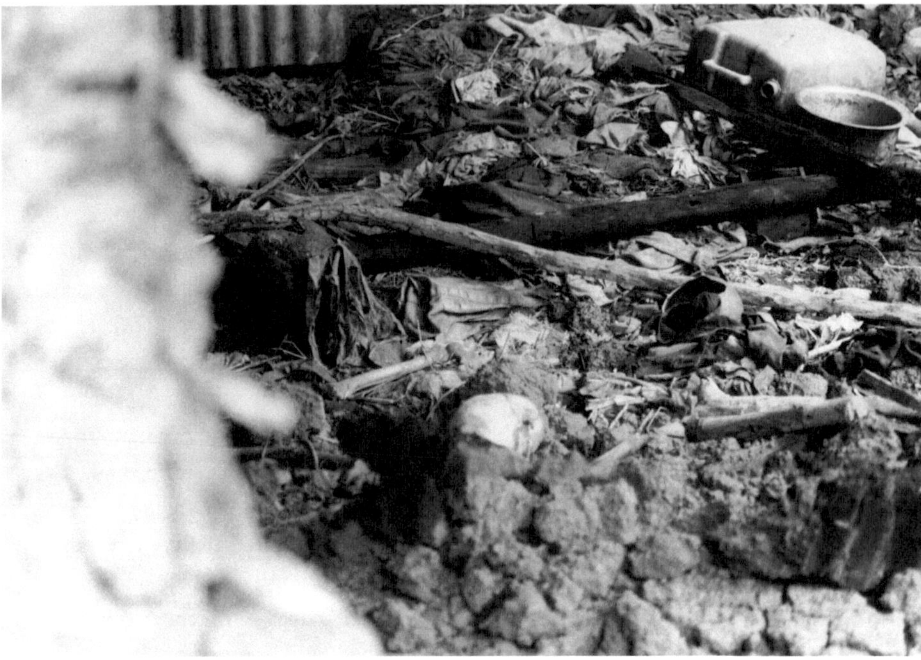

FIGURE I.1. Preservation of the Nyarubuye Church genocide site as it was found, 1994. Photo by Mario Ibarra, Ibarra archive, Chile.

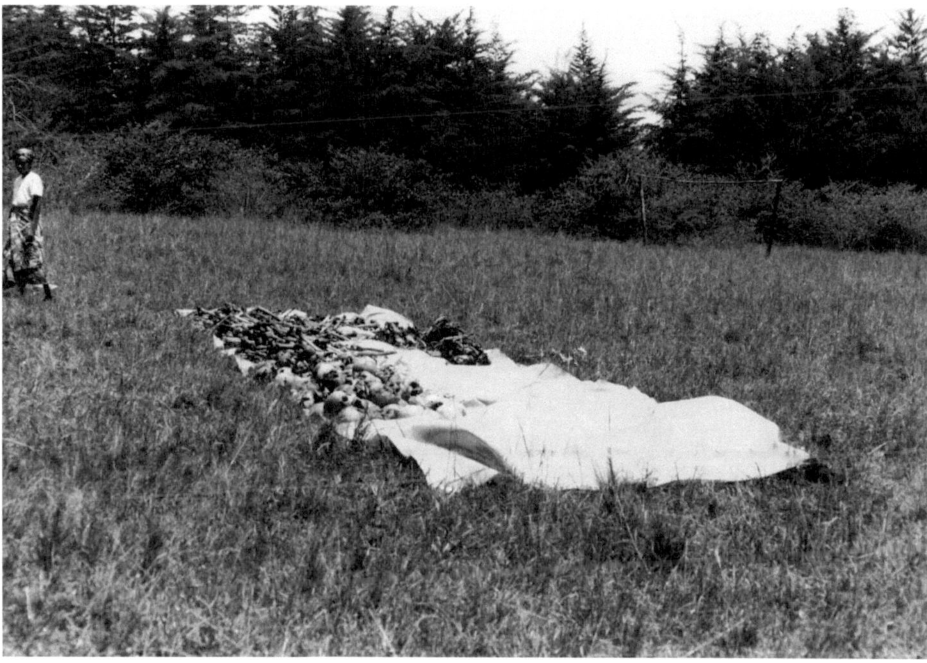

FIGURE I.2. Conservation of skeletal remains for display and reburial at the Murambi Genocide Memorial, 1996. Photo by Mario Ibarra, Ibarra archive, Chile.

luded to earlier, the sites triggered sadness, grief, and anguish for residents who lived nearby and whose relatives had been killed there.[6] Many residents decried the objectification of their relatives through display and related prohibitions on traditional burial rituals.[7] Still others believed that the display of bodies and bones was important to national remembrance, that the sites could educate future generations. As a result, the decision to make victims and massacres available to view was inextricably caught between the sites' value as material evidence of crimes and concerns about the places' effects on the living.

Louis had lost both of his parents to the genocide and was intimately familiar with those dilemmas. In 1996, aided by colleagues at the Genocide Memorial Commission, he found the bodies of his father and mother in western Rwanda. His parents were subsequently interred in marked graves, so he did not have to directly confront the question of whether he wanted his "people to be exposed" in a memorialized massacre site. Despite his personal experience of loss, Louis supported the conservation of victims' remains and their display in places of killing. Still, his familiarity with countless scenes of genocide across the country made the choice to conserve sites doubly heavy with responsibility. Ultimately, he remained steadfast in his view that displaying victims' remains was necessary to communicate the gravity and extent of genocidal violence. He reflected on that work twenty-four years later, musing, "I was convinced *then* that it was important. I still am today."[8]

Louis's convictions and tensions of conscience were not unique. They were echoed by others who worked to maintain those sites of memory, both before Louis was involved and thereafter alongside him. In this book I primarily draw from oral histories with individuals who had on-the-ground roles in that memory work to reconstruct the origins of genocide memorialization in Rwanda (see "Methods for Seeing and Listening" in this chapter). My interlocutors are not directors of ministries in the central government. They are individuals with local knowledge of the challenges and ambitions associated with "making history known." Some led investigations of massacre sites and violent crimes. Others were residents of communities who elected (and were paid) to conserve the bodies of victims and genocide sites. Still others were local government leaders who assumed their new roles immediately after the genocide and authorized the first preservation acts and conservation experiments. I also spoke with individuals who had lead roles in developing conservation techniques and curating memorials.

The historiographical contributions of this book are indebted to these individuals—especially Louis Kanamugire and Mario Ibarra—who played central roles in developing Rwanda's genocide heritage. Mario investigated genocide crimes immediately after the genocide as a human rights field officer for the United Nations. He led conservation experiments at massacre sites, working initially for the United Nations and later directly for the Genocide Memorial Commission. He brought camera equipment to the country and the documentary sensibility that made a photographic record of genocide memory work possible. Despite these pivotal roles, Mario has not previously been identified as a central figure in early memorialization processes. Louis joined the work of genocide conservation one year after Mario. For close to a decade (from October 1995 until 2003), he directed the Genocide Memorial Commission and was responsible for organizing and curating national memorials and commemorations. A third key figure in this history was Dr. Célestin Kanimba Misago, an archaeologist and director of the National Museum of Rwanda.[9] As a result of his academic training and the museum's location in Butare town, Dr. Kanimba was centrally involved in the conservation experiments that Mario conducted (supervised by Louis) at the Murambi memorial site.[10] Dr. Kanimba died in 2010, and I did not have the chance to interview him, so I primarily draw insights from Louis and Mario and their respective archives. In addition, both men's involvement in this work preceded Dr. Kanimba's.

Louis, Mario, and Dr. Kanimba shaped how and why state genocide memorials display the bodies of the dead at sites of killing (figures I.3 and I.4). They were critical intermediaries between local approaches to memorialization and those of the national government. They developed the institutional framework and conservation procedures for Rwanda's genocide memory, experimenting with and eventually codifying new approaches to representing targeted mass violence. Mario and Dr. Kanimba had hands-on roles in genocide conservation experiments. They drew both from residents' early initiatives to retrieve bodies and preserve evidence of massacres and from their individual expertise in human rights investigation and archaeology, respectively. Together with Louis, they built a set of conservation practices for a range of genocide evidence, including victims' remains, their belongings, weapons used in attacks, and the massacre sites. The work demonstrated what was possible to government officials, evolving Rwanda's genocide heritage by experimentation. In other words, top-level government officials were not the only, nor the primary, architects of the country's genocide conservation strategy. Instead, the production of a distinctly material and spatial memory of mass violence was propelled by both human rights *and* state interests.

This book holds several such paradoxes in tension. We see ethical and political conflicts in the backstage memorialization work of Louis, Mario, and others to construct a form of representation for the genocide. We draw closer to those individuals' emotional, affective, and physical labor: to the coexistence of trauma and justice seeking; to social connections built alongside grief; and to the preservation of human remains as collective memory through difficult, dehumaniz-

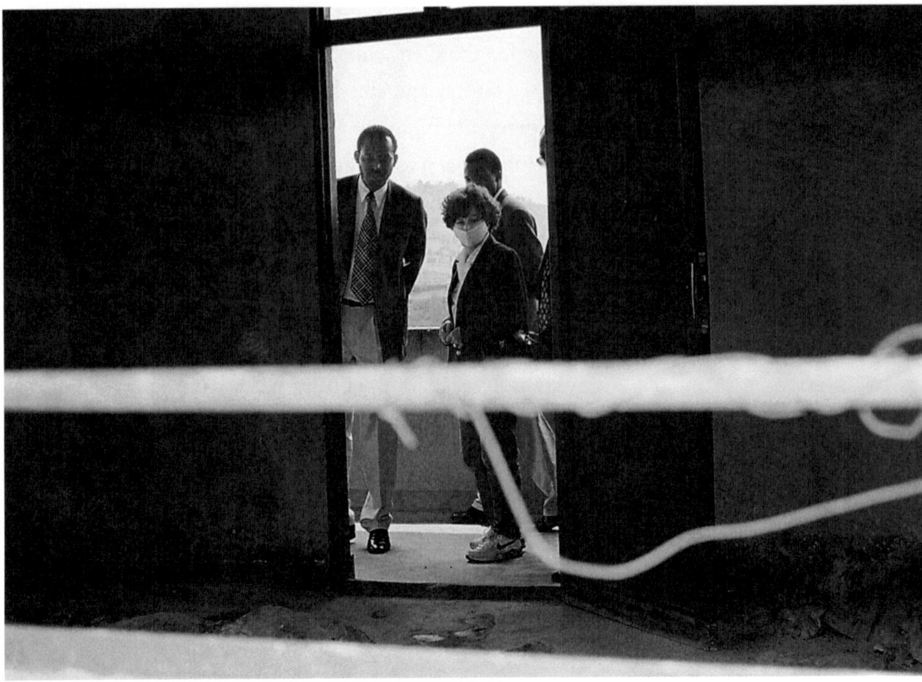

FIGURE I.3. Louis Kanamugire (*left*), Director of the Genocide Memorial Commission, leads Louise Arbour (*masked*), chief prosecutor of the United Nations International Criminal Tribunal for Rwanda, on a tour of conserved victims at the Murambi massacre site, 1996. Photo by Mario Ibarra, Kanamugire archive, Rwanda.

ing work. In the following sections, I lay out the relationships of paradox and connection that trace through the chapters. We encounter a genocide memorial landscape that today represents efforts in memory justice alongside those of state sovereignty and sociopolitical control. Yet early genocide memorial development demonstrates that state interests did not exclusively shape genocide history's representation in the landscape. A range of other influences—kin attentive to the humanity of victims as well as the growing (and global) practice of human rights—were also impactful. Those conflicting interests remain in tension at Rwanda's genocide memorials.

Thus, this book concerns not merely memorial monuments but a whole body of initiatives to represent violence—especially violent acts that are actively hidden or normalized—in public spaces. I call this phenomenon *trauma heritage* and call a subset of related initiatives in Rwanda *genocide heritage* to explore the affective landscape that exceeds the symbolism of memorial monuments.[11] Trauma heritage

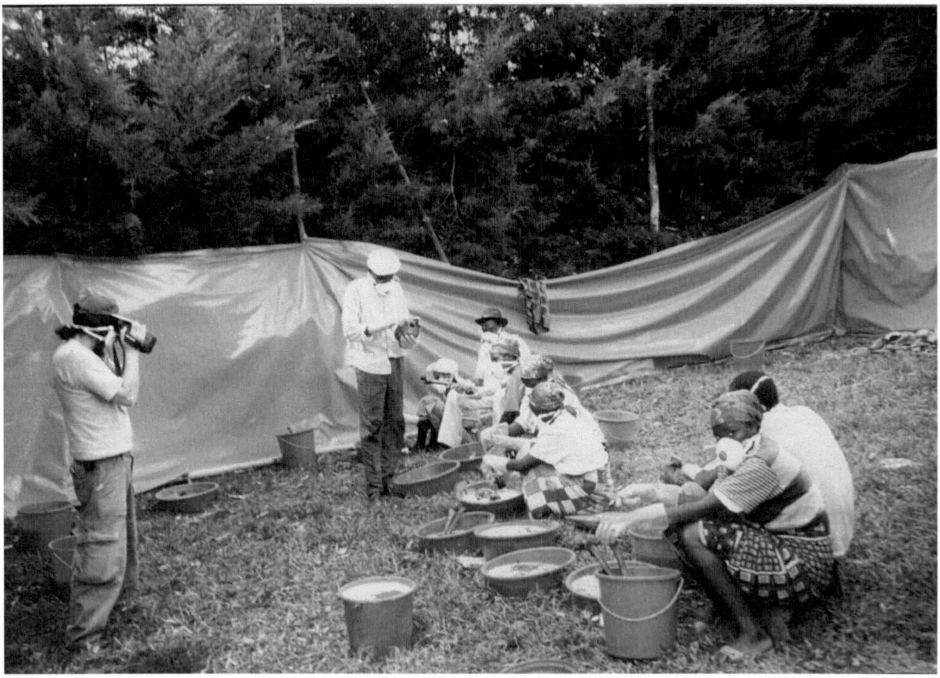

FIGURE I.4. Mario Ibarra (*left*), Dr. Célestin Kanimba Misago (*standing*), and local residents employed by the Genocide Memorial Commission clean and conserve the bones of genocide victims for reburial and display at Murambi, 1996. Courtesy of Mario Ibarra, Ibarra archive, Chile.

comprises the spatialization of traumatic experiences. It forms strategic challenges to erasure, inattention, and obfuscating rhetoric, replacing narratives with landscapes, amplifying words with images. But trauma heritage is not merely a representational tactic; it aims to be historiographical and reparative. It seeks to codify harms and violence as part of the historical record—and therefore offer evidence for judicial processes, initiate forms of social recognition and healing, and prevent recurrence. Motivated thus, trauma heritage comprises a distinct form of memorialization, distinguished by its concern with revealing acts of violence and its subaltern status (at least to begin with). That work is rife with irresolvable paradoxes to do with representing violence and its aftermath in communities.

My hope is that this book provides grounding for my interlocutors' calls to witness human rights and justice claims in Rwanda. Moreover, and especially as the country's stories draw in parallel experiences worldwide, I also hope that it begins to demonstrate a method for countering abstraction and inhumanity. Learning to "read" trauma heritage substantiates an ethics of seeing violence and listening to struggle. The following sections unpack the stakes and objectives of this form of remembrance. I also attend to the ethical dilemmas inherent in making violence known to wider publics, especially the challenges faced by survivors and kin, and the distinct demands that viewing places on others, like you, the reader. Oriented thus, the landscape of trauma heritage in Rwanda contains important lessons for understanding relationships between memories of injustice and forms of empowerment and repair.

## Trauma Heritage

In Kinyarwanda, the language spoken throughout Rwanda, *heritage* translates as *indangamurage*. The term is typically employed in museum settings in Rwanda but is conceptually much broader. Etymologically, *indanga-murage* is composed of two words. The verb *kuranga* refers to making something known, often through display. The noun *umurage* is an inheritance or something passed down from a familial elder. In the first years after the genocide, the government used the term *indangamurage z'itsembabwoko n'itsembatsemba* (heritage of the ethnic killings and massacres) to refer to all manner of material memory of violence—including sites of massacre, the bodies of victims, their belongings, weapons, and memorials to the genocide.[12] Central to the concept in Kinyarwanda, as in English, is the notion of making the past known and visible in the present.

Relatedly, my definition of *heritage* is "a past made present."[13] I emphasize the temporal and ontological aspects of the memory work that produces heritage. Temporally, *heritage* refers to ways that the past becomes relevant for, or at least drawn into, a present time. References to the past are important. People venerate and narrate significant experiences through heritage such as family lands, cultural customs, and mementos. Ontologically, *heritage* also refers to the *presence* of the past, which alludes to the importance that many societies accord to material representations of history, evident in memorials, monuments, or sites of cultural importance. My view of materiality is broad and ranges from something conceptualized and named to visual representations, physical objects, and places.[14] For example, material representations of the past include ancient ruins, aboriginal song lines, customary practices, religious rituals, and folklore. But as this book argues, a certain kind of empowerment is sought through memory's spatialization. Implicit in heritage's temporal and ontological registers is the perpetuation of a past made present. Spatializing the past seeks permanence and, by extension, future representation and relevance.

Heritage conceptually belongs to a category of memories that take material and spatial forms to become known and persist. Sociologist Maurice Halbwachs claimed that "collective memory," or how groups remember their past, requires localization in or reference to place. Halbwachs believed that all memory is socially constructed around some concept of space: He argued that only spatial imagery had the necessary stability to allow groups to discover their past in the present.[15] In Rwanda the idea to transform massacre sites into memorials echoes Halbwachs's view, underscoring that memories are not just possessed by people but are edified in landscapes. These *lieux de mémoire*, to expand on historian Pierre Nora's term, are not mere repositories of memory. They are sites of discourse in which historical narratives become tangible and are passed on to others.[16]

Trauma inflects memory in particular and powerful ways, affecting the ways it is spatialized. In her seminal work on the subject, Cathy Caruth defines trauma as injuries that are "doubled": felt by both bodies and minds but not simultaneously nor in ways fully knowable.[17] Trauma heritage identifies a third site where wounds are felt: the places and landscapes associated with traumatic experiences and their afterlives.[18] Those memories of violence become collective—located and remembered by groups that share traumatic experiences—in part through their presence in the landscape. Yet trauma is a particular type of past representation: It haunts, recurs, persists unceasingly, and is fleeting, in turn and at once. The representation of violence is often enigmatic. It is not always fully available to understanding. Trauma is often known only through the voice, body, or place that communicates, paradoxically, through pain. Nonetheless, as Caruth reminds us, traumas constitute a particular form of truth telling, relaying a reality "that is not otherwise available."[19]

Trauma heritage tells truths in distinct ways: as spatial stories of collective violence that are wrought by individual experience and intense feeling. The desire to compel acknowledgment of a group's trauma is particularly acute for those whose experiences of violence are erased or marginalized from public representation. And yet representing violent experiences is impossible. The effort to render pain legible takes an incalculable toll on the body and mind and affects how individuals navigate environments laden with difficult memories. Victims and activists nonetheless endeavor to find ways to make traumatic histories known to wider publics. They seek trauma heritage as a means to counter the abstraction and concealment of violence.

What I call an *ethics of nonerasure* propels these efforts, within trauma heritage, to make history known in spatial forms. Partly informed by human rights discourse, this ethic holds that the representation of genocidal crimes contravenes the purpose of such violence: the targeted destruction of a people. Spatialized memory retrains the averted gaze and tells otherwise ignored or hidden truths. There is an element of reparative—if not procedural—justice in those ambitions. Revealing and telling violent memories aims to defend the human rights of the individuals who have been persecuted, harmed, and killed. The ethics of nonerasure seeks to render that history indelible, never to be forgotten.

The ethics of nonerasure is not merely conceptual. It refers to values that guide material and spatial practices. In Rwanda the ethics of nonerasure motivated memory workers to seek recognition for genocide victims and forms of repair for a society split and traumatized by brutal mass violence. It continues to animate efforts to substantiate violent disappearances or violations that are not apparent. As a spatial form of memory evolving from this ethics of nonerasure, therefore, trauma heritage does not stop at mere remembrance. Trauma heritage seeks justice, empowerment, and repair. The ethics of nonerasure situates trauma heritage with an affective excess that anticipates future commitments.

Psychologist Pumla Gobodo-Madikizela spent years listening to witnesses of apartheid crimes as a former commissioner in South Africa's truth and reconciliation process. She writes of a "language of mourning" that she began to recognize there, one that represented both individual and shared, even transgenerational, experiences and memories of violence.[20] That language is often visceral, laced with emotion and traumatic memories. It is also recognizable by others who share similar, largely unacknowledged experiences. Gobodo-Madikizela describes the representation of trauma in testimony, therefore, as a process of giving public voice to silenced pain. In doing so, she underscores the social, sometimes liberatory, impacts that come with representing shared experiences of harm that are actively silenced.

Trauma heritage, extending Gobodo-Madikizela's salient observation about the language of trauma, makes public *space* for silenced pain. In this regard, trauma heritage demonstrates how spatialized memory can be a form of empowerment. To break through silence is to compel a society to recognize violence that is hidden from view or normalized in the background. It is to seize back control of the representation of self and others in life and history. It is an approach to justice and repair. I return to this more fully in the following sections, but note here, in a discussion on tensions, that trauma heritage locates opposing forces. It seeks to control memory as a form of power, and it also represents marginalized memories (in the context of that control) as a form of empowerment. Each of those forces loosely refers to the politics and ethics, respectively, of trauma heritage. Those politics and ethics are, in turn, critical to understanding the origins and legacies of authorized genocide representation in Rwanda.

### Repair

In trauma studies the *secondary witness* is a spectator or bystander who sees and hears the testimonies of others; they are not a participant in traumatic events but in accounts of them.[21] Trauma heritage produces secondary witnesses out of viewers, compelling them to see crimes erased or marginalized from view in the hope of seeding forms of repair. In this regard, trauma heritage is associated with initiatives in memory justice. *Memory justice* refers to the active remembrance of injustices to enact forms of repair, including accountability, restitution, and empowerment.[22] Facilitated by the evidentiary and social processes that preserve and share memories, it requires those who remember and witness alike. Central to the work of trauma heritage and memory justice, then, is an affront to indifference and abstraction. Instead, the very possibility of repair is predicated on drawing closer to listen to and see inordinately difficult stories and scenes of violence.

Political theorist W. James Booth claims that remembering and witnessing crimes are moral obligations. Memory—of the crime, its perpetrators, and its victims—is bonded to justice as debts and duties that each of us holds in societies broken by injustice.[23] The practice of justice, then, is grounded in an individual's everyday ethical engagement with the past. The search for retribution becomes one of societal responsibility through public representations of those memories. In other words, we know of our obligation to do justice to the past through material and narrative traces, which act as representatives for victims who can no longer speak.[24] By extension, spaces that hold memories of violence comprise part of a moral landscape of witnessing that helps to activate forms of justice.

Similarly, anthropologist Victoria Sanford, in reflecting on the aftermath of La Violencia, the Guatemalan army's massacres of Mayan communities in the 1980s, has argued that witnessing is both an individual and a social act. Sanford participated in investigations of clandestine state violence by the FAFG (Forensic Anthropology Foundation of Guatemala): excavating mass graves and interviewing survivors.[25] She asserts that acts of witnessing are not merely contained by the interests of individual and familial restitution. Sanford writes, "Witnessing is necessary not simply to reconstruct the past, but as an active part of community recovery, [it is] the regeneration of agency and a political project of seeking redress through the accretion of truth."[26] When vanquished memories are expressed in public, they serve at minimum to correct absent representations of injustice in history. Public disclosure can also support forms of individual and social healing.[27] Speaking about one's experiences demands reciprocation: the recognition of victims' suffering and forms of accountability from perpetrators and society at large. With truth and redress as central objectives, individual remembrance does critical social work.

Conceptualizing the witness with Booth and Sanford underscores the ethics of remembrance and its social impacts. But for both, efforts to repair are neither linear nor neat. Holding memories of crimes and harms is unruly, laden with trauma and righteous anger, and insufficient to guarantee justice alone. Attention to that unruly affect recenters the views of individuals affected by injustice. It enlivens the personal and intergenerational stakes of memory justice.

Those dimensions are rendered palpable by sociologist and filmmaker Colin Prescod, who in 2017 described the intense fury that he and other Black Britons feel in response to historical and ongoing racialized violence. Prescod declared his "rage against 'othering'; rage against 'White-washing' the record; rage against systemic, institutionalized denial; rage against continuing, intransigent, irritating, debilitating, distracting and destructive racism. This is rage about the necessity of transformation, a million miles from mere toleration. This is rage about making curatorial interventions into curative interventions."[28] Prescod enumerates violence enacted on individuals through systems and institutions and in representations of lives and histories. His rage is thus "about the necessity of transformation" in historiography and social life alike, led by Black voices and actions. With those memories central, he insists on finding forms of repair, not merely new forms to represent histories of violence.

In doing so, Prescod draws from a Black radical tradition that substantiates a need for reparations, not as individual payments, but as forms of communal restitution.[29] This is a point made by historian Robin D. G. Kelley who situates reparations within the US civil rights movement. Kelley argues that historically reparations were "never entirely, or even primarily, about money": they were part of communal strategies to advance social justice, racial reconciliation, and the autonomy, economic empowerment, and thriving of Black communities.[30] Kelley recounts "freedom dreams" imagined through forms of material retribution, symbolic restitution, the restoration of dignity, and equitable socioeconomic improvement.[31] Historically, then, the notion of repair has been inspired by dreams for freedom made necessary by the denial of basic rights and opportunities for whole groups of people.

But the scholarly discourse on repair does not always foreground redress for past injustices as the central impetus for reimagining the future. In a twenty-first-century essay on the philosophy of repair, STS scholar Steven J. Jackson challenges teleological views of the world that are concerned with technological progress, endless development, and everlasting nature.[32] His view has had particular purchase for those of us reflecting on a world vulnerable to anthropogenic climate change and coded biases unchecked within the rapid development of artificial intelligence. For Jackson, "broken world thinking" brings with it a renewed sensitivity to the "fragility of the worlds we inhabit."[33] Broken world thinking, in other words, reorients our progress-obsessed societies to the myriad needs for repair. And yet, Jackson's view is less attentive to the human sacrifices, entrenched inequalities, and harms done in the pushes for technological advance, racial capitalism, and power. By contrast, the efforts at repair foregrounded by Kelley, Prescod, Sanford, and Booth demand more of the past: They seek accountability and restitution for injustices that have occurred. Doing so also disrupts linear-progress narratives by drawing attention to silenced pasts, their legacies, and ongoing cycles of violence that remain.

Though separated by continents and distinct histories of violence and struggle, Rwanda, Guatemala, Britain, and the United States are linked by ardent commitments to radical forms of repair, built on histories and living memories of injustice. In each, memory serves as a precursor to any possibility of equality. The very histories that have been erased, dismissed, or devalued must be restored through forms of public recognition as a precondition to reparative efforts. But as Booth reminds us, with reference to Walter Benjamin's "Theses on the Philosophy of History," forms of justice that merely confront the wreckage of history are insufficient to "make whole what has been smashed."[34] Something more than remembrance is needed to attempt repair for brutal and systemic violence.

Nobel laureate and Nigerian writer Wole Soyinka underscores that the "something more" desired is in fact a future shaped by memory. He writes, "Memory—of what has been, of acts of commission and omission, of a responsibility abdicated—affects the future conduct of power in any form. Failure to adopt some imaginative recognition of such a principle merely results in the enthronement of a . . . culture of impunity."[35] For Soyinka, justice is tied to memory because what we acknowledge about the past makes possible either a future of continued injustice or a future of human rights and possibility. Memories of the past hold the potential to either uphold a culture of wrongs or form the basis for imagining restitution. In other words, forms of repair require both memory and imagination.[36]

Precedent forms of repair range widely. Some approaches seek material compensation for harms and their social, economic, and psychological effects in the form of monetary payments and redistributive policies. Other approaches are symbolic in nature, including truth-telling forums and the public recognition of victims and crimes committed. Still other efforts at repair are social in their attempts to mend relationships in divided societies and restore dignity to harmed and devalued groups. Despite their variety, each of these proposals for repair seeks to establish bridges between what has been and could be done, demanding that the historical and psycho-social dimensions of injustice inform the social and material propositions for redress.

When situated in relation to repair, and not merely remembrance, memory justice becomes a powerful cognate for both the recognition of past wrongs and related forms of restitution. The reparative efforts that derive from memory justice seek to address violence and its aftermaths in various ways. At minimum, memory provides testimony for procedural justice. But too often governments and legal systems fail to hold perpetrators accountable for their crimes. Moreover, a range of wrongs are not easily redressed through law, including psychosocial injuries, state terror, and structural oppression. A maximal form of memory justice demands a relationship to the future by imagining forms of social recognition and reparation. Repair, in this way, actively brings together moralistic needs, such as the imperative to right wrongs, advance justice, restore dignity, and recognize a people erased or forgotten—with discrete actions like political reform, equitable policies, the reconstruction of homes destroyed, and public acknowledgments of wrongs and the humanity of harmed groups. This is a reparative sensibility informed by peace and urban studies—one that views memory justice as critical to community empowerment and development. It is one that extends beyond broken world thinking to attempt to make things "right" for affected people in the present, concretely shaping future possibilities.

Nonetheless, it is important to remember that as a response to violence, repair cannot be considered inevitable, immediately accessible, or driven by technoscientific fixes. It also cannot reasonably be the first order response to historical injustice. Slavery, genocide, state terror, and colonialism have been so nearly normalized or erased from national and global consciousness that the outsize task is first to return memory to the legacies of that violence. Moreover, achieving repair is rarely conceivable for acts of violence that are, frankly, irreparable.[37] The individual and intergenerational experience of pain and trauma—the *rage* against it all, in Prescod's words—is incommensurable with any proposed corrective.

Memory, too, has limits. As a form of truth telling, it can only approximate a historical record, because violence literally destroys individual remembrance, and trauma complicates it further still.[38] Consequently, the multifaceted incompleteness of memory justice is a product of its inadequacy to redress violent acts. When striven for, memory justice remains necessarily unfinished, an aspiration. It requires continual work to approximate repair. Despite its difficulties, individuals and communities seek repair to fulfill desires for the acknowledgment of wrongs, restitution, and perhaps healing. Endeavoring to repair recognizes both the impossibility and necessity of those aims.

Situated as an endeavor in memory justice, trauma heritage enacts a distinct, if similarly inadequate and corruptible, form of repair. More on this follows in chapter 1, but in short, trauma heritage initiates the work of repair as spatial acts of historiography. The sites that make violent experiences known are a form of history representation. They constitute an othered history—a reparative historiography—that seeks to reveal and communicate marginalized and hidden experiences of violence. Not merely oral or written, the reparative histories that trauma heritage "writes" rely on material and spatial forms of representation to compel attention in the context of significant power imbalances and inattentive publics. In doing so, trauma heritage expands the field of historiography, itself a reparative act.[39] Additionally, by its presence in the landscape, trauma heritage intends change beyond remembrance. The sites hold space for justice, repair, and empowerment—making those objectives tangible and possible—for the harmed and their descendants.

Memory justice work in Rwanda was not purely an effort at victim advocacy. It was also tethered to contradictory state objectives that have evolved into the government's control of residents today. Furthermore, memory justice in Rwanda was not a local endeavor alone; genocide heritage referenced global efforts to spatialize hidden violence. Those efforts were intimately tethered to the development of human rights practice in the late twentieth century. Both of those aspects—forms of national politicization and entanglements in global movements—do not dilute the significance of memory justice as a driving force for Rwanda's genocide heritage. But they do suggest the need to more closely understand the actors and contexts involved in memory justice initiatives. Attention to Rwanda's early genocide heritage development along with its legacies three decades later provides a unique vantage on memory justice not as some romanticized effort, but as one embedded in a messy politics of repair, searching for seemingly impossible redress for injustice.

## An Ethics of Viewership

The images shown in the pages of this book document the discovery of genocide massacres and the work involved in preparing bodies, weapons, belongings, and sites for conservation. Many of the images are difficult to see. They form a historical record of violent experiences. I am deeply aware of their conflictual nature: their potential to be read as sensational representations of violence and to reproduce power and privilege in the relationships of viewer and viewed. Throughout, I endeavor to contextualize who made the photographs and videos, why, and, critically for the bulk of this uncaptioned historical documentation, what they portray. My request of the reader, following theorist Ariella Azoulay, is not merely to look at these unbearable images but to *watch* them. To watch images of violence is, as Azoulay claims, to "read them both out of and into the space of the political relations instated by photography."[40] That is, the images included in this book, like the landscapes of memory they reference, require an ethics of viewership for deep understanding. The ethics that guides watching invites viewers both to critically examine the regimes of meaning that condition the images' interpretation and also to radically see the agency and claims of the individuals pictured.

### WATCHING IMAGES

Azoulay builds out what is required of watching. She suggests that images of harm initiate a civil contract between the individuals pictured and us, the viewers. They compel us not only to bear witness but also to see others' claims for citizenship. Such is the "civic space of the gaze": one that rejects such terms as *empathy*, *shame*, *pity*, and *compassion* as organizers of one's view and instead begs a certain ethical imperative to reconsider one's own assumptions.[41] Both the act of watching and the reconfiguration of the gaze as a civic space enable an ethics of viewership.

Readers of this book may not be willing to see all of the images I include. That aversion is understandable. Images of violence are never easy to receive. For those who have experienced the pain of harm, especially, trauma heritage opens up landscapes of association and memory that one cannot help but see and feel. I am, however, appealing especially to those of us who are unaccustomed to experiences of violence; an ethics of viewership asks for your considered engagement. At the very least, my hope is that the images—and the histories they provoke—begin to open a larger set of questions about personhood and political circumstances beyond the image of suffering.

Two photographs demonstrate the watching required of an ethics of viewership. Both were taken by Mario Ibarra near the Murambi genocide site in 1996. They document what it was like to conserve evidence of genocidal violence (figures I.5 and I.6). One photograph shows a woman's arms gently encircling a toddler. They watch an infant playing with the grass at their feet. Blankets to keep the children warm are close in case comfort is needed. A long cloth for carrying them is also at hand, draped on the grass. The woman is resting and looking off into the distance, where another woman sits partially out of frame. She, too, holds a baby to her chest, nestled in a blanket on her lap. The women are conservation workers and also caregivers for their and others' children. They sit in the very field where the work of conserving victims' remains is taking place.

A second photograph documents what was out of frame in the first. The camera centers in on a multitude of hands suspended over a sheet of plastic that tenuously holds soapy water. The hands rub human skulls to wash the dirt and remaining bits of hair, blood, and flesh from genocide victims found in a mass grave. Other images in the series show several groups engaged in similar work, conserving hundreds of bones and skulls. Some of the remains will be displayed at the newly established Murambi Genocide Memorial. Others will be buried in consecrated graves.

Photographs of this backstage work of conservation and mothering challenge reading genocide memorials solely as commemorative monuments. They instead invite questions as to the dilemmas and emotional and physical labor inherent in that memory work. The scenes forestall hasty assumptions regarding the sites' political sensationalism. They likewise trouble the connections of that emotionally challenging work to memory justice. In place of both conclusions, the images ask viewers to contemplate the process of making trauma heritage and the people involved.

## METHODS FOR SEEING AND LISTENING

In the research for this project, an ethics of viewership served as a methodological guide. It formed part of my philosophy of seeing, one that resisted horror and anguish as my only reactions to the photographs of this memory work and the bodies and bones displayed at memorial sites. An ethics of viewership required that seeing led to watching the process of how these sites came to be, and deeply listening to the individuals involved and their struggles.[42] Attending to the memories of individuals who did and do memory work in Rwanda retrieves a more precise history of genocide memorials' ad hoc development and their politicization. Considering those individuals' ethical and social commitments traces their vast local and global associations across discrete practices of genocide heritage. I do not seek to resolve or romanticize those efforts. I aim to recuperate a sense of the tensions inherent in them.

In this book my aim is to read genocide heritage "both out of and into the space of political relations" instated by the postgenocide governing regime. To read genocide heritage into its political context is to recognize the lived experience of state power and social control that memorials reproduce. To read genocide heritage out of those forces is to be sensitive to the ethical imperatives and kinship that *also* produced those sites of memory. It is to attend to a diverse and marginalized memory landscape in Rwanda, aligned with genocide heritage in a search for repair but unable to gain similar public recognition.

Arriving at the watching required of an ethics of viewership was an iterative process. Research for this book developed within a larger project that explored government peacebuilding programs enacted through the design of new villages and rural landscapes.[43] Research took place over multiple visits to Rwanda in 2011–18, with my longest period of residence lasting for twenty months during 2012–13. My initial purpose was to understand rural residents' experiences of those

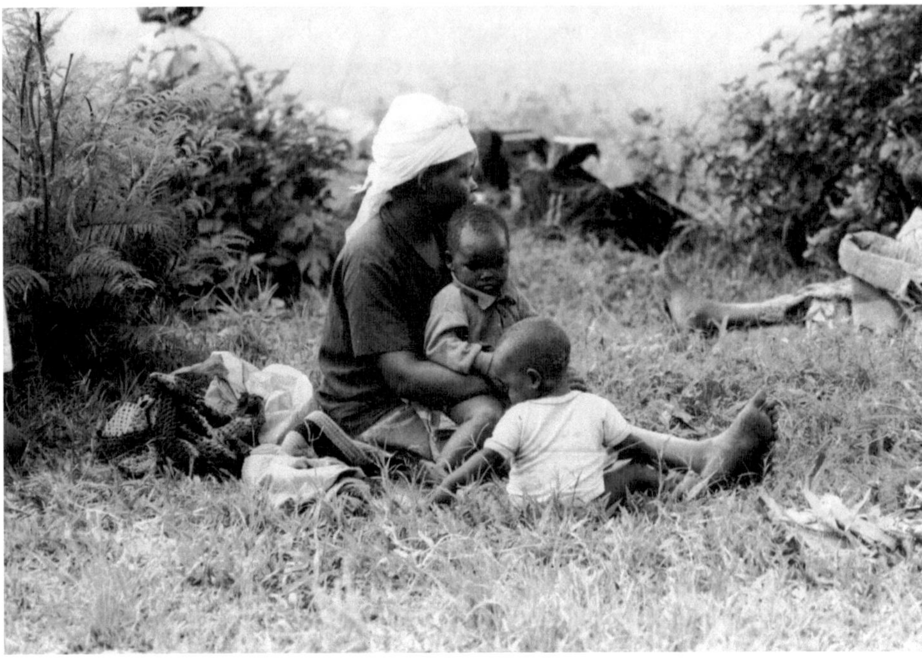

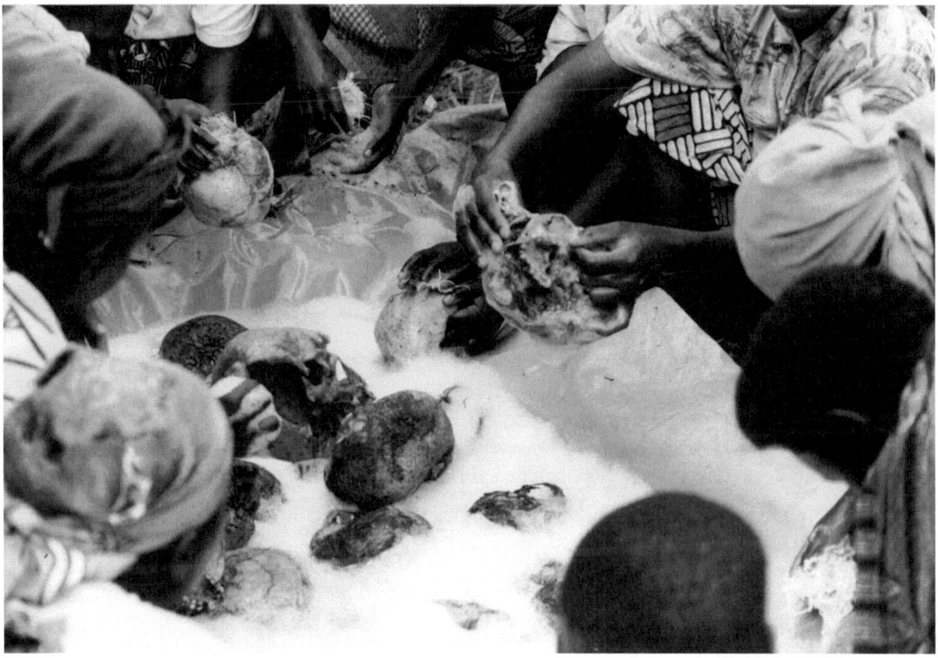

FIGURES I.5 AND I.6. Genocide Memorial Commission workers care for their children and clean the bones of genocide victims retrieved near Murambi, 1996. Photos by Mario Ibarra, Ibarra archive, Chile.

projects and the significant challenges that "building" peace posed. I came to this research with training in cultural geography and architectural history and a keen attention to socio-spatial phenomena—the interaction of people and their environments. Along the way, I encountered genocide memories codified in neat narratives by the government that were often repeated by rural residents. I also became privy to the unruly ways that those memories are embodied and navigated by a range of residents, including survivors and perpetrators, but also their relatives, bystanders, those who fled violence, and subsequent generations of Rwandan youth.

Government archives contained little information to indicate the roles that the military, the government, its partners, and local actors played in genocide memory conservation. Two primary factors explain this. First, relevant government documentation had been unevenly archived in the midst of the emergency postgenocide response, with much lost in subsequent years. The government archive that is most accessible to registered researchers, the former National Commission for the Fight Against Genocide (CNLG) Documentation Center, contained a wide-ranging photographic collection with no identifying information and a patchy repository of documents and ephemera related to memorialization from 1995 to 2008. Much of that historical record is retained ad hoc by individuals rather than by institutions. More generally, it was difficult to access politically sensitive topics in the country. This is a methodological and structural challenge well documented by scholars of Rwanda.[44] Second, much information related to the genocide, the aftermath, and the two governing regimes' operations during both periods was strategically withheld from public view by the government for various reasons related to protection—to avoid incrimination or to provide security or narrative control. Genocide heritage formed part of that larger politicization of available information because it formed the substance of opposing regimes' attempts to reveal and hide gross violations of human rights.

Similarly, most of my initial interviews were not ready avenues for discerning either the early history of genocide memorialization or individual views on state approaches to genocide remembrance. In 2012 and 2013, on the eve of the twentieth commemoration, genocide remembrance had become so dominated by state-authorized narratives and memorialization that most Rwandans I spoke with believed that they could not freely express their opinions on the subject outside of trusted circles.[45] Many rural residents were reticent to disclose views of memorials that did not align with state policies. Individuals involved in early genocide conservation—including those close to government decision-makers at the time and others who were employed to do the work—were often hesitant to disclose dilemmas inherent to conserving bodies and bones or the ad hoc nature of that approach. Genocide site and victim conservation was and is highly controversial within communities. It is also ethically muddied by government restrictions on free speech, prohibitions on customary burial practices, and state violence. It is furthermore entangled in long-standing critiques of the postgenocide regime by foreign scholars and international media and controversies regarding the state's own representations of history and its democratic governance.[46] This meant that the majority of my initial interviews with former and current government representatives and rural residents reinforced pithy official histories and perspectives without a sense of the process, local stewardship, or tensions of genocide heritage development. With repeat visits, space for more sprawling conversation, and, in some cases, guarantees of anonymity, many individuals did explore some of the doubts surrounding this work and the social, procedural, and political messiness it entailed. Those aspects had been increasingly filtered from official histories by 2014.

Several related structural factors troubled open discussions on the origins and effects of genocide memory representation. The strong public presence of Rwanda's genocide heritage—both in the capital and in rural communities throughout the country—mirrors government laws that regulate free speech and private remembrance and punish critics of the regime. By 2003 Rwanda's approach to genocide heritage conservation was bolstered by the involvement of Holocaust memory organizations, including Aegis Trust, which organized an archive of genocide survivor and witness testimony and a national memorial museum to victims in the capital, Kigali. Those efforts amount to a publicly conserved, state-authorized aesthetic and account of genocide history. In Latin America sociologist Elizabeth Jelin refers to similar phenomena as the "master narrative" of the nation: a version of history, and its accompanying symbolic landscape, that anchors national identity in state legitimacy and sovereignty.[47] A series of laws passed in 2008 reinforced the role of genocide memorials in conveying state-authorized histories and the government's reach in punishing genocide ideology and regulating free speech.[48] Since then, Rwandans have witnessed progressively tighter control over speech critical of the government, political opposition, and narratives that complicate state genocide histories. This has included the imprisonment of political dissidents, including Victoire Ingabire, an opposition party leader, in 2010; Paul Rusesabagina, manager of the Hôtel des Mille Collines during the genocide and whose actions to safeguard Tutsi were portrayed in the film *Hotel Rwanda*, in 2020; and of a widely popular musician and genocide survivor, Kizito Mihigo, whose music was a national standard at genocide commemorations before he questioned government national unity programs and omissions from authorized histories.[49] A 2016 law ratified existing government consolidations of memorial sites and the relocations of genocide victims buried at them.[50] Consolidations allow the government to manage fewer memorials, render their aesthetics and narratives more uniform, and provide better access to foreigners. But the practice has been highly controversial—especially for victims' families.

By my second year in this research process, I began to actively follow the silences I encountered in archives and interviews. Some of those silences indicated a lack of institutional memory within government ministries regarding the origins of genocide memorials. Other narrative gaps could be described as *amplified silences*, a term that anthropologist Jennie Burnet developed to refer to both the governing regime's control over civil liberties and the pervasive self-censorship that results from it, especially regarding a range of impermissible positionalities and topics related to the genocide and violence in the 1990s.[51] Many other silences did not represent government coercion at all but forms of everyday resistance—withdrawal, even—from participating in state narratives, policies, and expectations for citizenship.[52] Still other omissions reflected a language of trauma: emotionally burdened silences that stand in for the unspeakability of violent experiences.[53] Those silences required special care, including my attentiveness to speakers' feelings and a reinforcement of their boundaries. I came to understand all of these silences less as absences than as the "metadata" that Lee Ann Fujii followed in Rwanda. Fujii's research on what motivated the genocide relied largely on oral testimony.[54] In doing so, she came to understand that a range of silences in interlocutors' stories indicated "conditions in the present [that] shape what people are willing to say about violence in the past, what they have reason to embellish or minimize, and what they prefer to keep to themselves."[55] Those silences, then, tell us a great deal about how the present shapes the past.

Following silences led me to bring diverse source material together. My research turned to oral history and visual and spatial ethnography to grapple with the gaps and varied challenges of reading this memory landscape. Oral history is an approach to interviewing individuals that privileges their memories of life events, families, and communities to inform the historical record. Visual and spatial ethnography take images and places, respectively, to be central subjects and methods for ethnographic inquiries. Centered as subjects of conversations, sites of memory and photographs of conservation work provided concrete referents for uneven remembrance. As ethnographic methods, sketching, mapping, and walking through landscapes invited access to finer-grained details, feelings, and associations. For example, Mario often drew while he talked, illustrating sequences of his genocide investigations and approaches to conservation work. For some interlocutors, it was important to either describe meaningful places from memory or show me locations where violent events had happened but were no longer visible. My use of both methods attempted to restore individual voices and views to the origins and legacies of genocide memorialization that had been lost owing to the various structural, personal, and methodological factors I outline above.

In the study of trauma heritage—efforts to represent hidden or minoritized violence—visual and spatial evidence are especially critical communicative modalities in the context of restricted speech. Those nonverbal representations can harbor what can't be said, challenging singular or inordinately clear state narratives. Suppressed from public expression, those stories in Rwanda have taken refuge in a folded and annotated field map, a sharp-edged rock obsessively photographed in a genocide investigation archive, and the mummified body of a child—as the following chapters elaborate. Memories are also held in tension with the ways they are received today. Such is the case with the busy marketplace that today bears no marker noting a state reprisal attack, and the collective reburials of genocide victims at sites that no longer register the punitive labor of the prisoners who dug them. Those stories don't disappear when marginalized from inhospitable publics; they imbue places with feeling.

When speaking is possible, survivor oral histories are key sources of truth in the aftermath of violence that reveal details actively hidden by the powerful. Many interlocutors represented voices and narratives that are typically not recognized by state-authorized histories because they are too complex or deviate from or challenge official views. Often, however, respondents' narratives extended far beyond testimonies of fact. Those individuals linked past remembrances to present-day impacts, opening onto the social relations, aspirations, fears, and symbolic meaning situated by genocide memorials and photographs of memory work. In the less structured format of an oral history interview, they had more autonomy in how they replied to my questions and what they included (and when). I learned a great deal from those conversations about listening—especially to the sensitive and disjointed nature of traumatic remembrance.

In this research oral, visual, and spatial sources informed each other. Because of the relative lack of written documentation on early memorialization, I relied primarily on oral histories with people who first worked on genocide memory conservation. Finding those individuals and establishing grounds for more open conversations was also iterative: predicated in large part on multiple conversations over several years, establishing some measure of trust (including with Louis) and locating Mario in the first place (see chapter 1). Louis's and Mario's personal archives in Rwanda and Chile hold photographs and videos of exhumations, massacre conservation, and reburials that record the process of making genocide heritage from 1994 to 1998. Interviews with them and others were helpful in identifying the contents and describing the contexts of those photographs. Some of that visual material is publicly available in government repositories, but there is no index listing which places, dates, and activities they picture. I located other people involved in conservation work through Mario's and Louis's recollections and written documentation and by showing their photographs in rural communities near the sites pictured. Images, in turn, often prompted more detailed recollections in conversation. Places, both visible and hidden, served as mnemonic devices during conversations. Without these visual and spatial sources, I had limited understanding of the feelings and backstage work associated with memory conservation, or of relationships to early exhumations and reburials. As a result, I came to understand oral histories, visual documentation, and places as not mere source material for developing more "accurate," balanced, or grounded histories. These stories, images, and sites form a visceral archive of deeply emotional remembrance.

## LOCATING POSITIONALITY

This visceral archive—the process of assembling it and the experiences it represents—situates several ethical dilemmas I grappled with in this research. Among them, the single most challenging was the range of wrenching emotions that my questions evoked, balanced tenuously with my commitment to do no harm.[56] In such instances, consent to ask questions on the subject matter seemed a woefully minimal standard to permit my intrusion. Returning to conversation after a flood of grief or anger was never easy. I trod carefully in those instances, inviting interlocutors to stop, pause, or express only what they felt comfortable saying. The individuals who continued to speak with me acknowledged my apologies. They also stated what they thought was important for me and others to know about this history and why. A related ethical challenge has been writing the complexity of those encounters. I struggle with both relaying the deeply personal and violent memories told to me and weighing the political ramifications for interlocutors in doing so. Moreover, questions of relevance and judiciousness in representing experiences of trauma are critical to considering how readers receive these stories. Examining my positionality has been central to navigating both dilemmas and, similarly, to the methods of watching and listening that resulted in this book.

In most of my interviews, mention of the violence that occurred in the 1990s was first introduced at a remove. Understandably so—these were intimate memories that were not easily shared with others, especially outsiders. I was largely received as an outsider in this research. In rural areas in Rwanda, I was often teasingly called *akazungu* (small foreigner), a layered name that was simultaneously a diminutive, a commentary on my relatively short stature, and a term of endearment. In cities, residents were more likely to call me *Chinoise* (a francophone reference to my mixed Asian-Caucasian ethnicity). In both settings, both my privilege as a foreigner with the ability to travel and ask questions and my disadvantages as a foreigner with none of the knowledge and expertise possessed by Rwandans were raised by nearly everyone I spoke with. Foreigners' lack of situated understanding is so well known that it has long been codified in a genre of Kinyarwanda riddles (*inshoberamahanga*). I took my newfound monikers to be humbling, if slightly cringeworthy. I understood my diminution while conducting research to be part of a Rwandan "infrapolitics" of establishing agency in the context of historically unwanted foreign intervention.[57] It reinforced the partiality of my knowledge (and that of my interlocutors) in the process of encountering complexity and making sense of it.

To listen and watch in this context required relating to interlocutors as both a partial insider and an outsider. Scholars often conceive of researchers' positionalities in binary terms: either as insiders who have advantages in accessing information because they belong to the groups they study or as outsiders who retain objectivity and distance in the interpretation of data. Yet positionality is rarely static. Geographer Beverley Mullings made this point in her research with Jamaican company managers. She argued that individuals rarely remain insiders or complete outsiders.[58] Instead, Mullings suggested that "positional spaces" more aptly describe the process of creating a shared, if transitory, space of trust and cooperation within interviews in which power and class differentials, politically sensitive settings, or emotional topics challenge both. Within this framing, positionality is the product of an interaction of persons, and holding insider or outsider status is only ever partial. Trust is contingent on an appreciation of the situated knowledge of both parties, which is only ever approximated through mutual questioning.

In my case, developing a positional space for conversation was not a shortcut to access nor a subversion of power dynamics. I embraced my *akazungu* status because it humbled me. I sought some measure of social relation by gaining Kinyarwanda language proficiency.[59] Speaking in the local language was most appreciated by government officials, who took it as a marker of willingness to hear what they, and Rwandans in general, think. With rural residents, I conducted interviews in Kinyarwanda to meet them in the language in which they felt comfortable. I also partnered with a Rwandan translator in those interviews. Though certainly more familiar with the culture and language than I, they were also a relative outsider to the communities we visited as someone who did not grow up in those places. They prefer not to be identified. I consider ours a collaboration animated by questions regarding interpretation, un/ease, what was narrated, and what possibly was left unsaid. Without their humanity and insight, this work would have been both less joyous and less meaningful.

Our partnership and our collective partial insider and outsider statuses were critical to creating positional spaces where individuals explained commonly held local knowledge. In 2018, during a return visit with a couple living in the east of the country, our conversation shifted to my status as an outsider. I had asked if they had questions for me. In response, the husband asked where I was from, returning the conversation to where I began the interview.[60] I foregrounded my university affiliation and my US citizenship to reinforce my impartiality (and nongovernmental status). That my research was not sponsored by the government but could inform state policies was especially important to them. In response, the husband turned to my colleague, "*You* see us, we're part of the masses and we're at the bottom. *Urumva*? [Do you understand?] But she, she doesn't know. She cannot see what a Rwandan does, what Rwandans need."[61] We all nodded in agreement. The wife added, "It takes effort for someone from there to come here and learn what needs to be done. She will listen and give that knowledge to someone who has the means to do something about it."[62] The conversation was similar to others I had in rural areas throughout the country, where ordinary folks living with modest means were willing to explain their situations to me because, as an outsider, I did not have their knowledge or know what Rwandans know. That I might possibly be able to do something in response was not assumed to be immediate. It is, for me at least, an expectation that remains to be fulfilled.

Not everyone I spoke with wanted to talk about the past. Often, the harrowing nature of exhumations, conservation, and reburials—not to mention the violence that each followed—produced abstract narratives where details were withheld and replaced with procedural observations. I respected those boundaries. Those strategies kept difficult memories at a distance. I often navigated political and emotional sensitivities by employing the built environment as a form of distancing. I learned about the importance of those positional spaces from individuals residing in rural villages. Oftentimes, residents were most comfortable talking about worries about poisoned water wells as an analogue for conflicts with neighbors or speaking openly about the failures of electricity provision rather than deriding government policies. In some cases, walking together in landscapes supported more open storytelling. Out in the world, memories about the genocide and its aftermath were articulated at a relatively safe distance: not held inside but somehow elsewhere at the interface of self and environment. Other times, homes were more protective of memories contested by the government, and those landscapes would unfold within a safe interior where no one could be observed speaking, let alone to the *akazungu*. Often, conversations organized around photographs, memories of places, or walking in landscapes would shift our conversations from more general accounts to deeply personal reflections and experiences. The individuals who did speak about their experiences taught me about the complex temporalities of traumatic memories—at once contained or locked away in the past and yet easily triggered in ways that flood the present. I was consistently taken aback by how precipitously difficult pasts, relegated to a distance, spilled over into our conversations. In those moments when photographs were explained or experiences relived, I learned a great deal about the presence of the past.

I could not be a researcher at a remove in these instances. I cried after interviews. I felt wretchedly guilty for asking questions that evoked others' tears. Writing of research in Bosnia and Herzegovina and Rwanda, oral historian Erin Jessee rightly warns that there are limits to a researcher's "deep listening."[63] This is particularly the case when interlocutors recount experiences of harrowing violence. In the context of those stories especially, it is doubly difficult to then hear others' justifications for harms they inflicted. The deep listening that Jessee speaks of, like the ethics of viewership, comes with personal costs. Even acknowledging this, I needed to be able to quiet my own emotional reactions to listen to the many individuals who shared their experiences. The majority of my interviews took place in respondents' homes, in the midst of daily routines and everyday landscapes. As a result, rarely were remembrances relegated solely to the past. Those quotidian "distractions" grounded traumatic experiences in the present, providing context and a sense of life beyond. In rural Rwandan villages especially, I remember the *akana* (small child) that one of us was bouncing, the sounds of dry beans being sorted on flat baskets, and the giggles of neighborhood children just outside the door. Situated there, I listened not only to traumatic pasts but also to the present—and especially *why* interlocutors spoke with me. Whether responses were organized from the outset by a need to "make history known" or not overtly conditioned by personal or political motivations, I came to understand that the individuals who ventured to speak of their experiences intended their words to have some measure of transformative effect. They opened tentative positional spaces to foster others' understanding and, perhaps, their own empowerment.

The ethical dilemmas I encountered in research were echoed in writing. I struggled with writing emotionally and politically difficult experiences while remaining faithful to interlocutors and the ways they represented their memories. By way of attempting some balance, I offer an intimate history, not distant or evacuated of its emotional excesses, that also responds sensitively to individuals, their often-intense feelings, and significant concerns—including community dynamics and regime repercussions. Examining my positionalities as a partial insider and outsider has been helpful to navigating my roles and responsibilities in this regard. I have also found it helpful, in the writing of this book, to retrospectively consider my positionalities as a custodian and witness. As a custodian, a term that derives from archive studies, I highlight my responsibility as a researcher to hold, organize, and represent interlocutors' knowledge. That responsibility is not neutral, as critical archive studies scholars attest.[64] Feminist perspectives on custodianship emphasize the importance of not just an ethical responsibility to individuals and documentation of them but a relationship of care, as archivists Michelle Caswell and Marika Cifor put it, "about and for and with subjects."[65] Putting this in practice—in writing—is not easy. Folklorist Henry Glassie has described a similar challenge: how a feeling of responsibility for individuals and their histories translated into his writing about Northern Ireland during the Troubles. His "problem" was, as he put it, "to create an ethnography strong enough to cause disquiet in my world, but gentle enough to cause no discomfort among the people I wrote about."[66] Thinking feminist custodianship and Glassie together situates this book as primarily for an audience of outsiders—whether in Rwanda or elsewhere—not privy to the experiences I recount.

What began for me as an empirical observation of the ways that individuals spoke about experiences of violence and the aftermath of the genocide has become both a method for writing this history and a central narrative force in this book. I regard the uneven, sometimes removed, other times deeply personal, nature of the histories that result to be faithful to the book's fraught subject. Those perspectives offer a more intimate engagement with the silences and narratives of genocide memory under strict state control today. Time lapses also play an important part in the book's narration. Several decades passed between the events and their description. More than context for my research, that passage of time demonstrated the persistence of difficult memories, sometimes clear and other times hazy. In response, the chapters telescope from the first years after the genocide to lived experiences almost three decades later. In writing an intimate history comprising images, places, and stories that endure and slip in time, I attempt to represent the myriad ways in which the past is present in Rwanda.

When moving from recording individual histories to the stakes involved in documenting experiences of violence, I found myself functioning not merely as a custodian of interlocutors' stories but also as a witness. In earlier sections I situated the importance of witnesses—primary and secondary alike—in the context of reparative and memory justice work. Here, positioning myself as a researcher-witness seeks to highlight not only my ethical responsibilities to the individuals I spoke with but also the importance of not denuding the stories they told. Anthropologist Allen Feldman has reflected on the dilemmas and stakes of representing research on violence to wider publics.[67] He asks, "How do we translate the dead, the dying, the terrorized, the disappeared"—a social and emotional landscape of trauma, grief, and terror—"to a condition of historical actuality?"[68]

To contend with this question, I connect the writing of history to the sites in which it is located. Doing so has opened up the reparative history that this book documents and attempts—a history inscribed in landscapes to enact forms of repair in living communities. This is an expanded understanding of historiography, "written" in place, made material, and read visually. Writing reparative histories in and through place locates the excesses of feeling and experience that interlocutors recount. The history that this book attempts, like those developing from myriad sites of trauma heritage, demands an ethics of viewership attentive to individual agency and a willingness to engage sites and stories of violence.

As a result, this book is about making public space for silenced pain, as a form of empowerment and repair—and as a critique of the spaces in which no such acknowledgment exists. It is also about an ethics and method of listening and watching, one that draws close to trauma as an intimate form of acknowledgment and resists violent erasures by sharing feelings, aspirations, and lessons heard. The hope is that doing so proliferates the number of custodians and witnesses—those who care about, and for, and with individuals seeking justice, repair, and empowerment.

## The Chapters

This book documents an exceptional form of trauma heritage that emerged after the 1994 genocide against Tutsi in Rwanda to render scenes of massacre as visceral places of witness. It contributes new research on the initial memory work and dilemmas entailed in those efforts in making Rwanda's genocide heritage. In doing so, it traces connections to a global geography of trauma heritage practices, informed by the human rights movement developing in the late twentieth century. *Rwanda's Genocide Heritage* also explores the history of the sites' evolving state control and politicization. Genocide heritage continues to shape social and political life today. The sites exist alongside other struggles for memory justice embedded in unauthorized and prohibited trauma heritage in the country. As an extreme example of a local and global phenomenon, then, Rwanda's genocide heritage reveals the tensions inherent in confronting violence along with trauma heritage's potential and unruliness as sites of repair.

Chapter 1 introduces two of the first curators of Rwanda's genocide heritage—Louis Kanamugire and Mario Ibarra—who developed a *practice* of reparative history. They sought to formalize genocide memory in preserved and conserved killing sites, photographic and cartographic documentation of the scale of the killings, and commemorative ceremonies. In doing so, they worked to transform traumatic memories into history—an authoritative form of knowledge from which the genocide would be more likely to be recognized. Tracing the spatial and material forms of the truth telling they attempted, the chapter explores a central tension in trauma heritage, in which memory workers and witnesses navigate a distinctly affective—an inescapably sensorial and emotional—experience of aftermath landscapes to produce objective, historiographical representations. Louis's and Mario's memory work demonstrates the challenges of practicing a reparative history, up close and for wider recognition. Their work also contributes to conceptualizations of reparative history, furthering our understanding of the stakes, dilemmas, and modalities of such endeavors.

Chapter 2 traces the formalization of Rwanda's genocide heritage, detailing how and why the government decided to publicly display victims' remains and other material evidence as collective memory. The chapter updates precedent literature on the early development of genocide memorials, emphasizing the knowledge exchanges among the first preservation and conservation experiments at Nyarubuye, Ntarama, Murambi, and Nyamata. It also traces the local and global forces that led to the institutionalization of an extreme aesthetic in the representation of the genocide, which, rather than evolving from Holocaust memorialization templates (those influences would be more prominent a decade later), drew from a global human rights movement, including memory justice activism in Latin America. Those influences underscore that early genocide heritage exceeded state control both on the global scale and on the scale of local experiences of trauma.

Chapter 3 details the practices to preserve the country's first genocide heritage site at Nyarubuye Church (in eastern Rwanda). It follows three actors critical to Nyarubuye's preservation—the rebel Rwandan Patriotic Army, which took control of the country, ending the genocide; the regional office of the United Nations Human Rights Field Operation in Rwanda (UN HRFOR); and newly appointed local governing authorities. The chapter considers what these actors did to preserve the site, why they did so, and what ethical dilemmas and political pressures they faced. It also explores the phenomenon of secondary witnessing that emerged at the site and its outcomes. Regular tours by international observers positioned Nyarubuye as a metonym for the genocide. Nyarubuye centers the irresolvable tensions of Rwanda's genocide heritage: The misalignments between the ethics of nonerasure and state sovereignty, preservation and witnessing, and authorized heritage and its growing body of omissions.

Chapter 4 shifts to the Murambi Technical School, Rwanda's largest genocide heritage conservation operation. It follows both the formalization of that visceral aesthetic and the backstage work, and individuals, that developed it. Foregrounding the emotional, affective, and physical labor that produced genocide heritage, the chapter draws from photographs and videos of conservation work that were recorded in 1996–97 and oral histories with memory workers decades later. Those sources reveal genocide memorials less as monuments than as intimate and fraught engagements in reparative processes, driven by ethical and communal commitments. The chapter concludes by discussing the multiple temporalities and paradoxes inherent in forms of repair, evident in individual engagements in making genocide heritage.

Chapter 5 explores the interplay of exhumation, display of victims' remains, and reburial ceremonies to explore relationships between the visibility of violence and forms of social and political order instated by the new regime. The chapter draws primarily from photographs, taken in series from 1995 to 1997, of the work to recover genocide victims from mass graves, prepare their remains for reburial, and commemorate them in public ceremonies. Those photographs document the backstage and social dynamics of multiday events. In them we see accused prisoners laboring in processes of victim exhumation, temporary display, and reburial. The photographs also reveal the social hierarchies and socialization processes that emerged through new and old burial rituals in which mourning and campaigns for state sovereignty and justice coexisted, often in contradiction. The chapter concludes by considering how conservation and ceremonies for reburial and commemoration ordered aftermath landscapes and shaped how the state controls the future of the past.

Chapter 6 explores Rwanda's uneven landscape of memory, in which official genocide memorials sit side by side with less dominant forms of trauma heritage. Drawing from contemporary oral histories with rural residents across the country, it brings the country's authorized genocide heritage into conversation with marginalized memories and the places associated with them, noting the breaks, silences, and omissions that come into focus as a result. The chapter reveals a diverse memory landscape in Rwanda where underrecognized, unauthorized, and prohibited memories remain latent in terms of their public visibility. The move that genocide heritage shares with reparative history, from truth-telling to action, is not equally available to all. The stakes of Louis's and Mario's work in developing Rwanda's genocide heritage become more apparent as a result. The chapter explores the marginalized memories in the country that are not afforded the same opportunities for spatial representation and thus justice and empowerment.

The conclusion contextualizes the memory work that occurred in postgenocide Rwanda within an *era of trauma heritage*. My conceptual periodization describes a late twentieth-century phenomenon in which activists spatialized memories to reveal, and call attention to, hidden and normalized violence in the Global South. Such acts of trauma heritage continue to have resonance today—from the claims to existence and brutal erasure made by the fervent documentation of destroyed Palestinian homes to the collection and preservation of soil at lynching sites in the southern United States.[69] Those initiatives make public space for silenced pain, calling for recognition, justice, and repair. The era of trauma heritage traces a global geography of memory justice activism and its origins within the then-emerging international human rights movement. In this context, following one of the world's most devastating periods of mass death, Rwanda crystallized global shifts toward a distinctly *spatialized* form of memory justice.

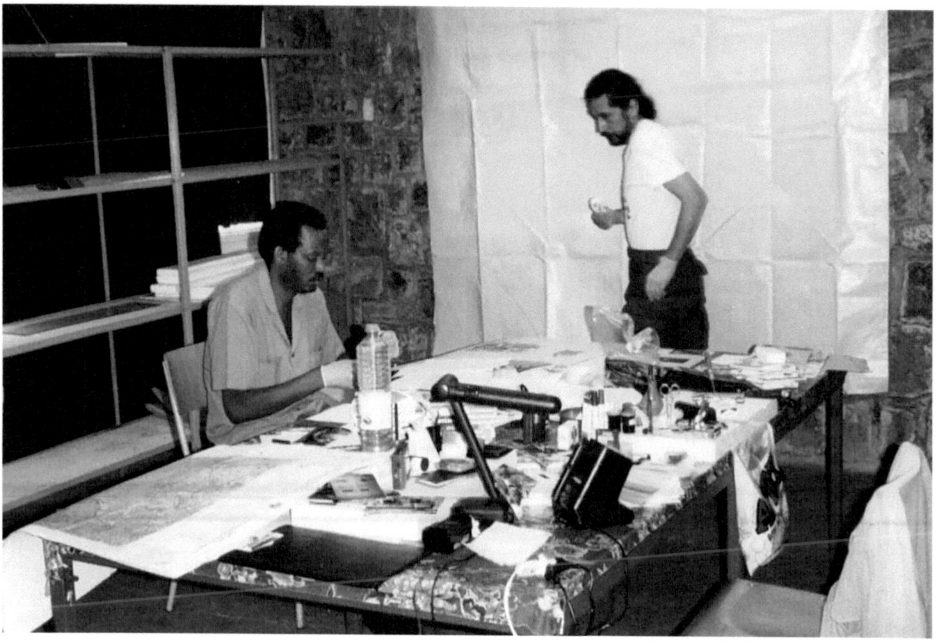

Louis Kanamugire (*left*) and Mario Ibarra select photographs and artifacts to display as evidence of the genocide at the Institut Français (French Cultural Institute) in Kigali, 1996. Courtesy of Mario Ibarra, Ibarra archive, Chile.

1

# *EL OLOR Y EL DOLOR* (THE SMELL AND THE PAIN)

## THE PRACTICE OF REPARATIVE HISTORY

When I visited the National Commission for the Fight Against Genocide (CNLG) in 2012, it was housed in a large repurposed villa in Kigali. I was looking for source material to explain how and why genocide victims and sites were first conserved as genocide memorials. What I found was an archive in fragments, incomplete in terms of information yet excessive in the affect it provoked. The lower-level documentation center contained, among other written materials related to the genocide, photographs in around twenty bound albums. The images primarily show victims discovered in fields, buildings, and hasty graves. They also show individuals at work documenting evidence at massacre sites, conserving victims' remains, and preparing for and attending reburial ceremonies. The photographs are not labeled or organized by subject, location, or date. Those data were misplaced: When copies were first placed in the previous office at Amahoro Stadium, the photographs were indexed and marked with identifiers.[1] Without this information, cut loose from the context that would make them intelligible, they present a seemingly endless, and yet excruciatingly nonspecific, view of the aftermath of atrocity.

Upstairs in the CNLG offices, an employee retrieved a large map that had been rolled up and stashed in the back of a bookshelf near his desk. If the photographs overwhelm through the dehumanizing repetition of death, the map offers only a dispassionate overview. Titled in French *Les grands sites du génocide et des massacres* (hereafter the *Genocide Sites Map*), it provides a countrywide accounting of major massacre sites overlaid on a tourist map of Rwanda.[2] The *Genocide Sites Map* includes 118 locations coded in three colors: red for religious sites, blue for public places, and green for "hills of resistance" (defensive positions where people fought against their attackers). A second, letter-size copy of the map was similarly tucked away, out of immediate view, in one of the three-ring binders downstairs in the documentation center. Both versions are representations of the genocide that identify locations of significant massacres. The CNLG retained no record of how the map was produced or who codified, selected, or represented the sites of death with such restraint. Printed in April 1997, both versions of the map represent the earliest comprehensive overviews of the genocide.

In the ground-floor reception office in which all CNLG visitors were required to register, a small drawing hung on a side wall (figure I.1). The sun had faded the colors. On a white background, an amorphous shape traces three capsule-like areas that are held in suspension within concentric rings. One shows a person standing, and the other two depict scenes of killing. The abstract realism of the image is discombobulating: The rings are hypnotic fields that alternate purple (now faded to a purplish blue), yellow, orange, and black and render the scenes placeless. The bodies are anonymous, simple forms that raise their hands with weapons, stand mute, and lie on the ground dismembered. The subject matter is psychically arresting and potentially refers to Rwanda but only because of the context in which it was found. No one knew who the artist was or how the drawing came to be there.

I put my many related questions to Louis Kanamugire. As inaugural director of the Genocide Memorial Commission from 1995 to 2003, he had intimate knowledge of the first eight years of the agency's challenging work, including why and how genocide heritage sites came to display the remains of victims. I brought documents and photographs I retrieved from the CNLG documentation center to our first meetings. I had seen Louis's signature alongside that of an individual named Mario Ibarra on several invoices and proposals for genocide memory conservation in the archive. I wanted to know if photographs of a foreigner, often shown photographing scenes of massacre or inspecting skeletal remains, sometimes wearing a hat with a United Nations (UN) logo, showed that individual. Louis was not sure, and he was not interested in elaborating.

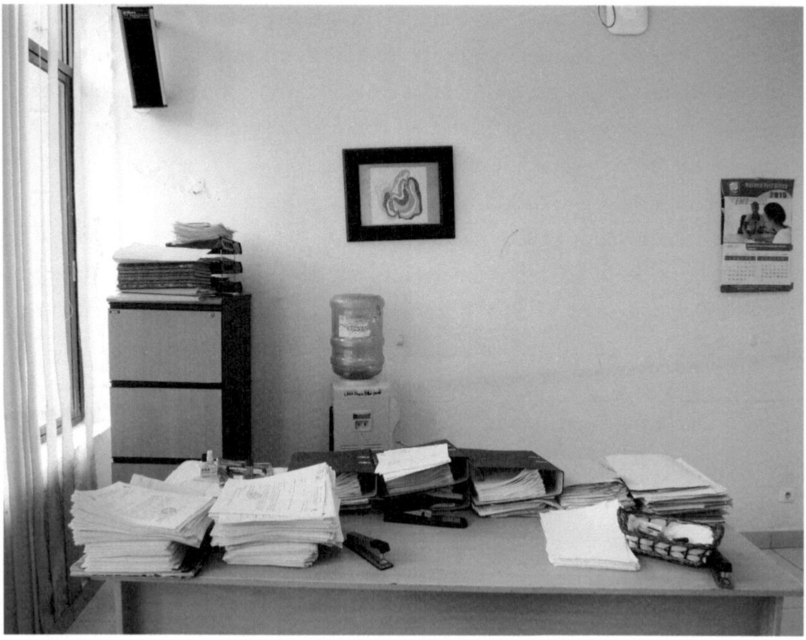

FIGURE I.1. Mario Ibarra's painting hangs, unattributed, above a desk in the CNLG reception office, Kigali, 2015. Photo by Erin Mosely. Courtesy of Delia Duong Ba Wendel.

Looking back, I think it was a matter of trust. Over six months passed, with near-weekly meetings at the same café near the CNLG offices, before Louis began to discuss details of early genocide memorialization that were not already widely known. Even then, his were partial recollections. I regularly asked if he had photographs or other documentation of that early memory work and never had any indication that he did. One day, he let me borrow his copy of the *Genocide Sites Map*; he emphasized the importance of the three different types of sites that it located. But he did not recall who authored the map or how it came to be made. A few weeks later, he shared a draft memoir about the Genocide Memorial Commission that he had been writing. It began to fill in some of the gaps. He asked me to translate it from French to English; I encouraged him to write a Kinyarwanda version. We edited his manuscript translations together, and I asked follow-up questions about the history he recounted and especially about his summaries of significant genocide massacres. In one of those conversations, Louis slid a stack of envelopes across our table at the café. They were filled with sleeves of photographic negatives in the sequence in which they were taken. The envelopes included brief notes giving the photographs' dates and locations along with the name of the person who had them developed. Mario was listed as the contact person on over half of the envelopes. The photographs caught me completely off guard: Many of the images were duplicates of those in the CNLG archive, but most were new to me, and all had some indication of provenance and context. I could start to piece together the work involved in genocide investigations, conservation work at killing sites, reburial ceremonies, and the relationships among them.

I asked Louis about Mario's name on the negative envelopes. Louis shared his copy of a document I had had difficulty obtaining in its entirety. "Copie du travail, MARIO" (Working copy, MARIO) was scrawled on the front in red ink, and the same handwriting had penned questions and notes for follow-up throughout. The *Rapport préliminaire d'identification des sites du génocide et des massacres d'avril–juillet 1994 au Rwanda* (Preliminary Report on the Identification of Genocide Sites and Massacres from April–July 1994 in Rwanda; hereafter *Preliminary Report*) was a written summary of the genocide investigations conducted by the Genocide Memorial Commission in late 1995, published in February 1996. It references photographs now in the CNLG archive, but those images no longer retain the call numbers indexed in the report. The *Preliminary Report* was one of the first documents to synthesize diverse forms of photographic, witness, and forensic evidence to ascertain what happened during the genocide. The Genocide Memorial Commission is listed as the author, but Louis drafted it in January 1996. The red ink comments throughout confirmed that he worked closely with Mario Ibarra as he wrote. Shortly after evidence of their collaborations was in front of us, Louis wrote Mario back into his memoir. Mario had been a member of the original Genocide Memorial Commission convened in October 1995. His expertise in human rights investigations had been pivotal to the group's own investigatory work. But Louis did not know where Mario had gone. And Mario did not want to be easily found.

It would take a great deal of fruitless inquiry, a long series of cold calls, and a trip to southern Chile to determine that the photographs, the framed painting in the CNLG office, the *Genocide Sites Map*, and the *Preliminary Report* were all produced during genocide investigations and conservation work that Louis Kanamugire and Mario Ibarra led throughout Rwanda during 1994–98. Following leads from former UN colleagues, in late 2013 I finally reached a relative of Mario's, who dubiously agreed to contact him on my behalf. Mario replied to my emails only in formal French, despite my communication in Spanish. His email's sender name was not his. He later told me that it was a pseudonym for a former colleague who had originally helped him set up the account. Like Louis, he initially kept a wary distance, unsure of my motivations. At that stage, I did not have a sense of the extent of his involvement in early investigations nor of his leadership in genocide heritage conservation.

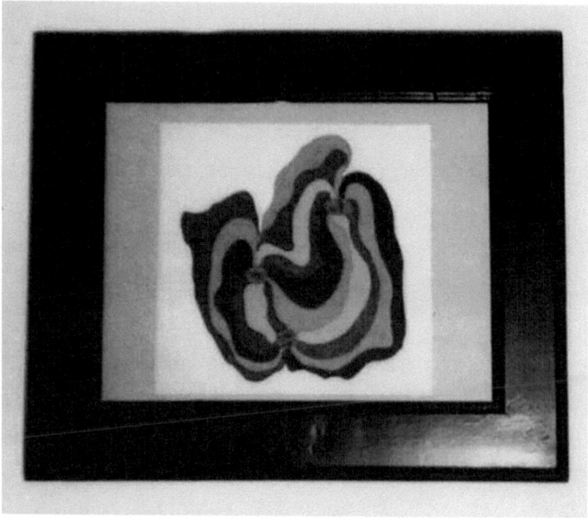

FIGURE 1.2. A Polaroid photograph that Mario Ibarra took of his painting before he left it with the Genocide Memorial Commission in 1998. Ibarra archive, Chile.

Two years after we began corresponding over email, Mario agreed to meet with me in southern Chile. We had been speaking for several days in a study room at a local university when Mario invited me to his home to see what he had brought back from Rwanda. The front room of his small apartment was striking. His library, which covered every wall, was dedicated to carefully held memories. Shelves were stacked neatly with rows of books. Mementos, many from Rwanda, were attentively placed throughout. His artwork punctuated the room: Most striking were delicate metal sculptures on large, orange-painted wood mounts that were made from stiff wire and bent into insects and the figures of individuals in the midst of attacks. These were artistic interpretations of what he observed in the country; his photographs and films similarly intermixed images of the landscape and natural life with those of death and violation. At least, that's what I came to understand over the next years.

In several boxes located below his bookshelves was a trove of photographs from Rwanda that extended far beyond those housed in the CNLG documentation center and Louis's personal archive. The photographs documented his work with the UN Human Rights Field Operation in Rwanda (HRFOR) in 1994 and 1995, including his investigations of killing sites and mass graves. They also documented his work, from 1994 to 1998, to preserve and conserve genocide sites, victims' remains, and the belongings and weapons found at the sites. Among the photographs was a Polaroid of the drawing I had seen hanging in the CNLG office (figure 1.2). The drawing was originally part of a series that Mario drew in 1994 as catharsis, to reflect on his own experience of the genocide's aftermath in Rwanda. Mario gave the drawing to the Genocide Memorial Commission in 1998 when he left the country. Others in the same style were framed in his apartment. The boxes also contained 8 mm videocassettes that he recorded of weddings, landscapes, genocide investigations, and conservation experiments from 1995 to 1997. And there were other ephemera, including a copy of the monthly journal published by the Rwandan Department of Defense. His investigations and interest in preserving genocide memory were the subject of a Kinyarwanda feature article in 1996. Mario spoke fondly of Louis (as Louis later did, in his more reserved way, of Mario), often inspired by his photographs to tell stories of their friendship and work together.

The visual archive from which this book primarily draws comprises the personal archives of Louis and Mario, located in Rwanda and Chile, respectively. The majority of the photographs and videos in both archives were taken by Mario or by associates using his equipment.[3] The images document investigations of hundreds of mass graves, the work of preparing bodies and sites for memorialization, and interactions in some of the most trying circumstances. Louis's and Mario's notes and recollections are the only reason these vignettes are legible. In most cases, images from their personal archives were encased in envelopes that include contextual information, such as place names, dates, a brief mention of what most of the roll documents, and the name of the person who delivered the film to be developed in Kigali (figure 1.3). Inside are continuous strips of numbered photographic negatives (figure 1.4). As a result, we gain a sense of the temporal sequence of Louis's and Mario's teams' investigatory and curatorial work process. We also learn more about how they moved from site to site in their genocide investigations, where conservation experiments began, and how they evolved. But the experiences to which those images refer are incomprehensible without the stories and circumstances that Louis and Mario relayed.

The absence of Louis and Mario from current historiography on Rwanda's genocide memorialization is surprisingly complete. Even when Louis Kanamugire is mentioned, he is rarely identified as the lead author of the *Preliminary Report* and the government official in charge of early genocide heritage development and commemorations. He is often portrayed as a background bureaucrat. Mario Ibarra has only recently begun to be associated with genocide investigations and memorial curation in Rwanda.[4] This is despite his imprint throughout the CNLG documentation center: in handwritten comments on the *Preliminary Report*, as the coauthor of the *Genocide Sites Map* and the main creator of photographs that fill shelves of albums, and in receipts, budgets, and proposals for conservation strategies.[5] Most of the documents kept in the CNLG archive are from 1996–98, when Mario worked directly for the Rwandan government. But by then Mario had already been investigating sites, taking photographs, and experimenting with genocide site preservation for two years (beginning in June 1994 while working for the UN). This work preceded the formation of the Genocide Memorial Commission in October 1995. When Mario began working with Louis in mid-1995 (first seconded from the UN, then directly for the commission), they traveled throughout the country to document the genocide in photographs, witness testimonies, and their own descriptions of sites.[6] Louis summarized their findings in the *Preliminary Report*, which also included an index of the photographs that Mario took during those investigations. Alongside the photographs and report, they developed a field map that was later formalized as the *Genocide Sites Map*. That we have a synthetic—and demonstrably visual—account of the geography of genocide violence in Rwanda is the result of both Louis's and Mario's efforts. Today these artifacts' co-origins and relationships are forgotten in institutional memory and genocide historiography.

The genocide archive codeveloped by Mario and Louis was not merely concerned with documentation. They also produced prototypical approaches to preserving and conserving victims' remains and sites of killing—as genocide heritage. These, too, can be regarded through the lens of the archive, on two distinct but related registers. The first regards the creation of social, political, and interpretative order through spatial organization: the putting of things in their proper place. The second concerns the types of reparative actions that result from historical truth telling. Archivist Michelle Caswell resists the idea that archives are mere repositories for historical records. Instead, she sees archives as intimately involved in the work of memory justice: recovering histories of injustice and related forms of resistance—to inform present-day activism.[7] On this view, archives (especially those held by communities) protect minoritized groups' histories and generate justice movements; they inspire a dialogue between the past and present along with future possibilities. The work that Mario and Louis did to transform memories of the genocide into historiography is linked: Their truth telling aimed to create pathways for repair and empowerment.[8] This chapter reconnects the documents they produced: with each other, with the context of their making, and with the affective geographies of violence that they rendered intelligible. In doing so, it seeks to carry out its own work of repair.

This chapter also positions Mario and Louis as early historians of the genocide, working not only to compile evidence of atrocities across the country but also to transform traumatic experiences and memories into history—a more stable, impersonal, and widely recognized form of knowledge. Early investigations in and of

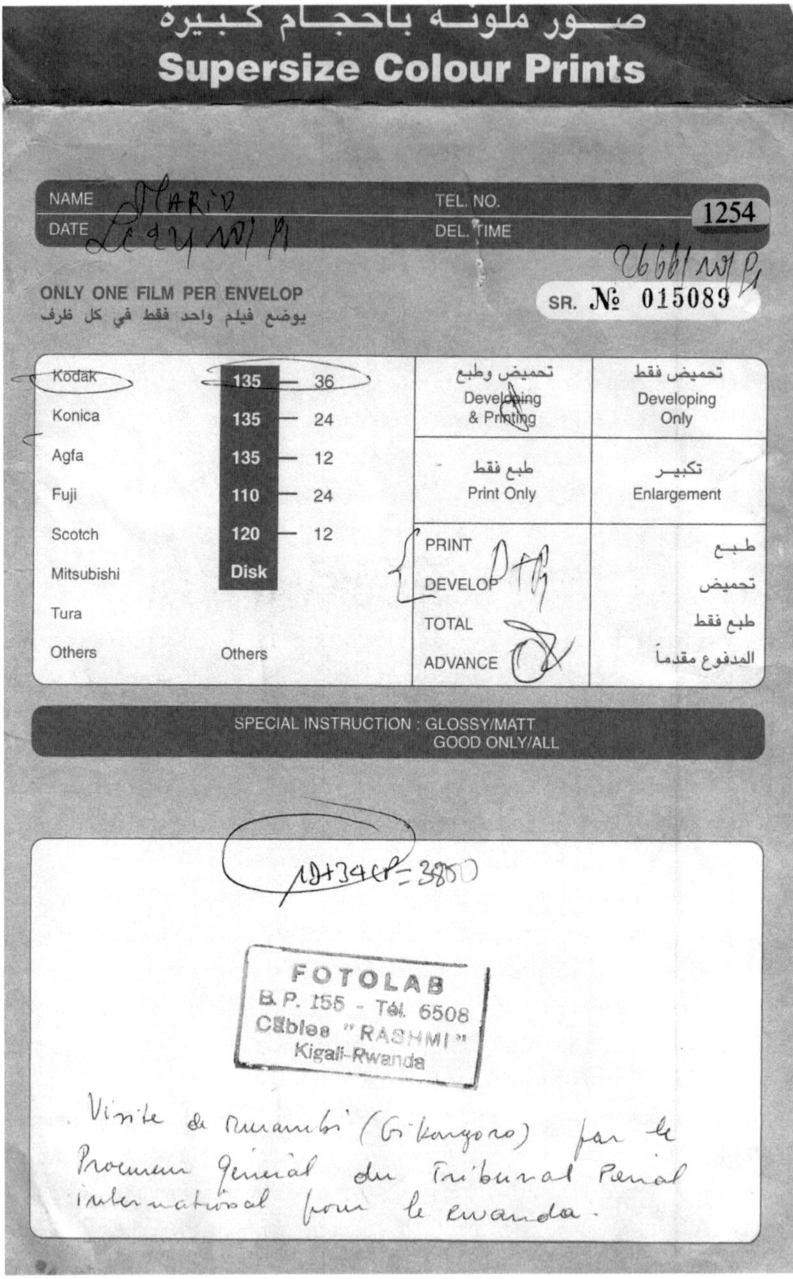


FIGURE 1.3. Envelope of photographs taken by the Genocide Memorial Commission with the negatives' development date (October 24, 1996), contact person (Mario [Ibarra]), identification number (1254), and notes on contents. Photo by Delia Duong Ba Wendel, Kanamugire archive, Rwanda.

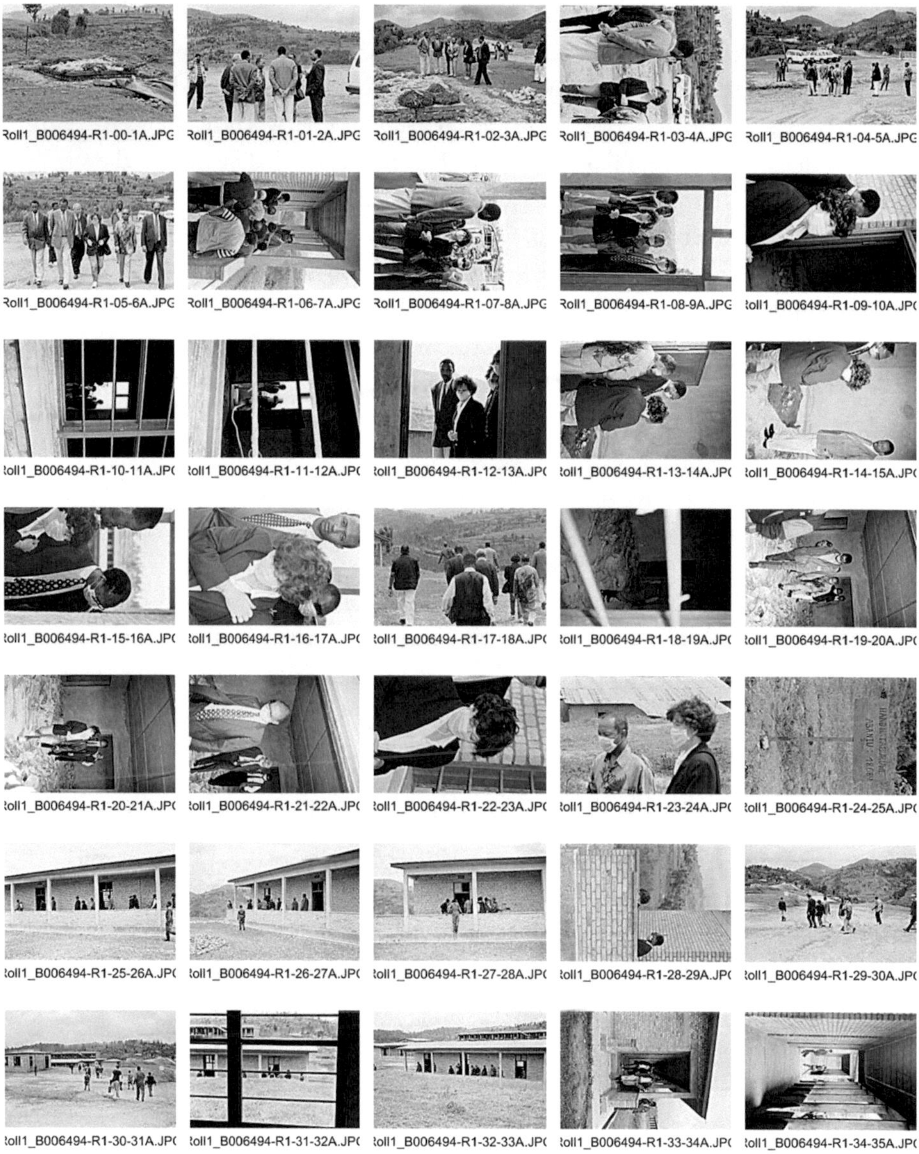


FIGURE 1.4. Contact sheet for photographic negatives from envelope 1254 documenting the United Nations International Criminal Tribunal for Rwanda's Murambi massacre site visit, led by Louis Kanamugire for the Genocide Memorial Commission, October 1996. Photos by Mario Ibarra, Kanamugire archive, Rwanda.

mass graves drew on the legitimizing power of systematic methods and visual and descriptive objectivity. Through the *Genocide Sites Map* and *Preliminary Report* in particular, Mario and Louis generated a rational, serial, and distanced approach to representation in the very moment that the genocide itself was being apprehended.

But these forms of representation were also personal. The archive they assembled can be seen as a starting point for understanding core tensions that run throughout this book. Like genocide heritage itself, this archive deploys dehumanizing representational forms in the name of human rights and grapples with the irreconcilable demands of human remains treated as evidence (displayed to establish truth) and as deceased persons (removed from sight out of decency and respect). The images and sites were not merely recorded and preserved for a historical record; they were intended to have impacts on the world, in real time. Genocide heritage was initially mobilized to convince foreign states that a genocide had occurred, that the violence was not a "mere African conflict."[9] Mario and Louis employed conservation, photography, and cartography as forms of truth telling that had a dual purpose as acts of repair—as means to witness injustice and initiate forms of redress. Yet we can see the paradoxes in Louis's and Mario's reparative historiography. We see the ways in which their earnest and objective documentation of the genocide was laden with resolute outrage and deep compassion. Their practices of repair were not restrained to writing. Mario and Louis sought to restore, not only to history but also to social landscapes, the people who had been erased by the genocide, to make the brutal crimes demonstrably evident. For survivors and relatives of victims, however, the material presence of the dead in the communities in which they live comes with indescribable pain. The individuals doing this memory work felt these conflicts deeply and personally.

The experiences of Mario and Louis themselves represent one major gap in the historical understanding of Rwanda's genocide heritage, which has been filled only through discussion and correspondence with them over the course of ten years. Rather than seeking to tell a story of investigatory triumph, I note Louis's and Mario's initial reticence to disclose details of genocide memory work and their roles in it to underscore their care and humility. Louis's and Mario's routes to memory work in Rwanda followed institutional pathways as well as personal commitments. Their earliest efforts to document massacre sites took place in a context of ongoing violence and attempts by perpetrators to hide and destroy the evidence of crimes. The precarity and vulnerability of the sites lent urgency to their work, mingling with the emotions and burdens that were sublimated in the records they produced. Their engagements were instead born from exceedingly cautious and traumatizing efforts to reveal the brutal details of mass violence, in the context of significant insecurity. That the conserved massacre sites, the photographs, the *Genocide Sites Map*, and the *Preliminary Report* are all linked—that they complement each other as aspects of genocide heritage and that they were coauthored by Louis and Mario—is an important historical clarification. But more important, I think, are the reparative ambitions and practices of their historiography.

When we listen to the *why* of their work, we hear much more than genocide histories. We feel the grief, rage, dedication, and kinship that animate their efforts in repair. As I was leaving Mario's home for the last time in 2015, he asked me to convey something through the history I was attempting to write. Speaking in Spanish, the language of his emotions, through which he recalled his many memories of Rwanda, he said, "*Pequeña* [a term of endearment], I never thought that other people would know of my Rwanda—about how it was to be in the *fossas* [mass graves]. This history is very important because it tells the story of the suffering of humanity, so that it will never happen again. This is an important battle. If you were to remember only two things—just two things from our conversations—please let it be *el olor y el dolor*."[10]

*El olor y el dolor* translates as "the smell and the pain." It refers, quite literally, to the stench of death and the wrenching sadness and anger that came from being among the bodies of victims. The smell and the pain refer, moreover, not to a discrete site but to knowledge of countless traumatic memories embedded in the landscape. Mario employed the phrase to emphasize what it felt like—both physically and emotionally—to document killing sites and interview survivors and witnesses throughout the country. Those affective experiences form the substrate of Louis's and Mario's reparative history. They are the substance, the ethical imperative, of the actions they hoped would result from their work.

## Reparative History

The case for repair necessarily begins with a historical accounting of the harms that forms of reparation might redress. This outsized task is typically not simply an act of archival retrieval. It is a rather more challenging endeavor in historical reconstruction. Documenting acts of violence is notoriously difficult, especially when crimes are committed by those in power, when evidence is occluded and unrepresented in official archives. It is, moreover, an accounting of individual and cultural trauma, an emotionally wrenching history of the present.[11] Reparative histories such as these are not all instrumental, nor oriented solely to prosecutions or individual compensation.[12] They carry a broader charge: a moral imperative to correct the historical record and, in the process, support a wide imaginary of forms of community repair. Such histories are reparative, in anthropologist David Scott's view, when they reconstruct "evil and unjust pasts in ways that potentially enable us to rethink the moral responsibility that the present owes in respect of them."[13]

Where Scott emphasizes the ethical stakes of such endeavors, historian Catherine Hall *practices* a reparative history. In the Legacies of British Slave-Ownership Project, Hall created an archive to track diffuse traces of racial capitalism evident in material wealth generated from enslavement.[14] In doing so, she followed "the money and the people" to make "visible the legacies of slave ownership, excavating what has been suppressed and marginalized, [and] re-inscribing the slavery business in modern British history."[15] The project's archival database resurfaces and reorganizes existing historical evidence as source material for a history that enacts repair. Hall's aim was not only to correct the omissions of slavery and colonialism in British national histories and social consciousness.[16] It was also to identify those who were responsible for and have benefited economically from historical and ongoing racialized violence. Hall's practice of reparative history preserves knowledge of harms—and their beneficiaries—to connect archival work to the aspirations of communities in need of redress. Reparative histories that are oriented to repair—that go beyond merely correcting the historical record—reshape social relations with a recognition of past wrongs. They provide justifications for future course correction and material forms of restitution.

Without such relationships between historiography and action, reparative histories risk being read as performative. This was historian Walter Johnson's warning when commenting on the historiographical turn to recenter the agency, knowledge, and experiences of historically marginalized individuals.[17] While sympathetic to the effort, Johnson cautions against the rhetorical posturing of histories disclosed in "closed circuit" conversations comprising only historians and their audience. The outcome is an insular, self-congratulatory commiseration on "the knowledge that they [historians] have transcended the past" rather than meaningful engagements in modes of redress.[18] In contrast, Hall's work exemplifies a reparative history that seeks societal impacts, that has shaped public histories and awareness of social responsibility. Johnson and Hall would likely agree that the purpose of such an endeavor is not to remake history for history's sake. Rather, the task of a reparative history is, returning to Scott, to rethink the moral responsibility that the present owes in respect of unjust pasts: to do something about ongoing forms of exploitation, incarceration, and oppression in the present.

This book is concerned with trauma heritage as a practice of reparative history. Attending to the work of Louis and Mario, it aims to understand how historical representation enacts repair and the challenges inherent therein. Louis and Mario effectively extend the views of Scott, Hall, and Johnson. They innovate on the form that reparative histories take by "writing" them into landscapes. Louis's and Mario's turn to the conservation of genocide evidence—in places, maps, and images—aimed to locate and make visible a history of violence. That historiography developed outside of academic circles, in living communities, and aimed to have real social impacts at both local and global scales. Making and receiving those histories of violence was agonizingly difficult. What Louis's and Mario's work demonstrates, more so than that of most other historians, is the deeply human dimensions—the emotional and affective labor—that are part of the practice of reparative history.

Trauma heritage is a strategic practice of reparative history. The turn to spatial, rather than oral or written, representation is a tactical circumvention of the normalization of violence and the suppression of related evidence. Trauma heritage demonstrates the reality of violence in public space. In making public space for silenced pain, trauma heritage declares the existence—the value—of those disappeared, harmed, and killed. It bolsters the memories of those individuals and injustices. It is not that written histories have no utility. Instead, the amplifying effects of emplacement and visualization respond to both the urgency of crimes' erasure and their persistent nonacknowledgment. Spatial representation is a critical communication tactic.

Trauma heritage also takes spatial form to inspire local responses. Trauma heritage manifests the location or material evidence of harms. It becomes a defiant representation of violence that resists normalization or concealment. Extending beyond representation, trauma heritage also seeks place-specific, reparative actions. Located in and experienced by living communities, as the trace, marking, or reconstruction of violence, it calls out for recognition and action. Making trauma heritage visible in public spaces elicits emotional and social connections. Its aim, as a result, is to enact forms of empowerment and repair for remembering communities.

For Louis and Mario, the spatial representation of genocide evidence transformed memory justice into a reparative historiography. Intrinsic to this move is not a devaluation of memory justice so much as an acknowledgment that historiography comprises a more widely recognized, and accepted, record of reality. Much of their work can be understood as an attempt to transform traumatic memories into history, to create an undeniable and authoritative form of knowledge from which the genocide would be more likely recognized. In doing so, they drew from marginalized evidence, including witness testimony, material traces and places of violence, and shared experiences of collective trauma. Louis's and Mario's reparative history established a place for the representation of those pasts, substantiated (and translated) testimonies by enabling people to experience and see evidence of crimes, and, through mapping, related instances of massacre to their occurrence at a national scale. In doing so, their turn to reparative history exceeded the mere representation of harms and injustice. Their work disrupted linear conceptions of time: The past persisted, uneasily, in place. The presence of the past sought to unseat dominant histories and cycles of oppression. Their approach to Rwanda's genocide heritage aimed to consider the future of the past as a reparative endeavor.

The durability of a reparative history written in landscapes, requiring encounter, opens the unruliness of repair initiated through trauma heritage. The recurring break between the making and the receiving, the life and the after, is the extended temporal site of intervention for reparative histories. It has to grapple with uneven afterlives, for repair is not instantaneous or easy work. Neither is it removed from corruptibility. Repair takes place within an extended temporality for which there is no horizon. It happens iteratively, with constant return, until perhaps victims and their descendants can be assured of rectification or that the violence they experienced will never happen again.

## Commitments and Pathways to the Work

Mario Ibarra never intended to be involved in genocide memorialization in Rwanda. A human rights expert from Chile, Mario first visited Rwanda in March 1994, one month before the genocide started. He traveled for the International Indian Treaty Council (IITC) investigations into violations of the Batwa Indigenous group's human rights. Mario began working for the IITC in January 1978 as an intern at their Geneva office while completing his undergraduate studies. A year prior, in 1977, Mario sought asylum in Switzerland after being subjected to torture and unlawful detention under Augusto Pinochet's dictatorship.[19] He subsequently earned a master's degree and recognition as an expert in international human rights protection and Indigenous rights and advocacy.[20] He served for several years as the IITC's permanent representative to the UN, a consultative status through which he participated in sessions of the Commission on Human Rights and the Sub-Commission on the Promotion and Protection of Human Rights (hereafter the Sub-Commission), a UN body tasked with studying human rights violations and discrimination, especially those affecting minorities, Indigenous peoples, and other vulnerable groups (figure 1.5).[21] Members of that consultative body are independent experts who make recommendations to the Commission on Human Rights. As a member of the Mapuche Indigenous community from territories now within Chile's borders, Mario was intimately familiar with land dispossession and targeted oppression. Indigenous rights were his most personal and enduring professional commitment, originating in a politics of his own identity and continuing in his scholarship and rural development work.[22] His personal experiences with structural and direct violence fundamentally shaped his professional engagements.

In May 1994, with violence related to the genocide fully underway, Mario left Rwanda to attend a UN meeting in Geneva; by this time, he was also concerned for his safety. He returned to Rwanda in June. He traveled to Switzerland again in August. Each of his travels to Europe was to attend meetings of the Sub-Commission, for which Mario was elected in February 1994 as an alternate representative of Chile (an alternate to José Bengoa) for a term of four years.[23] He held this post alongside his employment with the UN Human Rights Field Operation in Rwanda (HRFOR). His periodic travels to Geneva during 1994–98 provided a consistent conduit to relay his field observations in Rwanda to colleagues at UN headquarters.

When Mario returned to Rwanda in June 1994, his human rights work shifted from the capital, Kigali, to the east. Michele Wagner, a historian who trained under Jan Vansina (a renowned scholar of Central Africa at the University of Wisconsin), was then leading the HRFOR field office in Kibungo Préfecture in eastern Rwanda. She tapped Mario to join her there.[24] With field experience in Mozambique, Angola, Somalia, East Timor, Eritrea, Ethiopia, Guatemala, Bolivia, and Peru, along with his appointment to the Sub-Commission, Mario had earned a reputation as a seasoned and dogged human rights practitioner. Critically, however, he was not a forensic analyst or criminal investigator. Mario's expertise was instead shaped by personal experiences with injustice, including as a Mapuche and in Pinochet's Chile, and by professional skills learned in his postgraduate studies and work for the UN and IITC. When Wagner relocated to the HRFOR's Kigali headquarters in November 1994, she recommended that Mario take over her position as head of the HRFOR's Kibungo Préfecture field office.[25]

From the end of the genocide in July 1994 until April 1996, Mario investigated human rights violations in Rwanda for the HRFOR. His mandate primarily included investigating crimes related to the genocide but also those associated with the treatment of prisoners and Rwandan residents by the rebel army and the associated new postgenocide regime.[26] Genocide investigations entailed interviewing witnesses, locating and documenting hundreds of graves and killing sites in eastern and central Rwanda, and ascertaining who committed crimes, how, and who the victims were (to the extent possible). His work in Kibungo Préfecture, especially his quasi-forensic preservation of the Nyarubuye Parish massacre, garnered the attention of the new government in 1994. This led to his official secondment from the UN to the Rwandan Ministry of Higher Education, Scientific Research, and Culture (MINESUPRES) in mid-1995. The ministry established a new agency, the Genocide Memorial Commission, in October of that year. Thereafter, in a rare move for an international human rights worker, in April 1996 Mario chose to ter-

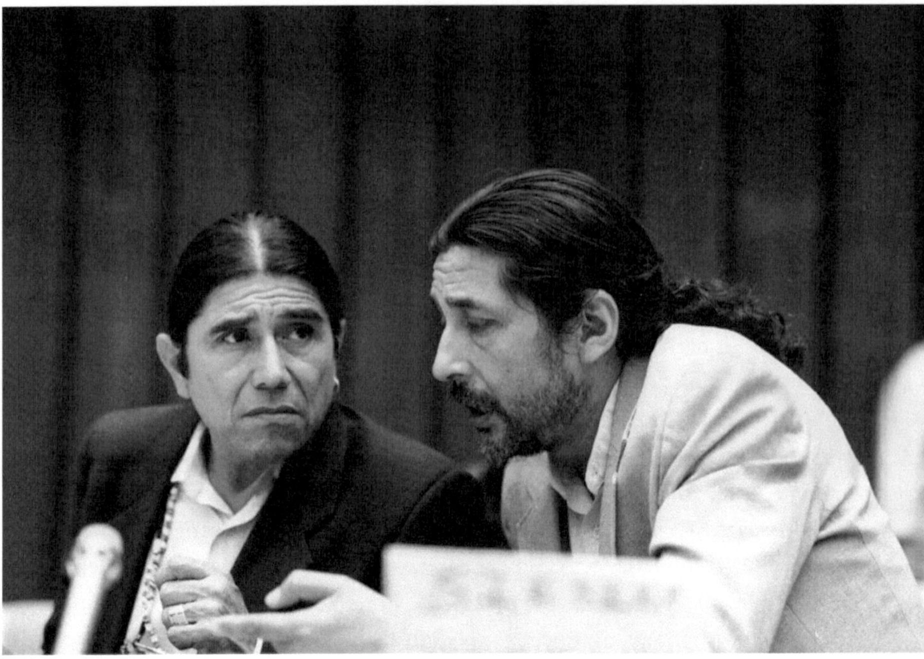

FIGURE 1.5. Mario Ibarra (*right*) speaks at a UN Commission on Human Rights session as the International Indian Treaty Council permanent representative (undated). Courtesy of Mario Ibarra, Ibarra archive, Chile.

minate his contract with the HRFOR to work directly for the Genocide Memorial Commission. Mario retained his position with the UN Sub-Commission and periodically attended meetings in Geneva through 1998. He continued working with the Rwandan Genocide Memorial Commission until March 1998, when he left the country for the last time.[27]

From mid-1995 to March 1998, Mario and Louis worked together to gather evidence of the genocide, curate memorials at killing sites, and organize reburial ceremonies. They were friends as well as colleagues. Their close relationship is evident in countless photographs of killing sites and conservation experiments. A particularly poignant series shows both men working at a long table in May 1996 (figure 1.6). The photographs capture the process of selecting items for display at an exhibition of genocide evidence, which the Genocide Memorial Commission organized at the Institut Français (French cultural institute funded by France's Ministry of Foreign Affairs) in Kigali. Wearing latex gloves, they examine photographs and artifacts from genocide sites. The images they hold in their hands, point to across the table, and examine through a magnifying glass are graphic but

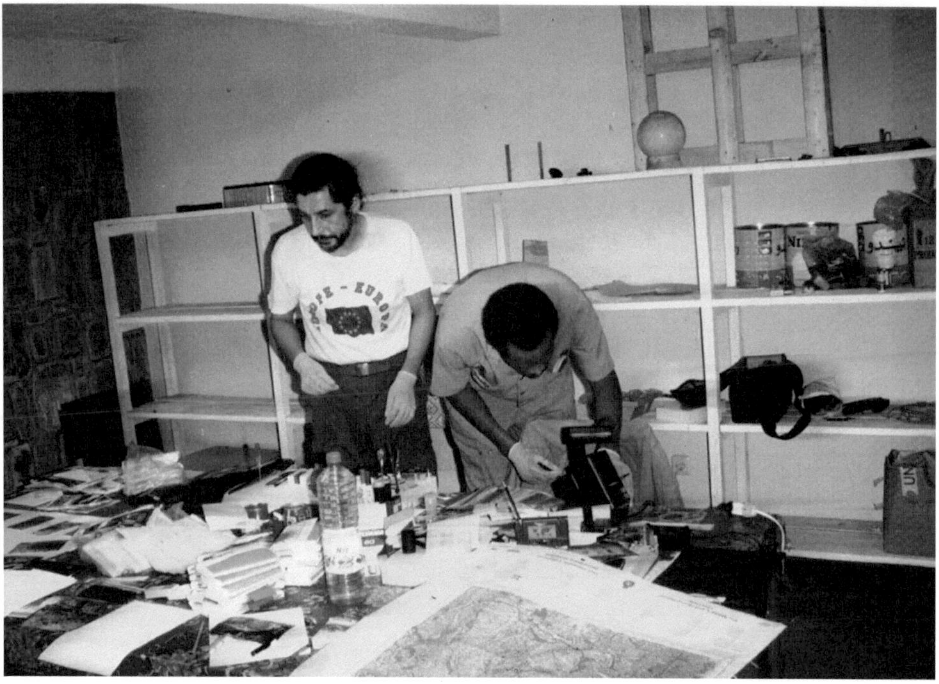

FIGURE 1.6. Mario Ibarra (*left*) and Louis Kanamugire prepare photographs, maps, and artifacts collected from genocide sites for display at their Institut Français exhibition in Kigali, 1996. Courtesy of Mario Ibarra, Ibarra archive, Chile.

familiar documentation of the killings they investigated. They are lost in seriousness but are also smiling, joking, and drinking beer. The scenes do not suggest any lack of respect for victims. Louis and Mario were both deeply committed to their work, fiercely defending it decades later. As I show in later chapters, the individuals who transformed massacre sites into memorials shared a rare intimacy. Their sociality in the context of this memory work was a means to reinforce their collective humanity amid the onerous task of confronting mass death.

Despite their close friendship, Louis and Mario had clearly defined work roles. Louis was in charge, as Mario noted in videos he filmed in 1995–97 and told me countless times in conversation. Louis was also the Genocide Memorial Commission's lead liaison to the central government, although the affiliations of the other six members of the task force that initially comprised the commission afforded access to other key ministries. As a government institution, the Genocide Memorial Commission had the authorizations necessary to conduct interviews and site investigations throughout the country in an insecure time. Because Louis was from Rwanda, he had more direct access to individuals' views. By contrast,

Mario, as a foreigner, relied on interpreters to make sense of what he heard. His was a close, though cautious, partnership with the Rwandan government. His HRFOR work to preserve the Nyarubuye massacre site inspired state memorialization practices and policy. Working alongside Louis, Mario was a source of technical expertise, contributing protocols and skills related to investigating genocide crimes (in witness interviews and at grave and massacre sites) and documenting what he found (in photographs and reports).

Although local resident groups and Mario's HRFOR team originally initiated genocide site preservation efforts in 1994, they did not have the financial capital or political authorization, let alone the workforce, to maintain and extend their work in the country. It was only with the support of government leaders that Louis, Mario, Dr. Célestin Kanimba Misago, and the workers they employed were able to further develop and formalize conservation techniques.[28] Many of the preservation and conservation approaches they developed from 1994 to 1998 were subsequently used at other memorial sites throughout Rwanda.

Louis was deeply private and preferred not to discuss his personal history.[29] The few details I mention are included in his draft memoir on the Genocide Memorial Commission. Prior to the genocide, Louis lived and worked in Burundi, where he had been in exile since 1966. In August 1994, a few weeks after the genocide ended, he returned to Rwanda. Louis worked for one year at UNESCO's Rwanda office, first as the head of the Sub-Commission on Culture, Humanities, and Social Sciences and later as the director of cultural heritage. While the UNESCO post exposed him to issues of heritage protection, the majority of his time there was more narrowly focused on education, his area of expertise. Like many employees of the new government after the genocide, Louis was selected to direct the Genocide Memorial Commission because he had university qualifications and some professional experience in related work and was also physically available.

Although his appointment as the director of the Genocide Memorial Commission was largely opportune, Louis considered it his civic duty to educate Rwandans and foreigners about what had occurred during the 1994 genocide. His larger dedication to pedagogy is significant in understanding his steadfast belief in the value of making history known. While in exile in Burundi, Louis taught philosophy, history, French, and geography for two decades in the secondary school system. These subjects are material to Louis's own approach to genocide memory curation, rooted in place-based historical representation in service of justice and the restoration of humanity. Improving school-age children's proficiencies in reading and writing was a primary focus of his work in the latter part of his career with MINESUPRES and in the private sector after 2011. Before and after his government work, Louis was the president of the Burundi Association of French Instruction

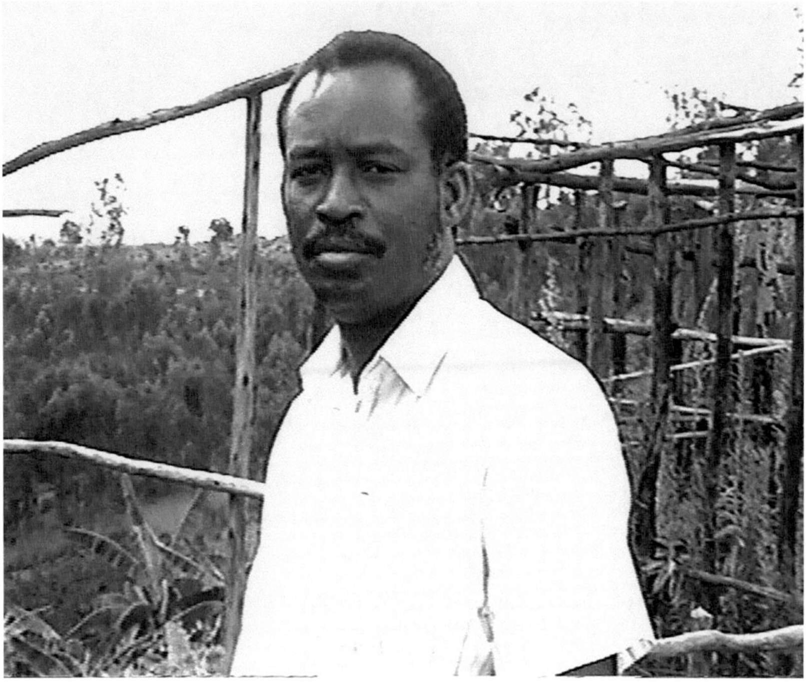

FIGURE 1.7. A video still from an interview Mario Ibarra recorded with Louis Kanamugire, who explained the rationale behind the conservation of victims at Murambi. Mario Ibarra, "Pepe (2)," video recording, June 6, 1997, cassette C44B6223, at 5:54, Ibarra archive, Chile.

and a founding organizer of several private schools there and in Rwanda. In these roles Louis valued teaching as a professional and civic responsibility.

Louis's commitments to the Genocide Memorial Commission were also deeply personal. In a 1997 video recorded at the Murambi genocide site, he stands uncomfortably in front of the camera, shifting his weight and looking off into the distance (figure 1.7). Mario is in the background and calls out to Louis in French, "Would you like to say a few words about the work that you, or we, do?" Mario was filming a series of video messages for José Bengoa and the UN Sub-Commission.

Louis begins, "We are here to see Murambi near Butare. It was a genocide site. We have been trying to identify and develop techniques for long-term conservation. I am with Mario Ibarra, who works for the Genocide Memorial and Massacres Commission. We have begun work in these 'slaughterhouses' to see how we can conserve material evidence long-term. What we are hoping to do now is to continue this work in the entire country. We want to know what happened and who committed genocide—

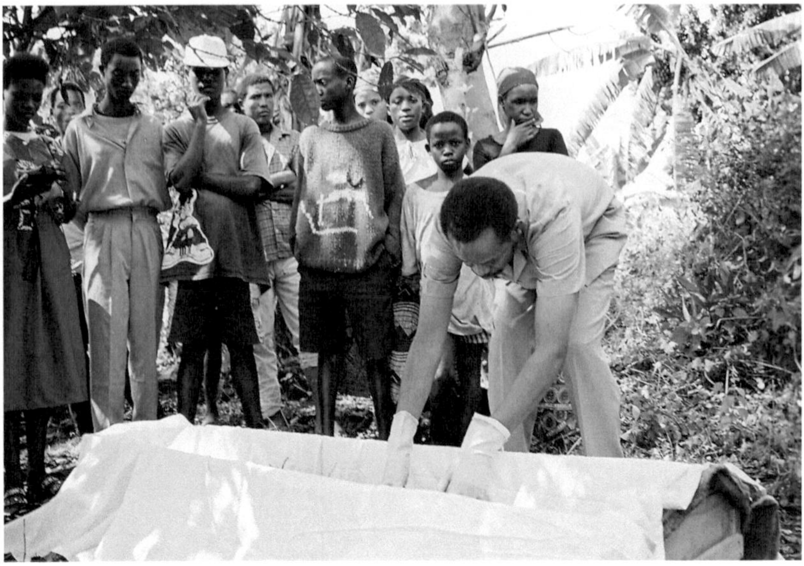

FIGURE 1.8. Aided by Mario Ibarra and local residents, Louis Kanamugire recovers the remains of his parents for reburial, western Rwanda, June 1996. Photo by Mario Ibarra, Kanamugire archive, Rwanda.

and to know this for each of the *préfectures* where more than two thousand people died."[30] Louis speaks deliberately and formally in French. He is a representative of the government describing the situation in Rwanda to a foreigner, with care, it seems, to present a factual and objective account.

Louis pauses. He then concludes his remarks with intensity: "Between April and July 1994, the country lost around one million people who were massacred and killed. They were innocent victims—killed in barbarous acts—by *génocidaires* who were aided by the former government and foreign powers." The camera lingers on his face for a few moments. He looks straight at the camera and then glances down to the ground. We hear the loud sounds of a motorcycle engine in the background. The video cuts to the inside of a building at Murambi that shows the results of conservation experiments. Several mummified bodies are displayed on high wooden tables.

Louis's fairly dispassionate and even scientific description of his team's conservation efforts quickly gave way to a bitter condemnation of the brutality of the genocide and those responsible. In that moment, we understand this violence not as some abstract concept or distant historical event. The genocide was deeply tied to personal experience (figure 1.8). Several of his family members, including his parents, were killed during the genocide. Louis felt his words.

Louis came to this work seeking justice for genocide victims and those, like himself, who had experienced structural discrimination as Tutsi in Rwanda. Born in Kibuye Préfecture in western Rwanda at the end of the colonial period, Louis reached university age under the first postindependence regime. He qualified for entry in the well-regarded National University of Rwanda in Butare but was not permitted to attend because of his Tutsi ethnicity. The prohibition exemplified the oppression that he and others like him endured on a daily basis. It was the last straw that forced Louis into exile. In 1966 he sought higher education in the nearby Democratic Republic of the Congo and Burundi. His experiences growing up in Rwanda and in a politically organized expatriate community in Bujumbura drew him to membership with the Rwandan Patriotic Front (RPF) in 1988. That affiliation also brought him back to Rwanda after the genocide, where he worked for the new RPF-dominated government. Both his teaching and his personal history drove the strident ethical sensibility that Louis brought to his directorship of the Genocide Memorial Commission in 1995.

Both Louis Kanamugire and Mario Ibarra helped to shape how and why state genocide memorials display the bodies and bones of the dead at sites of killing. They served as intermediaries between residents who organized early on to retrieve and care for victims' bodies and those in the national government who were authorized to make decisions. Louis and Mario also drew from their particular expertise in education and human rights practice, respectively, to conserve evidence of genocide massacres and curate those sites as memorials. As a result, they demonstrated what was possible to high-level state officials. They were not the only individuals pushing genocide heritage forward. However, they had pivotal on-the-ground roles in attempting to figure out what form it might take. In doing so, they grappled with central paradoxes: the diverging politics and ethics of genocide heritage and its unavoidably personal impacts.

In this context, Mario's and Louis's efforts to document and preserve evidence of the genocide—in the sites themselves, photographs, the *Preliminary Report*, and the *Genocide Sites Map*—attempted to make sense of difficult-to-know and seemingly senseless circumstances. In the first years after the genocide, those details were revealed primarily through encounters with the dead and information from the few available witnesses. Figure 1.9 shows a photograph from one of Mario's 1994 HRFOR investigations of a mass grave in Kibungo Préfecture; Louis and Mario selected it for the 1997 Institut Français genocide exhibition in Kigali.[31] For them, the image was emblematic of the work needed to document the genocide. I turn to it to illustrate the formative influence that Mario's HRFOR investigative method had on viewing, and locating, Rwanda's genocide heritage.

Mario and his HRFOR team found the site in the photograph with the help of local residents who suspected that there was a mass grave in the area. He typically worked with between four and eight individuals to locate genocide victims, document the sites, ascertain the manners in which they died, and, where possible, determine the identities of victims and perpetrators. They were often accompanied by local authorities or members of the military (figures 1.10 and 1.11). It was challenging because evidence had frequently been destroyed—by perpetrators who wished to hide their crimes, residents who returned to their fields to resume farming, local government officials who buried victims, and the passage of time.

At the mass grave, Mario first identified the extent of the disturbed earth, brushing the soil aside to reveal the edges of a tarp the killers had used to cover the hole. Soil had been thrown over the top to disguise the grave's location. He dug into the loose ground, uncovered a mass of bodies at the bottom, and pulled them out of the ground. A photograph (figure 1.9) shows Mario standing over a pile of the dead: Bloated bodies are barely discernible from each other and the layer of wet, soil-covered clothes that clung to all of them. He is wearing a face mask to filter particulates and the smell. Other photos of genocide investigations show him with pipe in hand; the fragrant tobacco helped to mask the stench (figure 1.12).

After the bodies were pulled from the ground, they were separated. The HRFOR team worked to catalog their gender, approximate age, location and size of wounds, and personal belongings. At this time in Rwanda, there was no possibility of DNA analysis—due to the number of dead and the lack of technology and funds—so most investigations could not conclusively identify victims. Still, relatives would often accompany the team and watch them work. Where possible, the HRFOR team tried to identify the residents' family members or neighbors from recognizable clothing or discernible physical features in skeletal structure. Killing instruments were also retrieved, cataloged, and stored as evidence.

Mario reiterated the importance of teamwork in all aspects of his genocide investigations. That work demanded immense physical labor and emotional endurance. But though they faced the challenges of sites together, team members bore the emotional tolls of their work alone and in diverse ways. Listing common reactions, Mario recalled, "There was the colleague that cried in her room, the colleague that could not get up from his room, the colleague that would not eat meat again because of what they saw, those that would pray, and those that drank."[32] Rwandans' firsthand experiences of violence and loss were considerably more jarring and upending than those of foreigners.

Mario spent an inordinate amount of time working within mass graves. He reflected on his struggles:

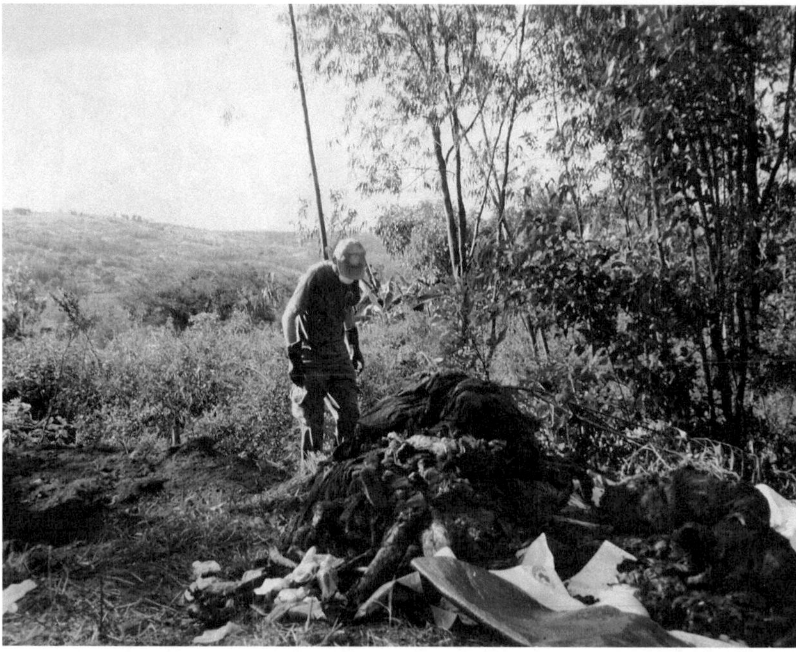

FIGURE 1.9. Mario Ibarra investigates and exhumes a mass grave site hidden in a tree grove as part of the UN HRFOR, Kibungo Préfecture, 1994. Courtesy of Mario Ibarra, Ibarra archive, Chile.

> One way to proceed is with many tears, crying all the time. The other is to bring an aseptic manner, without any sentiment [draws on paper to mimic taking notes during his investigations], to note what's here, to take the stories, and three to four photos. This was my way, because on one hand I was angry that there was no memory or path to justice. How would it come? I did not believe we should cry because of these experiences and conversations. There were things to do—to take testimonies, look for the motives [for the killings], and justice—both Rwandan and international. That was how I coped with this situation: to provide an idea of what happened.[33]

The rational proceduralism of his work—and its reparative ambitions—was Mario's way of processing traumatizing experiences. It resulted from his moral commitment to account for the dead. And yet, ultimately, making sense of the genocide was impossible. Reflecting in 2015, Mario told me that the longer he did that work, the more his doubts expanded, particularly in regard to the possibility of "knowing" the genocide with any certainty. The way he elaborated on this one day was

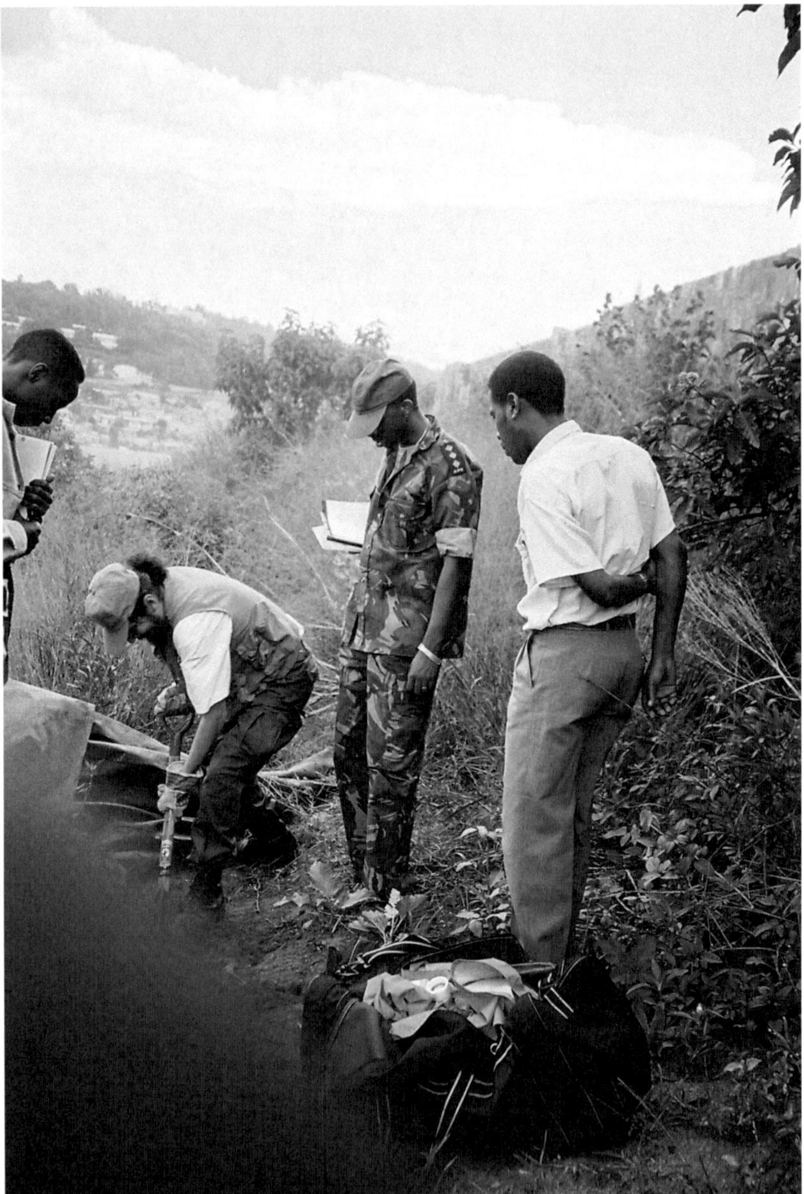

FIGURE 1.10. Mario Ibarra investigates a suspected mass grave outside Kigali with his UN HRFOR team and the Rwandan military observing, 1994. Courtesy of Mario Ibarra, Ibarra archive, Chile.

## HIRYA NO HINO

bahungira muri za Irani n'Uburusiya. Ubwo rero baziraga ko bari igitotsi hagati y'Abaturikiya,

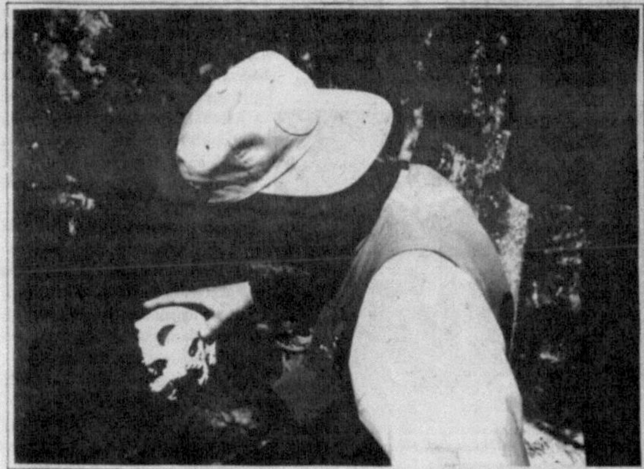

*Mario IBARRA: Umwe mu banyamahanga bashavujwe n'itsembabwoko.*

guhera muri 1908. «Interahamwe» zaho zari zimeze nka CDR bitaga «Ittihad» maze sinakubwira birara muri abo banyarumeniya barararika. Byasubiriye muri Silisiya, agace kamwe ka Armeniya, aho bishe 300.000 muri 1909. UBwo abandi bazungu cyane cyane b'i Burayi bica amatwi, bati biragayitse gusa. Uburusiya ndetse n'ibihugu by'Aziya birahigima. ng'uko kwa kudahana icyo kubyara.

Nk'uko tuzi ko abantu biyemeza gukora itsembabwoko bari bananiwe kubona umuti w'ibibazo ahubwo bagahungira mu kubihererezaho abandi no gushaka kubamara, ubwo Abaturukiya bari bambuwe hose mu duce bari bafite ku Burayi. Akagabo kitwaga Enver kajya muri Kokaze (Caucase) kati murwanye Abarusiya, naho kashakaga uko kica Abanyarumeniya Uburusiya burebera.

Muri 1915, abasirikare b'Abanyarumeniya bari mu ngabo z'Abaturiki bambuwe intwaro. Urwitwazo ari uko ngo hari Abanyarumeniya bafasha Abarusiya kurwanya Turikiya. Twibuke ko ibi byabaye mu ntambara ya mbere y'isi yose ubwo Abafaransa n'Abongereza bari mu ntambara barwanya Abadage, Abanyatrushe (Austria) n'Abaturiki. Ubwo rero babonye akanya ko kumaraho ntawe ubyitayeho.

Ku itariki ya 7/04/1994 mu Rwanda, isa na 24/04/1915 muri Armeniya, ni bwo itsembabwoko ryatangiyeyo maze abanyabwenge, abasirikare, abantu bose bari hagati y'imyaka 20 na 40. Ku ya 30/07/1915 nibwo byari bihosheje ariko bishe abantu nka miliyoni ebyiri. Tariki ya 10/02/1920 nibwo habayeho agace bise Armeniya. Bisa n'uko ino nyuma y'amahano kuri 19/07/1994 hagiyeho Guverinoma y'ubumwe mu Rwanda.

Ubu rero Abanyarumeniya basandaye ku isi yose kandi n'ubu baracyahagwa nyuma y'imyaka 80! Abuzukuru babo bamwe baba muri Amerika abandi i Burayi ariko hari udusigisigi tuba muri Aziya. Ntibataye umuco, idini baracyashakana hagati yabo. Benshi baragira bati «Itsembabwoko ryatubayeho risa n'iryanyu» kuko nta bucamanza, ubutabera bwigeze bubaho kuri twe. Twizere ko ibyacu bitazasa n'ibyabo n'ubwo na byo bigenda buhoro kuko ibihugu byose birebera abateguye itsembabwoko bigendera. Ariko hari abariho bagerageza bari bakwiye kubera urugero abandi.

Twizere ko umuntu kuba ari ikirura kuri mugenzi we,bizagera ubwo bishira!

***Capt. Firmin GATERA.***

INGABO N° 010 Werurwe 1996 Page.33

FIGURE 1.11. The Rwanda Ministry of Defense journal, *Ingabo*, features an article on Mario Ibarra's work for the HRFOR, March 1996. The photo's Kinyarwanda caption reads: "Mario IBARRA: One of the foreigners deeply affected by the genocide." Firmin Gatera, "Hirya no Hino," *Ingabo* 10 (March 1996), 33 (translated by author), Ibarra archive, Chile.

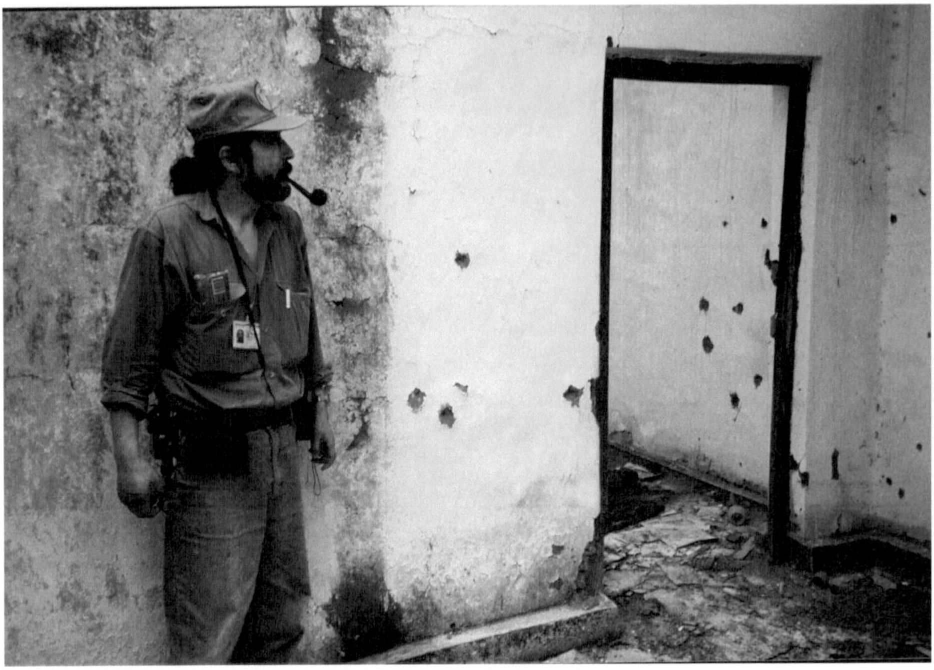

FIGURE 1.12. Mario Ibarra smokes a pipe to mask the stench of a killing site, Kigali, 1994. Courtesy of Mario Ibarra, Ibarra archive, Chile.

helpful to understanding what he meant: "I never accepted the *blanquitos* [white people] who arrived in Rwanda and, at the moment that they put their feet on the ground of the airport, knew the causes of the genocide, the effects of the genocide, and the solutions for the genocide! I lived there for four years, in the mass graves, speaking with people, and I still don't understand the causes, the origins, the consequences, the effects, and why."[34]

For Mario, repair and justice entailed, from one mass grave to the next, from one killing site to another, dogged work "to provide *an idea* of what happened." It was fundamentally opposed to the assumptions and totalizing views of most foreign aid workers—and the epistemic imperialism of the *blanquitos*—which delivered simplified, and fundamentally racialized, explanations and solutions for the mass violence that had occurred. It was dizzying work, burdened by what it felt like to see and touch the dead, to represent victims and name killers.

In the midst of the uncertainties and distressing experiences of Rwanda's aftermath landscape, Mario and Louis contributed evidence of the genocide: in situ, in images and films, and in a representation of its geography. With the exception of the International Criminal Tribunal for Rwanda (which was established only in November 1994), visual documentation of genocide sites was not a priority for other NGOs and HRFOR teams (see chapter 2).[35] It was expensive, required equipment, and was not the primary focus of most organizations' work, which was to collect the testimonies and observations of potential witnesses. If there was a fundamental perspective that shaped Mario's approach to genocide documentation, it was his intimacy with a personal and global geography of violations of the rights of individuals and groups, and the erasures of those histories of violence by those with power. Those experiences and commitments were mirrored by Louis and others involved in this work. By holding material evidence still, Mario and Louis rendered genocide sites as manifest evidence to communicate pain, violence, and injustice resoundingly outward. Such an approach understands the visual and spatial registers as powerful, and necessary, alternatives to the difficulty of representing violence.[36]

## The *Genocide Sites Map* and *Preliminary Report*

The excesses of incomprehension, acutely understood in the *olor y dolor* of killing sites and mass graves, drove Mario and Louis to render their experiences of the genocide aftermath sense-able. The photographs, conserved sites, *Preliminary Report*, and *Genocide Sites Map* that resulted have previously been understood as distinct artifacts with little relation to each other except for their content and government sponsorship. Among them, the photographs and sites are similar in their visceral representation of the deaths that occurred, whereas the report and map present more systematic overviews of the genocide. Stripped of information about their place, time, and subject, the photographs remain relatively mute without an explanation of their contents. Similarly decontextualized, or otherwise minimally narrated, conserved genocide sites reproduce intense experiences of mass death, as mass death. The *Preliminary Report*, which collected data from every *préfecture*, reads as a seemingly undifferentiated list of atrocities. The *Genocide Sites Map* offers a critically comprehensive understanding of where killings took place but renders them as points of interest across a territory. Restoring the links among these written, spatial, and visual records of genocide investigations is critical to reinforming the denuded representations we have today. These sources were co-constitutive of each other: Each was intended to supplement the representational constraints of the other. Together they demonstrate that feeling and ordering, closeness and distance, are inseparable but opposed aspects of trauma heritage work.

Of the four types of archival evidence, the *Preliminary Report* (figure 1.13) and the *Genocide Sites Map* (figure 1.14) have a distinctly distanced approach to genocide representation, resulting from Louis's and Mario's efforts to transform

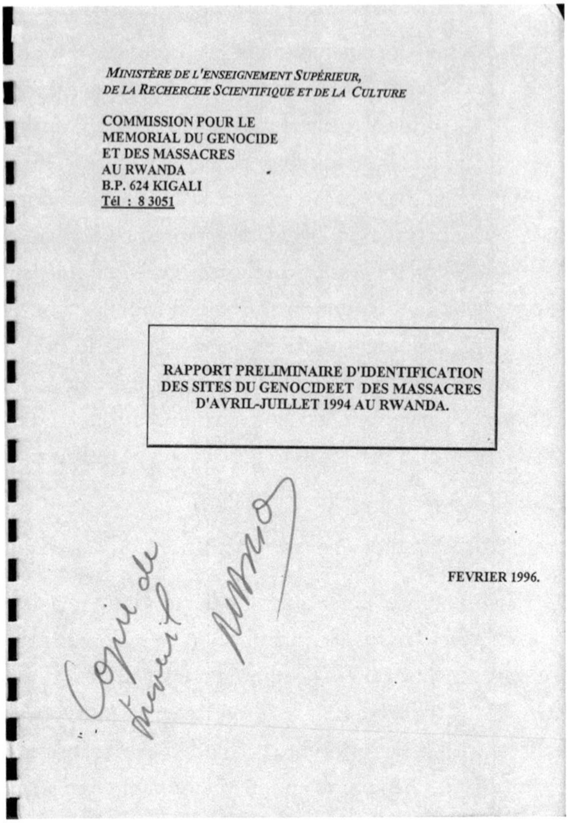

MINISTÈRE DE L'ENSEIGNEMENT SUPÉRIEUR,
DE LA RECHERCHE SCIENTIFIQUE ET DE LA CULTURE

COMMISSION POUR LE
MEMORIAL DU GENOCIDE
ET DES MASSACRES
AU RWANDA
B.P. 624 KIGALI
Tél : 8 3051

RAPPORT PRELIMINAIRE D'IDENTIFICATION
DES SITES DU GENOCIDEET DES MASSACRES
D'AVRIL-JUILLET 1994 AU RWANDA.

FEVRIER 1996.

FIGURE 1.13. Mario's "working copy" of the Genocide Memorial Commission's *Preliminary Report*, with red handwritten notes in French on the cover and throughout. Photo by Delia Duong Ba Wendel, Kanamugire archive, Rwanda.

genocide memory into objective history. The report and map were published in February 1996 and April 1997, respectively. Both sources originated as field notes and way-finding sketches from investigations that Mario and Louis conducted (independently and also together) from June 1994 to May 1996.

THE REPORT

The *Preliminary Report*'s writing is restrained and bureaucratic. We read Louis Kanamugire's voice, in French. In the report, Louis documented the genocide investigations conducted by the interministerial task force that comprised the Genocide Memorial Commission at its founding. Mario Ibarra was both a key task force

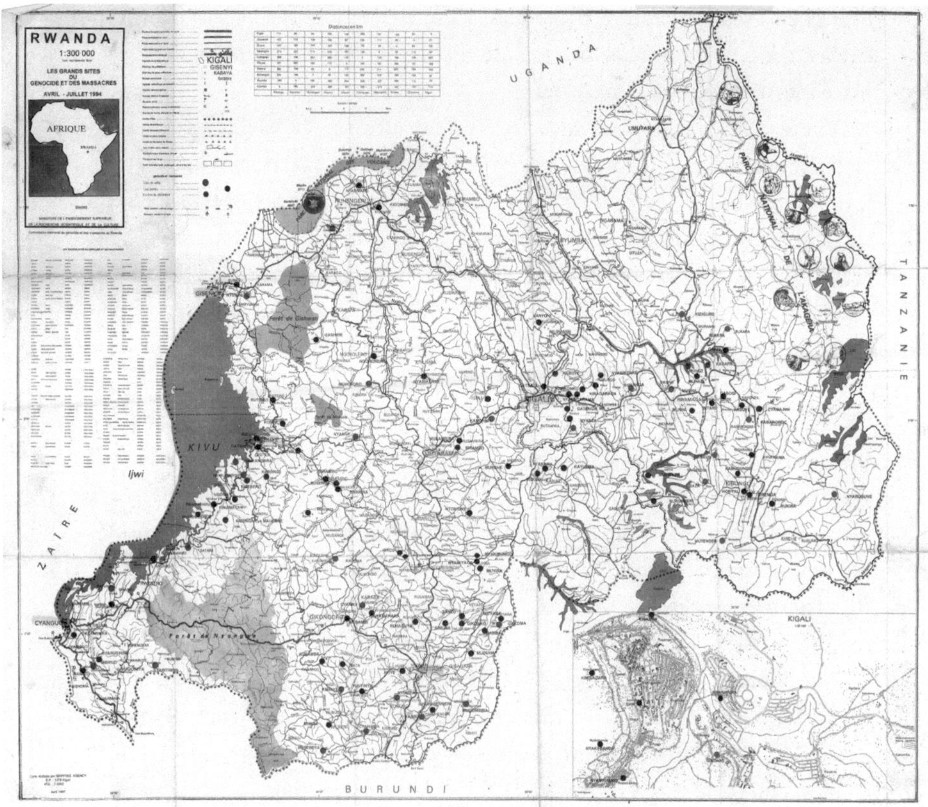


FIGURE 1.14. The third (and official) version of the *Genocide Sites Map*, printed by Captain Firmin Gatera and delivered by Mario Ibarra to colleagues in Geneva, Switzerland, in 1997. The map includes 118 locations coded in three colors: red for religious sites, blue for public places, and green for "hills of resistance" (defensive positions where people fought against their attackers). Courtesy of Marc Bossuyt, Belgium.

investigator and an adviser in the report's writing. Organized geographically by region, the *Preliminary Report* provides a site-by-site accounting of the number of people who died, those who survived attacks, the perpetrators and organizers of the killings, and the community members who protected the persecuted.

One of the entries in the *Preliminary Report* documents a location near Lake Muhazi in eastern Rwanda (which I introduce in the prologue). Louis's summary begins with a description of the killing site: "A mass grave about 12m deep and approximately 1.5m × 1.5m located 25m from the road crossing, one heading toward the Gishali Sanatorium and the other toward Muhazi Commune, on the property of well-known Smaragde Munyaneza. It was to serve as a septic pit. It had not yet been used. Nearby is a stone that still bears traces of blood."[37] Like so many other entries, the report begins with a technical and restrained account of an everyday place transformed into a mass grave.

The second paragraph in the entry is more arresting in its description: "The victims, some still living, were thrown into the pit. Children aged five years and less were first smashed against this rock, then thrown in the hole. The bodies had not been disinterred. The pit was covered with soil up to 2.5 meters below ground."[38] These spare few lines are burdened with the portrayal of a most horrendous scene. In the margins, Mario wrote "*details*," indicating that he and Louis had collected more information about the young victims, the manner in which they were killed, and perpetrators' identities that they should add to the terse entry. Their investigations included multiple trips to the mass grave in 1994–95 and the witness testimony of two adult survivors who narrowly escaped the attack and were unable to save the children. The *Preliminary Report* entry also indexes the photographs that Mario and colleagues took of the site. The image descriptions are similarly abbreviated, in stark contrast to what they saw: "Photos I, 26–27: Rock of torture and the interior of the pit. Photo I, 28: Rock of torture and surrounding area."[39]

The depiction of the killing site and mass grave near Lake Muhazi was not distinctive; the *Preliminary Report* catalogs hundreds of such sites in the same way. Each entry is predominantly structured by distant, scientific descriptions of the commission's findings. Periodically, almost as if Louis can no longer contain his contempt for the perpetrators and sorrow at the loss of so much life, more impassioned details make their way into his writing. In the above entry, Louis add details on the local government representative who was suspected of organizing the murders of the children on his property in 1994. He names him and his occupation, adding a chilling last sentence: "To the friend who came to seek refuge at his house, he [the genocide organizer] must have replied with a macabre quip, thanking him for coming to say goodbye before he died."[40] Louis's personal memoir of his first years working for the Genocide Memorial Commission is written similarly to the *Preliminary Report*.[41] Reading them together, I had the sense that the process of drafting summaries of genocide scenes was fraught with personal challenges. This is not to say that the veracity of the *Preliminary Report* should be questioned; as both Louis and Mario expressed earnestly, there were severe time and budgetary constraints on the investigations and writing. The report was as complete as they could achieve but not nearly as comprehensive as they wanted. Rather, it is to acknowledge all that had to be suppressed in the course of rendering the genocide into history, into a believable representation of excessive senselessness.

The original *Genocide Sites Map* was, as Mario told me, "not a map."[42] It was, instead, "only organized information."[43] Mario recalled that he and Louis began to mark locations and add field notes on a weathered and folded tourist's map of the country in late 1995.[44] Mario stored it in his boot during their investigations. It was not polished or formal, but it was nonetheless instrumental "to locate the testimonies, the points of interest that [residents] told us, and to know where to find the mass graves. It was ugly, but it worked! It was not a perfect document—we were sure it was not precise—but it was a good foundation for what [information] we could find at the time."[45] What began as a way-finding device to identify killing sites and mass graves throughout the country ended up being a key resource for developing a more comprehensive understanding of what happened during the genocide. Along the way, Louis and Mario annotated the map with quick observations from their investigations. In some cases, they noted the numbers of bodies found and the names of key local contacts. Elsewhere, they added directions for how to navigate to sites from main roads. One day, Mario distinctly remembers scrawling "*¿Qué puta ha pasado aqui?*" (What the f*** happened here?) on the map in frustration. Their copious notes quickly began to overwhelm the map's utility for navigation.

A second map, taped to a wall in Mario's home office in Kigali, provided means to distill the information gathered in the first. In that version, red marker was used to highlight seventy-six genocide sites that Mario and Louis considered significant because of the numbers of dead found, the type of place, or the manner of killing. They used it as a working aid to visualize the locations of significant massacres. Mario took photographs of it in May 1996 to chart his and Louis's progress (figure 1.15).[46] The timing of the photographs confirms that they were continuing to add and refine the sites selected to be representative of the genocide long after the Genocide Memorial Commission concluded its 1995 investigations and Louis wrote the *Preliminary Report* in early 1996. Moreover, in the first half of 1996, Louis and Mario were actively involved in some of the first experiments in conservation of genocide victims and sites, undertaken as part of the Genocide Memorial Commission. Their concurrent memorialization efforts on the ground and cartographic depiction of the killings demonstrate the importance they accorded to spatial representations of genocide history. It was paramount that a wider public read the witness testimonies and details of the massacres—but equally so that they *see* the killings, both up close and to understand their extent from a distance.

As soon as the second map was available to view, shifting from Mario's boot to the walls of his home office, it opened to politicization. Firmin Gatera was central to the map's transformation in this regard. An army captain in 1995 (previously a

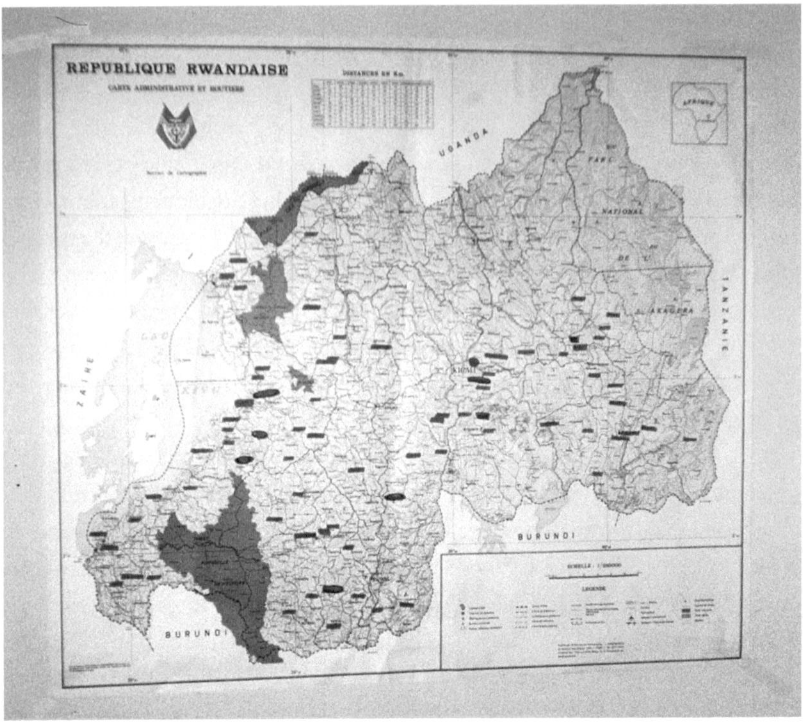


FIGURE 1.15. The second permutation of the *Genocide Sites Map*: a field map taped to the wall of Mario Ibarra's home in Kigali, May 29, 1996. Photo by Mario Ibarra, Ibarra archive, Chile.

high-ranking officer within the rebel Rwandan Patriotic Army), Gatera was the director of information and public relations for the Ministry of Defense within the postgenocide regime. In that role, he was one of the highest-ranking members of the interministerial task force that first comprised the Genocide Memorial Commission. Gatera's position within the Ministry of Defense provided authorizations for task force members, like Mario Ibarra, to travel throughout the country and conduct genocide investigations.[47] In late 1996 Gatera saw the second draft of the map hanging in Mario's house. He and Mario were friends and colleagues: They had already worked together on several investigations while Mario was with the UN. Gatera was also the editor of *Ingabo*, the Ministry of Defense journal, which featured Mario's work and photographs of genocide investigations in March 1996 (figures 1.11, 1.16, and 1.17). By Mario's telling, in late 1996 Gatera borrowed the map hanging on his wall to make a copy, claiming it was the most representative geographic index of the genocide that he had seen.

The final version of the *Genocide Sites Map* was created on instructions by Gatera, and by extension, the Rwandan Ministry of Defense. It had by then been significantly edited by Louis and Mario, who located 118 significant genocide sites that they categorized as one of three types: massacres that took place at religious sites, killings that occurred in public places, and key resistance efforts by communities under attack. Still, like the *Preliminary Report*, Louis and Mario felt their map to be woefully inadequate in representing the genocide. As Mario put it, "All of the places were more than could be contained by the map, and more than could be counted."[48] To produce and print the final map, Gatera used some combination of the US military demining team's equipment (to scan the large-format map) and facilities at the Rwandan government's mapping agency.[49] In the process, a smaller A4-sized version of the map was produced, which included a list naming all of the sites and a detailed inset on genocide sites in the capital, Kigali.

In 1997 Gatera printed three large copies of the reformatted map and gave them to Mario at the Kigali airport. Mario was traveling to attend the Sub-Commission meeting in Geneva. That meeting was convened in part to discuss the situation in Rwanda and weigh whether it should be categorized as a genocide. Mario showed the map to Sub-Commission members during meetings. He delivered one copy of the map to a representative of the High Commissioner for Human Rights on his request. He gave a second copy to Cardinal Giuseppe Bertello, then permanent observer of the Holy See to the UN (1995–2002) but previously the Apostolic Nuncio for Rwanda (1991–95). From his home in Butare in southern Rwanda, Cardinal Bertello had witnessed the civil war and the genocide that followed. But as he told Mario, he could only see what happened around him. The map provided him with a sense of the magnitude and geographic extent, beyond his limited view.[50] Mario gave the third copy of the map to Marc Bossuyt, a jurist and professor of law at the Université d'Anvers (University of Antwerp). Bossuyt was also a longtime resident of Rwanda who worked for the Belgian development agency in the 1990s and a fellow member of the Sub-Commission. From Belgium, Bossuyt sent me a scanned version of his copy of the map in 2015 and verified the details provided by Mario regarding its dissemination (figure 1.14). Bossuyt's copy confirms that the 1997 version printed by Gatera and carried by Mario to Geneva is identical to the large-format version circulating today.

Both the *Genocide Sites Map*'s medium as a visual representation and its expanded geography (produced in Rwanda for international distribution) were politically important as means to confirm and recognize what had occurred in Rwanda. Until 1998 the UN and its member states did not officially acknowledge that the violence of 1994 constituted a genocide.[51] Bossuyt documented the Sub-Commission debates and special rapporteur presentations to which he was privy.[52] He noted that

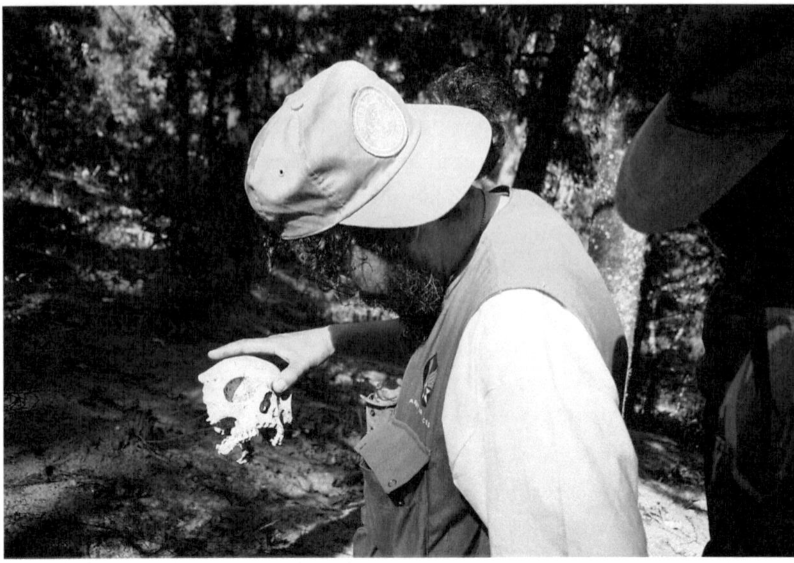

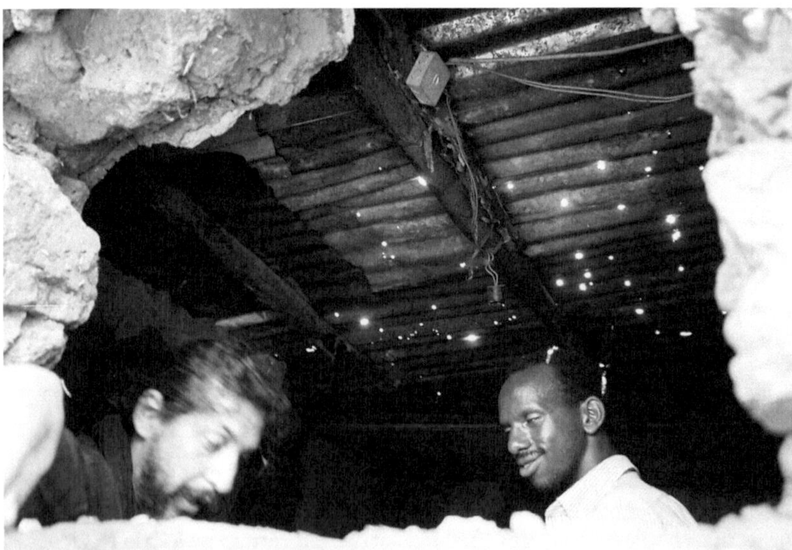

FIGURE 1.16. (*top*) Mario Ibarra investigates the genocide for the HRFOR, accompanied by the new governing regime's military, 1995. Courtesy of Louis Kanamugire, Kanamugire archive, Rwanda.

FIGURE 1.17. (*bottom*) Mario Ibarra and Captain Firmin Gatera investigate a killing site in Kigali, 1994. Courtesy of Louis Kanamugire, Kanamugire archive, Rwanda.

the UN's withholding of *genocide* from official declarations was internally disputed by officials conducting investigations in Rwanda, who repeatedly insisted that their findings merited that designation. The *Genocide Sites Map* was one of many mounting sources representing the incontrovertible evidence of genocide in Rwanda. The map's visual and cartographic modes of representation were critical to collect and geo-locate that evidence at a national scale. Gatera, with the prescience and savvy of the government's head of public relations, formalized and reproduced the original map so that Mario could distribute it in Europe for this express political purpose.

By contrast, the *Preliminary Report* was used as an evidentiary source primarily for judicial purposes. This was due in large part to its capacity to provide written summaries to locate places where the dead were found and gather related testimonies to identify organizers (and victims where possible) along with manners of death. It provided several courts with an extensive body of evidence. It was used to compile the Rwandan Supreme Court's August 1996 list of "First Category" perpetrators of the genocide (those identified as organizers and leaders). The report was also employed as prosecutorial evidence by the UN's International Criminal Tribunal for Rwanda.[53] Later, it provided background information for the 2002–12 National Service of the Gacaca Courts, a series of community-based trials that loosely followed customary practice.[54] The *Preliminary Report*'s use in these settings indicates both the overall dearth of genocide documentation in Rwanda and the document's continued significance.

## A Visceral Archive

The *Preliminary Report* and the *Genocide Sites Map* were Louis's and Mario's primary means of making sense: expanding from local knowledge to an account of the entire country and, in the process, translating the intensity of the smells, sights, and emotional weight of that aftermath landscape into a factual record. These sources, along with the photographs involved in their making and the conservation work Louis and Mario initiated at several sites, were created to archive the history of the genocide. In contrast to the report, the map is a spatial representation, one that establishes the reality of a genocide that took place. But for Mario and Louis, the map signifies much more. Dot after dot, the repetitive notation of genocide marks discrete experiences of injustice and massacre in Rwanda. Together these records constitute an experiential cartography of Rwanda's aftermath landscape: one traced inside countless mass graves and by the dead bodies they encountered. The map reverberates with the intensity of those experiences.

This is why, when I inquired into the politicized legacy of this memory work today, Mario's passionate indignation caused me to hold my breath. The *Prelim-*

*inary Report* and the *Genocide Sites Map* became political instruments through the processes of their formalization. Mario and Louis anticipated only part of their subsequent use: They developed both as investigatory tools to make political claims in service of justice. But the Rwandan government was also interested in the memorial sites, map, and report to substantiate the new regime's sovereignty. In the first years after the genocide, Rwandans experienced the tumult of insecurity caused by cross-border attacks from *génocidaires* in exile, counterattacks by the new Rwandan army (many of which targeted civilians), and the large-scale exodus and return of residents. The government's aggressive persecution of genocide organizers and deniers, which included a wanton disregard for civilian casualties, as well as obfuscation regarding those reprisal attacks, made for a volatile environment. The government was especially concerned with asserting its sovereignty and contesting the authority of foreign governments and organizations to intervene. The latter was a particularly sensitive issue in the wake of foreign countries' abandonment of the country during the genocide. The government mobilized its genocide archive to recognize victims and survivors, facilitate the trials and punishments of genocide perpetrators, and establish the ruling RPF party's legitimacy and right to rule. Amply evident at genocide memorials today, state ambitions for genocide evidence complicate the memory justice aims of Rwanda's genocide heritage with those of social and political control.

In 2015, Mario and I had been speaking for several days in southern Chile when I unwittingly provoked his anger on this topic. I asked what he thought of critics' claims that the state sensationalizes genocide memory. Given how widely known the Rwandan government's politicization of genocide history is today, I certainly didn't expect his reaction. Mario paused, livid—not so much at me as at the distortions of his and Louis's truth telling. He held my gaze, pointing adamantly to a copy of the *Genocide Sites Map* we had laid out on a table, and asserted: "They said that there was a massacre here. The massacre was there, *MIRA* [*LOOK*], IT WAS THERE. There, there, there, there, THERE. Look, here at the map! Here we have the names that gave us their testimonies. This serious crime [of nonacknowledgment] denied the *pueblo's* [people's] suffering. We are all, all, responsible in some part for this."[55]

I was taken aback, but I understood. For Mario, the map is a record of heinous crimes. It registers the brutal violence against individuals and families. The *Genocide Sites Map* is also representative of a greater geography of atrocity: one that linked Rwanda to his personal experiences of persecution under Chile's dictatorship, historical violations of Indigenous peoples' rights, and multiple investigations of gross human rights violations throughout the world. Motivated by an ethics of nonerasure, it calls out for acknowledgment and recognition. "Look," he said, "the genocide took place there, THERE. Look, here, at the map!" I wished I hadn't upset Mario so deeply with my question; the intensity of the moment still reverberates with me for his fervent commitments to the victims. His rage is also clarifying, compelling us to critically acknowledge the intention of this archival work—its urgent appeal to witness—along with the politics that would propel it into the realm of state interests. Both are part of this history.

### The Unnamed Site

Speaking with me on separate occasions—Mario in Chile in 2015 and Louis in Rwanda in 2013—both recalled the same site to describe what it was like to investigate the genocide. The septic pit next to the *ibuye* (rock) where they had discovered the forty-seven dead children, near Lake Muhazi, could not be forgotten.[56] What remains in national collective memory, by contrast, is paltry. As I noted earlier, the *Preliminary Report* includes a glancing summary of the evidence Mario and Louis found there. And although Louis recommended the site for national recognition as one of "*les places plus commémoratives*" (a shortlist of places identified for national commemoration), the *ibuye* does not appear on any official list of national or subnational genocide sites.[57] In the community where it is still remembered today, the site bears no state markings as a memorial. It also does not appear on the *Genocide Sites Map* nor in state historical narratives. But the *ibuye* and mass grave continued to haunt both Mario and Louis, to epitomize the brutality of the genocide and their countless encounters with violence. And yet the children are absent from genocide historiography. So, too, is any evidence in the landscape that the killings occurred. Today, without such demonstrable references to the victims, the commemorative enclosure of tall plants around the mass grave is legible only to those who already remember. But their memories are not rendered into history; no one else remembers the children. The site represents the stakes of Louis's and Mario's reparative history along with the dilemmas that exist, then and now, around the persistence and erasure of traumatic memory.

During our conversations, years apart and oceans away, Mario and Louis referenced near-identical photographs to insist on the rock's existence and importance. One, a black-and-white photograph, was taken in late 1994 when Mario led his HRFOR team in area genocide investigations (figure 1.18). It was one of several in Mario's possession in Chile. Another, a photograph in color, was taken in late 1995 on Mario's second visit to the site with Louis as part of their Genocide Memorial Commission investigations (figure 1.19). It was part of a set that Louis had in Rwanda. Louis referred to the site as the *ibuye*, using the Kinyarwanda word for the rock located near the mass grave. Both images place a large and cragged

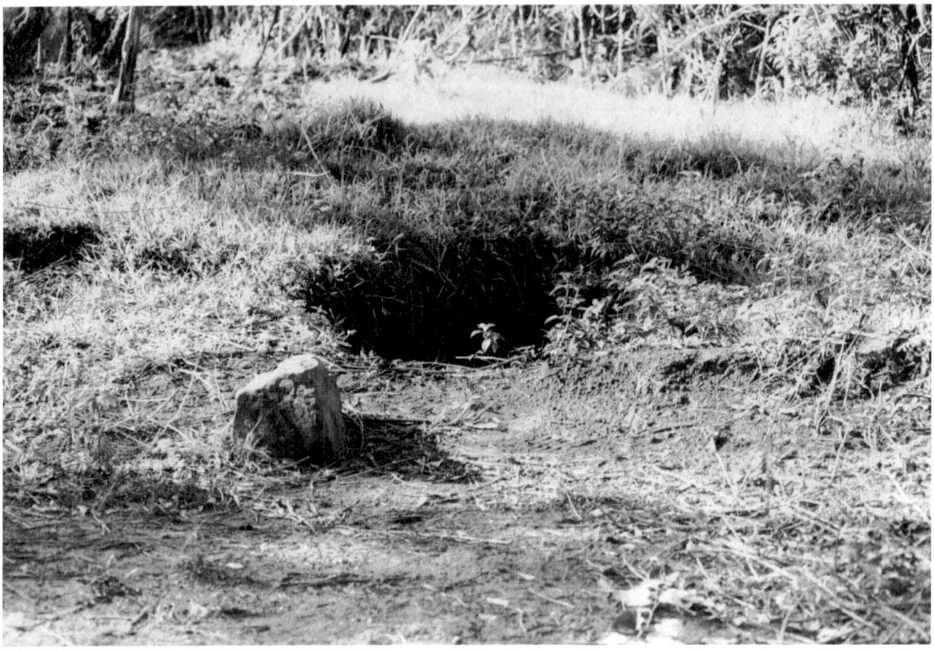

FIGURE 1.18. The *ibuye* (rock) near the mass grave where forty-seven children were found near Lake Muhazi in Rwamagana District, 1994. Photo by Mario Ibarra, Ibarra archive, Chile.

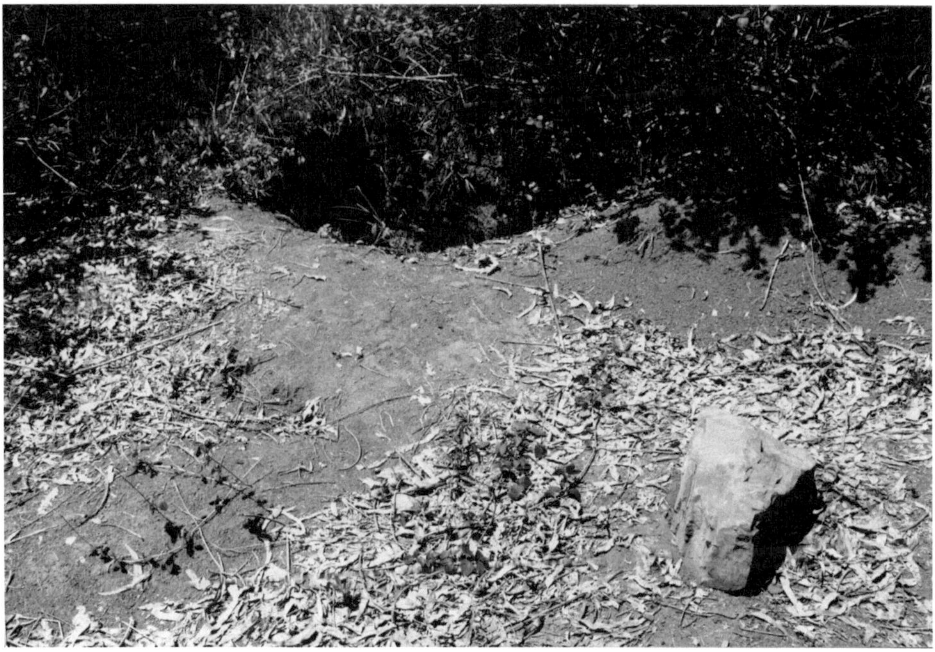

FIGURE 1.19. The *ibuye* and mass grave site one year later, in 1995. Photo by Mario Ibarra, Kanamugire archive, Rwanda.

*ibuye* in the foreground; the dark hole in the ground is a mere few steps behind it (see also figures 1.20 and 1.21). The photographs are underwhelming in their banality: They show the mute aspects of a landscape that are completely lost to sense without narration.

Attempts to reassemble Louis's and Mario's genocide archive restore a sense of the content and provenance of these photographs and the "*détails*" missing from the *Preliminary Report*. Doing so reconnects the ethics of nonerasure, which arose from their affective experience of genocide investigations, to what they wanted us to see: the objective documentation of genocide evidence. Together this archive comprises the foundations of their reparative work.

When Mario first encountered the property in 1994, he didn't see anything. An older woman who lived nearby told his HRFOR team to look near a rock in the field behind the house for her grandchildren. The rock was not remarkable. It was two feet long and ten inches high, its top surface was cragged, and its edges were sharp. When he looked closer, grooves in the rock were still stained with blood and brain matter despite recent rainfall. Mario noticed a shallow depression in the ground nearby. He prodded the rust-colored earth with the thin metal rod he typically carried and identified a five-by-seven-foot area where the soil was loose and had recently been disturbed. His colleagues cut the grass and removed leafy branches and other plants that covered the area. Small pieces of crania and tiny teeth lay scattered in the soil. The team began to document what they found. They sketched, mapped, took notes, and photographed the circumstances of the deaths and the locations in which they occurred.

Having excavated the soil, they prepared to access the subterranean space. Stabilizing his body with a rope, Mario hovered inside the hole to explore what lay at the bottom. He lifted one edge of a plastic tarp with his rod, revealing dozens of small skulls. When they pulled the bodies up, the team counted forty-seven children, aged five years or younger. In mid-April 1994 the attackers had separated the children from others seeking refuge in a nearby building. Unlike many of the killings during this time, the *génocidaires* did not use machetes. Most of the children died from blunt force trauma to their heads caused by repeated strikes against the rock. The killers then threw their tiny bodies into the septic pit. One year later, a field team led by Louis determined that the rock and mass grave were located on the property of a local politician who helped to organize the genocide in Muhazi Commune.[58]

A few days after they exhumed the bodies in 1994, Mario and his colleagues transported the children to another site for burial. They saved any remaining possessions and clothing for possible identification. Interment was intended to restore some measure of decency to the victims. However, the relocation was controver-

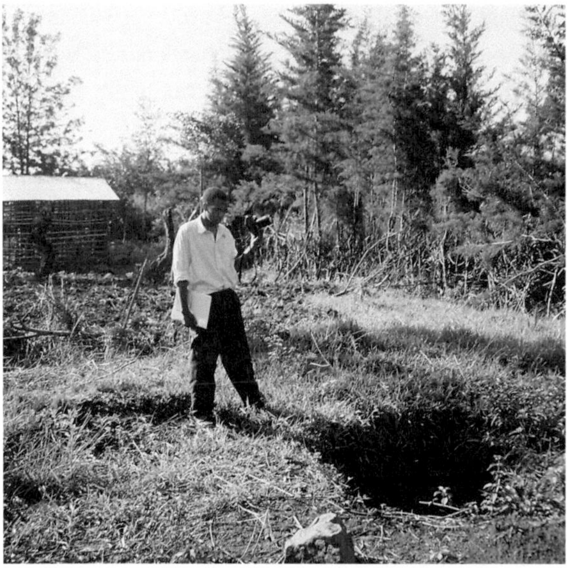

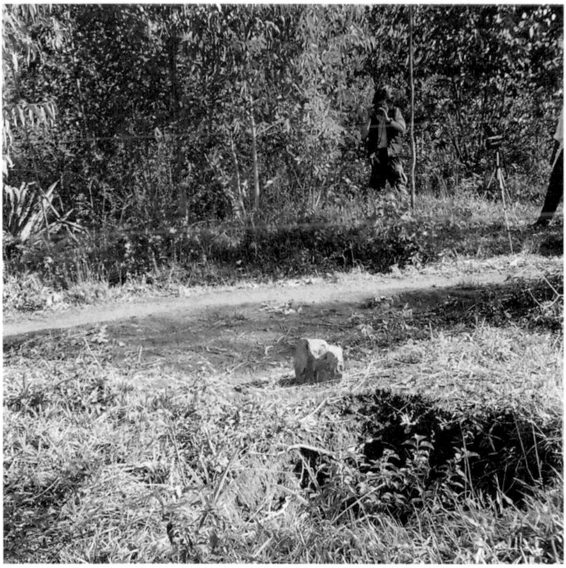

FIGURE 1.20. (*top*) A Genocide Memorial Commission affiliate stands near the *ibuye* and mass grave, poised to take a photograph, 1995. Photo by Mario Ibarra, Kanamugire archive, Rwanda.

FIGURE 1.21. (*bottom*) Mario Ibarra photographed documenting the rock and Muhazi mass grave, 1995. Courtesy of Louis Kanamugire, Kanamugire archive, Rwanda.

sial because the bodies were also evidence. Reburials such as these pitted humanity against historiography. These were not abstract conflicts. They were embodied and felt by the individuals performing this work. Mario put it this way, recounting his drive to the new burial site:

> I had a Nissan Patrol jeep and we covered them in plastic sheets and filled it—with the bodies, the skulls. We had the agreement of the Muhazi *bourgmestre* [commune mayor]. The other members of my team could not fit in the jeep because it was so full. I went maybe two kilometers, and I said to myself, driving alone, thinking about what I was driving in my car: Look at what they did, these evil people. That's the feeling I had, in a country that is not yours but that you take in your soul. And I think that it was the same for everyone, because what was most hurtful afterward was the silence of the interpreters. It was their country, these were their bodies, and my colleagues—no one said anything. I was in the same situation, driving, and I couldn't do anything. Please say something! It left something, a feeling, a sense that it's not finished. The things that one felt at that time cannot be written. But the most terrible thing was that you had to write a report [to the UN about the genocide investigation]. You had to write it and send it to a colleague far away, and when you receive a reply, the only thing that he says to you is "This is an interesting report," or "This report is well written."[59]

The logistics of the task—transporting human remains to a new location, obtaining authorization—gave way to moral outrage, sadness, desperation, helplessness, irresolution, and cynicism. Situations like these exceeded representation—they were experiences that "cannot be written"—and yet they had to be documented to account for what happened. In the next weeks, Mario's HRFOR team wrote reports to catalog and document this mass grave among many more. Their reports were aggregated along with others in the country and sent to the UN Office of the High Commissioner of Human Rights office in Kigali and to headquarters in Geneva. These processes of bureaucratic rationality were unaccommodating to individual reflection but nonetheless necessary as summary documentation. Altogether the team's efforts reconstructed the work of genocide, place by place. But a gulf remained between written representations and the experience of encounter. Visual and spatial documentation were meant to fill the gap, to mediate between moral restoration and information gathering.

For Mario in particular, visual and spatial forms of representation were methods for traversing scales, for moving between the intimate details of each site and a total view of the genocide. Both scales had distinct ethical motivations: to bear witness to individual victims and to represent atrocity in its entirety—to make it comprehensible and actionable in forms of justice. A visual record also primed spaces for reconstruction. Once evidence of the genocide was documented, the churches, schools, homes, hills, and fields that these sites occupied could be released to some semblance of everyday life, farmed for subsistence, or ordered in the new village forms that the government and its partners were beginning to construct. Today, in their separation both from each other and from the histories of their production, the photographs of genocide sites and the *Genocide Sites Map* provide divergent affective and objective representations of the work to understand the aftermath of mass violence.

By the time Louis and Mario began working together, the ministry in charge of the Genocide Memorial Commission had begun to privilege a more direct experience of atrocity. As I detail in the following chapter, the shift to conserving human remains and building damage in sites of killing was a result of both happenstance and curation. The *ibuye*'s lack of legibility—its inability to be conserved and to present lasting ruins of genocide as evidence to outsider-witnesses—omitted it from historiography. The rock needed narration, the bodies had been removed, and, as a result, the site was ultimately not selected as a national genocide memorial.

Today, over two decades later, photographs and individual memories are the only records of mass violence there. The *ibuye* figures an absence to tell a history of the politics of site selection and presentation. At the same time, those traumatic memories were not lost to Louis and Mario, who bore the weight of the *ibuye* and that of many other sites as individuals who retain minute, visceral knowledge of mass graves. For them, the *ibuye*, the young victims, and the manner in which they died signify and summarize, in a single site, the brutality of the genocide. Excluded from the list of national memorials, it is nonetheless emblematic of a compulsion not only to document but to move from witnessing to searching for a form of repair. The need to involve as many people as possible in this shift from perception to action underlies their archival work.

In "The Site of Memory," novelist Toni Morrison discusses the ethical imperative driving her writing, evoking parallels to Mario's and Louis's own practice of reparative historiography. Her fictional stories read as historical truths—as corrective representations of the past and present—drawing, as she does, from collective memories of American slavery and its legacies. Her objectives in writing as she does are twofold. She seeks to narrate the "interior lives" of enslaved people and their descendants: to represent the complex personhood of those individuals and restore their humanity for readers. Morrison also challenges whitewashed histories of slavery. She draws moral commitments to kin into that effort, providing full, unflinching accounts of the violence of slavery to challenge its purported neutrality. Morrison claims the image as a critical foundation for that reparative work. The image provides a key medium for conveying the intensity of collective memories and associated feelings. Moving "from the image to the text," as she put it, allows one to access "the remains . . . at the archeological site" that surface with a strikingly compelling vividness, providing her with guides "to a reconstruction of a world, to an exploration of an interior life that was not written and to the revelation of a kind of truth."[60]

In doing so, Morrison argues that sites of memory are sites of discourse. Sites of memory tell truths about histories of injustice. The real and conceptual places to which those memories attach open up shared stories and compel wider recognition of those experiences. In Morrison's framing, sites of memory register and evoke embodied, transgenerational practices of repair. The move from image (the site of memory) to text that she describes is analogous to the move from the encounter with the unreadable rock to a reparative historiography of it.

## Repair and the Writing of History

When the *ibuye* and its related mass grave were discovered, they did not figure as history. They represented an archaeological site—a site of forensic analysis—similar to many others where investigators aimed to identify the locations of victims and the means by which they were killed. At the same time, the site was excessively significant because of both its singular affect as the gruesome scene of child homicide and its symbolism of the genocide's barbarity. Still, despite the profound impacts that this site and so many other unmarked, unnamed massacres had on Mario and Louis, it is illegible in Rwanda's genocide historiography precisely because little remains apparent to view. Conditions of visibility and spatiality were so critical to the representation of the genocide that its historiography was understood expansively, in written as well as cartographic, photographic, and geographic forms.

Both visceral experience and rational distance were critical to representing the earliest histories of the genocide. Mario's and Louis's attempt to gain complete knowledge at every level, from the whole country to each victim, their identity and their manner of death, constituted an attempt at repair. They and their colleagues internalized the pain of doing this work but left it unrepresented in the written, photographic, and cartographic documentation they produced. Instead, they emplaced the horror and grief of the mass killings, putting genocide victims and sites on display. Their work to document, and later conserve, genocide massacre sites throughout the country reveals the subjective and traumatic labor of ordering that rendered the past representable as history. This is what it meant to translate recent traumatic memory into history, into a wider public's understanding of the past.

In *The Writing of History*, Michel de Certeau notes that historians often remain at a distance, physical and temporal, from the sites, past occurrences, and people that form the subject of their writing. And yet, he argues, "historians can only write by combining within their practice the 'other' that moves and misleads them and the real that they can represent only through fiction."[61] In other words, affective connection plays an active, subjective, and analytic role in closing that distance; historians are "moved" to represent the past and can often relay marginalized truths only by resorting to fabulation.[62]

In their reparative approach to historiography, Louis and Mario, like Certeau, demonstrated the role that feeling and subjectivity have in a reparative writing of history. Louis and Mario sought to, as Morrison put it, "rip that veil drawn over" the crimes of genocide, forcing public acknowledgment of the violence.[63] Theirs is a historiography that simultaneously pulled back—that sought to render the whole picture of violence—and pulled alongside, closer still, to challenge the abstraction of killing. By contrast, histories attentive to the battle but indifferent to the smell and pain of the trenches abound. They represent methods and approaches that would rather immortalize the strategy of war than represent the excesses of feeling and death that proceed from an aggregation of data rather than a sense of lived experiences and histories. Instead, Louis's and Mario's genocide documentation constituted an effort—in cartography, photography, and place—at recognizing the humanity of individuals whose lives had been erased.

In seeking to understand the *why* of their work, we confront repair as no easy process. Repair is a vigilance for, an active search for, injustices and their correctives. Striving for repair is an insurmountable task, oriented to impossible forms of healing and redress, and searching for wider recognition of that which has been silenced. Through their work we see the practice of reparative history as agonizing, indignant, sorrowful, and purposeful, centered as it is on harms and loss in its search for justice and restitution.

Commenting on Certeau's approach to critical historiography, philosopher Paul Ricoeur argues that the writing of history might more aptly be analogous to an "act of sepulcher."[64] In doing so, he claims that historiography not only is affectively driven but, more specifically, is an act of writing about the dead. It is thus an exercise in mourning and remembrance. For Ricoeur, the sepulcher refers to both the physical place of burial and the act of burying, and each resists—through reference to the space of lived experience, grief, and memorialization—the notion that historiography should be a distant and abstract representation of the past.

Louis's and Mario's reparative historiography demonstrates the virtues of active remembrance that Ricoeur extols even while it reveals irresolvable tensions arising from a history written by acts of sepulcher. Genocide sites and their documentation occupy the distinct but connected registers of affect and reason, immediacy and distance. Louis and Mario were navigating a critical dilemma for trauma heritage: How does one counter the abstraction of violence (and therefore its dismissal) and restore a sense of lives erased, when a direct view of violent erasure is itself a dehumanizing representation with the potential to retraumatize? Their attempts to produce rational written and cartographic representations of brutal mass violence appealed to a wider, inattentive public at a distance from Rwanda. But it sat at odds with the deep and traumatizing feelings that the massacre sites evoked. Their turn to trauma heritage sought a phenomenological representation of loss, death, grief, and rage rather than a purely didactic or descriptive one. That mode of communication, which emerged in the photographic record and the conservation of massacre sites themselves, turned to a distinctly dehumanizing form of representation. But it was done out of the will to show what had happened.

The demand placed on viewers was to respond in kind, witnessing and taking action toward justice. Impatient for criminal adjudication, genocide heritage is unwilling to adhere to the temporal constraints of building a case for trial. It is supportive of prosecution but more committed to publicizing knowledge of crimes. It is less concerned with the perpetrators' motives and means and more attuned to the experiences of those affected: to what was done to individuals. In this regard, documenting, preserving, and conserving—remembering, in material and spatial ways—places of death represent acts of caring for the dead. And yet the affective excesses of places of massacre and their representations are traumatizing for individuals, foremost among them the survivors of the genocide and relatives of victims. Still, those reparative histories exercised different types of agency as they sought to write and reinforce the history of targeted erasure in Rwanda.

An ethics of nonerasure motivated the development of maps, reports, photographs, and conserved sites. And yet those reparative historiographies simultaneously fed into forms of political power that legitimized the governing tactics of the new regime. The state's co-optation effectively disempowered citizens. But the material and spatial form of those histories matters. Through it all, even in the context of the politically uneven landscape of trauma heritage in Rwanda, a reparative historiography is sustained by a visceral archive.

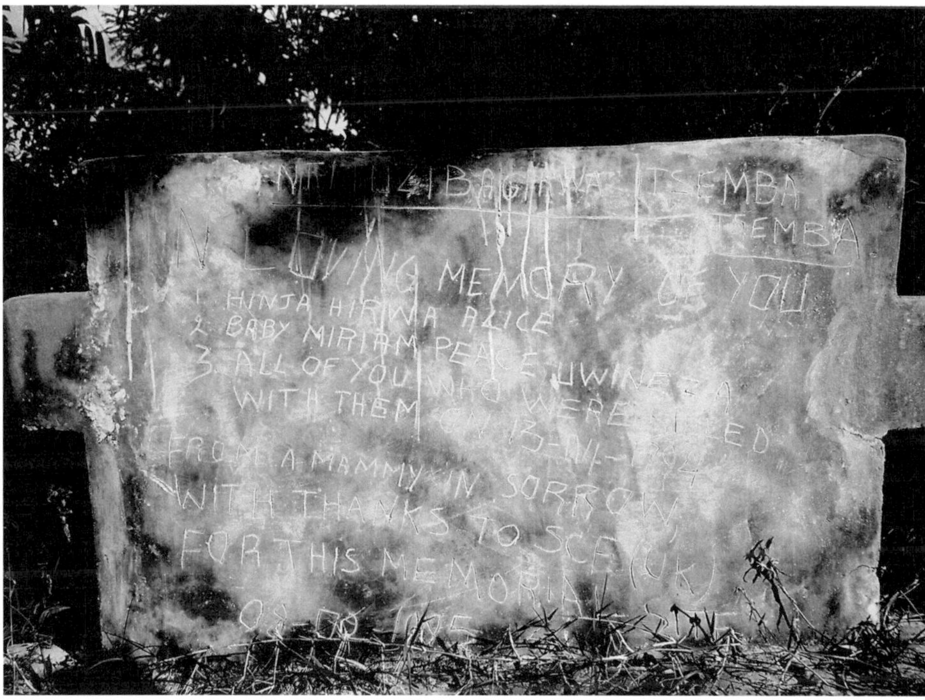


A communal grave marker, erected on September 8, 1995, that reads: "*Nti tuzi bagirwa itsembatsemba* [We don't know the killers]. In loving memory of 1. Hinja Hirwa Alice; 2. Baby Miriam Peace Uwineza; 3. All of you who were killed with them on April 13, 1994; From a Mammy in sorrow; with thanks to SCF [Save the Children] (UK) for this memorial site." Photo by Mario Ibarra, Kanamugire archive, Rwanda.

2

# BEYOND STATE CONTROL

## GLOBAL DIALOGUES AND LOCAL EXPERIENCES

Mario Ibarra's and Louis Kanamugire's work to document and conserve massacre sites—and the genocide heritage it gave rise to—reveals repair and empowerment as central ambitions of trauma heritage. And yet most scholars understand genocide memorial development to have been, at the least, steered by the government, if not explicitly politicized to strengthen state sovereignty and control. But even if the ability to authorize approaches to memorialization rested with the newly formed national government, this power was diffusely held. Though highly influential, the state was one of many parties interacting around genocide memorialization in the politically unstable context of conflict and its immediate aftermath. The situation exceeded state control both in terms of its global entanglements and on the scale of local experiences, initiatives, and memories of trauma.[1] Practical decision-making on a local level, as well as the knowledge that informed it, came from a range of actors, including genocide survivors, recent returnees, novice local government leaders, and foreigners working for international nongovernmental organizations (NGOs). The process of institutionalizing conservation practices as genocide heritage reveals the complexities of authority and control as various people with differing priorities and perspectives responded to recent and overwhelming violence. By asking who held decision-making power in these situations, this chapter seeks to make determining factors in the formation of Rwanda's genocide memorials newly visible.

Notably, architects, artists, and professional conservationists were not an influential part of early decisions regarding genocide memorial curation. Their absence further underscores the ad hoc and experimental nature of memory work in this period. Genocide heritage was steered by multiple state ministries, the military, civil society groups, and foreign organizations in the country. The new government and military were keenly aware of the strategic role genocide memory could have in judicial and nation-building processes. But it also learned from on-the-ground actors, formalizing their nascent preservation practices in memorial policies and in new institutions to authorize and manage genocide memory. Local experts and organizations and international groups filled a vacuum left by a government responding to the chaos and violence that continued after the genocide.

The deeply affective work of conserving sites of massacre produced lasting places of memory. It also shaped early government discussions regarding national representations of genocide history. State institutions followed and steered the work of postgenocide repair unevenly, working with and parallel to those groups in the first months and eventually taking up the mantle of decision-making and leadership. Throughout that early period and since, the appointment of Rwandan Patriotic Front (RPF) and government representatives to civil society organizations has brought state critics in line with the regime.[2] The processes by which genocide heritage became authorized, then, involved significant shifts in and muddying of the loci of power over time.

To illustrate this, I begin by describing four massacre sites that were the subject of discussions—among foreign and government leaders—on how to represent the genocide and make that history known to global and local publics. The earliest preservation and conservation practices took place at the Nyarubuye, Ntarama, and Nyamata churches and the Murambi Technical School. The sites were primary locations in a wider network of site-specific experiments that developed and formalized a strategy for conserving genocide evidence. Those relationships suggest seeing the sites less as memorial monuments from the start than as places of genocide heritage practice. In the context of an inordinately visceral aftermath landscape, the four sites also locate key dilemmas around how to represent mass violence. In the film and photographic documentation of that memory work and the oral history reflections of diverse individuals—including local, government, and international actors—we see and hear how challenging it was to both represent the genocide and live with its memory. In other words, preserving and conserving victims' remains and sites of killing was not easy, smooth, or top-down, government-directed work. It was rife with ethical, political, and personal predicaments.

The chapter continues to discuss the uncanny role of the United Nations Human Rights Field Operation in Rwanda (HRFOR) in genocide heritage development. Along with the armed forces of the RPF, the HRFOR provided the technical apparatus that made the earliest approaches to genocide evidence preservation possible. Critically, for both the state and this NGO, a discourse of human rights was a primary justification for the decision to put places and victims of massacre on display. Although HRFOR involvement in genocide memorialization was largely a result of Mario Ibarra's individual work, his involvement complemented late twentieth-century debates on the definition and scope of global human rights practice. That context had significant influence on Rwanda's genocide memorials and emboldened similar forms of trauma heritage elsewhere in the world.

The human rights justification for Rwanda's genocide memorials was not Mario's alone, and this chapter also considers two early plenaries that independently substantiate the influence of related discourses and practices. The first, a conference oriented to the theme "Rwanda: Reconstruire" (Rwanda: Rebuild), was co-convened by Swiss and Rwandan human rights organizations in Kigali in October 1994. It is one of the few documented early discussions regarding state and international responsibilities for (and interests in) defining collective memory of the genocide. The conference also reflects the early influence of memory justice and human rights objectives in genocide heritage curation. One year later, the national government organized the "Genocide, Impunity, and Accountability" conference, which also took place in Kigali, in November 1995. That plenary sought to leverage human rights discourse to support national government policies and approaches to genocide remembrance. Along with Mario's work for HRFOR, both conferences demonstrate the role that late twentieth century human rights discourse and practice had in developing a justification for and approach to Rwanda's genocide heritage.

The chapter concludes by following the formation of the Rwandan government's Genocide Memorial Commission, under Louis Kanamugire's direction, which consolidated disparate ministry and military practices and discussions related to the display of victims' remains, exhumations, and reburial and commemoration ceremonies. The commission's work and structure provide insights into how the government formalized local conservation experiments as state policy, authorizing the display of victims' remains as a form of national memory.

The following sections demonstrate the ways in which Rwanda's genocide heritage developed iteratively and from a dialogue across diverse sites—including at the locations of the massacres themselves, within (new) government institutions, and in plenaries that formalized connections between local and global influences. In doing so, the chapter contributes to the historiography of early genocide memorialization by clarifying the origins of decisions to conserve genocide massacres for public viewing. I highlight the localized memory work that responded, in the immediate aftermath, to a landscape of victims and violence that overwhelmed sense. I also call attention to the shaping influences of a global discourse on human rights along with the national government's concerns about sovereignty amid continued insecurity. When those sites and knowledge exchanges are understood together, we see the role of affect in grounding both human rights practice and the sovereignty aims of the new governing regime. As a result, the chapter retrieves a sense of the tensions in the—sometimes competing, other times aligned—local, state, and global forces that constituted Rwanda's genocide heritage.

## The First Genocide Memorials

Immediately after the 1994 genocide, massacre sites were preserved out of an urgent need to protect evidence of crimes. The idea to "fix" the sites as they were found responded to the removal of victims' bodies by perpetrators who sought to dispose of evidence and by church leaders who were keen to reconsecrate places of worship. Preservation became a strategy to make evidence available to view, especially for foreign journalists and government representatives who had been slow to respond to the violence and for international and national prosecutions. Within local communities, too, there was a sense that calling attention to crimes committed in churches, government offices, marketplaces, and homes would inhibit the impunity of perpetrators and their supporters. But by 1995, as massacre sites began to deteriorate in the sun and rain, preservation practices became untenable. Approaches to maintaining genocide memory shifted to conservation: from the preservation of whole scenes of massacre to techniques for preventing the deterioration of discrete evidence, such as victims' remains, their belongings, and the weapons used in attacks. The work of conservation involved recovering victims—from preserved killing sites and mass graves—and defleshing and cleaning skeletal remains for display at sites of killing. Preservation and conservation were part of a larger set of initiatives including exhumation, commemorative ceremonies, and reburial that sought to order Rwanda's aftermath landscape by managing views of the dead.

Nyarubuye, Murambi, Ntarama, and Nyamata locate the first experiments in preservation and conservation in the sites where the targeted mass killing of Tutsi occurred. Each has been pivotal to developing Rwanda's genocide heritage aesthetic, and today they make up four of six national genocide memorials. Nyarubuye Parish and the Murambi Technical School are significant as the locations of the first preservation and conservation practices, respectively. Those initiatives in eastern and southwestern Rwanda complemented, and then reinforced, a geographically dispersed network of related experimentation. The Ntarama and Nyamata Parishes, near the capital, Kigali, were important early testing grounds for the expansion of those practices into a national memorialization effort. The four sites' evolution as protomemorials took place in a context of insecurity marked by governing transitions, significant population movement, continued violence, urgent basic needs, and reprisal attacks. The work of preservation and conservation was, moreover, emotionally and physically brutal. By 1996 conservation work was proceeding at each in tandem, managed by the newly created Genocide Memorial Commission. Those experiments evolved alongside growing state control over the sites and collective memory in the country.

In the east, near the border with Tanzania, Nyarubuye Parish held the bodies of three thousand individuals who sought refuge there and were killed on April 15–17, 1994. It was one of the first killing sites to be preserved in Rwanda and was doubly significant for the international attention its preservation garnered. The rebel Rwandan Patriotic Army (RPA) first publicized Nyarubuye's location when it brought embedded journalists to the site during the genocide. Nyarubuye subsequently became a global reference for what was occurring throughout Rwanda. From July 1994 onward, preservation work was undertaken by Mario Ibarra and a small team of UN human rights officers. That work entailed protecting the crime scenes in the convent courtyard and annex buildings (and to a lesser extent, the main chapel, which had been cleaned up by the church) so that they could be documented, analyzed, and viewed by others (figures 2.1–2.3).[3] For over a year, Nyarubuye was preserved as a place of witness for a broad range of local, national government, military, and influential foreign government and NGO representatives. When the bodies were subsequently interred in July 1995, photographs of Nyarubuye's preservation continued to circulate in news media and political and human rights campaigns calling for the recognition of the violence as a genocide. Throughout its short but impactful history as a preserved genocide site, Nyarubuye catalyzed the methods, aesthetic, institutions, key actors, and knowledge transfers that constituted Rwanda's genocide heritage. The individuals involved in Nyarubuye's conservation later guided and physically contributed to memory maintenance work at other sites, including at Ntarama, Murambi, and Nyamata. Those relationships, and the disproportionate publicity that the site received, rendered Nyarubuye ground zero for conceiving what an authorized genocide historiography might look like and entail.

Ntarama Parish was among the longest preserved genocide sites in Rwanda. A considerably more modest parish complex than Nyarubuye, the small compound comprised a one-room chapel, classroom, and rectory (figures 2.4–2.6). On April 15, 1994, around five thousand people seeking shelter at the parish were killed by an extremist Hutu militia who attacked them with grenades and machetes.[4] It is not entirely clear who first preserved the massacre.[5] But by 1996 it was managed by the Genocide Memorial Commission, which preserved the Ntarama massacre for a decade.[6] The chapel was maintained as it was found with bodies, bones, mats, clothing, and other belongings decomposing on and in between low wooden pews (figure 2.5).[7] In 1996 a small and temporary wood shelter was erected between the chapel and rectory as a makeshift memorial. The shed structure displayed conserved skulls, bones, and clothing, raised up on tall tables, echoing approaches piloted at the Murambi massacre site (figures 2.4 and 2.6). During that first decade, the preservation of the Ntarama chapel massacre progressively shifted to the conservation of victims' remains and belongings, including, most iconically, the display of rows of conserved skulls and long bones on shelving that spanned the width of the church. Ntarama became a heavily frequented state memorial because of those displays and because it was centrally located near the capital. In the following decade, bodies and bones were progressively moved out of sight. When I first visited Ntarama in 2011, the display of victims' skulls and bones remained, but when I returned in 2018, only a few representative skeletal remains were on display (figure 6.17). More prominent was victims' clothing, conserved and hung from most available surfaces in the chapel. The memorial had added a wall of names, a meditation garden, and steel structures to protect the parish buildings. These changes marked Ntarama's transformation from a place of witness to a state representation of genocide memory rendered in the style and curatorial approach common to global memorial museums.[8]

The Murambi Technical School, located in the southwest of the country, was the first site where evidence of genocide was not preserved as a scene encountered but rather conserved and *reconstructed* in a site of killing. Murambi is furthermore exceptional among Rwanda's genocide memorials for displaying mummified bodies (figures 2.7–2.9). That unprecedented approach to memorialization—to making the bodies of the dead visible—arose from the total erasure of evidence. After the massacres the *génocidaires* removed an estimated thirty-five thousand people killed from the sprawling school complex. The operation, like the killings themselves, was not hidden but brazen: The perpetrators used large construction equipment to move thousands of individuals into nearby mass graves. Six months later, a local community group formed from Tutsi returnees (individuals formerly exiled from the area) exhumed hundreds of bodies and placed them back in the school, using a chemical preservative. By 1996 Mario and Dr. Kanimba had taken over and extended that conservation work in efforts organized by the Genocide Memorial Commission. If Nyarubuye could be considered a starting point for Rwanda's genocide heritage aesthetic, at Murambi it became institutionalized and paradigmatic. It was the largest conservation operation in Rwanda: There, the commission not only conserved victims' bodies but also piloted, developed, and formalized the conservation of skeletal remains, clothing, and other artifactual evidence of the killings. Mario's and Dr. Kanimba's memory maintenance work extended well beyond Murambi, occurring in tandem with several sites in the region and extending to Ntarama, Nyamata, and Bisesero in the west of the country (another national memorial site).[9] Today the vast displays of victims' skeletal remains at both Nyamata and Bisesero, their ordered and systematic organization, demonstrate both the knowledge transfers facilitated by Murambi and the scale of genocide heritage conservation operations.

Nyamata was the first memorial site where victims' bones were exhibited in a museological manner (figures 2.10–2.12).[10] Ten thousand people died at the parish on April 14–16, 1994.[11] Like at Murambi, Nyamata Church was emptied of victims' bodies within weeks of the killings. Returning the remains and belongings of the dead to the buildings where they were killed, and displaying them there, sought to restore some indication of the massacres' occurrence. Curation tentatively began in 1995 by exhuming the dead from the area and building new crypts to house them.[12] By late 1995 Louis and Mario were directing the site's conservation as part of the Genocide Memorial Commission and documenting the process in photographs (figures 2.13–2.14). During that time, a pyramidal display case and metal shelving were installed in newly dug, underground concrete crypts beneath the chapel. On the grounds adjacent to the church, several rows of belowground sepulchers also were created. By August 1997 conservation work on skeletal remains at Nyamata was proceeding apace.[13] As they did at Murambi, Mario, Dr. Kanimba, and Louis worked with local Nyamata residents to conserve the skeletal remains of victims. The chapel was a staging ground in the process of its ordering: Dr. Kanimba's photographs document large piles of bones and clothing throughout, which reached heights of at least five feet.[14] They filled the Nyamata crypts built adjacent to the chapel with coffins of intact victims and conserved skulls and bones neatly grouped by size (figure 2.12). Row on row and tomb after tomb were densely filled, conveying the scale at which Tutsi were massacred.

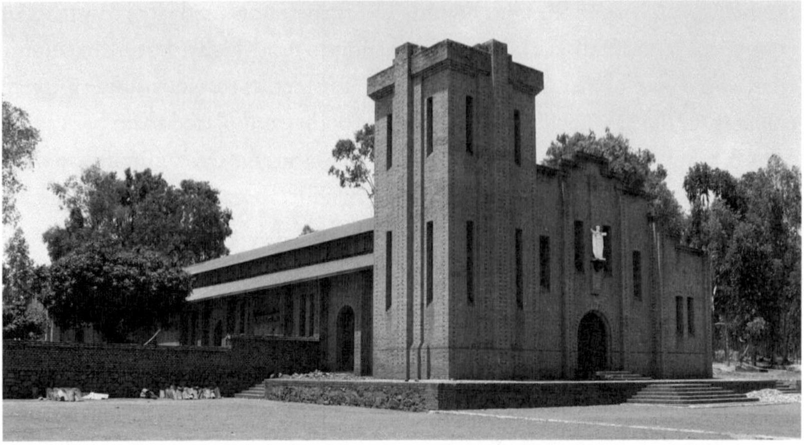

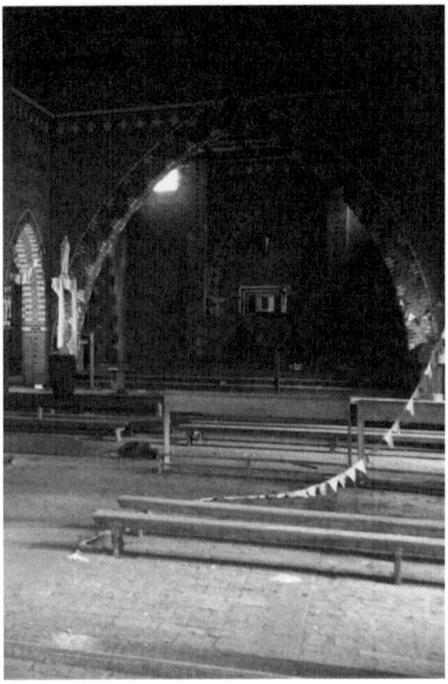

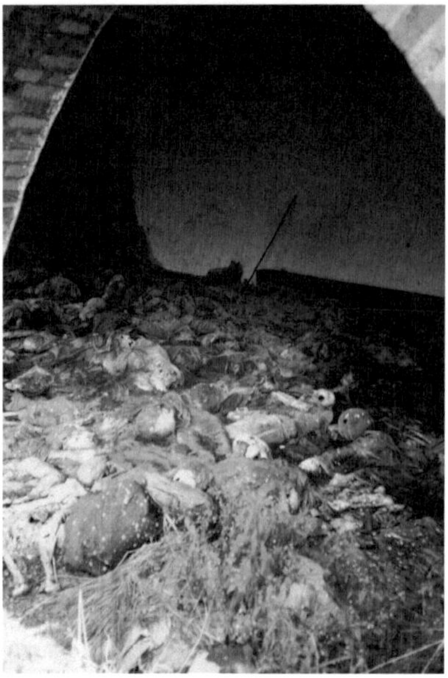

Nyarubuye National Genocide Memorial (figures 2.1–2.3)

FIGURE 2.1. (*top*) Contemporary view of Nyarubuye Church, in eastern Rwanda, the site of a national genocide memorial, 2013. Photo by Delia Duong Ba Wendel.

FIGURE 2.2. (*bottom left*) Nyarubuye Church in 1994, after Catholic officials emptied the building of the victims' bodies. Photo by Mario Ibarra, Ibarra archive, Chile.

FIGURE 2.3. (*bottom right*) By contrast, victims' bodies were preserved as they were found in the Nyarubuye Parish courtyard and rear convent buildings, 1994. Photo by Mario Ibarra, Ibarra archive, Chile.

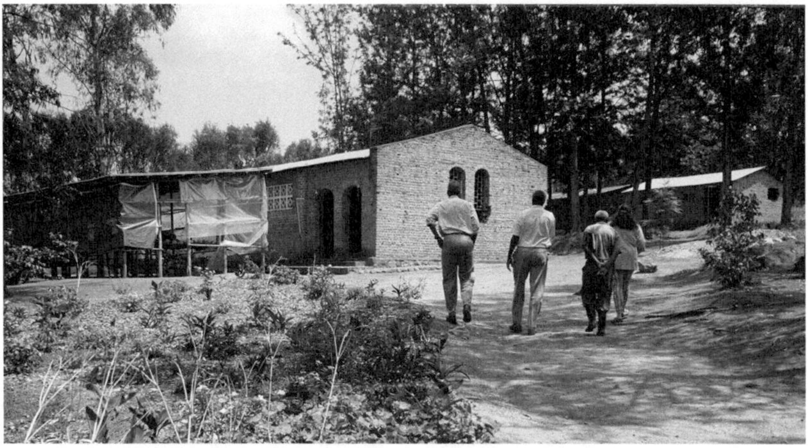

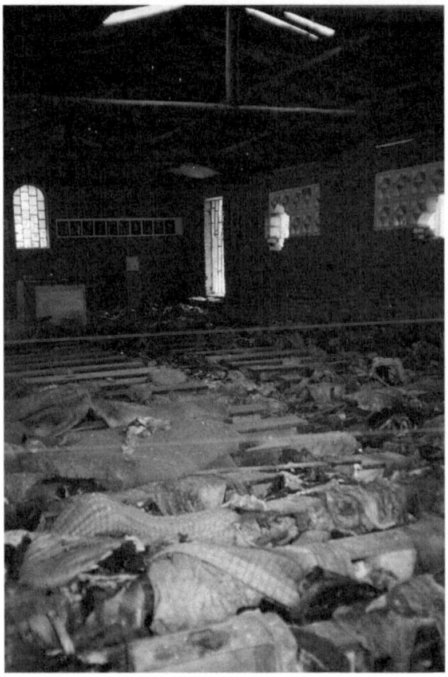

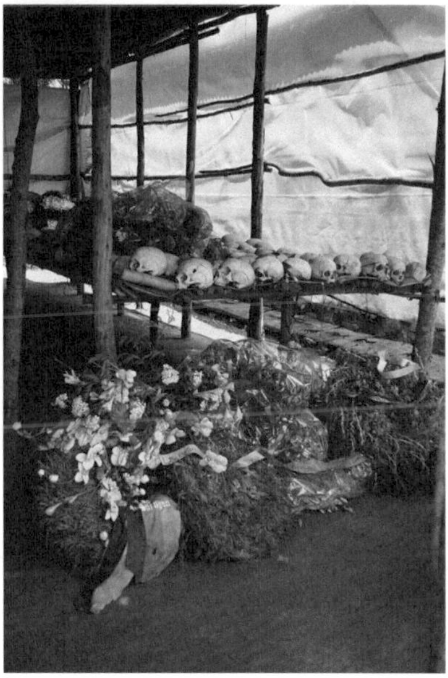

Ntarama National Genocide Memorial (figures 2.4–2.6)

FIGURE 2.4. (*top*) A United Universalist Church delegation visits the preserved Ntarama Church massacre site in September 1996. United Universalist Church Collection, Harvard University Andover Theology Archive, Cambridge, Massachusetts, Folder BMS16201/7 (5), "Africa-General, 1996–97."

FIGURE 2.5. (*bottom left*) The massacre inside Ntarama Church, preserved as it was found, September 1996. United Universalist Church Collection.

FIGURE 2.6. (*bottom right*) Victims' conserved skeletal remains displayed in a temporary shelter next to the Ntarama chapel, September 1996. United Universalist Church Collection.

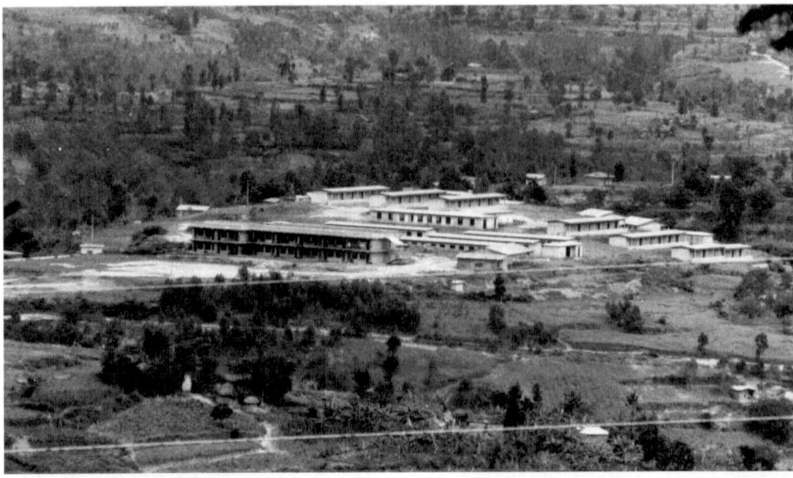

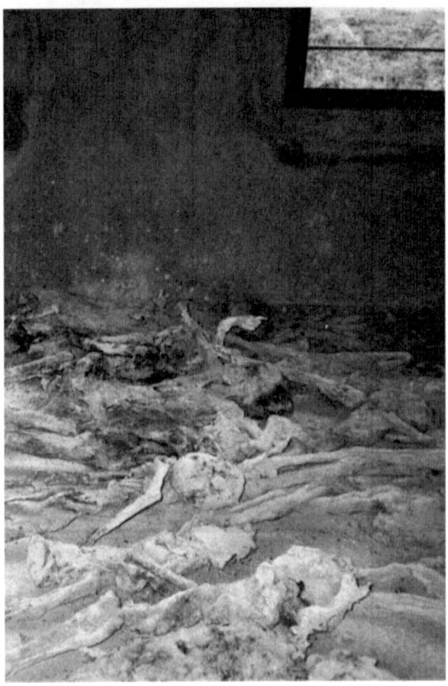

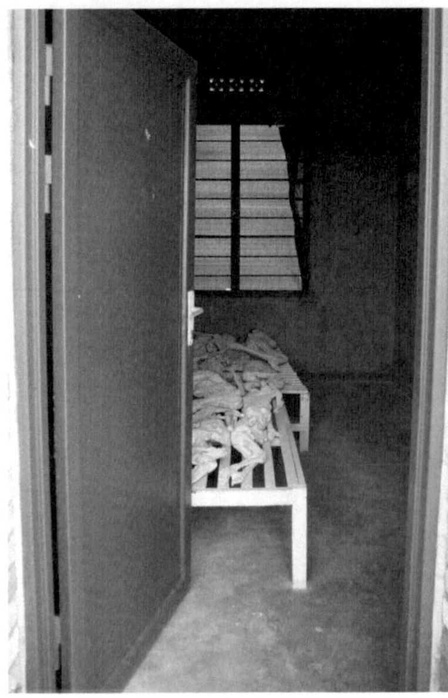

Murambi National Genocide Memorial (figures 2.7–2.9)

FIGURE 2.7. (*top*) The Murambi massacre site viewed from a helicopter, 1996. Photo by Mario Ibarra, Ibarra archive, Chile.

FIGURE 2.8. (*bottom left*) When Murambi genocide victims were first conserved in 1995, their bodies were exhumed, returned to the floors of buildings, and sprayed with lime preservative. Photo by Mario Ibarra, 1996, Ibarra archive, Chile.

FIGURE 2.9. (*bottom right*) In subsequent conservation work, the bodies were cleaned, chemically preserved, and placed back inside buildings on raised beds, where they remain today (photographed in 2013). Photo by Delia Duong Ba Wendel.

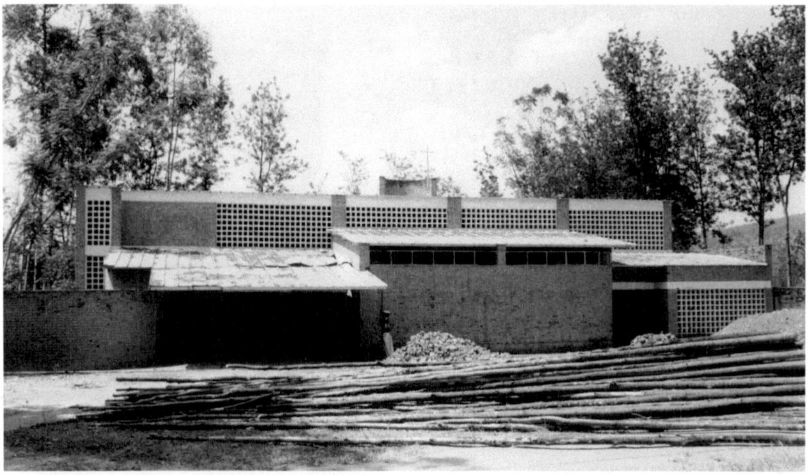

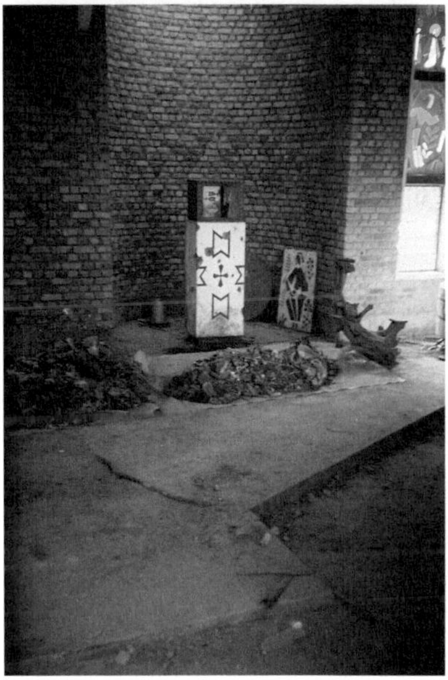

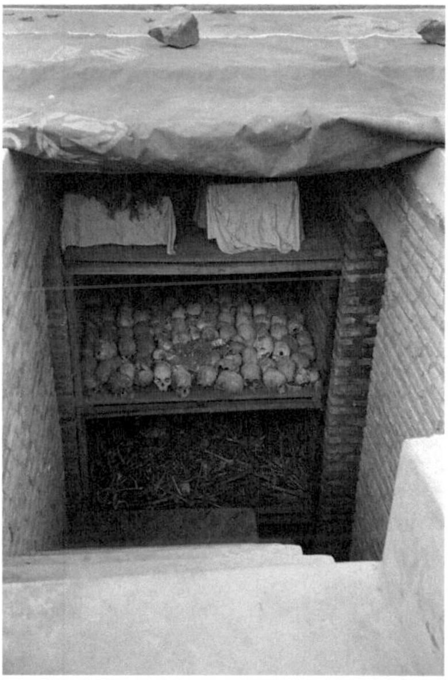

Nyamata National Genocide Memorial (figures 2.10–2.12)

FIGURE 2.10. (*top*) Construction of crypts to hold victims' bones underway both beneath and adjacent to Nyamata Church, 1997. Photo by Mario Ibarra, Ibarra archive, Chile.

FIGURE 2.11. (*bottom left*) Victims' belongings and remains gathered below the Nyamata Church altar before their display on pews and in new crypts, 1997. Photo by Mario Ibarra, Kanamugire archive, Rwanda.

FIGURE 2.12. (*bottom right*) New crypts built adjacent to Nyamata Church to hold conserved victims' bones, 1998. Photo by Mario Ibarra, Kanamugire archive, Rwanda.

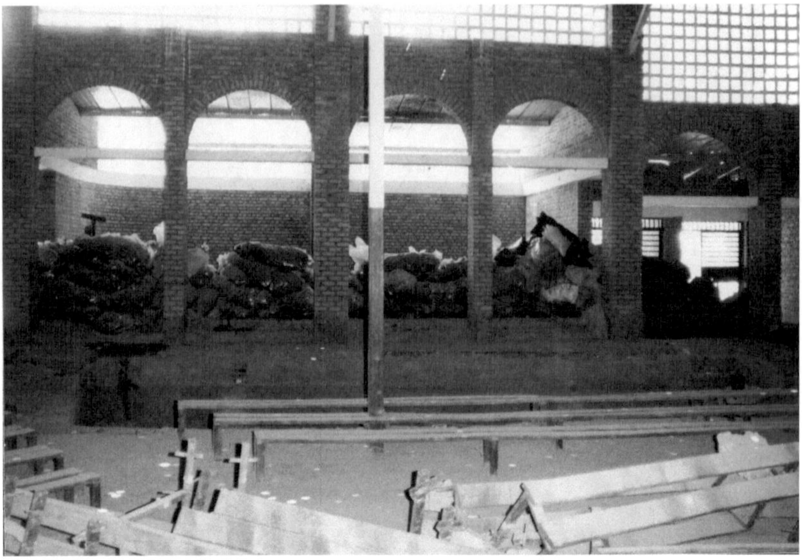

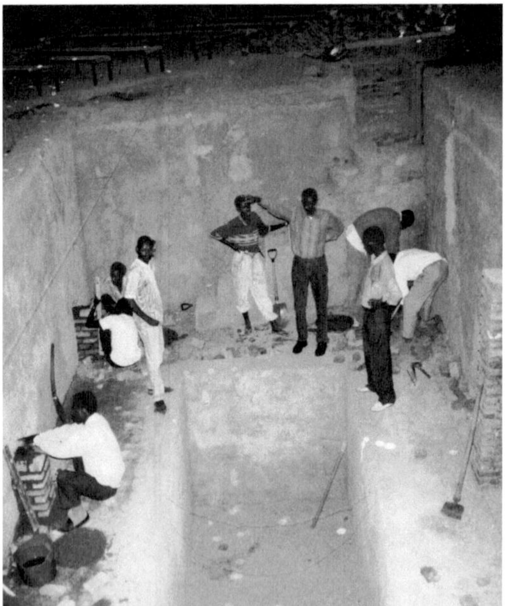

FIGURE 2.13. Large plastic bags along a wall in Nyamata Church hold the remains of genocide victims exhumed by the Genocide Memorial Commission for conservation and display, 1995. Photo by Mario Ibarra, Ibarra archive, Chile.

FIGURE 2.14. Workers build a belowground crypt inside Nyamata Church to hold conserved genocide evidence, 1995. Photo by Mario Ibarra, Ibarra archive, Chile.

In tandem with these first memorialization efforts—distinctly characterized by the preservation, conservation, and display of victims' remains—Rwanda's genocide heritage was also constituted by large-scale exhumations and reburials. Some exhumations were undertaken by human rights workers, like Mario Ibarra, who unearthed victims from hasty mass graves to investigate their identities, manner of death, and those responsible. Other exhumations were directed by the Genocide Memorial Commission and local authorities, which tasked prisoners (alleged *génocidaires*) with removing victims from the first mass reburial sites and sorting those remains. Some disinterred victims' remains were conserved for display at genocide memorial sites. But most of the exhumed victims were reinterred in reburial ceremonies organized by the commission. Display, if only temporary, was still an integral part of those ceremonies. Similar to the rows of skulls and bodies at Nyamata and Murambi, the ceremonies typically included the public exhibition of victims' skeletal remains before interment. At their conclusion, reburials attempted to return victims to some measure of dignity in consecrated mass burial sites and through communal rites.

Exhuming mass graves, reburying victims, and preserving, conserving, and displaying remains at killing sites were attempts to order a memory landscape and shape Rwanda's genocide heritage. In those efforts the approach to register lives erased was decidedly not subtle, nor without substantial labor and emotional turmoil. The conservation enterprise associated with Rwanda's genocide heritage, then, was no easy task. Ultimately co-opted by state interests in sovereignty and social control, the work nonetheless remained driven by individual commitments to a place, its people, and justice. This is one of the central paradoxes of Rwanda's genocide heritage with which this book grapples in its bid to understand why the display and emplacement of traumatic memories were considered so critical.

## The UN Human Rights Field Operation in Rwanda, 1994–1998

The idea to preserve and display material evidence of the genocide emerged in part from attempts to *practice* human rights investigations and protections in situ. Viewing the aftermath in Rwanda was, as a result, a delayed witnessing. Preservation and conservation permitted international observers, prosecutors with the newly formed International Criminal Tribunal for Rwanda, and related human rights and judicial investigators to see the genocide for themselves. The killing sites were maintained to recognize the existence of victims' human rights and charge perpetrators with crimes. And yet preserving victims' bodies and bones was a controversial human rights practice. Nyarubuye was a significant pilot site for

Rwanda's genocide heritage aesthetic. Nyarubuye also situates important debates on the purpose and methods of localized human rights practice that arose from the HRFOR's preservation, and display, of genocide evidence. The ability of the protomemorials to attract such wide attention, to prolong seeing the massacres—and the involvement of the UN in maintaining Nyarubuye as one such critical site—galvanized preservation and witnessing as core practices associated with Rwanda's genocide heritage.

In May 1994 the UN Office of the High Commissioner for Human Rights (OHCHR) launched its first field mission, the HRFOR, one month after the genocidal killings began.[15] The HRFOR operated in the country until the Rwandan government limited its mandate in July 1998.[16] A central motivation for the mission's creation was the notion that human rights did not merely exist as a set of universal principles. Rather, it was driven by the belief that human rights could be *practiced*. Less clear was how.

The Rwanda mission was preceded by substantial issues that were not easily resolved by the HRFOR's creation.[17] Paramount among them was the question of what human rights protections entailed, beyond advocacy, in contexts plagued by ongoing crimes. In addition, the issue of unclear hierarchical distinctions between multiple UN agencies engaging in human rights work hindered the authority of the OHCHR both at headquarters and in the field.[18] This was further complicated by the OHCHR's initial lack of dedicated financial support, which seriously hampered operations on the ground (and when the United Nations Development Program and United Nations High Commissioner for Refugees received disproportionate funding). Each of these issues undermined the OHCHR's new coordinating role, with serious impacts on human rights protection and promotion in Rwanda.

Drawing from recommendations provided by the 1993 Vienna World Conference on Human Rights, the newly appointed High Commissioner of Human Rights, José Ayala Lasso, interpreted the OHCHR mandate as necessitating the in situ presence of human rights officers.[19] Only then, he suggested, would the new OHCHR effectively deliver on two primary areas: human rights monitoring and technical assistance to incorporate a culture of human rights in local law, governance, and citizen treatment.[20] The emphasis on the field presence of human rights officers signaled a shift in the way that human rights were operationalized. Human rights officers were no longer conceived as monitors at a remove, objectively documenting violations. They were rather observers *and* technical advisers who worked closely with local officials to improve human rights protections. As a result, officers were embedded and entangled in complex sociopolitical dilemmas, charged with finding imperfect solutions.

The HRFOR did not launch to prevent the genocide from occurring; its role was mainly after the fact. The agency took responsibility for three huge tasks relating to human rights investigation, protection, and prevention.[21] Foremost among them was to ascertain the facts of crimes that occurred during the genocide, from April to July 1994. The field operation's second task was to monitor human rights *after* the genocide, including the treatment of refugees and returning populations, those suspected of genocide crimes, and prisoners in substantially overcrowded penal facilities.[22] The HRFOR's third area of work was technical assistance for the newly established transitional government and judiciary—to support the incorporation of human rights in prosecutions, governance, and the rule of law. The HRFOR set out to achieve these three objectives without adequate funding or staff.[23] The majority of those deployed to Rwanda did not have adequate human rights or field experience, let alone in conflict settings. And yet, through these three objectives, the HRFOR sought to localize human rights practice.

The HRFOR was certainly not the only human rights organization in the country.[24] Nonetheless, this UN field mission represented an innovation in global human rights practice. Through its presence and technical assistance to the transitional Rwandan government, the HRFOR defined human rights practice in the late twentieth century—a critical time when the implementation of international human rights law was evolving. At the local scale, the agency also amplified a focus on human rights advocacy, accountability, and protection. It sought to practice those objectives in communities torn apart by genocide. Given the failures of the UN to protect against human rights violations during the genocide, the HRFOR was aware of the ironies embedded in its objectives. But those tasks were, nonetheless, pursued in earnest.

### CHALLENGES IN SITU

In the east of the country, the Kibungo Préfecture field office was cited by HRFOR leaders as exemplary for demonstrating the potential and limits of localized human rights practice.[25] From November 1994 to June 1996, Mario Ibarra was head of that field office and led an HRFOR team of between four and eight people. In 2015 he described what it was like to "monitor" human rights and related violations in mid-1990s Rwanda:

> When I was the chief of the Kibungo team and I saw something that was not correct in the region—suppose it was taking prisoners out into the road, working and being beaten—the only thing that I could do was write a report. This report would be passed to one boss, and then another, then to Geneva, then to New York, taken to the embassy, and maybe the secretariat

would forget and nothing happened. While I was working for the ministry, I could talk to the *bourgmestre*. I could say: "*Señor Bourgmestre*, you are silly, this thing is imbecilic! Look at what you are doing. What if the Red Cross and the OHCHR came to see what you are doing; you'd be screwed!" I was not protecting the [Rwandan] government. I was protecting human rights.[26]

A cumbersome bureaucracy, understaffing, and meager funding and infrastructure set severe limits on what the HRFOR mission could do. Related frustrations eventually led Mario, a career human rights officer, to leave the HRFOR in 1996 and work directly for Rwanda's new Genocide Memorial Commission. Disillusionments with the HRFOR were not Mario's alone. They were shared by employees of the field mission at all levels in the hierarchy.[27]

The stakes were high. During the first months after the genocide, the situation in Kibungo was far from secure. The few surviving and returning residents were terrified of their neighbors. The scale and brutality of genocide attacks against Tutsi in the region had been immense and severe. There was also a high prevalence of revenge actions by both residents and new regime officials that ranged from extrajudicial killings to harassment, beatings, disappearances, and imprisonments without due process.[28] Further complicating the HRFOR's work in the region, the failures of the UN peacekeeping force (the UN Assistance Mission for Rwanda or UNAMIR) to prevent the genocide and protect civilians perpetuated distrust of the UN's subsequent local engagements (figure 2.15). In Kibungo, local authorities threatened residents with arrest if they provided UN genocide investigators with information or requested security protection.[29] Understandably, Rwandans were skeptical about the UN's and HRFOR's commitments to human rights concerns, and their abilities to act on them, after the civil war and genocide.

To address the climate of distrust in eastern Rwanda (between residents and toward the UN by the government) and improve the human rights situation there, Mario's Kibungo Field Office engaged several "tactical strategies," to use the first HRFOR chief of mission's phrase.[30] The strategies underscore the Kibungo Field Office's contribution to human rights practice: to engage locally—an obvious but nonetheless undervalued and underutilized principle of international organizations' action (figure 2.16). Key to this shift was the view that monitoring and calling out evidence of human rights violations were not enough. Kibungo staff met regularly with local authorities and residents, increasing their familiarity with the conditions, people, and problems of the area. By interacting with local authorities, other NGOs, and residents, HRFOR field officers could call attention to cycles of human rights abuse.[31] With knowledge of local needs, they could then design specific projects to address group vulnerabilities, cultures of impunity, judicial

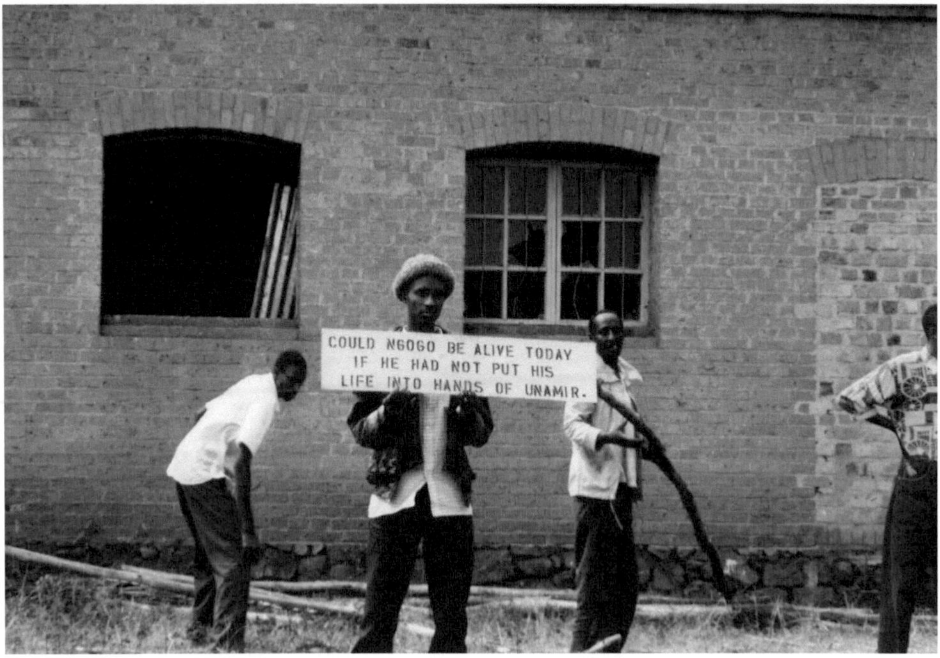


FIGURE 2.15. A protester holds a sign condemning the UN at the Nyarubuye genocide site during Secretary-General Boutros Boutros-Ghali's visit, July 14, 1995. Photo by Mario Ibarra, Ibarra archive, Chile.

and penal reform, or human rights education and steer donor funds to those enterprises.[32] Local projects, in turn, demonstrated the indivisibility of economic, social, political, civil, and cultural rights. This bottom-up methodology amplified the value and the range of a rights-based approach to rebuilding society and governance after the genocide—in the very communities in which threats to life, violence, economic deprivation, and distrust were experienced.

The Kibungo Field Office's advancements notwithstanding, the HRFOR's inadequacies stymied the fullness of its potential to affect the human rights situation in Rwanda. The HRFOR's institutional failures also, inadvertently, motivated the rights-based practices and advocacy that ultimately developed into genocide heritage. Both direct local engagement and work to bring attention to victims and crimes sought to bolster weak human rights institutions. Both were approaches to the local practice of human rights. When seen in this context, the preservation of Nyarubuye Church by Mario's Kibungo HRFOR team can be understood as a crucial effort in the localized practice of human rights investigation and advocacy.

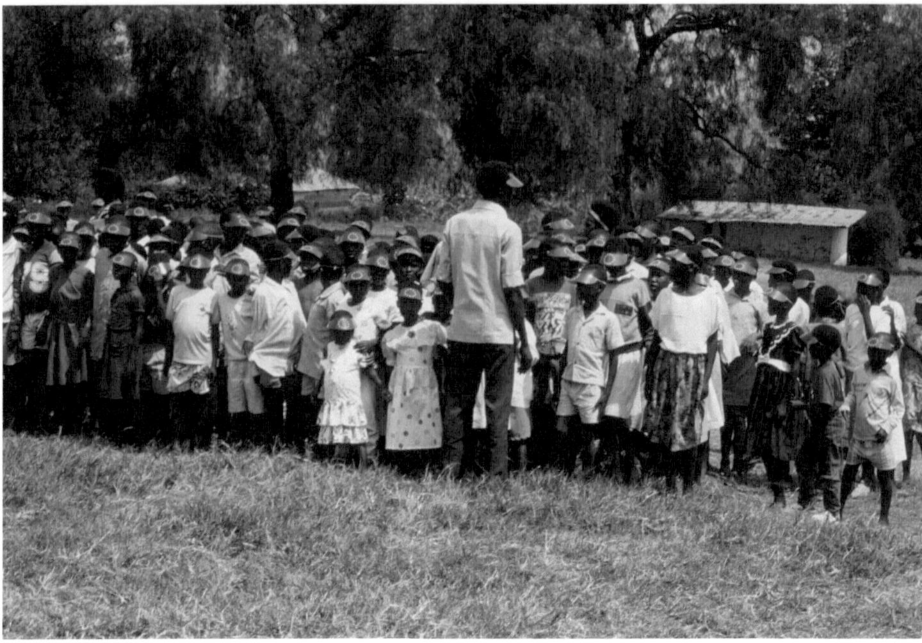

FIGURE 2.16. The HRFOR interpreted local human rights practice as community engagement, organizing a Children's Day festival for genocide orphans, who wore visors with the logo of the European Union (the sponsor), June 16, 1995. Photo by Mario Ibarra, Ibarra archive, Chile.

## QUESTIONS OF EVIDENCE

One of the HRFOR's lasting influences was establishing the preservation of massacre sites and victims' remains as a human rights practice. The connection transpired from one of the HRFOR's primary mandates: to collect "evidence of grave violations of international humanitarian law committed in the territory of Rwanda, including the evidence of possible acts of genocide."[33] Documenting evidence of massacres in situ, locating mass graves, and ascertaining the nature of attacks and the identity of those killed amounted to the de facto preservation of the details of that violence. Those efforts subsequently shaped Rwanda's genocide heritage aesthetic. Altogether, those engagements create an opening for thinking about the role of memory, narrative, and disclosure as a form of justice seeking that is far more immediate than criminal trials with their procedural, evidentiary, and custodial requirements.

The HRFOR's views on evidence and disclosure contrast with those of other UN bodies tasked with the criminal investigation and prosecution of genocide crimes. Chief among the latter were the special rapporteur for Rwanda, the subsequently appointed Commission of Experts, and the Special Investigations Unit (SIU), which was initially part of the OHCHR and later of the International Criminal Tribunal for Rwanda (ICTR). Among them, the HRFOR and SIU were the two primary bodies that investigated the genocide for extended periods of time in Rwanda.[34] When the SIU became the Legal Analysis and Coordination Unit of the ICTR in November 1994, its mandate became more explicit: to collect prosecutorial evidence. But from the start, the SIU's focus and methods of data collection remained consistent with prosecutorial aims. They were fundamentally opposed to those of HRFOR human rights investigations. In essence, the SIU aimed to be unbiased in its work, to remain distant from local experiences of violence. That remove was not easy to maintain in the genocide's aftermath, in a landscape upended by, and with residents reeling from, mass violence.

In April 1995 the SIU compiled a report on its genocide investigations that included descriptions of its investigatory methodology. The report established clear distinctions between its approach and that of the HRFOR. The SIU differentiated between three types of genocide evidence: documents related to the planning of the genocide, witness testimony (including from survivors, nontargeted residents, and perpetrators), and investigations of mass graves and massacre sites.[35] Each had challenges in factual reliability and prosecutorial viability. But for the SIU, documents and other hard evidence of the genocide's organization were the most credible for prosecutions. Witness testimony and massacre sites tended to be viewed as less reliable. The SIU's views on evidence were underpinned by errant cultural assumptions. For example, it considered local witnesses undependable because "the oral tradition in Rwanda can render it extremely difficult to distinguish between what a witness has seen and . . . has been told by other people."[36] The SIU investigators also determined that genocide perpetrator testimonies would likely be inadmissible in court, noting that "Rwandan arrest procedures, conditions of detention, and questioning of suspects fall short of international human rights standards and constitute a 'serious violation' thereof."[37] The SIU's assessment of in situ evidence at massacre sites and mass graves was similarly unfavorable. Those places were not only deteriorating because of rain and sun but also forensically contaminated. Many killing sites had been disturbed by genocide organizers who attempted to remove evidence of their crimes or by local residents who moved and buried the bodies of relatives.[38] For the SIU, therefore, spatial evidence had little value other than a representation of the genocide's occurrence: Environmental and custodial circumstances thwarted its reliability in criminal prosecutions.

Accordingly, the SIU made a critical operational distinction between two primary types of genocide evidence: that used for criminal prosecutions and that employed for "traditional human rights work."[39] The SIU focused mainly on building trial cases against higher-level organizers of killings. They kept their findings and investigatory processes confidential. They also did not privilege the collection of victim testimonies because those individuals were typically not firsthand witnesses to efforts to organize the genocide. By contrast, other, non-ICTR investigations were rather more interested in the details of genocide crimes gained from witness testimony and in situ evidence of the massacres. The purpose of the HRFOR's work, for example, was to make experiences of violence *known* at and beyond the local scale—not to keep evidence confidential for later adjudication.

The differentiation in the HRFOR's and SIU's evidentiary priorities had an unintentional, though nonetheless significant, effect on Rwanda's genocide heritage aesthetic. It ultimately bolstered the association of human rights work with the preservation and conservation of genocide sites. Immediately after the genocide, HRFOR officers, other NGOs, and Rwandan government officials turned to the SIU's downgraded evidence—testimonies and material and spatial evidence of mass violence—to make a case for the scope and severity of massive human rights violations in 1994 (figures 2.17–2.18). In addition to the HRFOR, African Rights, Human Rights Watch, and Physicians for Human Rights (PHR) undertook the first investigations of genocide sites and witness testimony to determine what had happened.[40] Long before trials were convened, human rights organizations documented and disseminated that recent history to a global public. Other organizations initiated similar work: The genocide survivors' association Ibuka developed a *préfecture*-wide survey of remaining households in Kibuye to identify the names of sixty thousand victims in the area.[41] Writing retrospectively in 2001, Dr. William Haglund, the head of the PHR forensic team in Rwanda, and his colleagues recounted the objectives that motivated their work: "(1) to collect narrative and physical evidence that assists in establishing the accountability of those responsible and bringing them to justice; (2) to assemble information instrumental in identifying the victims in order that the remains might be returned to surviving relatives; (3) to create a record that will stand up to historical revisionists; and (4) to expose such atrocities to world opinion and provide an international standard that will deter such atrocities in the future. The cumulative effect of such investigations is to give voice to the victims, imparting their voices from the grave."[42] These four PHR objectives represent principles codified in the 1948 Universal Declaration of Human Rights. They connect human rights practice to investigations of sites and witnesses to the genocide.

The interest of PHR in collecting narrative and physical evidence, assembling information about victims, creating a historical record, and exposing mass violence to a global public constituted the "traditional human rights work" that the SIU op-

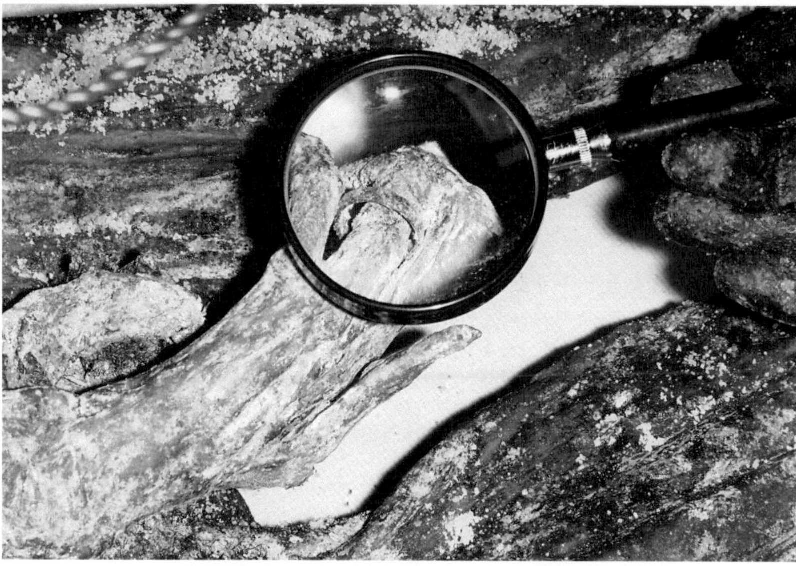

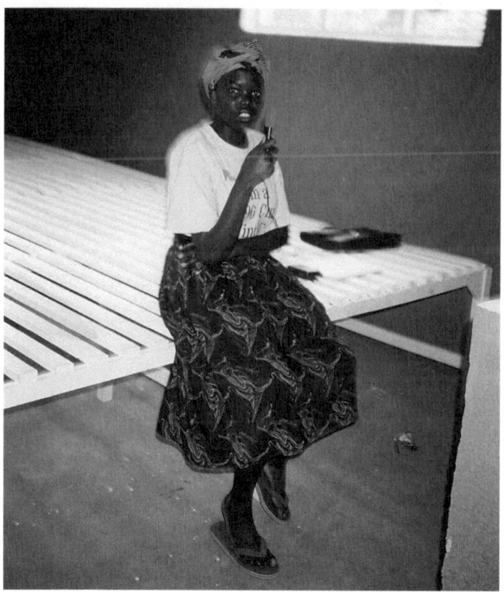

FIGURE 2.17. Material evidence: The Genocide Memorial Commission examines victims for identifiable belongings and causes of death, December 1996. Photo by Mario Ibarra, Kanamugire archive, Rwanda.

FIGURE 2.18. Survivor testimony: The Genocide Memorial Commission audio-records the experience of a survivor of the Murambi massacre, 1997. Photo by Mario Ibarra, Kanamugire archive, Rwanda.

posed. It was not strictly prosecutorial evidence; it was evidence of human rights violations intended for wide public distribution. Those objectives were shared by African Rights and Human Rights Watch, who relied on witness testimony and site observations to develop the first reports detailing the genocide. They were also shared by the Rwandan government and the HRFOR's Kibungo field team, who employed site preservation to perpetuate the visibility of the Nyarubuye massacre for visiting journalists and foreign government representatives. Paradoxically, the latter turned to dehumanizing representational forms to insist on the depravity of the perpetrators and the humanity of the victims. These are the diffuse but nonetheless significant legacies of in situ human rights practice for Rwanda's genocide heritage.

### "Rwanda: Reconstruire," October 1994

In the months immediately after the genocide, local, national, and international perspectives informed the aims and dilemmas of memorialization. Many of those conversations converged around notions of memory justice and its roles in establishing the facts of the genocide, rebuilding the nation, and preventing future violence. The "Rwanda: Reconstruire" conference demonstrates how widespread the interest in those themes was at an early stage. Neither Mario Ibarra nor Louis Kanamugire attended, but participants voiced concerns and priorities adjacent to theirs.

The "Rwanda: Reconstruire" conference was convened in the capital, Kigali, from October 22 to 28, 1994, by a Rwandan human rights organization, the Collectif des Ligues et Associations de Défense des Droits de l'Homme (CLADHO; Collective of Leagues and Organizations for the Defense of Human Rights in Rwanda) along with a Swiss partner, the Fondation Charles Léopold Mayer pour le Progrès de l'Homme (FPH; Charles Léopold Mayer Foundation for the Progress of Man). It was attended by 250 representatives of local civil society groups, international NGOs, the Rwandan government and the RPF, religious organizations, and foreign development agencies. Several attendees are of note for their roles in state, political party, and international NGO leadership, including Prime Minister Faustin Twagiramungu, Vice Prime Minister and RPF Executive Secretary Alexis Kanyarengwe, RPF founding member Tito Rutaremara, and Alison Des Forges of Human Rights Watch. This was an extraordinary gathering of a remarkable range of figures drawn into open debate at a time of continuing instability.

Over the course of seven days, participants discussed priority areas for rebuilding Rwanda. They compared other countries' experiences and proposed strategies for Rwanda's postgenocide reform. Among the topics discussed, memory was prominent. The Working Group on Memory comprised one of nine working groups that met on issues of judicial, media, civil society, land, and governmental reform along with specific challenges faced by youth, refugees, genocide survivors, and the government in attracting international aid.[43]

Discussions within the "Rwanda: Reconstruire" conference demonstrate a broad consensus among conference participants—three months after the genocide—on the importance of preserving evidence of crimes at massacre sites. Proceedings also outline the main motivations and characteristics of what would become authorized genocide heritage. At this early stage, memory emerges as a central concern in the task of building a future Rwanda.[44]

### JUST MEMORY

In their executive summary of the "Rwanda: Reconstruire" conference, co-convenors Pierre Calame and David Gakunzi differentiate between two types of memory in Rwanda. They use the term *constructed memory* to refer to the historically politicized constructions of social difference between Tutsi and Hutu groups that ultimately motivated genocidal violence. In this characterization, memory is mythology: weaponized for power and a politics of exclusion. By contrast, they employ *just memory* to refer to a new, postgenocide approach: one that would use the "history of the massacres themselves" as a foundation for the country's future history.[45] Here, just memory is not merely a form of truth telling but a means to recast the future of the past. The distinctions were elaborated by the Working Group on Memory, whose conversations are also documented in the conference proceedings. The participants' distinction between constructed and just memory foreshadowed the government's later condemnation of "bad" histories and promotion of "good" narratives.[46] Such binary distinctions have been central to national rhetoric and policy ever since.

However, the conclusions that the Working Group on Memory reached were not exclusively nationalist. Both national and foreign government representatives were part of the discussions. Participants who held or would later hold key Rwandan government positions included Joseph Nsengimana, who led the ministry that created the Genocide Memorial Commission in 1995 (the Ministry of Higher Education, Scientific Research, and Culture [MINESUPRES]), and José Kagabo, a Rwandan professor of history at the École des Hautes Etudes en Sciences Sociales (School for Advanced Studies in the Social Sciences) in France, member of the RPF leadership, and later senator of Rwanda's Southern Province. Prominent foreign participants in the Working Group on Memory included Jean-Pierre Gontard, a Swiss expert in conflict mediation; Ilan Halevi, a high-ranking Jewish member of the Palestinian Liberation Organization; and Chilean human rights lawyer Hernan Montealegre. The latter introduced the case study of Chile's violent dictatorship and politics of memory to the working group. Montealegre and others provided examples of memory projects developed within the global human rights movement as precedents for Rwanda's genocide heritage.[47] These participants were among a total of thirty-eight working group participants who brought diverse international experiences to bear on Rwanda's "problem of memory."

The Working Group on Memory suggested that a "just memory" for Rwanda would be achieved by privileging "objective" remembrance. The challenges to achieving a resolutely objective memory were not deliberated, nor were issues of what or who should be remembered. Instead, four conditions were identified to elaborate the concept of just memory: the form of memory, literal memory, exemplary memory, and memory and justice.[48]

The taxonomy was not analytically discrete. The "form of memory" concerned all categories in the list. It also emphasized the importance of material evidence to genocide heritage and, as a result, a visual and spatial mode of representation. Cast as memory-facts, "literal memory" referred to empirical observations of the genocide. The concept referred to evidence of the genocide's occurrence including documentation of the massacres' organization and related propaganda, sites of killing, weapons used, victims' belongings, and bodies. Perhaps more so than any other conceptualization, a "literal" memory justified the conservation efforts at sites of massacre to "document the recent history of the genocide . . . fixing the image of the genocide and planned massacres in memory."[49] Doing so substantiated the importance that material evidence and "objective" narratives had for achieving justice and safeguarding the future of the nation. However, the working group noted how insufficient "literal memory" ultimately would be in achieving "an objective and complete memory."[50] In other words, Rwanda's genocide heritage needed further intervention.

To those ends, "exemplary memory" and "memory and justice" emerged as critical amplifiers for seemingly self-evident, unmediated evidence of the genocide. Both types of memory emphasize state-authorized collective memories, which were considered of greater civic importance than individual remembrance. "Exemplary" memories emerged from the curatorial selection of particular genocide experiences for emphasis. "Memory and justice" reinforced the human rights foundations of the conference with the notion that individual testimonies speak truth to power and are pivotal to adjudication. The working group identified eleven examples of how the government and civil society could intervene to highlight exemplary memories for justice. Those eleven "concrete propositions" can be categorized in three broad fields of intervention: civic education, transitional justice, and heritage conservation.

Most of the civic education propositions have been adopted and elaborated over the past three decades, indicating the influence and resonance they had with government leaders. Prominent among them were efforts to reform—and develop state controls for—television and radio media, create a National Day of Remembrance, and review and standardize primary and secondary school history curricula. One suggestion—to identify a list of "rescuers" as a means to reconstruct "positive values" and the concept of "heroism" in relation to the genocide—gained early support but has been underemphasized in recent years.[51]

Another since-abandoned idea fit more squarely within human rights and transitional justice practice and involved the creation of a truth commission in advance of a reformed judicial system.[52] Notably, the proposal for a Rwandan truth commission precedes South Africa's Truth and Reconciliation Commission (1995–2002). The idea was modeled, as the summary document notes, on those that took place in Chile (1990–91) and El Salvador (1992–93) and informed in part by the challenges faced by some groups (Palestinians are explicitly mentioned) when engaging in truth-telling processes. The Working Group on Memory proposed that a Rwandan truth commission would investigate genocide crimes, identify perpetrators and other mechanisms that encouraged mass violence, and locate significant events and places for national commemoration. Though a truth commission was not ultimately formed, human rights and nongovernmental organizations, journalists, and the Genocide Memorial Commission took on the truth-seeking aspects of this proposition immediately after the genocide. The breadth of organizations involved in seeking facts reflects how little was known in the first years about how and why the attacks had occurred and who had been attacked amid the immense scale of genocidal violence.

## "FIXING" GENOCIDE MEMORY

A central concern of "Rwanda: Reconstruire" was how to "fix" genocide memory. The double entendre of the word was purposeful. On the one hand, to fix was to repair: to restore the omissions in genocide history, destroyed by the violence itself. On the other hand, to fix was to root, or preserve, the memories of the victims and the violations they suffered—both in place and in the minds of individuals in Rwanda and the world.

The conference participants conferred significant weight to obtaining and seeing evidence of the genocide. Memorials were mentioned twice in the Working Group on Memory proceedings: first as a general proposal to "fix the recent history of the genocide" and then specifically as a state policy to preserve evidence of the killings in situ.[53] No explicit mention is made of preserving victims' remains. But four of the eleven propositions by the Working Group on Memory propose, in general, that the government document and preserve "materials that illustrate the genocide and the planning of massacres."[54] Indicating what was lost by not doing so, the conference proceedings include the lament: "It is regrettable that the pile of machetes and other weapons used in the killings in Rusumo abandoned by fleeing militias were not left behind and carefully preserved."[55] In the context of the stated interest in manifest, visible, and "literal" evidence, the implication here was that some manner of maintaining scenes of massacre was paramount to producing a lasting memory of the genocide.

A lasting memory was also envisioned as a repository of witness testimony and records documenting the lives of the dead. The archive buildings at Kabgayi Catholic Parish, the baptismal records at Nyarubuye Church, and those of government offices and other parishes were targets of vandalism during the genocide. There, perpetrators purposefully destroyed birth and census records to erase records of Tutsi existence. The working group proposed a national repository dedicated to genocide history, which would include remaining records and documentation of witness testimony. From the beginning, a genocide archive was imagined in multimedia and in situ—dispersed among the multiple sites of the killings' occurrence.

The 1994 "Rwanda: Reconstruire" conference claimed genocide memory as a priority for rebuilding the country. It heard some of the earliest proposals by government and local and foreign civil society representatives to maintain genocide memory. The visibility of genocide heritage—comprising spaces of exception where killing sites were preserved and removed from the continuities of everyday life—demarcated both the enemy and the domain of the state. It also, paradoxically, established one of the earliest human rights justifications for Rwanda's genocide heritage. To those ends, the working group established the two main objectives of Rwanda's genocide heritage, dually conceived as evidentiary support for legal trials and means to fix "the image of the genocide and planned massacres in memory" (figure 2.19).[56] Those objectives flaunted the SIU's distinction between prosecutorial evidence and "traditional human rights work." The working group had a broader view of justice, one not merely tethered to criminal trials. The process of achieving justice was, instead, predicated on witnessing of the genocide, long after its occurrence, by publics near and far.

The proposals offered by the Working Group on Memory were certainly not the first nor the only such discussions regarding the role of conservation practices in genocide heritage. Notably, Mario Ibarra and Louis Kanamugire were not involved, which underscores that the human rights and nation-building

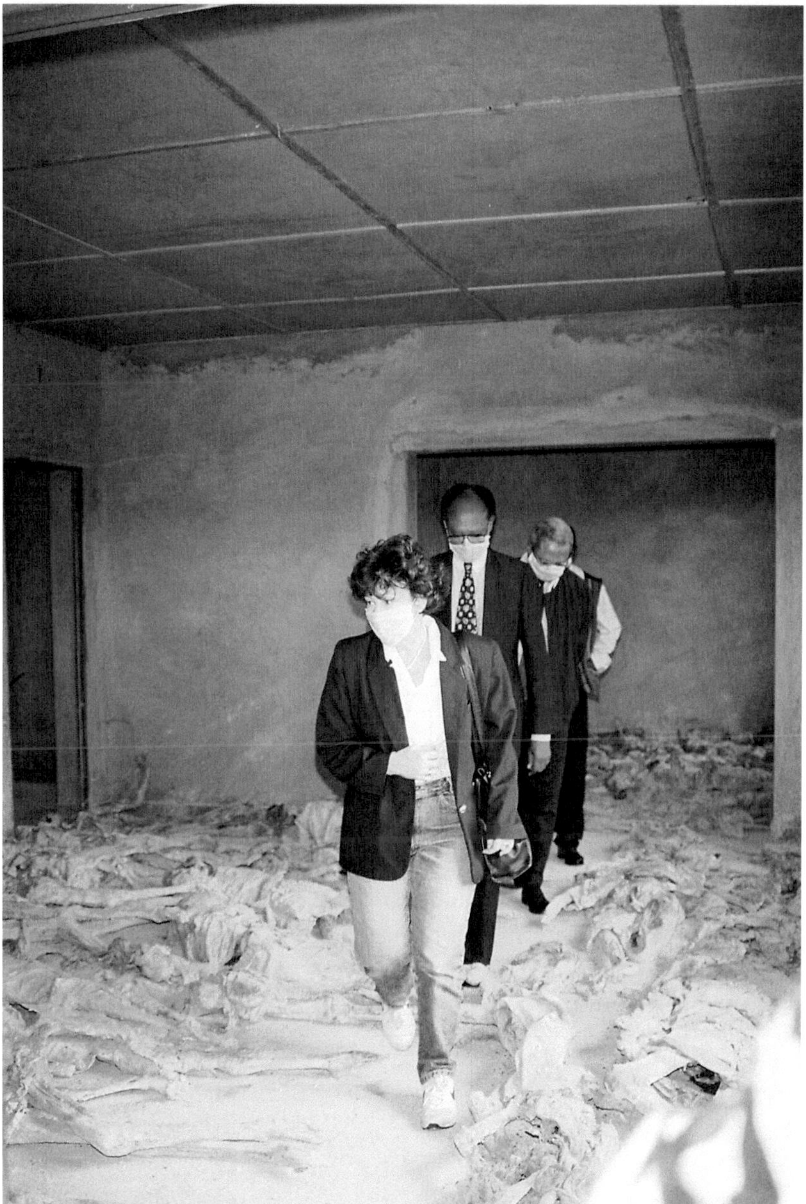

FIGURE 2.19. Chief prosecutor Louise Arbour and her ICTR team walk among conserved genocide victims at Murambi, 1996. Photo by Mario Ibarra, Kanamugire archive, Rwanda.

foundations for genocide heritage did not originate in nor stop at their particular engagements. Instead, the conference proceedings document official positions taken by higher-level representatives of the government who launched a Genocide Memorial Commission in charge of many of these aims one year later.

## The Genocide Memorial Commission, 1995–1998

State interests in genocide memorialization were marked by contradiction. Externally, the government was struggling to persuade the rest of the world to recognize the genocide. Internally, it was attempting to establish control by codifying evidence of the genocide as history while simultaneously suppressing challenges to the authorizing regime. These complementary yet incompatible interests were institutionalized in the Genocide Memorial Commission, which was formed on October 20, 1995, by MINESUPRES.

The Genocide Memorial Commission's mandate included four primary objectives. The first two were immediate priorities in the first year after the genocide: to collect basic information about the genocide and also to identify *les noblesses* (individual rescuers or heroic saviors during the genocide).[57] Both objectives were largely achieved by the first activities—the genocide investigations and related *Preliminary Report* and *Genocide Sites Map*—undertaken in 1995 by the commission. In 1996 and thereafter, it turned to a second set of priorities: to develop memorials in service of genocide memory and organize decent burials for victims throughout Rwanda.[58] The four objectives resulted in Rwanda's genocide heritage. In the process, the Genocide Memorial Commission associated national collective memory with a distinctive aesthetic derived from the preservation and conservation of genocide evidence. It also institutionalized paradoxical relationships among spatialized memory, state sovereignty, and human rights and justice.

### MULTIMINISTERIAL MEMORY WORK

In the year between the "Rwanda: Reconstruire" conference and the creation of the Genocide Memorial Commission, several government agencies initiated projects that later came under the commission's purview. Four ministries—the Ministry of Defense (MINADEF), Ministry of Labor and Social Affairs (MINITRASO), Ministry of Rehabilitation and Social Integration (MINIREISO), and MINESUPRES—were involved in matters related to genocide documentation, evidence preservation and conservation, and victim reburial and commemoration. The activities that those ministries led initially were ad hoc responses to local circumstances rather than coordinated strategies.

Before any other agency intervened, RPA forces were the first to be involved in safeguarding evidence of the genocide. Their protection of massacre sites made later preservation practices possible. The RPA also facilitated foreigners' access to massacre sites as the genocide took place, providing armed officers to accompany media correspondents and human rights investigators. In late April 1994, for example, military liaisons helped BBC correspondent Fergal Keane identify and then tour the Nyarubuye Parish massacre site, which was captured on film and broadcast to an international audience in late June.[59] Many RPA operatives also held key positions in the postgenocide government. Those individuals established critical connections between the Genocide Memorial Commission's approach to memory work and that of the military and MINADEF. An example includes the MINADEF Information and Public Relations Department, which built from similar liaison work during the genocide to provide access to genocide sites afterward, including investigations conducted by African Rights.[60] Captain Firmin Gatera, who was a member of the Genocide Memorial Commission's interministerial task force, was the head of MINADEF public relations. At Gatera's direction, his department codified Louis's and Mario's map of genocide investigations as the 1997 *Genocide Sites Map*.[61] He also claimed that genocide memorials were essential to national security.[62] The latter entailed an interest in protecting the country by preserving history as a preventative warning for future generations. Because most of the leadership of the newly formed government—at national, ministerial, and local levels—was affiliated with the RPA and RPF, it is difficult to delaminate either from the state genocide memory projects that followed. While military and high-level RPF affiliates were not always involved on the ground, those government actors were typically part of every authorizing decision.

Two other ministries—MINIREISO (oriented to demobilization and refugee return) and MINITRASO (dedicated to labor and social concerns)—were also involved in genocide memory projects, but the reasons are less clear. In particular, MINITRASO, especially its communications director, Silas Sinyigaya, was active in the first reburial and commemoration ceremonies and in the Genocide Memorial Commission's initial task force.[63] The involvement of the social affairs ministry with genocide memory was largely ad hoc: MINITRASO became the lead agency in charge of the first victim reburials by happenstance. In late 1994 Sinyigaya was approached by a resident living outside of Kigali, whom he knew, who requested state assistance to bury 150 members of her extended family and community.[64] According to Sinyigaya, this led to the first government-organized public reburial ceremony on November 13, 1994, which was presided over by the minister of health and attended by the local community, journalists, and government officials.[65] The World Health Organization and UNICEF (United Nations Children's Fund) provided plastic sheets to inter bodies. Decent burials (*gushyingura mu cyubahiro* in Kinyarwanda) continued to be conducted by MINITRASO until the Genocide Memorial Commission took over that role in 1996. In addition, MINITRASO took the lead in organizing the state's first national genocide commemoration at Rebero Hill in April 1995. The ceremony was pivotal in shaping Rwanda's genocide heritage: It commemorated the first anniversary of the genocide and, in doing so, connected the display of victims' coffins with state political messages that condemned the international community for its failures to act.

The reasons for MINIREISO's involvement are comparably less evident. Its head, Minister Jacques Bihozagara, was a founding member of the RPF and commanded significant influence in the postgenocide government.[66] Bihozagara helped to develop some of the first ideas regarding genocide memorials and provided logistical help for victim burials.[67] In 1997, two years after the creation of the Genocide Memorial Commission, Bihozagara took over as minister of MINESUPRES, to which it reported. Bihozagara authorized the experiments to conserve victims' remains that occurred in 1997 at Murambi, Ruhashya, and Nyamata, led by Mario Ibarra and Dr. Kanimba under Louis Kanamugire and the Genocide Memorial Commission.[68] Both posts, together with Bihozagara's status within RPF leadership, indicate the relatively early interest of the political party and government in genocide heritage and, in particular, the display of evidence and victims of massacres.

Another key player in MINIREISO genocide heritage initiatives was Eric Rousseau, a Belgian expatriate who curiously became involved in top-level discussions within the newly established government. The most detailed public record of Rousseau's involvement is available in transcripts of his testimony in the ICTR trial against Casimir Bizimungu and codefendants. Rousseau was a Belgian businessman who began volunteering for MINIREISO in July 1994, motivated by his earlier RPF fundraising efforts in Belgium and Jewish heritage. In his testimony for the ICTR in 2003, he notes that the latter compelled him to join government and respond, in some way, to the genocide.[69] At the trial Rousseau claimed that he had created the Genocide Memorial Commission.[70] Though it is possible that Rousseau first had the idea for the commission, Louis Kanamugire disputed that Rousseau had a significant role in developing the institution.[71] Rousseau's role in developing genocide heritage practices was rather more limited.[72] While at MINIREISO, he drafted a proposal for a genocide memorial in Kigali that "aimed to create . . . the tools necessary for a new national conscience, lasting reconciliation, an understanding of human rights, and a place to research the genocide."[73] Rousseau's February 1995 Kigali genocide memorial proposal preceded the commission's work and is significant for the correlations it established among genocide memorialization, human rights, and reconciliation. It was not the only precommission memorial proposal: MINESUPRES sponsored a Rwandan expatriate architect's plans for a genocide museum at Ntarama Parish outside Kigali that was submitted to the ministry in April 1995.[74] Athanase Ndutiye Kagahe's design notably and uniquely makes reference to the conservation of bodies, clothing and personal effects, weapons, and places of genocide massacre—which later was the hallmark of the Genocide Memorial Commission's approach to memorialization.[75] Rousseau's proposal did not include similar details but is nonetheless significant for its reference to the Yad Vashem Holocaust Remembrance Center and other Holocaust memorial museums, a connection that was only realized nine years later by the Holocaust memory organization Aegis Trust, which developed the national genocide memorial in Kigali. Rousseau served as the MINIREISO representative to the Genocide Memorial Commission's interministerial task force from October to December 1995.

These various cross-agency, pre-Genocide Memorial Commission activities reinforce several broader points about the Rwandan government's first genocide heritage engagements. First, given the range of ministries involved, it is clear that there was significant military and political support for genocide heritage immediately after the 1994 massacres. That support did not have clear origins. No single person or ministry was responsible for the state's stewardship of genocide memory in 1994. The only clear commonality of most—but not all—involved in state projects was their RPF or RPA affiliation.[76] Second, a consistent characteristic of the earliest genocide heritage projects was that they were iterative and ad hoc. This suggests that there was no clear plan from the start—nor a consistent aesthetic or method—for how to treat the collective memory of the genocide. Early genocide heritage work also relied heavily on individual expertise and those persons' relationships to local constituencies, international organizations, and/or the RPF. Last, the first preservation and conservation experiments at genocide sites were critical to the state's subsequent formalization of genocide heritage. In other words, the Genocide Memorial Commission was aware of and drew from these first site experiments and proposals to undertake a more coordinated approach. Others did as well. A collective memory and national history of the genocide thus developed iteratively at the nexus of international organizations, new state institutions, and local, site-specific practices.

Genocide heritage gained stature as a set of state-authorized approaches to "fixing" genocide memory with the formation of the Genocide Memorial Commission. Less than two weeks after the commission's creation, the Rwandan government sponsored a conference attended by prominent state representatives, human rights and other foreign NGOs, journalists, church leaders, and local and foreign academics. The proceedings of the November 1995 "Genocide, Impunity, and Accountability" conference primarily include written recommendations to the Rwandan government and international community. Under a section titled "The Determination of the Truth," organizers write, "The Conference believes it is imperative that the people of Rwanda and the world know how such a crime was conceived, planned, and executed. The Conference recognizes that, while criminal prosecution and gathering of information for . . . justice can be useful to this end, there remains an overriding need for a process whose sole and exclusive objective is the full documentation of the Rwandan genocide."[77] The statement clarified the need to separate a "memorial authority" from the judicial process, reinforcing the Genocide Memorial Commission's distinct and important role in representing genocide history. Organizers recommended that the MINESUPRES agency privilege seven tasks for the purpose of "memory preservation":

a. Construction of a National Memorial of the genocide;
b. Construction of monuments at the sites of the worst massacres;
c. Preserve the remains of the victims of genocide in at least every commune;
d. Carry out a thorough documentation of the genocide and publish it widely;
e. Draw up a map of Rwanda highlighting areas where the genocide took place;
f. Commemorate "Memorial Day" on the 7th of April each year;
g. Integrate the theme of genocide into cultural programs.[78]

The proceedings were published by the Office of the President, in the earliest and most explicit government statement regarding its approach to Rwanda's genocide heritage. By November 1995 building a national memorial and developing local memorials at major massacre sites had already gained widespread national and international consensus.[79] Rather less settled was the third recommendation—the preservation of victims' remains at local killing sites. Its inclusion represents a clear shift toward state endorsement of the controversial practice. By February 1996 Louis Kanamugire had completed the fourth recommendation by publishing the commission's genocide investigations in its *Preliminary Report*.[80] The *Genocide Sites Map* developed from Mario Ibarra's and Louis's investigatory work fulfilled the fifth recommendation in 1997. The latter recommendations were also steered by the commission and continue to be integrated in annual commemorations and media and education programs today. The creation of the Genocide Memorial Commission was pivotal, then, to the execution of state-authorized genocide memory preservation.

The Genocide Memorial Commission was initially organized as a task force representing the interests and participation of six different ministries. Louis Kanamugire, the commission's inaugural director, was employed by MINESUPRES. The five additional members were Captain Firmin Gatera from MINADEF; Silas Sinyigaya as the representative of MINITRASO; Eric Rousseau of MINIREISO; François Ntanganzwa for the Ministry of Gender, Family, and the Promotion of Women (MIGEPROF); and Deus Zabagabo from the Ministry of Interior and Local Development (MININTER). The primary role of the six members was to visit massacre sites and interview remaining residents. Mario Ibarra, Dr. Kanimba, and several lower-level government employees were involved as consultants and staff. Compared to the commission's six official members, Dr. Kanimba and Mario had rather more substantial roles in leading conservation experiments and genocide investigations. After the *Preliminary Report* was published in February 1996, the interministerial task force was disbanded, and the commission was staffed primarily by Louis Kanamugire and between one and eight associates.[81]

The first minister of MINESUPRES, Joseph Nsengimana, was a fervent defender of genocide memorialization and, as a highly influential academic and politician, had a significant role in authorizing Rwanda's genocide heritage aesthetic. Nsengimana served as MINESUPRES minister from just after the genocide to 1997, when he was appointed minister of MINITRASO, remaining there until the end of 1999. Nsengimana had grown up in Rwanda, earned a PhD in France, and was a professor of comparative literature at the National University of Rwanda before 1994. He lost his wife and two children in the genocide. When he took the position at MINESUPRES in 1994, he had already gained a reputation as a scholar and influential Labor Party (PL) leader. He wielded significant political capital within the new transitional government because of his academic position and scholarly knowledge, opposition party leadership, and personal losses and commitments as a genocide survivor.[82] Nsengimana's stature in the government shaped his ministry's ability to sponsor both the Genocide Memorial Commission and the conservation of human remains that began under his supervision at the Murambi killing site in 1996. He attended and helped draft the "memory preservation" objectives at the government's November 1995 conference. He also led government negotiations with the Catholic Church to memorialize prominent parish massacre sites instead of returning them to community worship.[83]

Under Nsengimana's leadership, the Genocide Memorial Commission took over the organization of national commemoration and reburial ceremonies. Louis organized the second annual commemoration at the Murambi massacre site in April 1996 in one of the commission's most prominent genocide memory projects. Activities associated with genocide heritage diversified and increased in scale after that national commemoration. In tandem, the commission assumed responsibility for the victim reburials that MINITRASO had conducted throughout the country. Reburial ceremonies were local community-oriented ceremonies distinct from the national and international exposure of commemorations. At the height of that work, the commission arranged 120 mass interments in a one-year period, averaging around two per week, from 1997 to 1998 (figure 2.20).[84]

During Nsengimana's MINESUPRES tenure, the Genocide Memorial Commission also ramped up its conservation efforts at major massacre sites, incorporating the display of victim remains and in situ evidence of killings into its approach to memorial curation. Though seemingly paradoxical, simultaneous efforts to bury and display victims indicate the significance that gruesome, deteriorating bodily remains had for constructing Rwanda's collective memory of the genocide. The sheer scale of barely recognizable human figures proclaimed humanity's loss and depravity at the same time, sending powerful ethical and political messages. In the earliest burial ceremonies, furthermore, bodies were often displayed for public viewing before they were interred. A few years later, in 2000, bodies were forcibly exhumed from Kigali-area burial sites and relocated to a new national memorial location in the capital.[85] The location of victims' remains holds high symbolic value in Rwanda's official genocide heritage landscape. Memorial consolidation has prompted decades of burial ground disturbance by the government and largely private expressions of discontent by survivors and relatives.

In 1997 the Genocide Memorial Commission was rehoused within a renamed Ministry of Youth, Sport, and Culture (MIJESPOC) under the new direction of Minister Jacques Bihozagara. The commission's stewardship under the then-influential RPF founding member reinforced the importance of genocide heritage to the state. In June of that year, the commission received additional, though modest, funding to continue its most ambitious experiments with the conservation of human remains at the three pilot sites of Murambi, Ruhashya, and Nyamata.[86] Conservation work on bodies was extended to an additional five sites by the end of the year, including at Nyarubuye, Ntarama, and Rwamagana and to a lesser extent at Mwulire in the east and Bisesero in the west. Those memory maintenance

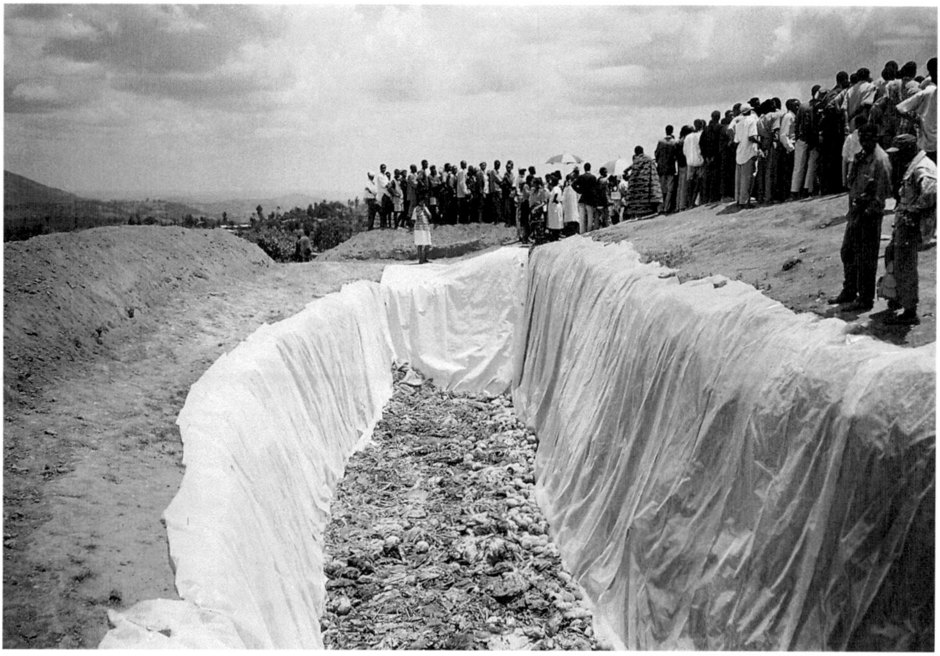

FIGURE 2.20. The Genocide Memorial Commission reburial ceremony for genocide victims in Mubuga Commune, Gikongoro Préfecture, October 24, 1996. Photo by Mario Ibarra, Kanamugire archive, Rwanda.

projects expanded the HRFOR's preservation experiments at Nyarubuye and the earliest conservation efforts initiated by resident groups and local authorities at large massacre sites. Those precedent efforts informed the preservation and conservation projects at Murambi, Ntarama, and Nyamata—led by Mario and Dr. Kanimba and directed by Louis for the commission—that institutionally bridged MINESUPRES and MIJESPOC, from 1996 to 1998.

Also in 1997, the government issued its first Draft Law on Genocide Memorials, further establishing collective memory of the genocide as within the state's purview.[87] It is the first official document to clearly establish the importance of a material, spatial memory as both *indangamurage* (heritage) and *ibimenyetso* (evidence). Although genocide heritage conservation paralleled judicial efforts to collect evidence of genocide crimes, and the *Preliminary Report* was widely referenced in national and ICTR trials, adjudication was not the primary objective of the Genocide Memorial Commission's work.[88] At most, memorialization aimed to document human rights violations and protect a collective memory of the genocide. To those ends, the 1997 Draft Law explicitly names the display of buildings, the bones of victims, tools used in the killings, and photographs and films as critical representations of the genocide.[89] The law conveys state authorization of the local conservation experiments conducted by the commission.

During the first years of its operation, the political importance of the Genocide Memorial Commission expanded while its budget remained meager and disproportionate to the scale of the tasks at hand.[90] As it attempted to wrest control in the face of unfolding existential threats, Rwanda's new government sought international recognition as a nation affected by a genocide. The state increasingly referred to a material and spatial memory to document evidence of genocide crimes, buttress the new regime's moral authority to rule, condemn foreign organizations and governments for not preventing the massacres, attract development funding, and argue for the state's right to national self-determination regarding its treatment of citizens and approach to genocide heritage.[91] Operating despite significant logistical obstacles, the commission's primary legacy remains the codification of conservation experiments as Rwanda's genocide heritage aesthetic. It did so through an iterative process, founded on a dialogue between local, site-specific responses; global commitments; and national policies that (often retrospectively) authorized those ad hoc initiatives.

A uniform genocide memorial curatorial strategy took more than a decade to achieve. Those efforts were reinforced with external funding and consultation from Aegis Trust, a British Holocaust memory organization that focuses on genocide education, documentation, and prevention. In 2004 Aegis Trust helped the Rwandan government establish the Kigali Genocide Memorial (KGM) in the capital, solidifying relationships between Holocaust and genocide memory curation ten years after preservation and conservation efforts throughout the country were initiated. Aegis Trust modeled the KGM genocide history exhibitions on its 1995 Beth Shalom Holocaust Centre in England, which was inspired by the Yad Vashem Holocaust Remembrance Center in Jerusalem. It also helped to establish the KGM Genocide Archive, which has been central to efforts to record individual testimony on genocide experiences. This effort developed in collaboration with the Shoah Foundation's Institute for Visual History and Education, one of several US-based history projects that were active in recording Holocaust survivors' testimonies. Since 2007 the Shoah Foundation has consulted for and trained archivists at the Rwanda Genocide Archive on the organization's interviewing, cataloging, and indexing methodology, establishing direct similarities between Holocaust survivors' testimonies and those in Rwanda.

In 2003, one year before Aegis Trust's involvement and in anticipation of related institutional changes in the curation of genocide memory, Louis was replaced as head of the Genocide Memorial Commission. The work of protecting genocide memory, maintaining memorials, and organizing national commemorations was again rehoused within a new institution, the National Commission for the Fight Against Genocide (CNLG), in 2008.[92] The first director of the CNLG was Dr. Célestin Kanimba Misago.[93] From 2008 to 2021, one of the primary objectives of the CNLG was to streamline the aesthetics and historical narratives at national-level genocide memorial sites. Almost thirty years later, the governing regime maintains a keen interest in genocide memory conservation and its close management within the organs of national institutions. As of 2021 the CNLG no longer exists, with most of its leadership relieved of their employment. The body was reorganized as the Memory and Genocide Prevention Directorate within a new Ministry of National Unity and Civic Engagement (MINUBUMWE). Despite the various shifts in the directorship of genocide memorialization and commemoration, organizations to manage genocide memory persist, demonstrating the enduring centrality of genocide memory to national interests.

### The Global Context for Rwanda's Genocide Heritage

Today a prevailing assumption is that the postgenocide regime directed Rwanda's genocide memorials in the RPF's interest from the outset and that those efforts were guided by the curatorial practices of Holocaust memory organizations. However, knowledge of Holocaust memorialization practices was uneven for the different groups that initiated preservation and conservation work. Moreover, the first individuals to undertake genocide memorialization were not exclusively agents of the new government. The new government had the power to authorize and fund those initiatives. But shifts in institutional involvement rendered the effort nonlinear and ad hoc, with diverse state representatives, and varying expertise and priorities, leading different aspects of the work. Those efforts occurred alongside independent genocide heritage experiments by international and local actors. The primary institutional connections and curatorial practices related to Holocaust memory developed ten years later, through the establishment of the purpose-built national genocide memorial in the capital, Kigali. Those relationships sought comparisons to the enormity and gravity of the Holocaust to foster increased recognition of targeted mass violence in Rwanda and support from the institutional and curatorial strategies of Holocaust memory organizations.[94] This is not to discount the power of the Rwandan state nor the influence of Holocaust memorialization but rather to situate both in the context of emerging global human rights practice and a local ethics of nonerasure, both of which drew on memory work to approximate justice and repair. Restoring this history to the first experiments and decisions related to Rwanda's genocide heritage articulates pathways interrupted. It presents ghostly reminders of the ethics and tensions eclipsed by state-managed genocide heritage.

Situating Rwanda's genocide heritage alongside Holocaust memorialization illustrates parallels and entanglements more than origins. It acknowledges the aesthetic similarities between Jewish and Rwandan genocide remembrance, including the earliest approaches to preserving victims' remains at Holocaust extermination centers and, later, the display of victims' belongings and artifacts. Key figures involved in the 1995 Genocide Memorial Commission—including Joseph Nsengimana, Eric Rousseau, Dr. Célestin Kanimba Misago, and Mario Ibarra—were no doubt aware of the Auschwitz-Birkenau Holocaust Memorial and the Yad Vashem Holocaust Remembrance Center. Rousseau and Athanase Ndutiye Kagahe referred to those precedents in their 1995 genocide memorial proposals. And prominent foreign advocates of Holocaust memory attended the government-organized "Genocide, Impunity, and Accountability" conference in November 1995, including Michael Berenbaum, the director of research involved in curatorial strategy for the US Holocaust Memorial Museum in Washington, DC; lawyer Arno Klarsfeld; and historian Efraim Zuroff, then director of the Simon Wiesenthal Center.[95]

And yet, as the next two chapters on the preservation and conservation of the Nyarubuye and Murambi massacre sites demonstrate, the first experiments in Rwanda's genocide heritage did not draw primarily or even exclusively from approaches to Holocaust remembrance. Aesthetic similarities to Holocaust memorials may have been purposeful in later cases, but for Nyarubuye, Murambi, Ntarama, Nyamata, and other sites of early genocide heritage experimentation, the preservation and conservation of massacre sites, victims' remains, and other material evidence of the crimes derived from site-specific conditions and the translation of an ethics of nonerasure in place.[96] This suggests that the individuals who initiated the conservation of massacre sites and victims' remains had similar motivations as the individuals who developed the first forms of Holocaust memory representation, even if they were not directly inspired by those efforts. Moreover, the 1994 "Rwanda: Reconstruire" conference proceedings indicate the influence of a wider geography of references to memory justice initiatives, including several from Central and South America. Many of those interventions drew substantially from human rights discourse and practice.[97]

Human rights influenced the turn to trauma heritage—to spatialized memory justice activism. The UN penned the Universal Declaration of Human Rights in 1948 to define and codify, for the first time, the fundamental human rights of all peoples. The subsequent question of how to *practice* human rights arose from efforts to translate the Universal Declaration and its challenges in diverse places. From 1994 to 1998, the HRFOR attempted to do just that in Rwanda: translate a set of universal principles into concrete activities that would support the investigation and protection of human rights while navigating substantial dilemmas. Holocaust memory representation and Rwanda's genocide heritage are, then, part of a larger geography and period of localized human rights practice. I call this an *era of trauma heritage* (a context I elaborate on in the conclusion).

But Rwanda's genocide heritage was also informed by local concerns and experiences that did not reference either Holocaust memory or global human rights discourses. Louis's commitments to family and Tutsi kin—and his interests in Rwandan civic education more broadly—represent the stakes of his imperative to make genocide history known. Mario's own lived history of state-sponsored violence in Chile—both as a result of the Augusto Pinochet dictatorship and against his Mapuche kin—further grounded the importance of and motivations for his own human rights practice. They are among many individuals who shaped genocide heritage through their personal commitments, work with local organizations and communities, and responses to the affective excesses of the genocide's aftermath. The new governing regime facilitated, and sometimes followed, those efforts, eventually endorsing the experiments as Rwanda's nationally authorized genocide heritage.

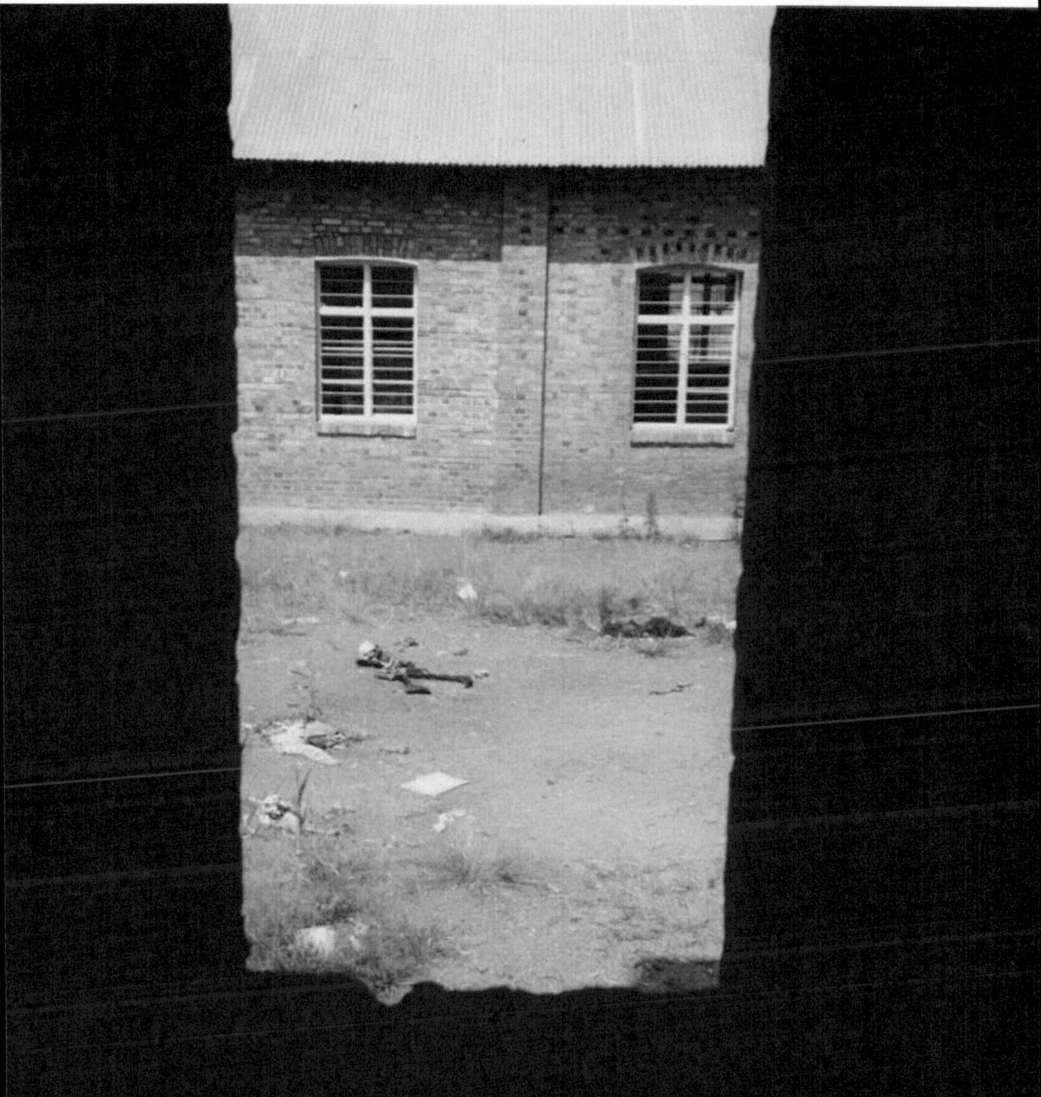

Witnessing the killings at Nyarubuye, 1994. Photo by Mario Ibarra, Ibarra archive, Chile.

3

# WITNESSING NYARUBUYE

## THE UNEVEN AFTERLIVES OF GENOCIDE HERITAGE

On May 28, 1994, Colonel Alexis Kanyarengwe, chairman of the Rwandan Patriotic Front (RPF), briefed regional and foreign journalists on the political party's military advancements and planned participation in a transitional government.[1] The press conference took place eight weeks after the genocidal killings began and seven weeks before the RPF declared its control over the country. Colonel Kanyarengwe spoke from Rusumo, a border town in Kibungo Préfecture near Tanzania. During the genocide the town was a key crossing point for thousands of residents fleeing Rwanda, many of whom sought shelter in refugee camps across the border. Concerned by the number of genocide organizers and perpetrators among them, the Rwandan Patriotic Army (RPA) was keen to control the border town. Kibungo Préfecture was therefore a significant RPA front for protecting Tutsi from subsequent attacks and finding and holding criminals accountable. That attention rendered the Nyarubuye massacre site, an otherwise remote location in the *préfecture,* critically important to demonstrating the existence, and brutality, of the genocide.[2] Colonel Kanyarengwe's press conference was an occasion to publicize the RPF's progress in halting the killings. Afterward, senior RPF representatives accompanied journalists to Nyarubuye Parish. The killings there had occurred fifty days earlier. The tour permitted journalists—and an international audience, through published descriptions and photographs—to view the aftermath.

The role of affect in that guided witnessing should not be underestimated. Nyarubuye was one of the first places where the mass nature of the genocide—the targeted killing of thousands of victims in a single location—was encountered by RPA troops.[3] Between April 15 and 17, 1994, around three thousand people died in the Nyarubuye Church buildings and grounds.[4] One month later, amid the ongoing killings, RPA forces secured the site. The church complex overwhelmed the senses with the visibility, smell, and tangibility of violent mass death.[5] For the next year, the customary burial of the dead was suspended. The visceral encounter was maintained as a scene of death. The bodies of the dead lying on the church grounds represented incontrovertible evidence of the immensity and harrowing nature of the physical and sexual violence associated with the genocide. Nyarubuye was preserved until July 16, 1995, and as a result garnered substantial international attention.[6] This, in turn, propelled preservation and conservation efforts at it and other massacre sites in efforts to establish Rwanda's genocide heritage.

The idea to preserve Nyarubuye Church as a scene of killing initiated an approach to remembrance that is activated and persists in spatial forms. Genocide heritage sites represent the violence that occurred during those three pivotal months in 1994. They make traumatic memories available to view and experience. Their preservation sought to reverse the nonacknowledgment of victims and prevent the destruction of evidence. But longer term, the mere recognition of the devastation caused by the genocide was not the sole objective of this memory work. By bringing witnesses to see the massacre site, those involved in the initial preservation experiments sought subsequent reparative actions, including forms of accountability, restitution, and empowerment (figure 3.1).

The witnessing that Colonel Kanyarengwe called on the international community to perform at Nyarubuye was a form of secondary witnessing—not of the violence itself but of the violence through its aftermath, preserved for viewing.[7] As leaders and journalists arrived on the scene, photographs and news coverage began to circulate globally, extending and reproducing means to "witness" the aftermath. Genocide heritage placed high demands on the witnesses it created, opening up the "civic space of the gaze" and its attendant responsibilities.[8]

But Nyarubuye's mode of address to the outside world also compelled ethical commitments that were rife with paradoxes. On the one hand, the ethics of

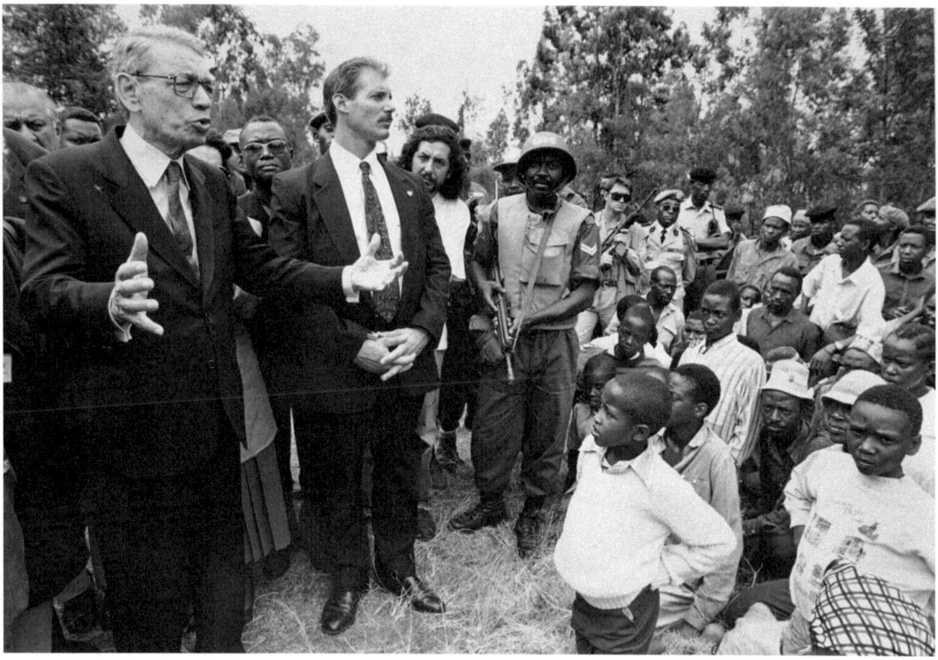

FIGURE 3.1. UN Secretary-General Boutros Boutros-Ghali (*far left*) speaks to residents at Nyarubuye Church. Mario Ibarra (*to the right of Boutros-Ghali*) is partly hidden by his security detail and is standing next to a UN soldier, July 14, 1995. Photo by Corinne Dufka (UN Photo, Digital Asset Management System).

nonerasure produces something that is difficult to see. Rwanda's genocide heritage is a challenging sight both for those who are very close (for whom it is inordinately painful) and for those who are distant (for whom it often becomes abstract and politicized). For outsiders in particular, the difficulty of seeing sites of massacre produces uneven responses to Rwanda's genocide memorials that tend to foreground shock encounters with the dead or the sites' political motivations. The display of victims' remains produces related challenges in understanding the complexities of what happened, placing limits on the communicative capabilities of material and spatial memory.

And yet, as Colonel Kanyarengwe's tour with journalists demonstrates, the affective power of Rwanda's genocide heritage was entangled, from the start, with the politics of state sovereignty. Sites like Nyarubuye were strategic references in a context of deep insecurity and uncertainty. Amid the widespread international and local disregard for the targeted mass killing of Tutsi, a new regime was asserting its legitimacy to rule. The preserved massacre was thus both a pivotal site of survivor testimony and material evidence to adjudicate genocidal and subsequent reprisal violence. In the years that followed, it was cited as such in both domestic and international court proceedings.[9] Viewing the scene at Nyarubuye provided incontrovertible evidence that mass killings of Tutsi had occurred.

More controversially, as I detail later in the chapter, the Nyarubuye Church massacre was erroneously used by an accused perpetrator to implicate the RPA in killings.[10] That accusation attempted to amplify reports of RPA-led reprisals against Hutu in the village surrounding the church and elsewhere across the country, which were initially suppressed for political reasons by the United Nations and the new Rwandan regime.[11] Thus, Nyarubuye Church became a significant early site of genocide heritage both for its historical importance as a visual archive of egregious acts of erasure and for its evidentiary value in highly politicized debates regarding the recognition of different groups' violent acts and the right to rule.

Understanding Rwanda's genocide heritage in the political context from which it emerged is also pertinent to considering the effects of genocide memorialization on citizens today. Over the past thirty years, the state management of genocide heritage has been characterized by attempts to control not just the gaze but the civic space of discourse on violence in Rwanda. The government's regulation of free speech and movement, along with its disciplining of memories, is amplified by a landscape of the genocide's nonerasure.

Thus, the tensions between the ethics and politics of Rwanda's genocide heritage are evident in its making and animated further in the sites' viewing. As one of the first preserved genocide heritage sites, Nyarubuye locates the origins and afterlives of those tensions. The church complex also forms part of a constellation of nascent memorial sites, exhumations, and centralized reburial that emerged after 1994 at the interface of site-specific practices and institutional formalization. Together, the work and organization of memory at these sites initiated and developed the approach to genocide heritage that we have today. And yet the sites' extended temporality—initiated in the preservation of a violent past and perpetuated through witnessing—reveals Rwanda's genocide heritage to be unruly. The history of making genocide heritage is marked by precipitous shifts in motivations, between memory justice and state sovereignty, and by the tendency of politics to eclipse ethics and personal commitments.

## Preserving Nyarubuye

Work to preserve the scene of the massacre at Nyarubuye Church preceded the formation of the Rwandan government's Genocide Memorial Commission by over a year. It was stewarded by Mario Ibarra, the director of the UN Human Rights

Field Operation in Rwanda (HRFOR) regional office in Kibungo Préfecture, who initiated the approach to memory maintenance together with Janvier Gasasira, the *bourgmestre* (mayor) of Rusumo Commune. Mario approached the work from a human rights framework and, in doing so, viewed site preservation as a means of establishing evidence of what had happened and publicize that proof for wider, global recognition. Gasasira came to endorse those memory justice efforts through a sense of national and communal responsibility. His turn to preservation was also inherently complicated by his traumatic loss of family members who were killed at Nyarubuye. Together Mario and Gasasira faced—and made—impossible decisions about the treatment of victims' remains and the place of genocide heritage in community life. Those decisions reverberated beyond the local, informing both national policy and global trauma heritage initiatives.

## PRESERVATION AS A MATTER OF HUMAN RIGHTS

In late July, after the RPF established control over the country, the HRFOR launched an investigation into the killings at Nyarubuye. The site's preservation resulted from that HRFOR investigation, not as a matter of its mandate but as a consequence of working relationships between local authorities and the HRFOR field office in Kibungo Préfecture. As I detail in chapter 1, Mario Ibarra had a significant role in shaping that effort, and he did so by drawing from his human rights practice, which informed the imperative and standards of evidence for publicly disclosing crimes related to the genocide. He regularly provided guided tours of Nyarubuye to visitors, including prominent foreign and national government representatives, relaying findings from the team's investigations. Concurrently, Mario was a member of the UN Sub-Commission on the Promotion and Protection of Human Rights, which met regularly in Geneva from 1994 to 1998. As a result, he made genocide history known both at the site of massacre—through the visceral experience of witnessing—and in Europe, at a substantial distance from *el olor y el dolor* (the smell and the pain).

In August 1994 Mario began to maintain and document evidence of the massacre at Nyarubuye. He described the scene from memory twenty years later, sketching a map of the grounds (figure 3.2):

> *Mira* (Look): The massacres occurred in a beautiful place. The central sanctuary was here, here was the repository, here was another small building, and behind was a large courtyard. This was the main building, the road passed from it down here toward the small village. Here were the trees and bougainvillea. And here were an enormous number of bodies in front of the church, and inside, here in the sacristy. When I entered for the first

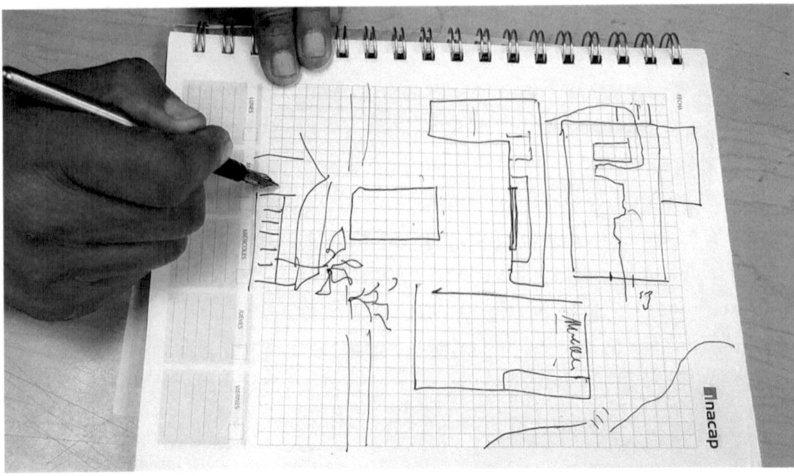


FIGURE 3.2. Mario Ibarra sketches the Nyarubuye Church buildings from memory in Chile, 2015. Photo by Delia Duong Ba Wendel.

> time, we found four to five hundred skulls here. Here at the door, there were bodies up to here [indicates to his shoulders]. They were stacked and left there. . . . There were also bodies in this area behind [in the courtyard, framed by the chapel, convent, and school buildings]. We began here [in the rear buildings and courtyard] because it was full of dead people who had not been moved. The grass had grown very high, and we could not clearly see what was there. First, we measured the grass, and then we cut it to see what was underneath. We made a plan to proceed: to not change the position of the bodies, to open a small path without touching the bodies, and after to work very slowly.[12]

When the HRFOR Kibungo office began its investigation, hundreds of victims remained in the annex buildings, courtyard, and surrounding grounds where they died (figures 3.3 and 3.4). Mario's team began by restoring visibility to the bodies hidden by grass and weeds in the courtyard, cutting away at the vegetation. They counted and photographed individuals to document the number killed in each location, sketching those spaces and conditions, cataloging personal belongings that might help to identify victims, measuring wounds, and identifying causes of death. The team documented every scene of death in the courtyard and surrounding buildings with precision. That attention to detail was critical as a matter of evidence and human rights: to account for what happened to each individual affected by mass violence.

In the paragraphs that follow, I relay the minute, and excruciatingly brutal, details that Mario recalled of Nyarubuye. As former members of his team recall, Mario was uniquely attentive to less visible evidence of violence and to deducing the manner of killings from crime scenes as a result of his previous human rights investigations and his own incarceration in Augusto Pinochet's Chile.[13] His observations permit us to see the violation of individuals and their struggles for survival amid the mass killings.

Mario and his team determined that most killings occurred on April 15, but genocidal attacks continued in the area around Nyarubuye Church until May 7. The *génocidaires* returned to the parish on April 16 and 17 to ensure that there were no survivors.[14] The killers used guns from a relative distance. They also wielded hoes, nail-studded clubs, and machetes in close and laborious acts of violence. Several women were raped before they were killed. They were found on the parish grounds with undergarments pulled to their feet. There was evidence of infanticide as well. One of the women Mario examined in the courtyard was carrying a baby in a cloth strapped to her back.[15] They were struck from behind, killed by machete blows to their skulls.[16]

During their first weeks at the site, the team noticed that a short wall located between the courtyard and the adjacent alley had been gashed repeatedly with thin cuts. Mario hypothesized that it had been used to sharpen machete blades so that the *génocidaires* could continue to kill. He confirmed his observation in interviews with prisoners held at the nearby *cachot* (prison). This detail is suggestive of the type of deduction needed to reconstruct scenes of killing. It is also indicative of the extent to which HRFOR investigations were dependent on the cooperation of local residents and prisoners to interpret findings. Access to both populations required maintaining relationships with local government officials.[17] Both access and cooperation were not guaranteed nor always amicable, which challenged interpretation.

Inside the main church building, victims had been removed from where they were killed and shifted to a high pile near the door. Local residents told the HRFOR team that the priest had attempted to remove the bodies and clean the nave (figure 2.2). The arrival of the RPA troops at Nyarubuye Church in May 1994 halted the priest's work. The differing scenes in the main church and rear courtyard represented opposing Catholic Church and RPA (and, later, government) views of the status of religious spaces transformed by massacre (figure 3.5). The number of parishes found as sites of massacre throughout Rwanda presented mounting evidence of the complicity of church leadership in the killings.[18] Churches were keen to downplay their roles in the genocide. They also resisted genocide conservation in places of worship.

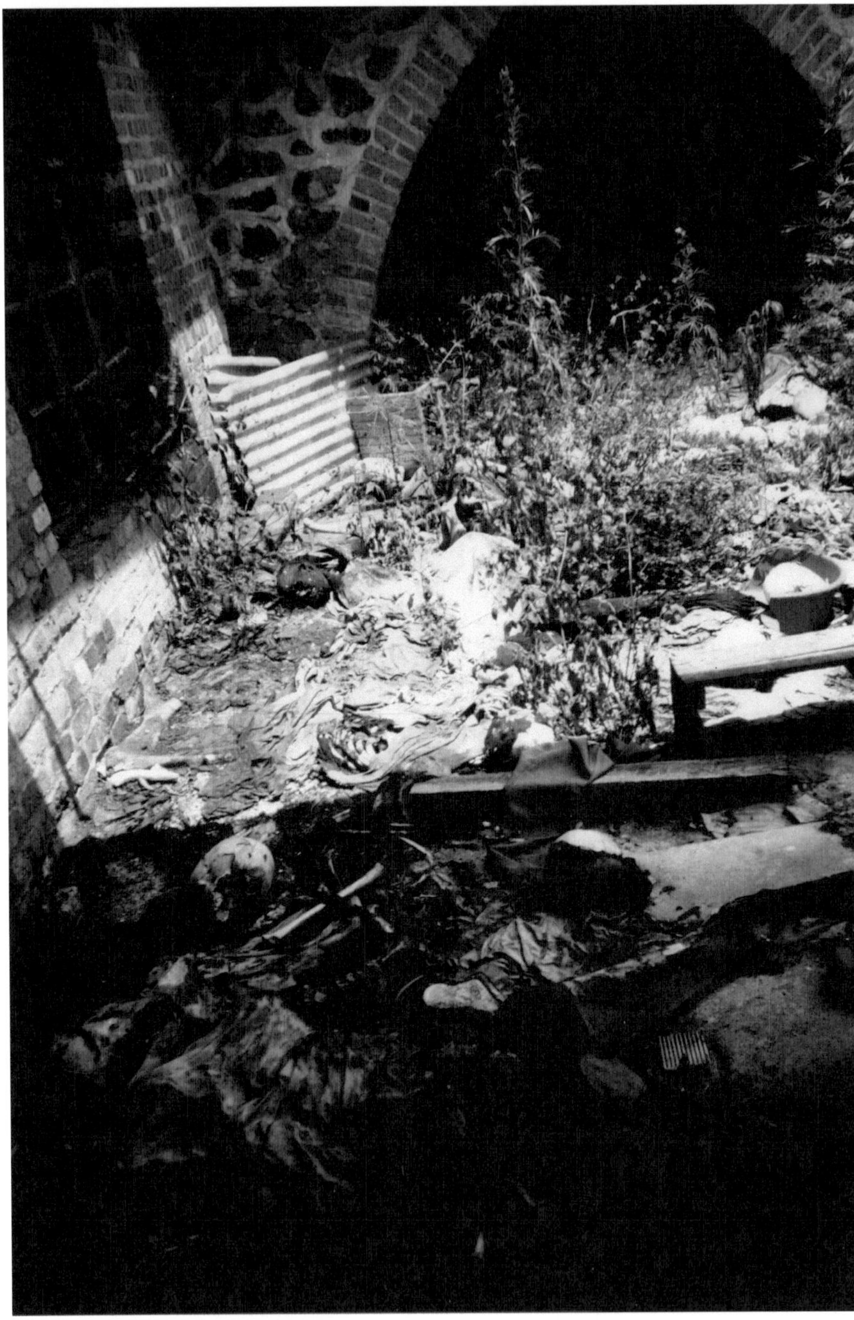

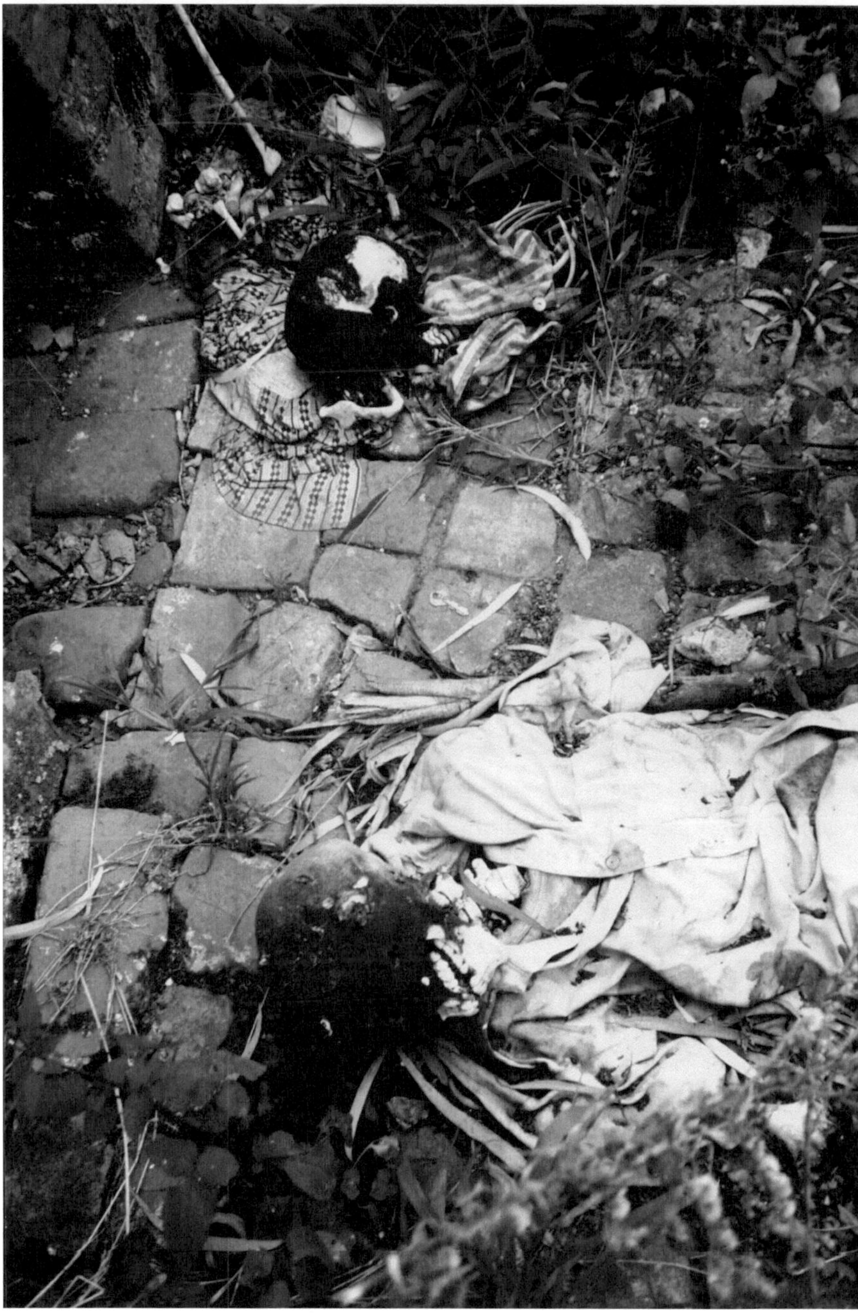

FIGURES 3.3 AND 3.4. Victims' remains and belongings Mario Ibarra preserved for the HRFOR in the Nyarubuye Church convent buildings and courtyard, 1994. Photos by Mario Ibarra, Ibarra archive, Chile.

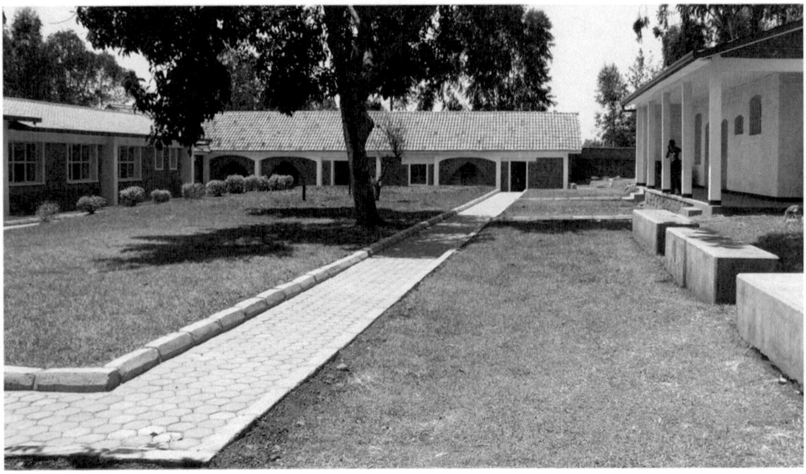

FIGURE 3.5. Today, the Nyarubuye Church courtyard and convent buildings (pictured here in 2013) are managed as a state genocide memorial; the church was returned to service. Photo by Delia Duong Ba Wendel.

Mario's HRFOR team was responsible for documenting and investigating the Nyarubuye massacre and determining the identities of victims, the manners in which they died, and the names of those involved in the killings. They also protected scenes of massacre and victims where they were found by establishing investigatory protocols. As a result, the HRFOR team's human rights work paralleled preservation practice. It took place in the context of a general reluctance, by foreign governments especially, to recognize the events in Rwanda as a genocide. For Mario and his team, documentation and preservation were means to challenge impunity and denial. Faced with scenes like Nyarubuye as a direct affront to the lack of international recognition, the team's moral imperative to represent the genocide effectively closed operational distinctions between human rights documentation, preservation, and memorialization.

### PRESERVATION DESPITE DEEP PAIN

Within the first days of investigating and documenting the massacre at Nyarubuye, Mario met Janvier Gasasira, the newly established Rusumo Commune *bourgmestre*. They established a working relationship despite issues of trust between HRFOR and government officials. Many Rwandan authorities deplored the deep contradictions that underlay postgenocide foreign assistance, asking where that aid and attention to human rights violations had been during the genocide. Conversely, for many foreigners working for nongovernmental agencies in Rwanda, the government's singular focus on genocide crimes often actively occluded other forms of violence—committed either during the rebel army's advance or in the identification or treatment of accused perpetrators. Gasasira and Mario's relationship generally kept such suspicions at bay—they formed a cautious friendship based on mutual respect and wry humor. Gasasira remembers Mario as direct and opinionated but thoughtful and genuinely open to working with local officials.[19] Mario remembers Gasasira as similarly pragmatic and straightforward, helpful in facilitating his access to local residents and prisoners for genocide-related investigations.[20] Their friendship became strained over issues related to more recent human rights violations (for example, Mario's inquiries into local prison conditions), but they nonetheless held each other in high regard.

Gasasira provided invaluable connections to the residents in his commune not just because he held a position of leadership but also because he was intimately familiar with the place and its people. He had grown up in a house near Nyarubuye Church. He attended primary school nearby, in the school where his father taught. There, as he recalls, he was routinely singled out and objectified by other students and teachers as Tutsi rather than called on by his given name.

After President Juvénal Habyarimana's plane was shot down, signaling the start of organized genocidal killings throughout the country, families from the surrounding region arrived at Nyarubuye Church to seek refuge. On April 14, 1994, Gasasira was twenty-six years old and living in the nearby settlement. Around 1 p.m., he saw a military truck carry soldiers to the market center near the parish. Thirty minutes later, he heard the rapid gunfire of automatic weapons. He ran away from the sound to look for his two younger brothers and three-year-old sister. They ran. Several days later, Gasasira and his three younger siblings managed to cross the border into Tanzania. While they fled, soldiers attacked the people living in the church parish. Gasasira and his brothers and sister remained in a Tanzanian refugee camp for several months, returning in late July after the ceasefire.

It was then that Gasasira learned that the military contingent that had descended on the area near Nyarubuye Church had been called there by the Interahamwe (a Hutu paramilitary group that perpetrated genocidal killings). Earlier that morning, residents had banded together to defend people attacked by the Interahamwe in a neighboring sector. In response, the soldiers rounded up all of the men in Nyarubuye and took them to the market center. The soldiers called on the Hutu in the group to stand aside. Tutsi men were instructed to remain sitting on the ground. They were killed with machine guns. Gasasira's father was among the dead.

Most of his immediate and extended family were killed either at the church or in the surrounding area. For Gasasira, Nyarubuye was saturated with loss. But he was painfully aware that his situation was not unique. In 2018 he reflected with me on his feelings of despair and grief in the immediate aftermath. "To me," he said, with heavy pause, "in '94, the whole country was dead. Dead, *dead*, dead. There was no hope for *anyone* who was there."[21]

In his mid-twenties and admittedly unprepared for the emotional toll and the immense responsibility of the job, Gasasira became the *bourgmestre* of Rusumo (figure 3.6). Taking the job was, as he put it, a matter of civic duty. It was his small contribution to the immense need for physical and social repair in the country: "Most of the young people of my generation entered the army [the RPA rebel forces]. So they had all given their lives to save this country. I needed to do my part, so when I was approached [for the job], I couldn't say no. My modest contribution was just to lead a small district to try to organize it in a period when the country was in need."[22] The newly instated government nominated him for the position because he was "somewhat qualified" as a university graduate but also because he had been a young member of the RPF since 1992 (not openly, as it was during the civil war). As *bourgmestre*, most of his work involved reestablishing basic access to health care, shelter, and water in the region. There were pressing social issues too, especially challenges of security, interethnic and government-resident trust, and equitable access to land and housing. Among these priorities, there was also the question of what to do about the dead lying in and around Nyarubuye Church.

Mario recalls that the idea to preserve the church as a massacre site came from one of his early conversations with Gasasira, who floated the idea that the church should remain "living" so that they would not lose what happened.[23] According to him, Gasasira petitioned the government to maintain Nyarubuye as a center of memory, and Mario included the suggestion in his UN report. Mario was not privy to higher-level Rwandan government decisions during this time; he knew only that the government approved of his work inasmuch as he was allowed to maintain the site as a ruin. The suggestion was controversial, not least because local clergy opposed it, but also because Nyarubuye's spaces were overwhelmed by the image, emotion, and smell of mass death. This was experienced on a daily basis by those living near the church—even at a distance. The church was surrounded by houses. The grounds were visible from the dirt main road, as were many of the bodies.

Gasasira did not openly admit that it was his idea to preserve the Nyarubuye massacre site. This was consistent with the ways I heard many people speak about the authorship of other postgenocide government programs in the country, including *gacaca* (neo-traditional, community-based trials) and villagization. Rarely would individuals (even much higher-ranking government representatives than Gasasira) claim responsibility for the initiation of an idea. Instead, Gasasira described the decision as one made by the government, discussed "at the highest

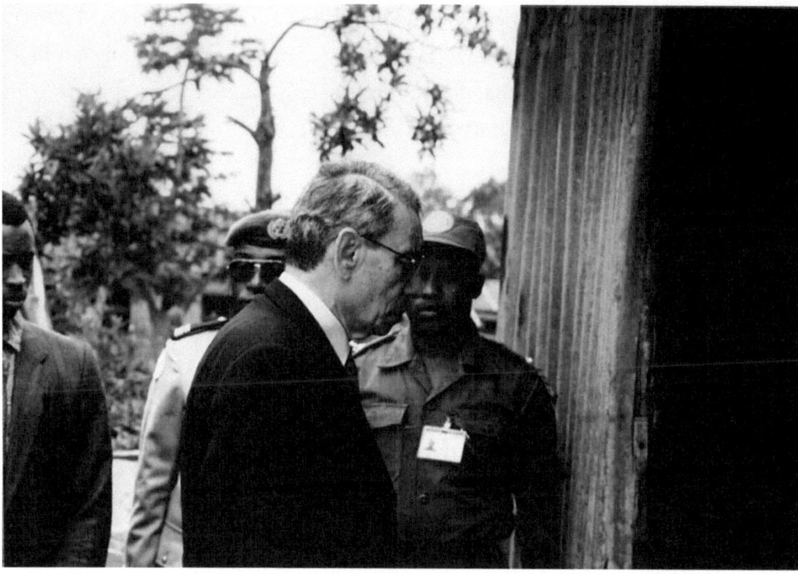

FIGURE 3.6. Janvier Gasasira (*left and partly cropped*), *bourgmestre* of Rusumo Commune, accompanies UN Secretary-General Boutros Boutros-Ghali on a tour of the preserved Nyarubuye Church massacre, July 14, 1995. Photo by Mario Ibarra, Ibarra archive, Chile.

level" but also felt, relevant to, and influenced "at the lowest level." The latter was "our level," where he admitted:

> It was a big pain for me and other survivors to see our family members lying there . . . it was a deep pain. And I have to confess that I was not—I did not like—seeing those bodies, lying there. You know: If you see someone from your family, how are you going to feel if you keep seeing that person? Day one, two, a year—lying somewhere? So, it was a big, big pain. But that's the cost to pay for building a country—and a memory—for building a memory of a nation that is more important than the deep pain you may suffer. You will build that nation for the new, upcoming generation, not for yourself.[24]

For survivors like Gasasira, a visit to Nyarubuye Parish meant confronting the decaying bodies of brutally murdered family members. Yet, despite that "deep pain," Gasasira insisted that the site should call attention to what happened to him and others. He returned to Nyarubuye Church multiple times throughout 1994 and 1995 to lead tours with international delegations and national government representatives. "All of those officials—I took them, we went to the site, we visited the bodies lying around Nyarubuye. For me, it is still very fresh as if it was yesterday. Because even the bodies at the church—I knew them—many were my family."[25] For Gasasira, building a national memory was deeply painful. It was an agonizing personal investment in the country's future.

## PRESERVATION AS NATIONAL MEMORY

By September 1994 the new government had refused multiple requests from the Catholic Church to remove the victims from Nyarubuye for reburial.[26] Representatives of the RPF justified the regime's decisions by claiming genocide sites as "testimony to the bitter months of murderous Rwandan minds."[27] Mario's HRFOR team continued to maintain the scene and the ability to view the massacre. The open field adjacent to the parish grounds facilitated easy landings for foreigners traveling by helicopter. Air travel allowed visitors to bypass the region's extremely rocky landscape and potential security threats in road transit. As a consequence of the site's identification by the RPA, subsequent government attention, preservation by HRFOR, and ease of access, Nyarubuye became one of the earliest and most prominent places to witness the genocide's aftermath. As a result, Nyarubuye became synonymous with a national memory of the genocide.

In early 1995 Mario and Gasasira met Silas Sinyigaya, then the Communications Director of the Ministry of Labor and Social Affairs (MINITRASO), at the parish.[28] Sinyigaya was accompanying a Belgian delegation to Nyarubuye. He asked Mario to provide a guided tour of his work there. Mario showed how the HRFOR team was working to estimate the number of victims and determine how they died. They examined the bodies, cataloged their belongings, and documented the places where they were found—to determine the details of their deaths. The work of revealing and maintaining the massacre as they found it yielded an almost archaeological, if not quite forensic, representation of the genocide. Through the lens of Nyarubuye—in situ evidence of mass violence and Mario's narration of it—both the gruesome details and the national scale of the genocide became legible.

The Belgian visit prompted subsequent conversations between Mario and Sinyigaya regarding possibilities for scaling up the approach to other sites in the country. Prominent midlevel ministry representatives, such as Sinyigaya, proved critical to the official sponsorship of genocide heritage because they facilitated knowledge exchanges between on-the-ground preservation and conservation experiments and conversations occurring among higher-echelon decision-makers. Another key figure in this regard was Dr. Célestin Kanimba Misago, an archaeologist who became the Director of the National Museum at Butare in 1996. Dr. Kanimba would later be central to the work that Mario Ibarra and Louis Kanamugire did in developing Rwanda's now-iconic Murambi Genocide Memorial. Those types of exchanges and encounters underscore the extent to which genocide heritage developed from interactions between local practices and national policy.

In situ interactions informed higher-level conversations. Publicly convened examples include the internationally attended October 1994 "Rwanda: Reconstruire" conference and the November 1995 government plenary on "Genocide, Impunity, and Accountability." At the "Rwanda: Reconstruire" conference, sites in Rusumo District, where Nyarubuye Church is located, were referenced to exemplify potential approaches to preserving genocide memory.[29] By the time of the government plenary one year later, a more extreme approach to genocide remembrance—the preservation of victims' remains, which had been piloted at Nyarubuye—had become an explicit national objective.[30] Both conferences are early examples of the prominence of genocide memory—among needs for governing reform, criminal prosecution, and reconstruction and reconciliation—as a national priority. References to Nyarubuye's preservation at the plenaries underscore the site's important role in shaping national genocide memory policy. Moreover, the conferences demonstrate that for the new government, finding a form for genocide memory that was convincing—as a matter of evidence and of emotional resonance—was as much a matter of national politics as it was of human rights.

Yet, in the first year after the genocide, authorship of Rwanda's national genocide memory strategy was not singular. As I detail in chapter 2, several discussions on genocide memorialization were occurring simultaneously across the military, multiple government ministries, foreign aid agencies, and human rights organizations. Acts of preserving genocide memory were not merely dedicated to nation building and sovereignty. For those undertaking them, preservation and conservation experiments evolved from iterative, deeply personal, and communal practices. Moreover, the decision to preserve evidence of the massacres, let alone conserve victims' remains, was controversial—among residents, those leading preservation work, and higher-level government officials alike.

The preservation, conservation, and display of victims' remains in sites of killing became a national government imperative as a result of the dialogue between individuals doing that memory work and government and foreign witnesses. Nyarubuye was one of the first, and most influential, sites to shape Rwanda's genocide heritage aesthetic. The preservation of the massacre there initiated a larger network of experiments in genocide site and victim conservation and preservation. That effort in turn led to the government endorsement of those practices as the representation of national genocide memory. Preservation work at Nyarubuye paralleled efforts at Ntarama Church near Kigali. Subsequent conservation practices developed at a number of places in tandem, including the Murambi massacre site near Butare and several locations near it, and later at Nyamata Church outside Kigali. The idea to make victims' remains permanently available to view also developed in the context of the government's early reburial ceremonies. Those occasions displayed evidence of the genocide to local communities and visiting dignitaries before interment. Early reburial ceremonies were critical precedents of contemporary genocide commemorations. By 1996 all three approaches to genocide memory—preservation, conservation, and commemoration—were led by the Genocide Memorial Commission. Increasingly from then onward, Nyarubuye and other proto-genocide heritage sites were managed by the government. The sites garnered widespread international attention through secondary witnesses who saw and experienced the genocide long after it occurred.

## Witnessing Nyarubuye

Rwanda's genocide heritage developed from an extended temporality produced by both the preservation of mass death and its image. One year before the Genocide Memorial Commission commenced its work, key experiments in maintaining memory of the genocide occurred at the Nyarubuye Church massacre site. The HRFOR Kibungo team's preservation of evidence at Nyarubuye enabled diverse visitors, especially foreign government representatives and journalists, to "witness" mass violence. Photographers produced a series of images that circulated internationally. Both the initial move to preserve the Nyarubuye massacre and the reproduction of its image in photographs are critical to understanding the ethics and politics of viewership that genocide heritage sites locate.

The UN's secretary-general, Boutros Boutros-Ghali, was one of the most prominent international visitors to Nyarubuye (figure 3.7). On July 14, 1995, Mario guided Boutros-Ghali on a tour of the parish grounds.[31] The two men walked together from building to building and into the courtyard. One year and three months had passed since the attack at the church. Three rainy seasons had hastened decomposition. The bodies seemed to melt into each other, vanishing into the ground and from their clothes. Discerning one from another was difficult, but once the eyes adjusted, individuals—including a contorted man against a wall, a baby near their mother, and the shapes of two women, one smaller huddled into the larger—could be seen. Bodies with more direct exposure to the sun had withered, skin stretched taut over skeletal frames. At the end of the tour, Boutros-Ghali and Mario entered the main church building alone to take shelter from the sun and reporters documenting the visit. According to Mario, the secretary-general was visibly shaken. He found the nearest surface to sit, took Mario's hand, and said a prayer.

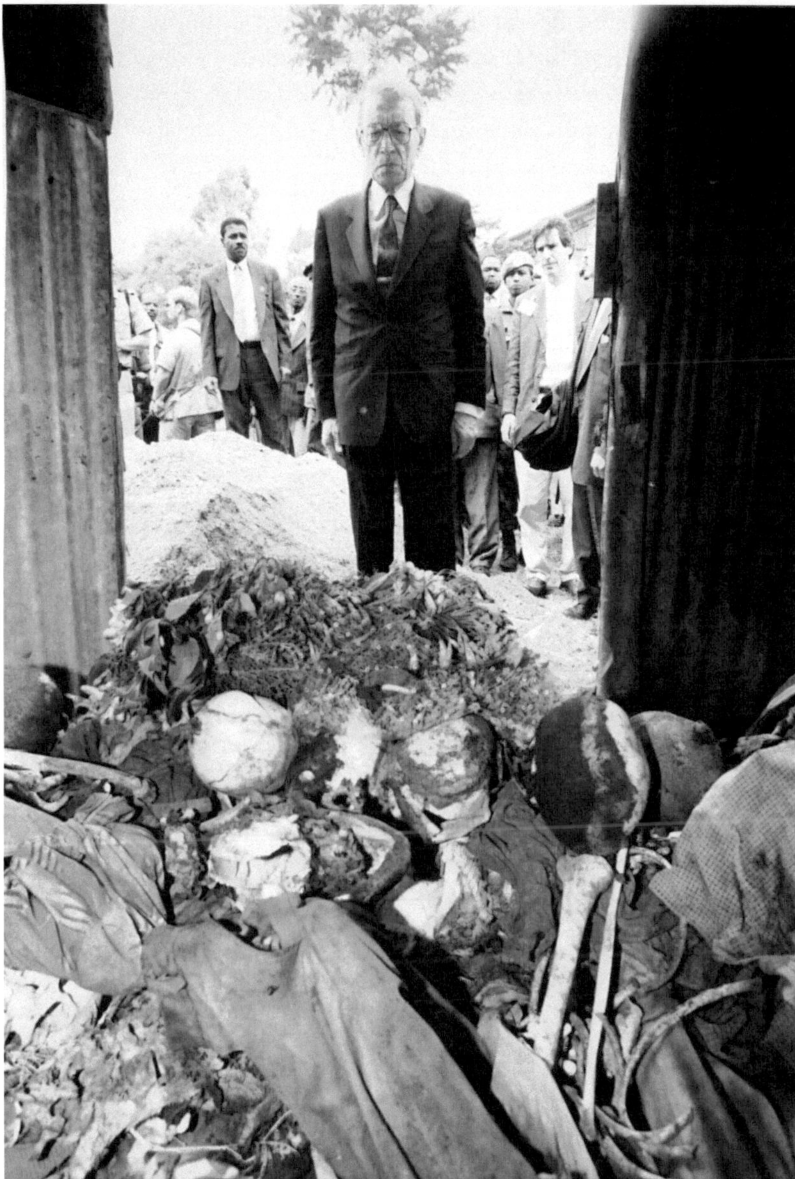

FIGURE 3.7. UN Secretary-General Boutros Boutros-Ghali photographed as a secondary witness of the genocide at the preserved Nyarubuye Church massacre site, July 14, 1995. Photo by Corinne Dufka (UN Photo, Digital Asset Management System).

Boutros-Ghali did not just visit Rwanda for himself, although by Mario's account, his reaction was sober and genuine. His presence conveyed the UN's recognition of the Central African country in the middle of the Bosnian War.[32] The latter was capturing the attention of a Global North preoccupied with sociopolitical precarity on Europe's periphery. Boutros-Ghali eventually left the quiet of the church to speak with international reporters and local residents outside. There, Rwandans (presumably organized by the government) held signs condemning the UN and the international community for its failures to stop the massacres that they knew were being organized (figure 2.15). The messages were written on large placards in English and French, to be photographed for an international audience. The secretary-general addressed the group of Rwandans gathered there, insisting, rather paternalistically, that locals should do more to combat the "culture of death" pervading Rwandan society in the wake of the genocide.[33]

During his visit, foreign photographers captured Boutros-Ghali viewing the dead. Photographs show him flanked by a crowd of journalists: by witnesses to the Witness. The images produce meta-representations of Nyarubuye's symbolic and social work as a place to view evidence of targeted mass violence. They not only convey a sober message from Rwanda to the world but also communicate the world's recognition (embodied in the head of the UN) of Rwanda. Shortly thereafter, journalists continued with the secretary-general's caravan to view other massacre sites in the region and a local prison.

By mid-1995 Nyarubuye was frequently featured in the international press.[34] The UN secretary-general's visit represents the height of the site's global exposure. Reporters toured the parish grounds, interviewing the same survivors time and again, describing the remains of victims, and emphasizing the sharp incongruity of the murdered dead in a church. This was a late response for a press corps that underreported the genocide as it was unfolding and misrepresented Rwanda's history of conflict and society afterward.[35] Nyarubuye and other sites were depicted in melodramatic portrayals of an inescapable present. One of these titles evokes the predominant tone in the reporting: "Legacy of Terror: Rwandans Are Still Suffering a Year After Tribal Tensions Exploded into an Orgy of Slaughter."[36] Such journalism reproduced erroneous representations of Rwanda and the genocide, recalling simplified Western understandings of Africanness. For the mass violence was not tribal: It was motivated by political elites who reinforced ethnic divisionism to gain power, mobilizing thousands to kill. Nonetheless, the atrocity reportage that emerged from photographers and journalists touring Rwanda exemplifies the rapidly developing globalization of news coverage in the late 1990s. A year after the genocide, global media networks had caught on to the news story, widely circulating images of the genocide's aftermath.[37]

Amid this attention, two days after Boutros-Ghali's visit to Nyarubuye, the Rwandan government ordered the interment of victims at the church.[38] It is not entirely clear why the dead were moved belowground at this time. As at other sites of mass killing, the bodies of the dead had putrefied and were deteriorating, rendering them untenable for longer-term display without a more aggressive conservation effort. In part, the interment represented the government's commitment to a countrywide "decent burial" program (called *gushyingura mu cyubahiro* in Kinyarwanda and *inhumation dans la décence* in French at the time), which the Genocide Memorial Commission was beginning to lead across the country.[39] Through the program, the commission also sought to suspend the work of local government authorities, residents, and returnees who had been expediently burying the bodies of relatives and neighbors that they found lying in fields and houses in their communities. Nyarubuye exemplifies the "pause" the government was attempting: to consolidate its control of killing sites and, in some cases, extend the viewings as recognition of the genocide (see chapter 5).

The Nyarubuye reburial also represents an early instance of the government's desacralization of church genocide sites. It was therefore not a response to Catholic Church protests about massacre preservation on parish grounds. On the day of the mass reburial, July 16, 1995, then Vice President Paul Kagame laid a foundation stone, designating Nyarubuye as a genocide memorial. This wrested control of the site away from the Church and was one of the first such designations, rendering Nyarubuye as a place of national significance within the state's purview.[40]

The date chosen for the government burial at Nyarubuye was significant, representing the one-year anniversary of the RPF's declaration of control over the country and end of the genocide.[41] Nevertheless, the relatively early interment of bodies was viewed suspiciously by RPF detractors. If, for many persecuted survivors and RPF affiliates, Nyarubuye Church represented a site of resistance and refuge attacked by genocidal extremists, for accused perpetrators and many critics of the RPF, the parish was staged to look like proof of genocide by RPA soldiers. The false claim locates the site as evidence not of genocide but of the RPF's extrajudicial killing of suspects in the area. These debates came to a head during the UN ICTR trial of the former mayor of Rusumo Commune, Sylvestre Gacumbitsi, in Arusha, Tanzania, in 2001–4. A decade after the genocide, ICTR judges ruled that Gacumbitsi had organized the genocidal killings at Nyarubuye Church and other sites in the region.[42] During his trial Gacumbitsi's defense team referenced the independent analyses of Human Rights Watch's Alison Des Forges and the UN's then-classified Gersony Report to argue that the RPF was responsible for the massacre at Nyarubuye Church. Those killed, they claimed, were not Tutsi but rather Hutu residents in the area targeted in retaliation for genocidal killings in the country. The defense team presented witnesses to corroborate its claims. Subtly refuting the defense's argument, Des Forges underscored that none of the victims at the church were found with their hands tied behind their back. According to her observations at diverse killing sites, RPA soldiers typically bound their captives before killing them. The defense's counterfactual account was debunked by the ICTR judges. The Gacumbitsi trial nevertheless revealed circumstantial evidence that the RPF had killed both armed *génocidaires* and civilians elsewhere in Rwanda. With rare exceptions (typically explained as the actions of rogue RPA soldiers), the RPF denies that it took part in organized, targeted executions.[43] That disputes regarding what happened at the church continue today demonstrates the discursive power of Nyarubuye in both the adjudication of genocide criminals and challenges to the RPF's right to rule.

Though these claims are factually incorrect, this history is still noteworthy for the multiple ways the site figures as evidence—of the genocide and crimes committed thereafter. I mention this controversy, then, not to perpetuate the claims but rather to suggest that the preservation of Nyarubuye Church produced two types of secondary witnesses. A general public that saw and experienced the site could be convinced of the genocide's occurrence. An adjudicating public leveraged the site further, using evidence from the parish to make judicial (and political) claims. Neither public was exclusively local. But for both, the importance of viewing was paramount to the claims being made.

The Nyarubuye burial ceremony was attended by Prime Minister Faustin Twagiramungu, Vice President Paul Kagame, President of the National Assembly Juvénal Nkusi, and other government officials. The ceremony featured the lowering of coffins (often with several victims in each) into tombs in a field adjacent to Nyarubuye Church. Bodies were also collected from Nyarubuye Sector and neighboring areas. Not all of these relocations were consensual: While many victims were retrieved from perpetrator-dug mass graves and sites of massacre, others were exhumed from private burial sites created by relatives and neighbors.[44] A month later, Germany provided RWF 10 million to assist in the government's nascent memorials program, and some of these funds helped to expand the Nyarubuye burial ground.[45] Germany's provision of funds for this purpose suggests an acknowledgment of similarities between Rwanda's mass violence and the Holocaust, which was one of the earliest of its kind by a foreign country. Within the next year, the tombs were reorganized as quadrants in a rectilinear garden and topped with purple-leafed plants arranged in multiple cross motifs (figures 3.8). Victims' skeletal remains, belongings, and other evidence of crimes committed at the parish were conserved for display inside the convent buildings (figure 3.9). Relocations and official inhumations at newly established memorial sites like Nyarubuye Church represent early efforts to centralize Rwanda's genocide heritage—to establish clearly defined and government-administered nodes of genocide memory in a diverse genocide landscape.

Burying Nyarubuye victims represented a shift in the development of genocide memorials in Rwanda: from the preservation of sites of massacre to images of them. After preservation efforts ceased and victims were reburied, images of Nyarubuye as a preserved massacre persisted in the foreign press. As a result, the transitional government's decision to move the material trace of the massacre belowground at the height of the site's recognition was inconsequential to its interest in publicizing Nyarubuye as an exemplar of genocide. Photographs of the preserved massacre effectively collapsed the witness-space into its image, diluting the site's forensic value and opening narration up further to sensational and politicized rhetoric. But the political power of the preserved site remained very much in memory. As a pilot site and protomemorial, Nyarubuye's preservation catalyzed subsequent efforts to extend the time of viewing Rwanda's genocide heritage.

## THE IMAGE

Photography played a complex role in the development of Rwanda's genocide heritage. In the hands of Mario and his team, photographs were crucial for documentation and as an alternative form of preservation. As human remains disintegrated and were removed from Nyarubuye and interred, photography enacted an ethics of nonerasure. While Mario practiced a studied objectivity, photojournalism from Nyarubuye tended to take a sensationalizing approach, feeding into false narratives of tribal violence and savagery. These accounts simultaneously widened the range of possible witnesses and collapsed other possible readings.

In December 1995 journalist Philip Gourevitch published a long-form essay in the *New Yorker* based on his travels to Rwanda after the genocide (expanded as the book *We Wish to Inform You That Tomorrow We Will Be Killed with Our Families* in 1998). He began by detailing what he saw at Nyarubuye Church: "Hundreds of bodies had been left where they were found, for commemorative purposes: tangled skeletons with weather-greened skin and flowered clothing patched over them; lone skulls in the grass; a pelvis with a sneaker stuck in it; and a lower jaw attached to a neck and torso with the rest of the head gone."[46] Gourevitch visited before the bodies were buried. He describes the church primarily as a scene of mass violence from which details can be discerned. He closes his essay with one of Gilles Peress's 1994 photographs from Nyarubuye, which offers a different type of representation in its focus on individual violence (figure 3.10).[47] The concluding image's black-

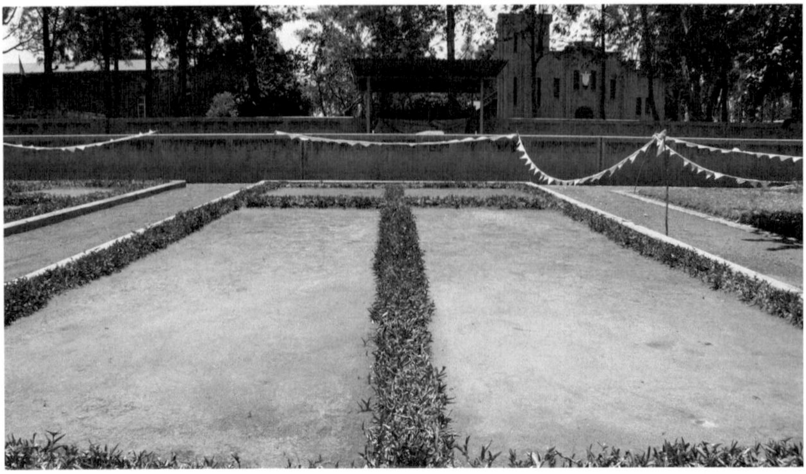

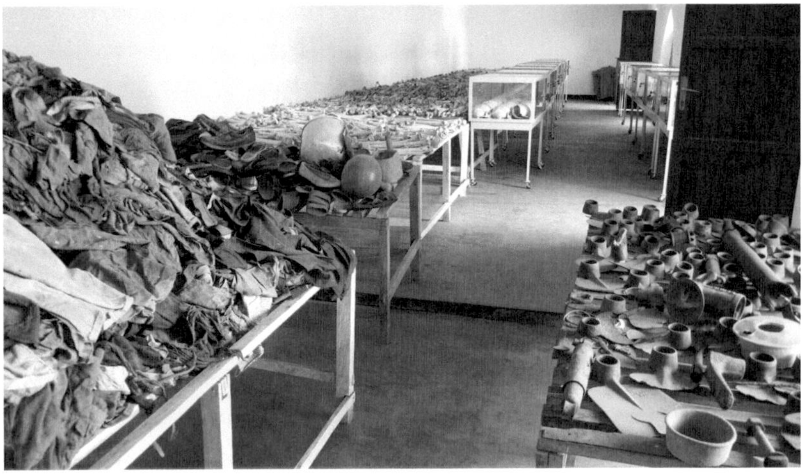

FIGURE 3.8. Genocide victims' burial ground and site of the 1995 reburial ceremony adjacent to Nyarubuye Church (convent and courtyard on left, church on right in background), 2013. Photo by Delia Duong Ba Wendel.

FIGURE 3.9. Temporarily relocated genocide evidence—victims' bones, clothing, killing instruments—on display tables during the Nyarubuye genocide memorial renovation, 2013. Photo by Delia Duong Ba Wendel.

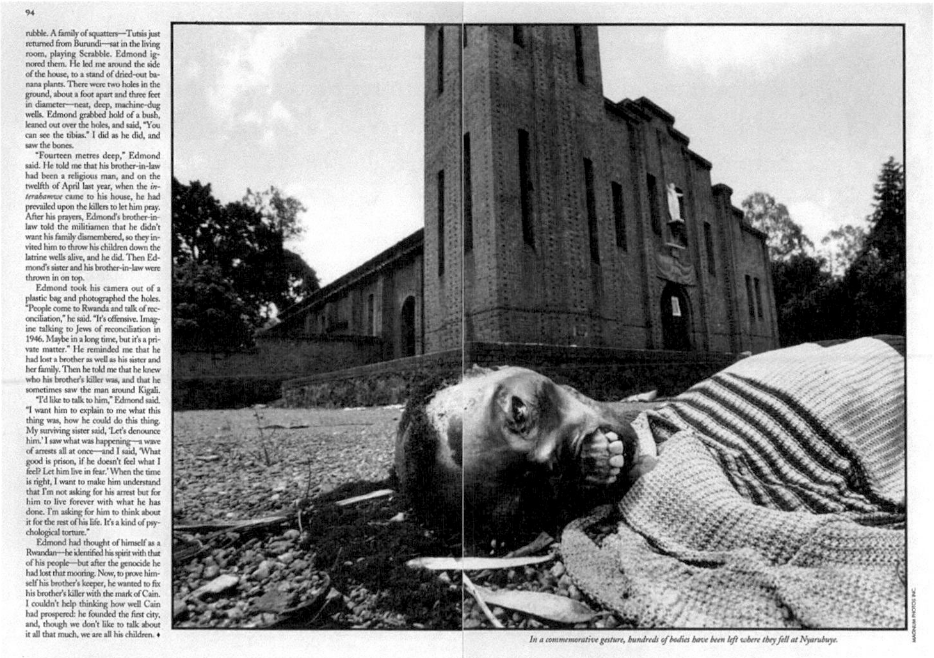

94

rubble. A family of squatters—Tutsis just returned from Burundi—sat in the living room, playing Scrabble. Edmond ignored them. He led me around the side of the house, to a stand of dried-out banana plants. There were two holes in the ground, about a foot apart and three feet in diameter—neat, deep, machine-dug wells. Edmond grabbed hold of a bush, leaned out over the holes, and said, "You can see the tibias." I did as he did, and saw the bones.

"Fourteen metres deep," Edmond said. He told me that his brother-in-law had been a religious man, and on the twelfth of April last year, when the *interahamwe* came to his house, he had prevailed upon the killers to let him pray. After his prayers, Edmond's brother-in-law told the militiamen that he didn't want his family dismembered, so they invited him to throw his children down the latrine wells alive, and he did. Then Edmond's sister and his brother-in-law were thrown in on top.

Edmond took his camera out of a plastic bag and photographed the holes. "People come to Rwanda and talk of reconciliation," he said. "It's offensive. Imagine talking to Jews of reconciliation in 1946. Maybe in a long time, but it's a private matter." He reminded me that he had lost a brother as well as his sister and her family. Then he told me that he knew who his brother's killer was, and that he sometimes saw the man around Kigali.

"I'd like to talk to him," Edmond said. "I want him to explain to me what this thing was, how he could do this thing. My surviving sister said, 'Let's denounce him.' I saw what was happening—a wave of arrests all at once—and I said, 'What good is prison, if he doesn't feel what I feel? Let him live in fear.' When the time is right, I want to make him understand that I'm not asking for his arrest but for him to live forever with what he has done. I'm asking for him to think about it for the rest of his life. It's a kind of psychological torture."

Edmond had thought of himself as a Rwandan—he identified his spirit with that of his people—but after the genocide he had lost that mooring. Now, to prove himself his brother's keeper, he wanted to fix his brother's killer with the mark of Cain. I couldn't help thinking how well Cain had prospered: he founded the first city, and, though we don't like to talk about it all that much, we are all his children. ♦

*In a commemorative gesture, hundreds of bodies have been left where they fell at Nyarubuye.*

FIGURE 3.10. Gilles Peress's jarring photograph of a man killed at Nyarubuye Church, included at the end of Philip Gourevitch's *New Yorker* article (December 10, 1995, 94–95).

and-white composition foregrounds the head of a man in an advanced state of decay: eye sockets empty, skin receded and tightened to the contours of his skull, with most of his hair crumbled into a pile on the ground. The camera is situated next to the man's face on the ground, casting back to a corner view of a looming church building in the background. The angle and perspective pull the eye, creating dynamic relationships between the decomposed man, intact brick church, and a white statue of Jesus above the front door to construct simple contrasts of the sacred and profane. In Gourevitch's article the image is captioned "In a commemorative gesture, hundreds of bodies have been left where they fell at Nyarubuye."

Both Peress and Gourevitch employ graphic vignettes from their personal experiences at Nyarubuye to bear witness to the occurrence of genocide in Rwanda. In doing so, they collapse the past into a present time, employing imagery of the aftermath of violence to represent what has already occurred. The images are similar to literary representations of the genocide in memoirs, novels, and travelogues published in the decade following 1994.[48] Although some of those texts are from survivors of genocide attacks, most are from visitors to sites and international observers of the mass killings. Their accounts develop from an urgent need to witness and testify to what happened in Rwanda, constituting what literature scholar Zoë Norridge has termed "testimonial narrative (non)fiction."[49] Norridge describes this literary genre as one that "reflects common authorial intentions (the commemoration and prevention of genocide), similar stylistic approaches (the interspersing of deeply personal narratives with contextualizing history), a set of common reference points (the Holocaust, specific Rwandan memorial sites) and international concerns (juggling reductive views of Africa with international conceptions of genocide)."[50] I suggest that this genre expands from that of literature and extends to both journalistic and photographic accounts that emerged in the first years after the genocide (that precede the publication of memoirs). Through both voice and vantage, these media testify to mass violence, reproducing witnesses in readers and viewers alike. The accounts primarily circulated in international news outlets (both mainstream and diasporic), given the closure of propagandistic national news sources and the relative lack of funding and infrastructure for local print media. The international circulation of these texts and images is critical, as well, to the nature of genocide heritage in Rwanda, which demands the attention of others and encourages global comparison to precedents like the Holocaust.

Among these forms of representation, the display of evidence and the visual documentation of genocide sites and victims have produced the extended temporality that has made the past present. The ability of a material and spatial memory to make a violent past visible and tangible, and therefore relevant for the present and future, is at the core of the ethics of nonerasure that drives Rwanda's genocide heritage. Examples include the photographs appended to news accounts and photo essays by professional photographers like Gilles Peress and Simon Norfolk, among others. Within this broadened testimonial genre, photographs are distinct from written accounts in their nonlinear, associative narratives and immersive visual imagery. But similarities derive from the ways that cameras are positioned as authorial, secondary witnesses.

Comparing the composition of two photographs of bodies at Nyarubuye—one from a collection by Gilles Peress (figure 3.11) and the other by Mario Ibarra (figure 3.12)—differentiates between testimonial and historical representations. Both images focus on a single victim who was killed apart from the others. The man in Mario's image is located at the side of the church. His skull had become detached at the neck. Investigators had repositioned it, jaw against the ground, to associate the mass of clothing nearby with a human form. The man's body had shrunk from his clothes, indicating the extent of its decomposition. The camera is set at a short distance, focused on the body from above, and frames the victim in the

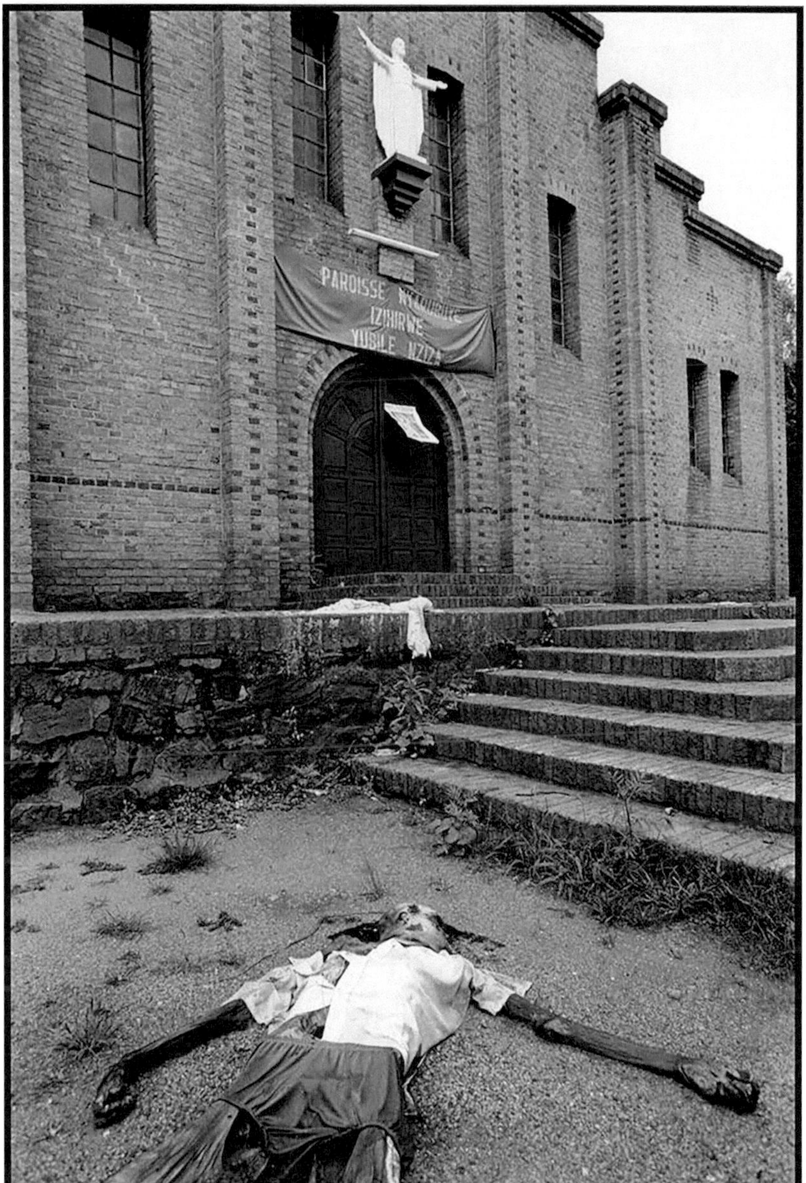


FIGURE 3.11. Photograph by Gilles Peress of a woman killed at the steps of Nyarubuye Church, 1994. Peress, Magnum Photos. Retrieved from Artstor Digital Library May 19, 2025, https://www.jstor.org/stable/community.9867128.

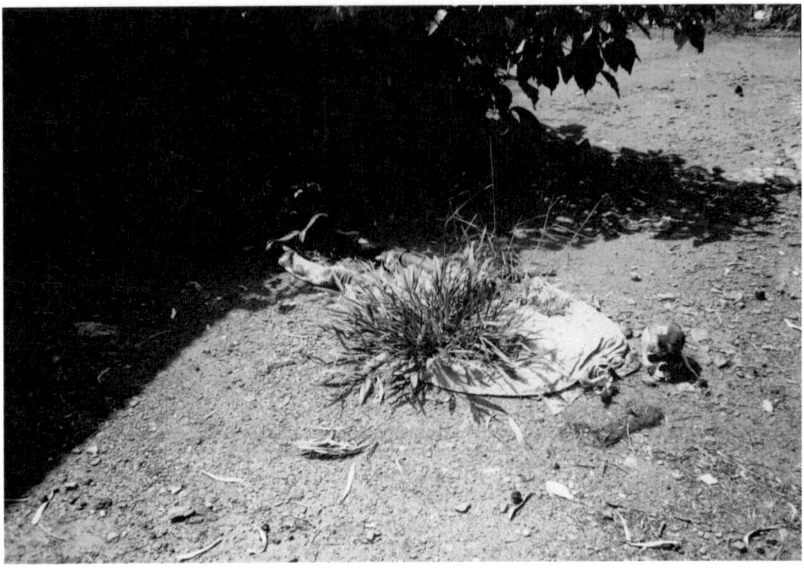

FIGURE 3.12. Photograph by Mario Ibarra of a body found on the Nyarubuye Church grounds, 1994. Ibarra archive, Chile.

center of the image. By contrast, Peress positions his camera at and between the feet of a woman found below the church steps. From that angle, we can see her undergarments and her torn clothing. The angle of view creates correspondences between the woman's extended, mummified arms and the whitewashed statue of Jesus with arms outstretched above the entryway to the church. The church looms vertically over the horizontal surface where the woman lies. Compositionally, her violation is doubled—eternally repeated—through Peress's image. The violence she suffered is also framed by the religious space in which her body was found.

While Mario's interpretation of significance privileged an incongruous image of death, Peress's artistry emphasized violation and immorality. Peress composed his image to preserve its significance without words, indexing meaning within the image itself. His stylization responds to the affective excess of scenes of mass killing. This is because, as journalist Fergal Keane reflected when he visited Nyarubuye Church in May 1994, "powers of visualization cannot possibly encompass the magnitude of the terror" that had been experienced by the individuals lying dead on the parish grounds.[51] To facilitate comprehension of a site that exceeds sense, Peress foreshortens relationships between nonspeaking victims and their context. This editorial approach is visceral and wrenching in the way that it pulls the viewer to details in the images: to look into the eyes of the bloated dead and to notice stiffened and clenched hands as last movements before death.[52] Peress is known for his conflict photography, and his image had a wide international audience in both artistic and news media worlds. Techniques of indexical compression were critical for viewers of Peress's images who were at a significant distance from Nyarubuye and Rwanda.

By contrast, Mario's photograph employs distance in his composition as means to record evidence of the violations. His images document the state of victims in terms of possible identity markers, manner of death, and relationships to where and among whom they were found. The objectivity revealed in Mario's photographs limits emotion to foreground a straightforward representation of the violence committed. The images thus make a claim to the kind of authoritative knowledge associated with objective representations. Mario's restriction of emotion was not for lack of empathy. It was a means to cope with his serial encounter with the dead (see chapter 1). The content and frames of most of Mario's photographs were carefully selected to record the circumstances of a particular subject and its immediate surrounds. His images are not immediately sensible in terms of why the subject was framed or how it relates to the site as a whole. That is because his photographs were typically taken in series and indexed to field reports and documentation of the details and context of each massacre.

Mario's photograph exemplifies a subset of photos and videos taken by Special Investigations Unit (SIU) investigators, Mario and his HRFOR team, and the Genocide Memorial Commission for the purpose of genocide investigations. I discuss this photographic record in the introduction and chapter 1, focusing on the systematic and prolific visual documentation by Mario and colleagues during 1994–98 investigations and conservation work. For them, photography was a specific epistemological and investigatory method used to record human rights violations for judicial and historiographic purposes.

Often, photographs were taken during investigations to document discrete moments in survivors' and witnesses' testimonies, especially those relayed at the sites of crimes. The places where genocide crimes occurred were particularly instructive mnemonic and verification devices in investigations.[53] Where possible, the HRFOR team would travel with (actual) witnesses of crimes to genocide sites to "unlock" memories that were challenging for them to recall. The sites' physicality grounded details that were often recounted in a dreamlike manner. In other cases, visiting the sites either confirmed or disproved witness stories in place. For these documentarians, photographs were motivated by human rights imperatives. They worked to establish the material evidence of crimes in service of those who were killed and could no longer speak.

Genocide investigators' visual methodology was oriented more to evidence collection than secondary witnessing. Sometimes, however, this was only a distinction of intention rather than reception. For example, *Ingabo*, a Kinyarwanda-language journal published by Rwanda's Ministry of Defense, used fifteen of Mario's photographs in a March 1996 "Genocide Special Issue" to illustrate findings from genocide sites and the views of top government officials on the massacres.[54] One of these photographs includes an image of Mario while he was working for the HRFOR, holding a skull in his hand to inspect it for wounds (figures 1.11 and 1.16). The caption, written by Captain Firmin Gatera, reads: "Mario IBARRA: *Umwe mu banyamahanga bashavujwe n'itsembabwoko* [One of the foreigners deeply affected by the genocide]."[55] The photograph's publication in *Ingabo* illustrates the ways in which Mario's representations were repurposed for state narratives. Recall also the state formalization of the *Genocide Sites Map* (via Captain Gatera) and the way in which it shifted from a field map recording locations of massacre sites to a convincing representation of the genocide at the UN headquarters in Geneva.

The distinction between testimonial and historical representations might seem trivial, especially in the context of Peress's and Mario's images' publication in the *New Yorker* and *Ingabo*. In each case, despite somewhat subtle distinctions in their intended use—for witnessing and evidentiary documentation, respectively—the images were reproduced to demand the attention of diverse secondary witnesses. The images figure doubly, then, as tools to politicize the gaze and to archive genocide memory.

Nyarubuye's development as a site of memory demonstrates how Rwanda's genocide heritage was co-constituted from spatialized memories and aftermath images. The HRFOR Kibungo team's early efforts to document and preserve conditions at Nyarubuye had a significant role in connecting human rights imperatives to that work and elongating a time of violence to allow witnessing to occur. The July 1995 shift from site preservation to the interment of the deteriorating bodies belowground did not dampen Nyarubuye's notoriety. Rather, images of the preserved site proliferated in written and visual testimonial accounts by such key secondary witnesses as foreign dignitaries, journalists, and photographers. Most of these representations, including one of the most popular—Gourevitch's *New Yorker* article with Peress's photographs—circulated after Nyarubuye had been emptied of bodies and erased as the site they portrayed. As a result, Nyarubuye Church was one of the first, but certainly not the only, examples of how genocide heritage developed from the collapse of witness-spaces and their images. Preserving genocide sites propagated an emblematic gaze, producing witnesses from visitors to killing sites and employing their personal observations to essentialize the complexity of the genocide. Through those shifts, witnessing became intimately bound to the ontology of genocide heritage in Rwanda.

### Uneven Afterlives

At Nyarubuye, as in Rwanda more generally, genocide heritage first emerged as a form of counter-memory, engaged in the pursuit of memory justice and repair. The site's preservation defiantly asserted the facts of the genocide to foreigners and local residents alike. At the same time, Nyarubuye's preservation laid the groundwork for what would become state-authorized genocide heritage. The establishment of authorized memory is a contested, relational, and contextual process, of which Nyarubuye offers an early example. Its brief preservation as a physical site, its circulation through photojournalism that both amplified and distorted the intentions behind preservation, and its simultaneous address to national and international audiences reflect many of the irresolvable tensions that are inherent to trauma heritage. Many of those tensions arise from the fact that Rwanda's genocide heritage today is authorized memory indelibly marked by its origins as counter-memory. The choice to confront the world with the unfiltered aftermath of brutality—as a means of compelling recognition of the genocide—resoundingly echoes in Rwanda's established national strategy for memorialization.

As a concept, counter-memory brings the distinction between authorized and marginalized accounts of the past into view. On one level, counter-memory refers to a negation of totalizing, closed, and hegemonic histories—a means to rewrite narratives of linear societal progress by attending to slavery, violence, and subjugation, for example.[56] Such a view sees counter-memory as oppositional and subversive in relation to common or shared interpretations of the past (in which gaps and power differentials are not always apparent). But this represents only a surface aspect of Michel Foucault's original concept of counter-memory. His is an approach to representation that simultaneously reinforces a "philosophy of difference" and suggests a methodology for historiography.[57] As such, counter-memory for Foucault is both negation and aspiration. It "refuses the certainty of absolutes" to disturb narratives that appear unified and immobile, ultimately showing "the heterogeneity of what was imagined."[58] Counter-memory is a vigilant, critical form of historical representation that both searches for omitted and marginalized histories and attempts to correct dominant accounts.

Counter-memory also, as American studies scholar George Lipsitz argues, situates truth telling as political praxis. Lipsitz writes, "Counter-memory surpasses history and myth . . . transcends the false closures of linear history and the destructive ruptures and divisions of myth to create an *active memory* which draws upon the pluralities of the past and present to illuminate the opportunities of the future."[59] Lipsitz underscores that counter-memory serves as a corrective representation for marginalized peoples' erasure from historical narratives.

By extension, I argue that counter-memory forms critical source material for reparative histories. In early versions of Rwanda's genocide heritage, counter-memory was constituted by unacknowledged narratives of the past told by and displayed in marginalized sources. The practices of reparative history that drew from those sources were "active" in their vigilance for a more inclusive representation of the past. They were also active in the sense of activating change. Temporality is crucial, for revising the past informs present-day values, which inflect future actions and knowledge. None of this counter-memory work was linear, nor without counter-interpretation. This is amply demonstrated in the history of Nyarubuye's development as genocide heritage.

The classification of genocide heritage as a form of memory justice, which evolved into practices in reparative history, is dependent on its claims relative to dominant representations of life and violence in Rwanda—in the country and the world. And yet the history of Rwanda's genocide heritage development exposes the somewhat tenuous status of counter-memory in its bid to oppose a hegemonic narrative. That is to say: the period of 1994–98 was critical to codifying counter-memories of Rwanda's violence as an internationally accepted, state-endorsed collective memory of the genocide. At the same time, some Rwandans' experiences during and after the genocide remain underrecognized and prohibited from national collective memory. Key to unpacking this shift and related omissions is to note that hegemony was characterized differently by the various human rights, mass media, and government witnesses involved. And yet, despite divergences in their motives, each drew inspiration from an ethics of nonerasure for different ends but with the same means: the preservation and depiction of the genocide.

Yet visual encounters with trauma heritage come with costs. Sites of traumatic memory can paradoxically serve the pursuit of human rights and justice for victims through jarring, if not dehumanizing, representations of violence. Rwanda's genocide heritage is thus defined by its contentious relationship to visibility: It seeks to display and compel attention to evidence—including human remains—of the targeted erasure of Tutsi and nonextremist individuals. Viewing the bodies and bones of victims in places where they were killed is emotionally challenging, to say the least, and differentially so for survivors, neighbors, and outsiders. Trauma heritage reframes aesthetics with a political and ethical set of considerations with which viewers are obliged to contend.

Nyarubuye serves as an extended temporal site of intervention characterized by a recurring break between the making of genocide heritage and its viewing. In this sense, Rwanda's genocide heritage is most clearly understood through its own processes of becoming. Its afterlives extend through the images, artifacts, and spaces that result. The afterlives of memory work at Nyarubuye have been complex and uneven. Various forms of misalignment have arisen between the ethics of nonerasure motivating the work and Nyarubuye's reception as a politicized and sensationalized approach to representing the genocide. Furthermore, as memorial sites were formalized over time, they produced a growing body of omissions—things left outside the frame, sites unrecognized in a landscape of violence, silenced. Consider, for example, the emotional conflicts endured by Janvier Gasasira, the evidence of reprisal killings witnessed by Alison Des Forges, or the unnamed rock (*ibuye*) that haunted Mario Ibarra and Louis Kanamugire. With Nyarubuye as a point of comparison, it becomes easier to grasp what is required of a viewer to read memory back into that single rock, standing inert and illegible in a landscape of rocks.[60] These are the uneven afterlives to which reparative histories must attend.

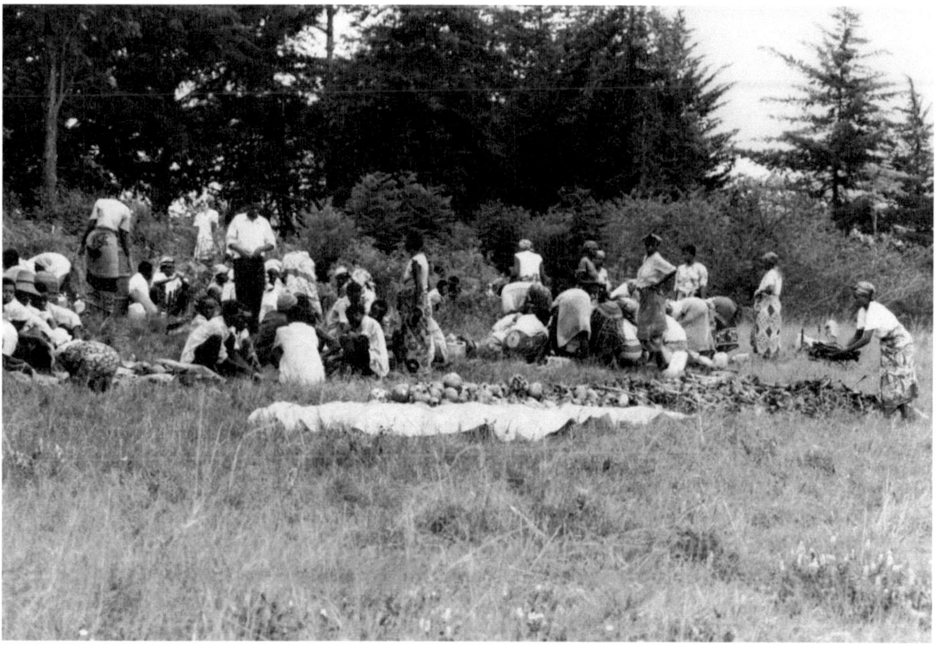

Memory workers clean and dry genocide victims' bones in a field near Murambi, 1996. Photo by Mario Ibarra, Ibarra archive, Chile.

4

# MEMORY WORK

## MURAMBI'S CONSERVATION

Today Murambi is Rwanda's most iconic genocide memorial. It stands out among all others for the mummified bodies available to view. While other sites display the disaggregated bones of victims, Murambi preserves their human forms. The memorial is a deliberately difficult, heartrending sight. Most exhibited bodies are contorted in the positions in which they died, flattened from the weight of others in mass graves. The bodies are covered in a white powdery lime preservative that was first applied in 1995. By 1998 the display of human remains was an integral part of the government's approach to genocide memorialization. The national imperative to witness the dead as part of Rwanda's genocide heritage was reinforced by the approach to representing the genocide at Murambi. And yet Murambi's conservation experiments were not singular: They developed together with memory work occurring at other sites in the country.

The permanent exhibition of victims required demanding physical and emotional work. The individuals who directed the conservation experiments at Murambi grappled with state interests, held strong ethical convictions, and attempted a clinical method for immortalizing the deaths despite the smell, the numbers found, and the work's psychic toll. Most workers had been displaced by the genocide and returned to the area in 1995 and 1996. Many were survivors of violence who had also lost relatives to the killings and later cared for others who remained. They were comparably more emotionally burdened given their personal encounters with mass violence but no less motivated by an ethics of nonerasure. To create the Murambi Genocide Memorial, these individuals exhumed and relocated victims' remains from mass graves and killing sites at and near the memorial. Intact bodies were examined, cataloged, returned to the school buildings, and preserved with chemicals. Those that began to deteriorate were defleshed and cleaned. The bones were either reburied or displayed. Other evidence was similarly conserved, including clothes and belongings found on the dead and tools that killers used in the massacres. That gruesome and tedious work was captured in photographs and videos during 1996 and 1997.

Despite being integral to the production of genocide heritage, this memory work remains largely unacknowledged in writing on Rwanda's genocide memorials. In 2003, philosopher Achille Mbembe reflected on Murambi, claiming the site as one of many examples of "necropolitics."[1] On his view, the preserved bodies of the dead communicate a contradiction. Anonymized by mass violence, they have little meaning other than a representation of atrocity. Yet they persist with a "stubborn will to mean, to signify *something*."[2] Mbembe offers a reading of the bodies at Murambi as a representation of the extreme outcomes of an exclusionary politics based on certain peoples' expendability. Literary scholar Sara Guyer extends this to a critique of Murambi's display of the dead, commenting on the "crisis of comprehension" that such representations of mass violence produce.[3] On her view, the exhibition of violent artifacts produces a "traumatic structure [that] interrupts the very possibility of narrative, memory, and knowledge."[4] Both interpretations are based on the overwhelming sensory experience of the site. In Guyer's reading, visitors' strong emotional reactions to the embodiment of deadly violence discourage further engagement with the historical context and individual experience of the genocide. Mbembe's characterization is similar but emphasizes that the bodies' anonymity—as unidentified, mummified forms—produces a singular message: that of mass death. The implied regret in both views is that the bodies of victims cannot communicate more beyond the shock associated with the visibility of death. Mbembe and Guyer are among many writers who claim the site as either a sensational representation of the genocide or one that is irreverent toward the humanity of the victims.[5]

An ethics of viewership demands more of the viewer. It implores witnesses to see the violent aftermath while also recognizing the lives and rights of victims that exceed the violence done to them. The bodies at Murambi are more than a symbol of mass death. While outsiders, and indeed many surrounding residents, may not know whose remains are on display, surviving relatives and memorial custodians regard them as kin. An ethics of viewership, then, requires "watching" scenes of killing through the memory work that made them, both governmental and individual.[6]

Moreover, Rwanda's genocide memorials are not "found" massacre sites. This is nowhere more apparent than at Murambi, which was initially emptied of victims and other evidence by the *génocidaires* and later reconstructed as a place of witness. The work of conservation was undertaken by individuals who were deeply affected by the substance of what they were doing and by memories related to their own experiences with violence. Transforming the Murambi massacre site into genocide heritage was part of a larger process—led eventually, but not initially, by the state—to progressively formalize the narration of genocide history. As other chapters in this book demonstrate, state interests are a central part of the authorization, curation, and afterlives of Rwanda's genocide heritage. However, this chapter does not engage at length with state motives for memorialization. Discussions of national politics were not as apparent at the scale of memory work, nor were they captured in the archival videos and photographs on which this chapter relies.

Instead, this chapter describes the backstage memory work that produced the Murambi Genocide Memorial. The following sections retrieve the processes by which victims' remains were conserved as genocide heritage. Oral histories in conjunction with photographs and videos that documented conservation reveal who prepared bodies for display and why that work was undertaken. The sources contribute to a reparative history of genocide heritage, providing a sense of how individuals managed the sight, smell, touch, and emotional substance of tasks associated with rendering genocide memory as authorized history—as recognizable genocide heritage. Without these intimate details, the bodies displayed at Murambi represent the genocide as immediately available symbols of atrocity. They foreclose reference to the affective experiences and narratives that the site locates. By contrast, a reparative history of genocide memory work seeks to retrieve the contradictions and ethics that were central to heritage making.

To resist an abstracted reading of the site, I endeavor to relay the intimate work of victim conservation and a sense of genocide heritage's iterative development. This is not a reading that is intended to be without politics but alongside it. The following pulls closer to those doing conservation and the victims they tended, to inform an ethics of viewership—one as much concerned with seeing the interior life of memory work as it is with developing a critical view of the state's control and politicization of genocide heritage.

## Murambi's Origins as a Genocide Memorial

On the *Genocide Sites Map*, Murambi is one of 118 dots that represent major massacre sites in the country (figure 1.14). It is color-coded: blue for civic spaces where killings occurred, red for killings located among sites of worship, and green for places of resistance. Murambi is located in the south of the country and at a significant remove from Nyarubuye in the east. Despite this distance, the two genocide sites are inextricably linked as places where the most significant conservation and preservation experiments occurred, respectively.

Memory work at both Murambi and Nyarubuye began through the initiative and labor of residents, local authorities, and nongovernmental entities that primarily worked or lived in the surrounding areas. At Nyarubuye, the local *bourgmestre* (mayor) and the field officers of the United Nations Human Rights Field Operation in Rwanda (UN HRFOR) were first involved. At Murambi, the earliest conservation activities were led by local *préfecture* authorities and a community development organization. At both massacre sites, the distinction between local groups' initiatives and national government involvement in the making of genocide heritage is critical, even if their roles are difficult to separate completely. As I document in preceding chapters, early genocide heritage work was tethered to national interests and required, at minimum, the authorization and support of the new Rwandan government and military. Notably, however, local and NGO actors identified the first sites and methods for preservation and conservation and were therefore responsible for the first approaches to genocide heritage. In other words, while those individuals did not have full autonomy, they had immense influence in demonstrating what was possible to national leaders. By mid-1995 their bottom-up work had evolved into a knowledge exchange regarding preservation and conservation experiments occurring at Nyarubuye, Murambi, and other massacre sites throughout the country. Many of the individuals initially involved led the subsequent conservation effort for the Genocide Memorial Commission. Much of that early work became codified as state-authorized genocide heritage. Attending to the memory work that transformed Murambi from a major massacre site to a national genocide memorial underscores the importance of collaborations to Rwanda's genocide heritage, especially between individuals who survived the massacre, those involved in the first ad hoc preservation activities, and those who conserved victims' remains at other sites in the country.

The first conservation activities at Murambi responded to conditions specific to the site and were then refined by methods developed at other places of massacre. The mummification of victims was the result of the soil composition in the mass graves that perpetrators dug to hide evidence of the genocide. Later the bodies were exhumed by local residents and authorities and returned to the Murambi school buildings for display. The bodies were sprayed with a lime solution to preserve them. That treatment created an extreme version of the genocide heritage aesthetic that had been developing in the country.

Though exceptional, conservation at Murambi did not develop in isolation. Preservation experiments at Nyarubuye and Ntarama preceded those efforts by almost a year.[7] By the time conservation work started at Murambi, Rwanda's genocide heritage had shifted from preserving places of massacre, which had become untenable given their deterioration, to conserving and displaying material evidence of the genocide. At Murambi and Nyamata, the shift to conservation was reinforced by the state of the sites after the massacres. At both killing sites, perpetrators had relocated victims to mass graves, removing evidence of the crimes from view. Both Murambi and Nyamata were, then, *reconstructed* as sites of killing. By the time work began in earnest at both sites, the Genocide Memorial Commission had been established—a substantial, if nascent, institution for the curation and protection of Rwanda's genocide heritage. As a result, the conservation of victims' bodies and bones at Murambi evolved in tandem with that at Nyamata and other sites, establishing a network of genocide heritage experimentation and knowledge exchange.

Murambi was initially not well known, nationally or internationally, as a site of genocide heritage. This was largely because victims' bodies were removed after the massacre occurred but also because, for one year thereafter, Murambi was controlled by the previous regime and foreign troops, then used for shelter by internally displaced people. Compared to other genocide sites, therefore, Murambi was less accessible to foreign journalists and Rwandan Patriotic Army (RPA) forces. It had less notoriety as a result. That status changed after the second national genocide commemoration was held there in 1996.

Before the genocide Murambi was a technical school under construction, comprising several brick buildings on a hilltop near Nyamagabe, a southern regional town in Gikongoro Préfecture. A genocide massacre took place on April 21, 1994, killing an estimated thirty-five thousand to forty thousand people who had sought refuge at the school.[8] The next day, local authorities affiliated with the previous regime cleaned up the site, employing bulldozers and prisoners to move thousands of victims' bodies from the school buildings and grounds into newly dug mass graves.[9] It was a two-week operation that managed to hide evidence of one of the most egregious acts of genocide from foreign journalists and the international community. At the same time, from April to May 1994, the rebel RPA advanced from northeastern to southeastern Rwanda, where they encountered Nyarubuye

Parish, and then to central Rwanda to support troops in the capital.[10] That offensive pushed extremists in the previous regime from Kigali to the southwest, where they stayed for several weeks before they moved northwest.[11] During and immediately after the massacre occurred, then, Murambi and the region were controlled by organizers of the genocide.

Thereafter, from June 21 to August 21, 1994 (two months that overlapped with the end of the genocide), French troops occupied the Murambi school complex. Under "Opération Turquoise" they set up a controversial western "humanitarian zone" where the school grounds became an encampment and their base of operations.[12] Today the Rwandan government and surrounding residents deeply resent French soldiers' irreverent inhabitation of Murambi.[13] French occupation also contributed to Murambi's less known status as a genocide heritage site, effectively delaying memory work there. When understood in the context of the removal of evidence and foreign disregard for the site as a location of mass killing, the move to return the dead to the school buildings resonates with ethical and political fortitude.

After the massacres Murambi was occupied by displaced Rwandan residents, extending the months of terror endured at the site and effectively delaying memory work there. Before, during, and after the French encampment and until late April 1995, Rwandan residents uneasily occupied the thirteen school buildings as an interim shelter. The first wave of relocations was forced.[14] Shortly after victims' bodies were removed by the *génocidaires*, local authorities moved women from the nearby Kigeme Hospital to the school compound.[15] The women identified as both Tutsi and Hutu, and most either had sought treatment at the hospital after fleeing violence or, more commonly, had just given birth. Living conditions were extremely dire. With walls and floors covered in congealed blood, Murambi was far from hygienic for new mothers, babies, and the ill. The women were forced to dispose of the few remaining bodies lying on the grounds and clean up fluids and evidence.[16] The complex did not have electricity or running water. Many women were repeatedly raped by Rwandan soldiers associated with the previous regime. The subsequent French occupation of the site afforded them some measure of protection. After the French left, refugees continued to occupy the site until the nearby Kibeho Camp massacre on April 22, 1995.[17] Some relocated from temporary shelter at the Groupe Scolaire, a boarding school in the nearby university town of Butare.[18] Others returned from immediate refuge and long-term exile in neighboring countries.[19] The extended occupation of the Murambi school complex—by thousands of victims of mass violence, foreign soldiers, and vulnerable refugees—muddies its symbolism as solely a genocide site. For the living, for the better part of a year, "being in Murambi was," as one Rwandan woman put it, "like being left in a mass grave."[20]

As a result, memory work at Murambi only began in mid-1995 as a series of ad hoc initiatives that evolved into a more systematic conservation process in 1996 and 1997. The first actions involved the revolting work of exhumation and the decision to place intact bodies in the school buildings. The conservation practices that followed were similarly physically and emotionally challenging. And yet, despite its personal toll, the work of revealing and conserving violated and decomposing human remains persisted. Many of the individuals doing genocide memory work saw it as a form of repair for the violent injustice that victims suffered.[21] Spatial representations of the massacre were integral to that effort. Returning the dead to a site of killing contested their erasure. The killing site's restoration sought to correct a historical omission—the existence of the victims prior to their deaths and the occurrence of the massacres—through the undeniable representation of the dead.

The individuals who led and participated in the conservation effort were acutely aware of the less principled aspects of this approach to genocide heritage. They personally felt the display of victims to be traumatizing and dehumanizing and knew that others also found it so. And from the second national commemoration of the genocide at Murambi in April 1996 to today, the same individuals have witnessed and experienced the site's progressive politicization by the government. Despite these contradictions, which set the ethics of nonerasure in opposition to its consequences, those who did conservation work maintain that the display of bodies and bones at Rwanda's genocide memorials is of utmost social and historical importance.

## THE SMELL AND THE SACRIFICE (*UKWITANGA*)

Gabriel (a pseudonym) was involved in the first conservation activities at Murambi, which occurred in mid-1995, before the Genocide Memorial Commission was formed. Then in his late thirties, he had returned earlier that year from exile in Burundi, where, coincidentally, Louis Kanamugire had been one of his secondary school teachers (with no bearing on Gabriel's involvement in memorialization). He took a job with the Nyamagabe Commune office near the Murambi genocide site. He joined the Amagaju Association, a small organization comprising mostly businesspeople who had recently resettled in Rwanda after long-term exile. The group originally formed to fund economic development in the Bufundu region, eponymously named for the chieftainship that controlled the area during monarchic times. The organization reprioritized its work in 1995 to address survivors' and victims' families' needs after the genocide. Specifically, the Amagaju set to work identifying the locations where perpetrators disposed of the people they killed. Most of the Amagaju leadership resided and worked in

Kigali, including the president, Gaspard Kajangwe, who was a managing director at Cogebanque.[22] Gabriel was appointed as the organization's local representative and directed its operations in the region, including exhumations, reburial efforts, and the first attempts to conserve bodies at Murambi.

The exhumation of bodies from mass graves at and near Murambi was initiated by the Amagaju for the purpose of locating victims and providing them with decent burials. The work of unearthing and recovering bodies from graves, fields, and buildings was done primarily by rural residents living near the massacre site, whom the Amagaju and local authorities employed.[23] The exhumations were a high priority for survivors and family members who did not know if their relatives were still living or had been killed, or where their bodies were. The Amagaju were mostly of Tutsi origin and had fled Rwanda in earlier pogroms that targeted Tutsi. Members were largely motivated by responsibility to kin and family, to the thousands of Tutsi murdered in the genocide.

In 2018 I asked Gabriel what it was like to oversee this work. When he responded, he shook his head several times while voicing a kind of guttural lament: "Oh . . . oh, oh . . . it was a sacrifice [*kwari ukwitanga*]. First of all, the smell was awful; you were in danger of getting sick. . . . Also, exhuming them was scary, really, because you could see a person when he was still fresh; you could see his clothes and say, 'I knew him.' You could recognize people there that you knew."[24] The word that Gabriel used, *ukwitanga*, was purposeful. In other contexts, it would not have meant sacrifice so much as a strong dedication to some person, thing, or cause. Gabriel used the term to emphasize what memory workers had to forgo to conserve bodies and sites of killing. The grief it reopened, fear of illness from breathing and touching the dead, and the putrid stench of death were all aspects of this work with which they contended to fulfill a responsibility to kin.

The Amagaju opened their exhumations to relatives searching for family members. A few identifiable victims were returned to their families for private burial. Thousands of others were reinterred in communal reburial ceremonies attended by survivors and kin, local government representatives, religious leaders, and national officials. Gabriel and the Amagaju continued exhumations and reburials into the first months of 1996, when the organization's funding ran out and they effectively disbanded. However, a key discovery in the process prompted a critical collaboration between the Amagaju, the National Museum in Butare (led by Dr. Célestin Kanimba Misago), the local Gikongoro Préfecture office, and eventually the Genocide Memorial Commission. Those partnerships led to the Murambi Genocide Memorial's distinctive aesthetic.

When the Amagaju exhumed victims from several mass graves, they found that the soil had acted as a kind of desiccant, effectively mummifying the bodies.[25] By late 1995 the Murambi school complex no longer hosted displaced persons. The *préfet* (government official) in charge of Gikongoro Préfecture, Félix Zigirinshuti, authorized the buildings' use to house the mummified victims. Mario Ibarra estimated that around two hundred bodies were placed on the floors of the buildings at that time.[26] Zigirinshuti both authorized and provided logistical support for the work and also contributed to genocide memory discussions occurring in the capital.[27] Records for the national government's November 1995 "Genocide, Impunity, and Accountability" conference show Zigirinshuti in attendance. Given his involvement in the first decisions to display the bodies of victims at Murambi, Zigirinshuti likely informed and endorsed the government's charge to "preserve the remains of genocide victims in at least every commune."[28]

The smell of the mummified bodies' decomposition was overwhelming in the Murambi school buildings, and the Amagaju did not have the expertise to maintain them. Gabriel recalled that Gaspard Kajangwe, the Amagaju president, reached out to Dr. Kanimba, whom he knew from university in Zaire (now the Democratic Republic of the Congo), to solicit his archaeological expertise in late 1995. In January 1996 Dr. Kanimba became the director of the National Museum of Rwanda, which is located near Murambi in Butare, a significant cultural center and university town. With Dr. Kanimba's involvement, the conservation operation at Murambi shifted from an ad hoc effort to one developed through systematic experimentation (figure 4.1). That the initial idea to conserve and display victims at Murambi was shaped by both the Amagaju Association and Dr. Kanimba underscores that the effort was not merely politically motivated by the new regime. Rwanda's genocide heritage also had significant ethical and reparative foundations.

## REVERSING A DOUBLE ERASURE

Dr. Kanimba was critical to developing the conceptual scaffolding for genocide heritage and the scientific basis for conservation experiments. His archaeological expertise and connections to the National Museum and the National University in Butare channeled significant knowledge and financial resources to the nearby site of Murambi. He was also at the center of genocide memory discussions within a wider network of academics, practitioners, government officials, and residents.[29] This included the Amagaju and local authorities, historians and other professors at the university, national government representatives, and members of the Genocide Memorial Commission. Not merely the resident expert, he is remembered with great fondness by several former guides and conservation workers at Murambi for valuing them as survivors and as conservators of genocide memory.

A decade later, Dr. Kanimba became more internationally prominent with a series of academic essays that argued for the importance of government-conserved

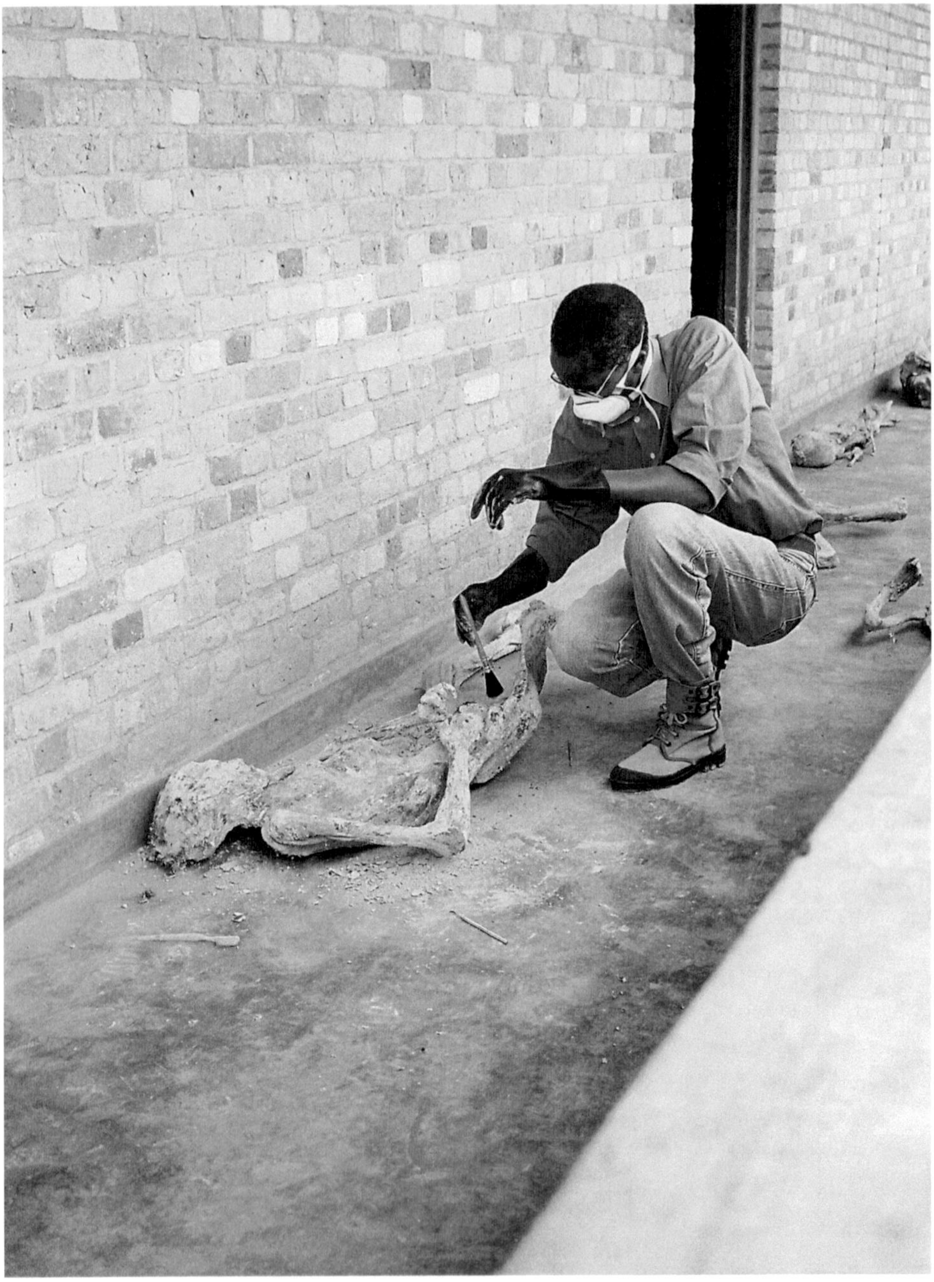

FIGURE 4.1. Dr. Célestin Kanimba Misago cleans the mummified body of a genocide victim at the Murambi massacre site as part of the Genocide Memorial Commission's third-phase conservation effort, December 1996. Photo by Mario Ibarra, Kanamugire archive, Rwanda.

genocide memory.[30] In one of his earlier writings, he notes that "the conservation of memory is not an end in itself," controversially eschewing the idea that Rwanda's genocide memorials serve as rigid and sensational symbols. He instead cites several domains, "historical, psychotherapeutic, social, political, and even economic," in which conservation had roles in addressing the postgenocide needs of individuals and the nation.[31] Dr. Kanimba continued to contribute to state genocide heritage institutions, becoming the first director of the National Commission for the Fight Against Genocide (CNLG), a new agency in charge of genocide memory, two years before his death on July 20, 2010.

Less widely recognized among Dr. Kanimba's contributions to genocide memory is his expertise and guidance in developing conservation techniques for victims' remains and other material evidence of the genocide. In response to the Amagaju Association's request for assistance at Murambi, Dr. Kanimba suggested spraying the bodies with hydrated lime or calcium hydroxide (figure 4.2). The substance acted as a preservative and dampened the stench of decomposition. Residents employed by the Gikongoro Préfecture office applied a hydrated lime mixture to the bodies with spray bottles. Photographs taken by Mario Ibarra in June 1996 provide a sense of what Murambi's spaces were like shortly after the first conservation efforts (figures 4.3–4.6). The images show concrete floors filled with bodies in several of the smaller buildings at the complex. The lower parts of the walls, the bodies, and the floor were covered in a dense, white, powdery substance. It is difficult to distinguish between different human forms, save for when light comes through the windows to cast stark shadows.

When I asked Gabriel why the Amagaju Association and the Gikongoro Préfecture office chose to display and conserve the exhumed bodies of genocide victims, his response was intensely emotional. "The killers dug and dug and *threw* them in there," he said, pausing for a moment to catch his breath. "They covered them with earth so that it [the killings] would be forgotten."[32] Gabriel's pauses were heavy with rage at both the killings and the removals.

He then went on to describe the Amagaju activities as a series of logical responses to those acts of erasure. Gabriel and other Amagaju Association members who returned from long-term exile were relatively distant from the killings compared to many survivors. Most had not directly experienced the recent attacks; they were not living in Rwanda when the genocide occurred.[33] Their conviction that genocide victims should be available to view was, perhaps, so resolute because they did not have to contend in the same way with the emotional conflicts and ambivalences the bodies provoked for many genocide survivors. By the Amagaju's logic, the display of bodies needed to be done to right a wrong on behalf of kin, to make visible that which could then never be forgotten. Gabriel continued to

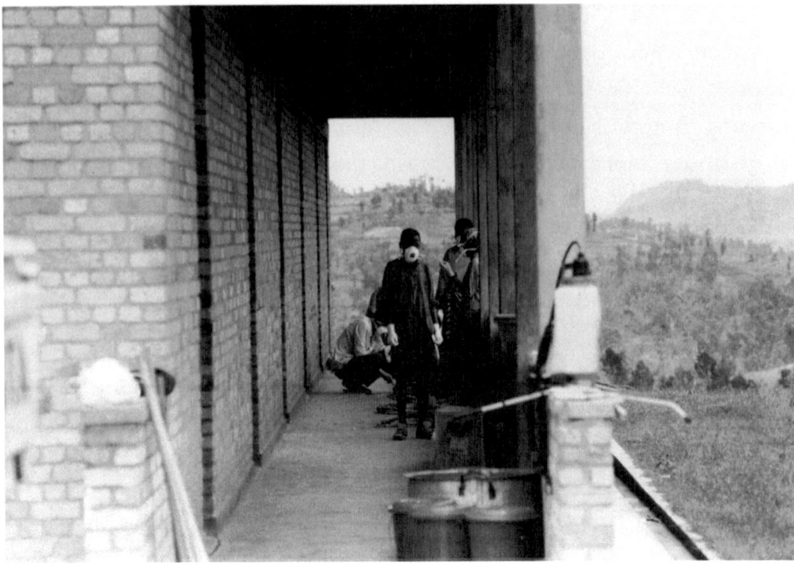

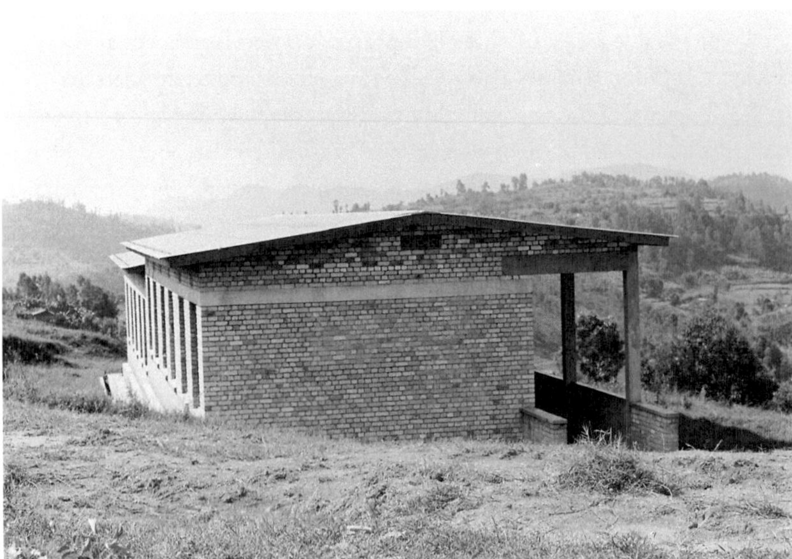

FIGURE 4.2. Genocide Memorial Commission workers begin the third conservation phase at Murambi, which involved cleaning victims' bodies and reapplying lime preservative (pump sprayer in foreground), 1996. Photo by Mario Ibarra, Ibarra archive, Chile.

FIGURE 4.3. One of thirteen buildings at the Murambi school complex where massacres occurred and the displaced later lived, photographed in June 1996. Today genocide victims' bodies are displayed there. Photo by Mario Ibarra, Kanamugire archive, Rwanda.

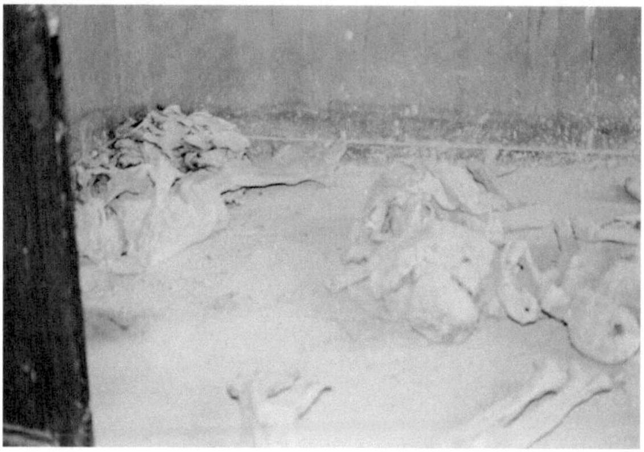

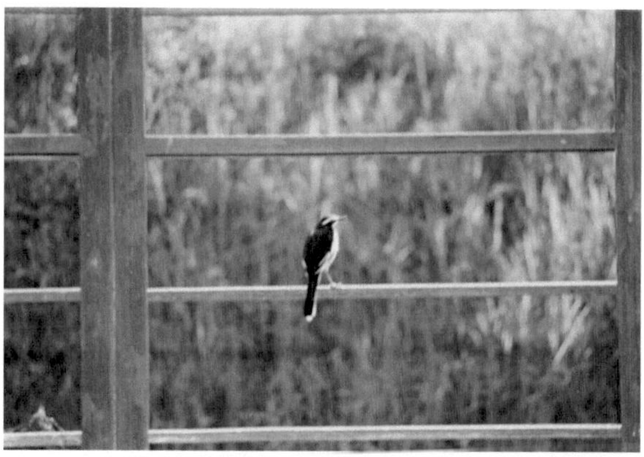

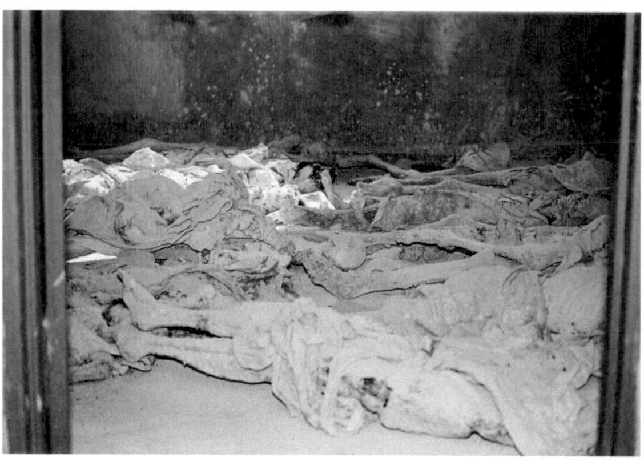

FIGURES 4.4 – 4.6. Three photographs from the same roll document the conditions of the Murambi school buildings after victims were first returned and conserved with lime in 1995. Mario Ibarra strove to capture some of the life (the bird perched on the window) amid the death. Photos by Mario Ibarra, June 1996, Kanamugire archive, Rwanda.

elaborate: "The reason that we applied *ishwagara* (lime) was to show the world that the genocide had occurred. By having them exhumed, we were showing the country—the world—that people died *here* and *here*. Then they [visitors] would be capable of seeing how many [victims] they were. It was a way of keeping evidence from being erased. Looking at those conserved with lime shows the world—the whole world that comes to visit memorials in Kigali and other places—that the genocide cannot be erased."[34]

In describing what motivated the conservation and display of mummified bodies at Murambi, Gabriel reinforced that it was important to show evidence of the mass killings where they occurred. The turn to spatial representation was also a consequence of the challenges with collecting and publicizing witness and survivor testimony of the massacres. Though testimony was critical to reconstructing what happened during the genocide, Mario, Louis, and the UN Special Investigations Unit (SIU) investigators noted that it was difficult to locate witnesses, gain their trust, and record reliable accounts in the immediate aftermath (see chapter 2). Many witnesses fled the areas near massacres or did not give testimony because they were worried about their security. Issues of witness access and reliability were compounded by the difficulties of Kinyarwanda translation for foreigners, the underrecognition of Rwanda and the genocide, and the removal of evidence. Together these challenges reinforced the importance of seeing and experiencing genocide sites and, as a result, the work of preservation and conservation.

At Murambi in particular, a material and spatial memory aimed to counter the *génocidaires'* double erasure (murder and disposal) of victims and a global public's lack of attention to the atrocities that occurred in Rwanda. In 1996 diverse actors, from government leaders to local organizations like the Amagaju, came to similar conclusions: the remains of the dead would be necessary to publicly represent the genocide. The sentiment was echoed by Louis in his aspiration to "make history known." It also related to Mario's belief—speaking specifically of Murambi and his conservation work elsewhere in the country—that "we would be able to maintain memory if we *showed* what happened."[35] It was a view shared by former Rusumo *bourgmestre* Janvier Gasasira, who spoke of the deep pain and simultaneous necessity of conserving the bodies of his neighbors and relatives in the Nyarubuye Church courtyard. And it was a point made, moreover, by Gabriel in relation to Murambi, who emphasized the central role that victims' bodies and bones had in representing the genocide. That Murambi was a retrospective conservation effort—the Amagaju did not preserve a killing scene; they reconstructed and approximated the killings—underscores the pivotal centrality of victims' remains as a metonym for Rwanda's genocide heritage.

The conditions at Murambi—the double erasure of victims, the soil composition that led to mummification, and the intervention of local groups—propelled an already existing view that the conservation of massacre sites and victims' remains was integral to Rwanda's genocide heritage aesthetic. Given the growing government consensus around the importance of display and witnessing, and the establishment of the Genocide Memorial Commission in late 1995, 1996 was a critical year in the evolution of these ideas. Three additional factors were critical to emphasizing conservation on a national stage and Murambi as its leading representation. These include Dr. Kanimba's role in genocide memory from late 1995 onward, the April 1996 national commemoration at Murambi, and Mario Ibarra's role as Dr. Kanimba's collaborator and as the Genocide Memorial Commission's main staff member at Murambi from 1996 to 1997.

### Genocide Memory Conservation

A video recorded on July 23, 1997, captures typical interactions between Mario Ibarra and Dr. Kanimba at Murambi (figures 4.7–4.9).[36] The film shows some of the conservation techniques they applied to the body of a small, flattened child. Merely a toddler when he died, the child had been crushed by the weight of other victims in a mass grave and mummified. In the video Mario adds a small plastic bag of salt to a conventional household bucket filled with warm water, mixing it to produce a cleaning and preserving solution. Without substantial resources, Dr. Kanimba, Mario, and their team worked with supplies that were readily available and otherwise used in domestic settings. In Kinyarwanda, Mario asks for more water. A third man, Emmanuel Murangira, enters the frame and pours water into the bucket. Mario gently submerges the child's body. Only his torso fits inside.

Using his hands to scoop and pour, Mario delicately saturates the rest of the child's body with the solution, noting to Dr. Kanimba in French, "It is ideal to clean most of it." Dr. Kanimba replies drily, "Uneasily, at the same time." Mario nods in agreement. The task is not physically difficult. They refer instead to their discomfort in conserving the body of a murdered child. The film documents several more minutes of Mario soaking the child's body, wearing a face mask and yellow kitchen gloves. Dr. Kanimba observes from behind the camera. The work is clinical yet respectful; the men are handling the dead but do so carefully and with purpose.

The conservation experiments video-recorded in 1997 are the culmination of several phases of memory work at Murambi. In the first phase, as I noted earlier, the Amagaju Association took the lead. Gabriel managed the exhumation of the victims removed from the site of massacre, their placement back in the school

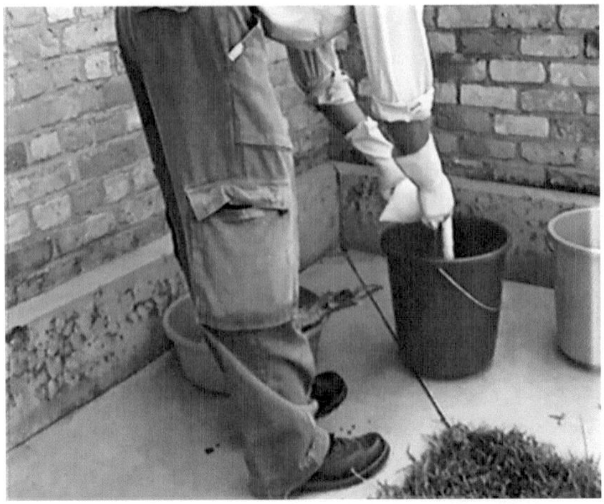

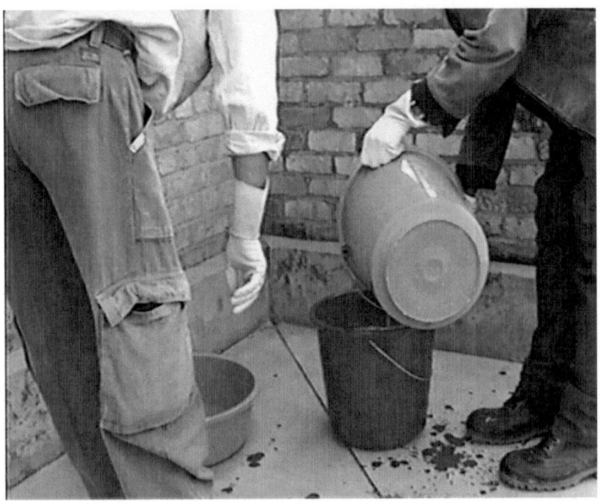

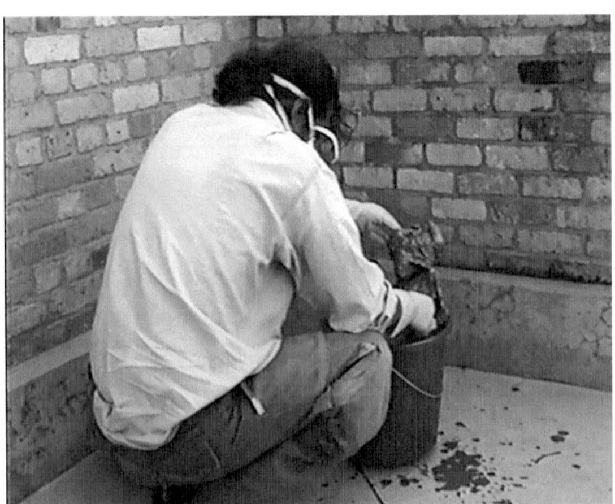

buildings, and their preservation with lime. The Amagaju were assisted in that effort by prefectural authorities associated with the new, postgenocide regime. In late 1995 both Dr. Kanimba and Mario became involved to consult on the Amagaju approach to conserving victims' remains.[37] The second and third phases of work were subsequently led by Mario and Dr. Kanimba as part of the Genocide Memorial Commission.

The second phase involved maintaining the initial conservation approach for the second national genocide commemoration, which took place on April 7, 1996. Work primarily entailed preventing further decomposition of the exhumed bodies and reducing the odors associated with their placement in the school buildings. Repeat applications of the lime solution, which Dr. Kanimba initiated in late 1995, began to slow decomposition. In early 1996 Mario began to focus on ventilation and climate control.[38]

The second commemoration had a catalytic impact on genocide memory conservation—both at Murambi, where the ceremony took place, and throughout Rwanda. It effectively legitimized, as state-authorized genocide heritage, the gravely unsettling display of victims' remains at killing sites. In doing so, the new governing regime reinforced witnessing as critical to combating genocide denial in local communities. In 1996, only two years after the killings occurred, *genocide denial* did not merely describe the rhetorical negation of mass violence; it referred to the removal of evidence of genocide crimes, of victims' bodies, from massacre sites. Both government documents and Dr. Kanimba remark on the role of memory preservation in contesting genocide denial and, more broadly, in contributing to the social work of national healing and reconciliation.[39] But the chemical preservation and exhibition of bodies were also oriented to a foreign audience, "to show the world," as Gabriel put it, what had occurred in Rwanda. By 1996, a year after the bodies were interred at Nyarubuye, the country's most iconic massacre site at the time, Murambi emerged as a critical stage for journalists and foreign state representatives to witness the genocide in its reconstructed form. The second national commemoration ceremony (which I discuss in the next chapter) at the school complex solidified that status.

Photographs taken by Mario in October 1996 show what the school buildings looked like during the second commemoration (as a result of the first and second phases of conservation) at Murambi (figures 1.4 and 2.19). His photographs docu-

FIGURES 4.7–4.9. Video stills of Mario Ibarra and Emmanuel Murangira experimenting with salt and warm water to conserve a child's body at Murambi. Mario Ibarra, "Mario Personal (3)," video recording, July 23, 1997, cassette G44D1046, at 56:38, 57:58, and 58:16, Ibarra archive, Chile.

ment the visit of Louise Arbour, then Chief Prosecutor of the UN International Criminal Tribunal for Rwanda (ICTR), and her team. Louis Kanamugire guided their tour as the director of the Genocide Memorial Commission, which was charged with maintaining the scene they were to witness. Photographs show the group peering timidly into the doorways of Murambi's smaller classroom buildings. Louis stood apart, describing what they see and what took place at the site. The group next ventured inside one of the larger buildings in the complex, which commission workers had named the *ibagiro*, or slaughterhouse. The ICTR visitors held masks to their faces. In each building they encountered, bodies were laid out across the floors, covering all available space. A dusty substance, left over from the lime preservative, covered the victims, much of the floor, and the lower half of the walls. It rendered the victims and room as one monochromatic entity, a view made more jarring by the recognition of bodies. In the larger building, a small path was carved to walk among the dead.

Arbour's ICTR team directed the international community's investigations and trials of genocide criminals in Rwanda. Their visit was not intended to provide evidence for the prosecutions of genocide organizers. Rather, it was a means to witness the aftermath. Murambi staged a deeply affective experience to inform their work. That viewership was significant for the relationship it established between Rwanda's genocide heritage and justice. After the second commemoration, Murambi was the primary government-authorized location for secondary witnessing.

A third phase of conservation work at Murambi commenced soon after Arbour's visit (and, more importantly, after the second national genocide commemoration that preceded her team's visit). It entailed the refinement of techniques to conserve victims' mummified bodies and identify approaches to prevent the deterioration of their bones and clothing (figures 4.10 and 4.11). It also involved more extensive coordination with massacre sites throughout the country to scale up the conservation of genocide victims' remains and evidence—in what was emerging as the official representation of genocide memory.

During the second and third phases, from 1996 to 1998, the Genocide Memorial Commission developed a geographically dispersed network of conservation experiments. The Murambi school complex became prominent for its conservation and display of mummified victims' bodies. But in exhumation processes at other sites, including those in the vicinity of Murambi, it was more common to encounter decomposed or disaggregated victims' remains. A significant part of the backstage work in Murambi's memorialization, therefore, was work to deflesh and clean thousands of skeletal artifacts. The skulls and discernible long bones of victims were then placed back into massacre sites or reburied in consecrated mass graves.

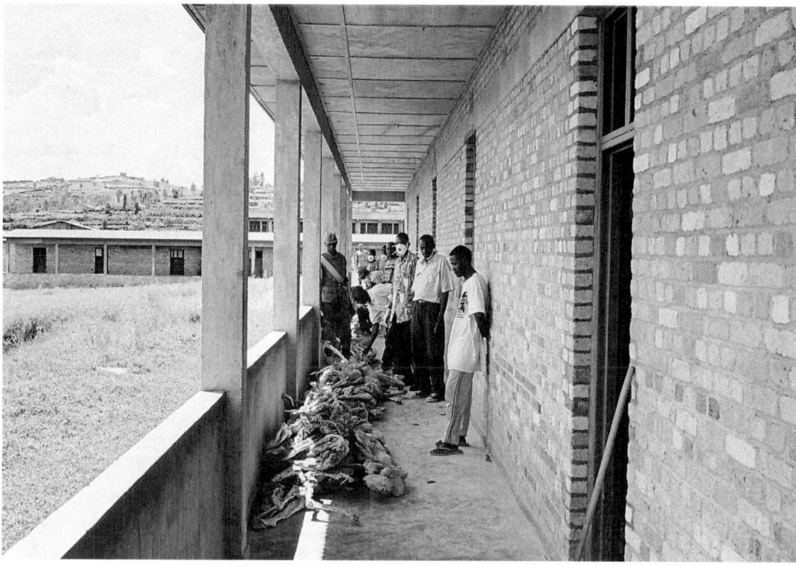

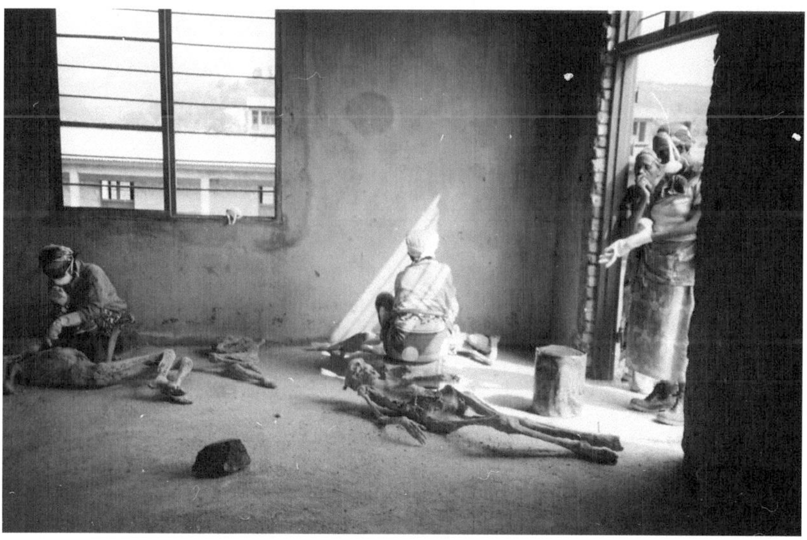

FIGURE 4.10. Emmanuel Murangira (*second from right*) and other Genocide Memorial Commission workers stand over mummified victims' bodies removed from Murambi classrooms to begin the third-phase conservation effort, December 1996. Photo by Mario Ibarra, Kanamugire archive, Rwanda.

FIGURE 4.11. Women working for the Genocide Memorial Commission clean victims' mummified bodies for longer-term display at Murambi, 1996. Photo by Mario Ibarra, Ibarra archive, Chile.

Murambi, and the three phases of conservation experimentation that took place there, were critical to establishing Rwanda's genocide heritage aesthetic. The process made conservation a feasible long-term strategy for maintaining genocide memory. It also scaled that effort throughout the country. Conservation maintained an unflinching, serial representation of mass violence in nearly every district in Rwanda. In doing so, it reinforced the significance of an extreme form of witnessing—not merely of any evidence of crimes but specifically of bodies and skeletal remains—for genocide representation.

## A NETWORK OF MEMORY WORK

From 1996 to 1998, Mario and Dr. Kanimba worked at five genocide sites that formed the core of their experimentation with, and development and scaling of, conservation techniques. Chief among those sites were the Murambi Technical School and Nyamata Parish (near Kigali), which were later designated as national genocide memorials. Three additional killing sites, which were originally government offices—in Mwulire Sector (located near Rwamagana in the East) and in Munini Sector and Ruhashya Commune (both located near Murambi in the south)—were not designated as national genocide memorials.[40] They were instead critical places of genocide memory work, connected in a network of conservation experiments directed by the Genocide Memorial Commission from Murambi (figures 4.12 and 4.13). The government offices were chosen because the sites contained tombs where thousands of genocide victims were reburied by local authorities and the commission. Louis, Mario, and Dr. Kanimba turned to those repositories of victims' remains to expand their nascent approach to genocide memorialization. In 1995, at the Ruhashya Commune office alone, local authorities entombed an estimated twenty thousand victims found in perpetrator-dug mass graves nearby.[41] In the third phase of conservation work at Murambi, workers employed by the Genocide Memorial Commission exhumed victims from Ruhashya, Munini, and Mwulire to advance techniques to conserve skeletal remains. The commission then repopulated memorials in proximity to those sites with deidentified, though symbolically representative, Tutsi victims.

Altogether, the memory work at the five sites (Murambi, Munini, and Ruhashya in the southwest; Nyamata near the capital; and Mwulire farther east) comprised the largest conservation effort in the country. It was a state-sponsored and -funded initiative directed by the Genocide Memorial Commission. Mario and Dr. Kanimba were the project's de facto technical conservation experts: Kanimba by his training in archaeology and Mario by his experience as a human rights investigator and his earlier work at Nyarubuye. Dr. Kanimba possessed knowledge of conservation techniques for material artifacts and provided a more systematic

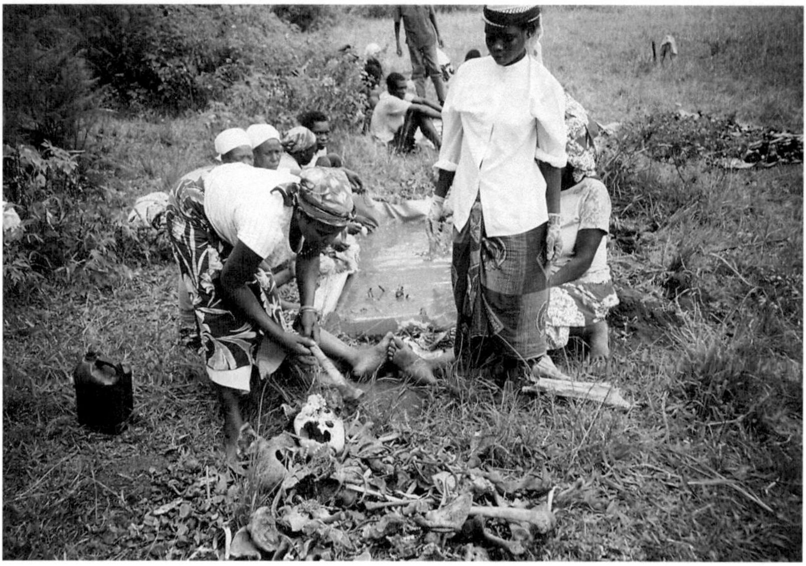

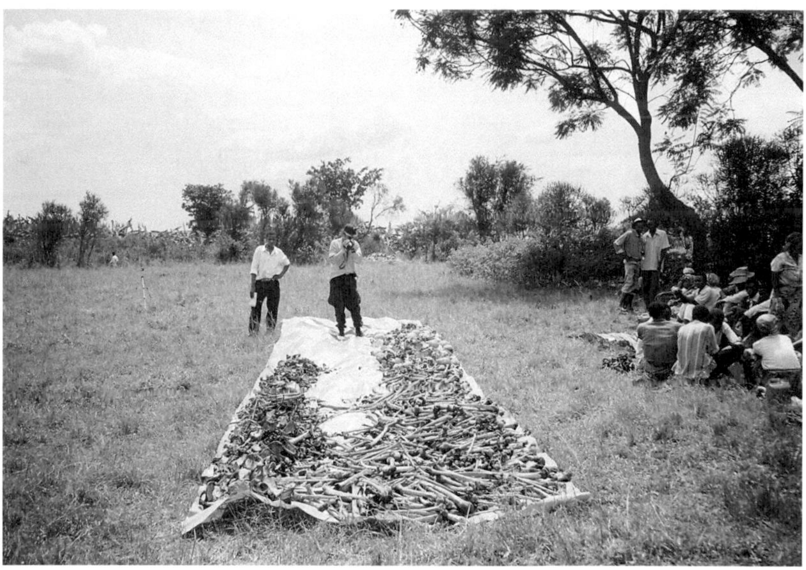

FIGURE 4.12. Genocide Memorial Commission workers sort and clean genocide victims' bones at the Mwulire Sector office in Gikongoro Préfecture near Murambi, 1996. Photo by Mario Ibarra, Kanamugire archive, Rwanda.

FIGURE 4.13. Mario Ibarra video-records the results of bone conservation, panning over victims' skeletal remains sorted on a tarp and drying in the sun, Mwulire Sector office, 1996. Kanamugire archive, Rwanda.

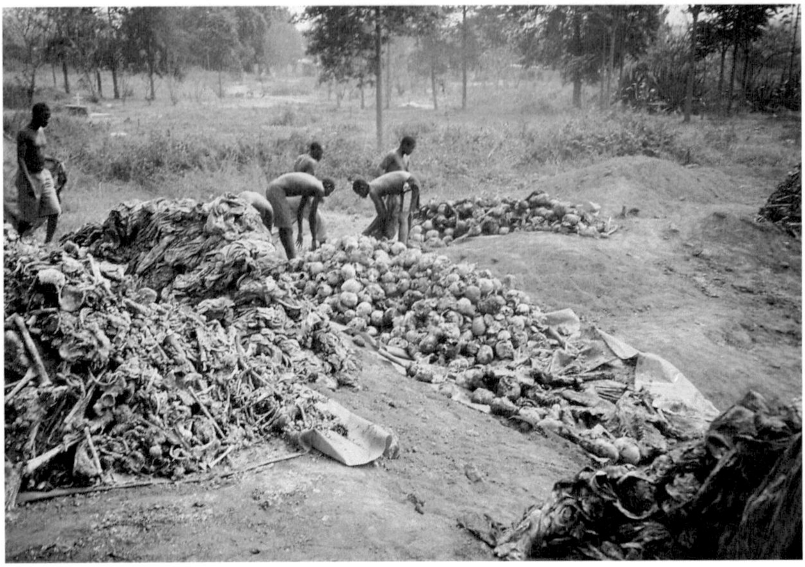

FIGURE 4.14. The Nyamata conservation process began with prisoners exhuming victims and sorting their skeletal remains and clothing, August 1997. Photo by Mario Ibarra, Kanamugire archive, Rwanda.

approach to their work. Mario worked to translate those techniques into practices that could be achieved with the minimal resources available to them. He also documented the process (see figure Int.4).

Three main tasks were part of the larger, systematic, and more organized conservation effort. Key among them was a series of experiments to find techniques to clean and conserve skeletal remains (figures 4.14–4.16). Conservation also involved finding a method to prevent the deterioration of mummified bodies at Murambi. Along with the work on victims' remains, the commission developed practices to sterilize and conserve their clothes and belongings, weapons used during the attacks, and damage to buildings. The memory work at the five sites prepared tens of thousands of bones and hundreds of mummified bodies for both display and reburial. Artifacts—including massive quantities of clothing and weapons—also were conserved for exhibition at memorial sites throughout the country. By comparison, initiatives to preserve the buildings damaged during genocidal attacks were considerably slower. Most of that work occurred after 1998 with the influx of foreign investment.

That human bones became the primary representation of Rwanda's genocide heritage was a direct consequence of this more systematic and scalable conservation

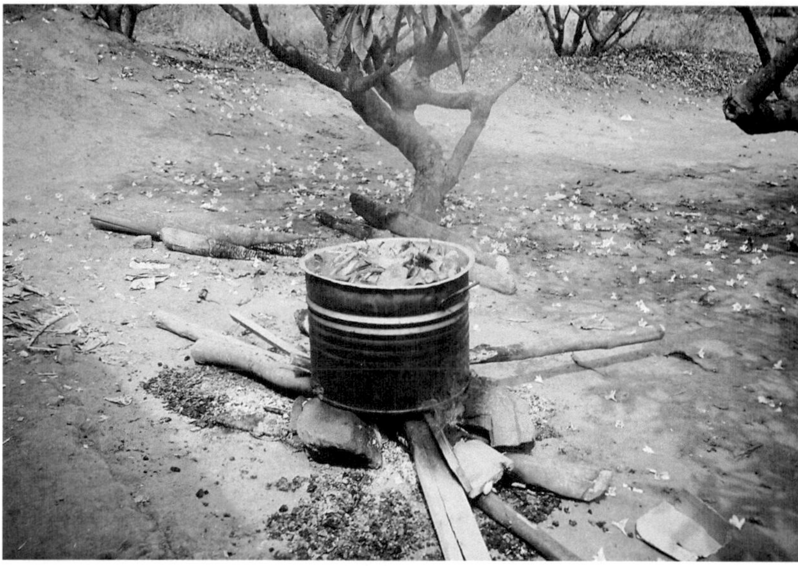

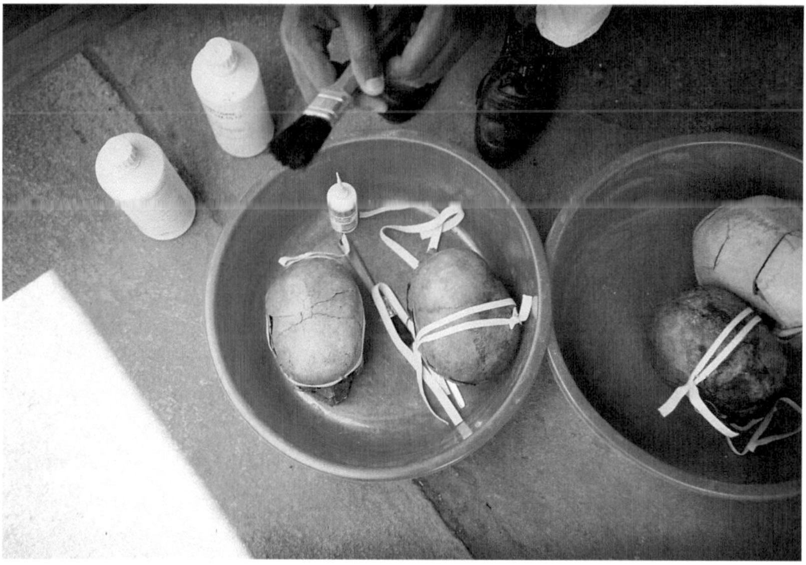

FIGURE 4.15. After exhumation, victims' bones are boiled in a large pot to begin conservation at Nyamata, August 1997. Photo by Mario Ibarra, Kanamugire archive, Rwanda.

FIGURE 4.16. Dr. Kanimba glues together skull fragments for display in the Nyamata crypt, August 1997. Photo by Mario Ibarra, Kanamugire archive, Rwanda.

effort. It began in earnest in 1996, eighteen months after the genocide occurred. Until then, victims had been lying either exposed in the open or interred in graves by perpetrators seeking to hide evidence of the genocide or by new authorities attempting to bury them with some decency. Months of decomposition revealed an excessive quantity of human bones, which provided a de facto visual representation of the scale of the genocide. Communicating the scale and extent of the killings became a high priority for the Genocide Memorial Commission's conservation efforts. They primarily chose skulls and long bones for display at genocide sites. Those parts were the easiest to identify as human and the most efficient to clean and conserve, respectively.[42] Local residents, mostly women, were employed by the commission to do that work (figures 4.17 and 4.18). The practices they developed for conserving skeletal remains became standard at most early memorial sites, and many concurrent reburial ceremonies, by late 1997 (figures 4.19–4.20).

## DETERIORATING MEMORY

Conservation work was necessarily iterative when it came to addressing the progressive decomposition of genocide memory. Finding a reasonable conservation approach came, as Mario recalled, from both Dr. Kanimba's training and what they learned from local initiatives and his investigations.[43] For example, as part of his genocide investigations for the UN, Mario was keenly aware of the ways in which the soil covering mass graves hastened decomposition. He observed other natural processes of decay that were cleaning bones quickly but eroding their surfaces. His investigations of bodies found in banana groves provided examples of expeditious cleaning by ants, prompting related experiments. Observing the attempts of local authorities in Gitarama Préfecture (in south-central Rwanda) to ventilate human remains in chicken coops prompted ideas for mitigating the smell. Ruhashya was the first site where Genocide Memorial Commission workers had the idea to use a combination of warm water and simple bars of hand soap. This was a cheap and readily available solution for cleaning the bones that had the added benefit of leaving a waxy film to protect their surfaces and a perfume to reduce the smell of decay. Rwanda's genocide heritage was made possible through simple innovations.

The conservation of mummified bodies at the Murambi school complex came with unique challenges. Unlike work with skeletal remains, the primary difficulty was not the volume. The two hundred or so intact bodies retrieved by the Amagaju represented only a small percentage of the tens of thousands killed at the site. Yet the mummified remains presented workers with distinct challenges because they looked human: It was possible to distinguish adults from children, find identifying features, and see injuries and causes of death. These were the paradoxes entailed in maintaining bodies for viewing.

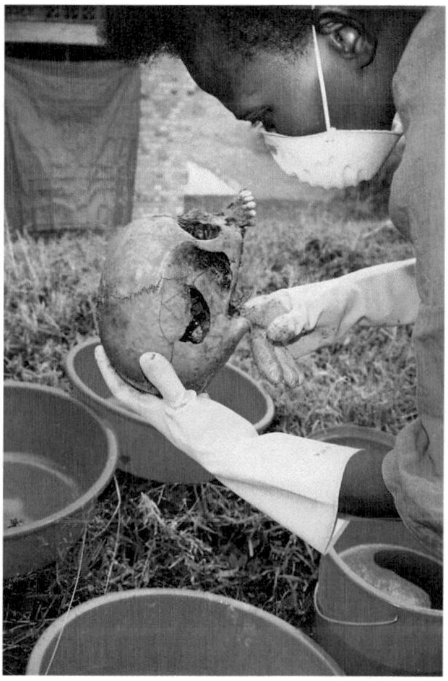 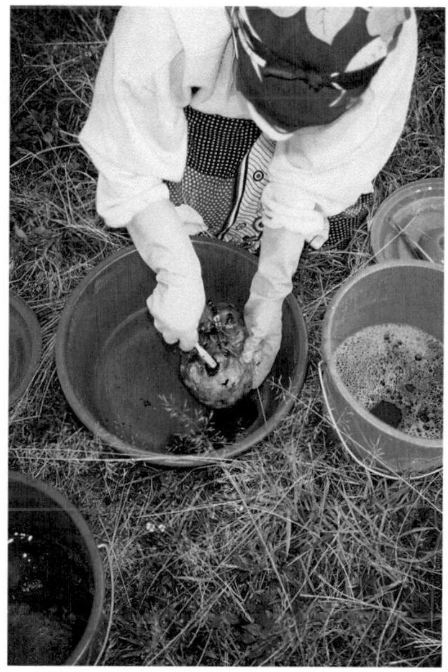

FIGURE 4.17. Conservationist working for the Genocide Memorial Commission cleans soil and matter from inside a genocide victim's skull, November 1996. Photo by Mario Ibarra, Kanamugire archive, Rwanda.

FIGURE 4.18. Conservationist cleans the inside of a genocide victim's skull with a toothbrush, bars of soap, and water, November 1996. Photo by Mario Ibarra, Kanamugire archive, Rwanda.

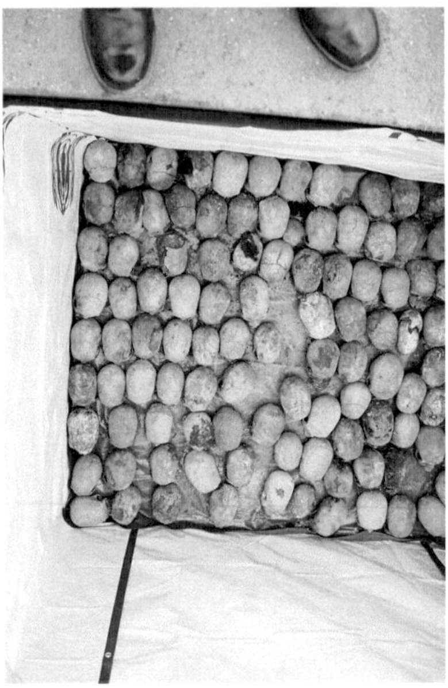

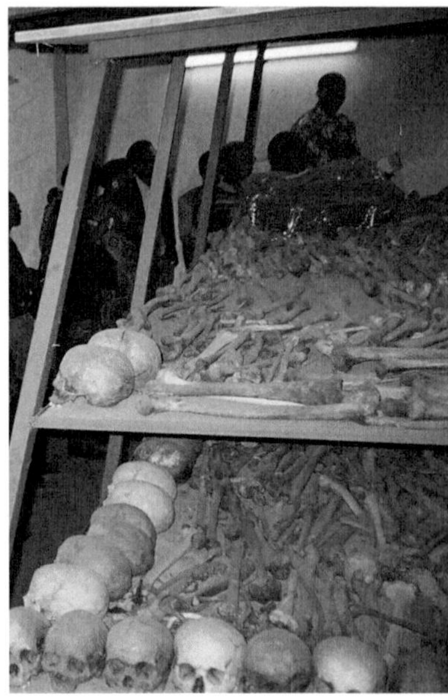

FIGURE 4.19. Genocide victims' remains were cleaned and sorted, to restore order and decency, before reburial near Murambi, November 1996. Photo by Mario Ibarra, Kanamugire archive, Rwanda.

FIGURE 4.20. Genocide victims' bones sorted and displayed in the subterranean crypt dug below Nyamata Church that visitors toured during the reburial ceremony on September 14, 1997. Courtesy of Louis Kanamugire, Kanamugire archive, Rwanda.

The third phase of the conservation effort, which the Genocide Memorial Commission began in late 1996, attempted to mitigate those tensions by developing systematic procedures. Commission workers first documented the victims. They identified gender and age and weighed and measured each body (figure 4.21). Each victim was photographed, with special attention given to injuries and personal items (figure 2.17). Commission workers then removed clothing and other belongings where possible and cleaned the bodies extensively. Cleaning involved scraping the bodies with toothbrushes and small picks to remove remaining hair, flesh, fungus, or soil. Workers also attempted to slough off the loose, chalky substance left by previous applications of the lime preservative. Bodies were then treated with denatured alcohol and saltwater baths to slow bacterial growth, and the lime mixture was reapplied.

Conservation work was also, importantly, communal; it was rarely done alone. It was also not a scientific effort undertaken in sterile working conditions with sophisticated tools. In 1997 Mario filmed some of that work inside one of the large halls at the Murambi school complex. The video shows several individuals, spaced several feet apart, each tending to a stiffened human form laid out on the floor. The desiccated bodies are light but unwieldy and petrified in rigor mortis. Speaking in Kinyarwanda, the workers comment on the hardened skin of the genocide victims and the challenges of cleaning them. They also joke with each other, maintaining running banter alongside the repetitions of their conservation work. Their chatter is followed often by silences accompanied only by the sounds of scraping and brushing. The seemingly endless and rote nature of their work is interrupted periodically by Dr. Kanimba and Mario, who are nearby to examine the injuries and identifying marks the workers discover.[44] The video depicts situations that are simultaneously serious and light, studious and social, in ways that seem strangely appropriate for the jarring and yet mundane work of conserving bodies as genocide memory.

When Genocide Memorial Commission workers completed those conservation tasks, the bodies were placed back in the school buildings on custom-built raised wood-slat platforms (figure 4.22). That simple innovation ventilated the bodies to help guard against further decomposition. The introduction of the platforms, along with rudimentary climate controls, derived from both the Gitarama chicken coop experiments and Mario's site studies. In the latter, using weighted string, Mario determined that at Murambi the winds changed direction significantly from morning to afternoon and during the dry and rainy seasons.[45] He covered several of the classrooms' windows with blue plastic tarps (with the UN logo) to shield the bodies from direct exposure to the sun and rain. He kept other windows unblocked for cross-circulation.

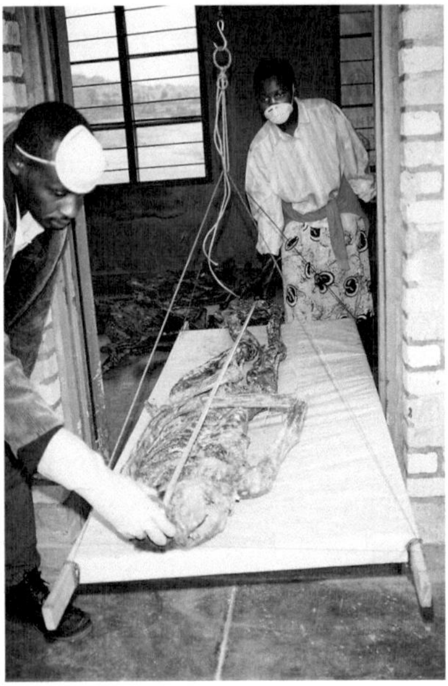 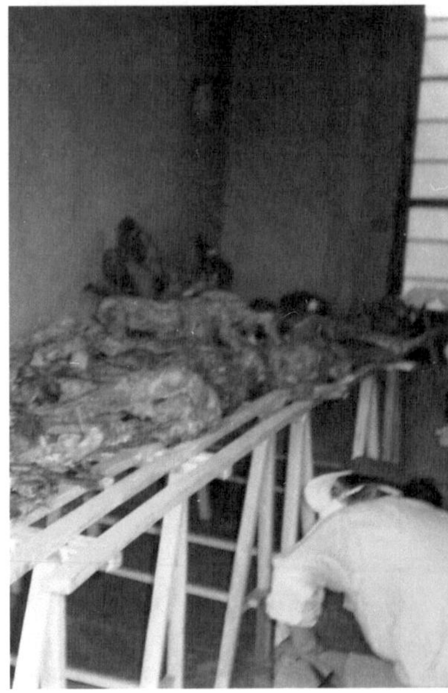

FIGURE 4.21. Emmanuel Murangira (*left*) and an assistant measure and weigh a genocide victim's body on a makeshift scale suspended from a Murambi classroom doorway, December 1996. Photo by Mario Ibarra, Kanamugire archive, Rwanda.

FIGURE 4.22. At Murambi, Mario Ibarra inspects conserved bodies to see if the newly built wood-slat tables provide adequate ventilation and protection from insects and moisture, late 1996. Courtesy of Mario Ibarra, Ibarra archive, Chile.

Victims' clothing held special status in the conservation effort (figures 4.23 and 4.24). This was particularly the case at Murambi because the perpetrators had ransacked the dead, taking their belongings, before they disposed of bodies in area mass graves. Those posthumous violations rendered the act of retrieving and preserving clothing an attempt to right yet another injustice. At other locations, in the absence of DNA technology, victims' belongings represented one of the few, albeit rudimentary, means to identify relatives in the first years after the genocide. Buttons, cloth patterns, and closed-toed shoes were particularly helpful for neighbors' and relatives' identification efforts. Subsequently, displaying victims' clothing and shoes strove to humanize their skeletal remains, for most were no longer recognizable as individuals. The artifacts proclaimed the dead as once living.

To conserve clothing at Murambi, the commission's workers first cleaned lime, blood, and soil from the fabrics. Those substances were dissolving the clothes and producing a putrid smell. They experimented with salt, denatured alcohol, and liquid antiseptic (cetrimide) diluted in water baths. Those approaches were ultimately less successful than boiling the clothes. The process of finding an appropriate clothing preservation method was documented in both photographs and videos. A series shows Mario Ibarra, Emmanuel Murangira, another young man, and a young woman in a black-and-white-striped sweater trying out the boil method (figure 4.25).[46] They stand around a large metal pot set on large stones above a fire in a clearing between Murambi's school buildings. Each of them wears a face mask and kitchen gloves. They simmer the clothes, stir the contents with large wood poles and sticks, and examine the results. Commission workers then dried the clothes on Murambi's grounds (figure 4.26) and hung them on cables across the width of the *ibagiro* (figure 4.23). Drying the clothes in that manner evolved into an approach for their display.

All of these conservation techniques reinforced the primacy of viewing evidence of mass death in Rwanda's genocide heritage. Victims' bodies and bones were critical to that representational effort. But the process of preparing them for display raised significant dilemmas and challenges for the workers involved. This did not merely concern the difficulties related to slowing decay; it was more importantly related to the embodiment of conservation work and the emotional, ethical, and physical demands that memory maintenance entailed.

## Memory Workers

In video recorded on July 17, 1997, inside the earthen vault near the Ruhashya Commune Office, a woman wields a long stick to pry skulls up and out of a large wooden crate (figures 4.27–4.29).[47] She wears yellow kitchen gloves, a headscarf,

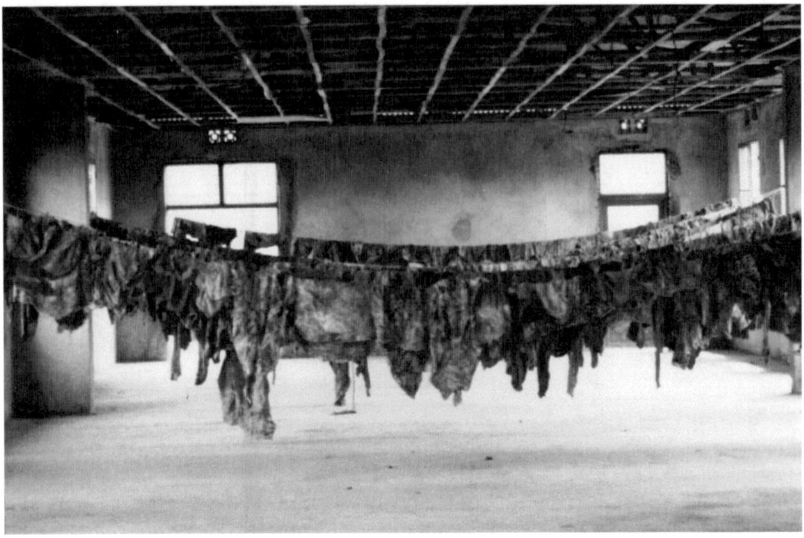

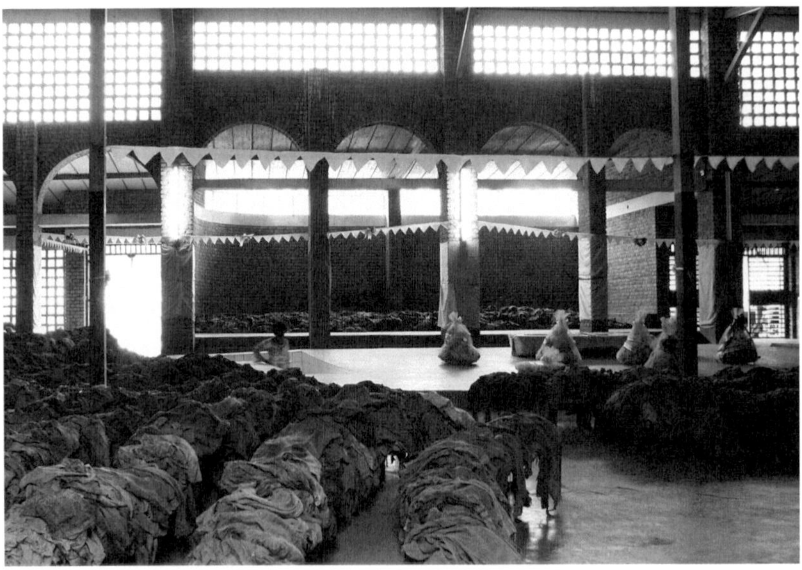

FIGURE 4.23. Victims' clothing dries on lines in a large building at Murambi after early conservation experiments by the Genocide Memorial Commission, 1996. Photo by Mario Ibarra, Ibarra archive, Chile.

FIGURE 4.24. The Nyamata Genocide Memorial in 2013, with conserved victims' clothing returned and piled on pews in the church. Photo by Delia Duong Ba Wendel.

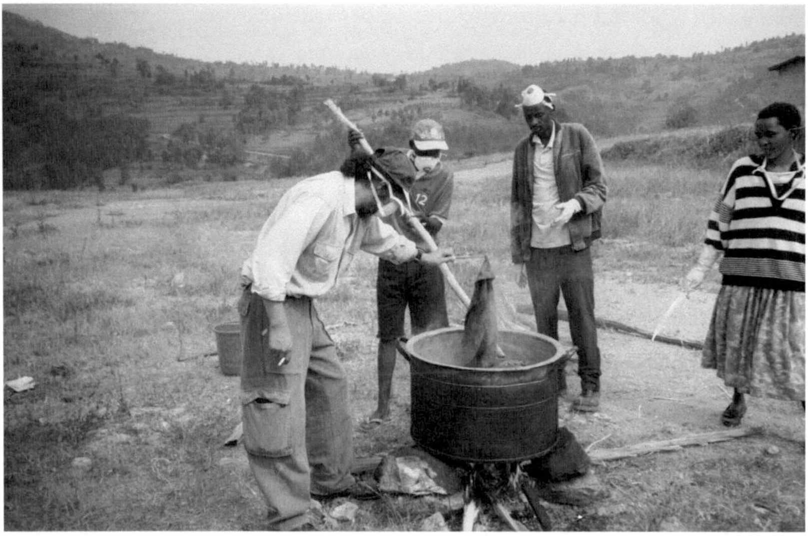

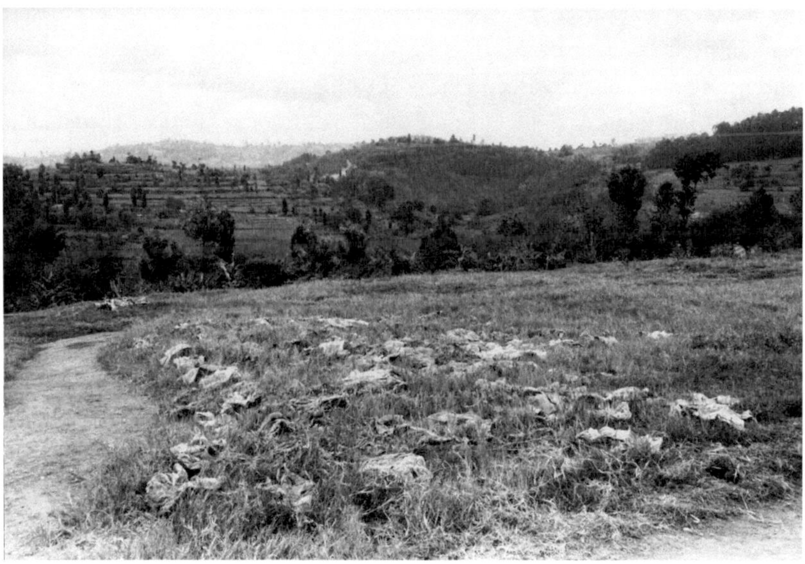

FIGURE 4.25. Mario Ibarra (*left*), Emmanuel Murangira (*center, in gloves*), and two other Genocide Memorial Commission workers experiment with boiling victims' clothing as a conservation approach at Murambi, 1996. Courtesy of Mario Ibarra, Ibarra archive, Chile.

FIGURE 4.26. After victims' clothing was boiled, Genocide Memorial Commission workers laid it out to dry on the Murambi school grounds, 1996. Photo by Mario Ibarra, Ibarra archive, Chile.

and a face mask but is otherwise dressed conventionally in a shirt tucked into faded cloth that wraps her waist as a skirt. Face masks were necessary to filter the decay, which was exacerbated by the humidity and heat inside the subterranean space. The smell significantly limited the amount of time she and others spent working inside the vault.[48] Another woman enters the camera's frame to pick up a shallow plastic tub filled with skulls. She ascends out of the tomb using a simple lean-to ladder constructed of wood poles.

Twelve crates are lined up against one side of the thirteen-foot-high vault. Each crate measures approximately nine feet wide by six feet deep and is four feet tall. Piles of bones are visible on top of the crates and are sorted by type: skulls on one, assorted long bones on another, and so on. Mario Ibarra enters the vault and examines a crate's contents. He picks up several skulls from openings at their base with forceps, examining the inside with a telescoping mirror. He and the first woman begin sorting the skulls by decomposition. Their work is silent, and the sounds of their movements are dampened in the large space dug into the soil. They put the skulls that require additional cleaning in buckets full of muddy water. Others are placed in dry buckets to be examined further for injuries. Long bones are similarly inspected and separated. Fracture patterns on the bones and skulls indicate the types of instruments used to kill—allowing the Genocide Memorial Commission to distinguish and catalog the use of nail-studded clubs, machetes, blunt objects, and firearms. Some of the weapons, especially those with ammunition, correlated to different groups responsible for the killings, including the former military-backed armed groups.

The video eventually shifts to the work occurring aboveground in an open area next to the Ruhashya office, screened from public view with vertically draped blue tarps (figures 4.30–4.32). The camera records the work of six individuals—four women and two men—sitting by green plastic tubs filled with long bones and skulls. They clean with toothbrushes, bars of soap, and water, brushing at joints and plying inside skulls to remove decomposing tissue. The sounds construct a rhythm of work from rasps, scrapes, and water plunges against the background of the workers' crying children.

The workers tease each other in Kinyarwanda, often glancing up in the direction of the camera, aware of its presence. Mario and Dr. Kanimba enter into view. Mario crouches down to inspect the bones to see if their experiments with household products are cleaning sufficiently with minimal damage. This prompts one woman to exclaim in Kinyarwanda, "You are working with the *muzungu* [foreigner]!" Another woman chuckles, replying, "*Sha*, stop laughing at me!" Dr. Kanimba is behind the camera and loosely translates the conversation into French for Mario, telling him, "They want to take you to their house for a meal."

Mario responds to the flirtation with a wry statement—"I could not possibly eat"—referring to his unease with the bones they are handling. Both men laugh as the camera zooms in on another woman as she uses one of the skulls to pour water into the other, flushing recent scrapings. The camera pans to an area behind the workers, where Dr. Kanimba and Mario discuss and inspect the cleaned bones and skulls that have been drying in the sun.

These scenes capture what it was like to do genocide memory work. Workers handled human remains just three years after experiencing mass violence in their own communities. A full range of emotions is not apparent in these vignettes, though the camera does document a sense of what conservation entailed. Residents employed by the commission treated human bones with ordinary domestic products to remove substances that were accelerating their deterioration. Individuals donned kitchen gloves to clean with water and bars of antiseptic soap; sterilize with rubbing alcohol and salt; and use toothbrushes, small metal trowels, and floor scrubbers to scrape remaining flesh and bodily fluids from the bones.[49] Maintaining genocide evidence for viewing was arduous work. It lasted for the better part of two years.

Far from irreverent toward the tasks at hand, the 1997 video of workers cleaning skeletal remains while joking and conversing represents the ambivalences of genocide heritage conservation. It is not a situation to be romanticized. Most conservation workers were struggling with significant losses and injuries while maintaining genocide memory. At Murambi, the majority were genocide survivors, most of whom were young, widowed mothers. The video reveals both a sense of that context and the workers' agency and humanity. This was not alienating labor, even if it was deeply painful for many. The intimacy of the scene is palpable in the ways that workers handled the remains of victims and connected with others in hopeful camaraderie. Their memories of violence coexisted with an ethos that was evident in the way they cared for victims and each other in the hardest of times. Such were the paradoxes inherent in the emotionally and physically difficult, and yet ethically and politically charged, imperative to conserve genocide heritage.

### EMMANUEL MURANGIRA

Most of the individuals who chose to work with the Genocide Memorial Commission at Murambi had already been involved in local efforts to locate and retrieve victims. When the commission took over that work and extended the conservation effort, Mario put measures in place to protect workers' physical and mental health: providing masks and gloves and requiring periodic breaks.[50] Conservation work was often a rare opportunity for employment in a context of scarcity and insecurity. Commission workers' compensation recognized the difficulties associ-

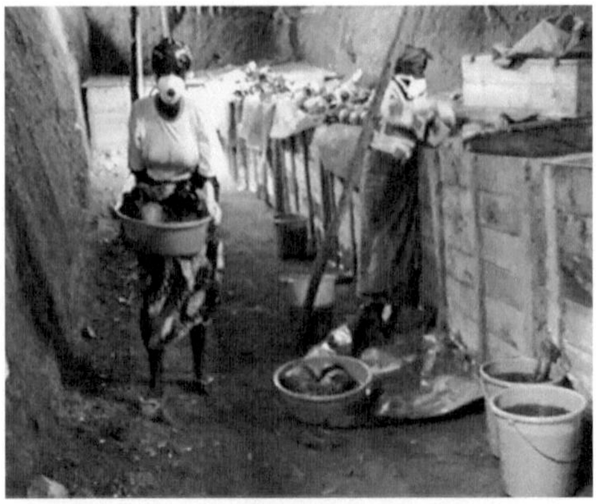

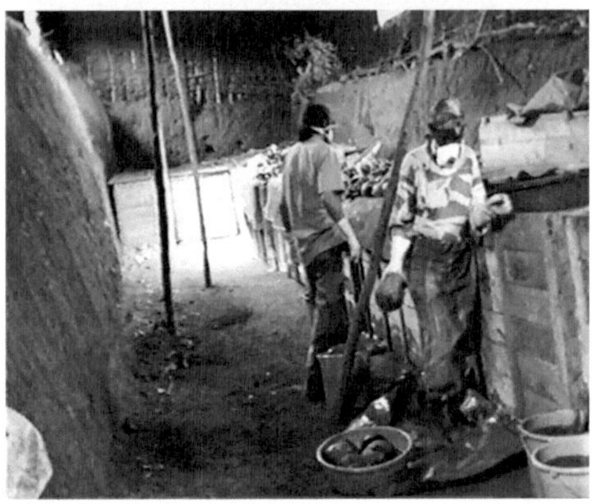

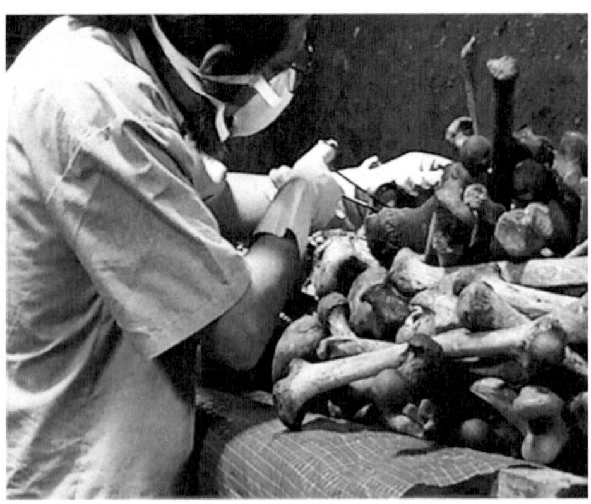

FIGURES 4.27 – 4.29. Video stills show Mario Ibarra and Genocide Memorial Commission workers sorting, inspecting, and removing victims' skeletal remains from the Ruhashya office burial vault for conservation. Mario Ibarra, "Mario Personal (3)," video recording, July 17, 1997, cassette G44D1046, at 06:58, 08:29, and 15:10, Ibarra archive, Chile.

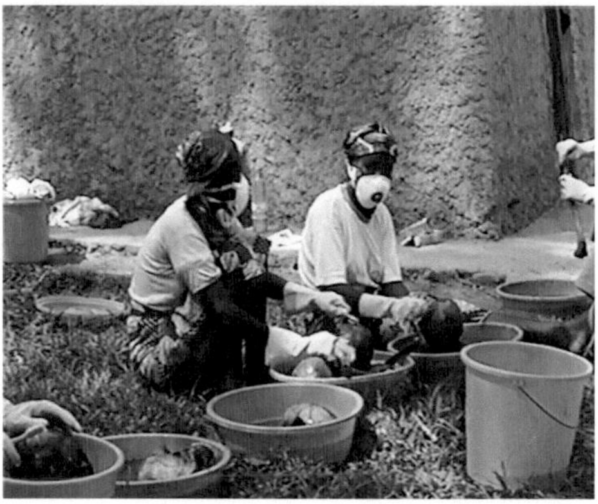

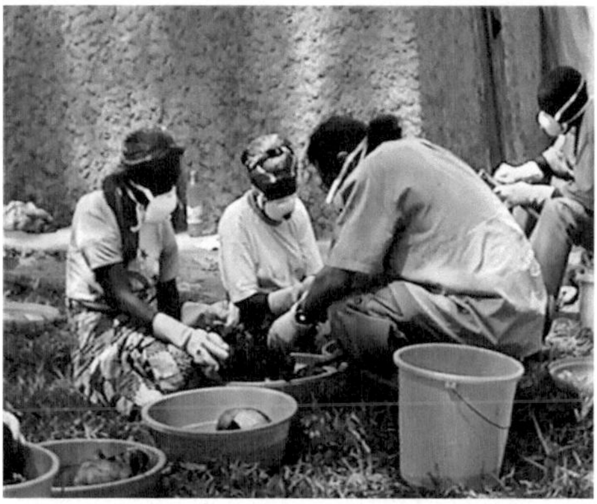

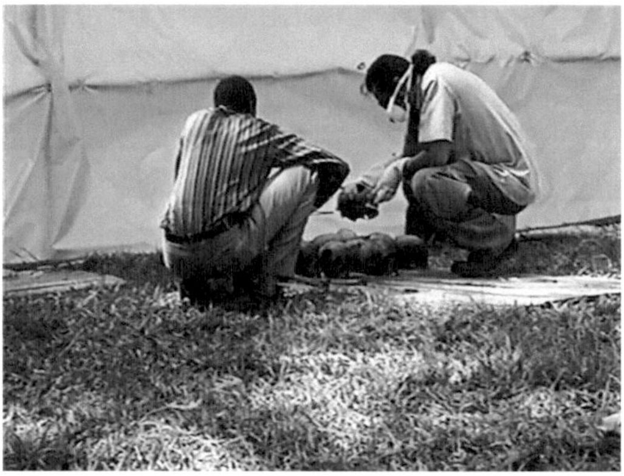

FIGURES 4.30 – 4.32. Video stills show Genocide Memorial Commission workers cleaning victims' skulls with toothbrushes and soap while Mario Ibarra inspects the progress and consults with Dr. Kanimba on the efficacy of the conservation experiments. Mario Ibarra, "Mario Personal (3)," video recording, July 17, 1997, G44D1046, at 17:00, 21:03, and 23:49, Ibarra archive, Chile.

ated with conserving human remains, and when there were lapses in government payouts, Dr. Kanimba compensated them through the National Museum's budget.[51] Those financial needs were not necessarily at odds with workers' grief and trauma. Many survivors were committed to conservation as a result of their own experiences during the genocide.

At Murambi, Mario worked most closely with Emmanuel Murangira, one of thirteen survivors of the massacre at the school.[52] Emmanuel lost his wife and five children to the killings, along with his sister, brother, and some forty other family members, narrowly surviving a bullet wound to his head. Immediately after the attacks, he fled to Burundi and returned months later to southeastern Rwanda, where refugees connected to the Amagaju Association helped him return to nearby Nyamagabe town in June 1995.[53] Aware of his losses and traumatic experiences, the Amagaju provided him with a house for two years. In return, Emmanuel began to work on their projects. He chose to be involved in the exhumations and nascent conservation work despite the immense emotional hardship it posed for him. His labor was not merely in return for shelter.

In 2008 interviews with genocide historian Samuel Totten and Rwandan genocide survivor and journalist Rafiki Ubaldo, Emmanuel described what it was like for him to be involved in work to recover the dead:

> To live in Murambi without my wife and my five children was . . . it was unbearable [begins crying]. Since 1996, when I was helping people to exhume victims' bones from sites of mass murder and witnessing again the inhuman ways people were killed, this is when I began to pray. . . . To bear to live with this situation, I prayed every day, asking God to give me enough strength to live. When I prayed, I prayed with other people, and after the praying, there was a kind of hope that we could continue living after what happened. I helped ten people locate their relatives. All of these people were refugees from 1959 who were searching for their relatives. I helped them to locate the bodies. . . . As for my wife and five children, I do not know exactly how they died. The women and children were inside the classrooms. What I do know is that they must have been killed in a very horrible way.[54]

Emmanuel's recollections are heartbreaking. He lays bare the intensity of his grief—and guilt for surviving. He reinforces, as well, his ethical commitments to finding the bodies of victims and bring those responsible to justice.

Soon after conservation work concluded at the site, Emmanuel became the Murambi memorial caretaker until his death in November 2011. During that time he remarried and established a modest home and farm nearby. He returned to the memorial daily, opening and closing the facilities and monitoring the humidity and the state of the bones and bodies displayed. He often, as Vestine Ndikuryayo, one of his coworkers recalled, was "the one who used to give testimony for this place. He would testify for visitors, and because of the language [barrier], Rwandans that came with foreigners would translate for them."[55] Photographs of his murdered wife and children were added to the memorial exhibition sometime after 2004. When, in 2008, Totten and Ubaldo asked why he continued to work there, Emmanuel responded, "I cannot miss being with my family. I have been with those bones for many years, fourteen, and it's like a habit. Those bones are like my neighbors."[56]

Emmanuel was a tall and lanky man who is present in many photographs and videos taken at Murambi by Mario in 1996–97 (figures 4.8, 4.10, 4.21, and 4.25). Rarely smiling or joking with others, he appears as a serious and calm individual who was integral to organizing and doing conservation work at the site. Most of that visual documentation is taken at a distance and contrasts with the up-close photographs of his face that proliferate in publications on the genocide.[57] Readers familiar with this imagery may know Emmanuel as the individual photographed at Murambi with a prominent bullet hole in his forehead, in images that Zoë Norridge has called "a prosthetic metaphor for wounding and death."[58] His visage is used time and again to symbolize survival from atrocity and to juxtapose his survivorship with the dead bodies in the school. As powerful as those images are, they parallel the memorial's disconnected symbolism today. They reinforce the image of atrocity in place of its lived experience. The latter persists in the memories of many who continue to work silently at memorials among visitors who do not recognize them and are shocked by what they see.

When Emmanuel's personal history and commitments are put in the context of his symbolism and the past three decades of state memorial management, those disconnects are ever more apparent. Today the Murambi Genocide Memorial is positioned more as a site of national importance than one embedded in local, lived experiences of genocide. This is evident in what the government and its partners have chosen to reveal about the site and whom they have chosen to value. The latter is especially apparent in the government's treatment of memorial employees. Like Emmanuel, many of the individuals first involved in conservation work at Murambi were later employed as guides and caretakers. In 2011 six were fired—either because other companies' cleaners were hired or because the guides did not fulfill new government civil servant requirements for holding university degrees and speaking fluent English.[59] Similar dismissals occurred at other national memorial sites.[60] Oral historian and genocide scholar Erin Jessee cites different reasons for turnover in this period, writing that the government "established a training program to identify and remove those memorial staff who were too emotionally and psychologically vulnerable due to their experiences of the genocide . . . and provide more resilient staff with coping strategies."[61] However, my interviews with memorial employees underscored, in ways that echo Emmanuel's daily duty, that working there was a choice. Many survivors found some measure of comfort for their personal losses in that work.[62] Their experiences of genocide-related trauma were not fully independent of their employment at memorials but also existed before and after it. Moreover, employment at the memorials was a critical source of income. The circumstances of the 2008–11 firings indicate that the state and its partners were not primarily concerned for the workers' well-being. Rather, they no longer recognized these individuals as valuable contributors to genocide memory.

### VESTINE NDIKURYAYO

In 2018 I returned to Rwanda with photographs of the 1996–97 conservation effort from Mario Ibarra's personal archive in Chile. A neighbor identified Vestine Ndikuryayo from one of those images and told me where she lived (figure 4.33). Vestine permitted my colleague and me to chat with her in the front room of her modest home. We sat on plush, upholstered chairs. She gazed soberly at the photographs from almost a quarter century ago (figure 4.34). One of them captured a young woman resting for a moment; she glances across her right shoulder toward the camera, face mask pulled down around her neck and hands still gloved. "Yes," she confirmed, "that's me."[63]

In the image Vestine sits on a wood stump with a mummified adult at her feet. Two other bodies are laid out behind her and to her left. A woman in the background works on a fourth. Taken in 1996, the image is one of many that document the commission's conservation work at Murambi after the second national commemoration, when workers were tasked with cleaning decaying matter from bodies previously displayed on the school's classroom floors.

I asked Vestine if she remembered who took the photo. She pointed to another of the photographs, which shows Mario, Emmanuel, and two others boiling clothing on the school grounds (figure 4.25). "It was this *muzungu*; I just don't remember his name. He is the one who came to show us how to clean the bodies."[64] Responding to my question about how she started that work, Vestine began by recalling where she was during and after the genocide.

Vestine and her family had previously lived in Kibeho, south of Murambi, an area known for visions of the Virgin Mary and Catholic devotion. It was also the location of a genocide massacre in April 1994 and, one year later, of a violent attack by the new military against suspected Hutu extremists in a displaced persons' camp. Most of Vestine's family was killed during the genocide. She saved two of her children, with whom she fled to Burundi; in early 1995 RPA forces repatriated

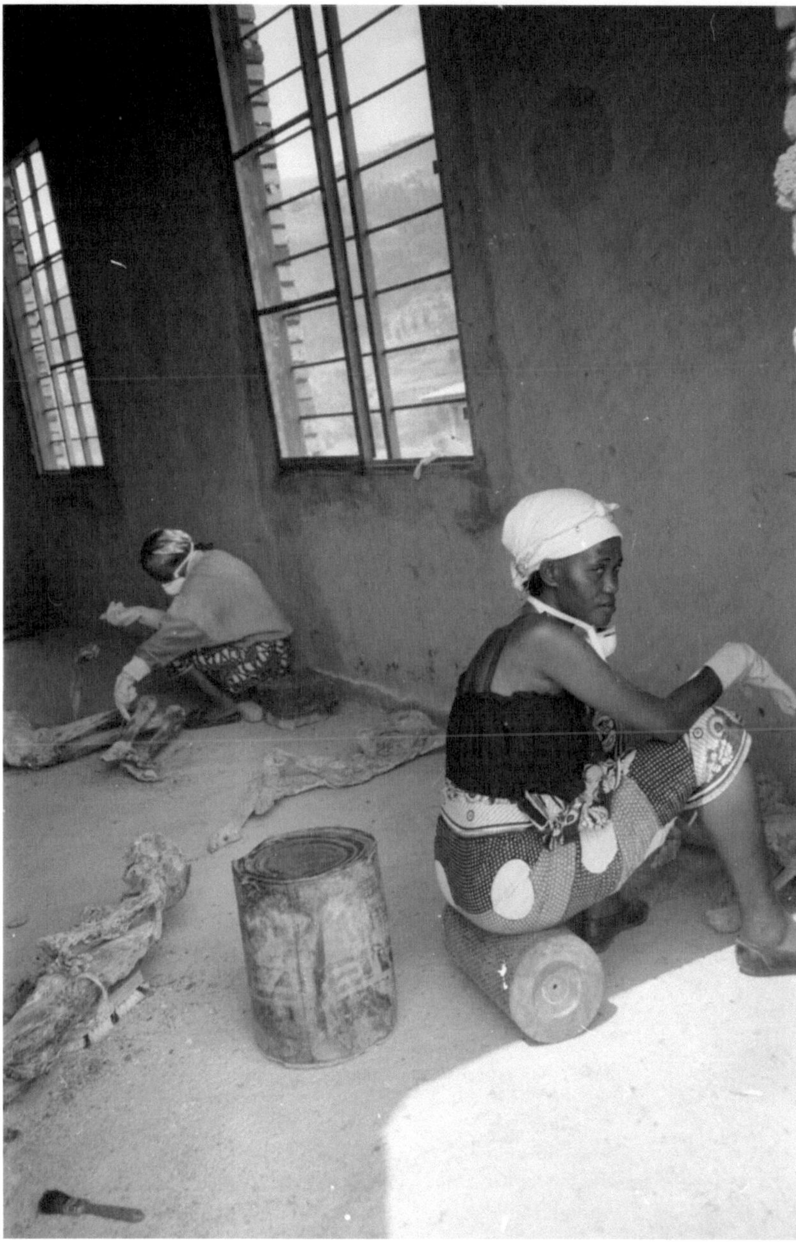

FIGURE 4.33. Vestine Ndikuryayo (*right*) rests momentarily while cleaning a genocide victim's mummified body for conservation at Murambi, 1996. Photo by Mario Ibarra, Ibarra archive, Chile.

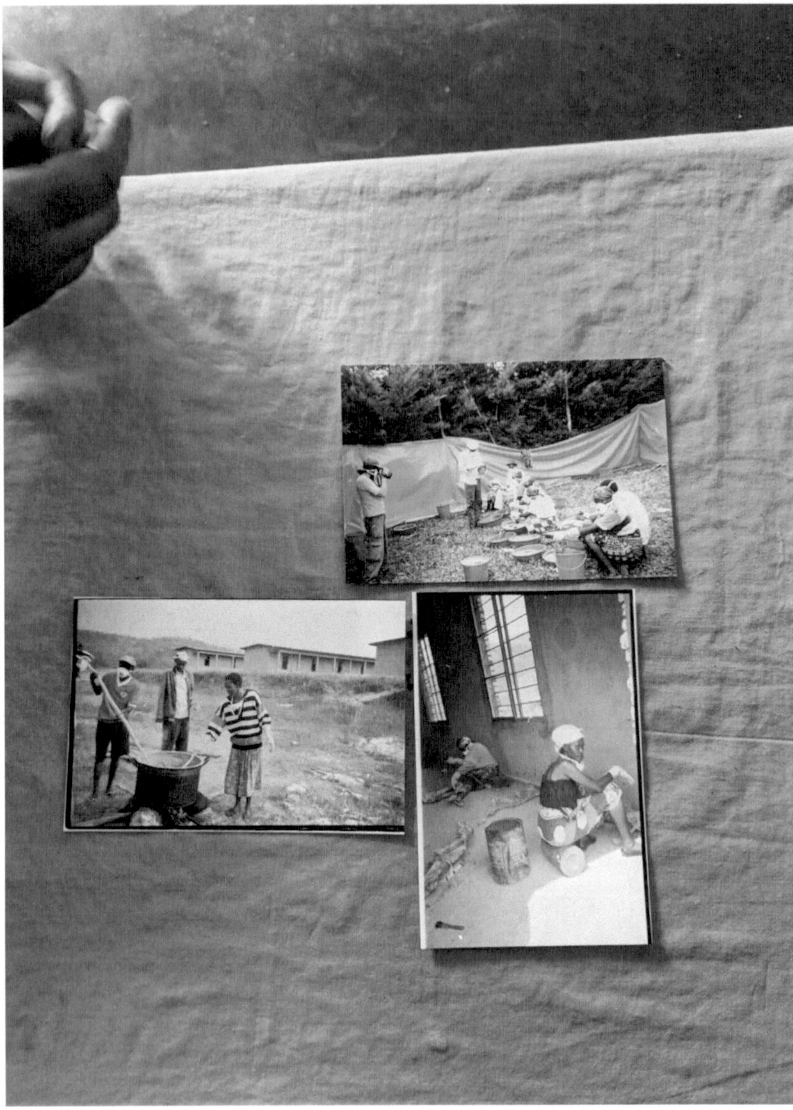

FIGURE 4.34. In 2018 Vestine Ndikuryayo described photographs, retrieved from Mario Ibarra in Chile and laid out on her coffee table, of the conservation work she did with the Genocide Memorial Commission. Photo by Delia Duong Ba Wendel.

them to Butare, the university town near Murambi, where they sheltered at the Groupe Scolaire boarding school. The RPA's closure of the Kibeho Camp and the killing of internally displaced people there in 1995 effectively forced residents to return to their homes in the area. Vestine did not; she felt unable to face what had happened to her there during the genocide. Instead, she joined several women to inquire about jobs at Murambi.

Vestine knew what kind of work was available at the massacre site. She recalled that after the Amagaju Association exhumed and placed the bodies back in the buildings, "We went to ask for work. And they gave it to me, to us."[65] Vestine described the work that she and others did at Murambi from late 1995 until the second national commemoration one year later: "We would clean the bodies and put chemicals on them. We'd also clean the buildings, the paths that led to them; we would sweep and mop after the rains because the rain used to go inside where the bodies were. We continued to clean until—until we put lime and chemicals on the bodies—there were bodies that still had—flesh. And others that had only bones, without bodies, like skulls that you can see."[66]

In that first phase, Vestine and others were hired by the Amagaju Association and Gikongoro Préfecture to minimally preserve the bodies placed on the floors of the Murambi classrooms and to clean and keep water out of the spaces. Both activities were conflated as normalized domestic work and paid equally. During that period most of the workers were women who had experienced violence, persecution, and the insecurity of temporary refuge at Murambi and regional sites nearby, like Kigeme Hospital.

When Gabriel, the local Amagaju representative, spoke with me about the individuals who worked with him, he referred to them as "Vestines." This moniker was not merely because Gabriel knew her. For him, Vestine represented the typical woman–survivor–widow–young mother who aided conservation efforts at Murambi (see figure Int.5). Once you look for it, women's care work is represented prominently throughout the photo and video documentation of genocide memory conservation. In the introduction I described two photographs from 1997 that documented the mothering—the caring for small children—that occurred adjacent to the cleaning of victims' skeletal remains. Earlier in this chapter, I relayed the audio recorded during a July 17, 1997, video of conservation work, where the sounds of children crying formed the background to the plunges and rasps of washing skulls and long bones. Though those instances of care work and memory maintenance occurred later, during the third phase, it nonetheless underscores that many conservation workers were mothers caring for small children while simultaneously negotiating the violence they had experienced and working to protect genocide memory. By that time, compared with the first phase, many more men were employed. But tasks were largely gendered. Women were organized to clean the bodies and bones, and men lifted and moved the bodies from and to the classrooms (figures 4.10–4.11).

But not every person working at Murambi was who they claimed to be. One of the first stories that Vestine told me, prompted by another photo I showed her, was of the young woman wearing a black-and-white-striped sweater working with Emmanuel and Mario on techniques for clothing conservation. She appears in other photographs as well, sweeping the classrooms and working with Mario to check the bodies for humidity after they were placed on the wooden platforms. Josie (a pseudonym) initially sought refuge at the Murambi site in 1995 with her one-year-old son. She told the other women that they had escaped the killings from their home in Butare and claimed that the scars on her son's body were from those attacks.[67] Sometime after the Genocide Memorial Commission's conservation work at Murambi concluded, she was identified by former neighbors as having participated in the genocide. Vestine and the women had believed that Josie was a survivor like many of them: "She used to pretend in front of us—even her face, you could easily think that she was a Tutsi like her mother."[68] But, according to neighbors who testified against her in a *gacaca* trial, Josie and her Hutu father joined the Interahamwe's attacks and were convicted for the murder of a young boy. They were both sentenced to fifteen years in prison. In recounting Josie's history, Vestine often shook her head in dismay, both conveying the betrayal that she and others felt and acknowledging the complexity of those postgenocide years. While I have not been able to independently verify Vestine's recollections, I include the anecdote as context for practices related to the ethics of nonerasure; insecurity, neighborly distrust, and personal survival also conditioned that work.

In 1996 conservation work at and near Murambi fell under the supervision of the Genocide Memorial Commission. It became more intensive after the second commemoration ceremony. Vestine recalled:

> At some point—it became necessary—to bring the *muzungu* [Mario Ibarra]. He showed us how to wash the bodies. We used to work with the director of the Butare museum too [Dr. Kanimba, director of the National Museum of Rwanda]. He used to show us things because he had a lot of knowledge, and he came [to Murambi] to work with the *muzungu*.
>
> We had to have those *uruhindu* [small spear-like knives used in tanning and basketmaking] forged. We would use them to find the soil and dirt inside—in some people, maybe due to drying or age or something—you could find some parts had sunk inside them and that dirt had gotten into those areas. On some of them you could see blood and flesh that was still

raw. We cleaned them well and put them in clean places; we put them on tarps, and later they had wooden platforms made, and we put the bodies on them. We would clean and fill one classroom and then clean and fill another one.[69]

At this stage, conservation workers were primarily employed to remove decaying organic material from the bodies and bones. Dr. Kanimba and Mario prioritized the cleaning to prevent their deterioration, which threatened the material representation of genocide memory.

But there was another motivation behind the cleaning, one connected to an ethics of nonerasure for victims who were killed in a violent and undignified way. Vestine broached the subject when she described her experience of the work. She recalled, "It was during the washing that it became very difficult—washing, lifting a person—that's when it was very difficult."[70] I wasn't sure at this point whether, by the somewhat vague phrase "it was very difficult [*byari bikomeye cyane*]," she meant that the work was emotionally or physically challenging. Hesitatingly, I asked how the work made her feel. Vestine reflected, "It was sad because actually—the bodies were still heavy—a person could not lift some of them; you had to lift the bodies with someone else. We were still sad. And the smell was very bad."[71] She paused at this point, lost in her memories, and I suggested that we stop or perhaps switch topics. Vestine shook her head, eyes watering, telling me, "Oya, nta kibazo" (No, it's not a problem), and held my gaze. Gingerly, I proceeded and asked why she did the work if it was so hard. She replied:

> Actually, to tell you the truth, even though I was poor and had those two children that I saved, that I survived with, and no other job—even though that is the truth, it [the work at Murambi] made me strong. I felt sad while I was working, but I also knew that there was no other way. You understood that if you didn't do it, someone else would—and with this type of work, there isn't an area of the body you don't touch—you touch everywhere. And when I thought about them being touched by . . . by those people who killed them . . . you knew that wasn't right either. And you knew that there was no other way. You had to clean them because they were your relatives. They were our people. And we didn't think that they should be touched by those people who killed them.
>
> You see, this genocide, it came as a surprise. Sometimes one can plan to bathe but get caught by surprise, the same way that the genocide came, and because of the surprise, you fail to clean yourself that day. Also, people used to talk, and there were those who used to say "Those Tutsi are dirty"—that kind of thing.

Vestine focused in minute detail on what it was like to touch and handle the dead—scraping, digging, brushing, and washing. It was gruesome, difficult, and saddening work. At the same time, she felt that cleaning and conserving victims' bodies was her duty. It was, in a way, a general cultural response, one that was distinctly Rwandan in its concern for personal comportment and cleanliness as an indicator of one's dignity. It was also a means to challenge the spurious derogations espoused by *génocidaires*: Tutsi were not inherently dirty, and she would not allow the state of victims' decomposing bodies to provide bigots fodder for such claims. Last, and perhaps most important, body conservation was intimate work, and Vestine chose to labor for her people, cleaning them closely to return honor to the murdered. With a rush of emotion, Vestine concluded her thoughts: "When you thought about all of the places that you had to touch—because soil had gone everywhere in the body and it required you to touch a person everywhere—you didn't want others to touch them. As someone who survived [Vestine paused, tears streaming down her face], you understood that you were the one who had to do it. Yes, but by doing it, it makes one . . . it made me stronger."

Vestine abruptly got up from her chair and left the room, sniffing back tears. She returned a few minutes later. I apologized for upsetting her, asking her *kumbabarira*, to forgive me. Vestine laughed, telling me, "I forgive you. It's OK; the emotions come, but there is no other way." I insisted, however, that I had caused her to remember by asking questions and apologized again. She responded matter-of-factly, "One doesn't get used to it," referring to the mix of feelings that her memories brought forward. We sat in silence for a few moments. I thought about what she had mentioned earlier: that almost every day for the past twenty-five years she opted to clean the classroom where the mummified bodies of children were located.[72] She suffers from searing migraines and hypertension that doctors diagnosed as related to the trauma of her experiences during the genocide. From the time that the bodies were first placed back in Murambi to today, she has acted with deep care for the victims, despite significant personal sacrifice. We spent the remainder of our time talking about her children, their successes in school, and their career ambitions. Her pride in them was exuberant. At the end of our conversation, Vestine returned to the memorial to complete her shift.

## The Paradoxes of Reparative History

Genocide memory work highlights the multiple temporalities and paradoxes inherent in forms of repair. A humanizing ethics of nonerasure produced both Rwanda's genocide heritage and the dehumanizing representational strategy intrinsic to its aesthetic. This dissonance was confronted directly and daily by those doing conservation work. The gruesome and emotionally debilitating work of preparing bodies for genocide heritage sat at odds with feelings of kinship and acts of care for victims. Individuals negotiated these central tensions in the process of making a lasting spatial genocide memory. The recent and violent past was made present in place and embodied forms—in the hope that memory would shape the future. Those paradoxes were never resolved. They were simply part of the genocide's exceptional aftermath.

Paradoxes were also apparent in the multiple temporalities that genocide memory work produced. As the videos show, the messy work of cleaning and exhibiting the dead was a profoundly ambivalent experience: emotionally distressing, repetitious, and mundane, yet replete with the joys of being with others, among the living. At the same time, conservation work was a radical reminder of the recent past, one of the worst examples of dehumanizing violence in world history. Its aftermath was quite literally at hand, especially for those conserving bodies, in present time. This was not a past that could easily be put away. Genocidal violence was a living memory for many of the individuals doing this work. It was a past relived through the work of maintaining the dead for the future. The legacy of the genocide, of the scores who died and were subjected to violence, represents a third temporality of genocide heritage. It is a liminal temporality, an intertwining of work to preserve past violence, its contemporaneous effects, and its aspirations for future. Conserving extreme dehumanization implored future generations to remember those who suffered and to prevent its recurrence.

On June 6, 1997, Mario Ibarra recorded a video within one of the small classrooms at Murambi.[73] Louis Kanamugire and Dr. Kanimba also are present, and the film captures them walking solemnly among and viewing the mummified bodies raised on tall platforms on both sides of the room (figures 4.35–4.37). Mario describes the scene from behind the camera. It was one of many video messages intended for "Pepe," Mario's nickname for José Bengoa, an anthropologist and historian who was his colleague at the UN Sub-Commission on the Promotion and Protection of Human Rights. Speaking in Spanish, Mario explains the Genocide Memorial Commission's conservation work along with the paradoxes it evoked:

> In this room we are in another phase of our work. At the right of the camera, one can see some of the bones of children. They are legal objects to be shown to the International Tribunal regarding what the criminals here did, and, on the other hand, they are artifacts to safeguard memory [*guardar la memoria*]—that is to say, to fix all of these things and create a museum for the genocide. That is the double objective.

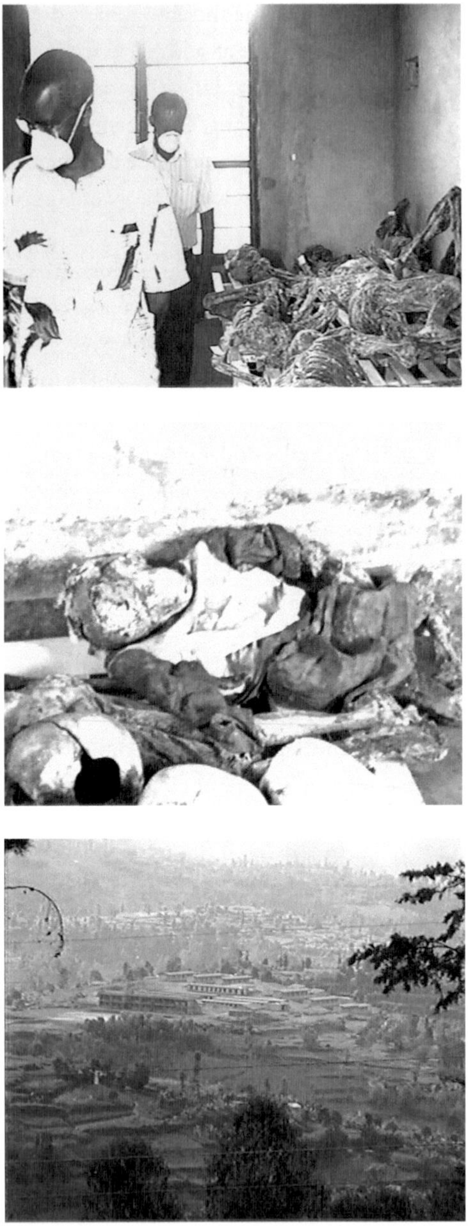

FIGURES 4.35–4.37. A video recorded by Mario Ibarra features Dr. Célestin Kanimba Misago and Louis Kanamugire touring the results of conservation at Murambi (*top*), zooms in to show the challenges of handling child victims (*middle*), and zooms out to a helicopter view of the school complex (*bottom*). Mario Ibarra, "Pepe (2)," video recording, June 6, 1997, cassette C44B6223, at 9:24, 16:47, and 19:38, Ibarra archive, Chile.

> I had said that we are in another phase; these bodies [on the left] were interred in a mass grave, and now we are cleaning them, adding lime, and raising them on these beds to prevent humidity and conserve the bodies. . . .
>
> Pepe, we are also trying to conserve these [Points to the bodies of small children] because they are particularly horrific. The analysis of the dentition shows that this child is no more than five years old. His head was completely bashed in, probably by a hammer blow. In the back there is a young girl in all of her clothes—everything—she was at the bottom of the grave. Her little legs were broken. It's the—how do I tell you this—this is the part of my work that is very, very hard.[74]

In Mario's narration, we have a sense of the emotional weight of the memories the commission was attempting to conserve in place. All of the victims mattered to the men in the video, but the presence of young children among them was especially distressing. Mario also clarifies the "double objective" of the work: to protect genocide memory for the future and preserve evidence of a genocide for pending judicial proceedings. Those acts of reparative history justified the dehumanizing aesthetic of the bodies and bones on display. For Mario and the Genocide Memorial Commission, victims' remains were an inescapable representation of that history. And yet the ethics of nonerasure and memory justice cannot fully compensate for the emotional burden carried by survivors and witnesses. Herein lie the paradoxes of reparative histories made from Rwanda's genocide heritage: Defiant against dehumanizing violence, they also represent and reproduce the image of dehumanization but in the name of history, justice, and human rights.

Like the paradoxes with which Gabriel, Vestine, and Mario contended, we—readers and secondary witnesses—too must grapple with the unruly affect and politics of Rwanda's genocide heritage. Not to experience the same. But to choose immersion over distance is to pull alongside, closer, to a more intimate history that demands repair.

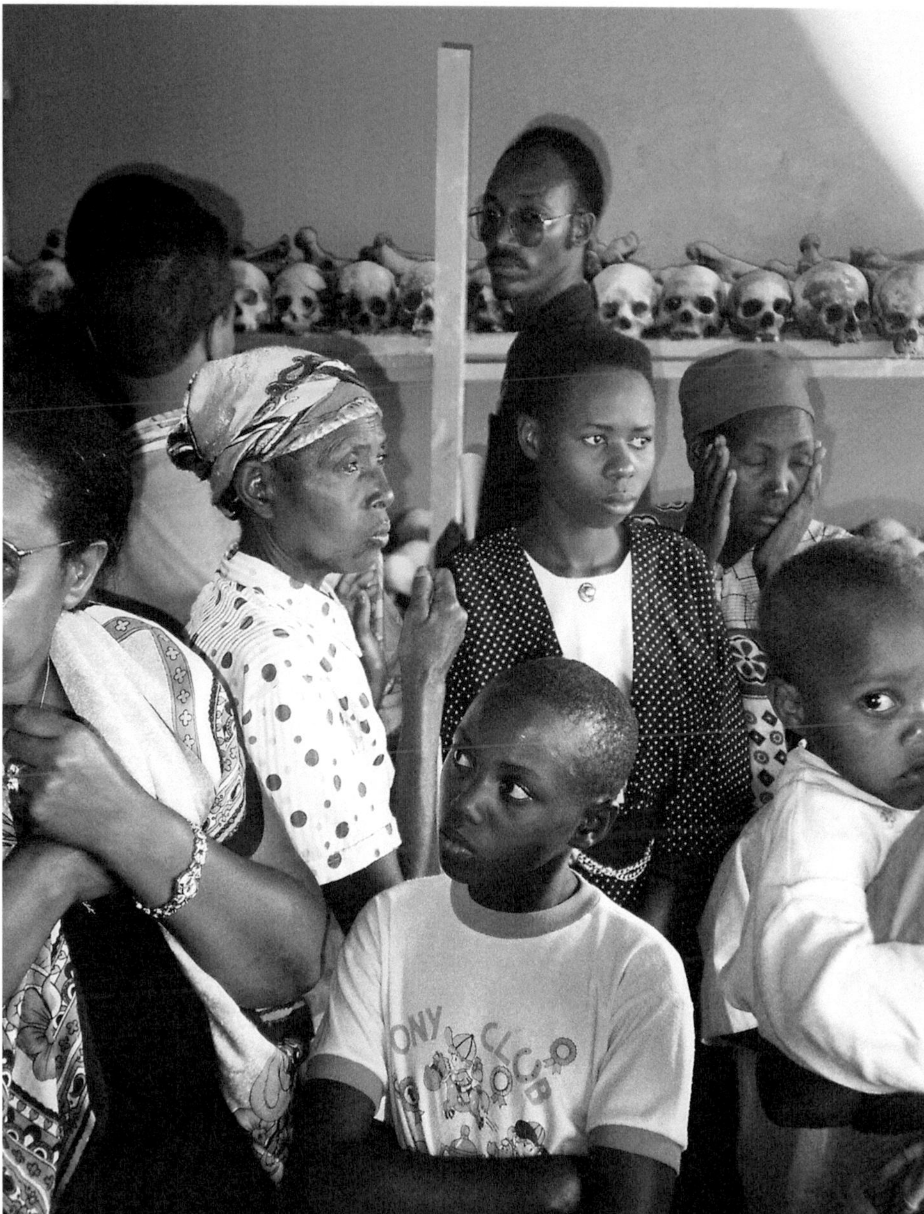

Survivors and relatives attending the Runha Church reburial ceremony visit a viewing room where genocide victims' skeletal remains are ordered and displayed in rows, November 3, 1996. Photo by Louis Kanamugire, Kanamugire archive, Rwanda.

5

# EXHUMATION, DISPLAY, REBURIAL

## ORDERING THE FUTURE OF THE PAST

While preservation and conservation efforts were underway at newly designated genocide memorial sites, ceremonies were also organized to rebury and commemorate the dead. Many ceremonies incorporated the display of genocide victims' remains (figures 5.1 and 5.2). Those acts were temporary testaments to the scale and impact of the mass killings. The exhibition of victims' remains typically lasted only for several hours or days before their reburial. Nonetheless, the imperative to render Rwanda's genocide heritage publicly *visible* evolved from and was reinforced at those sites of memory and ritual. So, too, were the ethical and political conflicts attached to exposing the dead and removing them from view.

As previous chapters have demonstrated, the display of victims' remains was motivated by human rights advocacy as much as by the civic and political interests of the new governing regime. Yet the visibility of violence, and its representation in bodies and bones, was deeply contested by residents living nearby and relatives concerned with victims' desecration. Those conflicts were palpable at memorials, within ceremonies, and in the backstage work of their making. Considering the

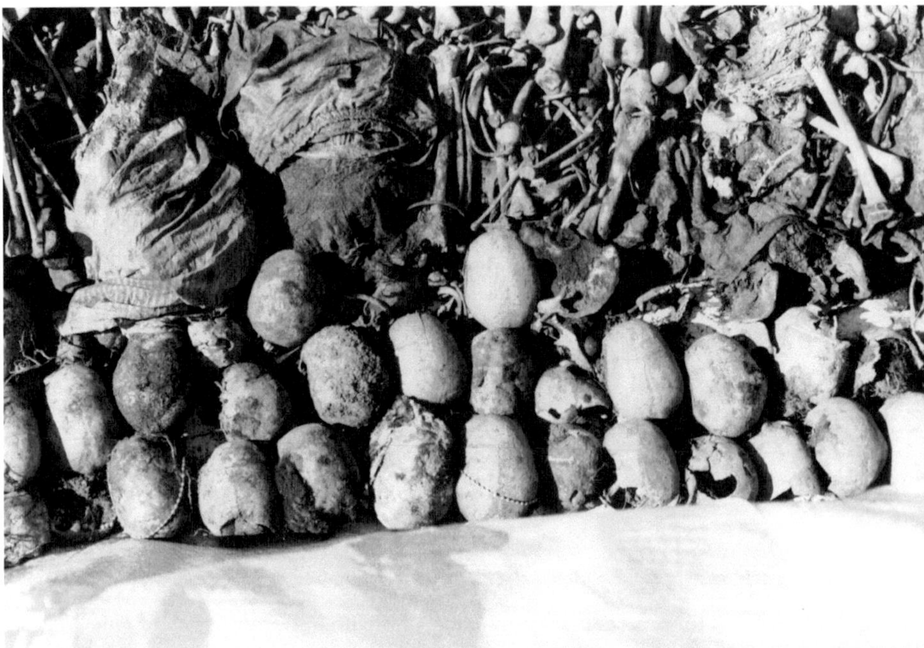

FIGURE 5.1. Genocide victims' bones grouped by type in a grave, photographed during the Mubuga Commune reburial ceremony, Gikongoro Préfecture, October 24, 1996. Photo by Mario Ibarra, Ibarra archive, Chile.

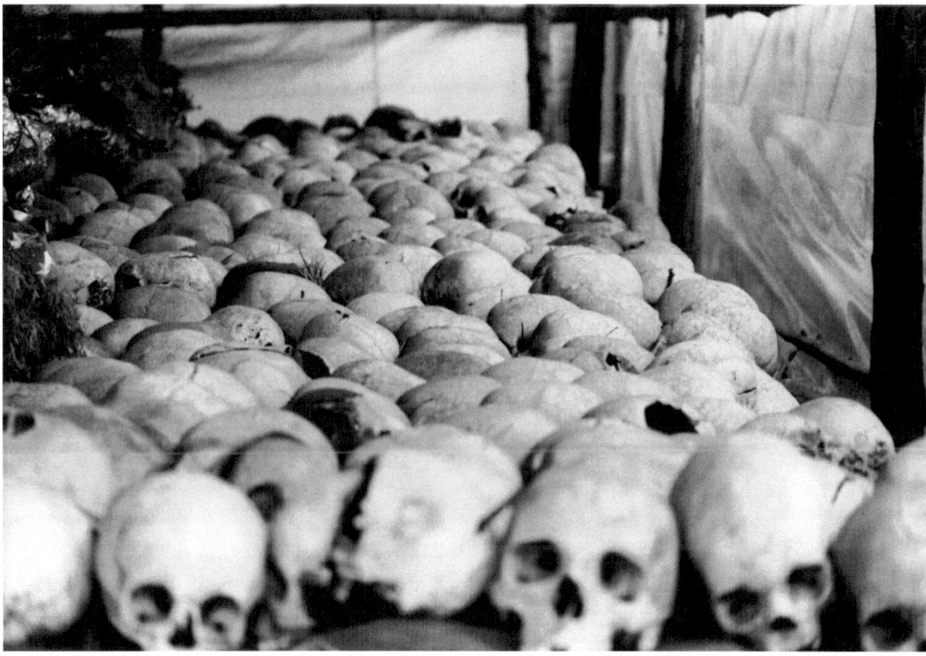

FIGURE 5.2. The temporary display of genocide victims' skulls during the Mwulire Sector reburial ceremony, November 6, 1996. Photo by Mario Ibarra, Ibarra archive, Chile.

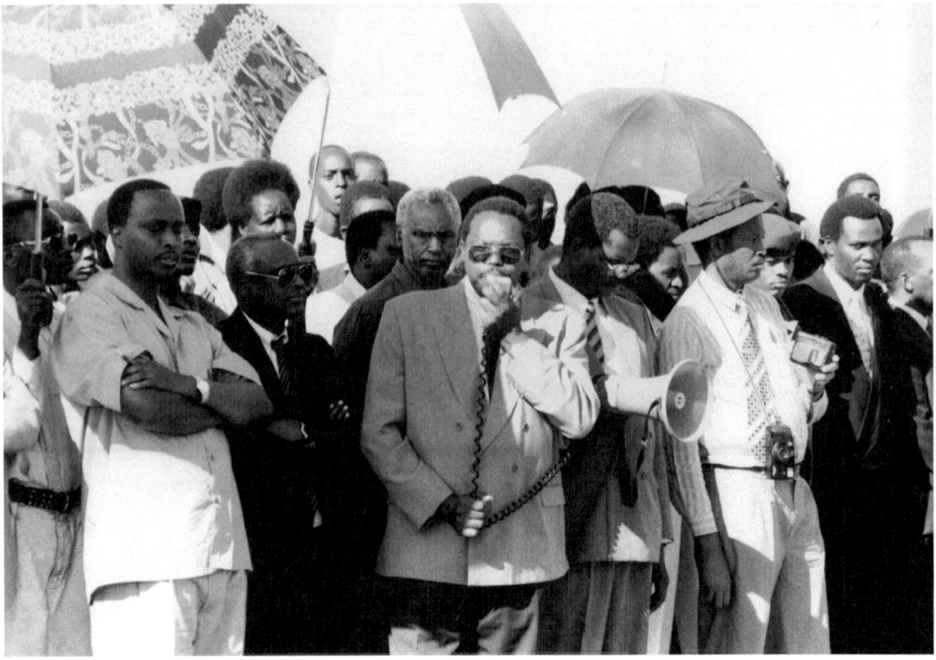

FIGURE 5.3. Speeches at the Mubuga Commune reburial ceremony with Louis Kanamugire (*right*) holding a camera, October 24, 1996. Photo by Mario Ibarra, Ibarra archive, Chile.

preservation of visibility alongside the interment of victims presents, then, not so much a study in contrasts as a persistent approach to genocide remembrance. It is to consider the role of viewing in ordering the past.

Exhuming, displaying, and reburying victims' remains were increasingly intertwined genocide heritage practices from late 1995 under the stewardship of the Genocide Memorial Commission (figure 5.3). Understanding these practices together emphasizes the conflicts that organizers negotiated to make the dead visible. The scale of genocide memory work undertaken from 1994 to 1998 was profound: hundreds of thousands of bodies and bones from massacre sites throughout the country were unearthed, examined, sorted, and cleaned. To prepare these remains for display at memorial sites or viewing at reburial ceremonies, memory workers, many of whom were genocide survivors motivated to care for their kin, undertook an excruciatingly emotional and physically demanding enterprise. The public and ritual display of bodies and bones, in communities still wracked by grief and insecurity and in many ways at odds with customary practice, was also not received with ease. Yet early organizers of both genocide memorials and reburial ceremonies shared an interest in unequivocally demonstrating that a genocide had occurred through material—and distinctly embodied—evidence of that violence, in place. Altogether, these conflicts underscore that the development of Rwanda's genocide heritage aesthetic was neither frictionless nor exclusively state led. Moreover, we see the display of the dead (whether permanent or temporary) as fundamentally connected to both exhumation and interment processes.

Today Rwanda's genocide heritage comprises several public-facing events and spaces, including genocide memorials and national commemorations, which represent the most prominent forms of state-authorized genocide memory. Both national commemorations and genocide memorials are practices that seek to establish temporal continuity by maintaining collective memory. Those approaches to maintaining permanent genocide memory are distinct but aligned: while genocide memorials conserve material evidence of the genocide, commemoration ceremonies maintain remembrance through annual repetition. Yet both national genocide commemorations and memorials ensure that genocide memory is visible—and therefore undeniable—in large public gatherings on days of remembrance and in public spaces within living communities.

Although less common today, and certainly not as prominent within genocide historiography, local reburial ceremonies were significant testing grounds for Rwanda's genocide heritage in the first years after the massacres. Like national commemorations, reburials are types of ceremonial remembrance. However, reburial ceremonies are relatively temporary as nonrepeated events with clear beginning and ending rituals. These aspects contribute to their less-known status. Nonetheless, reburial ceremonies are especially important to the history of genocide heritage development: hundreds occurred from 1994 to 1998, in contrast to only four national commemorations. Local reburial ceremonies became important staging grounds to test both the postgenocide communal rituals that would become central to national commemorations and the power of publicly displaying the remains of victims that persist at memorial sites.

Together, the first reburial and commemoration ceremonies reveal the role of performance in enactments of national sovereignty, social control, memory justice, and communal healing all at once. The first and second national genocide commemoration ceremonies (in 1995 and 1996) piloted the state rituals and messaging that endure as part of national genocide memory today. Those contributions are well-documented in the scholarly literature, and this chapter rectifies some of the discrepancies within it.[1] I also contribute analyses of newly discovered photographic and video documentation of the first reburial ceremonies to that scholarship. The "backstage" vantage that we gain is especially telling about state-citizen relationships—and the dynamics among government representatives, survivors and other residents, and prisoner-laborers. It foregrounds the original social and political ambitions—and the ethical dilemmas and controversies that existed then and persist in less public ways today—around the government's display, burial, and commemoration of the dead.

Rwanda's genocide heritage—and the first exhumation, conservation, and burial practices that produced it—ordered a landscape of mass death, shaping how the state maintains the future of the past and its control over it. Critical to that work has been the ordering of time through viewing. A large part of that ordering has involved the perpetuation of visible genocide memory. Much of this chapter unpacks the ways in which preservation and conservation practices became ritualized in reburial ceremonies and incorporated into annual commemoration ceremonies to extend the collective memory of the genocide into more lasting, and socialized, forms. Part of that socialization has entailed cultivating a national recognition of the genocide. It has also, from the perspective of many Hutu in the country, created distinctions in who is allowed to mourn the dead (Tutsi) and who is vilified for genocide deaths (Hutu).[2] Another significant impact of genocide heritage, then, has been to nationalize an ethnicized social order.

In the years immediately following the genocide, ordering also involved taming: creating a unitary temporal regime from the unruliness of the aftermath. For many individuals overcome by trauma and grief, genocide heritage superimposed a time of ceremony, longevity, and constant return that was out of step with lived experiences. It removed ancestral rites and other customary burial practices. The government claimed that the genocide was too exceptional an event to be mourned routinely and charged that many practices were either sponsored by religious bodies complicit in those killings or not sufficiently modern for a postgenocide time. Conservation suspended time through the viewing of the dead. Commemoration revived a particular moment in time, over time. The week (or, prior to 2004, month) of national mourning in which annual ceremonies take place interrupts daily routines. The ordering effects of reburial were slightly distinct: Those ceremonies ultimately contained the time of genocide, removing traces of violence from everyday life. Related burial places were dedicated, instead, to ritual return in ways that were often more elective and customary.

The creation of both places and ceremonies for genocide memory was not instantaneous. Viewing genocide memory required a multiyear process of preserving sites, locating and unearthing victims, and conserving their remains. It involved gruesome encounters with the remains of the dead by groups with widely varying positionalities and experiences of genocidal violence. Ordering Rwanda's genocide heritage also involved organizing bones and bodies by type, for display and reburial. Creating a unitary temporal regime for genocide remembrance took time and took over place, and this chapter also contributes to that understanding.

Rwanda's genocide heritage, like trauma heritage more broadly, makes public space for silenced pain by creating an extended time for witnessing. That spatial and temporal regime—practiced in the preservation and conservation of victims and sites, the performative rituals of reburial, and the annual return to commemoration—renders the future contingent on a recognition of the past. In those moves Rwanda's genocide heritage shares a core tenet of the transitional justice strategies that emerged in the late twentieth century to safeguard human rights in the aftermath of their violation. Rwanda's genocide heritage was not expressly shaped by transitional justice, but it does serve as a parallel case study of postconflict initiatives that develop, and tightly control, a space and time of permanent transition to prevent the recurrence of mass violence. It also raises significant cautions in that undertaking. Rwanda's genocide heritage has accrued irresolvable paradoxes associated with concerns for state sovereignty, sociopolitical ordering, and control over the future of the past that have layered onto evidentiary priorities derived from a human rights context. Early reburial and commemoration ceremonies situate a wider range of viewing practices involved in ordering the past. They provide a sense of what it was like to view the dead in the years immediately following the genocide. The ceremonies' preparation reveals, moreover, the work, affect, and social relations layered onto public spaces transformed by extended witnessing.

## The First National Genocide Commemorations

The first two national genocide commemoration ceremonies took place on April 7 in 1995 and 1996. The commemorations piloted two approaches to state ritual remembrance, each of which treated the dead differently: The first commemoration was primarily a reburial ceremony, while the second staged victims' bodies at a massacre site as a prelude to permanent genocide memorialization. Both shaped the scope and form of subsequent national commemorations.[3]

The 1995 ceremony notably did not display bodies or bones. Instead, it dramatically relocated victims' remains from various locations in the capital, Kigali, to a new and politically symbolic burial site. Prior to their interment, the ceremony organizers displayed closed coffins adorned with wreaths and political signs for public viewing. Along with the themes of "never forget" and guarantees of "punishment for *génocidaires*," the new governing regime produced signs that claimed foreign negligence in halting the massacres. The critiques relayed through commemoration slogans, speeches, and placards—at ceremonies honoring genocide victims—projected the moral authority of the new government. As a result, the first commemoration secured a lead role for the state in protecting genocide memory.

The first commemoration was organized by the Ministry of Labor and Social Affairs (MINITRASO) and the second by the Genocide Memorial Commission under the Ministry of Higher Education, Scientific Research, and Culture (MINESUPRES). On the surface, the institutional handover reflects a shift in the administration of genocide memory: from the domain of socioeconomic reconstruction to that of culture and education. However, this institutional rearrangement did not result in differences in the commemorations' objectives. Both ceremonies endeavored to recognize the victims of the genocide, communicate political messages, and establish places for remembrance.

In form, the second commemoration was comparatively more vanguard: It unveiled a permanent exhibition of victims' bodies at a killing site (Murambi) alongside the interment of skeletal remains in communal graves. Political messaging shifted from placards to the bodies of victims on display. The second commemoration effectively normalized the display of victims as a national approach to genocide memory. Thereafter, the viewing of material evidence and the transformation of massacre sites into places of remembrance became integral to the state's genocide heritage aesthetic.

The first and second commemorations also belong to the genre of reburial ceremonies. They are exemplary within that typology because of their national symbolism and catalytic reinforcement of an emergent genocide heritage.[4] Together, moreover, the ceremonies demonstrated the ordering role that the government assumed in its aesthetic and ritual treatment of the dead.

## APRIL 7, 1995

The first national commemoration ceremony was organized as an extended processional march through and south of the capital, Kigali, with stops at several significant sites of resistance, massacre, and burial. It was the culmination of a series of local reburials that Silas Sinyigaya organized for MINITRASO (his first such effort took place at Muyumbu Commune, outside Kigali, on November 13, 1994).[5] The 1995 commemoration commenced with a procession of genocide survivors and government and religious leaders from Amahoro Stadium toward Rebero Hill. Amahoro Stadium was a significant massacre site in a Kigali neighborhood east of downtown. During the genocide area residents sought United Nations protection there: Its UNAMIR peacekeeping force used the sports grounds as its headquarters. Along the way, the procession stopped at the nearby Remera Hero's Mausoleum, where Rwandan Patriotic Front (RPF) leader Fred Rwigema and former Prime Minister Agathe Uwilingiyimana were buried after they were killed in the civil war and genocide, respectively.[6] Thereafter, the attendees marched to the Kicukiro-Nyanza cemetery, where around six thousand

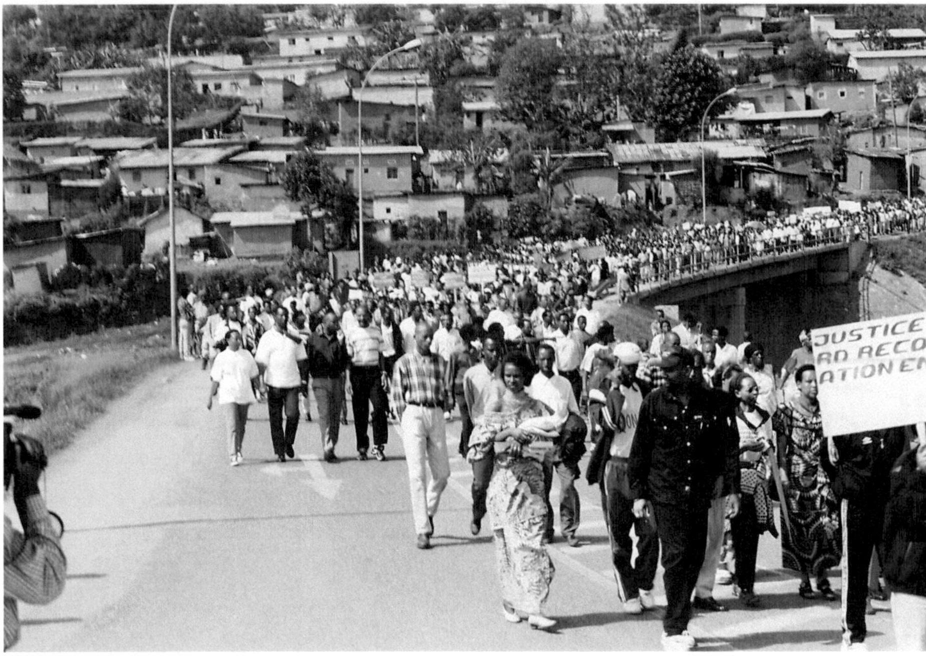


FIGURE 5.4. The 1999 national genocide commemoration, co-organized by the Genocide Memorial Commission and Ibuka, featured a procession through Kigali (between Gisozi Hill and St. Famille Church downtown). Courtesy of Louis Kanamugire, Kanamugire archive, Rwanda.

genocide victims were reinterred in marked communal and individual graves. The procession's culmination at Rebero Hill was significant, symbolizing both the RPF's 1994 military victory and subsequent regime change.[7] Rebero Hill was originally named for its panoramic view of the city of Kigali.[8] It was a strategic site in the RPF campaign to seize control of the government and end genocidal violence. Although fighting occurred there, genocide massacres did not. Rebero Hill was instead a symbolic battle site repurposed as a national memorial and cemetery, where fourteen thousand genocide victims were relocated from killings that took place in the capital and brought for burial.[9] All four processional stops were chosen to commemorate the genocide and recognize the founding of the new government. Although a ceremonial parade was not repeated at the second commemoration (which was also an anomaly among national ceremonies for its location in southwest Murambi rather than in the capital, Kigali), processions have been a consistent feature of subsequent annual state commemorations (figure 5.4).

The funerary scene at Rebero Hill was captured by several international photographers. Paul Lowe's images show a row of wooden coffins covered in purple cloth and adorned with flowers and wreaths (figures 5.5 and 5.6). In lieu of exhibited remains, individuals held large wooden crosses beside the coffins that listed the names of known victims. Twelve coffins held the bodies of former statesmen—both moderate Hutu and Tutsi politicians—who were targeted during the genocide. The remaining 188 coffins combined the bodies of thousands of victims gathered from throughout Kigali. The photographs also show several dump trucks and other vehicles on the periphery of the reburial ground that had been used to transport their remains to Rebero Hill.

Behind the coffins a series of black banners addressed a local, Kinyarwanda-speaking audience. The center two banners communicate two survivor organizations' statements of solidarity. Translated, they read: "ASRG-Mpore is with the genocide survivors in Rwanda" and "Avega-Agahozo will not forget ours [loved ones] killed in the genocide." The wooden placards to the far left of the image are in French, challenging an international audience: "Genocide: Why does the whole World keep silent? Sign of complicity?" and "The International Community ignored the genocide and today protects the killers." The placards conveyed the importance of national unity and collective remembrance to a local audience while international viewers received Rwanda's outrage. These signs were sanctioned (if not written) by the Rwandan government, which expected high international attendance at the first commemoration.[10] Few foreign dignitaries were present in 1995, however. For the government, this was a symbol of the world's inattention (and an issue the regime sought to remedy in the second commemoration). Nonetheless, the 1995 ceremony set a new standard: framing the commemoration of genocide victims in accusations of foreign inaction and complicity in the violence.

Despite these provocations the 1995 commemoration was the first state ceremony that attempted to bridge significant postgenocide societal ruptures—something only a few state ceremonies attempted. It venerated both Hutu and Tutsi victims, which also reflected the shared power structure of the transitional government. The ceremony was led by President Pasteur Bizimungu and Vice President Paul Kagame (Hutu and Tutsi members of the RPF, respectively). The recognition of all victims, regardless of ethnicity, was more than symbolic. The ceremony purposefully interred Hutu and Tutsi in the same memorial cemetery.

The first commemoration also represented the state's efforts to recognize religious diversity in the country. Unlike subsequent ceremonies, it included four religious services, conducted by a Catholic priest, an Adventist priest, a Protestant pastor, and a Muslim imam.[11] The different rites represented the religious diversity of people in the capital. The reburial ceremony was significant also for including

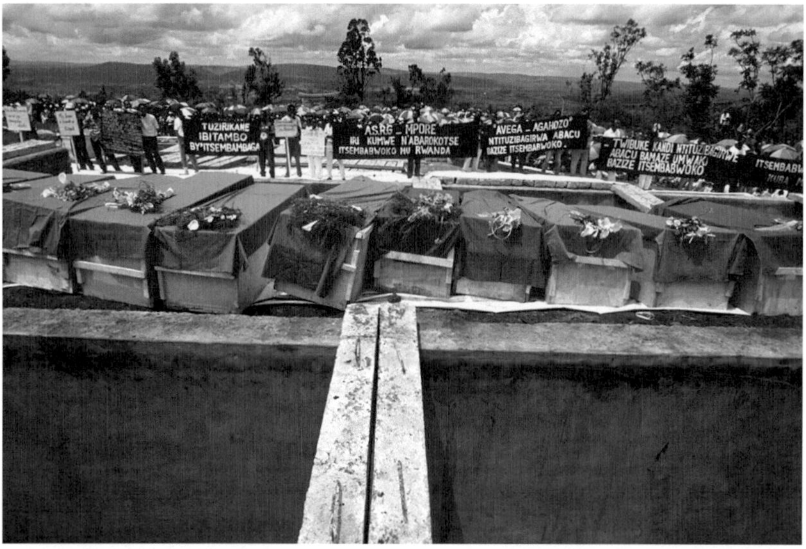


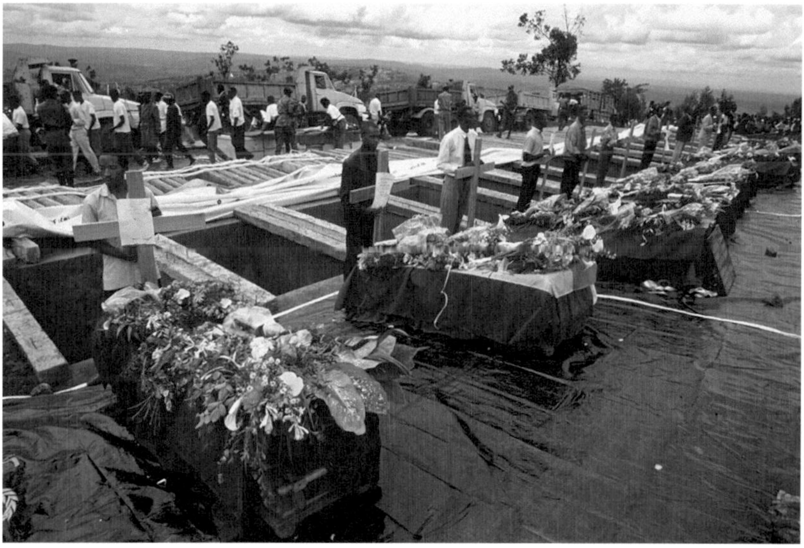

FIGURE 5.5. The first national genocide commemoration on Rebero Hill outside Kigali featured Kinyarwanda banners proclaiming solidarity with and justice for victims and signs in French accusing foreigners of negligence and complicity in the killings, April 7, 1995. Photo by Paul Lowe, Panos Pictures, https://www.panos.co.uk.

FIGURE 5.6. The first national commemoration on April 7, 1995, displayed the decorated coffins of genocide victims before interment. Victims were collected from massacre sites throughout the capital and relocated to the Rebero Hill burial ground. Photo by Paul Lowe, Panos Pictures, https://www.panos.co.uk.

the Catholic Church, many of whose priests were complicit in targeting refuge seekers for mass killing at places of worship. Subsequent commemorations have not explicitly acknowledged the ethnic and religious diversity of victims and have become progressively more secular ceremonies that primarily recognize Tutsi who were killed in the genocide.

### APRIL 7, 1996

The second national commemoration was organized by MINESUPRES and the Genocide Memorial Commission one year later. Bold in its aesthetics and content, the ceremony did not incorporate religious rituals, did less to acknowledge the diversity of victims, and put greater attention on the bodies of the dead as a representation of the genocide. It was again led by President Bizimungu and Vice President Kagame and presented a critical evolution in what anthropologist Jennie Burnet has called the "production of nationalized memory in postgenocide Rwanda."[12] In contrast to the ceremony at Rebero Hill, which was not a killing site and was located near the capital, the second commemoration took place at the Murambi Technical School complex. The site was chosen because of the Amagaju Association's and local authorities' independent decision to return mummified bodies to the school for display. Consequently, the second commemoration was the first national remembrance ceremony to exhibit victims' remains. However, it was not the first instance of this and should be seen in the context of the Nyarubuye and Ntarama protomemorial sites, which preserved scenes of massacre for secondary witnesses, and of local reburial ceremonies that had been including temporary public viewings of the dead.

When MINESUPRES Minister Joseph Nsengimana was interviewed by journalists during the second commemoration, he was asked why the government chose to display genocide victims. He began his reply with some bitterness, noting, "Some people say the genocide never took place; that we exaggerate."[13] He was referring in part to the disposal of evidence at Murambi, which, together with French troops' occupation of the site, prompted doubts as to the scale of killing and its classification as genocide. But by 1996 Nsengimana's words also reflected how the government felt the genocide was being represented in the world. As a result, Nsengimana was adamant: "The corpses will stay in this school as testimony to the genocide."[14] In doing so, he claimed the bodies as incontrovertible evidence of genocide, as an accusation of feckless neglect, addressed largely to representatives of foreign states and international organizations. Murambi was thus a strategic choice for the second commemoration, one that defended the government's moral authority in stopping the violence and publicizing the killings. To complement those government intentions, the ceremony eschewed religious rituals, even though the commemoration took place on Easter Sunday and the Catholic Church protested this decision in advance.

In place of placards, political messages were embodied by genocide survivors, victims' bodies, and secondary witnesses. Journalist Collette Braeckman observed the starkly performative aspects of that embodiment when a Tutsi genocide survivor was called in front of the crowd to recall his experiences during the massacre.[15] He then began to point at the local residents around him, accusing them of participating in the killings. Other members of the crowd applauded in response. Later, after speeches by politicians, the same genocide survivor walked up to the bishop of the Gikongoro Diocese, who was seated among foreign and local dignitaries, and accused him of participating in the massacre of Tutsi children and priests in the region.[16] Accusations of the Hutu individuals attending commemorations became a new ritual at subsequent annual ceremonies.[17]

During the second commemoration, the Genocide Memorial Commission led foreigners on tours of the classroom buildings after testimonies and speeches. They walked among the conserved bodies laid out on the floors. Bodies had been distributed among the many school buildings. Viewing them approximated the processional that debuted at the first commemoration. Local residents did not join foreign visitors. Seeing the dead was too emotionally difficult. Most Rwandans remained near the burial sites on the school grounds in collective mourning. The second national commemoration intensified the government's objective of bringing the genocide to the attention of a global public. It ordered the time and place of that attention by endorsing a reconstructed scene of violence in which the bodies of the dead were conserved and returned to where they were killed. Those returns—both the relocation of the bodies and subsequent witnessing—tethered memory maintenance and genocide remembrance together in the making of a national ritual.

The convergence of memorialization and commemoration at the Murambi massacre site galvanized what had until then been a series of experiments in developing Rwanda's genocide heritage. The bodies and bones of the dead were critical to anchoring genocide memory to place. They were not a mere symbolic index for the violence; they served a more performative capacity, reinstantiating the ethics of nonerasure, and the political status of Tutsi and Hutu, with every viewing. Unlike the first commemoration, which featured only the temporary viewing of coffins prior to reburial, the second commemoration's display of conserved bodies at the school produced a lasting site of memorialization. As a result, foreign witnesses and area residents could return to Murambi after April 7, 1996; the truth of the genocide and the forms of order that the state sought to establish could be continually reasserted. That extended temporality—enabled by the perpetual display of victims' remains—became a defining feature of Rwanda's authorized genocide heritage.

### Local Reburial Ceremonies: The In/Visibility of Violence

By virtue of their location and number, local reburial ceremonies provide insights into the spatial and temporal ordering processes of Rwanda's genocide heritage. Thousands of such ceremonies both preceded and followed the first and second commemorations. Their social and affective impacts are evident in the ceremonies' backstage production, organization, and effects on attendees grappling with the afterlives of violence.

The first local reburial ceremonies were massively larger than the private burials organized by family members. Collectively, they entailed the interment of hundreds of thousands of bodies and victims' remains. At that scale, their purpose was not only to reinforce a collective memory of the genocide but also to lay a community of victims to rest.[18]

The first ceremonies were not exclusively state led. Many were initiated by local residents and organized together with survivors' and religious organizations and local and national governing authorities. In rare cases, reburials were also initiated by international organizations. A prominent instance of the latter was a reburial ceremony near the Kibuye Catholic Church (in the west) organized by Physicians for Human Rights (PHR), a nongovernmental human rights organization that was conducting forensic investigations into the genocide.[19] For seven days, beginning on February 17, 1996, PHR provided public access to the bodies they had recovered from four mass graves at the parish.[20] The weeklong viewing enabled relatives to identify victims for private burials. Unidentified victims were interred by PHR and local authorities on February 24, 1996.

The national government's involvement in reburials preceded the formation of the Genocide Memorial Commission in October 1995, but by 1996 Louis Kanamugire had taken the lead in organizing the ceremonies and the rituals they included (see chapter 2). Under the commission, the government's first local ceremonies were expressly initiated for the purpose of *gushyingura mu cyubahiro*.[21] In Kinyarwanda the verb *gushyingura* refers to both archiving and burying. It connotes both immortalizing the dead in history and putting them in their rightful place, below ground. *Icyubahiro* means honor and respect and when used in relation to burials translates as "decency." A key priority of the ceremonies, then, was the respectful treatment and interment of the dead. In the process, the commission's *gushyingura mu cyubahiro* (decent burials) program involved a transformation, a reordering, of the aftermath landscape. Retrieving bodies from fields and hidden graves and locating them in a place of rest restored a sense of dignity to the victims and provided some semblance of order and safety for the living in everyday landscapes. Often, reburial also entailed transforming sites of killing or purpose-built burial grounds into commemorative places that could be reconsecrated and recognized. Knowing where victims were buried provided some measure of comfort to relatives and survivors. Retrievals and interments also removed the dead from the spaces of the living—homes, farm fields, churches, and streets—to which people were returning. Disentangling places of massacre from those of life allowed residents to begin to rebuild their lives without a constant emotional and embodied reminder of violence.

Though oriented in large part toward decent burial, the ceremonies were not composed of customary rituals. Reburial ceremonies replaced traditional Rwandan mourning and funerary practices, such as *guterekera*, which did not emphasize burial as much as rites to safeguard the deceased's passage to the spiritual world of ancestors (*abazimu*).[22] Such practices had initially been marginalized as pagan by the Catholic Church during the colonial period. Those rituals persisted, if discreetly, because they were critical to protect the world of the living, over which ancestors were believed to exert great influence. But the omission of ancestral communion and other such rites from reburial ceremonies amounted, together with government directives, to a state prohibition on their use. More broadly, Rwandan practices associated with the dead have historically varied regionally and according to class.[23] For the majority of Rwandans who did not belong to the monarchic clan, funerary rituals included wrapping the dead in mats or digging shallow graves within the family's domestic enclosure or nearby fields. Relatives added a few symbolic grains, medicinal plants, and animal products to safeguard passage to the world of *abazimu*. By contrast, in the Rwandan monarchic tradition, the body—of a dead Tutsi king (*umwami*)—was more central in funerary rites because of his symbolic and functional importance. In most cases, the *umwami*'s body was covered in butter or animal fat, milk, and blood; cured over a low fire and thereby mummified; covered in the skin of a bull; and transported to a necropolis. Final rites were performed in those architectural complexes, which had further significance as landmarks of monarchic power. They were often located on the kingdom's peripheries to guard a contested border or in sacred places to memorialize an ancient site.[24] The importance of kingly bodies to monarchic legitimation and territorial power evokes general parallels to the centrality of genocide victims' bodies to the founding of the new, post-1994 state. However, the government has never cited Rwanda's monarchic traditions as precedent for genocide memorialization.

Instead, for the government, the very historical rupture produced by the genocide justified new funerary and mourning rituals. Interviewed by a French journalist in 2000, Louis Kanamugire stated this succinctly: "Genocide is not in the African tradition. We want to discourage any attempt to return to considering it as such."[25] Louis's retort was made in defense of Rwanda's genocide heritage aesthetic more broadly. The controversies around the display of victims' bones and bodies at memorial sites echo the first oppositions to the temporary viewings at early reburial ceremonies. The public viewings of victims before interment were emotionally distressing, for survivors and relatives especially. Critics claimed that viewing the bones and bodies was a secondary form of violence, especially harmful for those who had experienced the genocide in 1994. These arguments dispute the necessity of visibility to genocide heritage. The viewings underscored, as historian Rémi Korman has put it, that the government interest in collective memory of the genocide took precedence over relatives' interests in identifying individual victims.[26] A decade later, in his memoir, Louis took pains to address critics' claims that genocide heritage desecrated victims.[27] He argued that the commission's display of bodies and bones at conserved massacre sites was necessary for history and, to a lesser extent, the forensic investigation of the crimes.[28] Louis represents the wider government view of genocide heritage as a form of representation suited to the exceptional nature of the violence. Reburial ceremonies produced those new, extra-ordinary traditions.

Local reburial ceremonies established some of the first communal rituals for genocide remembrance. They were widely attended by area residents, local government representatives, and civic leaders. Chief among the new rituals were public displays of the remains of the dead—both above ground and within newly dug mass graves. The displays aimed to both recognize the scale of the genocide—which was visually achieved by presenting multiple large piles of victims' remains—and restore some measure of dignity to genocide victims by aesthetically ordering their unearthed, disaggregated remains within graves in communal repose. But viewing was not always preferable, especially for survivors and relatives of victims, or even voluntary. For residents suspected of participating in killings, attendance was compulsory. Those new practices were introduced alongside the predominantly Christian rites that typically accompanied other burials in Rwanda. In doing so, the reburial ceremonies brought together rituals equally oriented to the exceptional—to making evidence of violent crimes visible—and to social convention, developing new practices for ordering the dead and living memory of the genocide. They provided spaces for a viscerally jarring form of witnessing, the grief and measure of the reprieve associated with burial rites, and the socialization of government norms and expectations. As a result, reburial ceremonies were hybrid and transitional practices. They negotiated tensions between an antagonistic visibility and restorative inhumation more acutely than other forms of genocide heritage.

The temporary display of victims' remains and their aesthetic ordering in communal graves were often not singular events. Those returns—to the time of genocide and to decent burial—were repeated and extended. This occurred, especially in the first decade after the genocide, in the work of prisoners or the use of *umuganda* (a monthly Saturday reserved for community work) to exhume the dead and rebury them. Exhumations, and victims' reinterment in annual ceremonies, continued well past the first decade. Throughout that period and more recently, it has also involved the relocation of genocide victims' remains from local to district-managed memorial sites. State television and radio channels host regular broadcasts of foreign dignitaries' visits to genocide memorials (including Murambi), reburial and commemoration ceremonies, and songs of genocide remembrance.[29] These broadcasts have aired most commonly during the national commemoration period over the past thirty years.

Early reburial ceremonies also enacted forms of social and political order, in ways distinct from the first national commemorations in 1995 and 1996. Then, Rwanda's sovereignty and critique of foreign states had been on view in protests at the events and speeches by new government leaders. National commemorations and reburial socialized residents by establishing the government's moral and political authority. Reburial ceremonies did so as well. But national commemorations were more overtly symbolic: they sought to communicate, to both a global and national audience, the strength of Rwanda's state sovereignty and critique of foreign countries through protests at the events and speeches by new government leaders. Although reburial ceremonies also included government speeches and state symbology, they emphasized practices for ordering the living and the dead within communities. These aspects are evident in the backstage preparations for the ceremonies and in the organization of the events, which in their sheer numbers and local orientations aimed to have direct impacts on surrounding residents.

The social dynamics at and in preparation for reburials helped reinforce binary postgenocide identities and relationships—both at the ceremonies themselves and well beyond, in the country more broadly. The Genocide Memorial Commission led the ceremonies' backstage preparations in coordination with state public works, military, and prison agencies. Prisoners suspected of genocide crimes were tasked with the gruesome work of exhuming and reinterring bodies. The large-scale retrieval of victims from mass graves and fields effectively rehoused the bodies of the dead within the domain of the state. During the ceremonies government and religious authorities gave speeches and led rites, survivors testified about their experiences, victims' remains were displayed, and other local residents were relegated to a watching public in the background. The organization of laborers, various attendees, and the dead reproduced distinctions between returnees (repatriates from long-term exile) and locals who had resided in Rwanda during the genocide, between survivors and perpetrators, and between Tutsi minority and Hutu majority residents. Reburial ceremonies staged the new and lasting social orders that transpired after the genocide, especially the power-structuring relationships among the living and between the living and the dead.

These rituals and ordering processes were documented in a substantial visual record, which includes photographs taken by professional photojournalists and a few video recordings by international observers of the first reburial ceremonies. Additional images retrieved from the personal archives of Louis Kanamugire and Mario Ibarra provide rare documentation of the public events and backstage preparations for reburials organized by the Genocide Memorial Commission. Louis's and Mario's personal repositories of photographs and videos were primarily intended for archival purposes rather than government use or news publication. Those images have not previously been reproduced in the news media nor analyzed as part of the literature on genocide commemoration and memorialization.

Louis's and Mario's photographs document the labor involved in exhuming bodies, the temporary display of victims' remains during ceremonies, the speeches and testimonies involved, and the interment of bones into newly dug communal graves. Most of their photographs were retrieved from undeveloped strips of negatives. As a result, the images do not merely record discrete moments; they also document longer sequences of activity. The extended temporality of the photographs reflects a fundamental aspect of genocide heritage and offers a way into thinking about the complex and nonlinear ways that visual evidence moves in time. They also render genocide heritage more personal and concrete, showing who was involved at various stages in the reburial process, including who prepared victims' remains and who led and attended the ceremonies.

## BURIAL ARRANGEMENTS

Every government-led reburial was preceded by a process of victim retrieval and preparation. This aspect of the ceremonies is the least widely known but one of the most controversial in communities. Describing those processes entails graphic descriptions of the minute and mass handling of victims' bodies; it is not easy to receive as a reader. That work was documented in films and photographs—many of which I include here. As I do in preceding chapters, I show that visual documentation to reveal both the process of making trauma heritage and the importance accorded to preserving a record of that work while it was being done.

After months and years of decay, the work of exhumation and victim recovery was unsettling and repugnant. It was assigned to prisoners, the lowest group in Rwanda's postgenocide social hierarchy, who were charged with a range of crimes, including identifying Tutsi neighbors as targets, stealing from them, and committing sexual violence and murder. In the first years after the genocide, human rights groups raised concerns regarding the presumption of prisoners' guilt based on evidence of varying quality, including the prevalence of false charges brought to settle other social conflicts.[30] Arrests were also made as forms of vengeance and broadly on the basis of Hutu identity. Mario Ibarra, in the context of his investigations as part of the UN Human Rights Field Operation in Rwanda (HRFOR), visited several local *préfecture* prisons to interview people who had participated in the killings for details on those massacres. He, along with people from several other organizations, remarked on the severe overcrowding, prevalence of disease, lack of adequate shelter, and malnourishment in Rwandan prisons.[31] Reburial preparations were an extension of those conditions. The rationale for prisoners' involvement as laborers was retributive justice: handling the putrid bodies of victims that they had presumably killed was a form of punishment.

Less publicly, genocide survivors and relatives, like Vestine Ndikuryayo, disapproved of prisoners handling the individuals they had killed, viewing it as a further sullying of their bodies.[32] The objection applied specifically to the work that immediately followed the retrieval of victims from fields and perpetrator-dug mass graves. That process was more intimate and included removing belongings like shoes and clothing from body parts, disaggregating and cleaning those remains, and sorting bones by type. The scale and extent of the violence—and the thousands of reburial ceremonies that followed—transformed a process that was initially handled with care, even quasi-forensically, into one that was massive and, depending on the context, tumultuous or mechanistic.

Some sense of that rough work was captured in video recorded by Jan Wilken, an International Criminal Tribunal for Rwanda (ICTR) investigator, during February 15–19, 1995. The video documents activities that took place before the first national commemoration and the formation of the Genocide Memorial Commission.[33] While investigating the genocide in southern Rwanda, Wilken observed reburial preparations at Kaduha Parish, a massacre site near Murambi in Gikongoro Préfecture. After the genocide the perpetrators had disposed of the bodies in and around the church in five shallow mass graves. Footage shows barely discernible graves, marked only by shallow depressions in fields, partly hidden by brush (figure 5.7).[34]

The filming begins by panning across a four-foot-high raised platform built from large branches tied together. The platform spans over fifty feet and is erected in the side yard of the church. Gikongoro's rolling hills frame the background. In the foreground we see a man's legs as he stands atop the wood scaffolding. It is partially covered with skeletal remains. Two men come into view to lift and empty a wheelbarrow with more bones and partially decomposed body parts on top of the wood platform to dry in the sun (figure 5.8). Given the labor required to lift and empty the wheelbarrow, it is not clear why the platform is raised so high above the ground. Wilken is in the background, documenting the work with his still camera. The video cuts to several more men shoveling tangled masses of bodies from a shallow grave into smaller piles. Another pushes a wheelbarrow up an adjacent incline toward the camera. A contorted adult body fits completely inside.

The next cut documents a man standing on the wooden platform, methodically lifting a hoe over the victims' remains as if tilling soil. He moves the body parts slowly from one spot to another. He makes little progress, and it is not clear exactly what purpose his actions serve; the victims' remains are already spread out evenly across the wood lattice (figure 5.9). None of this work is vigorous or fast-paced, and the workers move tools without reacting much to the bodies beneath them. Notes associated with the recording do not identify the workers as prisoners but rather as "local workers hired by RPF soldiers."[35] The workers seem inured to the substance of their work, emotionally distant but still focused on the tasks at hand, their mundane repetition and scale.

By the second national genocide commemoration in 1996, the labor required for reburial ceremonies was directed by the Genocide Memorial Commission, which commonly employed prisoners who were overseen by prison guards and military personnel. Louis Kanamugire was frequently on site to supervise the work (figure 5.10). Mario Ibarra photographed many of the victim recovery processes, reburial preparations, and local ceremonies that were organized by the commission (figure 5.11). When prisoners were involved, the exhumations and reburial preparations were typically larger in scale and more chaotic in pace and activity.

Three full rolls of film document a series of scenes and tasks prior to a reburial ceremony on June 30, 1996, near the Murama Commune office in Gitarama Préfecture in the west. The photographs begin with views of nine plastic tarps, some with UN logos, filled with heaping piles of bodies recovered from mass graves in the area (figure 5.12). The victims' remains are hardly distinguishable from each other: Decomposed flesh, clothes, tree roots, and soil fuse together in amorphous forms. Exhumed bodies were often kept for months in bags and tarps so that they could be interred together in reburial ceremonies.

The next photographs show over a hundred prisoners (mostly men, a few women) seated on the floor of a large room (figure 5.13). They are dressed in ordinary clothes, not prison uniforms. In another context, they would merely be individuals from the community gathered for a meeting. In a smaller room nearby, photographs show seven women sitting on the concrete floor. They are genocide survivors and have a range of reactions to being photographed. A few women

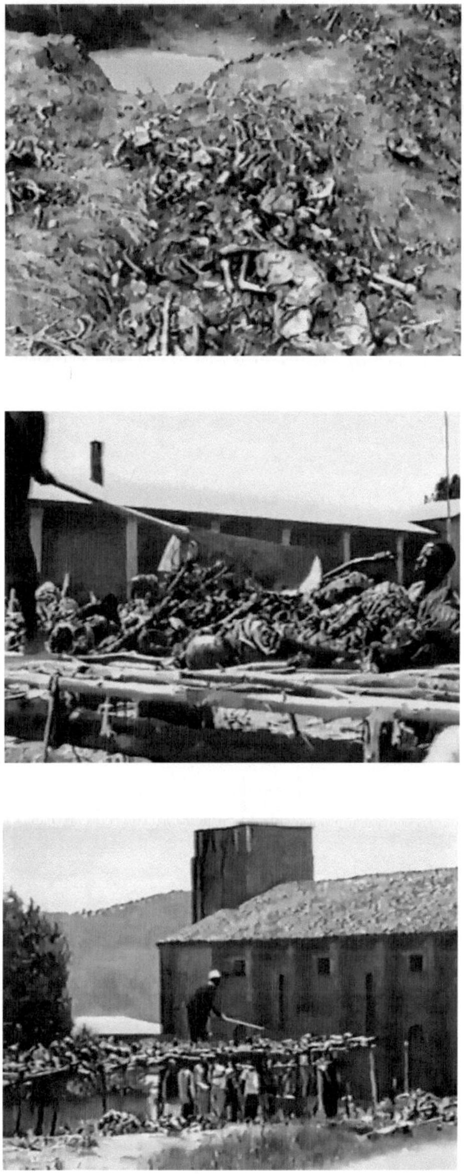

FIGURES 5.7 – 5.9. ICTR investigator Jan Wilken filmed the exhumation of a mass grave (*top*), the use of a wheelbarrow to carry victims' remains to a wooden scaffold to dry (*middle*), and a worker separating those remains for drying (*bottom*), at Kaduha Church in Gikongoro Préfecture, February 15, 1995. Jan Wilken, "Kabuha [*sic*]—ICTR Internal Video," box 118, videocassette RW031, at 09:24, 01:23, and 03:25, International Monitor Institute Collection, David M. Rubenstein Rare Book and Manuscript Library, Duke University, Durham, North Carolina.

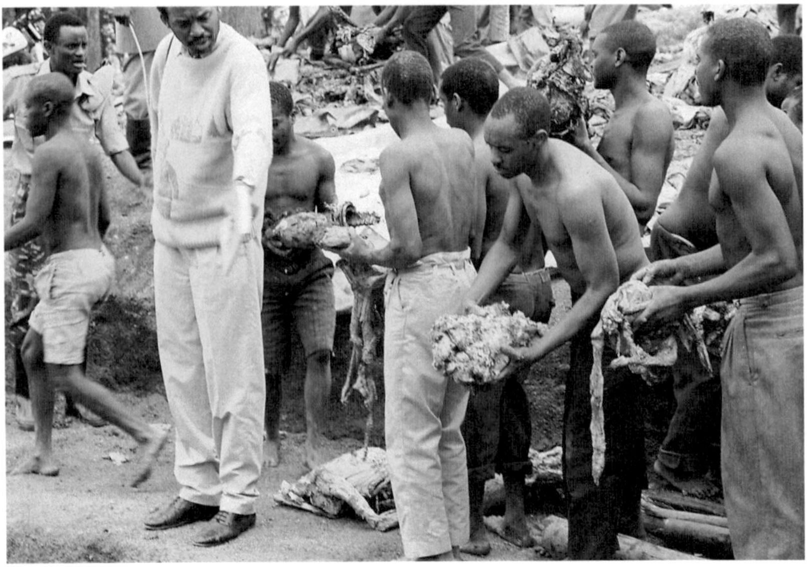

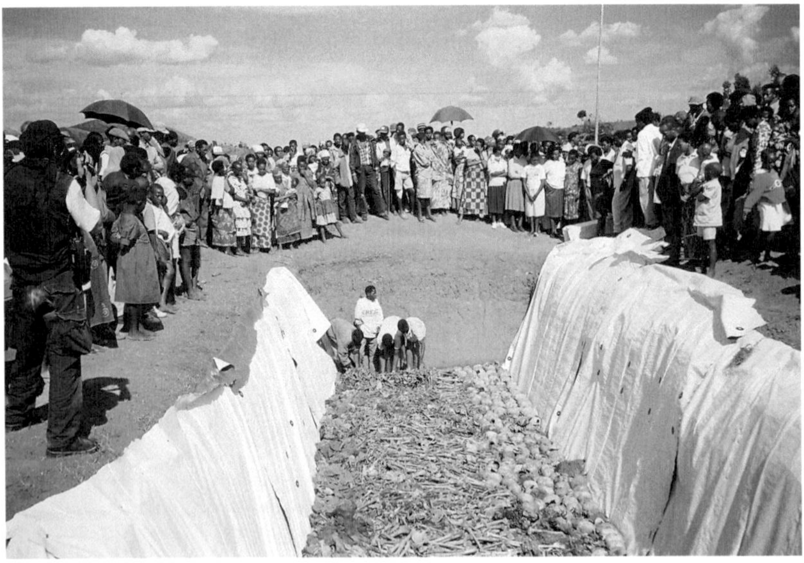

FIGURE 5.10. Louis Kanamugire (*left*) directs prisoners to move victims' bodies and bones to communal coffins for reburial, Murama office, Gitarama Préfecture, June 30, 1996. Photo by Mario Ibarra, Kanamugire archive, Rwanda.

FIGURE 5.11. Mario Ibarra (*far left*) photographs the Mubuga Commune reburial ceremony in Gikongoro Préfecture, October 24, 1996 (see also figure 2.20). Photo by Louis Kanamugire, Kanamugire archive, Rwanda.

smile at the photographer, some look away and into the distance, and others cover their faces. They await the reburial ceremony, where they will testify about the attacks they survived during the genocide and witness the interment.

The remaining photographs in the series show the ordering work that the prisoners did under the supervision of the Genocide Memorial Commission, several men in military uniforms carrying semiautomatic weapons, and uniformed guards holding long wood switches (figures 5.14–5.17). Shoes and shirts removed, pants rolled up high, the prisoners are immersed in piles of human remains. They pull apart the masses of bodies with their hands. Victims' clothes are put in one pile, skulls in another, long bones in a third; flattened and mummified corpses are gathered together; and ribs and narrow bones are sorted onto a fifth tarp. They build six large wooden crates, each approximately eight feet by seven feet and four feet deep, which are placed side by side in a long, continuous trench. Some prisoners work from inside the containers, standing on the jumble of skeletal remains as they are filled (figure 5.18). Others carry armfuls of chalky, desiccated body parts and bones to them.

The grisly, and yet taxonomic, categorization of human remains and belongings that took place at memorials was often reproduced in communal graves belowground. At the Murama Commune office, the contents of the six wooden crates were organized by type. In one photograph a man holds a pelvic bone that he adds to one side of a crate teeming with ribs and other smaller bones. The remaining half of the compartment is filled with defleshed skulls. Another image shows how that separation was maintained amid the dizzying multitude of victims' remains in the communal coffins (figure 5.19). Working in another wooden container, men build partitions with dimensional lumber to contain a few partially intact mummified bodies at one side. Clothing—all jumbled together, in hues of green, red, and brown—fills another crate nearly to the top (figure 5.20). In yet another, long bones are arranged neatly in a row, all oriented in the same direction and on top of the small rib and pelvic bones that fill the bottom of the crate, with a dozen skulls deposited neatly in a corner beside them.

In many other local reburial ceremonies, including one a few months earlier at Nyamasheke Church in southwestern Rwanda, organizers interred victims in one long communal grave lined with plastic rather than in distinct crates. In those circumstances, bones were separated, as at the Murama Commune interment, but then arranged to approximate a large group of human forms laid in a row (figures 5.1 and 5.11). The grave was ordered in that way to render its contents recognizable. Skulls were always laid at the top of a row because they were the most discernibly human of skeletal remains. Long bones were often positioned just below skulls; their size allowed them to be easily separated in the conservation process and also

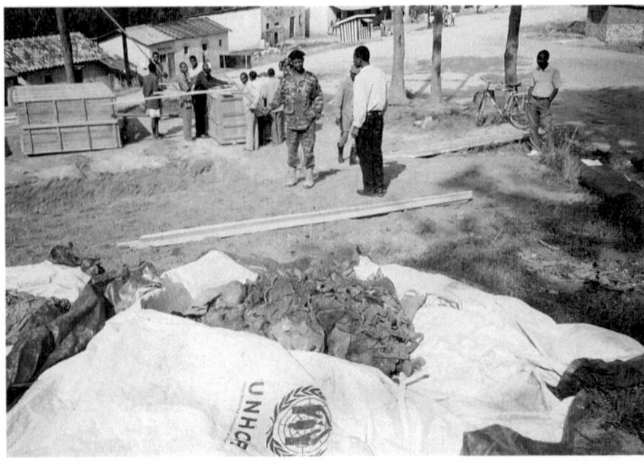

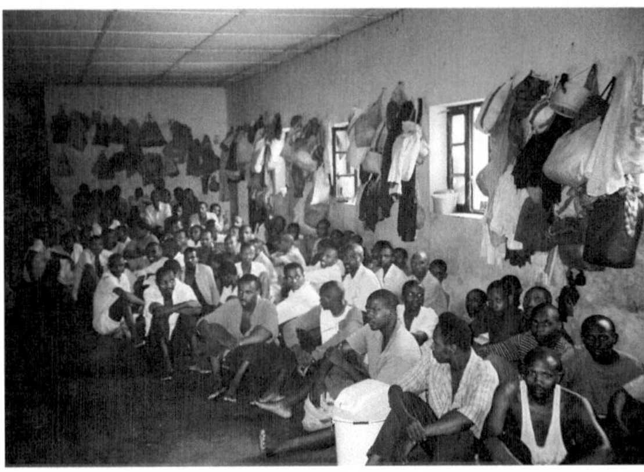

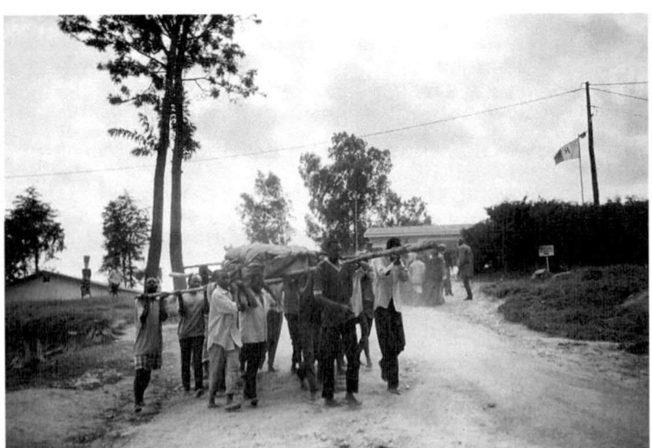

FIGURES 5.12–5.14. Sequence of photographs documenting preparations for the Murama Commune office reburial in Gitarama Préfecture, June 30, 1996. Reburial ceremonies gathered victims' remains (*top*) and often required the labor of prisoners (*middle*) to exhume and move (*bottom*) bodies and bones to grave sites. Photos by Mario Ibarra, Kanamugire archive, Rwanda.

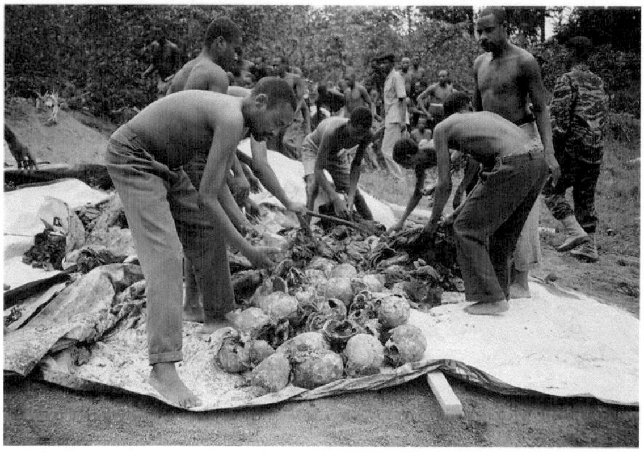

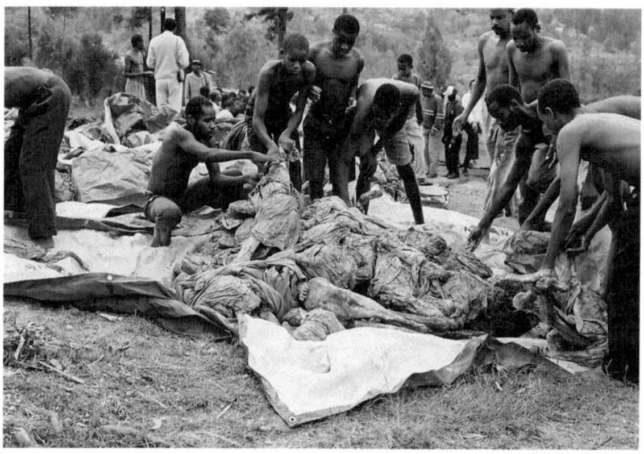

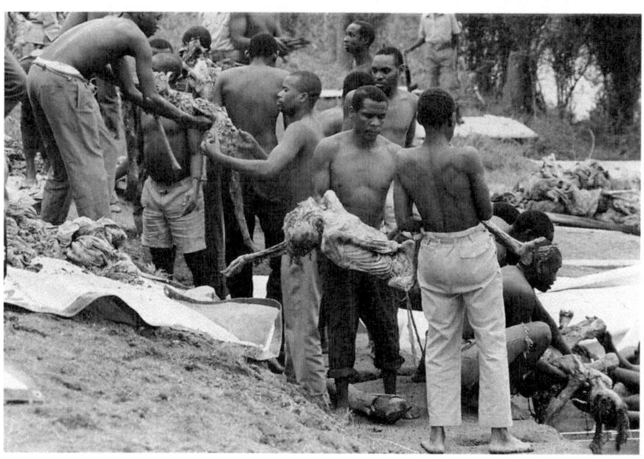

FIGURES 5.15–5.17. Prisoner-laborers separate and sort genocide victims' bodies, skulls, bones, and clothing to prepare for the Murama reburial ceremony in Gitarama Préfecture, June 30, 1996. Photos by Mario Ibarra, Kanamugire archive, Rwanda.

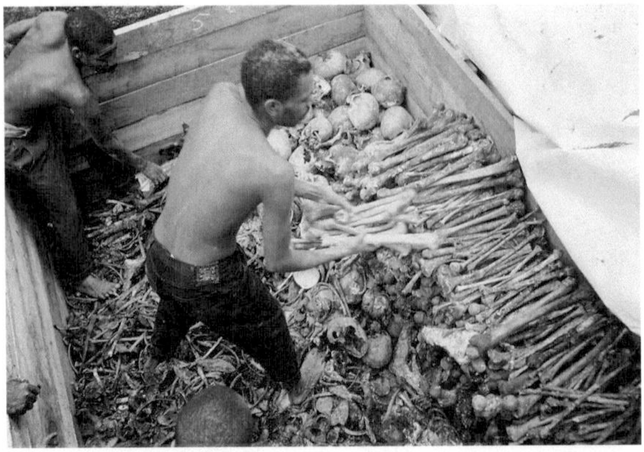

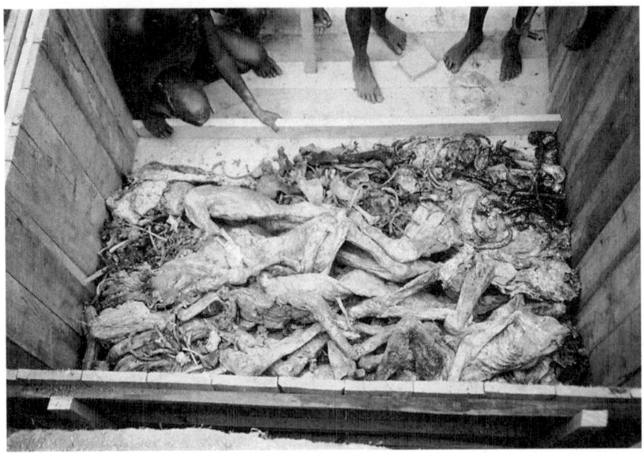

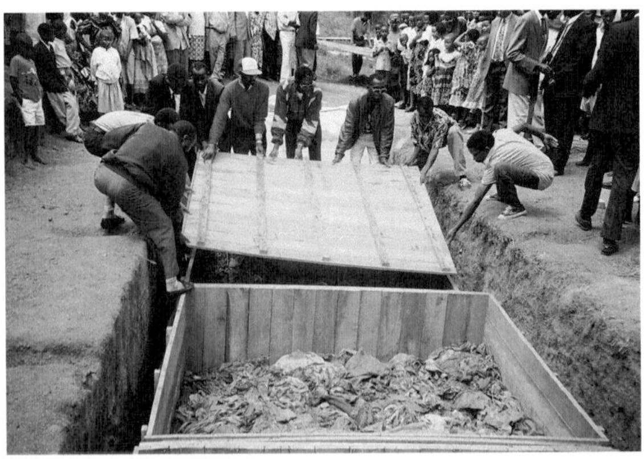

FIGURES 5.18–5.20. Outside the Murama office, conscripted laborers sort bones by type (*top*), place the few remaining intact victims' bodies on top of those piles (*middle*), and separate clothing into discrete coffins (*bottom*) before lids are placed on top, June 30, 1996. Photos by Mario Ibarra, Kanamugire archive, Rwanda.

permitted the bones' identification as human, especially for lay publics. Smaller bones and clothing were interred at the foot of the row. Mummified bodies, if they were found, were aligned with the skulls and placed on top of all the remains to signify the whole to which the parts referred. Photographs of reburial ceremonies throughout the country indicate that the use of coffins, wood crates, and large lined graves were all typical approaches to reburials, and in each, the taxonomic sorting of victims' remains also was common.

When understood in the context of *icyubahiro*—of honor and decency—the aesthetics of communal graves are meaningful. The genocide divided communities and the body politic in ways ideological, psychic, and physical. In both the Nyamasheke and Murama interments, burial arrangements were purposeful new rituals that gathered, deconstructed, and reconstituted the bodies of the dead. Ultimately, those practices attempted to retrieve a sense of order and humanity lost in the aftermath of dehumanizing mass violence. In doing so, it reproduced a new social order—one featuring witnessing and punishment.

## THE ARCHITECTURE OF PUBLIC VIEWINGS

After bodies were exhumed but before communal graves were closed, temporary public viewings of victims' remains often took place. In some instances, body parts were separated and arranged on tarps in aboveground pavilions. In other cases, remains were exposed inside subterranean graves. The viewings were only ever intended for ceremonial witnessing. When reburial ceremonies concluded, genocide victims were interred belowground: removed from view and everyday experience.[36]

In 1996, at the Murambi Technical School, Nyamasheke Church, and Murama Commune office reburial ceremonies (on April 7, April 27, and June 30, respectively), a range of attendees—including community members (never prisoners), politicians, religious authorities, and in some cases international visitors—gathered around open graves to view the reordered masses of victims' remains amid speeches and rites. The diverse attendees represent the varied purposes of the ritual viewings and reburials. In the national commemoration ceremony at Murambi, the display of mummified victims was predominately an assertion of national authority over genocide remembrance for a global audience. The presence of local genocide survivors and residents sought to perform the stakes of that remembrance in the naming of perpetrators among them. Local social dynamics were more prominent at the Nyamasheke Church and Murama Commune ceremonies, which were relatively smaller in scale and had minimal foreign attendance. Those ceremonies were more precisely attuned to ordering the local communities where they took place.

Photographs from the Murama Commune Office reburial ceremony show a large, diverse crowd assembled on all sides of a trench with all six crates fully open to view. Several local and national government representatives attended, including Louis Kanamugire and Captain Firmin Gatera; others gave speeches (figure 5.21). Religious rites were not documented in the photographs, but the ceremony did include other cultural practices, including a choral performance by local secondary school students. Afterward, survivors recounted their experiences of the massacres to the crowd. They did so graveside with victims' remains remaining in view, below. Mario Ibarra recorded several photographs of individuals standing and sitting near the communal graves during the testimonies and speeches. In one image, a young child stares resolutely at him, holding the camera's gaze (figure 5.22). She is part of a group, comprising mostly women, who are looking elsewhere: down into the crates, or holding their hands over their eyes. Their faces register numbness, anguish, and sadness. The public viewing concluded when wood covers were fixed to the top of the crates. Survivors, relatives, and state representatives laid wreaths and flowers on top of the closed coffins. The communal grave was then covered in soil and by large concrete slabs.

In other ceremonies, temporary public viewings were more provocative. The dead were not situated belowground but above—variously organized in large piles among which the living could walk. In those instances an extended time for the visceral witnessing of the dead (and in rare cases the identification of victims) was carved into the ceremonies themselves. The aesthetics of such public viewings were jarring, compelling viewers to see a mass representation of the genocide before, or instead of, the individuals who were killed.

The Nyamasheke Catholic Church reburial ceremony on April 27, 1996 (twenty days after the second national commemoration) exemplified such conditions. The ceremony was attended largely by Rwandan residents and therefore held primarily for a local audience rather than for foreign journalists and dignitaries. It was also a site of local cultural significance: Located on the southern shores of Lake Kivu on Rwanda's western border, Nyamasheke was one of the first Catholic missions built in the country. It was originally established in 1928 by White Fathers (Pères Blancs) priest Léon Delmas on the site of former King Rwabugiri's residence.[37] The brick church was built in 1947 and is one of the few remaining monumental buildings from the colonial period.[38] It rises to three stories with minimalist and rectilinear art deco lines traced in tall, narrow windows. The facade's stepped profile is echoed in the buttress pillars that repeat along its length, adding to the building's prominence in the landscape.

In 1994, like other churches throughout Rwanda, Nyamasheke became both a safe haven for area residents fleeing violence and a site targeted by killers. The

Genocide Memorial Commission estimated that eight thousand to ten thousand people died on the parish grounds during the genocide.[39] The 1996 reburial ceremony served a much larger population of victims. An estimated forty-five thousand people were killed in the surrounding region (Kagano Commune). Nyamasheke was a prominent cultural heritage site marked by the genocide, previous pogroms against Tutsi in the region, and a long history of monarchic, Catholic missionary, and colonial power and symbolism. For those various reasons, Nyamasheke Church was a historically significant place for *gushyingura mu cyubahiro*, though it was ultimately not named as a national-level genocide memorial site like Nyarubuye, Ntarama, Nyamata, and Murambi.

Three rolls of photographic film provide a sense of the nature and sequence of events during the Nyamasheke reburial ceremony. It did not occur inside the main church. In smell, state of destruction, and memory, the building was too close to the events that had occurred there. Instead, the Genocide Memorial Commission built two long and wide pavilions in the church's forecourt from plasticized tarps and wood poles (figure 5.23). Together with the space around them, the pavilions created three main zones. One pavilion provided reserved seating for invited guests—including Rwandan and foreign dignitaries, government officials, Catholic clergymen, and a Muslim imam—where commemorative speeches and witness statements were recorded (figures 5.24 and 5.25). Several coffins, draped in white and purple satin, adorned with Christian crosses, were positioned near the dais.[40] The second pavilion held jumbled piles of genocide victims' skeletal remains, loosely organized by size and type (figures 5.26–5.28). A crowd of local residents was cordoned off in a third zone, located outside the pavilions and uncovered by a tent structure, where they could watch the ceremony (figure 5.29). Military guards kept watch over the pavilion and peripheries. On the parish grounds some distance from the pavilion, several concrete vaults had been dug for victims' later entombment. A marker was erected next to a brick water well adjacent to the tombs to establish it as significant to the parish's local genocide history. In doing so, the Genocide Memorial Commission transferred the type of memory work it was doing at other massacre sites where evidence of the genocide—in this case, where perpetrators had hid victims' bodies after the killings—was conserved for public viewing.

At key junctures in the Nyamasheke reburial ceremony, the second pavilion became open to all attendees, converting it into a public space to witness the dead. In that space the attendees navigated an unwieldy collection of victims' remains that had been exhumed and moved from the church grounds and other massacre sites in the area. The piles were loosely sorted into long bones, skulls, and a smaller grouping of mummified corpses, which were all placed on plasticized tarps on the

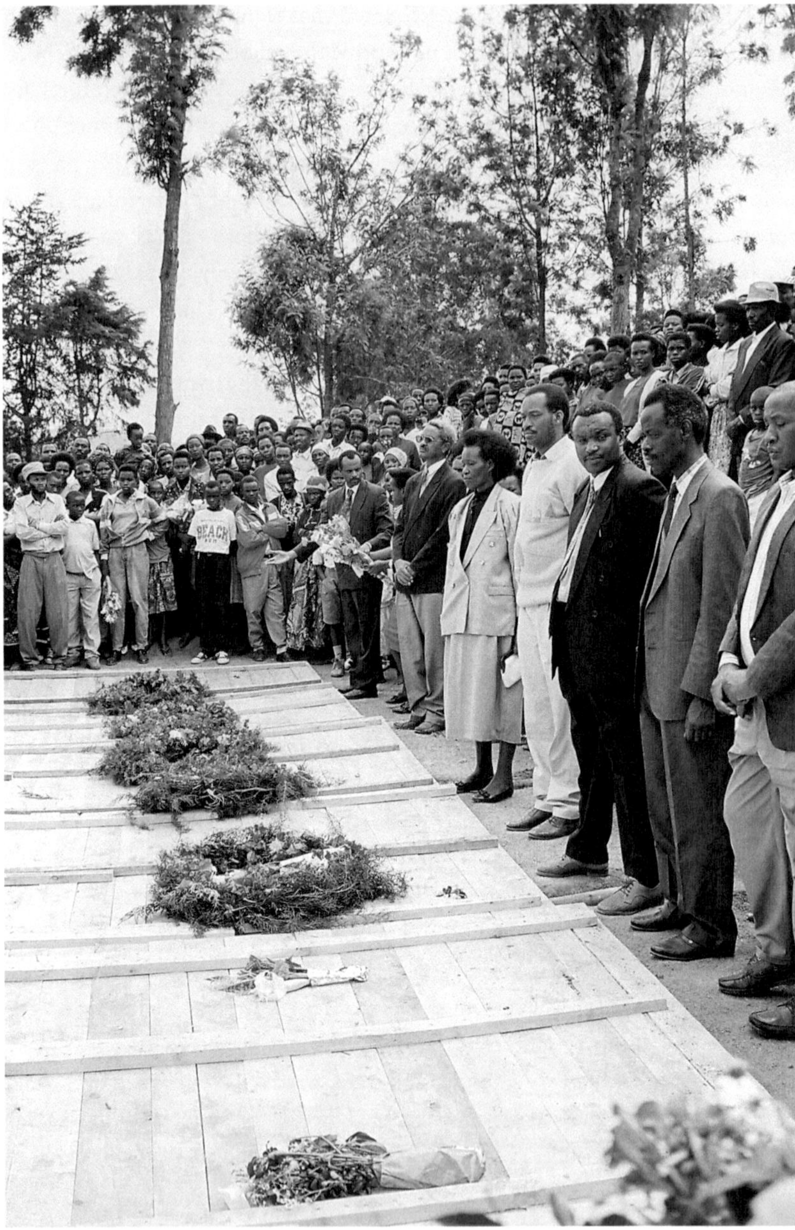


FIGURE 5.21. The Murama reburial ceremony concludes with speeches, survivors' testimony, and burial rites, June 30, 1996. Louis Kanamugire (*middle right, in a sweater*) and Captain Firmin Gatera (*far right background, holding a bouquet*) attended. Photo by Mario Ibarra, Kanamugire archive, Rwanda.

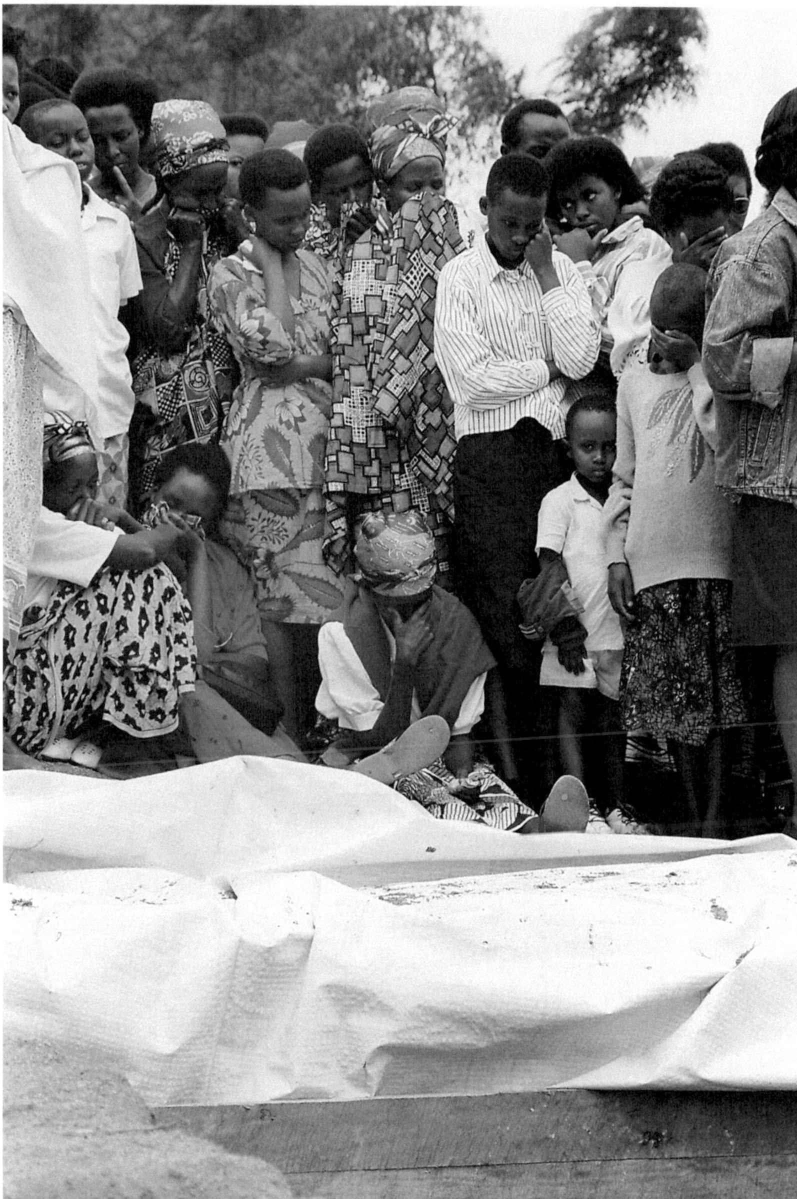

FIGURE 5.22. A child among survivors and relatives holds the camera in her gaze at the Murama reburial ceremony, June 30, 1996. Photo by Mario Ibarra, Kanamugire archive, Rwanda.

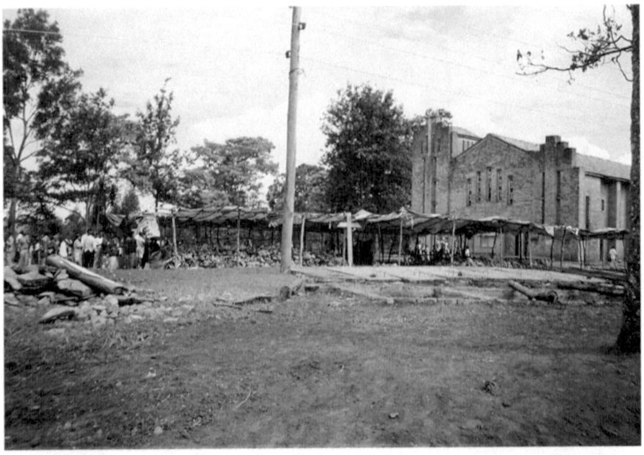

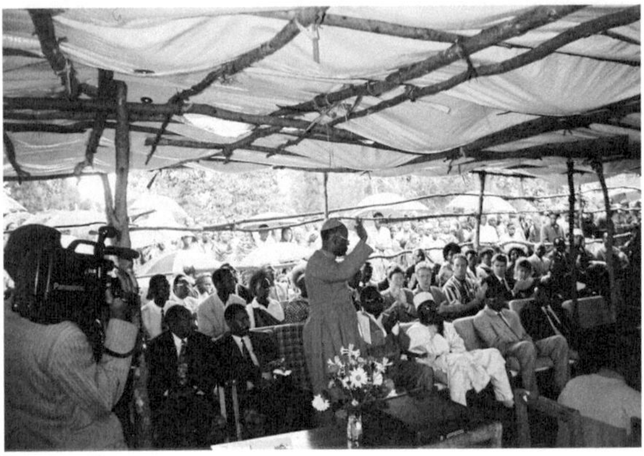

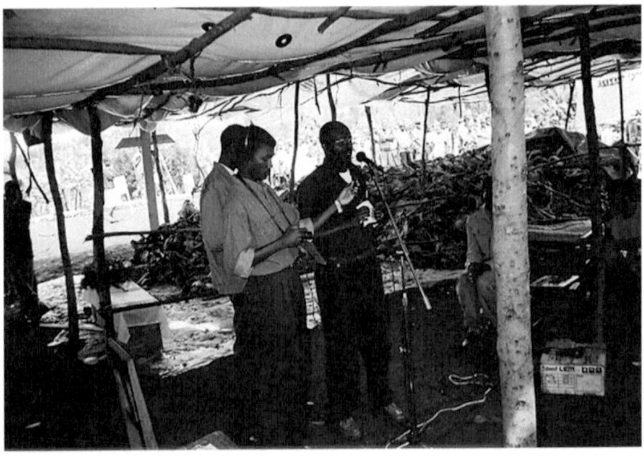

FIGURE 5.23–5.25. The Nyamasheke Church reburial ceremony featured temporary pavilions built in the forecourt (*top*), speeches by religious and government leaders (*middle*), and survivor testimony near the display of victims' remains (*bottom*), April 12, 1996. Photos by Mario Ibarra, Kanamugire archive, Rwanda.

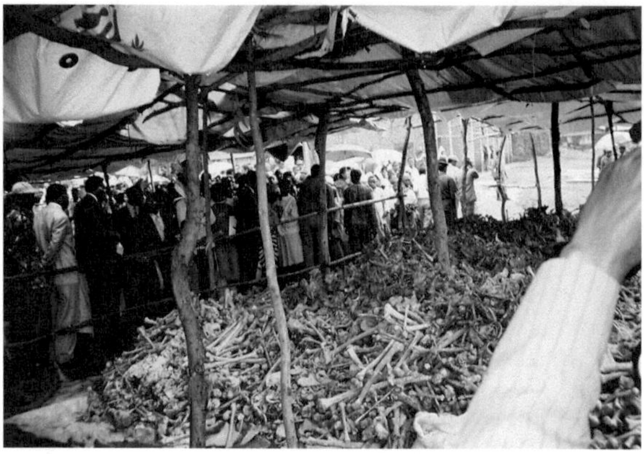

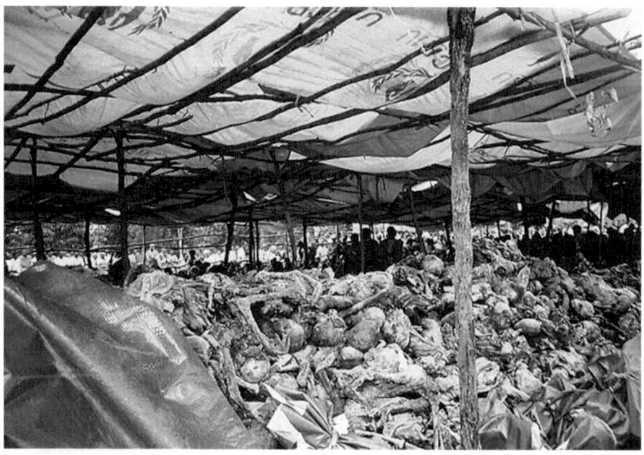

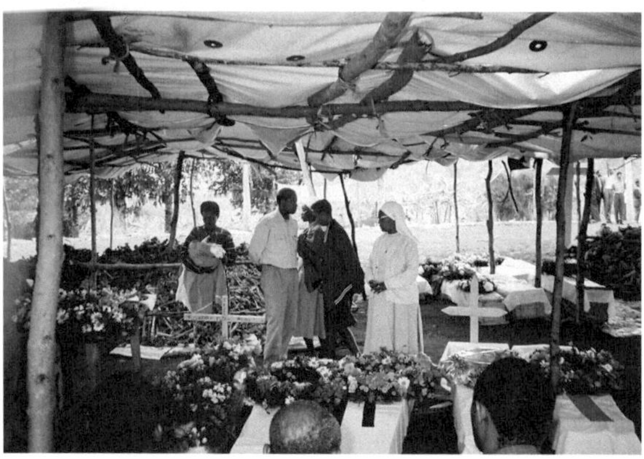

FIGURE 5.26 – 5.28. The pavilions built for the Nyamasheke reburial ceremony on April 12, 1996, featured distinct sections, including for the display of victims' bones (*top*), intact bodies (*middle*), and coffins for those identified (*bottom*). Attendees walked through those areas to witness embodied evidence of the genocide. Photos by Mario Ibarra, Kanamugire archive, Rwanda.

ground. The mounds of remains overwhelmed the senses and ability to contemplate the number of community members who had been killed. They embodied, as Mario Ibarra remarked decades later, the smell and the pain of Rwanda's genocide heritage. A large part of the aboveground display was organized as disorder to communicate the scale and effects of the genocide. When the victims were later interred in the communal grave, the commission arranged the victims' remains to approximate their human forms. That effort in organization had amplified significance, conveying, at last, some measure of order and repose to the mass violation.

Although political signs condemning foreign inaction were absent from the Nyamasheke reburial, the political messaging of the ceremony was clear. The embodiment of violence on display challenged denial of the genocide's occurrence and—through related feelings of shock and horror, relationships of kin to victims, and knowledge that the individuals who died were possibly among the masses—sought to involve attendees in contemplating the consequences of the aftermath. The shift from signposting to embodiment in order to represent the atrocities and demand attention followed the shift from the first commemoration ceremony, at Kigali in 1995, to the second, at Murambi in 1996. It was more broadly representative of the growing importance of victims' remains and spatial representation to Rwanda's genocide heritage aesthetic. At Nyamasheke, those displays communicated the moral, communal, and government condemnation of the genocide. The reburial ceremony was positioned to defiantly denounce the dehumanizing violence that preceded it, before the victims could be laid to rest. To those ends, only one sign, written in Kinyarwanda, hung from the pavilion that housed victims' remains. It announced the location and date of the reburial, along with an accounting of the forty-five thousand individuals killed in the commune. It was accompanied by three powerful statements: "Twamaganye itsembabwoko. Abacitse ku icumu nibitabweho. Ubutabera nibukurikira[ne] abicanyi bose" (figure 5.30). In English this translates as "We reject genocide. Survivors will not be left behind. All killers must be brought to justice." Those three sentences communicated outrage, solidarity, and commitments to justice to a local, Kinyarwanda-speaking audience. It was also a warning for anonymous genocide participants in the crowd.

The Nyamasheke reburial ceremony also incorporated several speeches by religious leaders and government representatives, who acknowledged the presence of a few foreign guests. Genocide survivors also publicly relayed their experiences of the targeted killings (figure 5.25). The speeches were projected through loudspeakers. Afterward, dignitaries filed through the center aisle of the pavilion to view the remains of the dead while residents watched from the peripheries (figure 5.26). Residents had opportunities to view the remains both before the ceremony

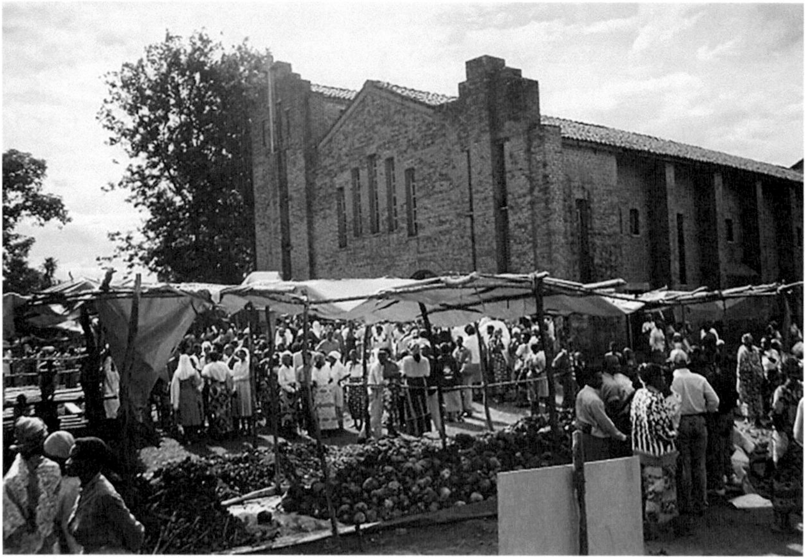

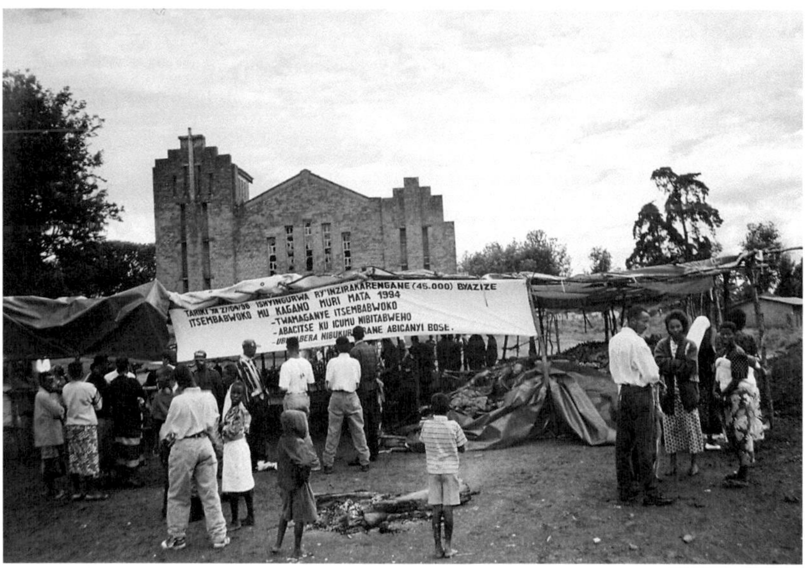


FIGURE 5.29. The periphery of the main pavilion at the Nyamasheke reburial ceremony, where local residents stood and additional victims' remains were displayed, April 12, 1996. Photo by Mario Ibarra, Kanamugire archive, Rwanda.

FIGURE 5.30. A banner hangs from the Nyamasheke Church reburial ceremony pavilion, identifying the forty-five thousand genocide victims killed in the area and vowing justice for victims and survivors, April 12, 1996. Photo by Mario Ibarra, Kanamugire archive, Rwanda.

and after the processions and speeches, but social hierarchies prevented copresence. Social stratification was comparably less stark during the interment, when the families of identified victims gathered at the edges of the burial sites next to the coffins along with government and religious officiants (figures 5.31–5.32). At the end of the ceremony, all victims' remains were removed from view and interred in communal graves. The temporary pavilions were then dismantled and the church returned to service (figure 5.33).

Through the public viewing of victims' remains, the Nyamasheke reburial enacted genocide heritage as a form of social, political, and affective order. It was an early instance of a now-prevalent process. According to Louis and Mario, most attendees supported temporary exhibitions as an opportunity to view "their" dead—somewhere among the many—before burial. In this generous interpretation, the viewings provided an emotional outlet for grieving and angry survivors and their families. From a comparably more neutral perspective, the attendees' promenade among the piles of remains in the long pavilion provided a sense of the scale and extent of the genocide. On a more intimate level, each bone and body part, collected en masse as they were, conveyed not only the number of individuals killed but also the loss of personhood to mass violence. But the public ceremony also had political value for a government galvanizing support for its right to rule. The use of the occasion for condemnatory speeches and displays of skeletal remains was similar to other ceremonies and produced a moral landscape of killers, saviors, and survivors. That stratification was on display in both the exhibition of victims (which implied the presence of killers) and the spatial separation of residents from elites during the event.

The Nyamasheke ceremony also exemplified forms of religious ordering in compromises reached between church and state. In this instance, the Catholic Church succeeded in restricting the display of remains in both time and space. The taxonomically arranged bones and body parts were available to view only on the day of the reburials. Thereafter, a permanent memorial was relegated to a small plot to the side of the forecourt rather than occupying the full church parish as in other national sites.[41] Today the Nyamasheke genocide memorial does not present overwhelming evidence of the killings; it is unlike the mummified bodies on display at Murambi and the belowground bone crypt at Nyamata Church (figures 6.14 and 6.15). Instead, most victims were reburied and remain out of view. The exception is the display of the skulls of twenty-two victims, who were later discovered in the area, in a curio cabinet at the burial site. When I visited in 2013, a roof structure had been erected over the tombs. The 1996 reburial ceremony allowed the Catholic Church to reestablish its moral authority in the area (after church leaders' complicity in killings throughout the country) and resume

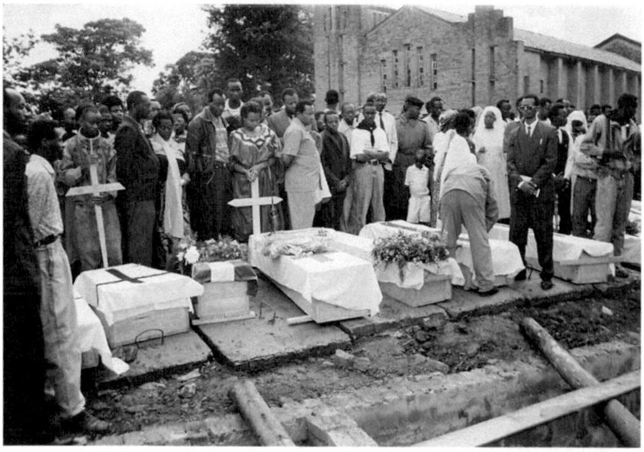

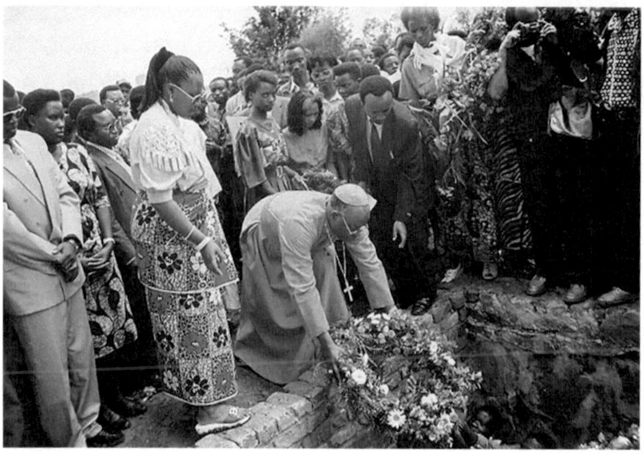

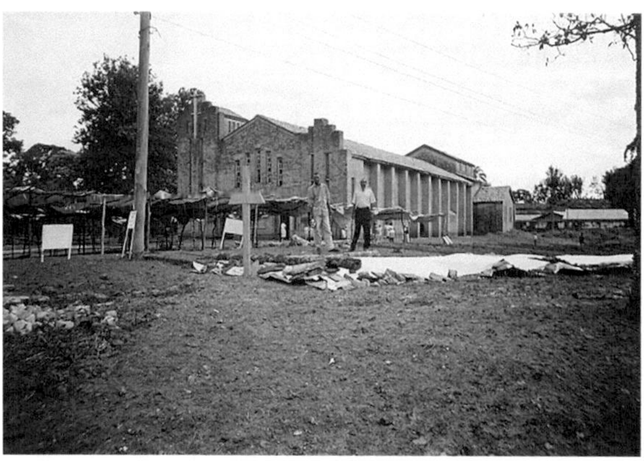

FIGURES 5.31–5.33. At the conclusion of the Nyamasheke reburial, victims were moved to a communal grave site at the side of the church where the crowd gathered (*top*), the bishop and others laid commemorative wreaths (*middle*), and the grave was covered (*bottom*), April 12, 1996. Photos by Mario Ibarra, Kanamugire archive, Rwanda.

social and cultural services at the parish. Moreover, the communal reburials had reparative value for attendees as ritual processes of death, grieving, and closure from which the work of rebuilding everyday lives could commence. Nyamasheke represents a rarely discussed instance of a compromise between viewing the dead as evidence of atrocity and burying victims *mu cyubahiro*, with dignity, belowground and out of sight.

The public viewings of genocide victims at reburial ceremonies piloted the display of bodies and bones at genocide memorials. In this sense, reburial ceremonies can be seen as protomemorials that helped define Rwanda's genocide heritage. Exhibiting victims ultimately became central to how memorial sites represent the genocide, proving pivotal to both a global image of the atrocities and the authorized historical narratives that reference and are reproduced at the sites. The practices of ordering, witnessing, and remembering that local reburial ceremonies staged underscore the spatial dimensions of genocide heritage—but not in a fixed or static sense. At the ceremonies' conclusion, burial grounds and marked killing sites formed enduring landmarks of Rwanda's genocide heritage. Annual commemorations stage public remembrance at those sites, reanimating the ethics of nonerasure in political messaging that has sharpened over the past three decades. Despite the temporary nature of the public viewings, reburial ceremonies highlight the temporal regimes that extend from those initial events, their repetition and return, and the lasting community impacts that genocide heritage engenders more broadly.

## Ordering the Future of the Past

The organizers of Rwanda's genocide heritage adopted a fundamentally visual and spatial approach to dealing with the aftermath of the genocide. Memorials and ceremonies were structures for ordering violent memory that involved displaying the bodies of the dead and removing them from public view. Before the reburials, hundreds of thousands of bodies lay in fields, abandoned homes, churches, offices, roads, and partially hidden mass graves throughout the country. Finding dead bodies was not merely physically jarring; it prompted troubling reckonings with fear, grief, enmity, and community futures. In the first years after the killings, those common and deeply personal encounters with death protracted the affective disorder of the genocide. Spatial representations of genocide memory enabled the organizers of Rwanda's genocide heritage to intervene in trauma's temporal dimensions too. Spatial ordering processes contained, and in most cases amplified and ritualized, the emotional flooding and temporal slippages endemic to grappling with traumatic experiences. The ceremonies' temporary public viewings of victims' remains—and their arrangement aboveground in representations of violence and belowground in communal repose—evolved alongside the conservation and display of bodies and bones at genocide memorials. Both approaches to ordering the dead stand in sharp contrast to the aftermath landscape and the messy and unenviable work of exhuming bodies from mass graves, and deliberately so. Putting victims to rest and reforming a social landscape devastated by violence required an aesthetic capable of ordering the future of the past.

These were the processes of making genocide heritage, whereby preservation, conservation, and ceremonial recognition of victims and violence tethered memory to place. That memory work organized the landscapes of the living and the dead. It also found lasting material and spatial forms for genocide memories that perpetuated their representation into the future.

Given individuals' experiences of the aftermath landscape, the Genocide Memorial Commission recognized that order was not some abstract goal untethered to affective experience. Ordering the past in postgenocide Rwanda was thus an inextricably sociopolitical and affective endeavor.[42] Rwanda's permanent genocide memorials and established practices of display evolved from the preservation and conservation of massacre sites and victims and more temporary, performative acts of commemoration as the government sought to develop state rituals for both remembrance and justice. The repetition of burial rites and the perpetual visibility of victims at newly designated memorial sites aimed to make that aftermath experience (and the ritual arrangement of bodies before interment) perpetually visible and visceral. The strategies extended the temporality of genocide and were intended to convey its repetition and scale to future witnesses. As a representation of that violence, the temporary display of bodies at early reburial ceremonies was an integral, if fleeting, part of the formation of Rwanda's more permanent memorialization of the genocide.

In this context, ordering the past was a primary and pressing national objective for a new government (figure 5.34). The new, RPF-led state attempted to generate sociopolitical order from Rwanda's genocide heritage beyond the mere perpetuation of the past (although ensuring future genocide remembrance was a central aim). In doing so, Rwanda's genocide heritage paralleled transitional justice strategies as a spatial manifestation of contemporaneous approaches to redressing conflicts.

During the late 1980s and early 1990s, transitional justice conceptually reframed postconflict analyses and policy, particularly around processes of regime change.[43] During that intense period of postcolonial and post–Cold War conflicts occurring predominantly in non-Western and Global South states, citizens demanded the disclosure of previous regimes' systematic abuses. Transitional justice strategies

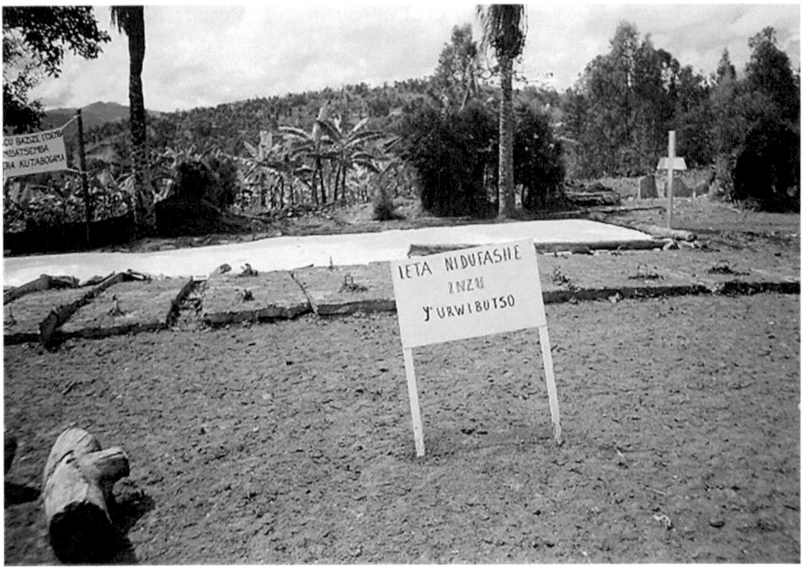


FIGURE 5.34. A sign placed next to the Nyamasheke Church communal grave site reminded visitors (in Kinyarwanda), "The government helped us build a memorial," April 12, 1996. Photo by Mario Ibarra, Kanamugire archive, Rwanda.

emphasized confrontations with past crimes in the present to engender more stable futures. Its advocates considered the representation of past wrongs to be a necessary precondition to granting legitimacy to new governments. The sharp break between the "before" period of violence and the "after" period of repair was attenuated as a result. By conceptually carving an interstitial space and time into peace processes, transitional justice proponents effectively dismissed the orthodox understanding of conflict as part of a linear progression toward peace. Wars were no longer representative of modernity's progress; instead, that violence might well reappear tomorrow. Both the desire for legitimacy and an attention to the fragility of peace created spaces to acknowledge wrongs and injuries, to negotiate for new beginnings and just living conditions. This conceptual space drew issues of structural and historical violence and future plans for rebuilding into a more contingent and dialectical relation.

But the practices of transitional justice are rarely politically neutral endeavors. That unevenness is apparent in the institutional reforms, the convening of truth commissions and judicial trials, approaches to reconciliation and reparations, and the memorialization initiatives and commemorative rituals that comprise transitional justice strategies. Critiques of transitional justice are wide-ranging.[44] They generally concern the power dynamics inherent in those strategies' implementation and priorities, which typically aim to reform structural violence rather than provide redress for acts of physical violence. Victors' justice is also a concern. Often, transitional justice mechanisms have been used by new regimes to gain legitimacy by associating crimes with past regimes, thereby accruing the social and political capital to govern.

Transitional justice was introduced in Rwanda in November 1995 in the context of the government-organized "Genocide, Impunity, and Accountability" conference, which aimed to facilitate a dialogue between Rwanda and the international community on issues of justice after the genocide. However, and as former Rwandan Prosecutor-General Gerald Gahima recounts of his involvement (from August 1994) in high-level government debates and policies on postgenocide justice:

> We [the RPF and transitional government] did not, however, consult and were not influenced by any literature or expertise on transitional justice as part of our search for an appropriate response to the legacy of the genocide. . . . Our engagement with transitional justice only really began with the convening of the ["Genocide, Impunity, and Accountability"] conference at the end of 1995 for the purpose of facilitating dialogue with the international community on the issue of accountability for the genocide. Our familiarity with transitional justice theory and . . . processes of other post-conflict societies grew from then onwards. However, Rwanda's policy makers never looked to transitional justice literature and the experiences of other societies for guidance. . . . We were always of the view that Rwanda's situation was unique and were focused on designing responses to address Rwanda's exceptional circumstances.[45]

Despite those disclaimers Gahima goes on to frame his and others' work within the RPF-led government retrospectively as ultimately engaging in transitional justice. His aim in doing so was to evaluate the country's legal responses to the genocide in comparison to a body of similar approaches to postconflict repair.[46] Gahima analyzes the judicial accountability mechanisms that transpired within the international criminal court, state trial, and neotraditional *gacaca* court systems that he helped develop or advised on in the new government. He adds little to no discussion, other than mentioning the government's keen attention to development and reconstruction, of places of memory and their role in state approaches to accountability and justice—despite the 1995 conference's explicit recommendation that the judicial process be reinforced by a "memorial authority" (the Genocide Memorial Commission) that would undertake seven priorities in service of "memory preservation."

This book's attention to memory justice provides a supplemental lens for the evaluation of transitional justice in Rwanda.[47] Genocide heritage can be seen to compensate for the shortcomings of criminal prosecutions, in both liberatory and regulatory ways. In Rwanda spatialized remembrance produces both memory justice and sociopolitical ordering processes that maintain the regime's control over everyday life. Implicit in the aesthetic regime of Rwanda's genocide heritage, then, was not so much a reference to transitional justice as a parallel endeavor: an ordering of time and space.

Transitional justice formed a larger context within which Rwanda's genocide heritage operated. As I discuss in chapter 2, the mechanisms of transitional justice—in particular, truth commissions, government institutional and judicial reforms, and memorialization efforts—and other instances of them (in places like Chile and El Salvador) were part of discussions of Rwanda's postgenocide "just memory" in October 1994. It was to those larger social and political processes that the ethics of nonerasure and national sovereignty concerns of a spatialized genocide memory were addressed. Genocide heritage was intended to safeguard memory—to protect a history of mass violence from being forgotten, diminished, and corrupted. The display of victims' remains at memorial sites formed a stalwart opposition to the previous geography of elimination and erasure. Early reburial ceremonies (including the first national commemorations) intervened with similar objectives and simultaneously developed communal rituals for grieving and remembrance.

In doing so, Rwanda's genocide heritage shaped temporal and spatial realities by imposing forms of order. Aesthetic ordering occurred in attempts to restore the spaces of the living (by removing dead bodies), reconstitute the human forms of the dismembered prior to interment, and display the dead in sites of massacre. Religious ordering provided anonymous victims with a decent burial and relatives and survivors with some solace through communal interments and funereal rites. Political ordering was prominent, especially at the national ceremonies, and included establishing the state's purview over genocide memory and creating new rituals for doing so that could be repeated annually. Postgenocide social ordering reproduced new hierarchies that were evident in the retributive exhumations done by prisoners, the spatial stratification of attendees, public viewings of the dead, and testimonial condemnations of perpetrators at ceremonies. Through such ordering, Rwanda's genocide heritage created a unitary spatial and temporal regime that projected social and political values. In the context of contemporaneous transitional justice strategies, it exemplifies the power, and limits, of similar efforts to order the past, and of the role of viewership in those endeavors.

The evolution of genocide heritage—from preserved scenes of massacre to the display of bodies and bones at reburial ceremonies, the development of annual commemoration rituals, and the conservation of victims' remains at memorial sites—has perpetuated memory of victims and genocide crimes. Throughout the country today, but especially in communities that more directly confront the visibility of victims' remains, Rwanda's genocide heritage has had lasting individual and communal effects. While government efforts to quell political unrest and replace it with a clearly defined sociopolitical order are appreciated by Rwandan residents, it can also stifle free expression, livelihoods, well-being, and relationships. In the case of Rwanda's genocide heritage, this bears out in a form of memory citizenship—which diminishes the importance of individual memory and diverse approaches to genocide remembrance, supplanting both with authorized historical narratives and memorialization.[48] The following chapter follows those conflicts to more extreme circumstances: unreconciled experiences of violence during and after the 1994 genocide.

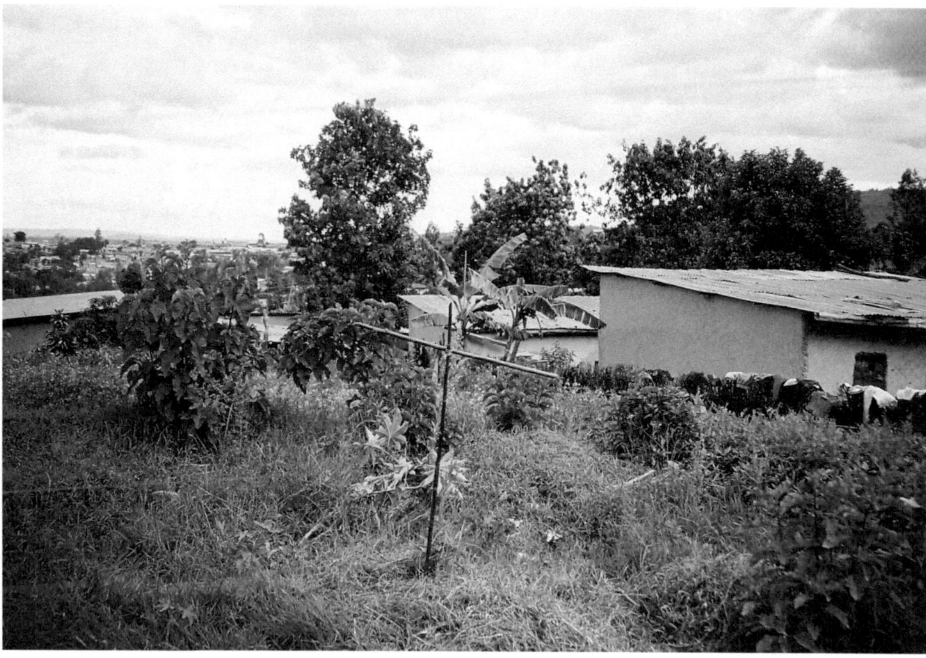

A simple bamboo cross locates the grave site of genocide victims—a local effort in remembrance—near homes on a hilltop in Kigali, 1994. Photo by Mario Ibarra, Kanamugire archive, Rwanda.

6

# MEMORY AND EMPOWERMENT

## *INZIBUTSO ZIGARAGARA, INZIBUTSO ZITAGARAGARA*

Rwanda registers a wide spectrum of trauma heritage: from state-authorized public sites and narratives to hidden ones of which it is prohibited to speak. Over the past thirty years, massacre sites' transformation into official *inzibutso za jenoside* (genocide memorials) has entailed a national effort in placemaking. As a result, genocide memorials are the most visible sites of trauma heritage in the country. Spatial presence conveys and reinforces collective memory of the genocide. Genocide memorials' visibility and ordering aesthetics also confer political legitimacy on the current governing regime and contribute to the regulation of genocide histories and related speech. By contrast, sites that are not clearly marked or codified as official genocide memorials locate experiences of violence that are personal, are known only locally, or have been denied and erased from national histories by the government. This unevenness results from the fact that trauma heritage is also a form of empowerment, and some are more powerful than others. The move from truth telling to action, a move that Rwanda's genocide heritage shares with reparative history, is not equally available to all.

Today the bulk of such power rests with the Rwandan state, which exerts widespread control over the country's landscape of memory. It has done so, in large part, through the spatial and temporal ordering processes of genocide heritage.[1] Those efforts have included conserving killing sites and victims' remains at clearly demarcated memorials, standardizing local genocide histories, and consolidating burial places in select government-administered locations. Annual state commemorations take place at genocide memorials as well, ritualizing acknowledgment of the sites and establishing authorized collective memory. At the same time, memorials' presence and narrative omissions reinforce government control over speech and acts. They represent state disregard for families' wishes concerning how victims' remains are displayed and where bodies are buried. They are locations for government-mandated annual commemoration ceremonies for which attendance by area residents is compulsory. Thus, while memorials provide symbolic and commemorative spaces for justice and healing, in this political context they are also sites of state sovereignty. The governing regime's control over the future of the past leads it to suppress other memories or punish individuals who revive them in public, producing a range of experiences that are underrecognized, unauthorized, or prohibited. A viscerally visible genocide heritage has attained dominance in this context. And yet the justice-seeking intentions of those sites of memory remain tempered by an uneven, and ultimately unruly, landscape of trauma heritage.

This chapter brings marginalized memories and the places associated with them into conversation with the country's authorized genocide heritage, noting the breaks, silences, and omissions that come into focus as a result. It builds on ethnographic and oral history research with rural residents living near genocide memorials two decades after the 1994 genocide. Rural areas are where the majority of Rwanda's population resides and represent a significant interface between authorized and other forms of trauma heritage. Rural landscapes have also been completely remade since 1994: Homes that were once located in hilltop kin clusters or scattered within farm fields have, over the past thirty years, been progressively moved to state-planned settlements. There, new neighbors live next to each other in often precarious conditions of trust and security. Despite the imposition of new settlements, a sense of place is maintained by farming practices that recall generational connections to land and home. Subsistence farming in plains, on hillsides, and in valleys also provides a daily rhythm of work for many, comprising planting, tending, and harvesting amid the dry and rainy seasons. Working the land comprises both an ancestral and quotidian time, which is experienced alongside (and not always informed by) that of genocide heritage.

What we learn from Rwandans living in rural areas is not just the interplay of domination and resistance but something more negotiated about the everyday nature of memory work and the different forms of power it enacts. Some of the individuals willing to describe their experiences to me relayed why they felt resigned to state control. Others talked about deferring resistance as a strategic choice, both protective and patient. And yet individual memories persist, registered in oneself and in encounters with place. There was a quiet in their stories, a refuge in domestic spaces, and the quality of stubborn defiance contained in the act of remembering differently. Their acts of remembrance constitute efforts at repair that diverge, in varying degrees, from the collective memory authorized by the state. Rwandans' memories challenge lived realities, creating the unruly patchwork of the country's trauma heritage landscape.

The people who inhabit Rwanda's uneven memory landscape perform acts of witnessing that refuse closure.[2] They resist forgetting—and do so in dialogue with the places that confirm and anchor their own accounts of traumatic experience.[3] Their intimate connections to landscape—as matters of livelihood, experience, and feeling—come to the forefront as a result. To reinscribe individuals in places of memory is to recognize the forms of empowerment they maintain, in defiance of ordered representations and as a challenge to hegemonic histories and actions. Seeing, or watching for, this unruliness is a crucial part of the ethics of viewership that Rwanda's trauma heritage demands.[4]

### *Inzibutso Zigaragara*

Almost everyone in rural areas with whom I spoke lived within close walking distance of a local government-administered genocide memorial.[5] This condition reflects the number of massacres that took place across the country. Most of those memorials are subnational: They are state authorized but typically managed by district or sector governments and are not among the six nationally recognized sites. They nevertheless maintain a substantial presence within local communities. Their primary purposes are to demarcate a place of genocide remembrance in those communities and to host the reburial of victims (figures 6.1 and 6.2). Most sites are clearly discernible, with signs that identify the site as a memorial to genocide victims and give the number of people who were killed at and near it. They comprise newly built roof structures over underground tombs as well as former civic buildings that were conserved and not returned to their former uses. Every local genocide memorial is fenced and therefore protected (desecration and vandalism were more common in the years immediately after the genocide). They are decorated in similar ways, usually with dry floral wreaths (from the most recent commemoration ceremony) and banners and ribbons evoking the government's official color of mourning (which shifted from purple to gray in 2012). At most

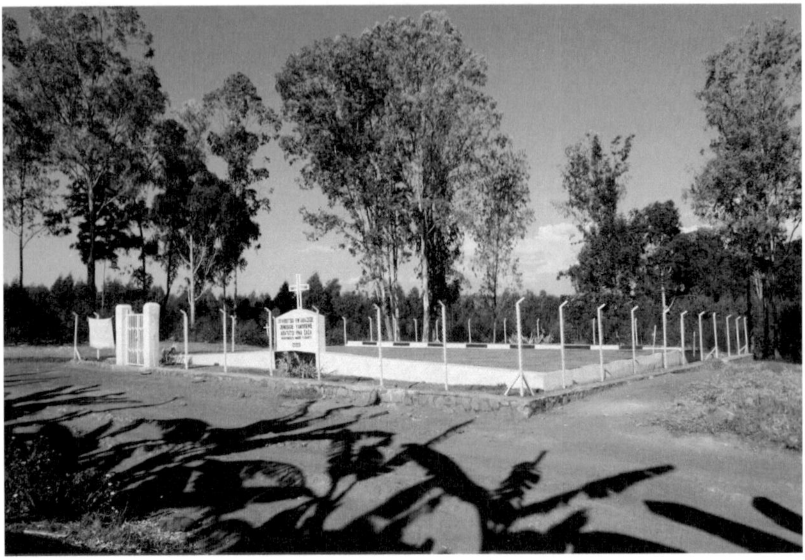

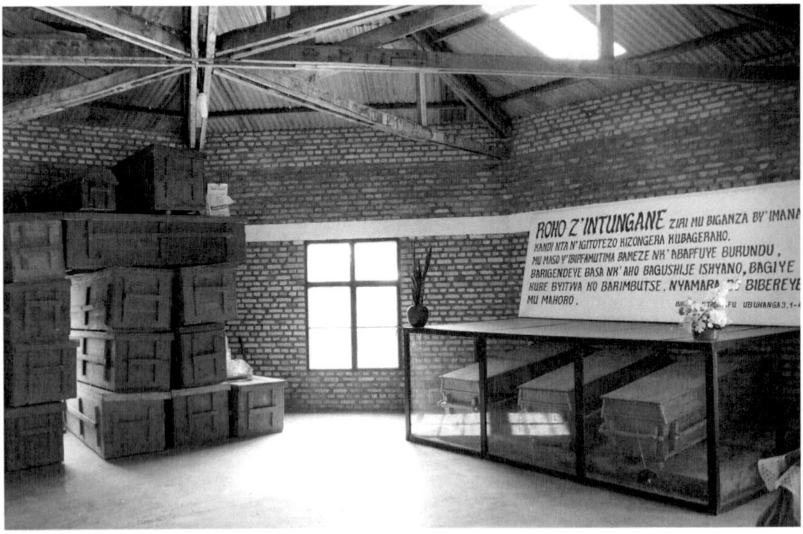


FIGURE 6.1. *Inzibutso zigaragara*: Zaza Catholic Seminary genocide memorial and grave site where 12,025 genocide victims are buried in southeastern Rwanda, 2013. Photo by Delia Duong Ba Wendel.

FIGURE 6.2. *Inzibutso zigaragara*: A pavilion and belowground crypt built for a genocide memorial next to Mugina Church in northeastern Rwanda display coffins to represent genocide victims, 2013. Photo by Delia Duong Ba Wendel.

local genocide memorials, the display of victims' remains is minimal: Typically, only a few representative skulls are exhibited in the aboveground structures; the majority of conserved remains are kept in tombs below.

The sites that host underground crypts are accessed by purpose-built stairs when commemoration ceremonies are held or, more generally, when people visit the site. The tombs are typically large concrete spaces filled with stacks of wood coffins draped in purple satin and white lace. Periodically, local authorities open the coffins for viewings by residents at commemorations or during visits by foreigners. Most of the coffins I was shown housed victims' remains: either skulls or larger bones loosely grouped by type. Entombing the remains in such ways approximated the mass reburial of victims when they could not be individuated. Altogether, a genocide heritage landscape comprising a widely distributed, and largely rural, complex of visible memorials and subterranean burial grounds has done important ordering work: It locates and contains the emotional and spatial messiness of mass murder (figures 6.3–6.11).

Throughout 2013, in interviews with rural residents, I asked, "Kuri mwe, ni ngombwa ko mugira inzibutso za Jenoside mu Rwanda?" (In your opinion, are genocide memorials important to have in Rwanda?) My question was inescapably conditioned by the preparations underway throughout the country for the twentieth genocide commemoration the following year. Local authorities had already begun to roll out new national policies and memorialization plans. A new campaign, "Ndi Umunyarwanda" (I Am Rwandan), was being piloted as both a public apology and a "unity and reconciliation" initiative.[6] Though it was formalized as a government policy only in November of that year, its socialization entailed months of television and radio broadcasts wherein public figures of Hutu ethnicity (who were not personally responsible) apologized on behalf of kin who had committed genocidal crimes. The phrase "Ndi Umunyarwanda" was meant to be repeated in public gatherings to foster notions of a singular Rwandanness after such performances of ethnicized responsibility. In this context, my questions for residents regarding their opinions of genocide memorials were entangled with government expectations of them and the suppression of free speech. Rarely did I hear the types of heightened emotional reactions to genocide site and victim conservation that were documented in the first years after the genocide.[7] Instead, most residents I spoke with consistently referred to genocide memorials as key sites of national and civic duty.

But when those individuals elaborated, a common descriptor emerged that revealed relationships among order, visibility, and state sovereignty in Rwanda. Most people I spoke with referred to genocide memorials as *inzibutso zigaragara* (established memorials). This phrase described the nature of these sites without directly

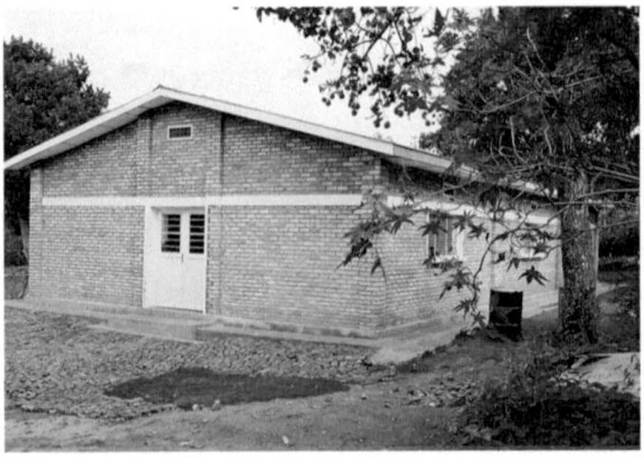

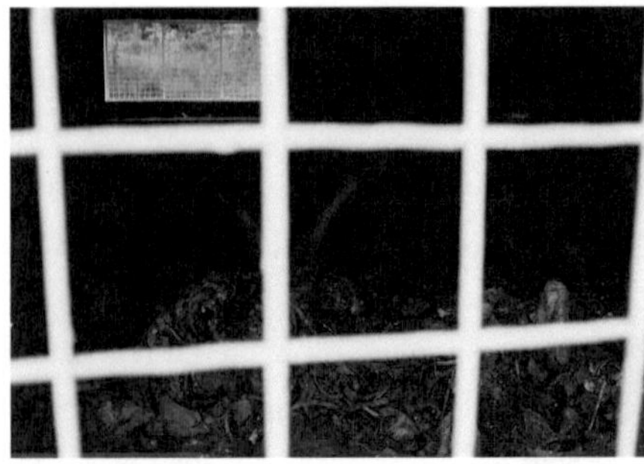

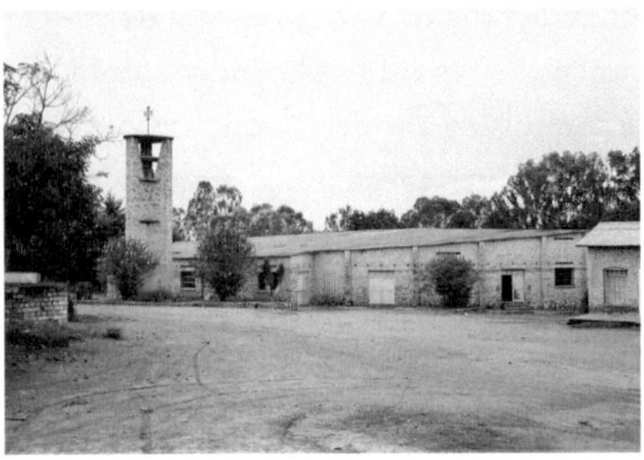

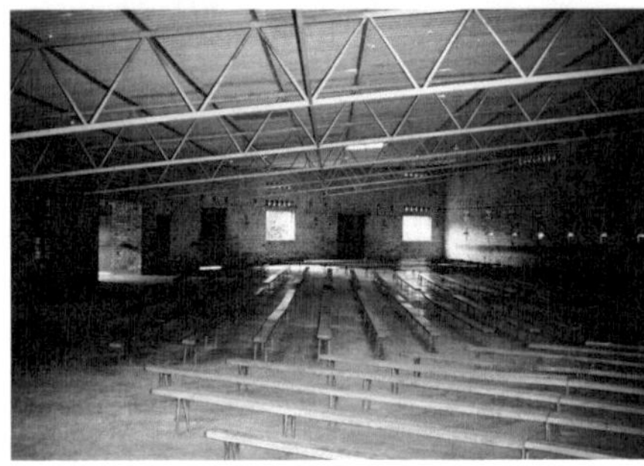

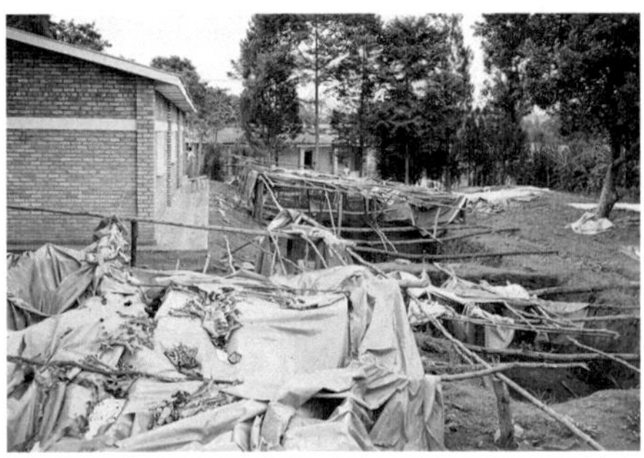

FIGURES 6.3 AND 6.4. (*top*) *Inzibutso zigaragara*: A building opposite Mugombwa Church, near the Burundi border, holds piles of victims' remains removed from the place of worship, 1996. Photos by Mario Ibarra, Kanamugire archive, Rwanda.

FIGURES 6.5 AND 6.6. (*middle*) Mugombwa Church, cleaned of genocide evidence, 1996. Photos by Mario Ibarra, Kanamugire archive, Rwanda.

FIGURE 6.7. (*bottom*) At the building opposite Mugombwa Church, the Genocide Memorial Commission developed a genocide memorial and burial ground for victims, 1996. Photo by Mario Ibarra, Kanamugire archive, Rwanda.

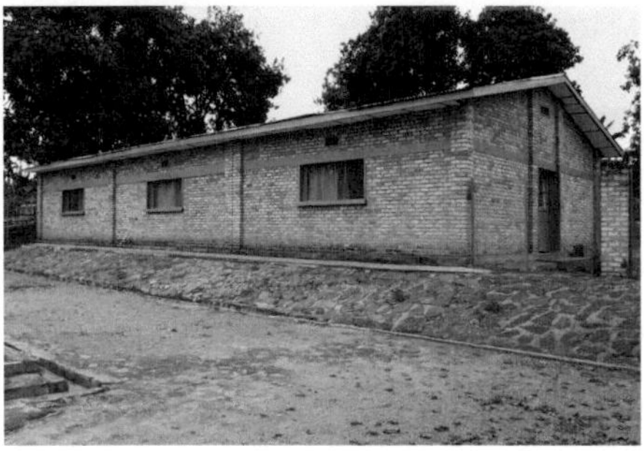
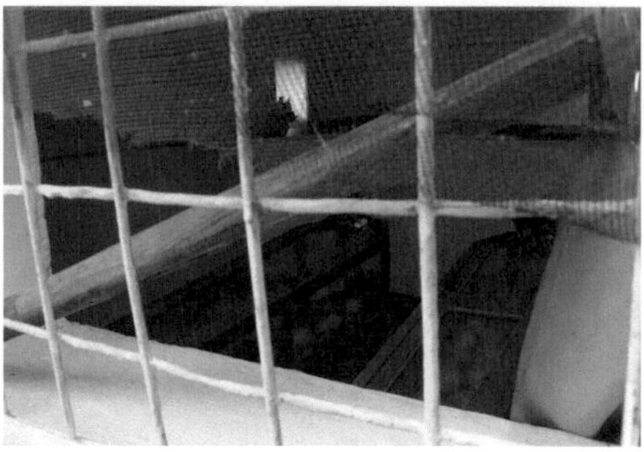

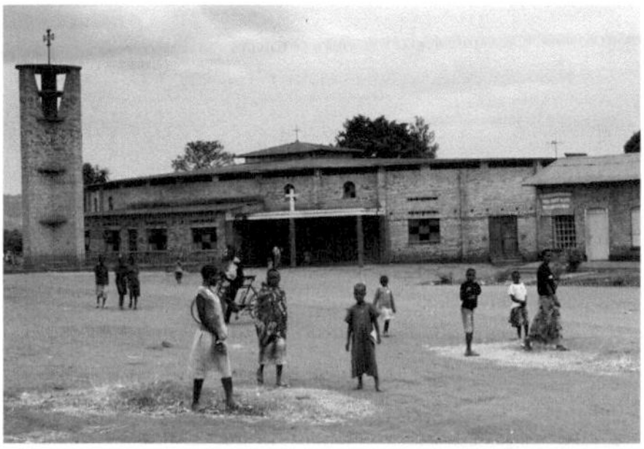

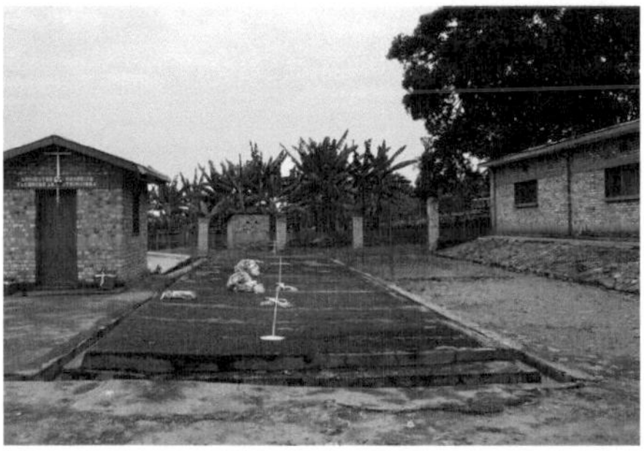

FIGURES 6.8 AND 6.9. (*top*) In 2013 the Mugombwa Genocide Memorial housed piles of victims' clothing in one room and displayed skulls in coffin-shaped glass-and-wood cases. Photos by Delia Duong Ba Wendel.

FIGURE 6.10. (*middle*) The church, opposite the Mugombwa Genocide Memorial, was restored to active service (pictured in 2013). Photo by Delia Duong Ba Wendel.

FIGURE 6.11. (*bottom*) The commemorative burial ground remains adjacent to the memorial (pictured in 2013). Photo by Delia Duong Ba Wendel.

referring to their politicization. It was used irrespective of how forthcoming residents were about their views of genocide memorials. *Inzibutso* is the Kinyarwanda term for genocide memorials. More generally, it refers to places or objects of memory. The adjective *zigaragara* (from the infinitive verb *kugaragara*) is multivalent in meaning. It is used to refer to things that are visible, ordered, and clearly demarcated. The alliteration in the repetition *gara-gara* reinforces the importance of order and visibility to what is described. The phrase suggests that today genocide memorials are "in their place": They are purposefully designated sites of memory that are known, regularly maintained, and available to view.

Some residents went so far as to say that because genocide memorials are *zigaragara*, their state-administered order and visibility helped to "prevent crimes before they occur."[8] This was a common view in the country, one specifically voiced by Ngoga, a thirty-three-year-old man (when I interviewed him in 2013) who fled the 1994 violence as a teenager and returned to live on his father's land near the Murambi Genocide Memorial a few years later. Many of the stories that I relay in this chapter concern the Murambi Genocide Memorial. Despite the site's exceptional aesthetic, interviews near Murambi were representative of opinions elsewhere in the country. The views of Murambi residents indicate the reach of state-authorized collective memory policies and their successful interpellation, despite the psychological and social impacts of the provocative memorial they live near.

Ngoga told me that he and his family visit the Murambi Genocide Memorial regularly during annual commemoration ceremonies. He explained that viewing victims' remains in a designated place of memory went a long way toward preventing crimes, including a future genocide. "People who see the bodies would not have the heart to wrong anyone," he claimed, "except people who have hearts as hard as stones."[9] On Ngoga's view, genocide memorial sites prevent the recurrence of mass violence by presenting material evidence of its consequences. They deter violence by appealing to viewers' humanity. Whether the sites are actual tools of crime prevention is debatable. But Ngoga's claims point to the moralizing narratives that public displays of victims at memorials generate. Viewing the dead is thought to separate those who are repulsed by the bodies and bones (and have a moral conscience) from those who are not affected (and are more likely to commit crimes).

In my conversations with rural residents, I also regularly asked what it was like to live next to memorials that display bodies and bones: "Utekereza iki kuri ziriya nzibutso zerekana imibiri n'amagufwa?" Even if not nearly as intense as Murambi, every local memorial that I visited had some dedicated place for the display of victims' skeletal remains, albeit typically minimal in number (figures

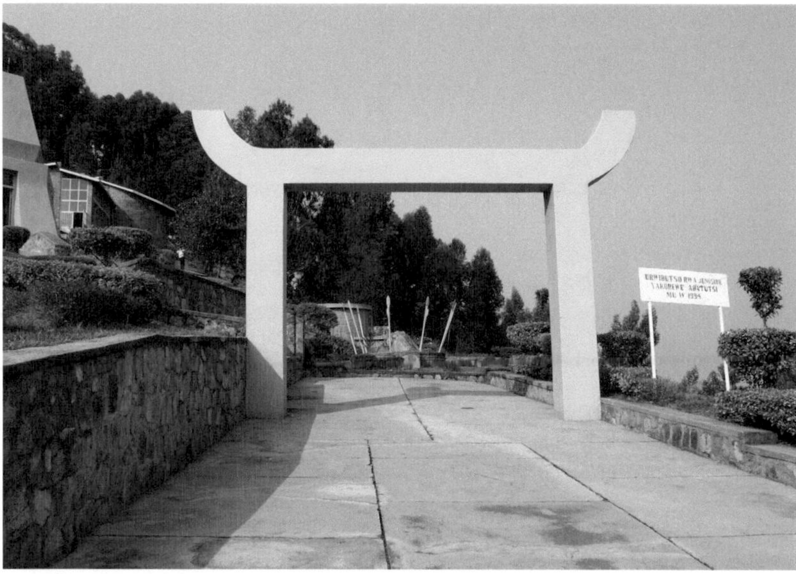

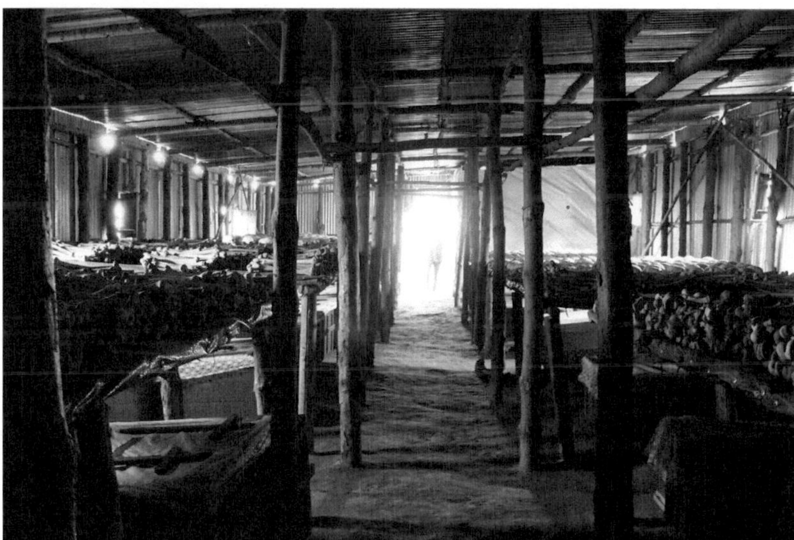

FIGURES 6.12 AND 6.13. *Inzibutso zigaragara*: Bisesero Genocide Memorial, in the west, was designed in 1995 by Vedaste Ngarambe and Athanase Ndutiye Kagahe but was completed only in 2018. In the interim, an annex structure displayed the bones of genocide victims (pictured in 2013). Photos by Delia Duong Ba Wendel.

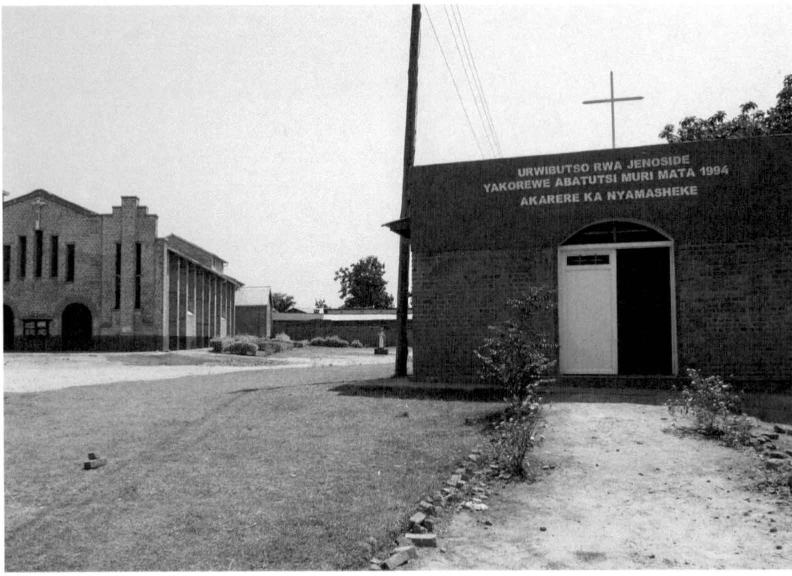


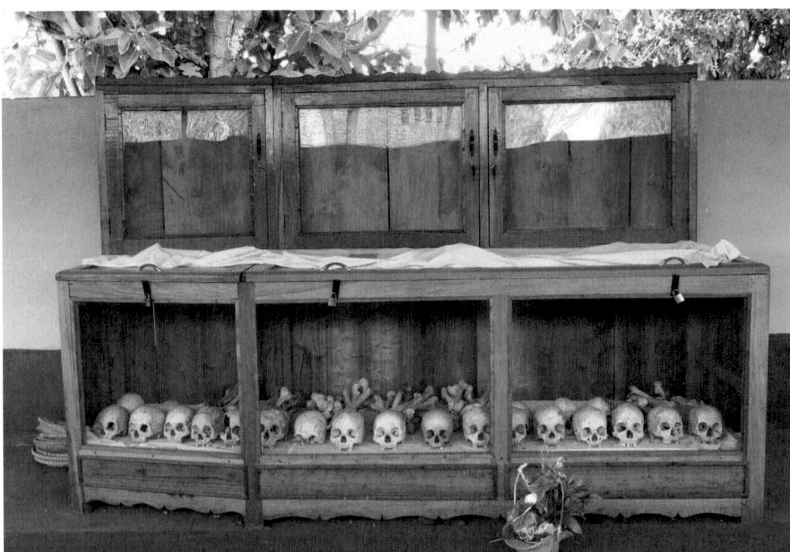

FIGURES 6.14 AND 6.15. *Inzibutso zigaragara*: The Nyamasheke Church Genocide Memorial comprises an open-air pavilion built over a concrete tomb for genocide victims; inside, a glass-and-wood cabinet displays a few representative skulls and long bones (pictured in 2013). Photos by Delia Duong Ba Wendel.

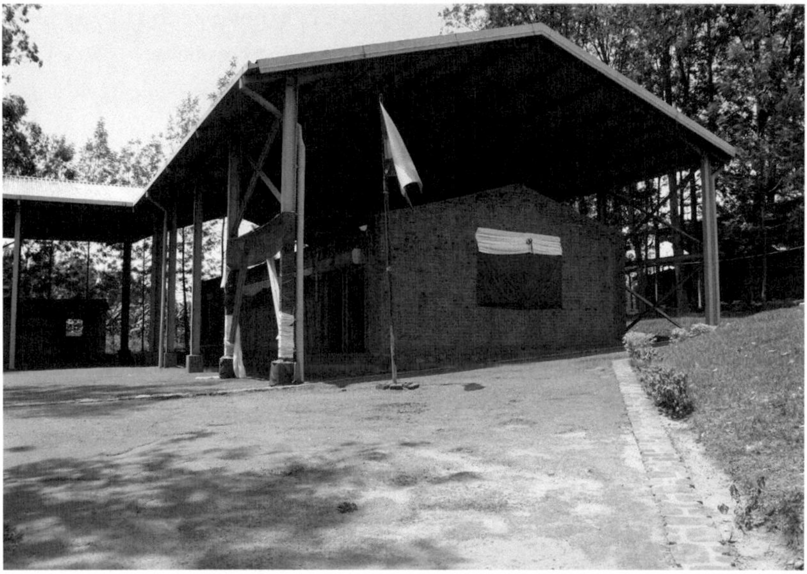

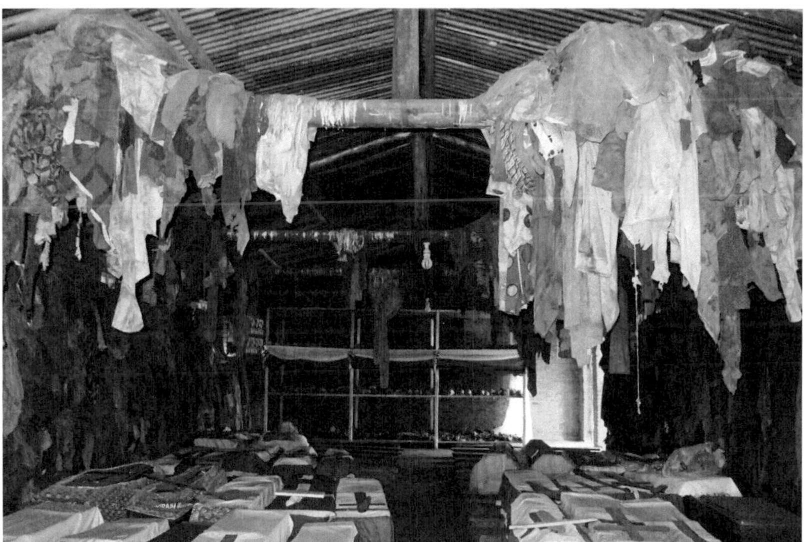

FIGURES 6.16 AND 6.17. *Inzibutso zigaragara*: At the Ntarama Genocide Memorial, the chapel today is protected by a steel structure. Inside, in 2013, shelving holding victims' skulls and long bones and coffins lined the floor, replacing the preserved massacre scene, while victims' clothing hung from the rafters. In 2018 only the clothing remained on display. Photos by Delia Duong Ba Wendel.

6.12–6.17). Most of the individuals I spoke with did not question the aesthetics of state genocide memorials. Their reticence to relay criticism was in part a result of the government's active vigilance for and punishment of genocide "revisionism, negationism, and trivialisation."[10] In this context, most people reflected instead, in less direct ways, on the nature of the sites as state-authorized public representations of genocide memory. They speculated rhetorically about the purpose of memorials, added some of their personal reactions to the display of victims' remains, and, to a lesser extent, described their own preferences for commemorating the genocide.

Esmée, a woman in her early thirties, viewed *inzibutso* similarly to others in the country. I spoke with her in her home on a plot downhill from the Murambi Genocide Memorial in 2013.[11] Like Ngoga, Esmée was fourteen years old during the genocide. She and her family were not targeted during the massacres. Esmée had grown up in the area but only moved next to the memorial in 2002 after she married. I asked her a question that I posed to every person I spoke with: "How do you choose to remember the genocide?" (*Ni ubuhe buryo mwahitamo bwo kwibuka ibyabaye muri jenoside?*) Esmée responded:

> How can I tell you that? I believe that the way that the government chose for us is enough for us. That way of always remembering during the month of April—it's when we remember ours [relatives], and those things are good because they prevent us from forgetting what happened in our Rwanda. I think there is no other way to remember . . . the bodies don't bother me. Because if they talked about it [the genocide] only in stories without it being visible—I was a child who saw what happened, but young people [today] will think they are just stories, and it will disappear. When you look at them [the bodies] in person, you say, "These things happened here."[12]

Not merely rhetorical, the question that began her reply, "How can I tell you that?" marked Esmée's difficulty in conceiving of individual choice in forms of genocide remembrance. Indeed, my question about individual preferences evoked the greatest confusion in respondents throughout the country. Most viewed decisions regarding genocide heritage as within the government's domain alone. Esmée's response was common: It stopped short of imagining alternative or nonstate forms of memorialization. Elaborating, Esmée claimed that the government was wholly competent to choose commemorative forms for its citizens. The government's way of remembering "is sufficient for us," she said, using the adjectival form of a verb (*guhaza*) that typically refers to common goods: That amount of water is enough for us; this food satisfies us. Her statement's phrasing communicated some combination of the instrumental nature of genocide remembrance and its personal challenges. As she noted, the work of remembering the genocide was difficult, but it must be done.

The views of residents living around the Murambi Genocide Memorial illustrated the negotiation between personal and national preferences for Rwanda's genocide heritage aesthetic. Their perspectives provided some sense of what it means to live near memorials that prominently display the remains of victims. When I asked what Esmée thought of the display of victims' bodies at the Murambi Genocide Memorial, she declared that they did not bother her. Rather, she underscored the important role that victims' bodies had in genocide remembrance: to ensure that the violence was believed, recognized, and remembered in future. Esmée worried that if the bodies were not seen, people (especially children born after the genocide) might not believe the histories that they represent. Those stories would then "disappear," unrecognized. This notion—that the display of victims' remains at memorial sites serves the education of future generations—echoes government objectives.[13] Taken together with her earlier claim, "ubwo baduhitiyemo bwari buduhagije" (what they chose for us was sufficient) suggested that if the state had selected those memorial forms to facilitate remembering, they were authorized and adequate to the task.

Esmée's state-mediated views of genocide memorials were similar to those voiced elsewhere in the country. Many noted the benefits they receive by publicly complying with government commemoration activities. Some individuals gain social capital or goodwill within their communities. Most enjoy, as a result of their public engagement in remembrance activities, less scrutiny by local authorities and avoid punishment or government aid withdrawal. Underscoring that point, relatively few individuals declared that they preferred to remember the genocide in private (79 of 620, or 13 percent). Most defined private remembrance either as a place for personal reflection or as family commemorations, both of which were contrasted with public ceremonies and official memorials. Only 31 of those 79 individuals favored private remembrance exclusively. The remaining 48 chose private forms of remembrance alongside annual commemoration ceremonies (37), genocide memorials (6), or songs (5).[14]

Of the 620 people I spoke with throughout the country, most named annual commemoration ceremonies as their preferred way to remember the genocide (410; 67 percent). Comparably, only around a third (173) preferred to remember the genocide at memorial sites. Despite the overwhelming preference for state-sponsored annual commemoration ceremonies, I do not think these responses diminish the importance of memorial sites as forms of genocide remembrance. Particularly telling in this regard is the number of people who preferred genocide memorials that displayed victims' remains (115) versus those who preferred to visit only places of burial (58). That imbalance indicates rural Rwandans' recognition of the government's genocide heritage aesthetic (the conservation of genocide victims, material evidence, and places of massacre) as a representation of national collective memory. Their endorsement of annual commemoration ceremonies further reinforces, at minimum, that residents recognize the importance of state performances of genocide remembrance. Both aspects demonstrate the governing regime's central role in establishing postgenocide social norms, particularly around public trauma heritage.

I did not find identity to be a significant determinant of differences in preferences about genocide remembrance. Of the 146 people I interviewed throughout the country who self-identified as genocide survivors, most valued state-sponsored forms of remembrance, such as commemoration ceremonies (104), memorial sites (36), and songs (44). Among them, only 21 genocide survivors chose private forms of remembrance; they make up around a third of the total number of respondents (79) with similar preferences. Of the scant 18 people who self-identified as genocide perpetrators, there was general agreement with this view: Most preferred state-sponsored commemoration ceremonies (14) and others preferred, in equal measure, memorial sites (4), songs (4), and private forms of remembrance (4). Demographics in Rwanda today suggest that the majority of the population living around genocide memorials has few clearly discernible relationships to the killings—identifying with Hutu lineages, most were neither targets of nor participants in killings, and a growing youth population either does not remember the events in 1994 or understands these events only through the deaths or actions of family members. This does not mean that mass violence does not profoundly impact those who experience its occurrence in a variety of ways—as survivors of genocidal violence, those who attempted to rescue victims, witnesses to those acts, neighbors who fled the country fearing reprisal, and family members (including now-grown children) who are related to both those accused of crimes and victims of them. Rather, this speaks to the inadvisability of making hasty assumptions regarding relationships between positionality or the direct experience of genocide and the impacts of memorials. As they are designed to do, the state's forms of genocide heritage perpetuate variable but lasting impacts on most Rwandans from a range of ages and backgrounds.

The relatively low preference for private remembrance, across all positionalities, is curious, however, particularly given the personal and enduring afterlives of this violence. Based on my conversations, I think it represents an acknowledgment of the dominant role of state-authorized forms of collective memory in addition to, or in place of, individual remembrance. The overwhelming diminution of private remembrance in the context of state-organized genocide heritage was partly related to my questions' proximity to the twentieth commemoration. Moreover, twenty years after the genocide, few private memorials remained, owing in large part to the government's demand that bodies in private grave sites be exhumed and incorporated into district and national burial sites. Respondents' lack of disclosure of private remembrance practices also follows decades of marginalization—by the Catholic Church and the colonial and postcolonial governing regimes—of customary practices like *guterekera* ancestor worship and related funeral rites. As a result, as Ngoga's and Esmée's reflections demonstrate, most people in Rwanda considered the state as the rightful steward of genocide heritage, with remembrance fulfilling either a civic duty or a national obligation.

Despite the consensus on the role of the government, there were substantial disagreements on whether genocide memorials should display the bodies and bones of victims. In 2013, 204 people I spoke with claimed that exhibiting victims' remains at memorials was important for civic education. A similar number of people (202) disagreed and did not prefer victims' remains to be visible. Many elaborated, claiming that seeing the displays of skulls, long bones, or bodies triggered painful emotions or bad memories. Few people (only 15) were willing to equivocate and support the educational value of victims' remains while enduring the sites' challenging emotional effects. To extrapolate from these views: most people in Rwanda—regardless of their identity or their history with violence—have strong views on the display of victims and see them as either necessary to genocide history or detrimental to personal well-being.

One last perspective from Albert, who was fifty-six in 2013, reinforces the social and behavioral effects of genocide memorials that Ngoga introduced earlier. Albert was imprisoned for genocide crimes. When he completed his sentence in 2009, Albert returned to the area near Murambi, where he had grown up and his father had owned land. Albert died from cancer a month before I returned to the settlement surrounding Murambi in 2018, so the following exchanges represent only his experience during the first four years after his prison release. At that time, he was adapting to living in the area as an *uwemeye icyaha* (reformed perpetrator), a phrase that literally refers to someone who has confessed to their crimes and, it is assumed, is engaged in some process of penance.

In 2013 Albert somberly and carefully responded to my questions about annual commemorations and the display of victims' bodies at Murambi. When I asked what he thought about the memorial, Albert reiterated aspects of *inzibutso zigaragara*: He thought the memorial was "good" because it was fenced and clearly defined, had security, and was kept up well. He then segued quickly to his visits to the memorial, underscoring that every year, when the government announces the date for the local commemoration ceremony, "we go there of our own free will—no one bothers us—we light a candle, and when the time runs out they tell us: You can go."[15] His rushed elaboration conveyed his procedural practice of genocide remembrance, which was carefully overseen by local authorities: His annual attendance at the memorial is socially obligatory, even if it is not legally compulsory. He is only allowed to leave Murambi's grounds when the allotted time for the ceremony is over. Commemorations at the memorial not only organize the local community's time but also reinforce a postgenocide social order.[16] During our conversation Albert repeatedly mentioned his family's voluntary participation in government-organized commemoration activities. It suggested his social precarity in relation to neighbors and government authorities. Annual commemorations presented both a reminder of his role in the genocide and a means to publicly atone for the actions that led to his social status.

When I asked how he preferred to remember the genocide, Albert responded in a roundabout way. First, he explained that he wasn't wholly to blame for the crimes he had committed: "For me, what happened in 1994—due to the fact that I had no leadership in it—it hasn't been good for me. . . . No, it hasn't been good for me."[17] But realizing that he had gone too far to elicit sympathy for the circumstances that led to his participation, Albert returned to acknowledge the gravity of the violence: "It happened of course, and it concerns us, and we realize that it is something really bad."[18] That last statement approximated what state and society urged Albert to say as an *uwemeye icyaha*. At that juncture, Albert shifted to more vociferously claim the transformative powers of genocide memorials and their exhibition of victims:

> But we appreciate that we have a place where we can commemorate it [the genocide]. Remembering is about being with people, discussing, sharing, laughing, asking for water from each other; and then you see that they are removed from us for no reason. That person who created that policy of remembering, of taking time to think about the victims and remember them: We found that it is very good, and we appreciate it. We can also show our own [our children], who are still young, that it [the genocide] is something awful, in a way that no one would consider doing it again.[19]

His statement seemed to be an embellished afterthought, but with it Albert claimed that commemoration ceremonies foster a sense of community that he does not usually experience in everyday life on the hillside. When he mentioned that the commemorations force others to realize that "they are removed from us for no reason," he referred to genocide survivors in particular who were suspicious and distrustful of him and his family (and perpetrators in general). Because of his social status, Albert appreciated his inclusion in the commemorative community that forms annually and the educational messages that the ceremonies and memorial communicate to future generations.

But the sociopolitical order that the memorial and annual commemorations reinforce cannot be easily excised from the circumstances of Albert's participation in state remembrance rituals. Remembering is required of all citizens, and the government especially expects it of genocide perpetrators like him. Albert participated because it was mandatory. Power differentials among citizens become more legible during performances of genocide remembrance and are especially impactful (and not merely symbolic) in ceremonies that take place in local communities.[20] Those effects were most clear when I asked Albert what he thought about the display of bodies uphill from his house. He prefaced his personal view by reiterating the government's sovereign control of genocide heritage: "For us, due to the power [*ubushobozi*] that we do not have, there is nothing we can do about it."[21] He then reflected on the bodies' impact on him: "I find that it causes me shame because I look at those many people there, lying like that, bodies there, and I realize that what was done in 1994 was something awful."[22] Given his previous statements, it was not clear whether the displayed bodies, his imprisonment, or other factors, including social stigma, prompted his realization that "what was done in 1994 was something awful." Regardless, Murambi's mummified victims presented Albert with a symbolic site from which to communicate his repentance to neighbors and authorities. At least annually and until his death in 2018, he performed genocide remembrance (and thereby his civic obligation) by viewing the bodies of the dead.

### *Inzibutso Zitagaragara*

Various sites of memory remain in tension with authorized genocide heritage—not because they challenge the need for and value of genocide remembrance but because they add to the history of violence in the country in ways that remain at odds with government priorities. I call these places *inzibutso zi-ta-garagara* to contrast how residents spoke about state-managed memorials. These sites of memory are *not* clearly defined, ordered, or publicly visible and acknowledged (the *ta* infix indicates the negative). *Inzibutso zitagaragara* exist within a particular realm in Rwanda, characterized by what anthropologist Jennie Burnet calls an "amplified silence."[23] Burnet cogently advances this concept to describe the Rwandan government's sublimation of certain experiences of violence and survival. Such experiences do not, as she says, "fit neatly into the dyadic Hutu perpetrator/Tutsi victim logic."[24] Burnet traces the variety of those embodied discourses:

> Many Hutu died in the genocide because they opposed the extremist regime that chose genocide as its policy, because they "looked" Tutsi, because they were married to Tutsi, or because they hid or protected Tutsi. Following the genocide, many Tutsi lived in the refugee camps in Zaire (now Democratic Republic of the Congo) and Tanzania alongside Hutu civilians, former government officials, soldiers, and Interahamwe militamen who fled Rwanda and the advancing RPF [Rwandan Patriotic Front].... Some Tutsi were married to Hutu either through marriages that preceded the genocide or through marriages that were forced upon Tutsi women and girls during the genocide. Others had succeeded in passing as "Hutu," had escaped the genocide, or were afraid to return to Rwanda, where they might be targeted by the RPF-led government or RPF soldiers. RPF soldiers killed Hutu and Tutsi civilians in individual acts of revenge for the genocide, in military operations to eliminate "perpetrators" who lived in internally displaced camps, in small-scale massacres, or in counterinsurgency operations to eliminate opposition to the new RPF-led government.[25]

Burnet notes that her summary does not convey a full range of experiences. However, it demonstrates the complexity of violence and its aftermaths along with the lack of representation that many individuals endure in Rwanda today. Silences are regulated both by the government's control over genocide-related narratives and by citizens' strategies for self-protection. The latter is effectively a self-silencing for those who fear that government-regulated public discourse is inhospitable to their experiences during the genocide and the violence thereafter.

Amplified silences are the result of the ways in which authorized genocide heritage dominates public landscapes and creates a duty to remember, which, in the context of punitive state control of historical narratives in Rwanda, suppresses choice and difference. When transposed to the analysis of social landscapes, amplified silences might be more aptly referred to as *amplified absences*. But they do not merely trace a lack; amplified absences in public trauma heritage provide trace evidence of persistent counter-memories held by individuals who do not "neatly fit." Barely visible but nevertheless enduring, those *inzibutso zitagaragara* are enlivened by what philosopher Nancy Fraser calls "subaltern counterpublics," where members of subordinated groups challenge the values and narratives upheld by dominant groups in unequal societies.[26] Trauma heritage sites remembered by counterpublics are not merely marginalized by hegemonic forces. They are key organizing spaces in which such groups "invent and circulate counter-discourses ... [and] formulate oppositional interpretations of their identities, interests, and needs."[27] I have come to understand this larger, less controlled landscape of counter-memory in Rwanda along three valences, as either underrecognized, unauthorized, or prohibited by the government.

*Underrecognized trauma heritage* refers to genocide memories that are not administered by government authorities. This is a geography of death and survival that is intimately known at a local level and is typically aligned with the government's own memorialization principles. Falling outside state management, underrecognized memories identify the limits of the government's ability to fully control genocide memory even while decentralized governance regulates permissible memorialization practices at the village level. The *ibuye* (rock) that I detail in the prologue and chapter 1 serves as a ready example (figures P.1, P.2, and 1.18–1.21).

*Unauthorized trauma heritage*, by contrast, refers to commemorative practices, places of memory, or narratives of experiences related to the genocide that are not sanctioned by the government. These include private burials of genocide victims that remain under the radar to thwart the forced relocation of loved ones' bodies to nationally managed burial sites. This category of counterpublic trauma heritage also includes the more controversial memories held by Hutu wives and husbands of Tutsi genocide victims who are not officially recognized as genocide survivors because of their ethnicity. Those memories take discrete forms in the personal memory landscapes of unauthorized survivors and remembrance; they are rarely spoken about or given public presence.

The last subcategory of counterpublic trauma heritage concerns prohibited memories of violence. *Prohibited trauma heritage* is distinguished from unauthorized places of memory by its content. Whereas unauthorized sites refer to memories of the genocide, prohibited memories concern reprisal violence during and immediately after the genocide, committed by the Rwandan Patriotic Army (RPA) during the genocide and by the RPF-led government military (comprising largely RPA troops) after the genocide. These memories are banned from public speech and are the most withdrawn from public view. Examples today consist of unmarked grave sites or places where that violence occurred, which have no autonomous forms of identification and can be interpreted only by individuals.

In the following I focus primarily on unauthorized and prohibited trauma heritage. Among the three counter-memory landscapes, they bring into strongest relief the work of repair yet to be done. Fewer political tensions remain in the interface of underrecognized and authorized trauma heritage. There will always be gaps between local and national remembrance, but keeping vigilant for subnational genocide heritage can inform and invigorate authorized collective memory in Rwanda. By contrast, the state's active forgetting and concealment of unauthorized and prohibited trauma heritage produce amplified silences and absences, reproducing forms of subjugation and unilateral power. These are the inequalities to which repair is addressed, driven by an ethics of nonerasure as a precondition for equal representation, citizenship, and opportunities for fulfillment.

South African psychologist Pumla Gobodo-Madikizela captures the struggle and hope of repair in the aftermath of historical violence. She advances an argument for a "reparative humanism," imploring affected parties to consider the objectives and impacts of approaches to repair amid past and ongoing brutality. Gobodo-Madikizela writes:

> The significance of the notion of "the reparative" lies in the fact that the work of healing after historical trauma must necessarily be an on-going process. "Reparative" suggests movement, an engagement in a constant search for the emergence of human moments that can create a sense of solidarity and transcend old dividing lines that promote othering. The quest for reparative humanism gestures towards transformative moments and new relational experiences. . . . This way of thinking about "the Other," even an other responsible for one's pain, arises out of concern for the broader societal goals of national healing.[28]

Gobodo-Madikizela draws examples from postapartheid South Africa to insist on both the unsettled and ongoing processes of repair that a history of racialized oppression and violence demands. In her case, the onus of repair is on state authorities and a wider society, with particular emphasis on white South Africans reluctant to confront their roles in and benefits gained from apartheid. On her view, victims of and witnesses to that violence, especially those willing to represent their experiences in public forms of truth telling, provide a "holding environment" that allows those responsible to face the violence and injustice they perpetrate.[29] Unauthorized and prohibited trauma heritage perform similar roles as places of witness: as anticipatory holding environments for the work of repair yet to be done.

## UNDERRECOGNIZED TRAUMA HERITAGE

There is no shortage of underrecognized trauma heritage in Rwanda. Sites of genocidal violence, and of victim retrieval, form a backdrop to everyday life. Those sites of memory are rarely made legible by governmental intervention. They are places that are, instead, cared for by local communities: tended, for decades, like the *imihati* (corn plants) that now encircle the location where forty-seven children were found near the *ibuye* (rock) in Rwamagana District. Of the many dimensions of individual and collective genocide memory in Rwanda that underrecognized trauma heritage elicits, one of the most resonant aspects for me has been the sites' relationality. I learned this through many conversations, but one stands out because it was least expected.

On the first day that I spoke with Mario Ibarra in person, a continent away from Rwanda in southern Chile, I prefaced our conversation by saying that I had brought copies of the photographs that Louis Kanamugire had given me in Kigali.[30] That mere mention of Louis prompted Mario to recall an experience he shared with him in western Rwanda, a few years after the genocide. They were there to try to find the mass graves where the bodies of Louis's parents, and most of his extended family, had been hidden. Mario recalled Louis's rare expression of vulnerability. "I will need you on this one," he remembered Louis saying. Despite their time working together, first in investigating massacre sites and then in conserving the bodies and bones of victims, Louis had never before been so shaken. Mario was also profoundly affected: Usually, he recounted, he would attempt to be more detached in his handling of remains and documentation of a genocide site. In this case, when they located the mass graves, Mario was just as methodical in his photographic and written documentation of the site, but he moved gingerly in his handling of Louis's loved ones. As our conversations continued over the next days, and Mario opened his personal archive to me, we located several photographs that Mario had taken during that trip (among them figure 1.8).

Years later, when I was able to return to Rwanda, I brought physical copies of those photographs to Louis. In our conversation I ventured into the topic carefully, unsure of Louis's emotional reaction. "Zana, ndebe" (Bring them, let me see), he told me. He immediately recognized the situation, "Ehh . . . turi i Murama" (This is us in Murama), he mumbled in Kinyarwanda, before switching into French: "It is my parents . . . it's . . . yes. Yes, I remember this well: It was Mario who took them [the photographs]. Oh, this is actually a good memory. It was in 1996, and I was able to find the bodies of my parents. So, this was the day of the reburial."[31] What I remember so distinctly about that conversation is the combination of sorrow and fondness that animated Louis's face as he narrated his memory of that day. For him, and so many others across the country who endure the afterlives of that violence, the places where his family were found and reburied remain palpably in memory.

And yet, returning to the *Preliminary Report* that Louis had written, I could not find mention of his family.[32] The reburial of approximately forty-five hundred individuals within the surrounding community in Murama Commune was, by contrast, well documented. It was also archived in Mario's photographic documentation of the Murama Commune reburial process and ceremony (figures 5.10 and 5.12–5.22). The area was clearly of personal significance to the authors, who had developed a comprehensive picture of mass violence in the country. But Louis's personal losses were nowhere registered. This is highly significant—not only for Louis's and Mario's efforts to render the collective memory of trauma as an objective, reparative history but also for the endurance of the site's significance in forms other than national recognition. In this context, some sites are reserved for personal memory rather than public recognition. They are also, in many cases, tacitly shared by individuals, worlds apart, connected by a bond born of significant trauma.

A range of similar underrecognized memories of genocidal violence form a rhizomatic substrate of local remembrance in Rwanda. Those sites sit quietly alongside more publicly performative genocide memorials and commemorations. They may remain underrecognized as authorized genocide heritage but nonetheless create a holding environment of relations among those who still remember.

## UNAUTHORIZED TRAUMA HERITAGE

Attention to unauthorized memories enables the recognition of very different spatial expressions of genocide heritage. For many older women in Rwanda today, especially those who survived their children and husbands, traumatic experiences are kept close: They are felt more in the body than in open landscapes. The embodied nature of traumatic memories is a common aspect of officially recognized genocide heritage, but often there is no other option for those whose grief has limited public reflection. Céleste, an older genocide survivor living in a village located an hour's drive southwest of the capital, once told me that her most difficult memories are not attached to places. Instead, she said, "I have them in my heart—they feel like small ants [*inshishi*]. I remember many things, and they feel like ants crawling on my heart. There are times that I feel like if I coughed, I would spit them up."[33] For Céleste and so many others I spoke with, memories, especially painful ones, do not exist out in the world. They are kept inside, in one's body, where you feel them like ants at your throat or crawling over your heart. The world outside is for making do—with one's neighbor, grief, and precarious livelihoods—all of which become harder with diminished family support.

Memories without a place in the world can remain internalized; they can also become ubiquitous, pervading entire landscapes because there is no single location where they belong. In the absence of the public recognition of one's pain, the embodiment of trauma can feel very lonely. Nkunzi was sixty-five when I visited her in 2018. From her home she had a prominent view of the Murambi Genocide Memorial (figures 6.18 and 6.19). She cared for a son and a grandson in a modest house that her husband's uncle had given them when they married in the 1970s. From that house, she had witnessed the demolition of houses on the hilltop to build the Murambi Technical School and later, in 1994, the genocide. I first spoke with Nkunzi in 2013, and when I did, she identified herself as someone who was not targeted in the genocide. Nkunzi explained, almost cryptically, "Those things

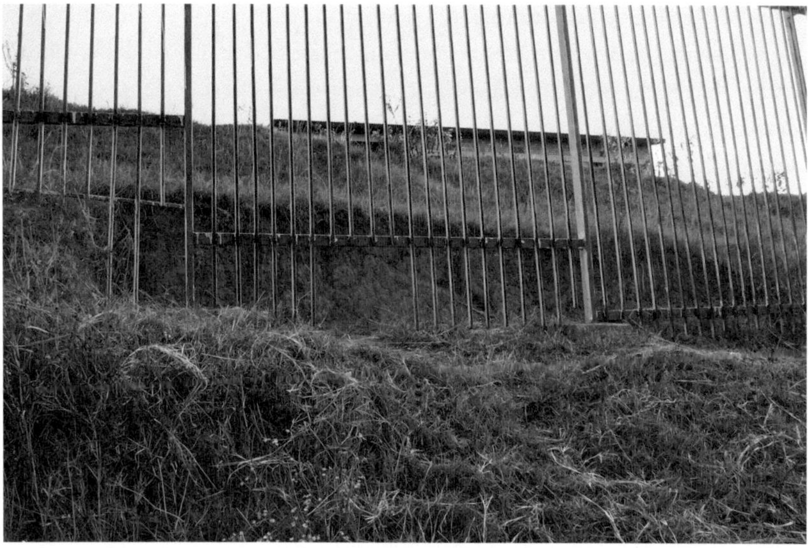

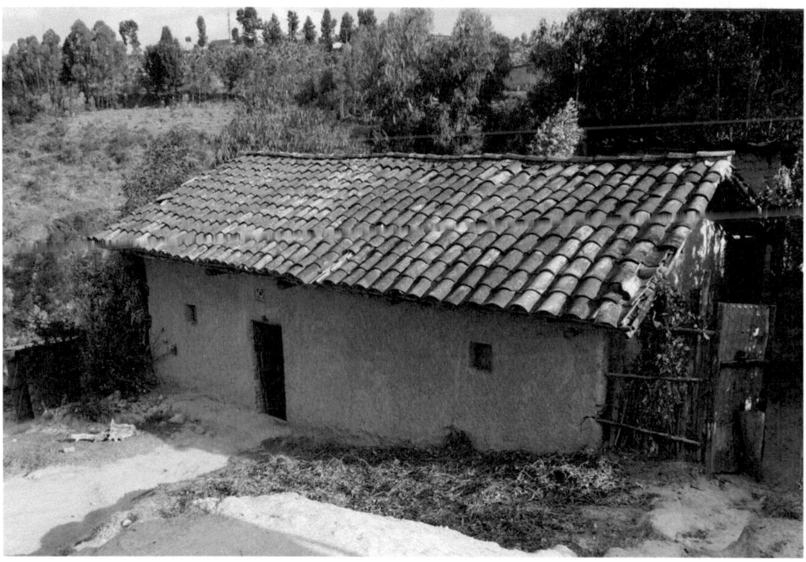

FIGURES 6.18 AND 6.19. *Inzibutso zitagaragara*: A home on the periphery of the Murambi Genocide Memorial (*top, on the hilltop behind the metal fence*), in 2013 and 2018. Photos by Delia Duong Ba Wendel.

that they [genocide perpetrators] did never made us happy—we suffered too."[34] By *we*, Nkunzi meant Hutu in her community, like herself, who did not commit crimes during the genocide. In context, I understood her statement to convey a deep compassion for victims and survivors of the targeted killings. She claimed strong solidarity with neighbors who died and their relatives. But I did not understand then that she also hesitatingly identified as a genocide survivor.

When I next spoke with her five years later, Nkunzi's body began to tremble visibly when we talked about the Murambi Genocide Memorial. This time, she revealed more about her own suffering, telling me, "I went through a lot of difficult times. I lost a husband, I lost a child; I lost others too. Those are things that hurt a person, and you don't tell them to others. You keep quiet because it's hard."[35] In addition to the pain of talking about her losses during the genocide, Nkunzi was reticent to disclose this information because as a Hutu, she is not officially considered a genocide survivor by the government.[36] Yet Nkunzi was married to a Tutsi husband and had a child and extended family who were killed in 1994. Her losses are just as real as those experienced by recognized survivors.

In our 2013 conversation, I had asked Nkunzi what she thought of the bodies on display at Murambi. She then mused, resignedly, "They make me sad of course, but when one is sad, what can we do? There is nothing else we can do. We go and look, and we say that those things should never happen again."[37] Without recourse to state and societal recognition given to others who lost family members in the genocide, Nkunzi felt powerless to choose how to commemorate them. Her statement indicated a pragmatic acceptance of the government's approach to genocide heritage. In 2018, however, she was more open about how the memorial provoked feelings of sadness: "When I go inside the memorial, I see them [the bodies] immediately, and I feel . . . I remember the fighting . . . and I say, 'God, may these things never happen again, may they never happen again or ever come back!' There is actually no place I could go and fail to remember something [about the genocide]."[38] The ambivalence that Nkunzi expressed through both statements was common among the many people in Rwanda whose suffering remains unacknowledged by local and national authorities. On the one hand, the presence of the Murambi Genocide Memorial did not matter to Nkunzi because the deaths of her family were always with her; she carried the burden of their loss every day. On the other hand, Murambi's proximity to her home was a constant reminder, pulling on her traumatic experiences and exposing them to view.

Between the isolation of memories felt only as bodily sensations and that of a landscape in which past traumas are everywhere, domestic life emerges as a vital site of repair. On this view, which attends in particular to women's experiences, a home can serve as a different type of memorial, a place that both symbolizes and enacts relationships with community, individual and family stories, and the struggles of everyday life. On the outskirts of a village in eastern Rwanda originally built by the United Nations Development Program (UNDP) after the genocide, Agathe described the ordinary environment of her home (figures 6.20 and 6.21). She evoked a domestic form of trauma heritage at the interface of public and private pain. From 1994 to 2001, Agathe was imprisoned without trial for genocide-related crimes. I spoke with her in 2013, twelve years after she was released from prison and moved near the UNDP village, and again in 2018 when she was eighty-eight years old.[39]

In 1994 Agathe's home was the location of a betrayal. Agathe was the second wife of a husband who died just before the genocide. After his death, her husband's son (from his first wife) insisted that Agathe marry him; she refused.[40] As retribution, her stepson accused her of cooking for the Interahamwe extremists who committed genocidal killings. In 2013, when I first spoke with her, Agathe insisted several times that she had remained in her house during the killings and, afterward, refused to join other neighbors fleeing the area.[41] Claiming that she stayed at home was her way of signaling that she did not participate in any crimes. She regarded not leaving the region as something a Hutu person who was not guilty of crimes would do. In 1994 the new governing authorities found her at home and imprisoned her. Jailed falsely for seven years for aiding and abetting *génocidaires*, Agathe was released only when her stepson died in prison. He was also accused of genocide crimes. The authorities were compelled to admit that they had no evidence for her alleged support of the Interahamwe.

After she was released from prison, Agathe received a new home. The house—a simple two-room mud brick structure with a corrugated metal roof—signified a return to ordinary life after its suspension. It was made possible through community acts of repair: Mud bricks and labor were contributed by Catholic and Protestant charities, and her son-in-law installed a government-provided metal roof to replace the grass thatch, which had been leaking in the rainy season. When I visited in 2013, the house was located on the periphery of the planned settlement, in a place of relative disorder where families desiring proximity to the village's infrastructure settled. Agathe's son-in-law called it "the place where people lost theirs" because the banana fields around them were where genocide survivors in the village found their dead relatives.[42]

In 2013 my sense was that despite having lived there for twelve years, Agathe did not feel like she really belonged. Immediately after she relayed that she had been falsely accused of helping *génocidaires* and imprisoned, Agathe reiterated that she had moved to the edge of a village that predominantly housed genocide survivors.[43] She felt tension with her new neighbors. Nonetheless, after several years in

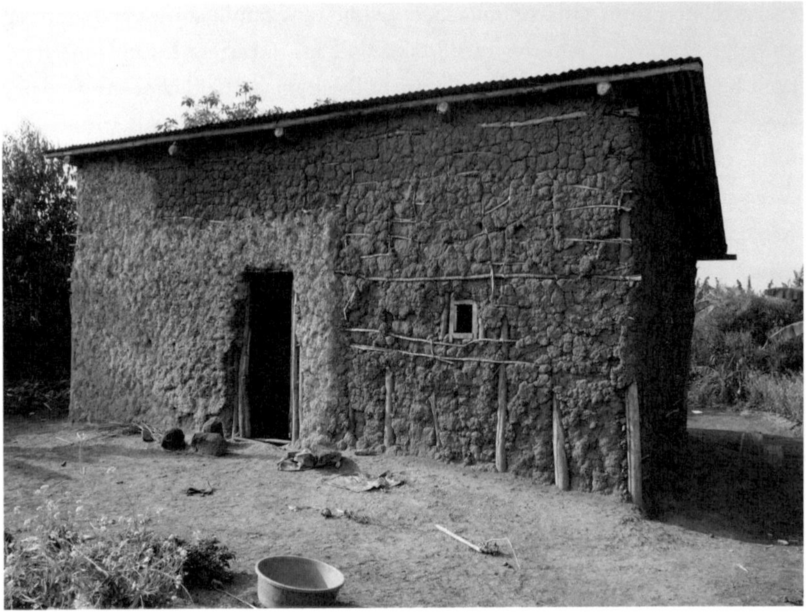

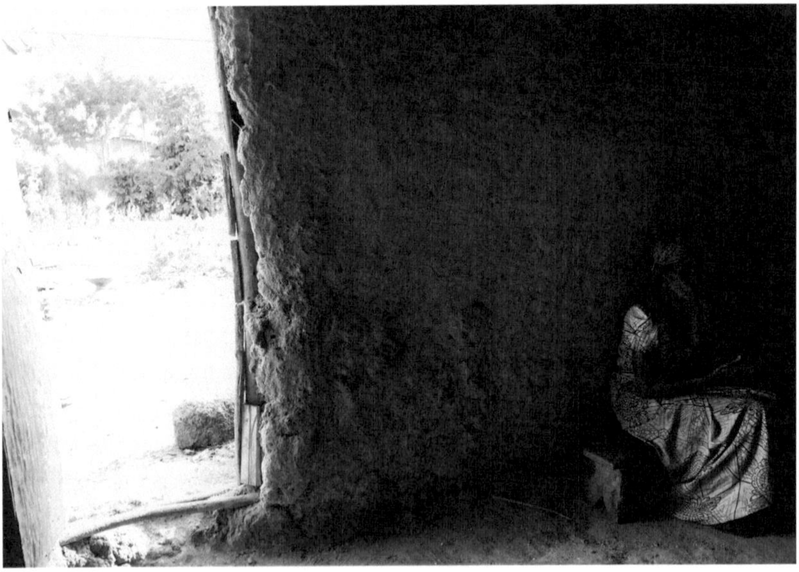

FIGURES 6.20 AND 6.21. *Inzibutso zitagaragara*: A home on the periphery of a village evokes a domestic form of trauma heritage at the interface of public and private pain. Inside sits Agathe (photographed with permission), 2018. Photos by Delia Duong Ba Wendel.

prison, Agathe's new home signified that she had one, that she had a place to which she could lay claim. When the prison authorities told her that she was free, she had been eating. "They made me drop the plate ... and I went home. God called me, and I went home."[44] In her telling, she left the place that fed and housed her to go to a piece of land that her husband left her that did not have a house. Once it was built, her new home signified her ability to be housed despite all that she had gone through. But her home was not merely of personal significance; it served as a symbolic interface between Agathe and her neighbors.

In 2018 I had trouble finding Agathe's house again: It was no longer on the periphery of the village but in the middle of a number of homes newly developed near the original settlement, attracted by the site's water and electricity. As a result, Agathe no longer lived on the edge of a community. I returned to the settlement's center and knocked on the door of the original village leader, an eighty-seven-year-old Tutsi man who had moved to the village with his wife from Uganda after 1994.[45] Four of their children had died while fighting with the RPA during the genocide. Our conversation focused largely on what he thought was required for reconciliation after the genocide. He then asked me if I knew the *umukecuru*, the old woman, living in the village extension. He was referring to Agathe, and though subtle, mentioning her at that juncture positioned her as a symbolic figure in the community's reconciliation process. Given her history, and his positionality as a veteran affiliated with the RPA and RPF, he seemed to say that it was possible for those falsely accused to live together with genocide survivors without resentment or antagonism. He took me to Agathe's home, where they embraced as if they were dear friends.

Agathe's home in this sense was an extension of her positionality and a reflection on larger social relations. She was the well-known *umukecuru* who had been accused of genocide crimes, had served time, and had been released to land where a community of mostly Tutsi returnees and survivors had settled. She was also an older widow, with a precarious livelihood and limited ability to take care of herself, whose social network was also sparse, at least initially, as a close relative of someone who had committed genocide crimes.

I read Agathe's home as a domestic form of trauma heritage because of the social work it does. Her home exists despite her false imprisonment; it registers the pain of that betrayal and loss along with her struggle and survival. It also represents a genocide history and her own familial relations, with which her neighbors in the village have had to reckon, personally and more broadly. In 2000 Amnesty International estimated that around 125,000 individuals had been detained in officially recognized state prisons, where an "overwhelming" number of prisoners were held without charge or trial.[46] Released without state compensation or acknowledgment, Agathe nonetheless exemplifies the best-case scenario of a deeply unequal judicial system. Her home is locally known in a landscape of injustice, sitting in tension between a reflection of unlawful government actions and the imperative for Rwandans to forget (certain things). As an unauthorized form of trauma heritage, Agathe's home registers these tensions quietly and personally while also politically symbolizing government achievements in reconciliation. The latter is ostensibly possible, at least in this case, by absencing, rather than resolving, conflict.

## PROHIBITED TRAUMA HERITAGE

Prohibited memories are difficult to see in the Rwandan landscape, especially for community outsiders, whether native or foreign. These memories are the most silenced and absenced: It is rare, if impossible, to find markers for the locations of reprisal killings and the burial places associated with them. This landscape becomes intelligible only when individuals are willing to share their stories. Those experiences are usually not relayed with ease. My interlocutors' cautious responses underscored that prohibited memories are trouble when expressed (and located) in public. When I set out to find the places they remembered, their hesitancies were mirrored in my own circuitous navigation and uncertain identification of prohibited sites of trauma. That transference said something profound about the importance of spatial forms of memory as the structure of collective remembrance: Without landmarks, trauma heritage is difficult for other people to know. In the context of the power imbalances that incur silences and absences in historiography, spatialized memories provide additional evidentiary support for narratives of violence and erasure, allowing that trauma to be recognized as real, as having occurred.

Disoriented yet again from all of the new houses built in a village in northwestern Rwanda in 2018, I asked a passerby if he could tell me when and for whom they were built. He was the village leader, it turned out: in his mid-thirties, affable and jocular. Unlike the first houses built in the area, the new homes were orderly and uniform. Each was covered in cement stucco and had blue shutters, doors, and wall vents. They sat high on concrete foundations with new, shiny corrugated metal roofs, spaced equidistantly on same-sized lots. He told me that the houses belong to the "Tanzanians," who returned to the country after the "*intambara* [fighting or war] of 1997." We were in a village near the Congolese border in the west. Identifying the new residents as returnees from Tanzania, at the far east of the country, was purposeful: It served to name them as distinct outsiders, if not actual foreigners. Returnees from the Democratic Republic of the Congo, merely an hour away, would not have been odd—most of the residents in the area had sought temporary refuge or exile there at some point in the 1990s. More germane to local parlance was the reference to the *intambara*, which, when dated to 1997 and 1998, was a colloquial reference to excessive force wielded by the RPF-led governing regime after the genocide. In the northwest especially, those military incursions did not discriminate between civilians and suspected extremist militants. Military attacks were spurred by an *abacengezi* (rebel) insurgency organized by previous government military (ex–Forces Armées Rwandaises, or ex–Rwandese Armed Forces) and Hutu Interahamwe paramilitary troops, who were responsible for perpetrating genocide crimes. Beginning in 1996, extremist forces returned to the region from exile in the Congo, embedded themselves in local communities in northwestern Rwanda, and began mounting attacks on Tutsi survivors and returnees and Hutu working with the new government.[47] In the course of suppressing that rebel uprising (1997–99), the new government's military killed tens of thousands of unarmed civilians in the northwest and the Democratic Republic of the Congo.[48] I asked the village leader where they had buried their dead from the *intambara*. He pointed to a hill in the distance (figure 6.22). Despite repeat attempts, I never found the exact location of the unmarked graves.

I originally learned about the burial hill from a local carpenter near whose home the houses for the "Tanzanians" were built. Alphonse's view of the *intambara* was complex, layered with his own personal losses in 1997 and veneration for the subsequent development and security gains the new government had provided to residents of the area. As I've detailed elsewhere, the houses that the government built for Alphonse and others were part of a "model village": an idealized rural planning experiment intended to provide modern infrastructure and standardized housing to the area.[49] But Ingurunguru Village residents did not refer to it as a model.[50] Instead, they were wary of the government's potential withdrawal of development aid and of repercussions for any voiced opposition to policies. Residents' social and economic inclusion felt precarious, contingent on their ability to transcend their ethnic affiliations (with Hutu *génocidaires* and *abacengezi* militants) and perform as compliant and dutiful citizens. Before the genocide, Ruhengeri Préfecture, where Ingurunguru Village is located, had a majority Hutu population.[51] As a result, few Tutsi genocide survivors live in the area, which, along with the region's long history of political separatism, and the more recent period in which *abacengezi* forces lived and organized in local communities, suggested to most of my interlocutors that they should not expect to be fully included in postgenocide development.[52]

To affirm their support of state development policies and not attract unfavorable attention, Alphonse and others living in Ingurunguru Village employed a number of strategies to render themselves "ordinary"—to appear aligned with

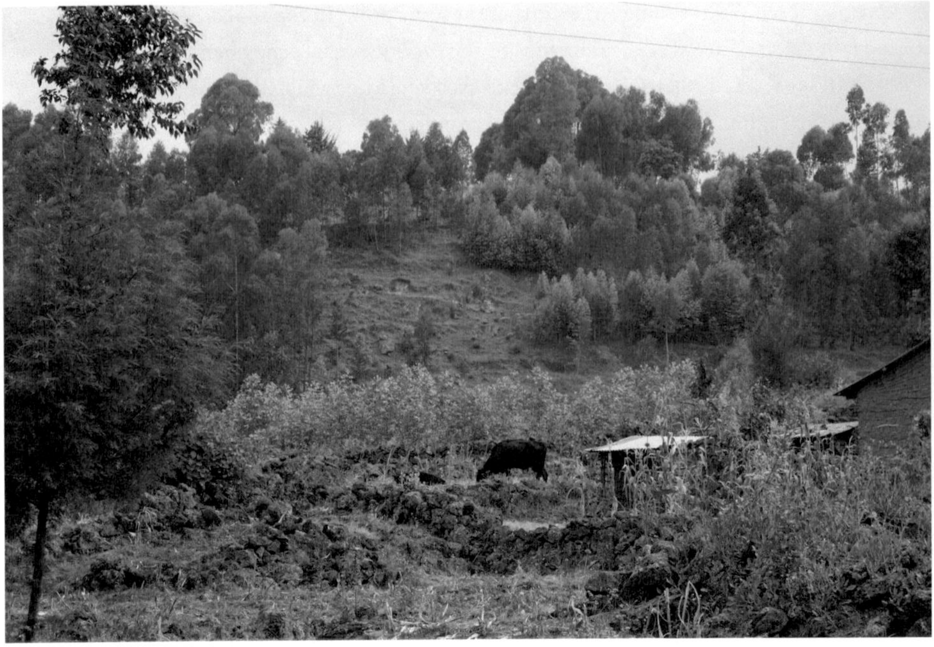

FIGURE 6.22. *Inzibutso zitagaragara*: A distant hill is the deliberately nonspecific place where Ingurunguru village residents buried their dead after the 1997 *intambara* (pictured in 2018). Photo by Delia Duong Ba Wendel.

the rest of Rwanda. The nonacknowledgment of Ingurunguru's exceptional model village status was one such practice. In another form of acquiescence to the state, residents did not complain publicly about undercompensated hard labor in service of environmental remediation, including land terracing, road building, and tree planting. In many of our conversations, too, Alphonse and other residents readily assumed the roles of genocide perpetrators, despite not actually having committed those crimes, rehearsing remorse and the terms by which genocide survivors might forgive them. This region saw relatively little genocidal violence because less than 1 percent of the population was Tutsi. Instead, the area is associated with the genocide primarily through the Hutu ethnicity of *génocidaires* and the *abacengezi* that returned there, not through most residents' actual commission of crimes. Strategies of ordinariness were also evident in repetitions of the phrase *tuvuga ururimi rumwe* (we speak one language) in our conversations. Residents' use of the phrase, which typically arose in response to my questions about the nature of conflict in the community, was purposeful: The phrase evoked state rhetoric and their agreement with the government's view that Kinyarwanda, the language spoken by all

Rwandans, provided the cultural basis for sociopolitical unity and postgenocide repair.[53] In each of these strategies, Ingurunguru residents positioned themselves as ordinary to compensate for national losses during the genocide and apologize for the wrongs of Hutu. Their subtle acknowledgments of authorized history sought to demonstrate that they were worthy of development benefits and inclusion in the country's future.[54]

This context of national expectations and local overcompensation explained why Alphonse described the killing of his parents in 1997 as understandable. His mother and father were shot at the local market, in government attacks on *abacengezi* in the area, in a place that today bears no mark of past violence (figure 6.23).[55] In 2013, in the course of my first questions regarding where and how he grew up, Alphonse told me about that formative incident: "Ababyeyi bahuye n'intambara barapf" (When my parents encountered the *intambara*, they died), leaving him to fend for himself and his siblings from the age of eleven.[56] I have translated *bahuye* (from *guhura*) as "encounter," but it more generally means "to meet." The phrase *bahuye n'intambara* is common in Kinyarwanda; in the context of speaking about his parents, however, his use of that verb renders passive how they met their violent deaths, without a sense of who was responsible. Later, he noted that his parents were running—trying to get away from active gunfire—when they were killed.[57] In 2018 he elaborated more on the context in which they died, explaining that when the *abacengezi* returned, the Inkotanyi (a colloquialism for the RPA, which in 1997 filled the ranks of the new regime's military) arrived to secure the region: "Because the *abacengezi* feared them [Inkotanyi], the *abacengezi* would run. Once they ran, the Inkotanyi would shoot. If a resident got mixed up in the crossfire, you understand that there was no crime—that's how it was."[58] In describing how his parents attempted to flee the fighting, Alphonse underplayed the government's fault in the killings at the marketplace.

I then asked if he or others in the village had a particular way of remembering his parents or other victims of the *intambara*. Alphonse replied, "Of course, one cannot *not* think about them, but because it was caused by the *intambara*, we try to keep it from happening again. Especially because they passed away [*bitabye Imana*] during the *intambara* . . . one might think that we would remember them, but we don't remember those that died because of the *abacengezi*. No, we never remember them. We remember the victims of the genocide: those who suffered an injustice in vain."[59] In his explanation Alphonse sublimates the violence suffered by his parents to that experienced by genocide victims. Though deeply personal, his father's and mother's deaths carry stigma. For him, public remembrance is contingent on national recognition and social acceptance. In response, my colleague, who was helping to translate our conversation, coughed uncomfortably and gently

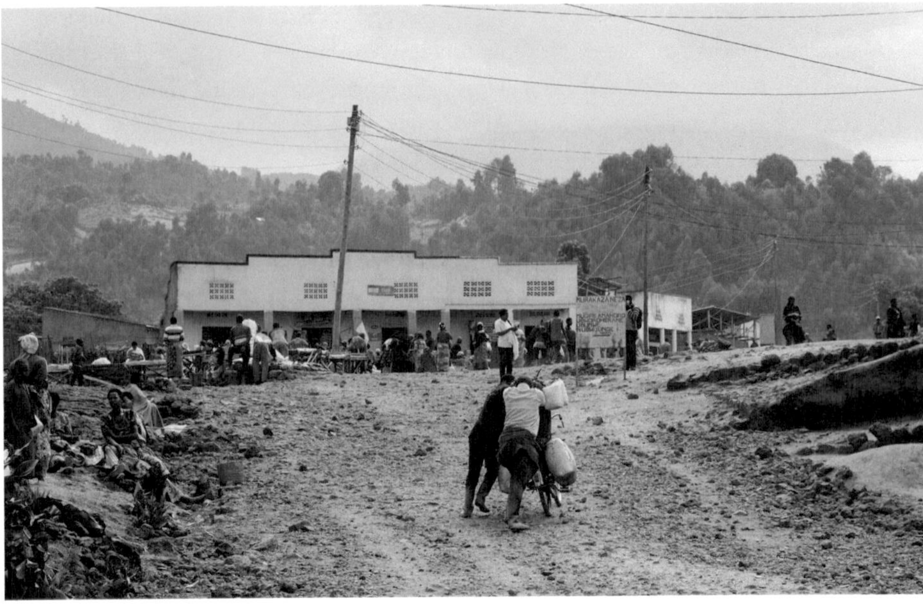

FIGURE 6.23. *Inzibutso zitagaragara*: The marketplace near Ingurunguru Village in northwestern Rwanda where Alphonse's parents were shot during the *intambara* (pictured in 2018). Photo by Delia Duong Ba Wendel.

pushed back: "Well, I don't know, but you have made me wonder: Weren't they [your parents] also victims of an injustice?" Alphonse replied matter-of-factly, "In their [my parents'] case, they were not killed out of cruelty [*ubugome*]. They died when we were being rescued. They [Inkotanyi] saved us from the enemies who attacked us."[60] Alphonse's views have a clear logic that allows him to process his traumatic experience and make a place for himself in the "new" Rwanda. As we were outsiders, my and my colleague's relative disbelief was related to the scale and intensity of the attacks that occurred in the region and the deeply personal effects we assumed it had on Alphonse and his family. We also came to our conversation with Alphonse having had exchanges with him and others in this village that indicated a heightened awareness of their vulnerability in an uneven national landscape.

Alphonse's views clarify the nature of prohibited memories in the country: Memories of the *intambara* are not so much silenced as absenced from ordinary landscapes. These memories are spoken, if in guarded ways, but their absences from view indicate that they have limited public recognition and little to no material evidence to verify them. Like the strategies that Alphonse and others undertake, "ordinariness" is conditioned by government expectations of citizens in a context in which ethnic distinctions have been banned, along with social difference more broadly, and order is maintained by the regulation of free speech. Alphonse did not hold back details of his parents' death—he was forthcoming to complete strangers that the attacks had happened, that killings had occurred in the marketplace, and that residents in the area had buried their relatives' bodies on the hillside. The government's use of excessive force to suppress the insurgency in Ingurunguru Village is not openly discussed by residents, but it is not fully erased from public discourse. Those prohibited memories are everywhere felt and referenced in Alphonse's environment, shared in others' memories of what happened and where. Those who remember keep the facts of the killings alive. But that violence is not officially recognized by the government, and there is no place for its commemoration or recognition in ordinary life. Authorized genocide heritage and punishments for genocide "revisionism, negationism, and trivialisation" have created a social order that sublimates prohibited memories, creating binary distinctions between socially un/acceptable narratives and in/visible landscapes. The ways that Alphonse shuns concern for injustice and his losses suggest critical coping strategies. His experience also indicates the state's reach in efforts to suppress prohibited traumas from ordinary collective memory. Like the reburial ceremonies immediately after the genocide, the hillside, wherever it may be, is where those memories are ordered, away from view.

Despite the social ordering processes that regulate the uneven landscape of trauma heritage in Rwanda, the past continues to shape the present and future in unruly ways. One of the most poignant examples of this came from two *abakecuru* (elderly women) living in the middle of Ingurunguru Village. When I first met Nyirashyaka in 2013, she was with Mukayiranga.[61] They were close friends of around the same age who were always together, finishing each other's sentences. Five years later, when I returned to the village, the women were again chatting in the back room of Nyirashyaka's house. They had propped the door open to let in the light; the walls provided some shelter from the cold northern winds. Nyirashyaka did not remember me or my colleague. Mukayiranga only vaguely remembered us. Nyirashyaka's words were often confusing to us—not only because of the linguistic particulars of the north but also because of her own patois, derived from Swahili and English.[62] Mukayiranga was a critical translator. Both women joked a lot, teased us, and drew multiple conspiracy stories from my body language. They didn't trust the *akazungu* (me, the small foreigner), but they did accord my colleague the treatment and respect they would give one of their adult children.

I asked how life, and their health, had been during the past five years. They were hungry. The soil was spent—they lacked fertilizer—and the corn, beans, and potatoes that they relied on for food had not yielded sufficient harvest that year.

Nyirashyaka, who was seventy, had been suffering from a stomach ailment. Mukayiranga's husband had died from an illness one month before our visit. When I asked what Nyirashyaka would like to see changed in the next five years, she referenced the past. Her aspirations for the future were both simple and profound: to have the help with farming and living that she would have had from her children, most of whom had died during the *intambara*.[63] Nyirashyaka also lost her husband in the fighting.[64] As a widow without any support from immediate family members, Nyirashyaka was classified within the "most vulnerable" socioeconomic category established by the government's *ubudehe* (loosely, "social welfare") rankings for local development assistance. She received a stipend from the government, but it was minimal, and she had no one to farm on her behalf. That help would typically have come from her husband and children. Nyirashyaka's world was completely upended in 1997 with significant effects on her ability to survive today. Her experience exemplifies the many ways that memories of the past are not just present, as lived traumas, but have concrete effects that shape individuals' well-being, livelihoods, and prospects for future. Nyirashyaka and Mukayiranga elaborated:

> NYIRASHYAKA: Seeing me at my age, after fourteen babies, imagine me living by myself, standing like this, without at least someone I can send to fetch me water?
>
> MUKAYIRANGA: She's been strong, yes.
>
> NYIRASHYAKA: Due to the *intambara*! [Pauses for a few seconds, then continues with tears in her eyes and in a quieter voice] I've now "hit the engine" [*nagonze miteri*].
>
> MUKAYIRANGA: Yes, she's now hit the engine.
>
> DELIA: I'm sorry, what did you say?
>
> BU (colleague): *Kugonga moteri* in Kinyarwanda: to hit the gas on a motor engine?
>
> MUKAYIRANGA: She is saying her mind is upside down. It means having no [clear] thoughts.
>
> NYIRASHYAKA: And many problems.
>
> MUKAYIRANGA: Yes, and many problems. Exactly as she is saying: All of those people died there, and her husband, and all of her children—all of this brings up too many thoughts. It's like she has hit the engine.
>
> DELIA: Please forgive us for bringing up these sad memories.

BU: Yes, please forgive us. We didn't mean to ask you about very sad things.

NYIRASHYAKA: Hmmm! [Laughs] No, not at all, we are not—you think you've made us sad? No, we were just discussing what happened. [Looks at Delia] This one is actually looking at me carefully.[65]

I was indeed worried about how precipitously our conversation on Nyirashyaka's desired future had turned into a flooding of the past, of the "engine" of traumatic remembrance. I was concerned with her feelings and the role my questions had in provoking distressing emotions. But as in so many other difficult conversations I had in Rwanda, Nyirashyaka took control and set the terms of our exchange. Nyirashyaka began to tease me, put *me* at ease, telling me that we were metaphorically walking together (*turajyana*). She turned it literal, telling me that she would go with me to Kigali, she would visit me, but she couldn't possibly fly by plane or go by boat. Mukayiranga jumped in, teasing both of us about Nyirashyaka's professed desire to go with me—could it be sincere, given that she did not understand me when I spoke? We laughed off the sadness, and Nyirashyaka's engine slowed.

I changed the subject. Given her emotional response to the *intambara*, I didn't want to push Nyirashyaka for further details on how her children and husband died and when. Instead, I asked if there were places nearby that she associated with happy memories. Nyirashyaka paused again, gathering her thoughts, and told me about the trees her children had planted in a field not far away. She had uprooted them so that the trees wouldn't remind her that her children were no longer there. Mukayiranga told me that similar trees were growing on the banks of a small river not far from the village, next to a primary school. They look similar and remind Nyirashyaka of her children too, sometimes in a good way.

After our conversation I was able to find the area they described but not the exact trees. Nyirashyaka used *ibiti* to refer to trees in general and did not specify the species. I assumed Nyirashyaka was referring to either the *intusi* (eucalyptus) or *gereveriya* (silky oak) groves; the *avoka* (avocado) trees would be far too valuable as food to cut down. The river and its banks were dotted with bright red canna lilies. The area was bustling: Women and men were soaking sacks of sorghum at the mouth of the cold stream, children were playing in the schoolyard nearby, and a local engineer was inspecting the canals the government had recently built to purify the water for drinking. This is the ordinary life to which most residents in the area aspire. I took a photograph of an *intusi* (figure 6.24). For me, the image provoked a double exposure, registering both the absence of material references to Nyirashyaka's grief and the *intambara*, and her choice to attach memories of her children to the trees.

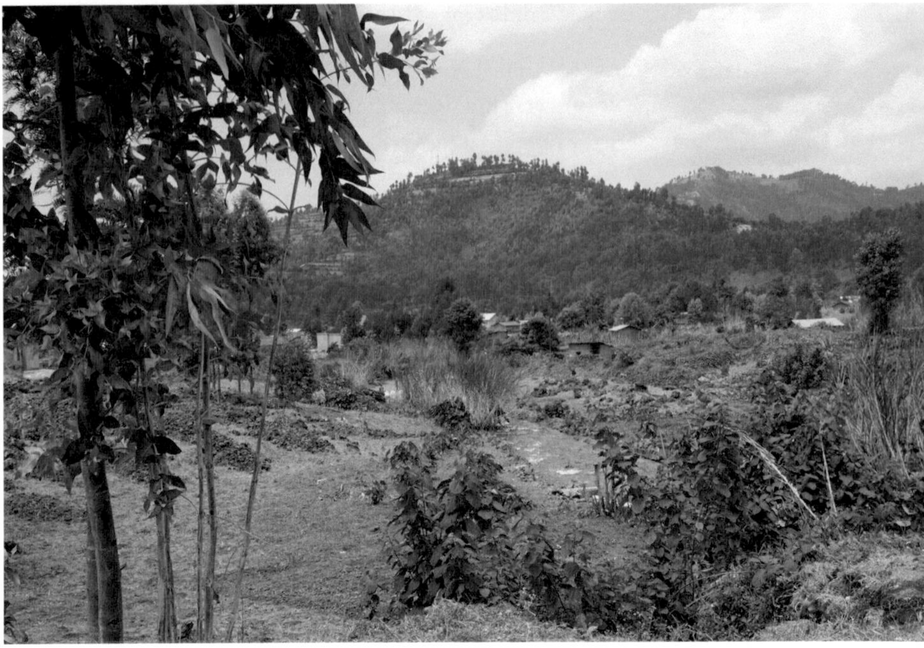

FIGURE 6.24. *Inzibutso zitagaragara*: An *intusi* (eucalyptus) tree growing next to the primary school and river near Nyira's home that reminds her of her children, 2018. Photo by Delia Duong Ba Wendel.

Nyirashyaka's experiences demonstrate just how unrulable prohibited memories are in Rwanda. Despite the government's regulation of ordinary life and provision of development assistance—efforts to establish social and economic order in the country—the past shapes the present in ways that remain outside the state's control. The losses suffered by survivors of the *intambara*, not unlike those experienced by genocide survivors, impact the present and future capabilities of individuals, especially those with meager means and minimal social support. The loss of family members handicaps their ability to survive and thrive in a context of severe scarcity, in turn rendering the country's social structure vulnerable. Moreover, feelings, especially those related to traumatic experiences, and individual remembrance exceed management by the state. When Nyirashyaka felled the trees that reminded her of her children, she removed symbolic reminders but was left with a daily embodied memory, in her hunger and thirst, of the lack of children to support her living. When Nyirashyaka steered our conversation, I was aware of the forms of empowerment she engaged in as she transformed sadness into laughter, ignored questions she did not wish to answer, or stated directly the real effects of her losses that she feels in her body, mind, and environment. These engagements with prohibited memories are forms of micro-empowerment that challenge the unilateral state regulation of trauma heritage. Nyirashyaka's choices to remember and forget provide some measure of control over how and when she feels, over how or whether prohibited memories are visible or subjects of conversation.

Prohibited memories are not confined to northwestern Rwanda. In the case of Ingabo Village in the southeast, near the Zaza Catholic Seminary founded in 1900 by White Fathers (Pères Blancs) missionaries, my attempt to follow up on an unauthorized memory led to the disclosure of traumatic experiences I had not expected to hear. Uwamahoro was sixty when I met her in 2013. Her house had personality: A bright-blue painted door and windows (unusually filled with glass) sat inside walls covered in coarse, gray-painted mud stucco. The avocado peel positioned atop a tall wood stick at the front edge of her plot indicated what she sold to neighbors (figures 6.25 and 6.26). Uwamahoro was the first person in the village to tell me that the government had been relocating the bodies of genocide victims from private grave sites to the memorial at Zaza (figure 6.1).[66] Memorial consolidation has entailed multiple relocations of victims from their original burial sites—first from private to state-managed sites and then from subdistrict to district sites.[67] The unauthorized aspect of that phenomenon is residents' (especially survivors' and victims' families') opposition to the uprooting and moving of loved ones, often to a new site at a substantial distance from their homes, which both obstructs individual choice regarding genocide victim remembrance and hinders visits to memorials.

Uwamahoro told me that she had fled the genocidal killings in 1994 after her husband and children were killed. She was Hutu, and he was Tutsi; the neighbors who perpetrated the killings knew that her children had a Tutsi father. She returned three years later and, with much pain and sadness, attempted to make a life for herself in the new village to which she was assigned. Village residents included released prisoners who had been jailed for genocide crimes but had now returned to their families, people who had committed crimes during the genocide but had not been brought to justice, and genocide survivors and families of victims. Given her ethnicity, despite her losses, Uwamahoro was not considered a genocide survivor by the government, which she relayed with some frustration: "You understand that they are ours, too, because we do not exclude ourselves; we go to the [Zaza] memorial to remember them too."[68] From Uwamahoro, I had a sense of the social dynamics in the village, but our conversation was somewhat rushed because she had other things she wanted to do that day. I did not want to

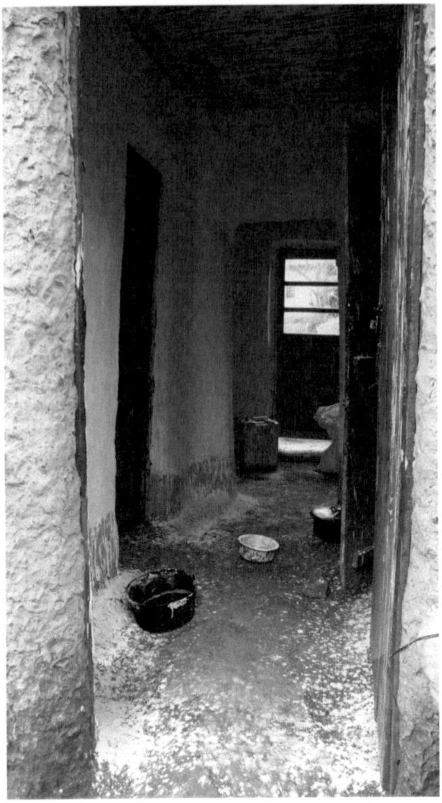

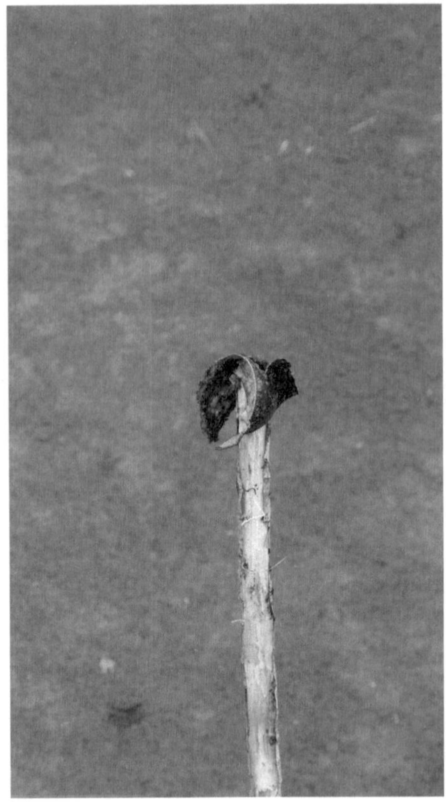

FIGURES 6.25 AND 6.26. *Inzibutso zitagaragara*: In 2013 Uwamahoro was painting her home's walls when she stopped to speak with me about genocide remembrance in Ingabo Village. An avocado peel on a stick outside her home indicated that she sold avocados. She died in 2016; the avocado marker is no longer there. Photos by Delia Duong Ba Wendel.

derail her by asking more about her husband and children. When I returned to the village years later, a neighbor told me that she had died in 2016. The avocado marker was gone, and the house rented.

I asked the neighbor if she knew of anyone who had lived in the village for a long time. She took us to a house on a road up the hill where an older man was sitting inside, readying some long, dry grasses to weave a mat (figure 6.27). He explained that the grass mat will cover the ceiling in their front room and was proud of the improvements to come. His wife came up from their farm field to join us. I noticed the water tap in front of their property near the road. The wife told us that the Japanese government had provided it but that the local authorities charge residents to use it. She was given the keys and asked to charge her neighbors. She laughed, claiming that she did at first, but with so many in need, she stopped charging herself and others.

We went inside their house to talk. Claver and Aurore were seventy-one and sixty-six, respectively; they were direct and humble, and from the start I had the sense that our conversation provided a rare space to share their stories of the past. I asked Claver how long he had lived in Ingabo Village. He leaned into the microphone attached to a voice recorder between us to make sure he would be heard. He had moved to the region in 1972, but he was not present when the village was built; he was in jail.[69] I asked if he felt comfortable telling us why he had been incarcerated.

After the genocide started, he and his wife had fled to Tanzania with their children. When he returned three years later, a woman living nearby accused him of killing Tutsi neighbors with the bow and arrow that he typically used to hunt. "During the *intambara*, they [police and military] gathered everyone together, and I said, 'They are accusing me wrongly; I did nothing.' I denied it, and that's why I was sentenced to jail for all those years."[70]

I asked what he saw and experienced during the genocide to try to evaluate his claims of innocence. Claver recalled that the killings happened suddenly: First, they heard the president had been killed, and then later that day, they heard that people were being killed in a nearby town. The young men living nearby began to organize themselves: "It was around 3 p.m., and they started 'to work,' to kill people. We were scared and hid and were plunged into total disarray—we had no idea what had just happened."[71] The next day, local authorities captured a man who had killed three Tutsi families living in the area. Claver thought the worst was over. But then local men organized again.

> They said that the *burugumesteri* [local mayor] had given them permission, that they needed to "go to work" for real. They came with whistles, saying that everyone had to stand up and "go to work," that everywhere across the country people were "working." We hid—we buried ourselves, actually, down in the marshes where we fetched water—we felt like everything was coming to an end around us. That's the way we saw it: they "worked" indeed; they killed people. Four days later, it was the Inkotanyi who got us back on our feet. That's when we left. Because you see, they [the Inkotanyi] didn't know who was what, and whenever they found people in the area, they made them explode with guns. So that's when we fled.[72]

Aurore picked up the story, telling us that as soon as they returned from Tanzania in 1997, they registered with the new local authorities in Zaza. The government

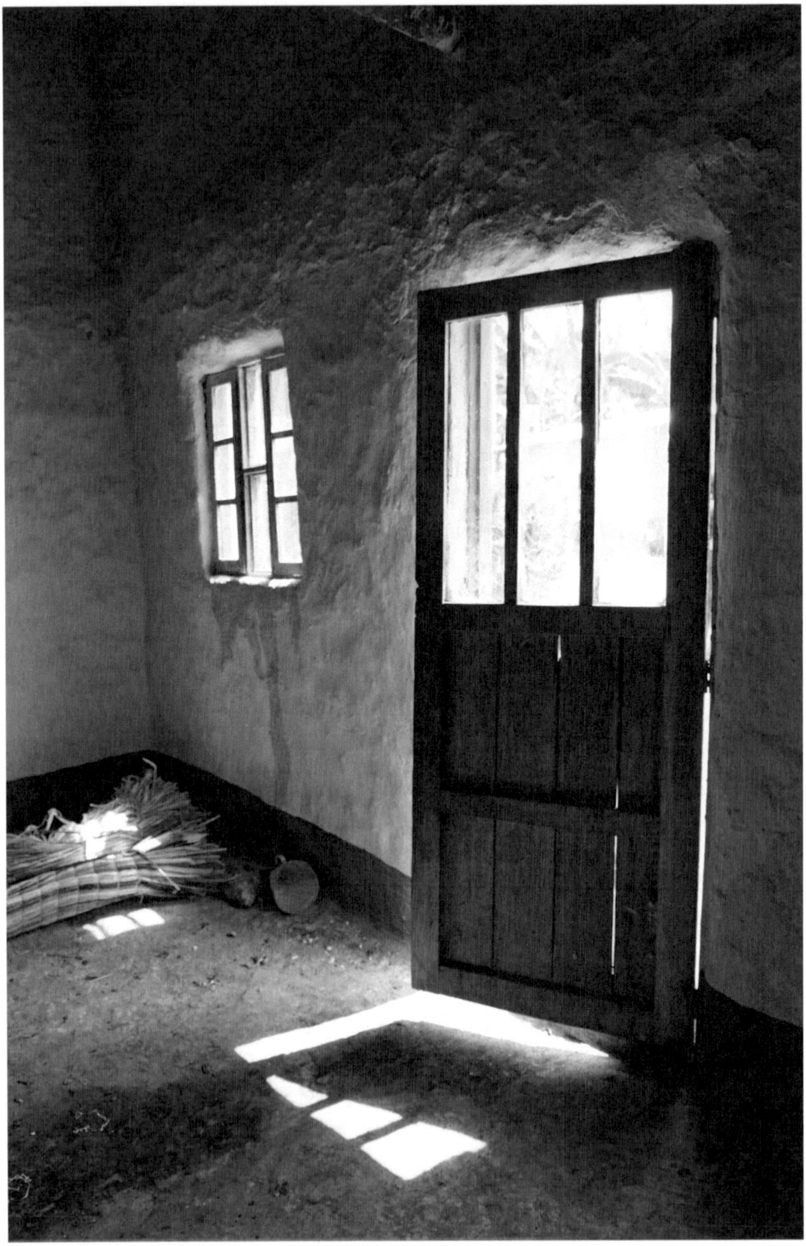

FIGURE 6.27. *Inzibutso zitagaragara*: The front room of Claver and Aurore's home in Ingabo Village, where we talked of reprisal killings and false imprisonment amid those events' erasure and denial, in 2018. Photo by Delia Duong Ba Wendel.

gave them corn, beans, and cooking oil and told them to return to their old home, which had been damaged in the fighting. Three days later, Claver was taken to prison. Aurore was left on her own with their ten surviving children. Though she had lived in the area all of her life, she was suddenly surrounded by new people, "the ones we call *abavuye hanze* [Tutsi returnees from long-term exile]."[73] To adapt, she said, "We humbled ourselves. We tried to be close to them, and that's how we got to know each other. We followed the new rules."[74] As Aurore told it, despite the jarring rupture of Claver's imprisonment, abiding by the "new rules" did bring some measure of fair treatment. While they were away for several years in Tanzania, their farming lands had been occupied by returnees. After Aurore returned, she petitioned the local *conseiller* (local sector mayor) to return some of her land so that she could feed her children. Her request was granted.

Yet in 2018 the family was still paying reparations for the looting crimes that their eldest son and Claver were accused of committing.[75] Their eldest had died in 1994, when he was twenty-two years old. He was picked up by the RPA with several other Hutu men, including neighbors' sons that Claver and Aurore remembered by name.[76] A genocide survivor identified men in the group as killers. Aurore's and Claver's stories differ slightly as to what happened next: The soldiers took the men either to the local cell office (a modest, two-room structure now in the center of the village) or to a neighbor's house next to it and killed them. Claver claimed, "They [the RPA] killed them with their guns—they pierced him [my son] in his heart."[77] Aurore followed by saying, "You cannot comprehend the things that happened here."[78] My conversation with Claver and Aurore had suddenly developed into one of the most graphic and forthright testimonies of reprisal and punishment that I heard in Rwanda. It was completely unexpected—we had no sense from our previous interviews that these types of prohibited memories were also present in this area.

Aurore told us that the RPA soldiers had thrown her son's and the others' bodies into a pit latrine behind the building where they were killed. In 2001 or 2002 local authorities had exhumed the presumed perpetrators' remains. They had reburied their bones at the Zaza Genocide Memorial. At Nyarubuye, which is in the same province as Ingabo, residents had told me that Hutu civilians or victims of reprisal killings had been reinterred at the genocide memorial burial ground as means for the RPA to dispose of evidence.[79] Claver's and Aurore's forthright and detailed account lent credibility to those rumors. In addition, Aurore relayed directions to the pit latrine where her son's body was thrown. Later I spoke with the woman who lived there. She was reticent to speak with me and conveyed no knowledge of those events. My colleague and I were strangers to her, and quite understandably, she engaged only superficially with my questions about what happened in the area in 1994. Though I am unable to independently verify Aurore's and Claver's story, what has become clear is that both everyday spaces in Ingabo Village and the local genocide memorial are focal points of prohibited memory.

It was not the only story of reprisal that Claver told me. Claver spent sixteen years in prison: He was first held at the commune office, but after an incident he was transferred to the larger Ntsinda Prison, where he completed his time. I asked what prison was like for him. He began by abruptly leaving his seat to search the other room for his prison release papers. He returned with a card inside a small booklet. With it, he could show us proof that he did not escape, served his time, participated in the local *gacaca* trial against him in 2007, and was allowed to return home in 2013.

Claver told me that when he was imprisoned in the smaller commune jail, they were first guarded by the police, but when the RPA soldiers came, the prisoners began to be beaten and taken away, to a house "*hariya haruguru* [up there] on the other side of the road."[80] Those prisoners were never seen again. Their bodies were found by accident several weeks later when a cow fell into a hole that had been dug for the bodies' disposal and then covered. One of the bodies was identified as that of a FAR soldier (a suspected *génocidaire*).[81] A team of *bazungu* (foreigners) who spoke English, led by a woman who spoke French and a little Kinyarwanda, arrived in the area to investigate. They interviewed Claver and other prisoners at the commune office jail and found the house where the killings had occurred. Claver said, "They checked and saw that it [the house] was full of blood. That's when we got some sort of reprieve. . . . That's when, on the following day, that white woman brought us *udukarita* [small cards]. *Udukarita*! I think I still have it here." At that juncture he again got up to search his belongings in the other room, desperate to show us evidence that would support his story.

The *bazungu* were investigators with a human rights organization, following up on reports of RPA-committed human rights abuses and reprisal killings in the local jails.[82] In return for the prisoners' testimony, the investigators provided "small [business] cards" that provided them with some measure of protection. As Claver put it, "Someone who had that card was safe; they [the soldier guards] could not call him outside and do anything to him."[83] The stakes of possessing that card were high, particularly given reports that local authorities had threatened residents in the *préfecture* with arrest if they provided UN human rights investigators with information or requested security protection.[84] Aurore told me that when their jailed relatives went missing, the governing authorities told her neighbors that those prisoners had "escaped." But their loved ones were disappeared and never heard from again.[85]

Although Claver and Aurore attached their prohibited memories to places in ordinary life and government-managed memorials, no proof remains of those revenge killings. When I looked, I saw that the house where their son was purported to have been killed, the other house near the commune jail where the prisoners were killed, the now-sealed latrine and field pits, and the Zaza Genocide Memorial do not bear any marker of the brutal events they described. Nevertheless, I recount our exchanges for two purposes: first, to bear witness to generally inaccessible testimony on human rights violations and erasures committed by the postgenocide regime, which have also been documented elsewhere;[86] and, second, and most pertinent to the nature of prohibited memories in Rwanda, to acknowledge that the absence of corroborating evidence—of material and spatial memory—in the context of those narratives' prohibition mirrors and extends the disenfranchisement experienced by Claver, Aurore, and others like them in the country. They told their stories with precision to compensate for that lack. Their gruesome descriptions of places all around them where killings and mass burials occurred, and Claver's agitated search for verifying documentation in the protective privacy of his home, conveyed the struggle and search for evidence as a laborious form of empowerment. Claver's extreme lack of power is registered in the fact that the only trace of the revenge killings remains in worn slips of paper bearing the official markings of his government and international organizations.

The memories that Uwamahoro, Aurore, and Claver recounted in Ingabo Village demonstrate the power inequalities around trauma heritage in Rwanda. As Mario Ibarra and Louis Kanamugire so clearly recognized, without corroborating evidence what is left is just memories. Evidence as a means of compelling recognition, and as a method of truth telling, is vital to individuals' and communities' abilities to move from remembrance to action. This unequal power not only prevents recognition but also causes real harm in daily lives. Traumatic memories and pain that are not afforded public acknowledgment continue to live in the body; they also manifest in real challenges to everyday subsistence and social support. These conditions of exclusion and erasure have effects on well-being and health. Acts of repair in Rwanda's uneven memory landscape address both affective and lived conditions. These are the circumstances to which memory justice and related actions are oriented.

## Trauma Heritage and Empowerment

Memory studies scholar Michael Rothberg poignantly argues that places of memory should more aptly be conceived as *knots* of memory.[87] As such *nœuds de mémoire*, "memory emerges from multidirectional encounters—encounters between diverse pasts and conflictual presents, to be sure, but also between different agents or catalysts of memory."[88] Accordingly, Maurice Halbwachs's concept of collective memory finds a new interpretation: not as the result of a unitary consensus so much as a patchwork of diverse, interrelated, and often conflicting accounts of the past.[89] In this reframing, the unauthorized and prohibited memories from Rwanda that I have been retelling might be understood similarly, in dynamic relation to a conflictual field of memories of traumatic experiences.

Authorized narratives on the past are inescapably knotted together with those that are prohibited. Each informs the other as perspectives on truth. But actively silenced and absenced within collective memory, unauthorized and prohibited memories have an antagonistic and activist status. They seek to repair collective memory and edify self and kin in society. In part, unauthorized and prohibited accounts of the past find refuge in knotted places—in the homes and landscapes of domestic life—that locate traumatic experiences in Rwanda. There, everyday trauma heritage stitches different temporalities together. Those who remember are compelled to navigate the past in their present. And when *inzibutso zitagaragara* are opened to view, those unauthorized and prohibited memories form stalwart resistance to authorized forgetting in the future. In these ways, the empowerment practiced through reparative historiography mirrors that which occurs in landscape.

Landscape becomes a critical index for memories that are unwritten and unspeakable. In a context of power imbalance, spaces serve to edify traumatic memories, to give some substance to unbelievable stories. Landscape has an evidentiary aura in the absence of evidence, but it is illegible without interpretation. In this regard, unauthorized and prohibited memory landscapes resemble Mario Ibarra's photographs with their missing index. The only way to unlock them is through the annotated negative sleeves and the oral histories of those involved. When the index is gone, when no markers exist in place, that history is relegated to the minds of individuals. But traumatic memories can't be easily put away, and that is particularly the case for experiences that have limited public recognition. In this sense, absenced memories remain ever present: They disrupt ordinary life and the government's management of it, in ways both small and large. Those unruly acts of remembrance, that landscape of compromised trauma heritage, reflect necessary and nearly impossible efforts at repair.

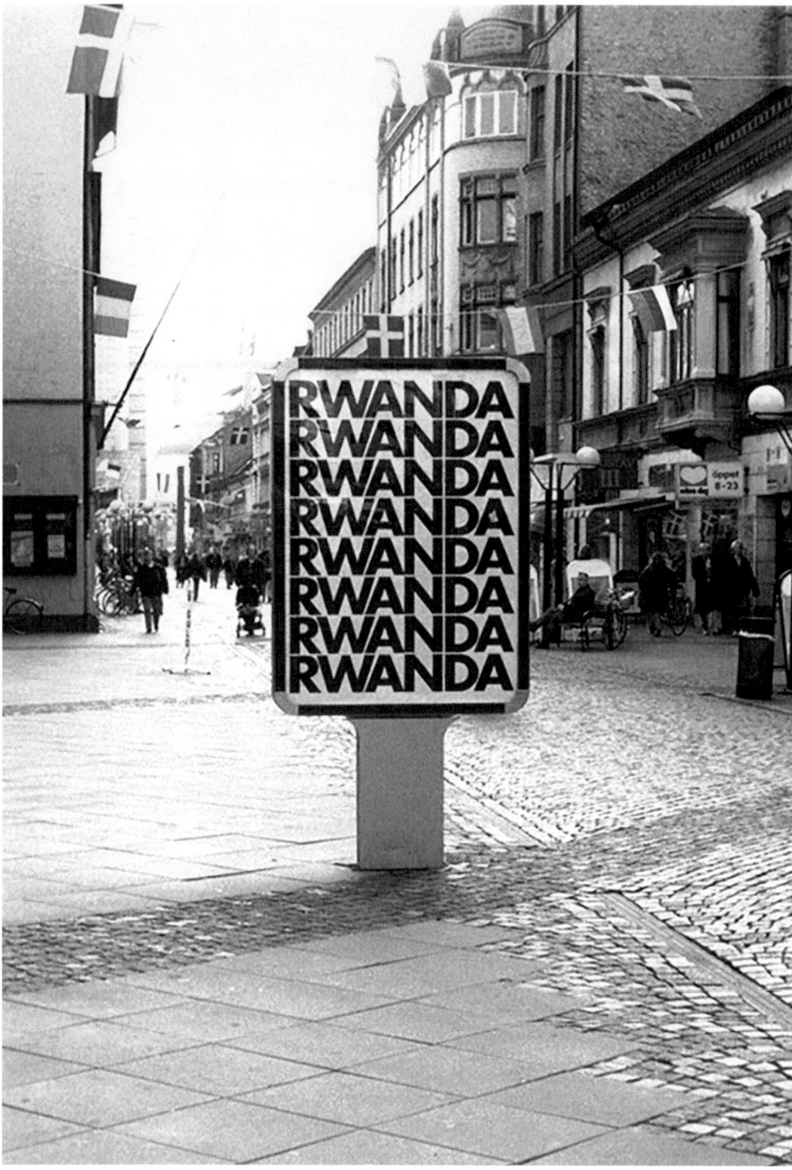


An example of trauma heritage: Chilean artist Alfredo Jaar disrupts everyday life in Malmö, Sweden, to recognize Rwanda and locate the genocide. Alfredo Jaar, 1994 (alfredojaar.net).

# CONCLUSION MEMORY JUSTICE IN AN ERA OF TRAUMA HERITAGE

In *Los trabajos de la memoria* (translated into English as *State Repression and the Labors of Memory*), Argentinian sociologist Elizabeth Jelin writes of memories that do urgent work. These are memories "of the oppressed and marginalized" and "about oppression and repression," which lay claim to experiences of "death, forced disappearance, torture, exile, and imprisonment" that remain otherwise erased or normalized.[1] Their urgency arises from those threats—of death/disappearance and erasure from memory/history—and the memories' double intent: to assert truths about the past and to demand justice. In those contexts, Jelin tells us, "memory, truth, and justice blend into each other, because the meaning of the past that is being fought about is, in fact, part of the demand for justice in the present."[2] I argue that the *spatialization* of violent memory—a phenomenon I call *trauma heritage*—has emerged as a response to the very conditions that Jelin describes. Trauma heritage emboldens memory justice with the demand to see, and therefore acknowledge, experiences of death, forced disappearance, and oppression.

Trauma heritage comprises practices that seek a material and spatial form for memories of violence that are underrecognized by larger publics or actively suppressed by those in power. It is a defiant truth-telling and justice-seeking type of memory representation that is substantiated by emplacement and visibility. The need to mark the place where violence occurred, to *show* that people were disappeared—to say that this happened *here*, that people were taken from and died *there*—is what the concept of trauma heritage refers to, in essence. Practices of trauma heritage derive from an *ethics of nonerasure*. This is my term for the moral imperative, partly informed by human rights principles, that seeks justice and repair by making violent histories known. To counter the disappearances, oppression, and destruction that are the objectives of violence, an ethics of nonerasure seeks to materialize and spatialize the hidden and erased. Locating and displaying evidence of crimes substantiates the existence—the humanity—of those violated. In doing so, trauma heritage locates material evidence—whether forensic traces or the locations of crimes—to support, and therefore to validate and make known, personal accounts of violence and ultimately compel wider recognition and collective action. Motivated thus, trauma heritage makes public space for silenced pain.

Rwanda's genocide heritage is a distinctive example of the spatialization of violent memory because, more acutely than in other cases, it reveals the ethical and political tensions inherent in the demand to witness. Furthermore, the origins of Rwanda's genocide heritage substantiate the concurrent influences—of local conditions and global human rights practices—that have shaped other examples of trauma heritage. The preceding chapters recounted the backstage processes and motivations involved in the first engagements in Rwanda's genocide heritage. From them we gain a more intimate and material understanding of memory justice work. Witnessing and placemaking became central tenets, evolving from efforts to publicize the existence of evidence of mass violence and then enlist national and global recognition of those acts as genocide. In the process, amateur conservationists navigated the "smell and pain" of aftermath landscapes, and their own traumas, to attempt reparative and caregiving work. The chapters also revealed the shifting loci of power in the making of genocide heritage over time: from local stewardship and uneven government involvement to subsequent forms of state authorization, nationalization, and co-optation of those memory initiatives. This lends valuable insights regarding the legacies, and evolving political contexts, of memory justice activism. Moreover, the Rwandan governing regime's use of genocide heritage to marginalize other pasts and regulate social and political life, though in many ways extreme, reveals the types of conflicts and effects that trauma heritage sites can produce in local communities. When genocide heritage is situated among other forms of trauma heritage in the country today, we see an extension and intensification of those conflicts. That more expansive contested-memory landscape is evident both in the range of disagreements in individual and state forms of remembrance and the real effects that uneven national commemoration has had on residents' lived experience of exclusion and disenfranchisement.

This conclusion sets the story of Rwanda's genocide heritage amid global efforts at memory justice and repair, as one exceptional and catalytic example among many. The tensions and forms of empowerment that we read in Rwanda's memory landscapes are not singular. They represent an *era of trauma heritage* comprising shared struggles against erasure in the Global South. At the same time, this era forces viewers to contend with the ethical and political contradictions inherent in memory justice. Those aspects are critical to understanding how trauma heritage is situated within larger political landscapes as forms of empowerment.

## An Era of Trauma Heritage

An era of trauma heritage refers to a time and geography of spatialized memory justice activism. It characterizes a historical period, particularly salient from the 1970s to the present, in which efforts to make crimes against humanity visible in public spaces proliferated. The struggles for recognition by advocates of Black communities killed and oppressed under apartheid in South Africa, Mayan communities murdered and persecuted in Guatemala, Bengalis violently suppressed in the movement for Bangladesh's self-determination, and the scores of Argentinian dissidents disappeared by the military junta exemplify what is at stake in claiming public spaces for absenced histories. Significant precedents, including those related to racialized violence in the United States and the Holocaust in Europe, had substantial influence in shaping both the human rights principles and the representational forms on which this approach to atrocity remembrance relies. Rwanda's genocide heritage exemplifies, in extreme ways, the core aspects of trauma heritage. However, trauma heritage is not confined to being a late twentieth-century phenomenon. It continues to be enacted, demonstrating—in efforts as diverse as the Equal Justice Initiative's Soil Collection project at sites of lynching in the United States and the detailed documentation of Palestinian homes and cultural landscapes destroyed since 1948—the enduring, urgent nature of struggles to break through dominant historical narratives and political regimes.[3] Recognizing an era of trauma heritage in world history foregrounds the spatial and material forms of representation that were thought necessary, by diverse groups under siege, to bring attention to terror, oppression, and mass death.

An era of trauma heritage also has a distinct geography: it developed primarily, though not exclusively, from a Global South landscape of underrecognized atrocities. The Global South to which I refer is not merely a southern hemispheric location. I invoke the term as a critical concept to refer to the postcolonial condition of economic subjugation and subaltern subjectivities that overwhelmingly correlate to places in a southern world geography. While the concept typically represents the ways that marginalized peoples and nations have endured the legacies of colonialism and racism, the deterritorialized dimensions of the Global South concept highlight how those experiences produce relational political and economic subject positions. In other words, as transnational solidarity movement scholar Anne Garland Mahler notes, "There are Souths in the geographic North and Norths in the geographic South."[4]

By locating origins in the Global South, I do not mean to say that violence is more endemic there or that trauma heritage originates in the memory traditions of Global South cultures. Neither is borne out by fact. Rather, spatial representations of violent pasts have gained ground in the Global South as a necessary amplification of speech. Turning up the volume on the representation of violence is conditioned by a lack of recognition (a mildly critical rendering of the situation) and more precisely by a long history of devaluation and subjugation of nonwhite, non-Western peoples. Spatial representations of that violence defy the silences imposed by powerful foreign and national regimes. They reveal both recent crimes and the legacies of historical violence, including the significant lasting effects of colonialism and enslavement. Trauma heritage is a provocative means to tell those marginalized truths in a form that transcends imposed barriers of language, bias, and power. In doing that truth telling, trauma heritage sites seek to both identify specific perpetrators and socialize responsibility for crimes through wider societal acknowledgment and accountability.

Global trauma heritage comprises a reparative historiography from the South: an expanded field of history representation, defiantly visible in material and spatial forms.[5] Conceptualizing this era underscores that histories of violence are relayed not only through written and testimonial accounts but, significantly, through spatialized forms of representation. Historiography in that expanded field seeks to cultivate an ethics of viewership. Seeing is distinct in its affective immediacy from histories that are heard and read; witnessing compels justice-seeking and reparative actions. Making public space for silenced pain, then, does distinct social and historiographical work.

## The *Atlas of Trauma Heritage*

Establishing the global reach of trauma heritage required new tools for visualization and mapping. To this end, I worked with Massachusetts Institute of Technology (MIT) student researchers to account for and represent trauma heritage established throughout the world.[6] The sites included in the resulting *Atlas of Trauma Heritage* (presented in this volume as appendixes 1, 2, and 3) are drawn from three sources: places of memory that we correlated to Matthew White's global accounting of the hundred most deadly (in terms of human casualties) events of war and forms of oppression from 1800 to 2000; a subset of sites registered with the International Coalition of Sites of Conscience that concern serious human rights violations; and *memorias situadas* (sites of memory) mapped by the Centro Internacional para la Promoción de los Derechos Humanos (International Center for the Promotion of Human Rights), a UNESCO-affiliated Argentinian governmental organization dedicated to remembrance and human rights protection.[7] The atlas has a reversed orientation (south up) in recognition of the preponderance of sites in the Global South and on the margins of the Global North. As the legend indicates, it tracks diverse forms of trauma heritage, including the conservation of evidence in the places where violence occurred ("event sites," marked with diamond symbols), memorials and museums that are not located where crimes were committed ("remote sites," identified by square symbols), and archives established to provide access to evidence of those atrocities (circle symbols). The *Atlas of Trauma Heritage* differentiates the affective range of those sites. It highlights the most visceral sites that display victims' remains at event and remote sites (black diamonds and squares, respectively). The atlas also identifies places that display other material evidence of human rights violations (gray-filled symbols of all types) and that mark the sites or the occurrence of crimes (outlined symbols of all types). Each of the symbols on the atlas emplaces an act of trauma heritage replete with affective resonance: Each marker locates violence experienced by individuals and communities along with survivors' and advocates' struggles for recognition.

The atlas is an incomplete representation. For example, it does not account for Wachira Waheire's efforts in Kenya to have the Nyayo House torture chambers in Nairobi, where he was held, designated as a heritage site.[8] Waheire's memory justice initiative is part of a larger, decades-long effort to publicly recognize Kenyan state violence against political dissidents in the 1980s.[9] A plethora of similar efforts are in the process of becoming; they are vying for spatial and material representation in the context of a lack of political will and funding. The *Atlas of Trauma Heritage* can locate only a limited number of efforts that have already been realized.

In 2021 we were able to identify a total of 271 trauma heritage sites (see appendix 1, the Concise Atlas of Trauma Heritage). Each symbol that we placed on the atlas carries an excess of feeling and purpose. The sites are immersed in struggles for memory justice against local histories of violence and oppression. In those contexts, trauma heritage engages uneven political landscapes as forms of empowerment. At the same time, each symbol articulates a range of tensions—between ethics and politics, human rights and state objectives, and the burdens and responsibilities of viewership—that are endemic to trauma heritage in its various forms. These are the types of commitments and tensions that are difficult to see on the *Atlas of Trauma Heritage*. And yet the aim, like that of Louis Kanamugire and Mario Ibarra's own *Genocide Sites Map*, is to begin to account for the scale and extent of trauma heritage—in this case, in the world.

The *Atlas of Trauma Heritage* shows the growing spatialization, over time and around the world, of marginalized memories of violence. The atlas does not track battle markers, burial grounds, and monuments, which are more common to public landscapes. Instead, it draws attention to memorials established in and dedicated to sites of violence that are involved in struggles to recognize those atrocities and victims. The Chronological Atlas of Trauma Heritage captures five-year intervals in trauma heritage development from 1875 to 2020 (see appendix 2 and the corresponding Chronological Index of Featured Trauma Heritage Sites in appendix 3). One of the first trauma heritage sites was established in 1879 on Zanzibar island off the coast of Tanzania in East Africa. It is an event site dedicated to remembering the dehumanizing transactions that trafficked human beings from East Africa to the Middle East at one of the largest slave markets in the region. Subsequent to those early engagements, an era of trauma heritage gains ground, so to speak, in diverse efforts to remember the Holocaust, Hiroshima, and racialized violence in the United States in the mid-1940s and 1950s. Trauma heritage dedicated to a wider range of atrocities and their victims emerges with greater frequency in the 1970s. That increase corresponds with the second wave of human rights discourse and related liberation and social justice struggles against colonial empires, dictatorships, genocidal attacks, and white supremacy.

Trauma heritage sites again pick up substantially in number and spread geographically in the 1990s, at a pace that continues today. Rwanda's genocide heritage emerges from that increase and expansion, which was influenced by the transitional justice "turn" around the same time and those practices' emergence from the field of human rights.[10] Critically, Holocaust memorialization continues to be a major force in the era of trauma heritage, but the atlas shows that those efforts were not the only center of such work. Moreover, iconic examples in Rwanda and Argentina, among others, demonstrate that trauma heritage efforts in other contexts did not originally reference Holocaust memory representations. A global history of trauma heritage activism locates, instead, the critical influences that the discourse and practice of human rights have had on memory justice.

## Trauma Heritage: The Local Practice of Human Rights

In 1948 the Universal Declaration of Human Rights was adopted by the newly formed United Nations (UN). The declaration articulated thirty basic rights that all individuals should expect to hold, anywhere in the world, in what historian Mary Ann Glendon has called "the single most important reference point for cross-cultural discussion of human freedom and dignity."[11] Despite its postwar emergence, the declaration was not solely a response to the Holocaust: It was a decades-long political project, led primarily by nonstate actors, that gained ground after the formation of the UN in 1945. Political scientist Susan Waltz notes that "Nazi horrors supplied a collective memory" and a gravely important, "ever-present reminder of the need to protect human rights" when the Universal Declaration of Human Rights was adopted.[12] But, she notes, lamentably, that "it was not the only experience of abusive human rights practice that participants [in the declaration's shaping] brought to the table."[13] In the years that followed, subsequent treaties, conventions, and criminal prosecutions progressively codified those thirty basic entitlements as international human rights law.[14] By the late twentieth century, the question of how to *practice* human rights—to develop actionable programs for protection, advocacy, and justice in communities in conflict—had become a pressing concern and a rather more difficult proposition to address (see chapter 2).

Liberation and social justice movements began to develop a response through localized activism. Historian Jean-Louis Cohen described this phenomenon as the "second wave" of human rights discourse, occurring from the 1960s to the 1980s within movements for independence from colonial control, the Soviet empire, and dictatorships in Latin America, among others.[15] In those contexts, activists turned to international human rights discourse to legitimate and galvanize local social justice claims. Their campaigns for criminal accountability demonstrated that universal treatises on the rights of all peoples could be applied and therefore could be actionable and locally specific rather than just idealistic and morally admonitory. Trauma heritage, arising from an imperative to publicize mass violence and gross violations taking place in communities, became a prominent Global South approach to the localized practice of human rights.

### THE ROLE OF MEMORY

Memories of violence played substantial roles in the second wave of human rights work. As human rights practice evolved and gained local specificity, so did its reliance on memories that harbored marginalized experiences under threat. Generally, remembrances of state terror and oppression informed the stakes of defining universal principles like human dignity and freedom. But more concretely, in this period witness testimony and journalistic accounts played particular roles as critical evidence in criminal prosecutions and public discourse.[16] Those sources served to oppose official histories and hegemonic narratives of the past: to counter the impunity of governing regimes. Making those memories public—making the history of the genocide *known*, to return to Louis Kanamugire's intentions in Rwanda—articulated those crimes for others to recognize, reinforcing human rights in the face of their violation.

The elevated status of memory in this period derived in large part from the pivotal roles that witnesses had in exposing and prosecuting anti-Semitic violence during World War II. Holocaust scholars Dori Laub, Shoshana Felman, and Annette Wieviorka describe this postwar period as a paradigmatic "era of testimony."[17] In doing so, they remark on the role of victims' voices and witness accounts in constructing a collective memory of the persecution, killing, and survival of Jews. The Nuremberg Trials (1945–46) were pivotal in this respect. Survivors testified from personal experiences of the crimes committed by the lead perpetrators of the Holocaust, bringing those deeds to the attention of a wider public. But the era of testimony does not just describe the proliferation of witness accounts in trials and recorded testimonies. It also refers to the diary entries and records of events that survived long after their authors were killed. In its many forms, testimonial accounts of Holocaust violence constitute an urgent practice of reparative history.

In his acceptance speech for the Nobel Peace Prize in 1986, Holocaust survivor and scholar Elie Wiesel reflected on the urgency with which he and other prisoners undertook that archival work: "The great historian Shimon Dubnov served as our guide and inspiration. Until the moment of his death he said over and over again to his companions in the Riga ghetto: '*Yidden, shreibt un fershreibt* (Jews, write it all down).' His words were heeded. Overnight, countless victims become chroniclers and historians in the ghettos, even in the death camps. . . . To testify became an obsession. They left us poems and letters, diaries and fragments of novels, some known throughout the world, others still unpublished."[18] To bear witness—to "write it all down"—was to write a history of genocide from the very places where it was experienced. The imperative to record every instance of that brutality was rooted in outrage over the world's indifference. It was also an act of nonerasure, testifying to the existence of victims, their humanity and rights, and witnessing of others. In the aftermath of the Holocaust, the public exposure of such deeply personal experiences of violence carried a moral imperative to speak and take responsibility for the truth, impressing it on a world of listeners.[19]

In the era of testimony, memory gained status as history. Witnesses became historians. Personal narratives challenged the inhumanity of mass violence. Survivors and witnesses also served as key translators, relaying fragmented and jarring memories of violence to a wider public. Testimonies about trauma are forms of recall that are notoriously difficult to recount, interpret, and verify. However, in the context of the dearth of information on the mass violence committed and the widespread destruction of material evidence, Holocaust survivors provided crucial information. Together, witnesses established the facts of crimes. Their testimonies produced a collective memory of the Holocaust that has had powerful implications for both justice seeking and historiography. The affective and evidentiary strengths of survivor voices established oral history archival practices as the primary model for the documentation of atrocities since.[20]

In their emotional and existential origins, there are parallels between an era of testimony and an era of trauma heritage. In both, survivors and witnesses are committed to rendering their memories as historical record. Both aim to produce an "urgent archive" from the details of the seemingly inconceivable, whether in written or spatial form, to enact forms of repair or prevention.[21] In these ways, the era of testimony does not supersede the era of trauma heritage so much as complement and evoke the intentions of spatialized memories.

And yet trauma heritage serves as a critical supplement to testimonial collective memory. An era of trauma heritage emerges precisely from contexts where speaking alone, or writing it all down, has not been enough to contest or dismantle dominant regimes and narratives. Moreover, the knowledge gained through viewing the aftermath of atrocity is visceral. It is a form of communication that survivors and kin have employed to convey, with gravity and force, stories of harm and survival: to ground them in experiential memory. Through spatialization, marginalized memories become incontrovertible. They gain amplified and powerfully affective representation.

## SPATIALIZED MEMORY: HOLOCAUST MEMORIAL MUSEUMS

Significant examples of global trauma heritage and human rights advocacy developed from Holocaust memorialization. The first Holocaust memory preservation efforts that occurred at concentration and extermination camps from 1944 to 1965, along with the establishment of the Yad Vashem Holocaust Remembrance Center in 1953, comprise significant precedents in trauma heritage.[22] Those memorialization efforts challenged the tepid acknowledgment of the violence that targeted European Jews during World War II: The term *genocide* was not commonly used until the 1960s, and it wasn't until the 1970s that the term *Holocaust* was used to refer to the Nazi killing campaign.[23] The process of defining a recognizable approach to Holocaust memorialization took place, then, over several decades, culminating in renewed global interest in the 1990s (at the fiftieth commemoration) in establishing Holocaust memorial museums worldwide.[24] That arc—from the ad hoc preservation of sites of killing to the development of global centers of Holocaust memory (and a recognizable memorial museum curatorial strategy)—mirrors the development, more broadly, of a global era of trauma heritage. As I detail more fully in chapter 2, situating Holocaust memorialization in an era of trauma heritage illustrates the parallels among diverse forms of the phenomenon more so than origins. In doing so, we see the influences the spatialization of Holocaust memory has had on the genre of memorial and human rights museums while also noting the occurrence of independent trauma heritage efforts in the Global South (with Rwanda and Argentina prominent among them).

From 1945 to 1995, three primary spatial approaches to Holocaust memory were piloted: the establishment of memorial monuments; the preservation of killing sites, victims' remains, and artifacts; and the development of memorial museums. Many of the first memorial monuments incorporated relics—material and symbolic references to Holocaust victims or sites of killing—including human ash and soil from the camps.[25] Other early initiatives to preserve material evidence of the crimes, victims' remains, belongings, and killing sites developed in tandem. The preservation of crematoria, gas chambers, housing barracks, and camp infrastructure opened sites of mass violence—and the atrocities of the Holocaust—to view by visitors. The preservation of victims' clothing, shoes, and belongings—and their display in aggregate at killing sites—conveyed the massive scale of lives lost. Some of the first preservation efforts at extermination complexes were led by Soviet-aligned governing regimes, including those of Poland and East Germany, which were keen to demonstrate the role of the Red Army in the camps' liberation.[26] The State Museum at the Majdanek concentration camp outside of Lublin, Poland, documented the main objectives of its preservation work: to maintain material evidence of Holocaust crimes and make those facts available to a wider public.[27]

But not all Holocaust memory preservation efforts were state led. Immediately after the liberation of Majdanek camp internees, residents of the nearby town gathered tons of human ash from the crematorium into a large pile on the grounds (figure C.1).[28] Many of the individuals who were killed at Majdanek were taken from Lublin and surrounding towns. Recuperating their remains was an act of nonerasure. It referenced the single largest mass execution of Jews during the Holocaust: Around eighteen thousand individuals were killed at Majdanek on November 3, 1943. Similarly, the first memorial tours of the Buchenwald concentration camp outside Weimar in East Germany also were not state led. In April 1945, the American soldiers who liberated Buchenwald marched neighboring Weimar residents through the camp to see and hear the circumstances of the killings and bury victims' bodies. Those acts, in historian James Young's estimation, "forcibly created German memory of the victims."[29]

Approaches to Holocaust memorialization underwent substantial debate and transformation in the decades following 1945, as survivors, advocates, and politicians searched for a collective memory representation appropriate to the gravity of mass violence against Jews. Documentation of those deliberations at various sites reveals consistent appeals by survivor groups to preserve more of the camp's structures as evidence of their imprisonment and the terror to which they were subjected.[30] By contrast, the majority of governing authorities favored the production of symbolic monuments that were decidedly more abstract in their reference to Holocaust atrocities. The state proposal for the Buchenwald camp memorial, for example, put forward a monument design that took the form of an inverted pyramid, a reference to the triangular badges camp prisoners were required to

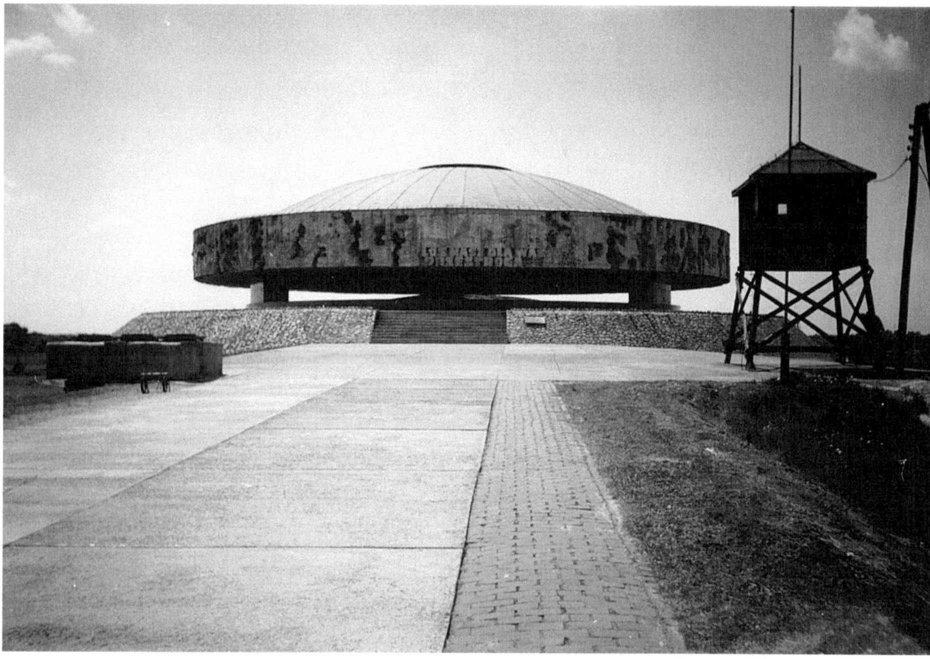

FIGURE C.1. Architect and Holocaust survivor Wiktor Tołkin designed a "floating" concrete memorial over victims' ashes at the Majdanek concentration camp in 1969, two decades after residents gathered and preserved them. Photo by Messer Woland, 2007 (Wikimedia Commons, CC-BY-SA 3.0).

wear. This more abstract representation of the Holocaust was highly contested by survivors.[31] Nonetheless, in the first decades after 1945, most state approaches supplanted realist site preservation with symbolic memorial monuments developed in the styles of heroic classicism or modernist expressionism.

It wasn't until the late twentieth century that the museological aesthetic now associated with Holocaust memorial museums—the unvarnished display of victims' clothing and belongings, the preservation of material evidence of crimes, and reconstructions of significant spaces or architectural elements of killing sites—returned as a representational strategy for Holocaust memory.[32] Similarly, a number of artistic interventions—also examples of global trauma heritage—were initiated to develop public consciousness of the Holocaust. Among them, Gunter Demnig's *Stolpersteine* (1992) has installed memorial stones on the sidewalks near the last residences of Holocaust victims in more than nine hundred cities across Europe.[33] Also in the 1990s, in anticipation of the fiftieth commemoration of the end of the Holocaust, a growing number of foreign nations sponsored memorial museums. Those efforts solidified the spatial approach to memory justice that is today associated with Holocaust memorialization, evident in diverse contexts, including the United States Holocaust Memorial Museum in Washington, DC (1993), the Holocaust Education Center in Japan (1995), and the Cape Town Holocaust Centre in South Africa (1999), among others.

Developments in Holocaust memorialization in the latter decades of the twentieth century influenced the global emergence of memorial museums, a phenomenon scholars also associate with "human rights museology."[34] Both human rights and memorial museums are significant forms of global trauma heritage. The museum genres prominently feature the material traces of atrocity that trauma heritage makes public. They include exhibitions of victims' belongings, killing instruments, portrait photographs of victims, recorded testimonies of survivors and witnesses, spatial reconstructions of sites of violence, and the artistic and literary creations of victims.[35] Alongside Holocaust memorialization, a significant shaping force of memorial and human rights museums has been transitional justice practices that emerged in the same period. Transitional justice strategies emphasized the need for public reckoning with the past—in memorials, truth commissions, and civic institutions, among other forms. As part of a localized practice of human rights, then, the museums controversially display forms of human suffering to, as peace scholar Terence Duffy puts it, "make a resounding appeal for the protection of human rights."[36] In doing so, the museums document and archive evidence of related crimes while providing forms of civic education and memorialization.[37] Increasingly, both museum types are part of global organizations, including the International Coalition of Sites of Conscience (a significant source for the *Atlas of Trauma Heritage*), that publicize memory justice practices to promote local and global human rights practice. Their significance to an era of trauma heritage, then, is both in their curation and display of material evidence of gross human rights violations and in the ways in which the museums share strategies for educating local communities and informing human rights practice.

## SPATIALIZED MEMORY: THE ARGENTINIAN PARADIGM

Trauma heritage also emerged as a form of localized human rights advocacy in Global South contexts during the last decades of the twentieth century. Social justice activists in Argentina were at the forefront of that work, establishing the value and force of trauma heritage within the "second wave" of human rights discourse and practice. They did so to combat the kidnappings, secret detentions, and torture committed by the governing regime from 1976 to 1983. State violence, which sought to quell opposition, targeted tens of thousands of Argentinians, including working-class men and boys thought to be prime agents of resistance, students of higher education considered to have a proclivity for subversion, and political activists and intellectuals.[38] The military junta denied that the acts occurred, and the press, under threat and control, remained largely silent. Anthropologist Antonius Robben has argued that the state's erasure of reporting and material evidence of its crimes relegated the junta's repression to the discursive domain, such that the struggle to make state terror known became "their word against that of the surviving victims."[39] To shift the battle for representation from the arena of discourse to the recognition of lives killed and harmed—from rhetoric to the facts of crimes—activists, human rights workers, and forensic scientists employed a range of trauma heritage practices. In other words, the military junta's brutal acts of erasure led to distinctly spatial approaches to representing those violent memories in public.

One of the most prominent of such efforts was steered by Las Madres (later, Las Abuelas) de Plaza de Mayo. The mothers and grandmothers who formed the ad hoc group in 1977 initially came together to demand information from Argentinian government officials about their disappeared children (both adult and young).[40] They formed a political organization that sustained a public protest of state terror for decades and advocated on behalf of victims with human rights organizations.[41] They are largely credited with helping to set the post-junta human rights agenda for the country.[42] The Plaza de Mayo is located in the center of Buenos Aires. Surrounding the square, state, civil, and economic seats of power are visible in the president's office, the city hall, the national bank, the Catholic Church of Buenos Aires, and various other buildings related to the military, state intelligence, and financial entities.[43] Among those buildings, at significant personal risk, a small group of women met weekly to challenge the silences that the government maintained to normalize disappearances.

In 1980 Las Madres de Plaza de Mayo organized the first public protest of state violence while the junta's terror campaign was ongoing. Weekly marches in the plaza continued every Thursday for decades. Not merely content with public demonstration, Las Madres insisted on establishing the presence of their disappeared children. They painted the ground with images of their signature headscarves, evocative of the diapers that had clothed their children, inscribing them with abductees' names and the dates of their disappearances. They marched in the Plaza de Mayo holding life-size photographs of the disappeared, plastering those images on the walls of buildings to show the scale and personal effects of the violence.[44] In 1983 Las Madres partnered with artist-activists Rodolfo Aguerreberry, Julio Flores, and Guillermo Kexel to lead *El Siluetazo*, transforming the plaza into a performance of trauma heritage (figure C.2). Protesters traced silhouettes of bodies on large sheets of paper, adding physical features and names to repre-

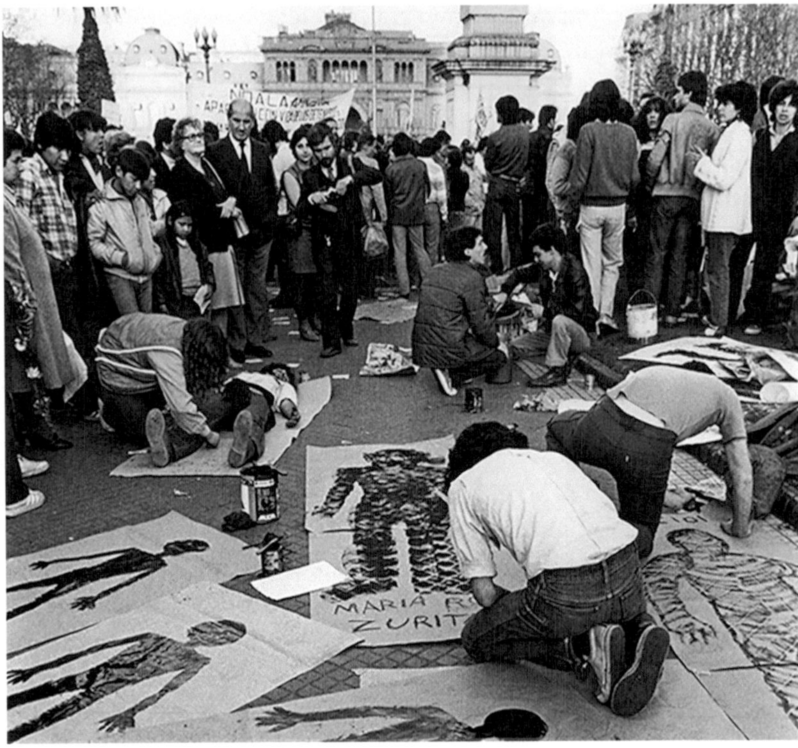

FIGURE C.2. *El Siluetazo*, conceived by artists together with Las Madres de Plaza de Mayo, defiantly claimed the existence of the disappeared by tracing their silhouettes on the plaza located in the center of Buenos Aires, September 21–22, 1983. Photo by Eduardo Gil (https://www.eduardogil.com/siluetazo.html).

sent specific individuals, affixing them to the ground and on walls throughout the plaza and city center. The drawings embodied the disappeared children, women, and men as a "graphic fact."[45] These trauma heritage practices made public space for silenced pain, leveraging emotional connections and affective relations for human rights activism.

The case of Argentina is furthermore instructive for the role of forensic anthropology in trauma heritage. After 1983 and the end of the military dictatorship, ad hoc exhumations of mass graves where the disappeared were suspected of being disposed were initiated in earnest by the state, the National Commission on the Disappearance of Persons (CONADEP), and Las Madres de Plaza de Mayo. In 1986 CONADEP and Las Madres called on the expertise of Clyde Snow, an American forensic anthropologist, who helped to form the Argentinian Forensic Anthropology Association and conduct more systematic investigations. The association's work not only was pivotal in efforts to identify the victims of state terror in Argentina but also led to related exhumations and forensic investigations of human rights violations in El Salvador, Ethiopia, Haiti, Rwanda, and East Timor and was part of a growing movement linking forensic science with human rights practice in the late twentieth century.[46] Those efforts aimed to find the disappeared and investigate hidden forms of violence, establishing that it occurred *there*, in *that place*, for a wider public to recognize. As a result, exhumations were not conducted for forensic evidence and criminal investigations alone. They were more broadly, like the work of Las Madres, part of a process of excavating memory and retaking public space.

Trauma heritage was a critical strategy of both Las Madres de Plaza de Mayo and Argentinian Forensic Anthropology Association investigations. Each is a hallmark case of contemporaneous efforts occurring across the Global South. Both Las Madres' demonstration of the existence of the disappeared in public spaces and forensic anthropologists' work to identify locations where violence occurred and was hidden demonstrated what global trauma heritage could achieve through spatialization and witnessing. In Argentina forty years later, strategic forgetting, impunity, and severely delayed truth telling have persisted in successive regimes' responses to the harms of the military junta. Trauma heritage is, as a result, not merely a response to the first acts of state terror. It persists materially to publicly register harms and serve as vigilant reminders of unredressed crimes. In this context, Argentinian trauma heritage continues to have relevance today as a form of repair: to advocate for victims, promote public awareness, and seek accountability and justice.

## TRANSITIONAL JUSTICE

By the end of the twentieth century, nascent transitional justice practices bolstered the very connections that trauma heritage activism was attempting: establishing public spaces for the recognition of violence as efforts at repair and redress. In 1988 José Zalaquett, the future commissioner of the Chilean National Commission on Truth and Reconciliation, called transitional justice "a new area of human rights practice" that emerged to respond to the specific sociopolitical challenges arising in the aftermath of repressive regimes.[47] As I discuss in chapter 5, transitional justice reframed analyses of postconflict settings, providing a radically different road map for changeovers from one governing regime to the next. Scholars and practitioners concerned with human rights in this intense period of civil conflict and political change responded to citizens' demands for the disclosure of previous regimes' systematic abuses. As a result, transitional justice refers to a number of strategies that demand accountability for the crimes of prior regimes, including truth commissions, criminal trials, and collective memory projects.[48] In each, the public representation of past wrongs became a precondition to not only granting legitimacy to new governments but also fostering the possibility of reconciliation, justice, and guarantees of those harms' nonrecurrence.

Important caveats, evident also in Rwanda's genocide heritage, remain regarding the role of memory justice work within transitional justice practices. Critics warn that, especially in the context of governing regime succession, trauma heritage tends to be used instrumentally as a tool of statecraft.[49] The nation-building functions of trauma heritage are wide-ranging. As a spatial representation of violent pasts, trauma heritage can be used to legitimize new regimes, thereby establishing unearned contrasts between previous and new political leaders, losers and victors. Memorialization in some cases has been used more technocratically: to expediently contain difficult pasts lest they spill over and shape reprisals and burden the present and future. In those cases, memorials truncate the time of mourning and transcend the past, producing myths that claim the nation's future as one of change and progress. In other examples, like in Germany and Rwanda, full national belonging is contingent on knowing and performing one's recognition of a state-authorized collective memory.[50] In those cases, the public spaces created by trauma heritage regulate social behaviors. Chapter 6 describes the state's disciplining of citizenship through authorized memory in Rwanda, which is evident in the ways that genocide memorials are used to condition the behavior of residents, especially Hutu and released prisoners. To *not* be seen attending commemorations or extolling the virtues of memorial sites is to be punished for genocide denial, at worst, or socially or economically ostracized by local authorities.

Nonetheless, trauma heritage—exhibiting evidence of crimes, establishing landmarks where they occurred, curating memorial museums, and convening commemoration ceremonies—has increasingly become an integral part of transitional justice processes. In those efforts, trauma heritage is not merely symbolic. Public forms of remembrance bear witness to structural and direct violence as cognates for truth commissions. They create public spaces for truth telling and its wider societal recognition. Trauma heritage also manifests actual spaces for the collision of past, present, and future temporalities. They hold collective memory narratives that recognize past crimes. And they have long-term effects. Trauma heritage has promoted civic education and dialogue, protected against cultures of impunity, and served, in some cases, as an important psychosocial space of mourning for victims and support for survivors and relatives.[51]

As the preceding sections and the *Atlas of Trauma Heritage* demonstrate, Rwanda's genocide heritage is not unique in foregrounding spatial evidence of violence—nor in preserving victims' remains, belongings, or sites of killing—as a form of memory justice. The gathering of ash from cremated Holocaust victims at the Majdanek concentration camp in Poland in 1944; the public display of Emmett Till's body in Chicago in 1955; the preservation of victims' remains and the Tuol Sleng prison and Cheong Ek killing fields in Cambodia in 1978; and the taking of public spaces to claim the existence of the disappeared in Argentina from 1980 all sought to establish, in visceral terms, the human impacts of ethnically and politically motivated mass violence. Memory justice work in Rwanda redoubled these types of efforts, located largely in the Global South, to reveal hidden violence so that it could be seen and felt. The spatial representation of brutal, marginalized memories continues today, building on these precedents, to leverage trauma heritage as forms of justice, empowerment, and repair.

## Rwanda in an Era of Trauma Heritage

The spatialization of genocide memory in Rwanda is emblematic of three general qualities of trauma heritage. The phenomenon emerged in large part as a human rights response to assert the existence, and value, of lives lost and harmed in contexts of oppression, terror, and mass violence. The spatial form that trauma heritage takes is important to how it supplants, contests, and circumnavigates the dominant narratives that occlude those crimes. In the process, spatialized memories proliferate the number of secondary witnesses who see the erased crimes and substantiate accounts of traumatic events. Witnessing is critically important to the objectives of justice, empowerment, and repair that trauma heritage activists seek. These three factors explain the frequent and sustained employment of trauma heritage around the world today. And yet, as the preceding chapters attest, Rwanda's genocide heritage also exemplifies the ethical and political caveats endemic to this approach to memory representation. Given that trauma heritage arises from uneven political landscapes, it must be understood in terms of both its intentions and its variable impacts: Both are relevant to understanding the wider phenomenon's legacies. Together, these core aspects—the human rights foundations, the significance of placemaking and witnessing, and ethical and political paradoxes—inform what constitutes an era of trauma heritage and, by extension, a reparative historiography from the Global South.

### RWANDA'S GENOCIDE HERITAGE AS HUMAN RIGHTS PRACTICE

Rwanda's genocide heritage derives, in large part, from the influence that human rights had on memory justice in the late twentieth century. Delving into the origins of decisions to conserve and display massacres—following the individuals who led that work and the conference discussions that connected parallel exam-

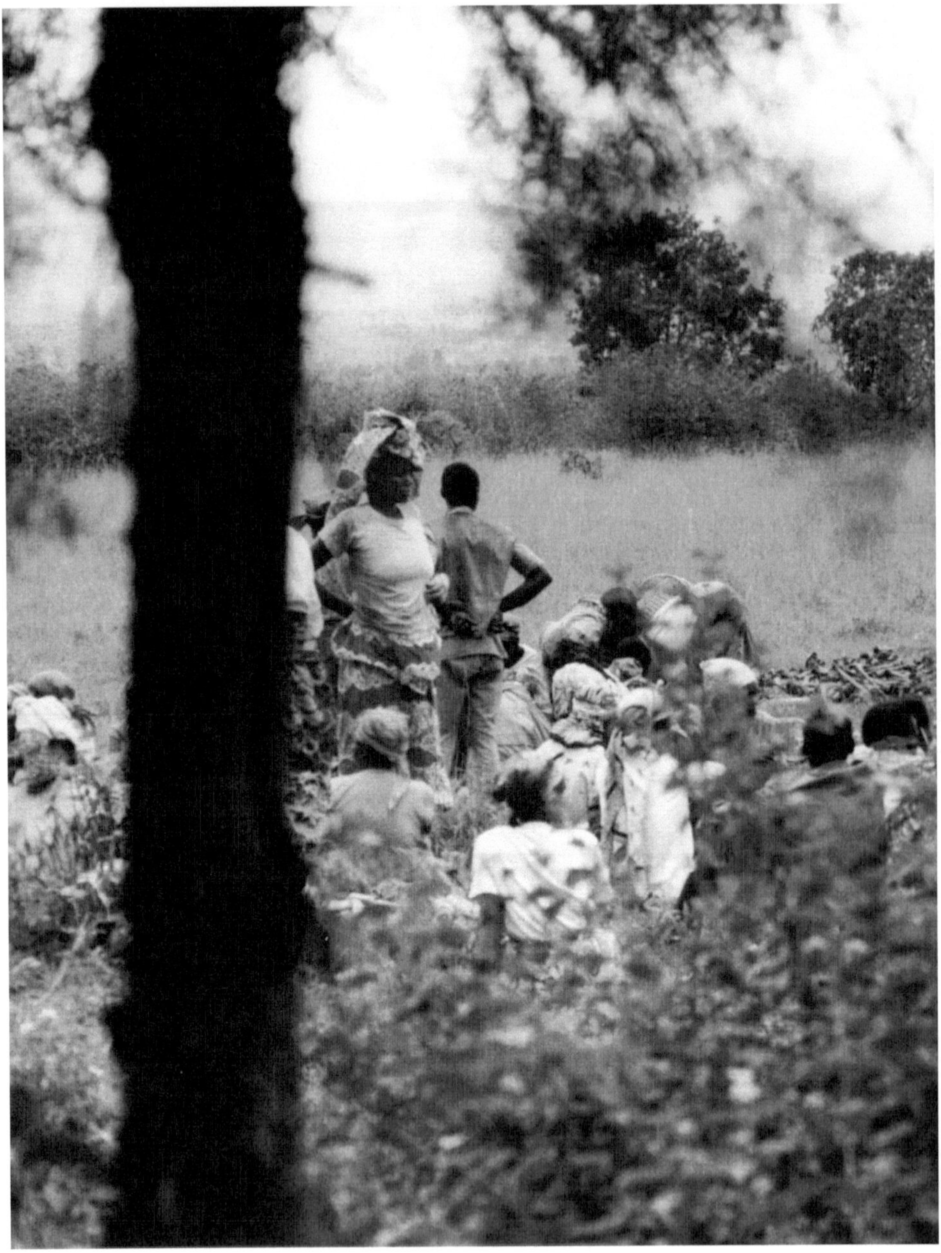

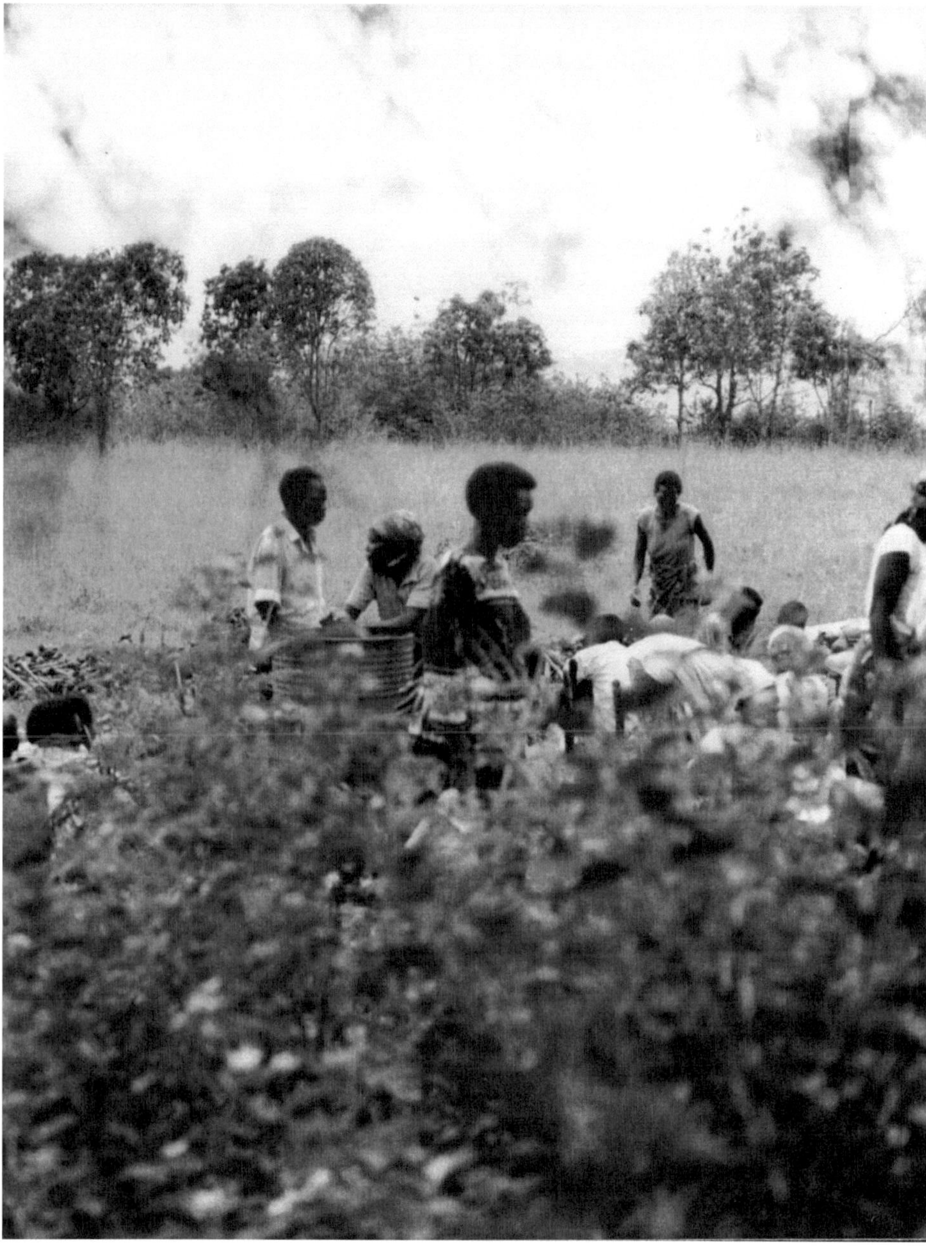

FIGURE C.3. "Watching" the memory work involved in memorialization: Conservationists clean and dry the bones of genocide victims in a field near Murambi, 1996. Photo by Mario Ibarra, Ibarra archive, Chile.

ples in the world—rendered that relationship in Rwanda visible. That exploration also made apparent the global geography of trauma heritage to which memory work in Rwanda was related. Overshadowed by analyses that have focused on state stewardship and politicization of memorialization and commemoration, nonstate influences (both local and global) have been less recognized as shapers of Rwanda's genocide heritage. The human rights foundations of Rwanda's genocide heritage are important to recovering a sense of the ethics and context of the enterprise (figure C.3). They are furthermore critical to resituating assumptions that Holocaust memorialization was the primary influence on the initial preservation efforts in the country; those connections were established a decade after the first genocide memorials were established. More generally, Rwanda's genocide heritage exemplifies the ways that trauma heritage grounds human rights practices in landscapes—not as principles to be applied but as projects of dignity restoration and justice that are lived.

As I detail in chapters 1, 2, and 3, the preservation of genocide evidence at massacre sites was technically and conceptually bolstered by human rights organizations and discourse and a reconceived view of its local practice. The preservation of the Nyarubuye Parish genocide site by the Kibungo Field Office of the UN Human Rights Field Operation in Rwanda (HRFOR) established one of the earliest such relationships and spurred subsequent conservation efforts in the country. Though not explicitly part of the HRFOR's mandate, Nyarubuye's preservation was an interpretation of the priority, established by the newly formed Office of the High Commissioner for Human Rights (OHCHR), to practice human rights *in situ*. In it, human rights complemented, and served as a stopgap to, criminal prosecutions by uplifting "downgraded" evidence, including witness testimony and sites where mass killings occurred. In a human rights context, for which the priority was to publicize crimes, both types of evidence proved highly compelling for lay publics: establishing emotional connections to victims of violence and means to hear and see the scope and severity of the human rights violations committed during the genocide. However, in the context of criminal prosecutions, witness testimony was deemed subjective and prone to error, and massacre sites were not considered real evidence (they were contaminated by weather and attempts to clean them up). Not content to abide by the evidentiary standards, lengthy time required to prepare for trials, and nondisclosure requirements of criminal prosecutions, localized human rights practice in Rwanda emphasized the value (and immediacy) of witnessing. The affective and political power of Rwanda's early genocide heritage—as a form of human rights advocacy—is evident in foreign dignitaries' visits to the Nyarubuye genocide site and the circulation of editorial photographs of it in prominent reportage in 1994 and 1995 (see figures 3.7 and 3.10).

Beyond the instance of Nyarubuye, and especially evident in conferences convened by the government and nongovernmental organizations (NGOs) immediately after the genocide, the global discourse on human rights served as a primary justification for the decision to preserve and display places and victims of massacre. For example, in the October 1994 "Rwanda: Reconstruire" conference in Kigali, organized by two human rights organizations, attendees referenced truth commissions in El Salvador and Chile to illustrate connections between collective memory and justice. In doing so, they defined memory as a form of truth telling and justice seeking: a means to reveal wrongdoing, acknowledge victims, and begin a process of repair for survivors. Participants also introduced three contexts where mass killings occurred—Cambodia, Chile, and Palestine—as examples of failed international intervention, a reconciliation process initiated without a mechanism for justice, and an ongoing genocide dismissed as such by a global public, respectively.[52] Those transnational comparisons emboldened Rwanda's genocide heritage organizers to adopt a different approach to memory justice in the country. The conversations echoed contemporaneous transitional justice practices that were being piloted in other contexts of reckoning with the past and regime change, demonstrating the extent to which trauma heritage was becoming integral to global human rights practice.

But Rwanda's genocide heritage was not merely the result of the local interpretation of global human rights discourse. It also emerged, independently, in local initiatives in victim caregiving and communal repair. The first preservation and conservation experiments in Rwanda that displayed material evidence of the massacres for public viewing were led simultaneously by genocide survivors, Tutsi kin (including returnees from long-term exile), representatives of the new governing regime, and international human rights workers. Those diverse individuals put victims' remains on display as part of an ethics of nonerasure, thereby shaping what would become Rwanda's genocide heritage aesthetic. Their intimate relationships between personal memories and collective action substantiate the reparative ambitions of trauma heritage. Though several of the first initiatives did not explicitly reference human rights or transitional justice, the efforts were nonetheless aligned, if not in name, by similar interests in publicizing the genocide, seeking justice and accountability, and remembering victims. Rwanda's genocide heritage derived, as a result, from both locally specific initiatives and an awareness of other memory justice efforts taking place around the world. Those practices trace a global geography of liberatory and social justice movements that amplified marginalized memories of violence through spatial representation.

Rwanda's genocide heritage exemplifies a paradigmatic shift in memory justice activism in which spatial representations of violence strategically supplemented the testimonies of survivors and witnesses. In Rwanda spatialized genocide memory comprised preservation and conservation practices along with ceremonies for commemoration and reburial. It also took form in the construction of a visceral archive—maps, photographs, and videos of genocide investigations and conservation work. Those varied initiatives in spatialized memory demonstrate the key relationships that trauma heritage has to action, at least in drawing attention to unrecognized violence, if not in connecting the acknowledgment of crimes to forms of justice.

Moreover, the spatial forms that Rwanda's genocide heritage takes demonstrate the power of placemaking. Placemaking is an urban design practice that strives to develop a sense of place—including feelings of belonging, way-finding, and affective connection. It initially emerged in the 1970s (coincident with an era of trauma heritage) to combat the estrangement endemic to modern, "placeless" cities and urban development.[53] In the context of trauma heritage, placemaking gains critical social and political dimensions.

Trauma heritage *makes places* for memories of violence. That act alone is critical in the context of those histories' silencing, denial, and normalization. In doing so, trauma heritage expands historiography—articulating in spatial forms what cannot be said or has not been written—as a reparative act. A spatial mode of representation also permits a transcalar understanding of violence. Rwanda's genocide heritage was aesthetically and politically exceptional in this regard. Louis and Mario employed both the conservation and mapping of genocide sites to convey both intimate feeling and the scale of mass violence. Through spatialized memory, and its reproduction in map and image, they attempted to cut through willful ignorance and genocide denial, demonstrating the existence, scale, and intimate effects of that violence in forms other than words.[54] That memory work was by no means easy; conserving evidence of violence took an immense emotional and physical toll. The affective knowledge that genocide heritage located was, in turn, powerfully tethered to its reception by viewers, who bear witness to others' memories of traumatic experiences and the feelings and people associated with them. In doing so, trauma heritage utilizes public space to edify personal accounts of hidden or marginalized violence. That aim of empowerment—of recognizing memory as history—is critical to the work of reparative historiography. Such declarations substantiate the existence—the humanity—of those violated.

Placemaking for memories of violence also holds time. In Rwanda, where massacres occurred in churches, government offices, homes, and the spaces between, holding time and place for memories of the genocide sought to intervene in local communities. It was also an act for a wider public: Placemaking expands the witnessing and experiencing of Rwanda's genocide heritage. Critical to the power of Rwanda's genocide heritage has been the extreme aesthetic associated with that placemaking and the ways in which conservation, photography, and ritualized commemorative return have extended the time of the aftermath for viewing. Spatialized memories are, then, not merely retrospective: Remembrances situated in place have both immediate and lasting impacts. Their extended temporality and demonstrable presence in public spaces serve to counteract strategic forgetting and unfulfilled redress.

Considering the making and witnessing of Rwanda's genocide heritage broadens what is meant by the social dimensions of placemaking. The process of making genocide heritage was not solitary work. Like human rights practice more broadly, it necessarily developed from networks of solidarity and resistance. It was motivated by kinship and developed from relationships of care, grief, and survivorship. The political and social impacts of Rwanda's genocide heritage have been contingent not merely on its makers but on witnesses that transform viewing into action. And yet genocide heritage is not merely relational; it also refers to the state institutions that have progressively formalized national genocide memory. Government policies have complicated the social impacts of genocide heritage, entangling justice seeking with the aims of state sovereignty.

## TRAUMA HERITAGE AS REPAIR

Relationships of memory and action have not always been considered reliable. Comparative literature scholar Andreas Huyssen has criticized human rights prosecutions for their reliance on fragile and difficult-to-verify memories.[55] This not only opens such judicial processes to evidentiary weaknesses but also undermines human rights as an enforceable or binding set of principles. As a result, in Huyssen's estimation, memories present few avenues to direct action in the context of human rights practice. Given these circumstances, we might conclude that trauma heritage has few means to directly support such actions as reparations, individual or group legal claims, or political and institutional change.

But twentieth-century liberation and social justice activists who engaged in spatialized memory justice work contended otherwise. Elie Wiesel concurred: Although memory justice had few immediately actionable capabilities, particularly in preventing targeted violence, it remained critically important. In 1986, in the context of his Nobel Peace Prize speech, Wiesel underscored this belief, declaring: "We must *remember* the suffering of my people."[56] He continued by situating the Holocaust within a Global South geography of atrocities: "*As we must remember* that of the Ethiopians, the Cambodians, the boat people, Palestinians, the Mesquite Indians, the Argentinian '*desaparecidos*' [disappeared]—the list seems endless.... There may be times when we are powerless to prevent injustice, but there must never be a time when we fail to protest."[57] With this powerful contextualization, Wiesel both acknowledges discrete experiences of terror and violence and refers to the global solidarity movement that emerges from human rights advocacy.

As a spatial and visible form of protest, trauma heritage provides important corroboration of testimonial memory in the context of severe power imbalances. Moreover, trauma heritage fills critical gaps in efforts by judiciaries and governing regimes to hold criminals accountable. Such work claims the presence of memories in the context of their silencing. Activists assumed that while trauma heritage might not directly enact reparations, it would form the foundation of further action in legal and political spheres.

The turn to spatialized memory in Rwanda and elsewhere in the world was a means to both amplify marginalized narratives and deliver actionable progress in attaining justice for victims and human rights advocacy and protections. As instances of localized human rights practice, trauma heritage practices did not merely call for recognition. It sought to *do something* within communities and institutions. That shift, which extended truth telling into placemaking, was critical to establishing tangible confrontations—in one's lived environment—with traumatic experiences that had been erased or normalized. The aim was to retrain the averted gaze, shatter the veil of denial, and, in the process, expand networks of solidarity among those who witness.

## The Paradoxes of Memory Justice

Rwanda's genocide heritage, perhaps more acutely than other forms of trauma heritage, reveals the inherent tensions in representing mass death as a form of memory justice. The sites open ethical tensions intrinsic to revealing violence, and personal traumas, for public viewing. In this regard, Rwanda represents an extreme case of both the visceral experience of witnessing and the politicization of collective memory. But it is not alone in this regard.

A potent trauma heritage site in the US city of Chicago animates those antagonisms. For four days in September 1955, and then in photographs published in *Jet Magazine* and the *Memphis Tri-State Defender*, Mamie Till-Mobley publicly displayed the body of her son, Emmett "Bobo" Till, in defiance of the silences surrounding his racially motivated murder.[58] She opened his casket, and Emmett's brutalized body, to hundreds of thousands of people. It was an act born of extreme pain and rage, a choice that no mother should have had to make. But Mamie Till-Mobley said of her decision:

> I could talk for the rest of my life about what had happened to my baby, I could explain it in great detail, I could describe what I saw laid out there on that slab . . . one piece, one inch, one body part at a time. I could do all of that and people still would not get the full impact. They would not be able to visualize what had happened, unless they were allowed to see the results of what had happened. They had to see what I had seen. The whole nation had to bear witness to this.[59]

The public viewing of her son was a remembrance of his individuality and humanity. It also opened a site of social mourning and political action—a site of trauma heritage—that further galvanized the civil rights movement in the United States (figure C.4).[60] Mamie Till-Mobley revealed Emmett's body so that a nation would "realize just how twisted, how distorted, how terrifying race hatred could be."[61] Through viewing, the affective power of her soul-wrenching loss gained an added dimension: demonstrable, incontrovertible evidence of racialized violence. This deeply personal instance of trauma heritage was established to advocate for the human rights of African Americans and seek justice for ongoing forms of racialized oppression and killing. The visceral act of seeing aimed to bridge from knowing and recognizing those crimes to doing something about them.

At the core of the era of trauma heritage—and specifically the appearance and viewing of spaces, artifacts, and images of violence in the public sphere—is an insistence on immediacy and a collapse of emotional and physical distance. Some semblance of the trauma embedded in memories of violence is exposed to strangers as a result.[62] Those memories flood the senses, commanding attention to the horrific. In Rwanda's case, collective memory is transfixed by the aftermath of violence in conserved scenes and victims of massacre. Those displays of evidence both tell us too much about the genocide and are insufficient to relay intimate details held in individual histories. It is an imperfect form of representation that situates several central contradictions, for genocide heritage is both inordinately difficult to see and has been designed precisely for viewing. As a result of their conservation and curation, the victims' remains and killing sites that demonstrate genocide heritage exceed fact and approximate spectacle. And yet genocide heritage's origins in human rights—despite formative entanglements in Rwanda's national politics—warn us against judging memorials solely as fetish sites of death.

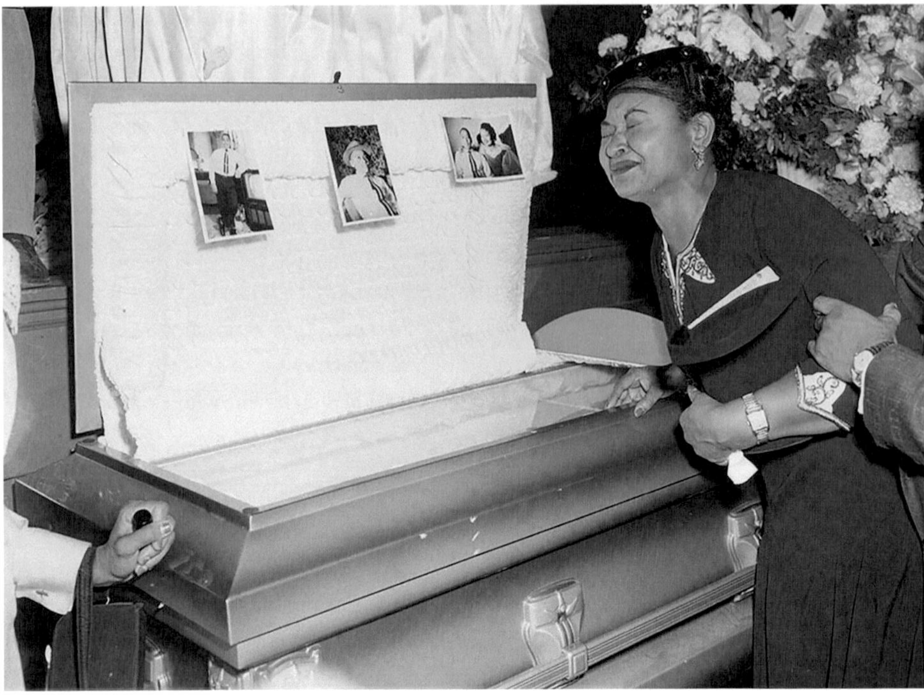

FIGURE C.4. A photograph that Mamey Till-Mobley, mother of Emmett Till, who was lynched in Mississippi in 1955, included in her memoir. She affixed photographs from her last Christmas with her son to his casket. *Chicago Sun-Times*/AP, Chicago, September 5, 1955.

In parallel analysis, art historian Georges Didi-Huberman writes of four clandestine images photographed in August 1944 from within the Auschwitz death camp. The photographs were taken by prisoners under profound duress and were smuggled out of the camp rolled up in a tube of toothpaste. Though not entirely clear, they attempt to document the murder of individuals in a rare visual representation of Holocaust gas chamber killings. Didi-Huberman describes the photographs as liminal and impossible. They both record an absence, in the "imminent obliteration of the witness," and document violence that exceeds representation in word and image.[63] The images capture a past made present, such that both the death of the witness and the overwhelming presence of death are preserved for the future. These, then, are "four images *in spite of it all*," Didi-Huberman writes; they exist "in spite of the risks, in spite of our inability to look at them today."[64]

The era of trauma heritage takes up the dilemma captured in those images of the unthinkable. Trauma heritage substantiates the facts of violence hidden or normalized. It gathers witnesses and, in doing so, casts those realities widely: to confront those who wish to look away or are ignorant of the crimes committed. This moral imperative notwithstanding, trauma heritage has complicated afterlives. It is the very substance of these memories that is difficult to see, especially for publics at a distance from the scene of the crime and for those who are too close, for whom the memories are personal.

The images collected in this book perpetuate Rwanda's genocide heritage for a global public. They make the past present. I do not show them as provocation; the images were originally created to archive details of the genocide's occurrence. They also document the labor and conditions that went into *making* Rwanda's genocide heritage. More broadly, they present evidence for this book's central argument: They explain why an era of trauma heritage developed across the Global South in the late twentieth century and continues to persist today. Yet the violence that Rwanda's genocide heritage preserves and circulates troubles many who view those sites and images. Their graphic nature persists, as Didi-Huberman notes, "in spite of our inability to look at them today."[65]

This is a central challenge for an era of trauma heritage tasked with exposing marginalized forms of violence. At the heart of the issue is the central contradiction that trauma heritage navigates, between truth and fetish, evidence and spectacle. It also speaks to the discomfort that many secondary witnesses feel, for Rwanda's genocide heritage is oriented primarily to the unfamiliar and those who do not wish to see. Those persistently visible memories reveal, as well, significant conflicts between the ethics of remembrance and the politics of national sovereignty. The violent images and spaces that enter the public sphere present these dilemmas without resolution. Instead, Rwanda's genocide heritage—and indeed trauma heritage more broadly—mobilizes its dual status as truth and fetish for political activism, trading shock for recognition.

The ubiquity of media, memorials, museums, and trials that have mobilized trauma heritage for such purposes suggests a shift in the role and regard of spatialized memory. Trauma heritage has become a critical means to advocate for memory justice and, in turn, forms of disclosure, empowerment, and repair. The prevalence of the phenomenon assumes an engaged global citizen—one capable, if only for a moment, of looking. The insistence on being there, observing with one's eyes—on anecdotal evidence, no less—directly confronts the digitization of seeing and the assumed contemporary obsolescence of material culture. But, as Rwanda's genocide heritage reminds us, the politics of trauma heritage sites suggest that they are not pure expressions of counter-memory. We must also be attentive to where representations of the dead haunt the living and bolster the powerful. Such are the paradoxes of memory justice enacted in an era of trauma heritage.

# ACKNOWLEDGMENTS

*Kuri mwese mwampaye impano y'igihe cyanyu n'ibitekerezo byanyu: nizere ko iki gitabo kigaragaza ukuri mwifuzaga gutanga*. This book was born from countless *impano*—gifts—that took the form of reflections and (measured) trust, rebukes and chiding, conveyed despite and because of struggles remembered and lived. I write in recognition of the many individuals who spoke with me and their experiences, wit, and fortitude. To Louis, Mario, Janvier, and Vestine especially: I hope I have portrayed your work, and your views on it, with the care and complexity that it deserves. That aspiration is redoubled with Louis's and Mario's recent passing. My hope is that this book affords others insight into the dilemmas and forms of justice that result from their efforts to "make history known."

The process of listening was one of partnership, shared lament, and laughter. To my dear and trusted colleague who accompanied me on nearly every encounter *mu cyaro*: thank you for the privilege of your insights and the pleasure of your friendship. Thank you, moreover, to our original research team and *umushoferi udasanzwe*, whose deft navigation of winding hills always kept us safe. To Erin Moseley and Lowell Brower, my family in research: thank you for your close reads, hard questions, and unwavering support in life. To Carola Velasco Hodgson, an exemplar of generosity and compassion: thank you for your sisterhood during those weeks in Chile and for years before and beyond. To the many more friends living then in Rwanda—Sam, Sara, Frances, Tomà, Elizabeth, Anna, Doudou, Jordan, Liz, Megha, and Sush: thank you for enlivening this work over shared meals and your stalwart support.

Research for this book was made possible by funds granted by the Harvard Weatherhead Center for International Affairs, the Social Science Research Council, the Harvard University Sheldon Fellowship, the Harvard Humanitarian Institute, the Harvard Rockefeller Institute for Latin American Studies, and the

Massachusetts Institute of Technology (MIT) Department of Urban Studies and Planning. I am furthermore grateful to the American Council on Learned Societies and a Mellon Postdoctoral Fellowship from the University of Pennsylvania Wolf Humanities Center for the time and space to write my first draft thoughts, along with the communities of scholars and friends that both convened. A Production Grant from the Graham Foundation for Advanced Studies in the Fine Arts made it possible for the book's images to be put in dialogue with its text.

Writing was done in (substantial and prolonged) iteration and through companionship. I am foremost grateful for the exceptional editorial assistance of Florence Grant: Thank you for your sensitive reads of my work and guiding me to express myself with greater clarity. Thank you, moreover, to the staff, editorial board, and editors at Duke University Press—especially Elizabeth Ault, whose belief in the book sustained it for the many years it took to develop. To the two anonymous reviewers who read *multiple* drafts of the *entire* manuscript: thank you for your time and energy amid the scarcity of both, and above all for your constructive feedback, which pushed this project to its significantly better version. Thank you to my MIT students, who read early drafts of chapters in my Cities of Contested Memory course and enlivened the idea of memory justice with their own pursuits. And thank you to my scholarly kin—my brother, Garnette Cadogan, whose indefatigable support and feedback emboldened my historiographical approach; dear friends and exemplary scholars Fallon Samuels Aidoo, Hiba Bou Akar, Sai Balakrishnan, Rania Ghosn, and Kian Goh, from whose research in spatial politics I've learned so much; Anooradha Iyer Siddiqi, an equally inimitable scholar and strident builder of community, who initiated the Columbia University Insurgent Domesticities working group and the collaborations that developed with Lilian Chee, Kush Patel, Jay Cephas, and many more in Caregiving as Method; and Assumpta Mugiraneza, from whose expertise in issues of trauma, collective memory, and cultural practice—and generosity of spirit—I continue to learn from in ways both scholarly and personal. Thank you to Mariana Arcaya, devin michelle bunten, Gabriella Carolini, Karilyn Crockett, Dayna Cunningham, Holly Harriel, Catherine D'Ignazio, Jason Jackson, Erica Caple James, Timothy Hyde, Taina McField, Monica Orta, Nasser Rabbat, Justin Steil, and Larry Vale, who provided feedback on early versions of chapters and a sense of home at MIT. Thank you to the faculty, organizers, and audiences at the departments of Architecture, Planning, and African Studies at the University of Buffalo, Columbia University, the University of Florida, the University of Michigan, Princeton University, and Harvard University for your invitations to speak about my research and for your questions—the latter heightened the stakes and pushed the implications of my work. Thank you, as well, to Barbara

Elfman, who opened her home to a wayward couple when they needed it most and provided a most scenic refuge for writing. As always, I bear sole responsibility for all mistakes made and views expressed.

Last but certainly not least, to my family, my most cherished writing partners: my most effusive and heartfelt thank yous. To my partner in life, Matthew Steele: thank you for encircling this endeavor with your love, penchant for absurdity, unrelenting patience and support, editorial acumen, and a home. To our daughter, to whose joy, impishness, and curiosity I turn for uplift: thank you for gifting me the privileges of motherhood and learning and laughing with you. To our child currently kicking around in my belly: I eagerly anticipate your lifetime of discovery and the memories that we will all make together. To my siblings, aunts, uncles, mother-in-law, and extended family-in-law: thank you for your thoughtful questions and encouragement throughout this long writing process. To my Vietnamese grandparents, aunts, uncles, and cousins: please know that I have been shaped, from a young age, by listening to your memories, attentive to your sacrifices and dreams for our generations to come. To my mother and late father: I owe you both a special debt of gratitude for the ways that you contended with war and inequality by developing commitments to justice and humanity. Thank you for leading by example and with humility. This book is also in honor of your pasts, and the futures they make possible.

# APPENDIX 1 CONCISE ATLAS OF TRAUMA HERITAGE, 1875–2020

MAPS 1–4. (*overleaf*) The Concise Atlas of Trauma Heritage locates 271 sites that spatialize memories of silenced and absenced violence from 1875 to 2020. Compiled by Delia Duong Ba Wendel (2024). Maps by Tyler Rivera. Art by Zac DeGiulio. The following sites are also represented chronologically to map their development over time (see appendix 2) and identified in an index of featured sites (see appendix 3).

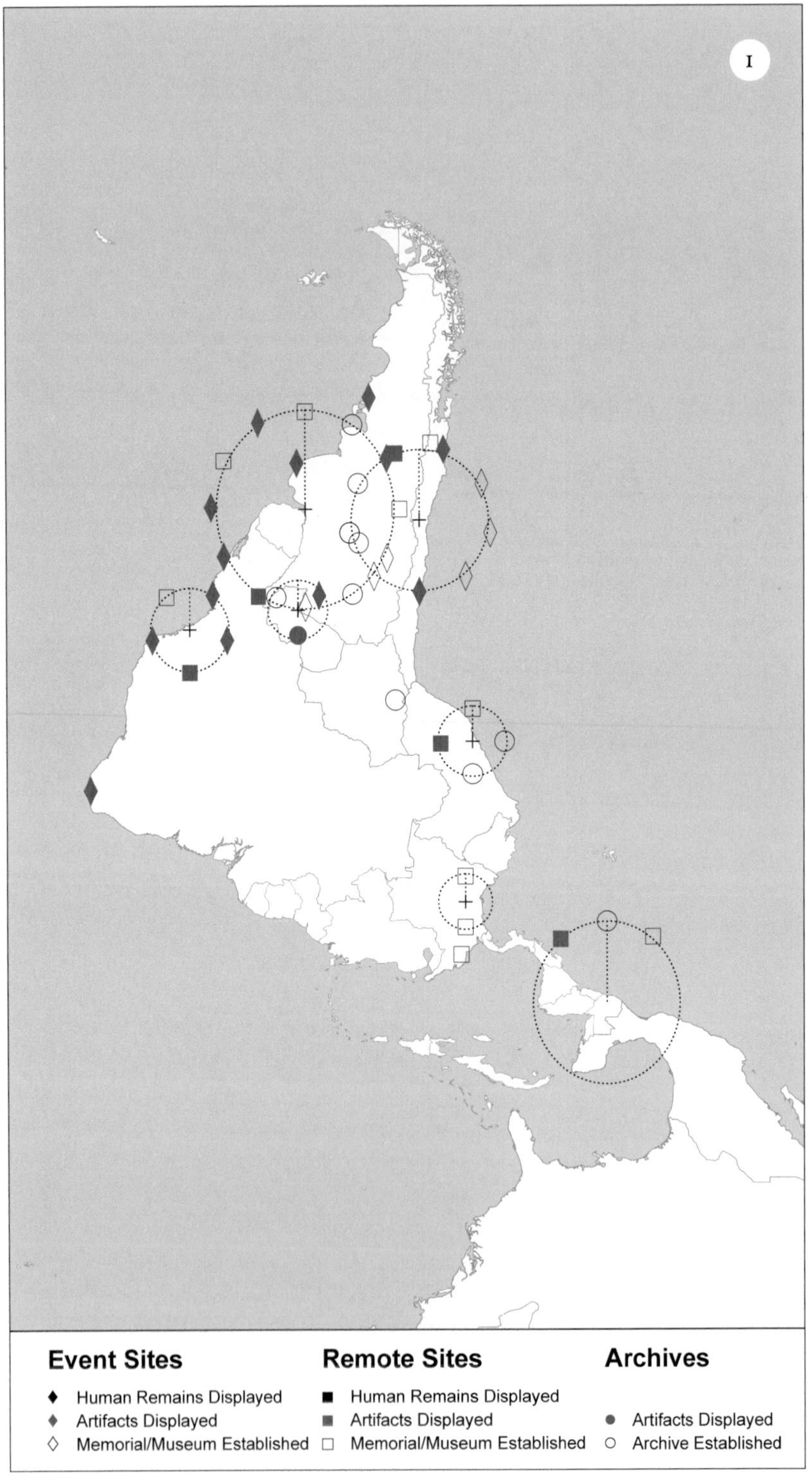
I
Event Sites
Human Remains Displayed
Artifacts Displayed
Memorial/Museum Established
Remote Sites
Human Remains Displayed
Artifacts Displayed
Memorial/Museum Established
Archives
Artifacts Displayed
Archive Established

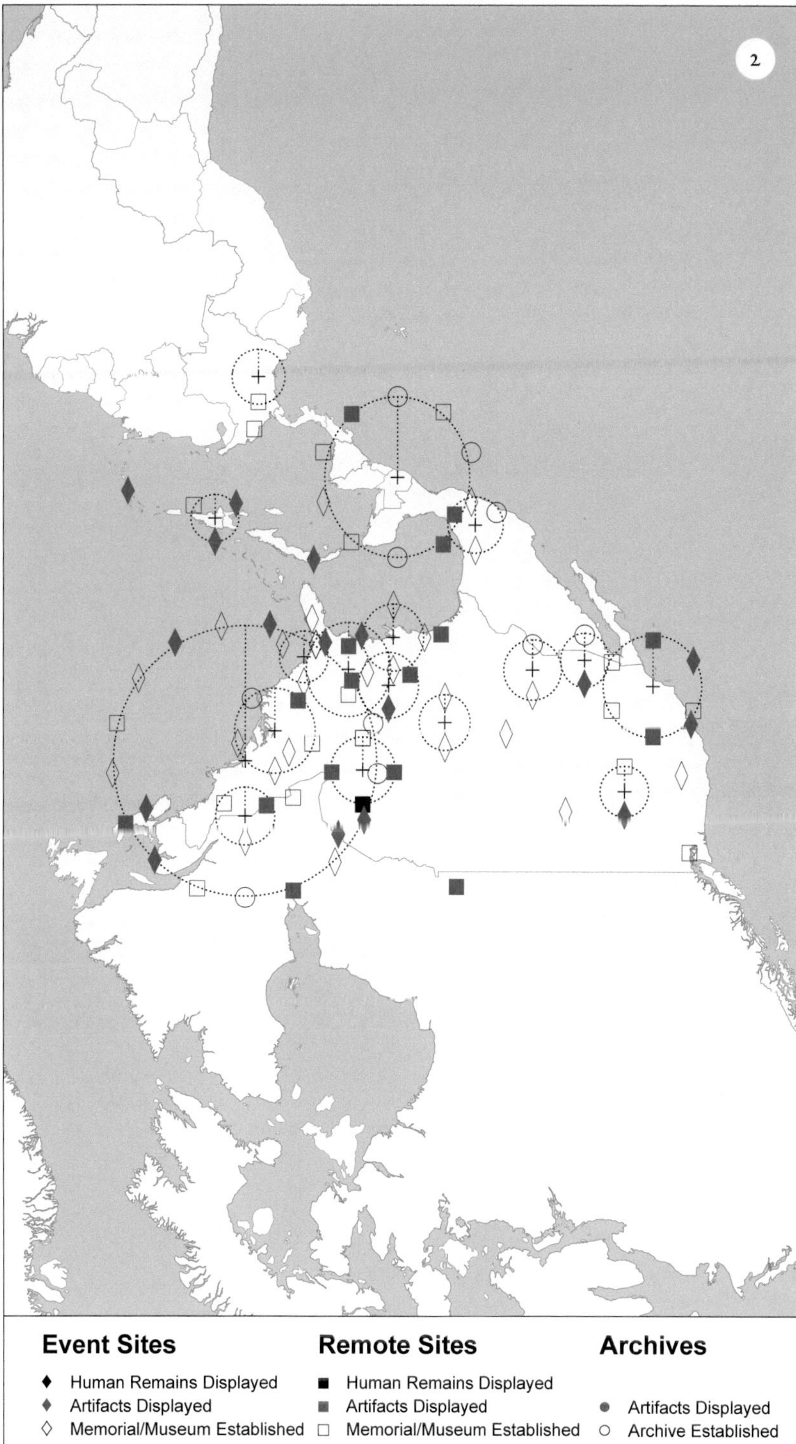
2
Event Sites
Human Remains Displayed
Artifacts Displayed
Memorial/Museum Established
Remote Sites
Human Remains Displayed
Artifacts Displayed
Memorial/Museum Established
Archives
Artifacts Displayed
Archive Established

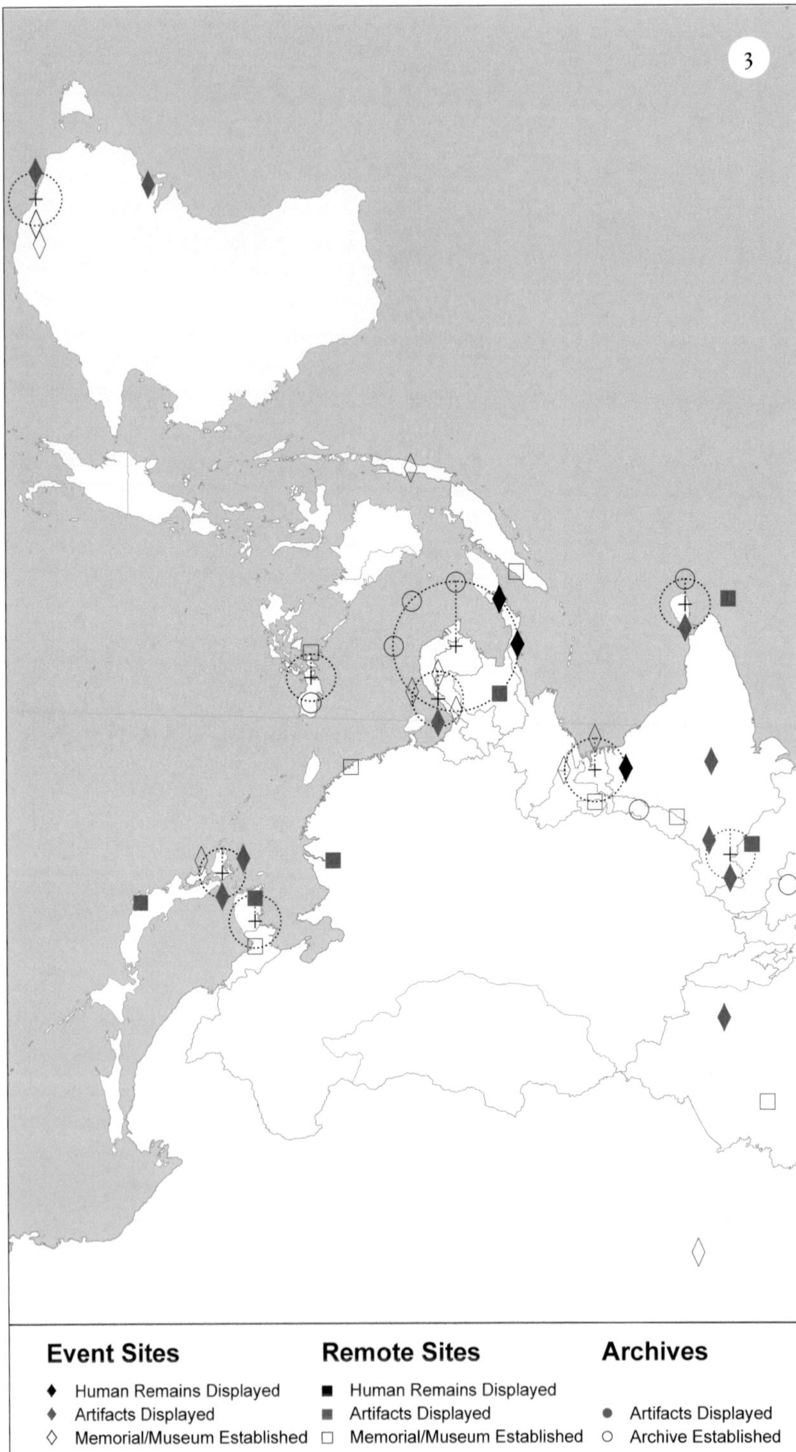
3
Event Sites
Human Remains Displayed
Artifacts Displayed
Memorial/Museum Established
Remote Sites
Human Remains Displayed
Artifacts Displayed
Memorial/Museum Established
Archives
Artifacts Displayed
Archive Established

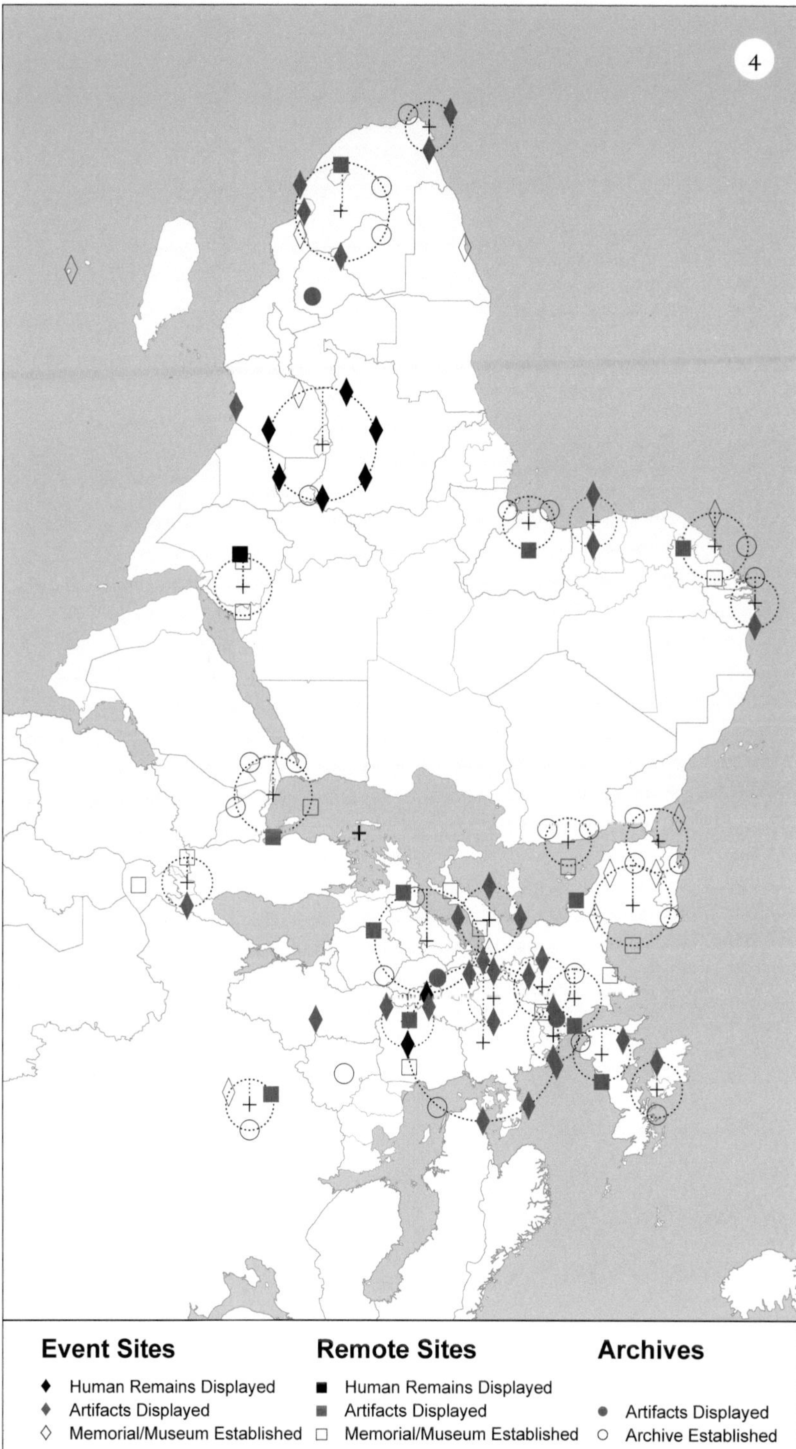
4
Event Sites
Human Remains Displayed
Artifacts Displayed
Memorial/Museum Established
Remote Sites
Human Remains Displayed
Artifacts Displayed
Memorial/Museum Established
Archives
Artifacts Displayed
Archive Established

# APPENDIX 2 CHRONOLOGICAL ATLAS OF TRAUMA HERITAGE, 1875–2020

MAPS 5–20. (*overleaf*) The Chronological Atlas of Trauma Heritage is organized by five-year intervals, locating sites as they were established between 1875 and 2020. Compiled by Delia Duong Ba Wendel (2024). Map by Tyler Rivera. Art by Zac DeGiulio. The Chronological Index (appendix 3) identifies featured trauma heritage sites.

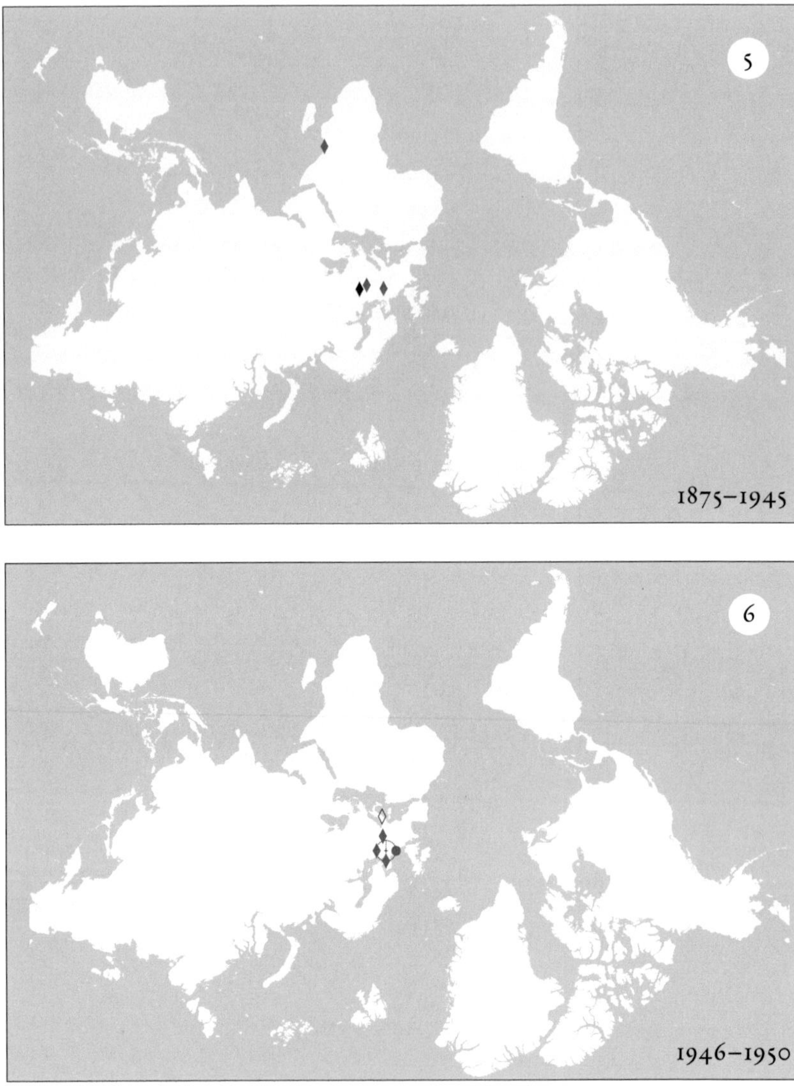


**Event Sites**

- ♦ Human Remains Displayed
- ♦ Artifacts Displayed
- ◇ Memorial/Museum Established

**Remote Sites**

- ■ Human Remains Displayed
- ■ Artifacts Displayed
- □ Memorial/Museum Established

**Archives**

- ● Artifacts Displayed
- ○ Archive Established

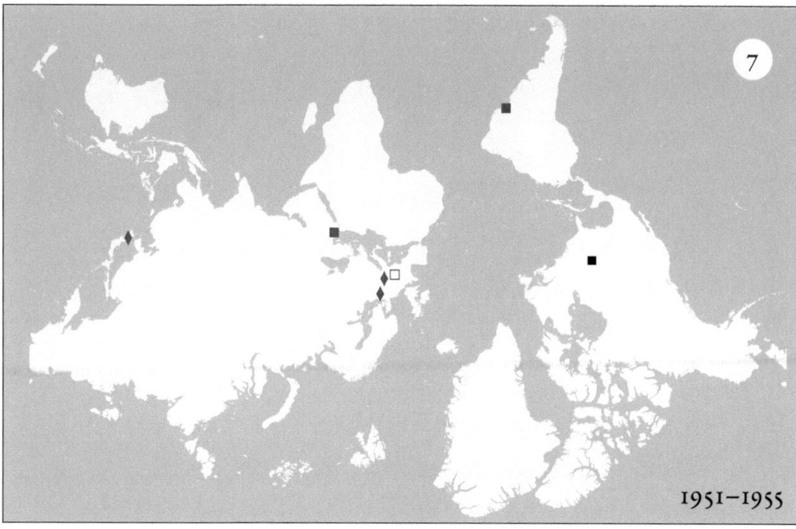


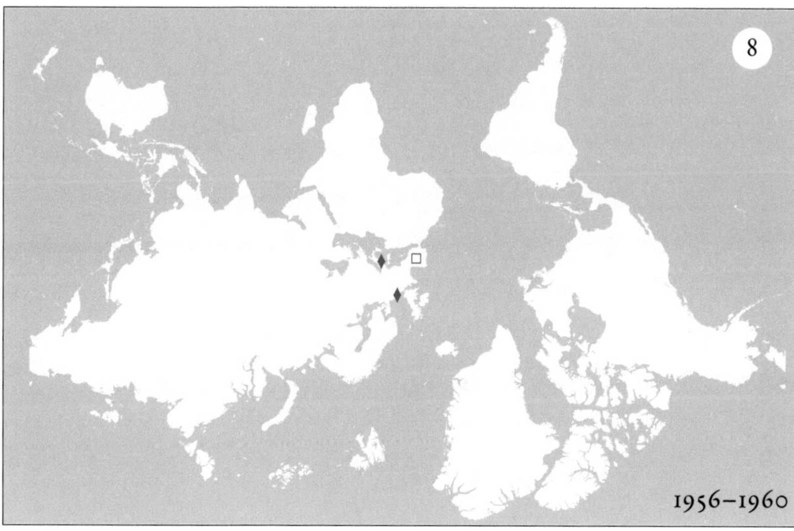


**Event Sites**
- ♦ Human Remains Displayed
- ♦ Artifacts Displayed
- ◇ Memorial/Museum Established

**Remote Sites**
- ■ Human Remains Displayed
- ■ Artifacts Displayed
- □ Memorial/Museum Established

**Archives**
- ● Artifacts Displayed
- ○ Archive Established

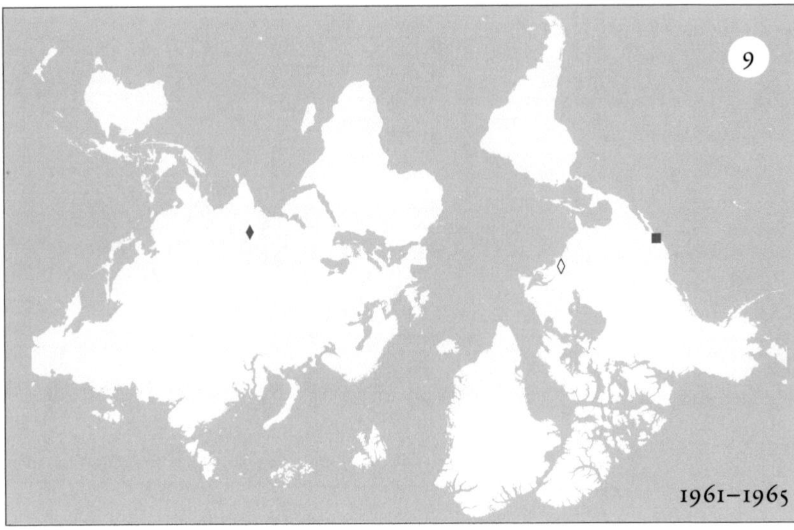


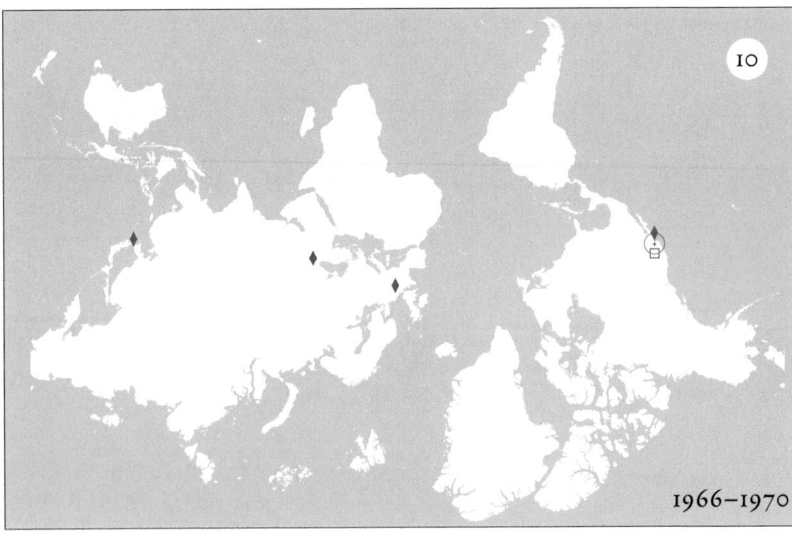


| Event Sites | Remote Sites | Archives |
|---|---|---|
| ♦ Human Remains Displayed | ■ Human Remains Displayed | |
| ♦ Artifacts Displayed | ■ Artifacts Displayed | ● Artifacts Displayed |
| ◊ Memorial/Museum Established | □ Memorial/Museum Established | ○ Archive Established |

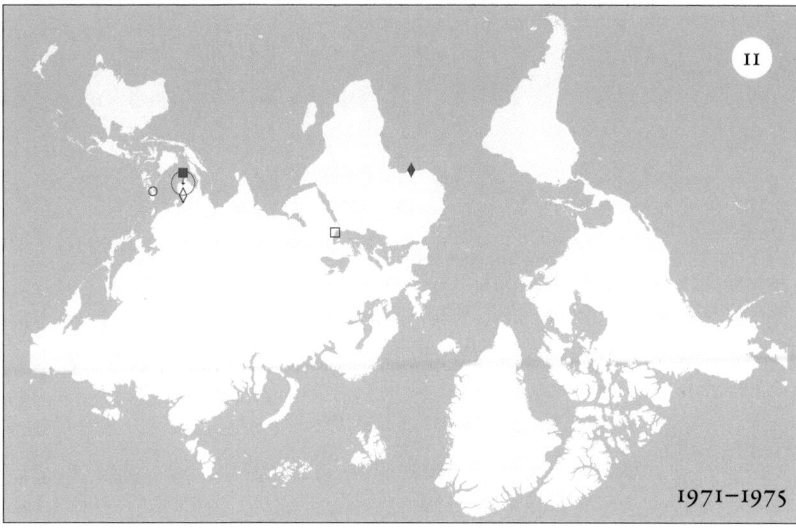


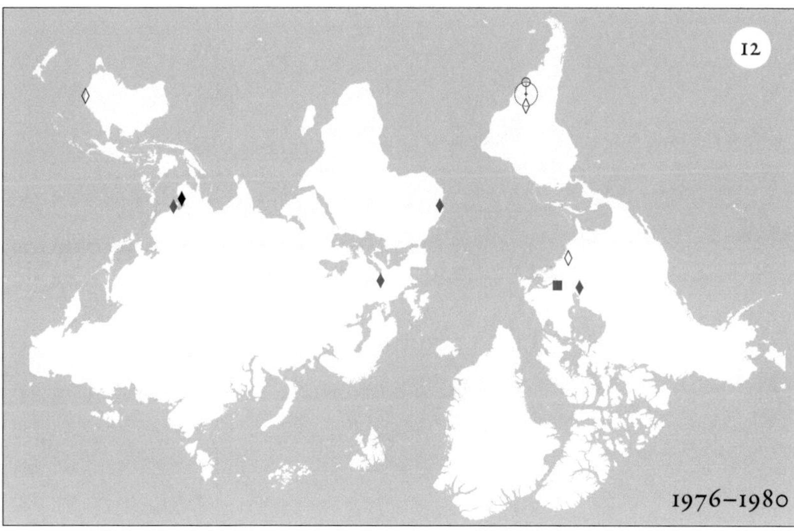


**Event Sites**

- ♦ Human Remains Displayed
- ♦ Artifacts Displayed
- ◇ Memorial/Museum Established

**Remote Sites**

- ■ Human Remains Displayed
- ■ Artifacts Displayed
- □ Memorial/Museum Established

**Archives**

- ● Artifacts Displayed
- ○ Archive Established

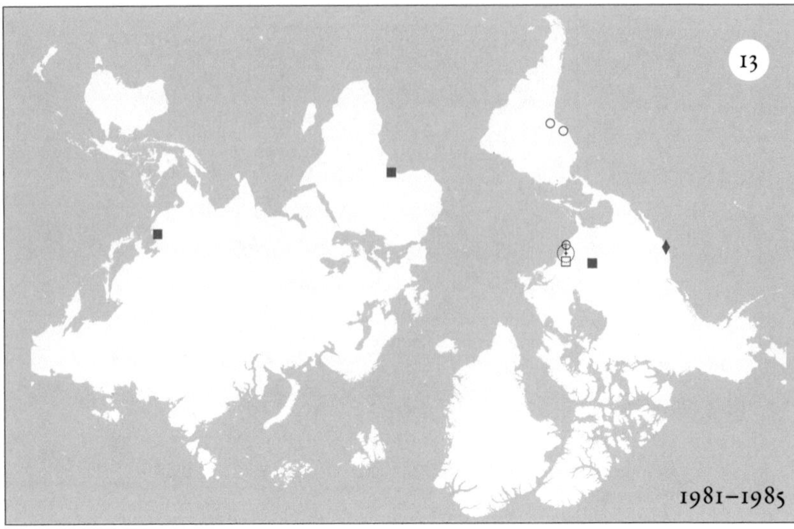


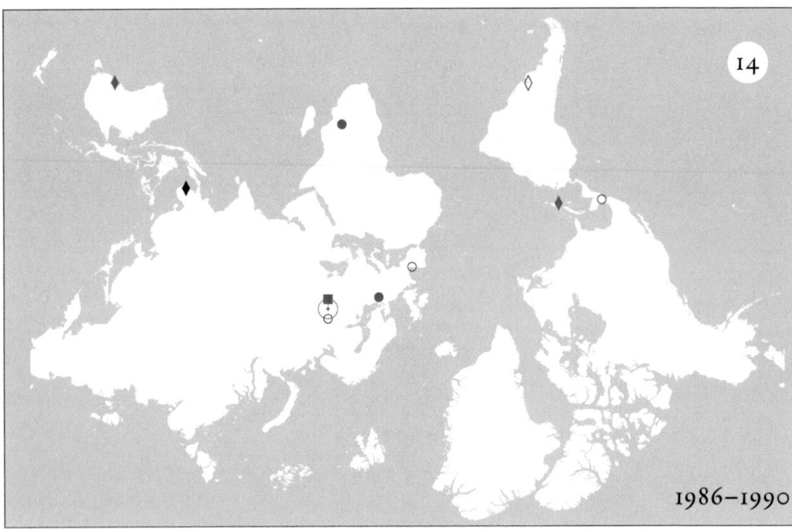


| Event Sites | Remote Sites | Archives |
|---|---|---|
| ♦ Human Remains Displayed | ■ Human Remains Displayed | |
| ♦ Artifacts Displayed | ■ Artifacts Displayed | ● Artifacts Displayed |
| ◇ Memorial/Museum Established | □ Memorial/Museum Established | ○ Archive Established |

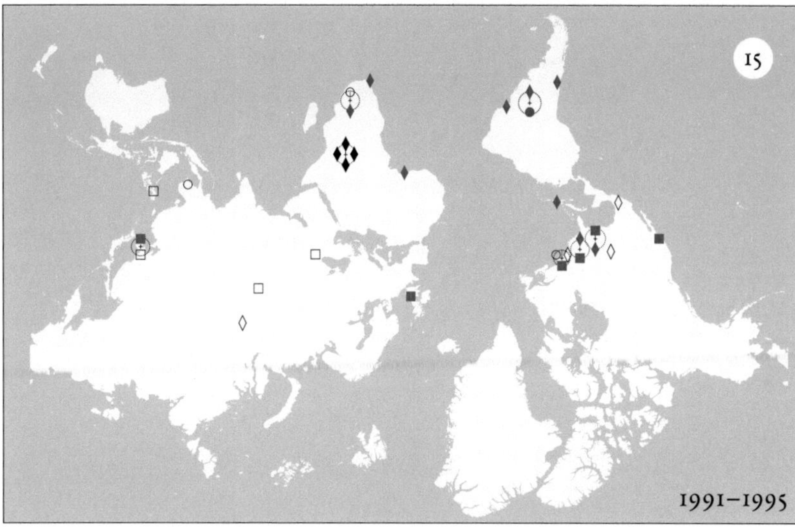


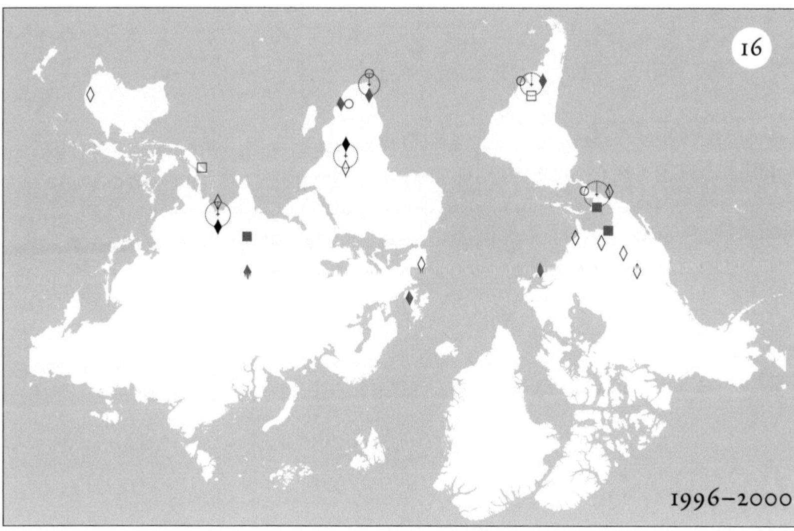


| Event Sites | Remote Sites | Archives |
|---|---|---|
| ♦ Human Remains Displayed | ■ Human Remains Displayed | |
| ♦ Artifacts Displayed | ■ Artifacts Displayed | ● Artifacts Displayed |
| ◇ Memorial/Museum Established | □ Memorial/Museum Established | ○ Archive Established |

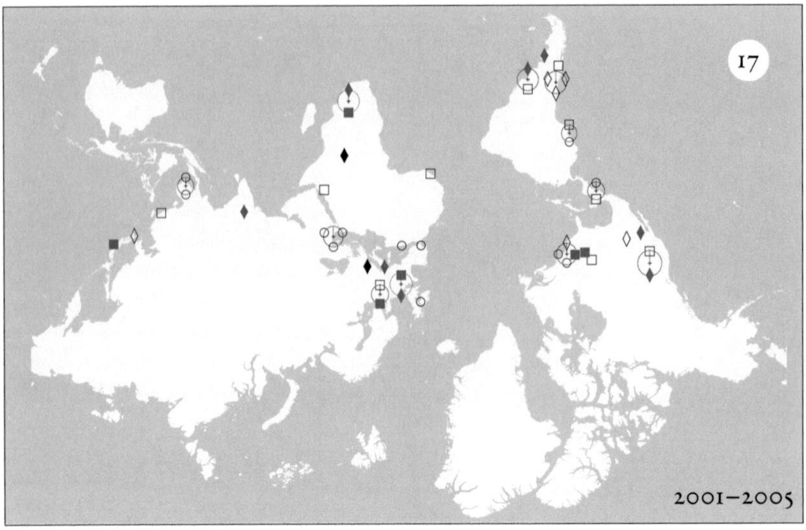
17
2001–2005

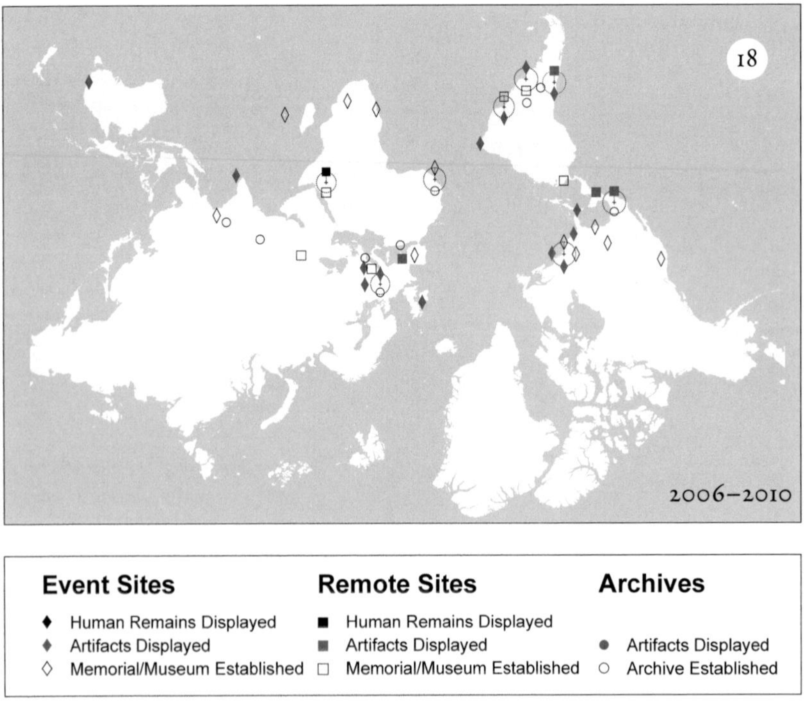
18
2006–2010
Event Sites
Human Remains Displayed
Artifacts Displayed
Memorial/Museum Established
Remote Sites
Human Remains Displayed
Artifacts Displayed
Memorial/Museum Established
Archives
Artifacts Displayed
Archive Established

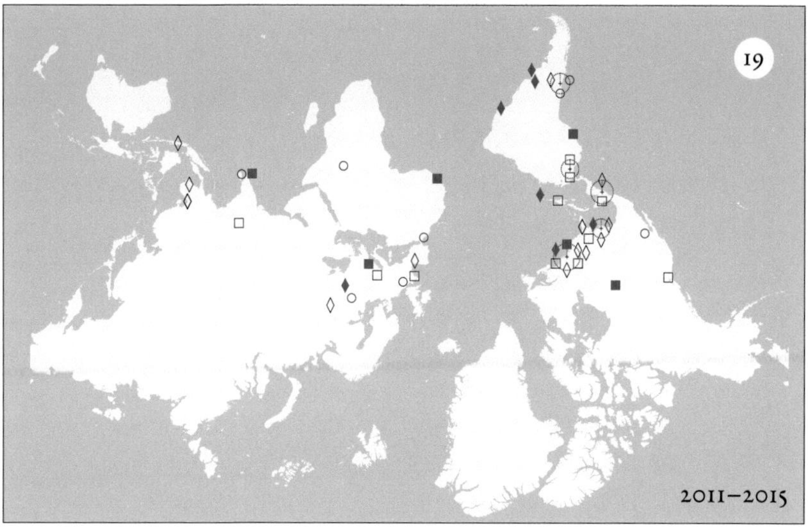


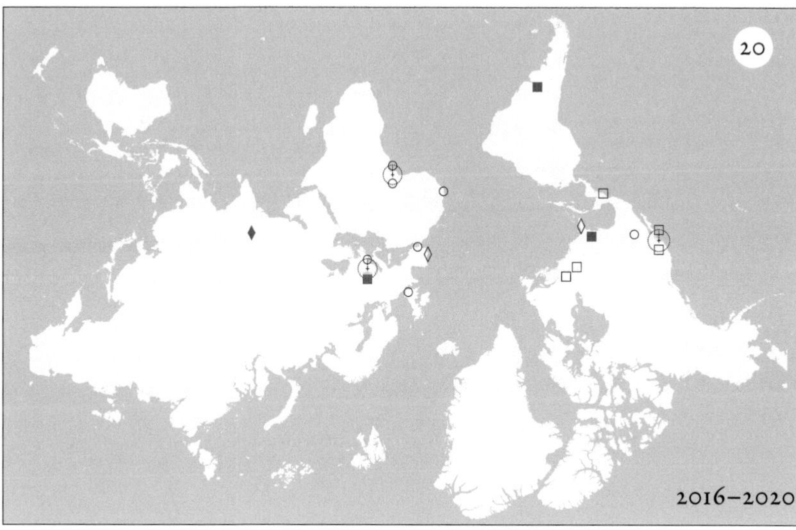


| Event Sites | Remote Sites | Archives |
|---|---|---|
| ♦ Human Remains Displayed | ■ Human Remains Displayed | |
| ♦ Artifacts Displayed | ■ Artifacts Displayed | ● Artifacts Displayed |
| ◇ Memorial/Museum Established | □ Memorial/Museum Established | ○ Archive Established |

# APPENDIX 3

# CHRONOLOGICAL INDEX OF FEATURED TRAUMA HERITAGE SITES, 1875–2020

The Chronological Index of Featured Trauma Heritage Sites (*overleaf*) identifies the trauma heritage sites included in the preceding Chronological Atlas of Trauma Heritage, 1875–2020 (presented in appendixes 1 and 2), organized by the year in which they were established. Delia Duong Ba Wendel (2024).

1875–1945

- ♦ Anglican Church Slave Market Memorial Zanzibar; Zanzibar, Tanzania 1879
- ♦ State Museum at Majdanek; Lublin, Poland 1944
- ♦ Auschwitz-Birkenau Holocaust Memorial Museum; Oswiecim, Poland 1945
- ♦ Buchenwald Memorial; Weimar, Germany 1945

1946–1950

- ♦ Bergen-Belsen Holocaust Memorial; Lohheide, Germany 1946
- ♦ Flossenbürg Holocaust Memorial; Flossenbürg, Germany 1946
- ○ Arolsen Archives of Nazi Persecution; Bad Arolsen, Germany 1948
- ♦ Ravensbrück Holocaust Memorial; Fürstenberg/Havel, Germany 1948
- ◇ Fosse Ardeatine World War II Massacre Memorial; Rome, Italy 1949

1951–1955

- ♦ Dachau Holocaust Memorial; Dachau, Germany 1952
- ■ Instituto Cultural Israelita Brasileiro; São Paulo, Brazil 1953
- ■ Yad Vashem Holocaust Remembrance Center; Jerusalem, Israel 1953
- ♦ Sachsenhausen Holocaust Memorial Museum; Oranienburg, Germany 1954
- □ Haitian Slave Revolt: Toussaint Louverture Mémorial; La Cluse-et-Mijoux, France 1954
- ■ Emmett Till's open-casket memorial; Chicago, Illinois, United States 1955
- ♦ Hiroshima Peace Memorial Museum; Hiroshima, Japan 1955

1956–1960

- ♦ Museo Storico Della Liberazione; Rome, Italy 1957
- □ Valley of the Fallen, Spanish Civil War; San Lorenzo de El Escorial, Spain 1959
- ♦ Anne Frank House; Amsterdam, Netherlands 1960

1961–1965

- ♦ Jallianwala Bagh Colonial Massacre Memorial; Amritsar, India 1961
- ■ LA Museum of the Holocaust; Los Angeles, California, United States 1961
- ◇ Rokeby Museum; Ferrisburgh, Vermont, United States 1961

1966–1970

- ♦ Nagasaki Atomic Bomb Museum; Nagasaki, Japan 1966
- ♦ Douaumont Ossuary at the Mémorial de Verdun (World War I); Fleury-devant-Douaumont, France 1967
- ♦ Tsitsernakaberd Armenian Genocide Memorial; Yerevan, Armenia 1967
- □ Armenian Genocide Martyrs' Monument; Montebello, California, United States 1968
- ♦ Manzanar Japanese American Concentration Camp; Inyo County, California, United States 1969

| | 1971–1975 | |
|---|---|---|
| ♦ | Cape Coast Castle; Accra, Ghana | 1974 |
| ● | Task Force Detainees of the Philippines; Manila, Philippines | 1974 |
| ◇ | Ben Duoc Memorial Temple; Ho Chi Minh City, Vietnam | 1975 |
| □ | Tel Aviv Holocaust Memorial; Tel Aviv, Israel | 1975 |
| ■ | War Remnants Museum; Ho Chi Minh City, Vietnam | 1975 |

| | 1976–1980 | |
|---|---|---|
| ♦ | My Lai Massacre Memorial; Quảng Ngãi, Vietnam | 1976 |
| ◇ | The Addison Road Living Museum; Marrickville, Australia | 1976 |
| ◇ | Madres de Plaza de Mayo; Buenos Aires, Argentina | 1977 |
| ◇ | Historic Stagville State Historic Site; Durham County, North Carolina, United States | 1977 |
| ♦ | Gorée Island Memorial to the Slave Trade; Dakar, Senegal | 1978 |
| ● | Comisión de homenaje a las víctimas de Vesubio y Proto Banco; Buenos Aires, Argentina | 1979 |
| ♦ | Montefiorino Republic and Italian Resistance Museum; Montefiorino, Italy | 1979 |
| ■ | Montreal Holocaust Museum; Montreal, Canada | 1979 |
| ♦ | Shingwauk Residential Schools Centre; Sault Ste. Marie, Ontario, Canada | 1979 |
| ♦ | Tuol Sleng Genocide Museum; Phnom Penh, Cambodia | 1980 |

| | 1981–1985 | |
|---|---|---|
| □ | Martyr's Memorial, Algerian War; Algiers, Algeria | 1982 |
| □ | National Martyrs' Memorial; Savar, Bangladesh | 1982 |
| □ | Vietnam Veterans Memorial; Washington, DC, United States | 1982 |
| ● | Asociación Nacional de Familiares de Secuestrados, Detenidos y Desaparecidos del Perú; Ayacucho, Peru | 1983 |
| ♦ | Angel Island Immigration Station Foundation; Tiburon, California, United States | 1983 |
| ● | Asociación de Familiares de Detenidos Desaparecidos; La Paz, Bolivia | 1983 |
| ● | Kupferberg Holocaust Center and Archives; Bayside, New York, United States | 1983 |
| ■ | America's Black Holocaust Museum; Milwaukee, Wisconsin, United States | 1984 |
| ■ | Biafran War Museum; Umuahia, Nigeria | 1985 |
| ■ | Nanjing Massacre Memorial; Nanjing, China | 1985 |

| **Event Sites** | **Remote Sites** | **Archives** |
|---|---|---|
| ♦ Human Remains Displayed | ■ Human Remains Displayed | |
| ♦ Artifacts Displayed | ■ Artifacts Displayed | ● Artifacts Displayed |
| ◇ Memorial/Museum Established | □ Memorial/Museum Established | ○ Archive Established |

1986–1990

- ◇ Equipo Argentino de Antropologia Forense; Buenos Aires, Argentina 1986
- ♦ Fort Dimanche Prison; Port-au-Prince, Haiti 1986
- ♦ Migration Museum; Adelaide, Australia 1986
- ○ Nehanda and Kaguvi Court Record; Harare, Zimbabwe 1986
- ● Gernika Gogoratuz Centro de Investigación por la Paz; Guernica, Spain 1987
- ♦ Choeung Ek Mass Grave and Memorial; Phnom Penh, Cambodia 1988
- ● Centro de Derechos Humanos Fray Bartolomé de Las Casas; Chiapas, Mexico 1989
- ● Memorial International Society; Moscow, Russia 1989
- ■ Solovetsky Stone; Moscow, Russia 1990
- ○ Stasi Records Archive; Berlin, Germany 1990

1991–1995

- ♦ National Civil Rights Museum; Memphis, Tennessee, United States 1991
- ○ Archives of Terror; Asunción, Paraguay 1992
- ■ Birmingham Civil Rights Institute; Birmingham, Alabama, United States 1992
- ◇ *Brown v. Board of Education* National Historic Site; Topeka, Kansas, United States 1992
- ♦ Hector Pieterson Memorial and Museum; Soweto, South Africa 1992
- □ Museum of Sexual Slavery by the Japanese Military; Gyeonggi-do, South Korea 1992
- □ Monument to the Victims of Famine; Nur-Sultan, Kazakhstan 1992
- ♦ Museo de las Memorias: Dictadura y Derechos Humanos; Asunción, Paraguay 1992
- ■ Holocaust Memorial and Tolerance Center of Nassau County; Glen Cove, New York, United States 1992
- ♦ Slave Route; Ouidah, Benin 1992
- ◇ Voices Against Injustice (formerly Salem Award Foundation for Human Rights and Social Justice); Salem, Massachusetts, United States 1992
- ■ Museum of Tolerance; Los Angeles, California, United States 1993
- ◇ Nazino Island Memorial; Nazino, Russia 1993
- ♦ Museu da Imigração do Estado de São Paulo; São Paulo, Brazil 1993
- ◇ Tlatelolco Stele; Mexico City, Mexico 1993
- ■ United States Holocaust Memorial Museum; Washington, DC, United States 1993
- ♦ District Six Museum; Cape Town, South Africa 1994
- ♦ Eastern State Penitentiary; Philadelphia, Pennsylvania, United States 1994
- ♦ Hermanas Mirabal Museum; Salcedo, Dominican Republic 1994
- □ Monument to the Disappeared; Manila, Philippines 1994
- ♦ Ntarama Genocide Memorial; Kayumba, Rwanda 1994
- ♦ Nyarubuye Genocide Memorial; Nyarubuye, Rwanda 1994
- ● The Hart Island Project; New York, New York, United States 1994
- ♦ Villa Grimaldi and Parque por la Paz; Santiago, Chile 1994
- ■ War Memorial of Korea; Seoul, South Korea 1994
- □ Armenian Genocide Museum-Institute; Yerevan, Armenia 1995

1991–1995 (*continued*)

| | | |
|---|---|---|
| ● | Genocide Documentation Center; Phnom Penh, Cambodia | 1995 |
| ● | Khulumani; Johannesburg, South Africa | 1995 |
| ♦ | Murambi Genocide Memorial; Murambi, Rwanda | 1995 |
| ■ | National Holocaust Centre and Museum; Newark, United Kingdom | 1995 |
| ♦ | Nyamata Genocide Memorial; Nyamata, Rwanda | 1995 |

1996–2000

| | | |
|---|---|---|
| ◇ | Heart Mountain Interpretive Center; Powell, Wyoming, United States | 1996 |
| ■ | Holocaust Museum Houston; Houston, Texas, United States | 1996 |
| ♦ | Liberation War Museum; Dhaka, Bangladesh | 1996 |
| ■ | Museo de la Palabra y la Imagen; San Salvador, El Salvador | 1996 |
| ♦ | Diefenbunker: Canada's Cold War Museum; Ottawa, Canada | 1997 |
| ◇ | Fundación de Antropología Forense de Guatemala; Guatemala City, Guatemala | 1997 |
| ◇ | Martyrs of the Fraternity Sanctuary; Buta, Burundi | 1997 |
| ♦ | Robben Island; Western Cape, South Africa | 1997 |
| ♦ | The Workhouse; Southwell, United Kingdom | 1997 |
| ♦ | Bisesero Genocide Memorial; Bisesero, Rwanda | 1998 |
| ◇ | Little Rock Central High School National Historic Site; Little Rock, Arkansas, United States | 1998 |
| □ | Parque de la Memoria—Monumento a las Víctimas del Terrorismo de Estado; Buenos Aires, Argentina | 1998 |
| ● | Centro de la Memoria Monseñor Juan Gerardi; Guatemala City, Guatemala | 1998 |
| □ | Monument to Victims of Suharto's Purge; Medan, Indonesia | 1998 |
| ♦ | Museo de la Memoria; Rosario, Argentina | 1998 |
| ● | Steve Biko Foundation; Johannesburg, South Africa | 1998 |
| ■ | The Tibet Museum; Dharamshala, India | 1998 |
| ♦ | Canadian Museum of Immigration at Pier 21; Halifax, Canada | 1999 |
| ◇ | Martyred Intellectuals Memorial; Dhaka, Bangladesh | 1999 |
| ● | Memoria Abierta; Buenos Aires, Argentina | 1999 |
| ♦ | Samora Machel Monument; Mbuzini, South Africa | 1999 |
| ● | Human Rights Media Centre; Cape Town, South Africa | 2000 |
| ◇ | McLeod Plantation Historic Site and Caw Caw Interpretive Center; Charleston, South Carolina, United States | 2000 |
| ◇ | Myall Creek Massacre Memorial; Myall Creek, Australia | 2000 |
| ◇ | Priaranza del Bierzo Mass Grave; Priaranza del Bierzo, Spain | 2000 |
| ◇ | Sand Creek Massacre Site; Kiowa County, Colorado, United States | 2000 |

| **Event Sites** | **Remote Sites** | **Archives** |
|---|---|---|
| ♦ Human Remains Displayed | ■ Human Remains Displayed | |
| ♦ Artifacts Displayed | ■ Artifacts Displayed | ● Artifacts Displayed |
| ◇ Memorial/Museum Established | □ Memorial/Museum Established | ○ Archive Established |

2001–2005

- ■ Apartheid Museum; Johannesburg, South Africa 2001
- ● Healing Through Remembering; Belfast, Northern Ireland, United Kingdom 2001
- ■ Jewish Museum Berlin; Berlin, Germany 2001
- □ Memorial for the Remembrance of the Disappeared-Detainees; Montevideo, Uruguay 2001
- ♦ Minidoka National Historic Site; Jerome County, Idaho, United States 2001
- □ Samay Development Organization; Monrovia, Liberia 2001
- ● Peace Institute of Cambodia—Youth for Peace; Phnom Penh, Cambodia 2001
- ♦ Bois du Cazier Coal Mine Disaster Memorial; Marcinelle, Belgium 2002
- ● Historical Memory Project; New York, New York, United States 2002
- □ Idaho Anne Frank Human Rights Memorial; Boise, Idaho, United States 2002
- ■ Lest We Forget Museum of Slavery; Philadelphia, Pennsylvania, United States 2002
- ◊ Memorial Paine; Paine, Chile 2002
- ♦ Fondazione Scuola di Pace di Monte Sole; Marzabotto, Italy 2002
- ◊ Nagasaki National Peace Memorial for Atomic Bomb Victims; Nagasaki, Japan 2002
- ● Zochrot; Tel Aviv, Israel 2002
- ◊ Estádio Nacional; Santiago, Chile 2003
- ● Fondo Kati; Cádiz, Spain 2003
- ◊ William C. Goodridge Freedom Center and Underground Railroad Museum; York, Pennsylvania, United States 2003
- □ Martyrs' Memorial Monument; Mek'ele, Ethiopia 2003
- □ Monument to Memory and Truth; San Salvador, El Salvador 2003
- ● Movimiento Ciudadano Para Que No Se Repita; Lima, Peru 2003
- ♦ Srebrenica Genocide Memorial; Potocari, Bosnia and Herzegovina 2003
- ♦ Constitution Hill; Johannesburg, South Africa 2004
- ♦ Centro Cultural por la Memoria de Trelew; Chubut, Argentina 2004
- ♦ Human Rights Memorial Museum; Buenos Aires, Argentina 2004
- ♦ Kigali Genocide Memorial Centre; Kigali, Rwanda 2004
- □ Memorial to the Murdered Jews of Europe; Berlin, Germany 2004
- □ Centro Cultural and Museo y Memoria de Neltume; Panguipulli, Chile 2004
- □ National Cambodian Heritage Museum and Killing Fields Memorial; Chicago, Illinois, United States 2004
- ■ National Underground Railroad Freedom Center; Cincinnati, Ohio, United States 2004
- ● UMAM Documentation and Research; Beirut, Lebanon 2004
- ● ACT for the Disappeared; Beirut, Lebanon 2005
- ♦ Bhopal Gas Tragedy Memorial; Bhopal, India 2005
- ◊ Bosque Redondo Memorial at Fort Sumner Historic Site; Fort Sumner, New Mexico, United States 2005
- □ Cultural Revolution Museum; Shantou, China 2005
- ● Damascus Center for Human Rights Studies; Washington, DC, United States 2005
- ♦ Jewish History Museum and Holocaust History Center; Tucson, Arizona, United States 2005

2001–2005 (*continued*)

| | | |
|---|---|---|
| ● | Kdei Karuna; Phnom Penh, Cambodia | 2005 |
| ■ | Mémorial de la Shoah; Paris, France | 2005 |
| ● | Archivo Histórico de la Policía Nacional; Guatemala City, Guatemala | 2005 |
| ● | National Coordination of the Families of the Disappeared; Algiers, Algeria | 2005 |
| ◇ | Comité de Derechos Humanos: NIDO 20; Santiago, Chile | 2005 |
| □ | The Eye That Cries; Lima, Peru | 2005 |
| ■ | Women's Active Museum on War and Peace; Tokyo, Japan | 2005 |

2006–2010

| | | |
|---|---|---|
| ♦ | African Burial Ground Monument; New York, New York, United States | 2006 |
| ● | Archivo de la Memoria de la Provincia de Córdoba; Córdoba, Argentina | 2006 |
| ● | Centro de Investigaciones Históricas de los Movimientos Sociales; Mexico City, Mexico | 2006 |
| ♦ | Memorial da Lutas e Ligas Camponesas; Sapé, Brazil | 2006 |
| □ | Neighborhoods for Memory and Justice; Buenos Aires, Argentina | 2006 |
| ♦ | The Parramatta Female Factory Project; North Parramatta, Australia | 2006 |
| ♦ | Charleston Old Slave Mart Museum; Charleston, South Carolina, United States | 2007 |
| ◇ | Jamalpur Gandhi Ashram; Jamalpur, Bangladesh | 2007 |
| ■ | Memorial Democràtic de la Generalitat de Catalunya; Barcelona, Spain | 2007 |
| ♦ | Centro Cultural y Museo de la Memoria; Montevideo, Uruguay | 2007 |
| ♦ | Museum of Free Derry; Derry, Northern Ireland, United Kingdom | 2007 |
| ♦ | B92 Fund—Museum of Tolerance; Belgrade, Serbia | 2007 |
| ◇ | Swakopmund Concentration Camp Memorial; Swakopmund, Namibia | 2007 |
| ♦ | Tea Plantation Workers Museum; Kandy, Sri Lanka | 2007 |
| ◇ | 9/11 Pentagon Memorial; Arlington, Virginia, United States | 2008 |
| ◇ | Càrcel de Carabanchel para la Memoria; Madrid, Spain | 2008 |
| ● | Dirección de Verdad, Justicia, y Reparación; Asunción, Paraguay | 2008 |
| ◇ | Le Morne Brabant Slavery Resistance; District of Rivière Noire, Mauritius | 2008 |
| ♦ | Memorial of Resistance; São Paulo, Brazil | 2008 |
| □ | Museum of Memory and Identity; Montes de María, Colombia | 2008 |
| ◇ | Pennhurst Memorial and Preservation Alliance; Spring City, Pennsylvania, United States | 2008 |
| ♦ | Remember the Triangle Fire Coalition; New York, New York, United States | 2008 |
| ◇ | Sophiatown the Mix; Johannesburg, South Africa | 2008 |
| □ | The Cry of the Mother; Baku, Azerbaijan | 2008 |
| ◇ | Tule Lake National Monument; Newell, California, United States | 2008 |

| Event Sites | Remote Sites | Archives |
|---|---|---|
| ♦ Human Remains Displayed | ■ Human Remains Displayed | |
| ♦ Artifacts Displayed | ■ Artifacts Displayed | ● Artifacts Displayed |
| ◇ Memorial/Museum Established | □ Memorial/Museum Established | ○ Archive Established |

2006–2010 (*continued*)

- ● Afghanistan Human Rights and Democracy Organization; Kabul, Afghanistan 2009
- ● Mish'al Association for the Children of the Disappeared in Algeria (Algeria-Watch); Algiers, Algeria 2009
- □ Amhara People's Martyrs' Memorial Monument; Bahir Dar, Ethiopia 2009
- ● Association des Victimes, Parents et Amis du 28 septembre 2009; Conakry, Guinea 2009
- ♦ Casa Memoria José Domingo; Santiago, Chile 2009
- ● Cultural Heritage Without Borders; Tirana, Albania 2009
- ● Gulag Association; Prague, Czech Republic 2009
- ◇ John Hope Franklin Center for Reconciliation; Tulsa, Oklahoma, United States 2009
- ◇ Leona Tate Foundation for Change; New Orleans, Louisiana, United States 2009
- ● National Network of Families of Disappeared and Missing in Nepal; Kathmandu, Nepal 2009
- □ Núcleo de Preservação da Memória Política; São Paulo, Brazil 2009
- ♦ Slave Route Museum; Matanzas, Cuba 2009
- □ Kozarac Genocide Memorial; Kozarac, Bosnia and Herzegovina 2010
- ■ Memorial para la Concordia; Guatemala City, Guatemala 2010
- ■ Museo de la Memoria y Tolerancia; Mexico City, Mexico 2010
- ■ Museum of Memory and Human Rights; Santiago, Chile 2010
- ♦ Nuremberg Trials Memorial; Nuremberg, Germany 2010
- ♦ Historical Museum of the City of Krakow, Schindler's Factory; Krakow, Poland 2010
- ■ Red Terror Martyrs' Memorial Museum; Addis Ababa, Ethiopia 2010
- ◇ Sierra Leone Peace and Cultural Monument; Freetown, Sierra Leone 2010

2011–2015

- ◇ 9/11 Memorial; New York, New York, United States 2011
- ● Human Rights Center for Memory and Archives; Rabat, Morocco 2011
- □ Memorial for the Disappeared; Khairichandanpur, Nepal 2011
- □ Museo Memorial de la Resistencia Dominicana; Santo Domingo, Dominican Republic 2011
- ◇ Middle Passage Ceremonies and Port Markers Project; Jacksonville, Florida, United States 2011
- ● Syrian Network for Human Rights; Paris, France 2011
- ♦ Valongo Wharf Slave Memorial; Rio de Janeiro, Brazil 2011
- □ Armenian Heritage Park; Boston, Massachusetts, United States 2012
- ● Belarusian Documentation Center; Minsk, Belarus 2012
- ◇ Carlisle Indian School Farmhouse; Carlisle, Pennsylvania, United States 2012
- □ Dobrava Memorial Park; Maribor, Slovenia 2012
- ■ Gallery 11/07/95; Sarajevo, Bosnia and Herzegovina 2012
- ● Global Society Initiative for Peace and Democracy; Arua District, South Sudan 2012
- □ Centro de Memoria, Paz y Reconciliación; Bogotá, Colombia 2012

2011–2015 (*continued*)

| | | |
|---|---|---|
| | Museum of Women's Resistance; Brooklyn, New York, United States | 2012 |
| □ | Memorial to the Abolition of Slavery; Nantes, France | 2012 |
| ● | The Herstories Archive; Colombo, Sri Lanka | 2012 |
| ◇ | Vitoria-Gasteiz Massacre Memorial; Vitoria-Gasteiz, Spain | 2012 |
| ● | Cantos Cautivos; United Kingdom/Chile | 2013 |
| ● | Colibrí Center for Human Rights; Tucson, Arizona, United States | 2013 |
| ◇ | Đồng Lộc Junction; Hà Tĩnh, Vietnam | 2013 |
| ♦ | Faro de la Memoria; Mar del Plata, Argentina | 2013 |
| ♦ | Gettysburg Seminary Ridge Museum; Gettysburg, Pennsylvania, United States | 2013 |
| ■ | Museo Casa de la Memoria; Medellín, Colombia | 2013 |
| ■ | Sierra Leone Peace Museum; Freetown, Sierra Leone | 2013 |
| ◇ | Robert Hicks Foundation; Bogalusa, Louisiana, United States | 2013 |
| ■ | Canadian Museum for Human Rights; Winnipeg, Canada | 2014 |
| □ | Casa de la Memoria "Kaji Tulam"; Guatemala City, Guatemala | 2014 |
| ● | Asociación por la Memoria y los Derechos Humanos Colonia Dignidad; Santiago, Chile | 2014 |
| ♦ | National Museum of the Revolution of Dignity Maidan Museum; Kyiv, Ukraine | 2014 |
| ◇ | Melinka Corporación de Memoria y Cultura de Puchuncaví; Puchuncaví, Chile | 2014 |
| ◇ | Memory Landscapes; Comalapa, Guatemala | 2014 |
| □ | National Center for Civil and Human Rights; Atlanta, Georgia, United States | 2014 |
| ◇ | Posledny Adres Foundation; Moscow, Russia | 2014 |
| ◇ | Sleuk Rith Institute; Phnom Penh, Cambodia | 2014 |
| ◇ | Whitney Heritage Plantation; Edgard, Louisiana, United States | 2014 |
| ◇ | Whitney Plantation Museum; Wallace, Louisiana, United States | 2014 |
| □ | Center for Reconciliation; Providence, Rhode Island, United States | 2015 |
| □ | Consequences of Radiation Exposure; Seattle, Washington, United States | 2015 |
| ◇ | Flight 93 Memorial; Stoystown, Pennsylvania, United States | 2015 |
| ◇ | Caribbean Center for Memory of the Slave Trade; Pointe-à-Pitre, Guadeloupe | 2015 |
| ◇ | Museo Sitio de Memoria; Buenos Aires, Argentina | 2015 |
| ■ | Place of Memory Museum; Lima, Peru | 2015 |
| ◇ | Plumbon Mass Grave; Plumbon, Indonesia | 2015 |
| □ | Red Colombiana de Lugares de Memoria; Buenaventura, Colombia | 2015 |

| **Event Sites** | **Remote Sites** | **Archives** |
|---|---|---|
| ♦ Human Remains Displayed | ■ Human Remains Displayed | |
| ♦ Artifacts Displayed | ■ Artifacts Displayed | ● Artifacts Displayed |
| ◇ Memorial/Museum Established | □ Memorial/Museum Established | ○ Archive Established |

2016–2020

| | | |
|---|---|---|
| □ | Armenian Genocide Memorial; Los Angeles, California, United States | 2016 |
| ○ | Biafran War Memories; Dakar, Senegal | 2016 |
| ◇ | onePulse Foundation; Orlando, Florida, United States | 2016 |
| ○ | UTEP Borderlands Public History Lab; El Paso, Texas, United States | 2016 |
| ◇ | Museu Nacional Resistência e Liberdade—Fortaleza de Peniche; Peniche, Portugal | 2017 |
| □ | National Holocaust Monument; Ottawa, Canada | 2017 |
| □ | Reflect Space; Glendale, California, United States | 2017 |
| □ | Sanctuary of the Fallen El Triunfo; Champerico, Guatemala | 2017 |
| ♦ | The Partition Museum; Amritsar, India | 2017 |
| ■ | War Childhood Museum; Sarajevo, Bosnia and Herzegovina | 2017 |
| ● | Asociación Pasaje Begoña; Malaga, Spain | 2018 |
| ● | Center for Memories; Enugu, Nigeria | 2018 |
| ● | Centre for Public History; Belgrade, Serbia | 2018 |
| ● | Museum of British Colonialism; United Kingdom/Kenya | 2018 |
| ■ | National Memorial for Peace and Justice; Montgomery, Alabama, United States | 2018 |
| ■ | Museo Internacional para la Democracia; Rosario, Argentina | 2019 |
| ● | The African Network Against Extra-Judicial Killing and Enforced Disappearances; Serrekunda, the Gambia | 2020 |
| □ | Flight PS752 Memorial; Toronto, Canada | 2020 |

| Event Sites | Remote Sites | Archives |
|---|---|---|
| ♦ Human Remains Displayed | ■ Human Remains Displayed | |
| ♦ Artifacts Displayed | ■ Artifacts Displayed | ● Artifacts Displayed |
| ◇ Memorial/Museum Established | □ Memorial/Museum Established | ○ Archive Established |

# NOTES

## PROLOGUE: A ROCK AMONG MANY

1. Both Mario Ibarra and Louis Kanamugire passed away while this book was in production (in March 2025 and December 2024, respectively). Louis's 2013 memoir (Kanamugire, "Temoignages recueillis") offers a significant overview of the memory work he directed for the Genocide Memorial Commission.

2. In 2021 the CNLG was replaced by a newly established Ministry of National Unity and Civic Engagement (MINUBUMWE).

3. Rutayisire passed away in December 2023. See Rutayisire, "Approche locale du génocide" (2014); and Rutayisire et al., "Kwandika amateka ya jenoside" (2022).

4. I use the term *authorized heritage* following Smith, *Uses of Heritage* (2006).

5. GOR, Law No. 15/2016 of 02/05/2016 Governing Ceremonies to Commemorate the Genocide Against the Tutsi and Organisation and Management of Memorial Sites for the Genocide Against the Tutsi, *Official Gazette*, no. 22 (May 30, 2016): 30–50. The 2016 law retrospectively granted state authorities discretion to consolidate memorial sites that would otherwise be considered "permanent" (Article 15, 43). It both legislated a practice that preceded it and suggested an amplified program of memorial consolidation and burial relocation in years to come.

6. Traditional religious practices include *guterekera*, a form of ancestral communion that is practiced with discretion today. See Bigirumwami, *Imihango n'imigenzo* (1984), 218–28; Burnet, *Genocide Lives in Us* (2012), 99–101; and Taylor, *Milk, Honey, and Money* (1992).

7. In Rwanda, ethnic identity is patrilineal.

8. The RPA was the armed force associated with the RPF political party. It seized control of Kigali on July 18, 1994, effectively stopping the genocide. The RPF has since dominated the national government and is the party associated with President Paul Kagame.

9. This view is espoused by critics of the postgenocide, RPF-led government who claim that reprisal killings of Hutu during and after the genocide amounted to organized, ethnically targeted mass violence similar to the 1994 genocide against Tutsi. That criticism was reprised in both a BBC documentary, *Rwanda's Untold Story* (2014), and journalist

Michela Wrong's book *Do Not Disturb* (2021). For work that parses related debates, see Beloff, "'Double Genocide'" (2022).

10. GOR, Law No. 18/2008 of 23/07/2008 Relating to the Punishment of the Crime of Genocide Ideology.

11. GOR, Law No. 56/2008 of 10/09/2008 Governing Memorial Sites and Cemeteries of Victims of the Genocide Against the Tutsi in Rwanda, Articles 3 and 11.

12. GOR, Law No. 56/2008, Article 10. The law listed eleven features that every national and district-level site should have. Key among them were state control over memorial curation, administration, and access. In addition to displaying skeletal remains, clothing, and weapons, the law stipulated that each memorial should host curated exhibitions on the history of the genocide and show photographs and the names of victims, perpetrators, and rescuers associated with crimes in each region.

13. CNLG, "Sites mémoriaux du genocide" (2012).

14. The situation evokes what Michael Rothberg and Yasmin Yildiz describe as "memory citizenship," in which full national belonging is contingent on knowing and performing one's recognition of a collective memory. Their concept arises from an analysis of migrants in Germany who experience the country's Holocaust commemoration and civic education programs. Rothberg and Yildiz, "Memory Citizenship" (2011).

15. Longman, *Memory and Justice* (2017); Nyirubugara, *Complexities and Dangers* (2013); Purdeková, *Making Ubumwe* (2015); and Vidal, "Commémoration du génocide" (2004).

16. Lemarchand, "Politics of Memory" (2008), 65–66.

17. Cook, "Politics of Preservation" (2006).

18. Brauman et al., "Rwanda" (2000); Vidal, "Commémorations du génocide" (2001); Vidal, "Commémoration du génocide" (2004); and Vidal, "Humanitaires" (2004).

19. Burnet, *Genocide Lives in Us* (2012); and Longman, *Memory and Justice* (2017).

20. Buckley-Zistel, "Remembering to Forget" (2006).

21. Notable exceptions are an article coauthored by human rights activist Théonèste Rutagengwa and the history of ethnicized vernacular memory by Olivier Nyirubugara. Longman and Rutagengwa, "Memory, Identity" (2004); and Nyirubugara, *Complexities and Dangers* (2013).

22. Misago, "Instruments de la mémoire génocide" (2007).

23. Bolin, "On the Side of Light" (2012); Brandstetter, "Contested Pasts" (2010); Davis and Bowring, "Right to Remember" (2011); Eltringham, "Bodies of Evidence" (2014); Guyer, "Rwanda's Bones" (2009); and Sodaro, *Exhibiting Atrocity* (2018), 84–110.

24. Bolin, "Imagining Genocide Heritage" (2020); Lischer, "Narrating Atrocity" (2019); Ibreck, "International Constructions" (2013); Selimovic, "Making Peace, Making Memory" (2013); and Wosińska, "Murambi Is Not Auschwitz" (2017).

25. Baldwin, "Constructing Identity" (2019); Breed, *Performing the Nation* (2014); Fox, *After Genocide* (2021); Grzyb, "Unsettled Memory" (2019); Jessee and Mwambari, "Memory Law" (2022); King, "Memory Controversies" (2010); Korman, "Politique de mémoire" (2013); Korman, "L'état rwandais" (2014); Korman, "Mobilising the Dead?" (2015); Korman, "Bury or Display?" (2015); Mwambari, "*Agaciro*" (2021); and Mwambari, *Navigating Cultural Memory* (2023).

26. Dumas and Korman, "Espaces de la mémoire" (2011); Korman, "Universitaires et intellectuels rwandais" (2022); and Mason, "Conserving Rwandan Genocide Memorials" (2019).

27. Burnet, *To Save Heaven and Earth* (2023); Jessee, *Negotiating Genocide* (2017); Selimovic, "Gender, Narrative, Affect" (2020); and Viebach, "Mediating 'Absence-Presence'" (2020).

28. Jessee, *Negotiating Genocide* (2017); Ibreck, "Politics of Mourning" (2010); Lakin, "Memory and Victimhood" (2022); and Major, "Unearthing, Untangling" (2015).

29. Jessee, "Micro-Politics of Remembering" (2022); Major, "Unearthing, Untangling" (2015); Nsabimana, "Genocide-Time" (2023); and Viebach, "Mediating 'Absence-Presence'" (2020).

30. Meierhenrich, "Topographies" (2011); Meierhenrich and Lagace, "Tropes of Memory" (2013); and Mwambari, "*Agaciro*" (2021).

31. Butler, *Precarious Life* (2004), xx–xxii.

32. With reference to Hannah Arendt's "space of appearance" and Giorgio Agamben's "bare life." Arendt, *Human Condition* (1958); and Agamben, *Homo Sacer* (1998).

## INTRODUCTION: TRAUMA HERITAGE AS REPAIR

1. Louis Kanamugire, interview, Rwanda, July 16, 2018 (translated from French and Kinyarwanda by BUK and the author).

2. Kanamugire, interview, July 16, 2018.

3. Kanamugire, interview, July 16, 2018.

4. Significant sources for understanding the origins and dynamics of the 1994 genocide against Tutsi include Burnet, *To Save Heaven and Earth* (2023); Des Forges, *Leave None to Tell* (1999); Fujii, *Killing Neighbors* (2009); Newbury, "Ethnicity" (1998); and Straus, *Order of Genocide* (2006).

5. Four of those national genocide memorials were established at killing sites (Nyarubuye, Ntarama, Nyamata, and Murambi), and two were purpose built (Bisesero and Kigali). Chapter 2 provides an overview of the first sites and their interrelated development, while chapters 3 and 4 focus on Nyarubuye and Murambi, the primary loci of preservation and conservation practices, respectively.

6. Interviews with residents in the first years after the genocide include reactions to genocide sites. See African Rights, *"Go"* (2007); Burnet, *Genocide Lives in Us* (2012); Schotsmans, *A l'écoute des rescapés* (2000); and Vidal, "Commémorations du génocide" (2001).

7. For burial practices and funerary rites in Rwanda, see Bigirumwami, *Imihango n'imigenzo* (1984), 218–28; Kagame, *Organisations socio-familiales* (1954); Sadruddin, "Death in an Ordinary Time" (2022); van't Spijker, *Usages funéraires* (1990); Taylor, *Milk, Honey, and Money* (1992); and Vidal, "Commémoration du génocide" (2004).

8. Kanamugire, interview, July 16, 2018.

9. I call him Dr. Kanimba, using his Rwandan first name, honoring how interlocutors who worked with him referred to him (with significant fondness).

10. Louis, Mario, and Dr. Kanimba were colleagues and friends. They worked together

from 1996 to 1998 to refine conservation techniques. Mario, a human rights expert, was subordinate to Louis. They were also close friends. Louis was the director of the Genocide Memorial Commission, but at particular memorial sites like Murambi, he often deferred to Dr. Kanimba and Mario with their respective academic and field expertise. After Louis was forced to retire, Dr. Kanimba became the first director of the CNLG, assuming control over the rehoused Genocide Memorial Commission for a brief period (2008–10) before his death.

11. My conceptualization of genocide heritage drew from my development of the concept of trauma heritage and is independent of other scholars' work on similar concepts. My framing emphasizes the material and spatial forms of genocide remembrance, along with the processes and work entailed in their development. Annalisa Bolin develops a parallel concept in archaeological research on contemporary Rwandan memorials in "Imagining Genocide Heritage" (2020).

12. Until 2008 the term *genocide* (*génocide* in French and *jenoside* in Kinyarwanda) was not officially used in Rwanda. The Kinyarwanda term *itsembabwoko n'itsembatsemba* (ethnic killings and massacres) was more common. That phrase recognized the thousands of Hutu who also were killed during the 1994 violence; it was later changed to the narrower "genocide of the Tutsi." In 1997 the phrase *indangamurage z'itsembabwoko n'itsembatsemba* appears in government documents to refer to the "heritage of the ethnic killings and massacres." GOR, "Umushinga w'Itegeko rishyiraho Ikigo cy'Igihugu cy'Urwibutso rw'Itsembabwoko n'Itsembasemba," PRIMATUR, January 1997, Article 4, CNLG Archive, Kigali. For a history of genocide terminology, see Ntakirutimana, "Génocide" (2017).

13. My definition of *heritage* bears similarities to Richard Terdiman's compelling definition of memory as a past made present. However, in further narrowing the conceptual implications of present/presence, I emphasize that heritage has particular material and temporal dimensions that distinguish it from the broader category of memory. I also situate the formation of an especially charged trauma heritage not within European modernity, as Terdiman does, but within a late twentieth-century Global South geography of atrocity. See Terdiman, *Present Past* (1993).

14. I follow Battiste and Henderson, *Protecting Indigenous Knowledge* (2000); Smith, *Uses of Heritage* (2006); and Smith and Akagawa, *Intangible Heritage* (2009), in calling for a broader definition of heritage that includes intangible cultural production. Intangible heritage includes forms of labor, oral culture, expressions, knowledge, and performances as valued cultural and historical references. In my view, all heritage, whether tangible or intangible, is material in the sense that it involves some form of objectification and classification.

15. Halbwachs, *On Collective Memory* ([1925] 1980), 167.

16. Nora, "Between Memory and History" (1989).

17. Caruth, *Unclaimed Experience* (1996), 4.

18. Trauma heritage resonates with what Karen Till calls "wounded places," which are "understood to be present to the pain of others and to embody difficult social pasts." Till, "Artistic and Activist Memory-Work" (2008), 108.

19. Caruth, *Unclaimed Experience* (1996), 4.

20. Gobodo-Madikizela, "Aesthetics of Memory" (2020), 126.

21. Felman and Laub, *Testimony* (1992), 75–76; and LaCapra, *Writing History* (2001).

22. Gould and Harris, "Memory for Justice" (2014); Booth, "Unforgotten" (2001). Several Rwandanist scholars refer to the concept of *memory justice* to locate a key objective of genocide memorials: Ibreck, "Politics of Mourning" (2010); Longman, *Memory and Justice* (2017); and Viebach, "Aletheia" (2014).

23. Booth, *Communities of Memory* (2006), 116.

24. Booth, *Communities of Memory* (2006), 113, 116.

25. Sanford, *Buried Secrets* (2004).

26. Sanford, "'What Is Written'" (2003), 73.

27. Speaking about traumatic experiences is not always desired nor conducive to individual healing, especially in the context of gender-based violence. See Ross, "Speech and Silence" (2001); and Theidon, "Milk of Sorrow" (2009).

28. Prescod, "Archives" (2017), 84.

29. Prescod, "Gaming the System" (2020).

30. Kelley, *Freedom Dreams* (2002), 114.

31. Kelley, *Freedom Dreams* (2002), 10.

32. Jackson, "Rethinking Repair" (2014).

33. Jackson, "Rethinking Repair" (2014), 221.

34. Walter Benjamin, paraphrased in Booth, *Communities of Memory* (2006), 112. As a precursor to repair, Benjamin's angel of history moves forward into the future by facing the wrongs of the past.

35. Soyinka, *Burden of Memory* (1999), 81–82.

36. Salamishah Tillet elaborates this as the "poetics of reparations." Tillet, *Sites of Slavery* (2012), 136.

37. Philosopher Margaret Urban Walker notes that while wider publics typically consider the worst atrocities impossible to repair, those are precisely the harms that reparations advocates most often invoke. Walker, "Making Reparations Possible" (2015), 211.

38. Levi, *Drowned and the Saved* (1986), 23–35.

39. In suggesting that trauma heritage expands the field of historiography, I reference Rosalind Krauss's canonic essay that reconceptualized sculpture in the postmodern period. Krauss, "Sculpture" (1979).

40. Azoulay, *Civil Contract* (2008), 16.

41. Azoulay, *Civil Contract* (2008), 17.

42. On the twin methodological concepts of "thick description" and "deep listening," see Geertz, *Interpretation of Culture* (1973), 3–36; and Portelli, *Death of Luigi Trastulli* (1991).

43. My research in Rwanda included historical and ethnographic research within government ministries responsible for rural development as well as research with 620 rural residents living in thirty-six villages that initially included semistructured interviews and mapping and later oral history and visual and spatial ethnographic research. The latter included return visits and oral histories with forty rural residents and others involved in preservation and conservation work, exhumations, and reburials in 1994–98. In rural villages I initially worked with a team of five recent Rwandan university graduates to conduct interviews. My primary research assistant and collaborator helped me to lead that team and worked with me as a translator on most interviews, which we conducted

in Kinyarwanda. Research also entailed two weeks in Chile in 2015 to interview Mario Ibarra, primarily in Spanish with the translation assistance of a dear friend (see chapter 1). Wendel, "Ethics of Stability" (2016); and Wendel, "Roof Politics" (2023).

44. The reflections of Rwandanist researchers are instructive to both doing research in the country and sensitively navigating the ethical dilemmas that arise in any field research. Burnet, *Genocide Lives in Us* (2012); de Lame, *Hill Among a Thousand* (2005); Fujii, "Shades of Truth" (2010); Ingelaere, "Learning 'to Be' Kinyarwanda" (2015); Jessee, "Limits of Oral History" (2011); Thomson, "Getting Close to Rwandans" (2010); and Thomson et al., *Emotional and Ethical Challenges* (2013).

45. See chapter 6 and similar observations of the same period in Baldwin, "Constructing Identity" (2019).

46. Purdeková, *Making Ubumwe* (2015); Reyntjens, "Struggle over Truth" (2015); Thomson, *Whispering Truth to Power* (2013); and Waldorf, "Censorship and Propaganda" (2007).

47. Jelin, *State Repression* (2003), 27–30. See also J. Scott, *Domination* (1990); and Smith, *Uses of Heritage* (2006).

48. GOR, Law No. 18/2008; GOR, Law No. 56/2008, Articles 3 and 11; and Jessee and Mwambari, "Memory Law" (2022).

49. Amnesty International, "Ensure Remedy" (2021); African Court on Human and Peoples' Rights, The Matter of Ingabire Victoire Umuhoza v. Republic of Rwanda, Application No. 003/2014, Judgment on Reparations, December 7, 2018, https://www.african-court.org/cpmt/storage/app/uploads/public/5fa/a78/40b/5faa7840b28df631183075.pdf; and Mwambari, "Music" (2020). Suppression also includes assassinations of dissidents in foreign countries: Human Rights Watch, "Repression Across Borders" (2014).

50. GOR, Law No. 15/2016, Articles 15 and 43; and Grzyb, "Unsettled Memory" (2019).

51. Burnet, *Genocide Lives in Us* (2012), 111.

52. Buckley-Zistel, "Remembering to Forget" (2006); Doughty, "'Our Goal Is Not to Punish'" (2015); Ingelaere, "Do We Understand?" (2010); and Wendel, "Roof Politics" (2023).

53. Caruth, *Unclaimed Experience* (1996); Eastmond and Selimovic, "Silence as Possibility" (2012); Malkki, *Purity and Exile* (1995); and Ross, "Speech and Silence" (2001).

54. Fujii, *Killing Neighbors* (2009).

55. Fujii, "Shades of Truth" (2010), 231.

56. "Do no harm" refers to beneficence, which, along with justice and respect for persons, are Belmont Report principles inscribed within codes of research ethics. National Commission for the Protection of Human Subjects of Biomedical and Behavioral Research, *Belmont Report* (1979).

57. J. Scott, *Domination* (1990).

58. Mullings, "Insider or Outsider" (1990), 340.

59. Kinyarwanda training was supported by three years of US Foreign Language and Area Studies grants. My research also required competency in French and Spanish.

60. I always introduced the purpose and topics of my research at the beginning of interviews. Midway through and at the end, I made space for respondents' questions of me—which is when these follow-up queries were usually broached.

61. "180731_12–10," interview, Rwanda, July 31, 2018 (translated from Kinyarwanda by the author). The majority of interviewees living in rural areas preferred not to be identifiable, so I instead reference the date and time of their interview transcripts (e.g., 180731_12–10, to make note of a recording begun at 12:10 p.m. on July 31, 2018) or provide a pseudonym.

62. "180731_12–10," interview.

63. Jessee, "Limits of Oral History" (2011), 291–92.

64. Custodianship is a fraught concept within archive studies that refers to the legal and social responsibilities for possessing, organizing, and preserving historical knowledge. The custodial tradition typically refers to the roles of institutions, like national archives, in that work. Critical archive studies scholars, particularly those with Indigenous, feminist, and Black perspectives, argue that custodianship has historically been a nonneutral, paternalistic, and selective endeavor. See Agostinho, "Archival Encounters" (2019); Buchanan, "Decolonising the Archives" (2007); Caswell and Cifor, "From Human Rights" (2016); and Stoler, "Colonial Archives" (2002).

65. Caswell and Cifor, "From Human Rights" (2016), 36.

66. Glassie, *Passing the Time* (1982), 13.

67. Feldman, *Archives of the Insensible* (2015).

68. Feldman, "Epilogue" (1996), 251.

69. Bshara, "Lifta's Ruins" (2022); Forensic Architecture, Tantura (2023); Khalidi, *All That Remains* (1992); Rajagopal, "Opinion—Domicide" (2024); Sharpe, "And to Survive" (2018); and Webber-Heffernan, "Remembering Differently" (2024).

## CHAPTER 1. *EL OLOR Y EL DOLOR* (THE SMELL AND THE PAIN)

1. Mario Ibarra, interview, Chile, January 9, 2015. The photographs are indexed in Genocide Memorial Commission, *Rapport préliminaire* (1996). Our conversations took place primarily in Spanish but also in French and English. A dear friend, native Chilean, and professional psychologist, Carola Velasco Hodgson, kindly helped to translate my broken Spanish for Mario and convey the depth of his thoughts where I lacked understanding. All Spanish translations are mine.

2. Genocide Memorial Commission, *Les grands sites du génocide et des massacres, avril–juillet 1994*, Mapping Agency MINESUPRES, Kigali, April 1997.

3. Documenting evidence of the genocide was a collective effort apparent in several photographs. Figure 1.20 shows a staff member of the Genocide Memorial Commission moments before he photographed Mario photographing the *ibuye* (rock) near the mass grave in Rwamagana Préfecture (figure 1.21). The proliferation of images was facilitated by equipment that Mario brought to Rwanda.

4. Shortly after Louis added a brief mention of Mario's involvement to his memoir, Rémi Korman, a prominent researcher of genocide memorialization for whom Louis was a key interlocutor, began to publish on Mario's role in early genocide memorialization efforts. Korman, "L'état rwandais" (2014); Korman, "Mobilising the Dead?" (2015); and Korman, "Bury or Display?" (2015). These exchanges underscore historiographical work as iterative, incomplete, and constructed in part through personal networks and partial recollections and narrations.

5. It was this documentation that led me to find Mario in the first place.

6. Until the country's territorial reorganization in 2001, *préfectures* (directed by a *préfet*) were the equivalent of provinces, followed in size by *communes* (led by a *bourgmestre*), *secteurs* (sectors, governed by *conseillers*), and *cellules* (cells, led by *responsables*).

7. Caswell refers to this as "liberatory memory work" in *Urgent Archives* (2021).

8. The relationships between truth telling and justice should not be considered immediate or linear but are part of an unfolding process of community-based repair and empowerment. Lykes et al., "Narrating Survival and Change" (2003).

9. Des Forges, *Leave None to Tell* (1999), 208–38, 492–500; Thompson, *Media* (2007), 145–76; and Straus, *Order of Genocide* (2006), 63–94.

10. Mario Ibarra, interview, Chile, January 11, 2015.

11. J. Alexander et al., *Cultural Trauma* (2004).

12. In the literature, distinctions between "reparative" and "reparatory" history are not conceptual but grammatical. I use the term *reparative history*, although David Scott ("Preface" [2017]) and Catherine Hall ("Doing Reparatory History" [2018]) refer to similar work as *reparatory*. More precisely, the *reparative history* that this book documents and advances gently departs from those precedents to foreground the turn to spatialized historical representation, which is evident in Louis's and Mario's work. Reparative histories manifest in public spaces are distinct, in both form and effect, from the written reparatory histories described by Scott and Hall.

13. D. Scott, "Preface" (2017), x.

14. Hall, "Doing Reparatory History" (2018).

15. Hall, "Doing Reparatory History" (2018), 16–17.

16. Bergin and Rupprecht, "Reparative Histories" (2018).

17. Johnson, "On Agency" (2003).

18. Johnson, "On Agency" (2003), 120.

19. In September 1977 representatives of Indigenous communities, dressed in traditional clothing and symbols, gathered at the UN's Palais des Nations for the first Conference on Discrimination Against Indigenous Populations in the Americas. It was an auspicious year for Mario to arrive in Geneva.

20. Mario's undergraduate studies in history and technical drawing at the University of Chile were interrupted by the Pinochet dictatorship. In exile in Switzerland, he completed an undergraduate and graduate degree in development studies and another master's in human rights law and protection in Strasbourg, France. His expertise in human rights practice was widely recognized by colleagues I interviewed. His Indigenous rights advocacy is documented in Minde, "Destination and the Journey" (2008).

21. Prior to 1999, this body was named the Sub-Commission on Prevention of Discrimination and Protection of Minorities. I use *Sub-Commission* throughout the chapter to refer to both the pre- and post-1999 names for this group of experts.

22. Ibarra, *I Mapuche* (1989); Ibarra, "Apuntes para una cronología" (1992); and Ibarra, *Notas sobre algunos instrumentos* (2007).

23. ECOSOC, "Election of Members of the Sub-Commission on Prevention of Discrimination and Protection of Minorities," February 7, 1994, E/CN.4/1994/85/Add.2, United Nations Digital Library.

24. Michele Wagner, interview, United States, December 1, 2017.

25. Wagner, interview.

26. Mario recalls that 70 percent of his time was spent investigating the genocide in eastern and central Rwanda. He also monitored the conditions of children in three orphanages, of accused perpetrators of genocide crimes in two Kibungo prisons, and of returning refugees.

27. Mario stopped working with the Genocide Memorial Commission at the end of his UN Sub-Commission mandate to pursue other employment. He was also aware of the deteriorating relationship between the OHCHR and the Rwandan government, which resulted in the termination of the HRFOR mission in May 1998.

28. See the introduction and chapter 4 for more on Dr. Kanimba's role and background.

29. I narrate the decisions and projects related to genocide heritage differently when I discuss Louis rather than Mario. Louis lived in Rwanda in a political context that limits expressions of individual agency. I attempt to be sensitive to this.

30. Mario Ibarra, "Pepe (2)," video recording, June 6, 1997, cassette, Ibarra archive, Chile, at 05:54 (translated from French by the author).

31. Though Louis and Mario stated that the exhibition they curated at the Institut Français took place in 1997, photographs of Louis and Mario selecting evidence and photographs for it are date-stamped May 6, 1996.

32. Mario Ibarra, interview, Chile, January 8, 2015 (this and all interview excerpts translated from Spanish by the author unless otherwise noted).

33. Ibarra, interview, January 8, 2015.

34. Ibarra, interview, January 9, 2015.

35. Louis's and Mario's efforts to investigate and document the genocide paralleled those of African Rights, Human Rights Watch, the International Committee of the Red Cross, Physicians for Human Rights, church groups, and the survivors' association Ibuka. See African Rights, *Death, Despair* (1994); Des Forges, *Leave None to Tell* (1999); Ibuka, "Kibuye Dictionary Project," unpublished document from 1996–99 survey research in Kibuye Préfecture, 1999, CNLG Documentation Center, Kigali; and Physicians for Human Rights, *Investigations* (1997).

36. Scarry, *Body in Pain* (1985).

37. Genocide Memorial Commission, *Rapport préliminaire* (1996), 94.

38. Genocide Memorial Commission, *Rapport préliminaire* (1996), 94.

39. Genocide Memorial Commission, *Rapport préliminaire* (1996), 94.

40. Genocide Memorial Commission, *Rapport préliminaire* (1996), 95.

41. Kanamugire, "Témoignages recueillis" (2013).

42. Ibarra, interview, January 8, 2015.

43. Ibarra, interview, January 8, 2015.

44. I have not been able to locate this original working map; a possible reason for this follows shortly.

45. Ibarra, interview, January 8, 2015.

46. To my knowledge, this is the only surviving record of the second draft of the map.

47. ICTR, "Case No. ICTR-99–50-T," trial transcript, Arusha, November 19, 2003, ICTR Digital Archive.

48. Ibarra, interview, January 9, 2015.

49. Process relayed by Firmin Gatera to Mario Ibarra. Ibarra, interview, Chile, January 8, 2015.

50. Ibarra, interview, January 8, 2015.

51. See speeches by US President Bill Clinton on March 25, 1998, and UN Secretary General Kofi Annan on May 7, 1998.

52. Bossuyt, "United Nations Human Rights Procedures" (1998).

53. Dumas and Korman, "Espaces de la mémoire" (2011), 12; ICTR, "Case No. ICTR-99–50-T," November 19, 2003; GOR, "Publication of the List No. 1 of the First Category Prescribed by Article 9 of the Organic Law No. 09/96 of 30th August 1996," *Official Gazette*, no. 17 of 1/9/1996 (November 30, 1996).

54. *Gacaca* was a controversial grassroots court that heard perpetrators' testimonies and initiated forgiveness rites and reparations for victims' families and survivors in Rwanda. See Clark, *Gacaca Courts* (2010); Geraghty, "Gacaca, Genocide" (2020); Ingelaere, *Inside Rwanda's Gacaca Courts* (2016); and Longman, "An Assessment" (2009).

55. Ibarra, interview, January 9, 2015.

56. The site where the children were found had a profound impact on me as a result. Finding the unnamed site became an objective of my return visits to the country.

57. Genocide Memorial Commission, *Rapport préliminaire* (1996), 102. In later conversations both men reiterated that they had recommended the site for a national memorial. Louis Kanamugire, interview, Rwanda, May 31, 2013; and Ibarra, interview, January 8, 2015.

58. Genocide Memorial Commission, *Rapport préliminaire* (1996), 92–93. In 1994 Smaragde Munyaneza was the president of the Mouvement Démocratique Républicain (MDR), or Republican Democratic Movement, which was previously known by the name MDR-Parmehutu, the primary political party supporting Hutu in the country. Witnesses identified him as a primary organizer of genocide killings in Muhazi Commune.

59. Ibarra, interview, January 8, 2015.

60. Morrison, "Site of Memory" (1998), 194–95.

61. Certeau, *Writing of History* (1988), 14.

62. Saidiya Hartman calls this "critical fabulation," independently extending this notion. Hartman, "Venus in Two Acts" (2008).

63. Morrison, "Site of Memory" (1998), 191.

64. Ricoeur, *Memory, History, Forgetting* (2004), 366.

## CHAPTER 2. BEYOND STATE CONTROL

1. A key finding from a 2001–2 study on the effects of government genocide memory policies on how Rwandans remember the past was that the government has limited ability to control collective memory despite its restrictions on free speech. Longman and Rutagengwa, "Memory, Identity, and Community" (2004), 168, 178.

2. Filip Reyntjens discusses CLADHO, a Rwandan human rights organization, and Silas Sinyigaya's appointment to lead it in the late 1990s to exemplify the progressive state control of civil society organizations. I discuss both in this chapter as early drivers of state-led genocide heritage. Reyntjens, *Political Governance* (2013), 57–63.

3. The preservation of the Nyarubuye massacre site occurred after several bodies had been removed by Catholic leaders eager to return the church to service.

4. Genocide Memorial Commission, *Rapport préliminaire* (1996), 171.

5. It is not entirely clear how the massacre at Ntarama Church was first preserved or by whom. Mario Ibarra knew of the Ntarama genocide site from his UN investigations but was not involved in the initial decision to conserve the massacre. Athanase Ndutiye Kagahe, the architect who developed one of the country's first genocide memorial designs for Ntarama, noted that minister Joseph Nsengimana of MINESUPRES selected the site. Athanase Ndutiye Kagahe, phone interview from France, June 17, 2017, in English, Kinyarwanda, and French. Kagahe's proposal for Ntarama was based on his early 1995 visit to the church, where he became convinced of the importance of a "*mémoire visuelle*" (visual memory) for representing the genocide. His proposal is also one of the first to recommend that material evidence of the genocide should be displayed in memorials and to draw connections to Holocaust memorial museums. Kagahe, "Étude d'un projet du musée du génocide Section Ntarama," April 1995, CNLG Archive, Kigali.

6. In 2000 political scientist Timothy Longman claimed that preservation efforts at Ntarama ceased in a rare state response to pressure by genocide survivors, local residents, and the Catholic Church. Longman, *Memory and Justice* (2017), 67. However, photographic journalist Larry Towell's images from 2005 show only a partial removal of victims' remains, with some bones and belongings still on the church floor. Larry Towell, Rwanda, Ntarama Church, south of Kigali, December 2005, Artstor Collections, accessed February 19, 2025, https://www.jstor.org/stable/community.

7. A video of Ntarama Church on October 7, 1996, documents the extent of the massacre's preservation. "Video IMI-027_Unknown-Ntarama_19961007," box 118, RW027, International Monitor Institute Collection (IMIC), David M. Rubenstein Rare Book & Manuscript Library, Duke University, Durham, NC.

8. Lischer, "Narrating Atrocity" (2019); and Sodaro, *Exhibiting Atrocity* (2018).

9. Bisesero is the first architecturally designed genocide memorial site in Rwanda. During the genocide the site was a storied "hill of resistance" where Tutsi residents were killed fighting *génocidaires*. The design process began in 1995–96 with Athanase Ndutiye Kagahe, the French-Rwandan architect who authored the Ntarama proposal, and Vedaste Ngarambe, an architect who remained in the country to supervise the project.

10. Though technically the conservation of skeletal remains at Bisesero and Nyamata proceeded in tandem, I make this claim because Bisesero was plagued by over two decades of construction delays and displayed bones in an annex shed during that time. Permanent crypts to hold victims' bones were built at Nyamata in 1995.

11. Genocide Memorial Commission, *Rapport préliminaire* (1996), 174. Other accounts put the estimated dead lower, at three thousand. Des Forges, *Leave None to Tell* (1999), 18.

12. Not much is known about who initiated the work at Nyamata. The government was not involved at the very beginning.

13. A report written by Dr. Kanimba for the Genocide Memorial Commission notes that bone conservation began on August 10, 1997, after the construction of the tombs. Genocide Memorial Commission, "Rapport d'activities sur les sites de Murambi et de Ruhashya du 18 au 31 juillet 1997; Dr. Célestin Kanimba Misago," August 4, 1997, 2, CNLG Archive.

14. Misago, " Instruments de la mémoire" (2007), 2.

15. The creation of the OHCHR represented the UN's renewed commitment to the protection of interrelated economic, social, and political rights by establishing a new high commissioner directly under the authority of the secretary-general in December 1993. High Commissioner José Ayala Lasso assumed his post one day before the onset of the genocide. As a matter of emergency response and as a demonstration of the nature and scope of what the OHCHR could do, Lasso immediately pushed to establish a field-based operation (HRFOR). It was an extreme objective in the context of ongoing genocidal violence.

16. The governing regime terminated the HRFOR's human rights monitoring activities in response to a December 1997 communique from OHCHR High Commissioner Mary Robinson critiquing its human rights violations and lack of reconciliation strategies.

17. Some of the most insightful evaluations of the HRFOR and OHCHR come from those in its leadership: Clarance, "Human Rights Field Operation" (1995); Clarance, "Field Strategy" (1997); Howland, "Mirage, Magic, or Mixed Bag" (1999); Martin, "New Frontier" (1998). See also African Rights, *"Waste of Hope"* (1995); and Alston, "Neither Fish nor Fowl" (1997).

18. Including that of the preexisting UN Centre for Human Rights, UN Department of Peacekeeping Operations, and UN Department of Political and Peacebuilding Affairs. Authority over UN human rights work was further muddled by the OHCHR's uneven funding and technical support in the field. Martin, "New Frontier" (1998), 121–23.

19. Lasso, "Defining the Mandate" (1994/95), 39; and OHCHR, "Report of the High Commissioner for Human Rights to the Commission on Human Rights: Building a partnership for human rights," E/CN.4/1997/98, February 24, 197, UN Digital Library, https://digitallibrary.un.org/record/238468?ln=en&v=pdf.

20. See debates on the role of human rights field missions. Howland, "Mirage, Magic, or Mixed Bag" (1999), 42–44.

21. OHCHR, "Human Rights Questions: Report of the United Nations High Commissioner for Human Rights, Human Rights Field Operation in Rwanda," November 13, 1995, 4, file S-1085-0015-05, doc. A/50/743, UN Archives, New York.

22. OHCHR, "Letter from the High Commissioner for Human Rights José Ayala Lasso to UN Secretary General Boutros Boutros-Ghali on his Mission to Rwanda," April 5, 1995, 2, file S-1085-0015-08, UN Archives New York.

23. The HRFOR grew from a July 1994 skeleton crew of 20—two human rights monitors per *préfecture*—to, at the end of 1995, 120 staff, most of whom were based centrally in Kigali. OHCHR, "Report on the Human Rights Situation in Rwanda and the Activities

of the HRFOR," November 2, 1995, 27, file S-1085–0015–05, doc. HRFOR/RPT/E, UN Archives, New York.

24. Among them were CLADHO (established in 1993), FPH, Human Rights Watch, Amnesty International, African Rights, and PHR.

25. Clarance, "Human Rights Field Operation" (1995), 298; and Howland, "Mirage, Magic, or Mixed Bag" (1999), 37–38.

26. Ibarra, interview, January 8, 2015.

27. Clarance, "Human Rights Field Operation" (1995); Clarance, "Field Strategy" (1997); Howland, "Mirage, Magic, or Mixed Bag" (1999); and Martin, "New Frontier" (1998).

28. OHCHR, "Update on the Activities and Findings of the Human Rights Field Operation in Rwanda (HRFOR) for the Period 25 February–10 March 1995," March 10, 1995, 3, file S-1085–0015–09, UN Archives; United Nations High Commissioner for Refugees (UNHCR), *Summary of UNHCR Presentation of Experts: 10 October 1994* [colloquially referred to as the Gersony Report], unpublished report, Geneva, October 11, 1994. https://richardwilsonauthor.com/wp-content/uploads/2010/09/gersony_report.pdf; and ECOSOC, "Report on the Situation of Human Rights in Rwanda Submitted by Mr. René Degni-Ségui, Special Rapporteur of the Commission on Human Rights," June 28, 1995, file S-1062–26–8, doc E/CN.4/1996/7, UN Archives, New York.

29. Clarance, "Human Rights Field Operation" (1995), 297.

30. Clarance, "Human Rights Field Operation" (1995).

31. Clarance, "Human Rights Field Operation" (1995), 298.

32. Clarance, "Field Strategy" (1997), 246.

33. UN Security Council Resolution 935, July 1, 1994, UN Security Council Resolutions Digital Archive, http://unscr.com/en/resolutions/935.

34. The HRFOR and SIU investigators spent more time in local contexts than the Commission of Experts or the special rapporteur did. The latter relied on shorter observational missions to Rwanda and investigations conducted by the SIU and HRFOR.

35. OHCHR, "SIU Final Report on the Genocide Investigation," April 12, 1995, 3, 16, file S-1085–0015–07, UN Archives, New York.

36. OHCHR, "SIU Final Report," 34.

37. OHCHR, "SIU Final Report," 36n 100.

38. OHCHR, "SIU Final Report," 41.

39. OHCHR, "SIU Final Report," 2.

40. African Rights, *Death, Despair* (1994); and Des Forges, *Leave None to Tell* (1999).

41. Verwimp, "Machetes and Firearms" (2006), 10–11.

42. Haglund et al., "Archaeology of Mass Graves" (2001), 57.

43. CLADHO and FPH, *Rwanda: Reconstruire* (1994); translated from French by author.

44. Organizers Pierre Calame and David Gakunzi took memory to be so critical to the task of *rebuilding* Rwanda that they discuss it prominently in the executive summary of the conference: CLADHO and FPH, *Rwanda: Reconstruire* (1994), 9–20.

45. CLADHO and FPH, *Rwanda: Reconstruire* (1994), 12.

46. For discussion of what constitutes *amateka mabi* (bad history) in Rwanda today, see Jessee, *Negotiating Genocide* (2017), 207–10.

47. CLADHO and FPH, *Rwanda: Reconstruire* (1994), 25.

48. CLADHO and FPH, *Rwanda: Reconstruire* (1994), 27–29.

49. CLADHO and FPH, *Rwanda: Reconstruire* (1994), 28.

50. CLADHO and FPH, *Rwanda: Reconstruire* (1994), 27.

51. See Burnet, *To Save Heaven and Earth* (2023).

52. CLADHO and FPH, *Rwanda: Reconstruire* (1994), 28–29.

53. CLADHO and FPH, *Rwanda: Reconstruire* (1994), 29.

54. CLADHO and FPH, *Rwanda: Reconstruire* (1994), 28.

55. CLADHO and FPH, *Rwanda: Reconstruire* (1994), 28.

56. CLADHO and FPH, *Rwanda: Reconstruire* (1994), 28.

57. Kanamugire, "Témoignages recueillis" (2013), 12–13.

58. Kanamugire, "Témoignages recueillis" (2013), 12–13.

59. Keane, "Journey into Darkness" (1994). See also BBC, "RPF Leader Kanyarengwe" (1994); and Gourevitch, "Letter from Rwanda" (1995).

60. African Rights, *Death, Despair* (1994).

61. Ibarra, interview, January 9, 2015.

62. ICTR, "Case No. ICTR-99–50-T," November 20, 2003: Exhibit "Firmin Gatera, RE: The Interministerial Commission about the Momorial [sic] of Genocide" (November 26, 1995).

63. Sinyigaya was communications director for MINITRASO from September 1994 until December 1995. He led the government's postgenocide civic education reform (1996–99) while also the executive secretary of CLADHO (1999–2007).

64. Silas Sinyigaya, interview, Rwanda, August 6, 2018.

65. Rémi Korman describes this burial ceremony and identifies its location in Muyumbu, a commune in greater Kigali Préfecture. Korman, "Mobilising the Dead?" (2015), 57. See also Ntirenganya, "Muyumbu" (2017).

66. Bihozagara left MINIREISO in a February 1999 government reshuffle to address corruption. Reyntjens, "Talking or Fighting?" (1999), 5. He served for four years as Ambassador of Rwanda to France and Belgium. In 2016 he died of suspicious circumstances in a Burundi prison while awaiting trial on charges of espionage.

67. Sinyigaya, interview, August 6, 2018.

68. Genocide Memorial Commission, "Rapport d'activités."

69. Dumas and Korman, "Espaces de la mémoire" (2011), para. 9; and ICTR, "Case No. ICTR-99–50-T," November 20, 2003, 11–12.

70. ICTR, "Case No. ICTR-99–50-T," November 20, 2003, 16.

71. Louis Kanamugire, interview, Rwanda, May 31, 2013.

72. ICTR evidence (Case No. ICTR-99–50-T, November 20, 2003: Exhibits P.8 and P.9) acknowledges Eric Rousseau's early role in developing genocide memorials (letter from MINIREISO Minister Bihozagara, August 14, 1994) that ran parallel to efforts at MINESUPRES (letter from Bihozagara to MINESUPRES Minister Nsengimana, August 2, 1994).

73. ICTR, "Case No. ICTR-99–50-T," November 20, 2003: Exhibit "Projet d'un Mémorial sur les Victimes de Guerre et de Génocide par Eric Rousseau (07 Feb 1995)."

74. Kagahe, "Étude d'un projet" (1995).

75. Kagahe, "Étude d'un projet" (1995), 2. Kagahe references the Auschwitz memorial museum as precedent.

76. For example, neither Kagahe nor MINESUPRES Minister Nsengimana were RPF affiliates.

77. GOR, "Genocide, Impunity, and Accountability: Dialogue for a National and International Response—Recommendations of the Conference Held in Kigali from November 1st to 5th, 1995." Kigali: Office of the President, December 1995, 24, University of Texas at Austin Digital Archive, https://repositories.lib.utexas.edu/server/api/core/bitstreams/6da68886-2bd2-4159-be14-2d99a71da94b/content.

78. GOR, "Genocide, Impunity, and Accountability" (1995), 27.

79. See parliamentary debates in Kinyarwanda: GOR, "Urwibutzo rwa Genocide na Massacres," Inyandiko Mvugo No 174/AN/96, Parliament, Government of Rwanda (PRIMATUR), Kigali, February 21, 1996; and GOR, "Kubaka urwibutso rw'itsembatsemba n'itsembabwoko," Inyandiko Mvugo No 181/AN/96, PRIMATUR, Kigali, March 7, 1996.

80. Genocide Memorial Commission, *Rapport préliminaire* (1996).

81. Kanamugire, "Témoignages recueillis" (2013), 16.

82. Nsengimana held positions of national political influence through 2006, including as special adviser to President Paul Kagame (2000–2006) and Rwanda's ambassador to the United Nations, African Union, Jamaica, Venezuela, Ethiopia, Djibouti, Egypt, and Israel.

83. Dumas and Korman, "Espaces de la mémoire" (2011), 16.

84. Genocide Memorial Commission, "Prévisions budgétaires de 1997–1998, MIJESPOC," 2, 1997, CNLG Archive.

85. Eltringham, "Exhibition, dissimulation et 'culture'" (2012).

86. Louis Kanamugire and Mario Ibarra, "Projet et plan de travail," Genocide Memorial Commission report to MIJESPOC, June 12, 1997, CNLG Archive.

87. GOR, "Umushinga w'Itegeko rishyiraho Ikigo cy'Igihugu cy'Urwibutso rw'Itsembabwoko n'Itsembasemba," PRIMATUR, January 1997, CNLG Archive, Kigali.

88. CLADHO and FPH, *Rwanda: Reconstruire* (1994), 27–29; and Genocide Memorial Commission, *Rapport préiminaire* (1996), 243. Reflecting on this purported relationship between genocide heritage and judicial prosecutions, Mario Ibarra stated the following: "The role of the Tribunal was to identify the principal authors of the genocide in order to take them to Arusha.... WE [the Genocide Memorial Commission] were focused on maintaining memory and bringing attention to "noble persons" [rescuers] to arm history with the context of the mass graves. For this we collected information that ultimately COULD BE useful for someone doing an investigation for a trial, but this was not our primary purpose." Ibarra, interview January 9, 2015. See also video recordings of Mario Ibarra and Louis Kanamugire at the Murambi genocide memorial on June 6, 1997, and July 8, 1997. Ibarra, "Pepe (2)"; and Mario Ibarra, "Pepe Carta Filmada," video recording, July 1997, cassette E44E0129, Ibarra archive.

89. GOR, "Umushinga w'Itegeko," articles 6 and 7.

90. Germany provided RWF 10 million in Genocide Memorial Commission start-up funds. Genocide Memorial Commission, *Rapport préliminaire* (1996), 134.

91. GOR, "Umushinga w'Itegeko" (January 1997); Longman and Rutagengwa, "Religion, Memory, and Violence" (2006); and Pottier, *Re-Imagining Rwanda* (2002).

92. The CNLG was created on February 16, 2007, but was not fully operational until

April 2008. GOR, Law No. 09/2007 of 16/02/2007 On the attributions, organization, and functioning of the National Commission for the Fight Against Genocide, *Official Gazette*, no. 46 special (March 19, 2007).

93. One year after assuming the new position, Dr. Kanimba published an overview of the CNLG's mission: Misago, "Commission Nationale" (2009).

94. A phenomenon that Holocaust scholars Daniel Levy and Natan Sznaider call "cosmopolitan memory" and that Aleida Assmann terms "global memory." Levy and Sznaider, "Memory Unbound" (2002); and Assmann and Conrad, *Memory in a Global Age* (2010).

95. Korman, "Universitaires et intellectuels rwandais" (2022); and GOR, "Genocide, Impunity, and Accountability" (1995), 33–45.

96. A 1996 Genocide Memorial Commission budget aspirationally lists travel to Israel as well as the United States, Cambodia, and Algeria—presumably to visit memorial precedents. Genocide Memorial Commission, "Ikigo cy'Urwibutso rw'Itsembabwoko n'Itsembatsemba mu Rwanda," Summer 1996, 6, CNLG Archive, Kigali.

97. A range of memory justice initiatives were discussed at the conference, situating those of the Holocaust among others taking place in Chile, El Salvador, and Palestine.

## CHAPTER 3. WITNESSING NYARUBUYE

1. BBC, "RPF Leader Kanyarengwe" (1994).

2. Other sites of killing, including at Ntarama and Nyamata near Kigali, would have been easier for the press to access. But in late May 1994, Kibungo Préfecture was relatively safer than the capital. The eastern *préfecture* was under the control of RPA troops.

3. The RPA soldiers had discovered the church only a week or so prior to the May 28 press conference. Keane, "Journey into Darkness"(1994); Huband, "Churchyard Slaughter" (1994); Wagner, interview; and Ulbrich, "Death of Peacekeeper" (1994).

4. Reports put the number of dead at Nyarubuye Church between three thousand and twenty thousand people. The numbers are imprecise because some bodies had been moved from the church by the time investigations started, interviewees' estimates vary widely, and many summaries count numbers killed in the entire sector, an administrative territory of around thirty square miles that also has the name Nyarubuye. I use the estimate of three thousand victims found on the church grounds because it was the number provided to BBC reporter Fergal Keane by RPF information officer Lieutenant Frank Ndore and corroborated by a survivor interviewed by African Rights in July 1994. African Rights, *Death, Despair* (1994), 284; and Keane, *Season of Blood* (1995), 76. However, there is a good deal of variation: The HRFOR Special Investigations Unit (SIU) counted 615 people dead in the church buildings and grounds in December 1994. OHCHR, "SIU Final Report." A nun who survived the attacks estimated that five thousand people had sought refuge there. Huband, "Churchyard Slaughter" (1994), 10. Louis Kanamugire listed ten thousand dead at the parish in the Genocide Memorial Commission's *Rapport préliminaire* (1996), 135, which was partly corroborated by a witness for the International Criminal Tribunal for Rwanda (ICTR) trial against Rusumo Commune Mayor Sylvestre Gacumbitsi. ICTR, "Case No. ICTR-2001–64-T: The Prosecutor vs. Sylvestre Gacumbitsi," trial transcript, Arusha, June 17, 2004. And RPF Colonel Kanyarengwe insisted in

May 1994 that twenty thousand people had been found at the church—the number of victims the *Rapport préliminaire* counted in Nyarubuye Sector. Kanyarengwe's estimate is cited in BBC, "RPF Leader Kanyarengwe" (1994).

5. Paraphrased from UN Special Rapporteur René Degni-Ségui, who visited Nyarubuye Church in October 1994. ECOSOC, *Special Rapporteur Report on the Situation of Human Rights in Rwanda*, E/CN.4/1995/70, November 11, 1994, 4 (UN Digital Archive, documents.un.org).

6. Rutazibwa and Rutayisire, *Génocide à Nyarubuye* (2007), photograph captions on front cover and p. 106; OHCHR, "Update on the Activities of the HRFOR 13 July 1995–28 July 1995," July 28, 1995, box S-1085–0015–07, 19, UN Archives, New York; and Ibarra, interview, January 8, 2015.

7. See Felman and Laub, *Testimony* (1992); and LaCapra, *Writing History* (2001).

8. See Azoulay, *Civil Contract* (2008).

9. See chapter 2 for examples, including the United Nations International Criminal Tribunal for Rwanda's (ICTR) reference of church massacres in the east for its prosecution of individuals accused of genocide crimes: ICTR, "Case No. ICTR-96–4: The Prosecutor *v.* Jean-Paul Akayesu," trial transcript, Arusha, September 2, 1998: Testimony of Cameraman Simon Cox.

10. ICTR, "Case No. ICTR-2001–64-T."

11. The Rwandan government explains reprisal killings as the result of a few bad military actors. Though their extent and calculated organization have been questioned by former US and Canadian military investigators, the existence of brutal reprisal killings is rarely disputed. In 1994 the Gersony Report documented UN investigations on reprisal violence. Though it was suppressed by the UN in consultation with Rwanda, the findings are approximated in the written comments Robert Gersony gave to the Commission of Experts in 1994. Des Forges, *Leave None to Tell* (1999), 553–56; and UNHCR, *Summary* (1994).

12. Ibarra, interview, January 8, 2015.

13. Ben Majekodunmi, phone interview, March 9, 2013; Wagner, interview.

14. There were some survivors, many of whom hid under the bodies of the fallen dead. Organizers returned to the site during this period for the express purpose of separating the living from the dead by using pepper spray.

15. Ibarra, interview, January 8, 2015.

16. A well-known survivor of the killings, Leoncia Mukandayambaje, was similarly struck on her head with a machete and her baby killed while strapped to her back. She regained consciousness among the dead in the courtyard and hid in the latrines for two days while killers returned.

17. This was a time of significant insecurity due to continued fighting and the mass exodus and return of people. Relationships between the new government and international nongovernmental organizations (NGOs) were not good: Thirty-eight international humanitarian NGOs were expelled in 1995, accused of "interfering in the country's internal affairs and a lack of cooperation." Associated Press, "Kigali" (1995).

18. Longman, *Christianity and Genocide* (2010); see also a scholarly anthology sponsored by the Aegis Trust: Rittner et al., *Genocide in Rwanda* (2004).

19. Janvier Gasasira, interview, Rwanda, August 4, 2018. Gasasira recalled the experiences that follow during our 2018 conversation.

20. Ibarra, interview, January 8, 2015.

21. Gasasira, interview.

22. Gasasira, interview.

23. Ibarra, interview, January 8, 2015.

24. Gasasira, interview.

25. Gasasira, interview.

26. Esipisu, "Only Dogs Remain" (1994). The "UN observer" mentioned in the article was likely Mario Ibarra.

27. Esipisu, "Only Dogs Remain" (1994).

28. Ibarra, interview, January 8, 2015.

29. CLADHO and FPH, *Rwanda: Reconstruire* (1994), 28.

30. GOR, "Genocide, Impunity, and Accountability" (1995), 27.

31. Mario Ibarra recalled these details of Boutros-Ghali's visit to Nyarubuye. Ibarra, interview, January 8, 2015. Mario's roles as guide and companion are corroborated in official UN photographs from the visit (see figure 3.1).

32. UN Secretary-General, "Programme of the Secretary-General on 13 July 1995 Follow-Up," July 13, 1995, file S-1088–0034–07, UN Archives.

33. Crossette, "U.N. Chief" (1995).

34. See Burkins, "Legacy of Terror" (1995); Burkins, "Past Tortures" (1995); Huband, "Churchyard Slaughter" (1994); Huband, "Holocaust" (1995); McNeil, "Ntarama Journal" (1995); and Susman, "New Horror" (1994).

35. Pottier, *Re-Imagining Rwanda* (2002), 53–108; and Thompson, *Media* (2007), 145–276.

36. Burkins, "Legacy of Terror" (1995).

37. Karnik, "Rwanda and the Media" (1998); and Réra, "Rwanda, de l'espace médiatique" (2016).

38. Rutazibwa and Rutayisire, *Génocide à Nyarubuye* (2007), colophon, 106.

39. Kanamugire, "Témoignages recueillis" (2013), 11.

40. By 1996 the Catholic Church negotiated a subsequent agreement to allow it to retain control over the main chapel. The Genocide Memorial Commission managed the annex buildings and parish grounds.

41. The ceasefire was declared on July 18, 1994.

42. ICTR, "Case No. ICTR-2001–64-T."

43. Des Forges, *Leave None to Tell* (1999), 535–60; and Guichaoua, *From War to Genocide* (2017), 313–17.

44. Views relayed by Rusumo, Ngoma, and Nyanza District residents and government employees off the record in 2013 and 2018.

45. Genocide Memorial Commission, *Rapport préliminaire* (1996), 134.

46. Gourevitch, "Letter from Rwanda" (1995), 81.

47. Gourevitch, "Letter from Rwanda" (1995), 94–95. See also Peress, *Silence* (1995).

48. Dallaire, *Shake Hands* (2003); Diop, *Murambi* ([2001] 2006); Gourevitch, *We*

*Wish to Inform* (1998); Hatzfeld, *Into the Quick* ([2000] 2008); Keane, *Season of Blood* (1995); Koff, *Bone Woman* (2004); and Umutesi, *Surviving the Slaughter* ([2000] 2004).

49. Norridge, "Writing Against Genocide" (2011), 256–57.

50. Norridge, "Writing Against Genocide" (2011), 256.

51. Keane, *Season of Blood* (1995), 80.

52. Peress, *Silence* (1995).

53. Ibarra, interview, January 6, 8, and 9, 2015; and Wagner, interview.

54. *Ingabo* 10 (March 1996).

55. Firmin Gatera, "Hirya no Hino," *Ingabo* 10 (March 1996), 33 (translated from Kinyarwanda by author).

56. Foucault, *Language, Counter-Memory* ([1977] 1980), 152–53.

57. Foucault, *Language, Counter-Memory* ([1977] 1980), 111, 146–47.

58. Foucault, *Language, Counter-Memory* ([1977] 1980), 147, 153.

59. Lipsitz, *Time Passages* (1990), 226 (italics mine).

60. Metaphorically, I note that Nyarubuye Church and Village are Kinyarwanda toponyms that refer to the rocky landscape (*nyar-ubuye*) that characterizes the region.

## CHAPTER 4. MEMORY WORK

1. Mbembe, "Necropolitics" (2003).

2. Mbembe, "Necropolitics" (2005), 35 (italics mine).

3. Guyer, "Rwanda's Bones" (2009).

4. Guyer, "Rwanda's Bones" (2009), 157.

5. Bolin, "On the Side of Light" (2012); Eltringham, "Bodies of Evidence" (2014); Meierhenrich, "Topographies" (2011); and Vidal, "Commémoration du génocide" (2004).

6. Azoulay, *Civil Contract* (2008).

7. Genocide Memorial Commission, "Rapport de depenses pour les travaux de conservation des ossements des victimes du génocide et des massacres," report sent from Dr. Kanimba to the Memorial Commission, Butare, August 4, 1997, CNLG Archive; and Genocide Memorial Commission, "Projet et plan de travail" (1997).

8. In 1996 the Genocide Memorial Commission estimated that 35,000 to 40,000 people were killed at Murambi—based on the 20,154 bodies found in nearby mass graves and witness testimony. Genocide Memorial Commission, *Rapport préliminaire* (1996), 55. Subsequent government and African Rights reports put the number higher, at 50,000. African Rights, "Go" (2007), 10, 134.

9. African Rights, *"Go"* (2007), 116–20

10. Des Forges, *Leave None to Tell* (1999), 154.

11. Des Forges, *Leave None to Tell* (1999), 212.

12. Prunier, "Opération Turquoise" (1999).

13. This sentiment is memorialized on Murambi's grounds in a plaque that the Genocide Memorial Commission placed to identify the mass grave on which French soldiers erected a volleyball court.

14. African Rights, *"Go"* (2007), 137–50.

15. Most Tutsi at Kigeme Hospital were killed by extremist militia after the Murambi massacre. Local authorities saved some Tutsi women and relocated them along with Hutu women to the school complex. Survivors and perpetrators interviewed by African Rights suggested that they were transferred to show the French soldiers that people of both ethnicities had survived—to minimize the reported violence.

16. Corroborating testimony collected by African Rights, one of my interviewees described having to mop the blood and clean the buildings to stay at the site in this period. Vestine Ndikuryayo, interview, Rwanda, July 23, 2018.

17. The April 22, 1995, massacre at the Kibeho Camp killed an estimated 1,500 to 2,000 internally displaced people, including some 100 Tutsi by the Interahamwe and over 1,000 Hutu by the RPA, who shot guns and mortars into crowds. See ECOSOC, "Report on the Situation of Human Rights in Rwanda Submitted by Mr. René Degni-Ségui, Special Rapporteur of the Commission on Human Rights," UN Archives, New York: File S-1062-26-8, Doc E/CN.4/1996/7, 28 June 1995: 23; Pickard, *Combat Medic* (2008); and Prunier, *Africa's World War* (2009).

18. "Gabriel" (pseudonym), interview, Rwanda, July 25, 2018.

19. Ndikuryayo, interview.

20. Interview with a woman relocated to Murambi from Kigeme Hospital after the April 22 massacre, in African Rights, *"Go"* (2007), 140.

21. Among the six individuals who were involved in early genocide conservation that I managed to locate this was the most common reason for doing the work despite significant emotional and physical discomfort.

22. Cogebanque (Compagnie Générale de Banque) is a bank with headquarters in Kigali.

23. Kanamugire, interview, May 31, 2013.

24. Gabriel, interview.

25. The role of the soil composition in producing the distinct conditions for mummification at Murambi was corroborated by Gabriel, Mario Ibarra, and Louis Kanamugire in separate interviews in 2018, 2015, and 2012.

26. In a video filmed at Murambi on June 6, 1997, Mario Ibarra notes that around two hundred bodies were being actively conserved at the site. Ibarra, "Pepe (2)," June 6, 1997, at 17:20. All videos translated by the author from French, Spanish, and Kinyarwanda, unless otherwise indicated. Later that year, a Genocide Memorial Commission report noted that by July 31, 1997, "167 full corpses, 51 skulls, and 61 long bones" were being conserved. Genocide Memorial Commission, "Rapport d'activités." In an August 2000 interview with a French reporter, Louis Kanamugire noted that the number of bodies on display at Murambi had increased to 1,864. Thorin, "Au pays" (2000). The discrepancies are likely due to distinctions between bodies being actively conserved, intact bodies that had been exhumed, and developments in subsequent conservation efforts, including at the nearby Ruhashya government office. By 2000 Louis estimated that twenty-seven thousand bodies had been reinterred in communal graves at Murambi.

27. I did not have the chance to speak to Zigirinshuti, but Mario, Louis, and Gabriel corroborated the central involvement of the Gikongoro *préfet* in the decision to place the bodies in Murambi's buildings—though none of them recalled his exact name.

28. GOR, "Genocide, Impunity, and Accountability" (1995), 27.

29. When the National University reopened in April 1995 (coincident with Amagaju exhumations at Murambi), Dr. Kanimba collaborated with university historians Aloys Rufangura and Joseph Jyoni wa Karega on the topic of genocide memory. Korman, "Mobilising the Dead?" (2015), 60.

30. Misago, "Préservation de la mémoire" (2005); Misago, "Instruments" (2007); and Misago, "Commission Nationale" (2009).

31. Misago, "Préservation de la mémoire" (2005), 135.

32. Gabriel, interview.

33. But as Liisa Malkki's study of Hutu refugees in Tanzania demonstrates, displacement often amplifies what she calls "mythico-histories" and identity-based sovereignty claims. Consequently, exile may be a place of physical distance but great emotional intensity. Malkki, *Purity and Exile* (1995).

34. Gabriel, interview.

35. Mario Ibarra, interview, Chile, January 6, 2015.

36. Ibarra, "Mario Personal (3)," video recording, July 23, 1997, cassette G44D1046 at 58:42, Ibarra archive.

37. Documented in videos taken by Mario Ibarra, indexed in Genocide Memorial Commission, *Rapport préliminaire* (1996), 55.

38. Ibarra, interview, January 9, 2015

39. GOR, "Genocide, Impunity, and Accountability" (1995); Misago, "Préservation de la mémoire"(2005), 137–39; and Genocide Memorial Commission, "Projet: Office National des Mémoriaux du Génocide et des Massacres au Rwanda," July 1996, CNLG Archive.

40. The Mwulire Sector office in eastern Rwanda (present-day Rwamagana district) deserves special mention because it was not located near Murambi; it was a key location of 1996–97 conservation work that extended the network of experimentation across the country. Approximately 28,600 victims were killed there. Mario knew of the site from his HRFOR investigations. Photographs from 1996 and 1997 show a shelter that the Genocide Memorial Commission built to display victims' remains (not unlike those at Bisesero and Ntarama; see figure 5.2), workers sorting and cleaning bones outside the office building, Mario filming, and the use of a vehicle from the Ministry of Higher Education, Scientific Research, and Culture (MINESUPRES) that indicates the ministry's logistical support for the endeavor.

41. Genocide Memorial Commission, *Rapport préliminaire* (1996), 19.

42. Ibarra, interview, January 9, 2015.

43. Ibarra, interview, January 9, 2015.

44. Ibarra, "Mario Personal (3)," July 21, 1997, from 37:44 to 45:24 (Kinyarwanda and French).

45. Ibarra, interview, January 9, 2015.

46. Ibarra, "Mario Personal (3)," July 23, 1997, at 45:32.

47. Ibarra, "Mario Personal (3)," July 17, 1997, at 26:03.

48. Ibarra, "Pepe Carta Filmada," July 10, 1997, at 9:18.

49. Genocide Memorial Commission, "Prévisions budgétaires" (1997).

50. Ibarra, "Pepe Carta Filmada," July 10, 1997, at 15:58; and Genocide Memorial Commission, "Projet et plan de travail" (1997).

51. Genocide Memorial Commission, "Projet et plan de travail" (1997), 5. A conservation worker elaborated that when they conserved bodies, they were paid RWF 1,000 per day, but otherwise their salary was RWF 15,000 per month. Ndikuryayo, interview.

52. Emmanuel's second name is documented as both Murangira and Muzengira in government and academic publications. I use the name his former neighbors and memorial coworkers used—Emmanuel Murangira. I did not interview him; Emmanuel died in November 2011.

53. Emmanuel Murangira, interviews, January 22, March 29, and April 9, 2008, documented in Totten and Ubaldo, *We Cannot Forget* (2011), 90. Samuel Totten and Rafiki Ubaldo write that Emmanuel returned in September 1995, but an interview with reporter Jina Moore puts it slightly earlier, in June. Moore, "Rwanda's Keeper" (2014).

54. Murangira, interview, in Totten and Ubaldo, *We Cannot Forget* (2011), 90–91. When Emmanuel refers to "refugees from 1959," he is speaking of Tutsi who were forced to live in exile.

55. Ndikuryayo, interview.

56. In Totten and Ubaldo, *We Cannot Forget* (2011), 97.

57. See, for example, images by photographers Sean Sheridan (*Testimony: Africa* [2010], cover) and Per-Anders Pettersson (2003): https://peranderspettersson.photoshelter.com/image/I0000y9UkgpkwoBE. Also see the cover photograph, taken by Ubaldo, of Totten and Ubaldo's book of survivor interviews, *We Cannot Forget* (2011).

58. Norridge, "Photography, Film" (2019), 55.

59. It is unclear whether Emmanuel was included in the firings; he was very ill with cancer by 2010, and his wife often worked on his behalf until his death in November 2011. The most common reasons for the firings in my interviews were lack of English language fluency, university degrees, or connection to new contractors. At Murambi, the private contractor charged with cleaning the memorial rehired a select few in 2016.

60. At Nyarubuye, my interviews with the former memorial caretakers revealed that firings occurred earlier, in 2008.

61. Jessee, *Negotiating Genocide* (2017), 87.

62. This point is also made in Moore, "Rwanda's Keeper"(2014); and Totten and Ubaldo, *We Cannot Forget* (2011), 97.

63. Ndikuryayo, interview.

64. Ndikuryayo, interview.

65. Ndikuryayo, interview.

66. Ndikuryayo, interview.

67. Ndikuryayo, interview. In actuality, Josie's son suffered from epilepsy; the injuries were from seizures.

68. Ndikuryayo, interview.

69. Ndikuryayo, interview.

70. Ndikuryayo, interview.

71. Ndikuryayo, interview.

72. Along with Emmanuel, Vestine is one of the longest-employed workers at the Mu-

rambi memorial—she is in charge of the cleaners and does that work herself. Vestine was among the six employees fired in 2011 and was later rehired by a private cleaning service in 2016.

73. Ibarra, "Pepe (2)," June 6, 1997.

74. Ibarra, "Pepe (2)," June 6, 1997, at 6:04–19:40

## CHAPTER 5. EXHUMATION, DISPLAY, REBURIAL

1. Brandstetter, "Contested Pasts" (2010); Burnet, *Genocide Lives in Us* (2012); Fox, *After Genocide* (2021); Korman, "Mobilising the Dead?" (2015); Dumas and Korman, "Espaces de la mémoire" (2011); Vidal, "Commémorations du génocide" (2001); and Vidal, "Commémoration du génocide" (2004).

2. Paraphrased from the reflections of a Hutu individual interviewed by Agence France Presse on October 20, 2000, in Vidal, "Commémorations du génocide" (2001), 46.

3. For studies of contemporary commemorations, see Baldwin, "Constructing Identity" (2019); Breed, *Performing the Nation* (2014); Ibreck, "Time of Mourning" (2012); and Mwambari, *Navigating Cultural Memory* (2023).

4. For analysis of commemoration ceremonies from 1995 to 2000, see Vidal, "Commémorations du génocide" (2001). For analysis of early exhumations, see Jessee, "Promoting Reconciliation" (2012); and Major, "Unearthing, Untangling" (2015).

5. The Muyumbu reburial, which I discuss in chapter 2, is also described in Fox, *After Genocide* (2021), 47–48; Korman, "Mobilising the Dead?" (2015), 57; and Ntirenganya, "Muyumbu" (2017). My additions to that history are from Sinyigaya, the government official in charge of the reburial, whom I interviewed in Rwanda on August 6, 2018.

6. Purdeková, *Making Ubumwe* (2015), 146.

7. Given the distance, the procession likely traveled by vehicle from the Amahoro Stadium area to Rebero Hill.

8. *Rebero* is a locative gerund of the verb *kureba* ("to see"). The hill's name means "a place where you see" or a vantage point for panoramic views of the wide hilltop (*ki-gali*) on which the capital city (Kigali) was built.

9. Louis Kanamugire recalled that most of those fourteen thousand victims were retrieved from the Centre Hospitalier de Kigali (CHK, today called the University Teaching Hospital of Kigali) massacre site. Kanamugire, interview, Kigali, March 1, 2013. Other sources note that the number buried at Rebero Hill was closer to six thousand people. Balzar, "Genocide Victims" (1995); and Vidal, "Commémorations du génocide" (2001), 6.

10. Balzar, "Genocide Victims" (1995).

11. Vidal, "Commémorations du génocide" (2001), 6.

12. Burnet, *Genocide Lives in Us* (2012), 95.

13. Quoted in Kaban, "Rwanda Remembers" (1996).

14. Quoted in Kaban, "Rwanda Remembers" (1996)

15. Braeckman, cited in Vidal, "Commémorations du génocide" (2001), 25.

16. The bishop was arrested by President Bizimungu but cleared of charges in 2000. Associated Press, "Rwanda Court Acquits" (2000).

17. Burnet, *Genocide Lives in Us* (2012), 101.

18. Attendees might have believed that their relatives lay among the dead, but individual identification was rare.

19. These PHR investigations near Kibuye supported UN International Criminal Tribunal for Rwanda (ICTR) prosecutions. Korman, "Bury or Display?" (2015), 210–12.

20. McKinley, "From a Grave" (1996).

21. Kanamugire, interview, March 1, 2013.

22. *Guterekera* is a form of ancestral communion that is practiced with discretion today. Burnet, *Genocide Lives in Us* (2012), 94–95, 99–101; Vidal, "Commémoration du génocide" (2004); and Viebach, "Mediating 'Absence-Presence'" (2020).

23. Bigirumwami, *Imihango n'imigenzo* (1974), 218–28; Chrétien, *Great Lakes* (2003), 121–37; de Lacger, *Ruanda* (1959), 203–37; and Taylor, *Milk, Honey, and Money* (1992).

24. Chrétien, *Great Lakes* (2003), 121–22.

25. Kanamugire, quoted in Thorin, "Au pays" (2000), 171.

26. Korman, "Bury or Display?" (2015), 206–7.

27. Kanamugire, "Témoignages recueillis" (2013), 44.

28. Kanamugire, "Témoignages recueillis" (2013), 101.

29. Mwambari, *Navigating Cultural Memory* (2023).

30. Bonner, "Rwanda Prison" (1995); and McKinley, "76,000 Still in Jail" (1996).

31. Amnesty International, *Troubled Course of Justice* (2000); and Lorch, "Rwanda Jails" (1995).

32. Vestine Ndikuryayo, interview.

33. Jan Wilken, "Kabuha [*sic*]—International Criminal Tribunal for Rwanda (ICTR) Internal Video," February 15 and 19, 1995, box 118, videocassette RW031, IMIC.

34. The mass graves are also enumerated in Genocide Memorial Commission, *Rapport préliminaire* (1996), 60.

35. Item notes, Wilken, "Kabuha" (1995).

36. Although reburial was assumed to be final, many victims' remains have been subsequently re-exhumed and reburied in state efforts to consolidate genocide memorials. This has painfully extended the time of burial and mourning.

37. Newbury, *Cohesion of Oppression* (1988), 66, 247n2.

38. Designed by White Fathers Belgian priest Father Joseph Gillessen, who built several churches in Rwanda.

39. Genocide Memorial Commission, *Rapport préliminaire* (1996), 50–52.

40. At the Nyamasheke reburial, victims' families were photographed by the open caskets as proof of relative identification. The piles of disordered remains formed a background in contrast.

41. A national-level commemoration ceremony took place at Nyamasheke in 2006 with the theme "Remember the genocide by telling the truth in the Gacaca courts."

42. The importance of time ordering and postgenocide experiences of time are discussed in Nsabimana, "Genocide Time" (2023); Sadruddin, "Death in an Ordinary Time" (2022); and Viebach, "Of Other Times" (2019).

43. Baines, "Spirits and Social Reconstruction" (2010); Barkan, *Guilt of Nations*

(2000); de Greiff and Duthie, *Transitional Justice* (2009); Elster, *Closing the Books* (2004); Graybill and Lanegran, "Truth, Justice" (2004); Hinton, *Transitional Justice* (2010; Shaw et al., *Localizing Transitional Justice* (2010); and Teitel, "Transitional Justice Genealogy" (2003).

44. Andrieu, "Civilizing Peacebuilding" (2010); Frankzi and Olarte, "Understanding the Political Economy" (2013); Leebaw, "Irreconcilable Goals" (2008); Lundy and McGovern, "Whose Justice?" (2008); Shaw et al., *Localizing Transitional Justice* (2010); and Vielle, "Transitional Justice" (2012).

45. Gahima, *Transitional Justice in Rwanda* (2013), 62.

46. Gahima, *Transitional Justice in Rwanda* (2013), xxxviii–xxxix.

47. See also Julie Viebach's discussion of the afterlife of human rights archives in transitional justice. Viebach, "*Transitional Archives*" (2021).

48. Rothberg and Yildiz, "Memory Citizenship" (2011).

## CHAPTER 6. MEMORY AND EMPOWERMENT

1. See also Jessee and Mwambari, "Memory Law" (2022).

2. To paraphrase W. James Booth, who compellingly argues that a witness can be both a person and a place: bearing witness is an act of refusal to forget and conceal. Booth, *Communities of Memory* (2006), 73.

3. For analysis of forgetting, see Ricoeur, *Memory, History, Forgetting* (2004), 412–56.

4. Azoulay, *Civil Contract* (2008).

5. This was true for 577 of the 620 individuals I spoke with in rural areas, in each of the country's thirty districts. The primary exception was thirty-seven residents living in the northeast, a region without genocide massacres (and therefore memorials) because it was controlled by the RPA.

6. Baldwin, "Constructing Identity" (2019); Blackie and Hitchcott, "'I Am Rwandan'" (2018); and Purdeková, *Making Ubumwe* (2015).

7. For resident reactions during the first years after the genocide, see African Rights, *"Go"* (2007); Burnet, *Genocide Lives in Us* (2012); Schotsmans, *A l'écoute des rescapés* (2000); and Vidal, "Commémorations du genocide" (2001).

8. "Ngoga" (pseudonym), interview, Rwanda, August 26, 2013. All interviewee names in this chapter are pseudonyms.

9. Ngoga, interview.

10. Article 13 of the Rwandan Constitution (2003) states, "The crime of genocide, crimes against humanity and war crimes do not have a period of limitation. Revisionism, negationism and trivialisation of genocide are punishable by the law." Constitution of the Republic of Rwanda, April 6, 2003, accessed online: https://ihl-databases.icrc.org/en/national-practice/constitution-republic-rwanda-2003.

11. "Esmée" (pseudonym), interview, Rwanda, August 26, 2013.

12. Esmée, interview.

13. Early internal documents from the Genocide Memorial Commission confirm that teaching genocide history to children, by making it visible, was an important priority for the curation of memorial sites. Genocide Memorial Commission, "Prévisions

budgétaires" (1997). Regardless, viewing bodies as a national obligation to genocide history is challenging for many adults in Rwanda, let alone children.

14. Music composed for genocide remembrance is a popular commemorative form in Rwanda. Mwambari, "Music" (2020).

15. "Albert" (pseudonym), interview, Rwanda, August 26, 2013.

16. For research on postgenocide time as a form of social ordering, see Baldwin, "Constructing Identity" (2019); Nsabimana, "Genocide-Time" (2023); and Viebach, "Of Other Times" (2019).

17. Albert, interview.

18. Albert, interview.

19. Albert, interview.

20. Baldwin, "Constructing Identity" (2019)

21. Certainly, *ubushobozi* can translate widely—as an ability based on resources, physical capability, or time, etc. I chose to translate this as "ability in terms of access to power," given the context of our conversation. Albert, interview.

22. Albert, interview.

23. Burnet, *Genocide Lives in Us* (2012), 111.

24. Burnet, *Genocide Lives in Us* (2012), 111.

25. Burnet, *Genocide Lives in Us* (2012), 111.

26. Fraser, "Rethinking the Public Sphere" (1990), 67.

27. Fraser, "Rethinking the Public Sphere" (1990), 67.

28. Gobodo-Madikizela, "Aesthetics of Memory" (2020), 138.

29. Gobodo-Madikizela, "Aesthetics of Memory" (2020), 136–37.

30. Ibarra, interview, Chile, January 6, 2015.

31. Kanamugire, interview, Rwanda, July 16, 2018.

32. Genocide Memorial Commission, *Rapport préliminaire* (1996), 85.

33. "Céleste" (pseudonym), interview, Rwanda, July 17, 2018. Céleste was eighty-seven years old when I interviewed her in 2018.

34. "Nkunzi" (pseudonym), interview, Rwanda, August 26, 2013, and July 23, 2018.

35. Nkunzi, interview, July 23, 2018.

36. Burnet, "Whose Genocide?" (2009); and Hintjens, "Post-Genocide Identity Politics" (2008).

37. Nkunzi, interview, August 26, 2013.

38. Nkunzi, interview, July 23, 2018.

39. "Agathe" (pseudonym), interview, Rwanda, August 9, 2013, and July 20, 2018.

40. Agathe, interview, July 20, 2018.

41. Agathe, interview, August 9, 2013.

42. Interjection by son-in-law, during Agathe, interview, August 9, 2013.

43. Agathe, interview, August 9, 2013.

44. Agathe, interview, July 20, 2018.

45. "Valens" (pseudonym), interview, Rwanda, July 30, 2018.

46. Amnesty International, *Troubled Course of Justice* (2000), 5, 8.

47. Longman and Rutagengwa, "Religion, Memory, and Violence" (2006), 247.

48. Human Rights Watch, "Search for Security" (2000); and OHCHR, "Democratic

Republic of the Congo, 1993–2003: Report of the Mapping Exercise Documenting the Most Serious Violations of Human Rights and International Humanitarian Law Committed Within the Territory of the Democratic Republic of the Congo Between March 1993 and June 2003," Geneva: OHCHR, August 2010. UN Digital Library, https://digital library.un.org/record/709895?ln=en&v=pdf.

49. Wendel, "*Duture Neza, Duture Heza*" (2025); and Wendel, "Umudugudu w'Ingunguru" (2018).

50. The seventeen individuals I interviewed also did not use other common terms for model villages, like *agasozi ndatwa* (a "praised hill") or *intangarugero* (an exemplary settlement). Ingurunguru Village is a pseudonym.

51. GOR, *Recensement general* (1994), 124. The Hutu population in Ruhengeri Préfecture was approximately 760,660 (99.2 percent) and only 0.5 percent Tutsi. However, previous censuses were not wholly accurate due to government inflation and strategic resident misreporting (i.e., Tutsi reported themselves as Hutu to gain the latter's socioeconomic and political benefits).

52. Northwestern Rwanda is historically prominent for its political autonomy from the Tutsi monarchy in the nineteenth century and the consolidation of political economic power in the region during the Second Republic (1973–94).

53. This was a key strategy of the "Ndi Umunyarwanda" (I Am Rwandan) campaign: The government claim that its citizens speak one language (Kinyarwanda) is a strategy of national unity and reconciliation, intended to socialize ethnic nonrecognition.

54. Though I introduced myself as an independent university researcher, my relative whiteness and foreigner status likely encouraged interlocutors to err on the side of proclamations of government support.

55. I can find no record of the marketplace attacks, but Amnesty International provides a sense of the violence of 1997 in Ruhengeri and Gisenyi (northwest). Amnesty International, "Report 1998" (1998).

56. "Alphonse" (pseudonym), interview, Rwanda, August 5, 2013, and July 19, 2018.

57. Alphonse, interview, July 19, 2018.

58. Alphonse, interview, July 19, 2018.

59. Alphonse, interview, July 19, 2018.

60. Alphonse, interview, July 19, 2018.

61. "Nyirashyaka" and "Mukayiranga" (pseudonyms), interview, Rwanda, August 5, 2013, and July 18, 2018.

62. A northwestern Kinyarwanda accent is typically characterized by a lilting, singsong cadence and the somewhat confusing (for me) use of "thing" pronouns for people nouns (*iki-/ibi-* are used in place of *umu-/aba-*).

63. Reminding herself of the *intambara*, Nyirashyaka subsequently wished to have *umutekano rwose* (complete security) amid the threat of renewed rebel attacks today. See also Ingelaere, "Living the Transition" (2009).

64. Nyirashyaka had fourteen children, all of whom died from miscarriage, childhood illness, or the *intambara*. Fetching water in jerricans, gathering firewood, and borrowing lighted kindling from neighbors for cooking fires are daily activities for survival that are particularly difficult for elderly and disabled persons.

65. Nyirashyaka, interview, Rwanda, July 18, 2018.

66. "Uwamahoro" (pseudonym), interview, Rwanda, September 3, 2013.

67. Eltringham, "Exhibition" (2012); GOR, Law No. 15/2016 of 02/05/2016 Governing Ceremonies to Commemorate the Genocide Against the Tutsi and Organisation and Management of Memorial Sites for the Genocide Against the Tutsi, *Official Gazette*, no. 22 (May 30, 2016): Article 15; and Gryzb, "Unsettled Memory" (2019).

68. Uwamahoro, interview.

69. "Claver" and his wife "Aurore" (pseudonyms), interview, Rwanda, August 2, 2018.

70. Claver, interview.

71. Claver, interview.

72. Claver, interview.

73. Aurore, interview.

74. Aurore, interview.

75. Claver left ambiguous whether he looted properties during the genocide alongside his eldest son. Aurore paid RWF 43,000 to one family (USD 50 in 2018), but RWF 42,000 remains on that debt; RWF 15,000 is owed to another family.

76. I did not transcribe our conversation because Claver and Aurore identify several people by name and describe where they live.

77. Claver, interview.

78. Aurore, interview.

79. Interviews with Hutu men (a nephew and his uncle, respectively) residing in Nyarubuye on July 31, 2018, and August 1, 2018). The nephew had been jailed and accused of genocide crimes. The uncle witnessed reprisal killings by the RPA and suspected that their bodies were buried at the Nyarubuye Genocide Memorial.

80. Claver, interview.

81. FAR, or the Forces Armées Rwandaises (Rwandan Armed Forces), was the national army of the former Hutu-led governing regime. They fought the RPA (armed forces of the RPF) prior to and during the genocide.

82. In 1995, Mario took photographs of the same commune jail that Claver references as part of his United Nations Human Rights Field Operation in Rwanda mandate. His photos show gaunt prisoners with injuries, crowded as large groups in small cells.

83. Claver, interview.

84. Clarance, "Human Rights Field Operation" (1995), 297.

85. Aurore, interview.

86. Amnesty International, *Rwanda* (1997); Des Forges, *Leave None to Tell* (1999); and U.S. Department of State, "Rwanda 2022 Human Rights Report" (2022).

87. Rothberg, "Between Memory and Memory" (2010); and Rothberg, *Multidirectional Memory* (2009).

88. Rothberg, "Between Memory and Memory" (2010), 9.

89. Halbwachs, *On Collective Memory* ([1925] 1980).

1. Jelin, *Trabajos de la memoria* (2002), 42–43. See also Jelin, *State Repression* (2003).

2. Jelin, *Trabajos de la memoria* (2002), 43.

3. For the Equal Justice Initiative project, see Fryer, "Heritage as Liberation" (2023); and Sharpe, "And to Survive" (2018). For Palestinian trauma heritage, see Azimi, "'Reduced to Dust'" (2024); Khalidi, *All That Remains* (1992); Rajagopal, "Opinion—Domicide" (2024); and Sa'di and Abu-Lughod, *Nakba* (2007).

4. Mahler, *From the Tricontinental* (2018), 6.

5. Considering historiography in an "expanded field" refers to Rosalind Krauss's reconceptualization of what constitutes sculpture in the postmodern period. Krauss, "Sculpture" (1979).

6. MIT student researchers Tyler Rivera and Gary Tran collected and analyzed the data used for the *Atlas of Trauma Heritage*, and Rivera and Yabework Abebe Kifetew developed visual representations for its various iterations. The maps in this book were designed by Zac DeGiulio. All work on the *Atlas of Trauma Heritage* was made under my direction, and all faults and inconsistencies are mine alone.

7. Schuessler, "Ranking History's Atrocities" (2011); White, *Atrocities* (2012); International Coalition of Sites of Conscience, "Institutional Members," January 2021, https://www.sitesofconscience.org/wp-content/uploads/2021/01/All-member-list.pdf; and Centro Internacional para la Promoción de los Derechos Humanos, *Memorias Situadas*, interactive map and database, accessed February 2, 2021, https://www.cipdh.gob.ar/memorias-situadas/.

8. Miriri and Houreld, "Moi's Kenyan Torture Victims" (2020).

9. Citizens for Justice, *We Lived to Tell* (2003).

10. Arthur, "How 'Transitions' Reshaped" (2009).

11. Glendon, "Knowing" (1998), 1153.

12. Waltz, "Reclaiming and Rebuilding" (2002), 439.

13. Waltz, "Reclaiming and Rebuilding" (2002), 439–40. Waltz refers to a global geography and history of atrocity, writing:

> The Spanish Civil War, and the ruthless bombing of Guernica, had deeply affected many Latin Americans. Well over 200,000 Chinese had been slaughtered when Japanese soldiers invaded and sacked Nanking in 1937. In South Africa the Nationalist Party was rising to power on a platform of racial and ethnic discrimination. Pakistan and India were at war that some called genocidal. Tensions were rife in Palestine, where Zionist leaders would soon claim a right to statehood, dispossessing and displacing thousands of Palestinian Arabs in the process. Lynchings in the USA were common and the humiliation of colonial rule was painfully familiar to many. Soviet intentions to limit individual freedoms had long been apparent, even if the scope of Stalin's brutal policies were not yet fully appreciated. Unfortunately, people who were ready to think about human rights, and the need to protect them, had many experiences on which to draw. (440)

14. De Schutter, *International Human Rights Law* (2019).

15. Cohen, "Rethinking Human Rights" (2008).

16. Levy and Sznaider, *Human Rights and Memory* (2010), 11, 18–19.

17. While Shoshana Felman and Dori Laub use the term *era of testimony*, Annette Wieviorka describes the same phenomenon as the *era of the witness*. Felman and Laub, *Testimony* (1992); and Wieviorka, *Era of the Witness* ([1998] 2006). I use the concept that was first articulated. See also Felman, "Era of Testimony" (1991); and Wiesel, "Holocaust as Literary Inspiration" (1990).

18. Wiesel, "Hope, Despair, and Memory" (1986).

19. Felman, "In an Era of Testimony" (1991), 39–40; and Felman and Laub, *Testimony* (1992), 204–5.

20. Huyssen, "Present Pasts" (2000), 24; Shenker, "Through the Lens" (2016); and Wieviorka, *Era of the Witness* ([1998] 2006), xiv–xv.

21. I use the term *urgent archive* in reference to Michelle Caswell's view of archival practice as that which informs present and future actions. Caswell, *Urgent Archives* (2021).

22. The first conserved Holocaust concentration and extermination camps opened as memorials at Majdanek (1944), Auschwitz-Birkenau and Theresienstadt (1947), Buchenwald (1958), Sachsenhausen (1961), and Dachau (1965).

23. Petrie, "Secular Word 'Holocaust'" (2000); and Zelizer, *Visual Culture* (2001).

24. Assmann, "Holocaust—A Global Memory?" (2010); Young, *Texture of Memory* (1993).

25. Holocaust heritage of this kind traveled internationally as well: When Buchenwald camp survivors left in 1945, they gathered human ash from the incinerators into eighteen urns for future memorials. Marcuse, "Holocaust Memorials" (2010), 56n11.

26. In 1947 the Polish parliament mandated the preservation of all remaining structures in Holocaust concentration camps. Marcuse, "Holocaust Memorials" (2010), 56, 64; and Young, *Texture of Memory* (1993), 49–154.

27. Young, *Texture of Memory* (1993), 121.

28. Young, *Texture of Memory* (1993), 124.

29. Young, *Texture of Memory* (1993), 75.

30. Holocaust survivors often diverged on these matters: Harold Marcuse documents a Dachau survivor protesting a statuary representation of camp prisoners because it "immortalized the horrors" of the Holocaust. Marcuse, "Holocaust Memorials" (2010), 72.

31. Debates regarding Holocaust memorial development are especially well documented at Buchenwald because of the number of survivors who remained near the site and were involved in the process. Marcuse, "Holocaust Memorials" (2010), 74.

32. Sodaro, *Exhibiting Atrocity* (2018), 30–57.

33. Demnig, *Stolpersteine* project website, accessed January 29, 2025, https://www.stolpersteine.eu/en/home.

34. On the global emergence of memorial museums, see Dickinson et al., *Places of Public Memory* (2010); Sodaro, *Exhibiting Atrocity* (2018); and Williams, *Memorial Museums* (2007). On human rights museology, see Carter and Orange, "Contentious Terrain" (2012); and Duffy, "Museums of 'Human Suffering'" (2001).

35. Fromm et al., *Museums and Truth* (2014); Huyssen, *Present Pasts* (2003); Schindel and Colombo, *Space and the Memories* (2014); Sodaro, *Exhibiting Atrocity* (2018); and Young, *Texture of Memory* (1993).

36. Duffy, "Museums of 'Human Suffering'" (2010), 10.

37. Carter and Orange, "Contentious Terrain" (2011), 117.

38. The 1984 report of the National Commission on the Disappearance of Persons (CONADEP) estimated that 8,960 individuals were disappeared. Argentina, CONADEP, *Nunca Mas* (1984), pt. 1, sec. B.

39. Robben, "How Traumatized Societies Remember" (2005), 131.

40. Fisher, *Mothers of the Disappeared* (1989), 52–70.

41. Bosco, "Madres" (2006); and Bouvard, *Revolutionizing Motherhood* (1994), 68.

42. Jelin, "Politics of Memory" (1994).

43. Cerisola, "Aparición con vida" (1995).

44. Page, *Memories of Buenos Aires* (2013), 3–16.

45. Longoni, "Photographs and Silhouettes" (2010), 10.

46. Doretti and Snow, "Forensic Anthropology" (2015)

47. José Zalaquett (November 1988), quoted in Arthur, "How 'Transitions' Reshaped" (2009), 323–24.

48. Chief among transitional justice strategies are truth commissions, which first convened in Bolivia (1982), Argentina (1983), and Uganda (1986) and continued through the 1990s in Chile (1990), Nepal (1990), El Salvador (1992), Guatemala (1994), South Africa (1995), and Sierra Leone (1999). Notably, truth and reconciliation commissions were not implemented in Bosnia and Herzegovina (despite attempts between 1997 and 2006) nor in Rwanda (which opted for *gacaca*, a neotraditional community adjudication system). More recently, a commission in Canada heard evidence of state crimes against Indigenous peoples (2008–15).

49. Hamber et al., "Utopian Dreams" (2010); Hobsbawm, "Introduction" (1983); and Sumartojo, "Memorials and State-Sponsored History" (2018).

50. Rothberg and Yildiz, "Memory Citizenship" (2011).

51. Buckley-Zistel and Björkdahl, "Memorials and Transitional Justice" (2020); Levy and Sznaider, *Holocaust and Memory* (2005); and Olick, *Politics of Regret* (2007).

52. CLADHO and FPH, *Rwanda: Reconstruire* (1994), 25.

53. C. Alexander, *Pattern Language* (1977); Jacobs, *Death and Life* (1961); Lynch, *Good City Form* (1981); Rossi, *Architecture of the City* (1982); and Tuan, *Space and Place* (1977).

54. Exemplifying this point, Chilean artist Alfredo Jaar developed *Untitled (Newsweek)* in 1995, comprising seventeen *Newsweek* covers from April 1994 until the magazine finally featured the Rwandan genocide nine months later.

55. Huyssen, "International Human Rights" (2011), 611.

56. Wiesel, "Hope, Despair, and Memory" (1986); italics mine.

57. Wiesel, "Hope, Despair, and Memory" (1986).

58. *JET Magazine* and the *Memphis Tri-State Defender* are primarily devoted to an African American readership.

59. Till-Mobley and Benson, *Death of Innocence* (2003), 139.

60. See Reverend Jesse L. Jackson's foreword to Mamie Till-Mobley's memoir: "More than 100,000 demonstrated their disgust at that casket. Each one of those people who saw how her son was defaced left telling their own story. They were never the same again.

Mamie's courage unsettled people of conscience into action." Till-Mobley and Benson, *Death of Innocence* (2003), xii.

61. Till-Mobley and Benson, *Death of Innocence* (2013), 172. The quotation reprises Mamie Till-Mobley's caption for the photograph of her son's casket in her memoir. The preceding photographs and the first chapters in her account take care to describe Emmett as a person: as a problem-solver, independent, loving, and curious.

62. Landsberg, *Prosthetic Memory* (2004).

63. Didi-Huberman, *Images* (2008), v.

64. Didi-Huberman, *Images* (2008), v.

65. Didi-Huberman, *Images* (2008), v.

# SOURCES

## ARCHIVES AND IMAGE SOURCES

Commission Nationale de Lutte contre le Génocide (CNLG; National Commission for the Fight Against Genocide) Documentation Center (now incorporated within the MINUBUMWE), Kigali, Rwanda

Genocide Archive of Rwanda, Kigali Genocide Memorial, Kigali, Rwanda

Ibarra, Mario. Personal archive, Chile

Photographs and videos held in the archive: part titles 2, 3, 5, 6, and 8; figures I.1, I.2, I.4–I.6, 1.2, 1.5–1.7, 1.10, 1.12, 1.15, 1.18, 1.20, 2.7, 2.8, 2.10, 2.13–2.16, 3.3, 3.4, 3.6, 3.12, 4.3, 4.7–4.9, 4.11, 4.22, 4.23, 4.25–4.33, 4.35, 4.36, 4.37, 5.1–5.3, and C.3

Institut de Recherche Scientifique et Technologique (Institute of Scientific and Technological Research), Butare, Rwanda

International Committee of the Red Cross, Library and Public Archive, Geneva, Switzerland

International Monitor Institute Collection (IMIC), David M. Rubenstein Rare Book and Manuscript Library, Duke University, Durham, NC

Photographs and videos held in the archive: figures 5.7–5.9

Kanamugire, Louis. Personal archive, Rwanda

Photographs held in the archive: part titles 1, 4, and 7; figures I.3, 1.3, 1.4, 1.8, 1.16, 1.17, 1.19, 1.21, 2.2, 2.3, 2.11, 2.12, 2.17–2.20, 4.1, 4.2, 4.4–4.6, 4.10, 4.12–4.21, 5.4, 5.10–5.34, and 6.3–6.7

Official Gazette of the Republic of Rwanda, https://www.minijust.gov.rw/official-gazette

Rwanda Parliament Archives, Kigali, Rwanda

United Nations (UN) Archives, Geneva

United Nations (UN) Archives, New York

United Nations (UN) Digital Library, https://digitallibrary.un.org/

United Nations ICTR Digital Archive, International Residual Mechanism for Criminal Tribunals, https://unictr.irmct.org/
United Nations Photo Archives, Digital Asset Management System, https://dam.media.un.org/
Photographs held in the archive: figures 3.1 and 3.7
United Universalist Church Collection, Harvard University Andover Theology Archive, Cambridge, MA
Photographs held in the archive: figures 2.4–2.6
University of Texas at Austin, Digital Archive, https://repositories.lib.utexas.edu
Wendel, Delia Duong Ba. Personal Archive, interviews with 620 rural residents of Rwanda, USA
Photographs and maps held in the archive: figures P.1, P.2, 1.1, 1.13, 2.1, 2.9, 3.2, 3.5, 3.8, 3.9, 4.24, 4.34, 6.1, 6.2, and 6.8–6.27; maps C.1–C20 in appendixes 1 and 2; and map index in appendix 3

## INTERVIEWS

*Note*: Unless otherwise noted, interviews are in English.

### *Anonymized*

"180731_12–10" [anon.]. Rwanda, July 31, 2018 (Kinyarwanda)
"Agathe" [pseud.]. Rwanda, August 9, 2013, and July 20, 2018 (Kinyarwanda)
"Albert" [pseud.]. Rwanda, August 26, 2013 (Kinyarwanda)
"Alphonse" [pseud.]. Rwanda, August 5, 2013, and July 19, 2018 (Kinyarwanda)
"Céleste" [pseud.]. Rwanda, July 17, 2018 (Kinyarwanda)
"Claver" (with wife "Aurore") [pseuds.]. Rwanda, August 2, 2018 (Kinyarwanda)
"Esmée" [pseud.]. Rwanda, August 26, 2013 (Kinyarwanda)
"Gabriel" [pseud.]. Rwanda, July 25, 2018 (Kinyarwanda)
"Ngoga" [pseud.] Rwanda, August 26, 2013 (Kinyarwanda)
"Nkunzi" [pseud.]. Rwanda, August 26, 2013, and July 23, 2018 (Kinyarwanda)
"Nyirashyaka" (with friend "Mukayiranga") [pseuds.]. Rwanda, August 5, 2013, and July 18, 2018 (Kinyarwanda)
"Uwamahoro" [pseud.]. Rwanda, September 3, 2013 (Kinyarwanda)
"Valens" [pseud.]. Rwanda, July 30, 2018 (Kinyarwanda)

### *Named with Consent*

Bossuyt, Marc. Phone interview (Belgium), March 10, 2015
Gasasira, Janvier. Rwanda, August 4, 2018
Howland, Todd. Phone interview (Colombia), April 15, 2013
Ibarra, Mario. Chile, January 6, 8, 9, 10, and 11, 2015 (Spanish, English, and French)
Kagahe, Athanase Ndutiye. Phone interview (France), June 17, 2017 (French, Kinyarwanda, and English)
Kanamugire, Louis. Rwanda, March 1, 2013; May 31, 2013; June 14, 2013; June 21, 2013; July 16, 2018 (Kinyarwanda and French)

Majekodunmi, Ben. Phone interview (USA), March 9, 2013
Ndikuryayo, Vestine. Rwanda, July 23, 2018 (Kinyarwanda)
Sinyigaya, Silas. Rwanda, August 6, 2018
Wagner, Michele. USA, December 1, 2017

## WORKS CITED


African Rights. *"Go. If You Die, Perhaps I Will Live": A Collective Account of Genocide and Survival in Murambi, Gikongoro, April–July 1994*. Kigali: African Rights, 2007.

African Rights. *Rwanda, "A Waste of Hope": The United Nations Field Operation*. London: African Rights, 1995.

African Rights. *Rwanda: Death, Despair, and Defiance*. London: African Rights, 1994.

Agamben, Giorgio. *Homo Sacer: Sovereign Power and Bare Life*. Stanford, CA: Stanford University Press, 1998.

Agostinho, Daniela. "Archival Encounters: Rethinking Access and Care in Digital Colonial Archives." *Archival Science* 19, no. 2 (2019): 141–65.

Alexander, Christopher. *A Pattern Language*. New York: Oxford University Press, 1977.

Alexander, Jeffrey C., Ron Eyerman, Bernhard Giesen, Neil J. Smelser, and Piotr Sztompka, eds. *Cultural Trauma and Collective Identity*. Berkeley: University of California Press, 2004.

Alston, Philip. "Neither Fish nor Fowl: The Quest to Define the Role of the UN High Commissioner for Human Rights." *European Journal of International Law* 8, no. 2 (1997): 321–35.

Amnesty International. "Amnesty International Report 1998—Rwanda." January 1, 1998. https://www.refworld.org/docid/3ae6a9f210.html.

Amnesty International. *Rwanda: Ending the Silence*. AFR 47/32/97. Report, September 25, 1997. https://www.amnesty.org/en/documents/afr47/032/1997/en/.

Amnesty International. "Rwanda: Ensure Remedy After Fair Trial Violations in Paul Rusesabagina Case." AFR 47/4753/2021. Public statement, September 20, 2021. https://www.amnesty.org/en/documents/afr47/4753/2021/en/.

Amnesty International. *Rwanda: The Troubled Course of Justice*. AFR 47/10/00. Report, April 2000. https://www.amnesty.org/en/documents/afr47/010/2000/en/.

Andrieu, Kora. "Civilizing Peacebuilding: Transitional Justice, Civil Society and the Liberal Paradigm." *Security Dialogue* 41, no. 5 (2010): 537–58.

Annan, Kofi. Speech to the Parliament of Rwanda. May 7, 1998. http://www.un.org/press/en/1998/19980506.SGSM6552.html.

Arendt, Hannah. *The Human Condition*. Chicago: University of Chicago Press, 1958.

Argentina, Comisión Nacional sobre la Desaparición de Personas (CONADEP). *Nunca Más: The Report of the Argentine National Commission on the Disappeared*. New York: Farrar, Straus and Giroux, 1984.

Arthur, Paige. "How 'Transitions' Reshaped Human Rights: A Conceptual History of Transitional Justice." *Human Rights Quarterly* 31, no. 2 (2009): 321–67.

Assmann, Aleida. "The Holocaust—A Global Memory? Extensions and Limits of a New Memory Community." In *Memory in a Global Age: Discourses, Practices, and Trajec-*

*tories*, edited by Aleida Assmann and Sebastian Conrad, 97–118. New York: Palgrave Macmillan, 2010.

Associated Press. "Kigali, Rwanda." *AP Worldstream*, December 6, 1995.

Associated Press. "Rwanda Court Acquits Bishop of 1994 Massacre Charges." *New York Times*, June 16, 2000. https://www.nytimes.com/2000/06/16/world/rwanda-court-acquits-bishop-of-1994-massacre-charges.html.

Azimi, Negar. "Opinion: 'Reduced to Dust': An Elegy for Gazan Life." Illustrations by Asma Ghanem. *Washington Post*, February 27, 2024. https://www.washingtonpost.com/opinions/2024/02/27/gaza-lost-bombardment-invasion-places-oral-histories/.

Azoulay, Ariella. *The Civil Contract of Photography*. New York: Zone Books, 2008.

Baines, Erin. "Spirits and Social Reconstruction After Mass Violence: Rethinking Transitional Justice." *African Affairs* 109, no. 436 (2010): 409–30.

Baldwin, Gretchen. "Constructing Identity Through Commemoration: *Kwibuka* and the Rise of Survivor Nationalism in Post-Conflict Rwanda." *Journal of Modern African Studies* 57, no. 3 (2019): 355–75.

Balzar, John. "Genocide Victims Mourned in Rwanda, Africa." *Los Angeles Times*, April 8, 1995.

Barkan, Elazar. *The Guilt of Nations: Restitution and Negotiating Historical Injustices*. New York: W. W. Norton, 2000.

Battiste, Marie, and James (Sa'ke'j) Youngblood Henderson. *Protecting Indigenous Knowledge and Heritage*. Saskatoon, Canada: Purich, 2000.

BBC. "RPF Leader Kanyarengwe Speaks to Journalists on Moves to End Fighting." BBC Monitoring Service Africa, May 28, 1994.

BBC. *Rwanda's Untold Story*. BBC2, October 1, 2014.

Beloff, Jonathan R. "'Double Genocide' or Revenge Killings? Did the Liberators of a Genocide Commit Their Own?" In *In the Shadow of Genocide: Justice and Memory Within Rwanda*, edited by Stephanie Wolfe, Matthew Kane, and Tamia Ansah, 132–49. New York: Taylor and Francis, 2022.

Bergin, Cathy, and Anita Rupprecht. "Reparative Histories: Tracing Narratives of Black Resistance and White Entitlement." *Race and Class* 60, no. 1 (2018): 22–37.

Bigirumwami, Aloys. *Imihango n'imigenzo n'imizilirizo mu Rwanda*. Nyundo, Rwanda: Diocèse de Nyundo, 1974.

Blackie, Laura E. R., and Nicki Hitchcott. "'I Am Rwandan': Unity and Reconciliation in Post-Genocide Rwanda." *Genocide Studies and Prevention* 12, no. 1 (2018): 24–37.

Bolin, Annalisa. "Imagining Genocide Heritage: Material Modes of Development and Preservation in Rwanda." *Journal of Material Culture* 25, no. 2 (2020): 196–219.

Bolin, Annalisa. "On the Side of Light: Performing Morality at Rwanda's Genocide Memorials." *Journal of Conflict Archaeology* 7, no. 3 (2012): 199–207.

Bonner, Raymond. "Rwanda Prison Fills with Targets of Political Vengeance." *New York Times*, January 1, 1995. https://www.nytimes.com/1995/01/01/world/rwanda-prison-fills-with-targets-of-political-vengeance.html.

Booth, W. James. *Communities of Memory: On Witness, Identity, and Justice*. Ithaca, NY: Cornell University Press, 2006.

Booth, W. James. "The Unforgotten: Memories of Justice." *American Political Science Review* 95, no. 4 (2001): 777–91.

Bosco, Fernando J. "The Madres de Plaza de Mayo and Three Decades of Human Rights' Activism: Embeddedness, Emotions, and Social Movements." *Annals of the American Association of Geographers* 96, no. 2 (2006): 342–65.

Bossuyt, Marc. "United Nations Human Rights Procedures Regarding Burundi, Rwanda and Zaire (1994–1997)." In *International Law: Theory and Practice; Essays in Honor of Eric Suy*, edited by Karel Wellens, 493–504. The Hague: Martinus Njihoff, 1998.

Bouvard, Marguerite Guzman. *Revolutionizing Motherhood: The Mothers of the Plaza de Mayo.* Wilmington, DE: SR Books, 1994.

Brandstetter, Anna-Maria. "Contested Pasts: The Politics of Remembrance in Post-Genocide Rwanda." Ortelius Lecture 6. Wassenaar, Netherlands: NIAS, 2010.

Brauman, Rony, Stephen Smith, and Claudine Vidal. "Rwanda: Politique de terreur, privilège d'impunité." *Esprit*, August/September 2000, 147–61.

Breed, Ananda. *Performing the Nation: Genocide, Justice, Reconciliation.* Chicago: Seagull Books, 2014.

Bshara, Khaldun. "Lifta's Ruins: The Presence of Absence." *Jerusalem Quarterly*, no. 90 (2022): 98–114.

Buchanan, Rachel. "Decolonising the Archives: The Work of New Zealand's Waitangi Tribunal." *Public History Review* 14 (2007): 44–53.

Buckley-Zistel, Susanne. "Remembering to Forget: Chosen Amnesia as a Strategy for Local Coexistence in Post-Genocide Rwanda." *Journal of the International African Institute* 76, no. 2 (2006): 131–50.

Buckley-Zistel, Susanne, and Annika Björkdahl. "Memorials and Transitional Justice." *An Introduction to Transitional Justice*, edited by Olivera Simic, 269–89. London: Routledge, 2020.

Burkins, Glen. "Legacy of Terror: Rwandans Are Still Suffering a Year After Tribal Tensions Exploded into an Orgy of Slaughter." *Toronto Star*, April 2, 1995.

Burkins, Glen. "The Past Tortures a Struggling Land." *Philadelphia Inquirer*, March 19, 1995.

Burnet, Jennie E. *Genocide Lives in Us: Women, Memory, and Silence in Rwanda.* Madison: University of Wisconsin Press, 2012.

Burnet, Jennie E. *To Save Heaven and Earth: Rescue in the Rwandan Genocide.* Ithaca, NY: Cornell University Press, 2023.

Burnet, Jennie E. "Whose Genocide, Whose Truth?" In *Genocide: Truth, Memory and Representation*, edited by Alexander Hinton and Kevin O'Neill, 80–110. Durham, NC: Duke University Press, 2009.

Butler, Judith. *Precarious Life: The Powers of Mourning and Violence.* New York: Verso, 2004.

Carter, Jennifer, and Jennifer Orange. "Contentious Terrain: Defining a Human Rights Museology." *Museum Management and Curatorship* 27, no. 2 (2012): 111–27.

Caruth, Cathy. *Unclaimed Experience: Trauma, Narrative, and History.* Baltimore, MD: Johns Hopkins University Press, 1996.

Caswell, Michelle. *Urgent Archives: Enacting Liberatory Memory Work*. New York: Routledge, 2021.

Caswell, Michelle, and Marika Cifor. "From Human Rights to Feminist Ethics: Radical Empathy in the Archives." *Archivaria*, no. 81 (2016): 23–43.

Cerisola, Roberto Amigo. "Aparición con vida: Las siluetas de detenidos-desaparecidos." *Razón y Revolución*, no. 1 (1995). https://razonyrevolucion.org/aparicion-con-vida-las-siluetas-de-detenidos-desaparecidos/.

Certeau, Michel de. *The Writing of History*. New York: Columbia University Press, 1988.

Chrétien, Jean-Pierre. *The Great Lakes of Africa: Two Thousand Years of History*. New York: Zone Books, 2003.

Citizens for Justice. *We Lived to Tell: The Nyayo House Story*. Nairobi: Friedrich Ebert Stiftung, 2003.

CLADHO (Collectif des Ligues et Associations de Défense des Droits de l'Homme) and FPH (Fondation Charles Léopold Mayer pour le Progrès de l'Homme). *Rwanda: Reconstruire—Séminaire international, Kigali, Rwanda (22–28 octobre 1994); Compte-rendu des travaux en atelier CLADHO-FPH*. Paris: Editions-Diffusion Charles Léopold Mayer, 1994.

Clarance, William. "Field Strategy for the Protection of Human Rights." *International Journal of Refugee Law* 9, no. 2 (1997): 229–54.

Clarance, William. "The Human Rights Field Operation in Rwanda: Protective Practice Evolves on the Ground." *International Peacekeeping* 2, no. 3 (1995): 291–308.

Clark, Phil. *The Gacaca Courts, Post-Genocide Justice and Reconciliation in Rwanda*. Cambridge: Cambridge University Press, 2010.

Clinton, Bill. "President Bill Clinton's Remarks to the People of Rwanda." Miller Center of Public Affairs, University of Virginia, March 25, 1998. https://millercenter.org/the-presidency/presidential-speeches/march-25-1998-remarks-people-rwanda.

CNLG (Commission Nationale de Lutte contre le Génocide). "Sites mémoriaux du génocide: Nyamata, Murambi, Bisesero et Gisozi." UNESCO World Heritage application brief, June 16, 2012. https://whc.unesco.org/en/tentativelists/5753.

Cohen, Jean L. "Rethinking Human Rights, Democracy, and Sovereignty in the Age of Globalization." *Political Theory* 36, no. 4 (2008): 578–606.

Cook, Susan E. "The Politics of Preservation in Rwanda." In *Genocide in Cambodia and Rwanda: New Perspectives*, edited by Susan E. Cook, 281–99. New Brunswick, NJ: Transaction, 2006.

Crossette, Barbara. "U.N. Chief Focuses on Africa's 'Underdog Conflicts.'" *New York Times*, July 23, 1995. https://www.nytimes.com/1995/07/23/world/un-chief-focuses-on-africa-s-underdog-conflicts.html.

Dallaire, Romeo. *Shake Hands with the Devil: The Failure of Humanity in Rwanda*. Toronto: Random House, 2003.

Davis, Shannon, and Jacky Bowring. "The Right to Remember: The Memorials to Genocide in Cambodia and Rwanda." In *The Right to Landscape: Contesting Landscape and Human Rights*, edited by Shelley Egoz, Jala Makhzoumi, and Gloria Pungetti, 211–26. London: Routledge, 2011.

de Greiff, Pablo, and Roger Duthie. *Transitional Justice and Development: Making the Connections.* New York: Social Science Research Council, 2009.
de Lacger, Louis. *Ruanda.* Kabgayi, Rwanda: A. Perraudin, 1959.
De Schutter, Olivier. *International Human Rights Law.* 3rd ed. Cambridge: Cambridge University Press, 2019.
Des Forges, Alison. *Leave None to Tell the Story: Genocide in Rwanda.* New York City: Human Rights Watch, 1999.
Dickinson, Greg, Carole Blair, and Brian L. Ott, eds. *Places of Public Memory: The Rhetoric of Museums and Memorials.* Tuscaloosa: University of Alabama Press, 2010.
Didi-Huberman, Georges. *Images in Spite of It All: Four Photographs from Auschwitz.* Translated by Shane B. Lillis. Chicago: University of Chicago Press, 2008.
Diop, Boubacar Boris. *Murambi: Book of Bones.* Translated by Fiona McLaughlin. 2001. Reprint ed., Bloomington: Indiana University Press, 2006.
Doretti, Mercedes, and Clyde C. Snow. "Forensic Anthropology and Human Rights: The Argentine Experience." In *Hard Evidence: Case Studies in Forensic Anthropology,* edited by Dawnie Wolfe Steadman, 303–19. New York: Routledge, 2015.
Doughty, Kristin. "'Our Goal Is Not to Punish but to Reconcile': Mediation in Post-genocide Rwanda." *American Anthropologist* 116, no. 4 (2015): 780–94.
Duffy, Terence. "Museums of 'Human Suffering' and the Struggle for Human Rights." *Museum International* 53, no. 1 (2001): 10–16.
Dumas, Hélène, and Rémi Korman. "Espaces de la mémoire du génocide des Tutsis au Rwanda: Mémoriaux et lieux de mémoire." *Afrique Contemporaine,* no. 238 (2011): 11–27. https://francegenocidetutsi.org/KormanDumasEspacesMemoire2011.pdf.
Eastmond, Marita, and Johanna Mannergren Selimovic. "Silence as Possibility in Postwar Everyday Life." *International Journal of Transitional Justice* 6, no. 3 (2012): 502–24.
Elster, Jon. *Closing the Books: Transitional Justice in Historical Perspective.* Cambridge: Cambridge University Press, 2004.
Eltringham, Nigel. "Bodies of Evidence: Remembering the Rwandan Genocide at Murambi." In *Remembering Genocide,* edited by Nigel Eltringham and Pam Maclean, 200–218. London: Routledge, 2014.
Eltringham, Nigel. "Exhibition, dissimulation et 'culture': Le traitement des corps dans le génocide rwandais." In *Cadavres impensables, cadavres impensés: Approches méthodologiques du traitement des corps dans les violences de masse et Les Génocides,* edited by Élisabeth Anstett and Jean-Marc Dreyfus, 93–105. Paris: Éditions Petra, 2012.
Esipisu, Manoah. "Only Dogs Remain in Rwandan Massacre Village." *Reuters News,* September 30, 1994.
Feldman, Allen. *Archives of the Insensible: Of War, Photopolitics, and Dead Memory.* Chicago: University of Chicago Press, 2015.
Feldman, Allen. "Epilogue: Ethnographic States of Emergency." In *Fieldwork Under Fire: Contemporary Studies of Violence and Culture,* edited by Carolyn Nordstrom and Antonius Robben, 224–53. Berkeley: University of California Press, 1996.
Felman, Shoshana. "In an Era of Testimony: Claude Lanzmann's *Shoah.*" In "Literature and the Ethical Question," edited by Claire Nouvet. *Yale French Studies,* no. 79 (1991): 39–81.

Felman, Shoshana, and Dori Laub. *Testimony: Crises of Witnessing in Literature, Psychoanalysis, and History*. New York: Routledge, 1992.

Fisher, Jo. *Mothers of the Disappeared*. Boston: South End, 1989.

Forensic Architecture. Tantura: Executions and Mass Graves in Palestine. Accessed May 24, 2023. https://tantura.forensic-architecture.org/.

Foucault, Michel. *Language, Counter-Memory, and Practice: Selected Essays and Interviews*. Edited by Donald F. Bouchard. (First published in the UK by Basil Blackwell, 1977.) Ithaca, NY: Cornell University Press, 1980.

Fox, Nicole. *After Genocide: Memory and Reconciliation in Rwanda*. Madison: University of Wisconsin Press, 2021.

Frankzi, Hannah, and Maria Carolina Olarte. "Understanding the Political Economy of Transitional Justice: A Critical Theory Perspective." In *Transitional Justice Theories*, edited by Susanne Buckley-Zistel, Teresa Beck, Christian Braun, and Friederike Mieth, 201–21. New York: Routledge, 2013.

Fraser, Nancy. "Rethinking the Public Sphere: A Contribution to the Critique of Actually Existing Democracy." *Social Text*, no. 25/26 (1990): 56–80.

Fromm, Annette B., Viv Golding, and Per B. Rekdal, eds. *Museums and Truth*. Newcastle upon Tyne, UK: Cambridge Scholars, 2014.

Fryer, Tiffany C. "Heritage as Liberation." *American Anthropologist* 125, no. 2 (2023): 420–34.

Fujii, Lee Ann. *Killing Neighbors: Webs of Violence in Rwanda*. Ithaca, NY: Cornell University Press, 2009.

Fujii, Lee Ann. "Shades of Truth and Lies: Interpreting Testimonies of War and Violence." *Journal of Peace Research* 47, no. 2 (2010): 231–41.

Gahima, Gerald. *Transitional Justice in Rwanda: Accountability for Atrocity*. New York: Routledge, 2013.

Geertz, Clifford. *The Interpretation of Culture: Selected Essays*. New York: Basic Books, 1973.

Genocide Memorial Commission. *Rapport préliminaire d'identification des sites du génocide et des massacres d'avril–juillet 1994 au Rwanda*. Kigali: MINESUPRES, February 1996.

Geraghty, Mark. "Gacaca, Genocide, Genocide Ideology: The Violent Aftermaths of Transitional Justice in the New Rwanda." *Comparative Studies in Society and History* 62, no. 3 (2020): 588–618.

Glassie, Henry. *Passing the Time in Ballymenone: Culture and History of an Ulster Community*. Philadelphia: University of Pennsylvania Press, 1982.

Glendon, Mary Ann. "Knowing the Universal Declaration of Human Rights." *Notre Dame Law Review* 73, no. 5 (1998): 1153–90.

Gobodo-Madikizela, Pumla. "Aesthetics of Memory, Witness to Violence, and a Call to Repair." In *Post-Conflict Hauntings: Transforming Memories of Historical Trauma*, edited by Kim Wale, Pumla Gobodo-Madikizela, and Jeffrey Prager, 119–49. Cham, Switzerland: Palgrave Macmillan, 2020.

GOR (Government of Rwanda). "Genocide, Impunity, and Accountability: Dialogue for a National and International Response—Recommendations of the Conference Held in Kigali from November 1st to 5th, 1995." Kigali: Office of the President, December

1995, 24. University of Texas at Austin Digital Archive, https://repositories.lib.utexas.edu/server/api/core/bitstreams/6da68886-2bd2-4159-be14-2d99a71da94b/content.

GOR (Government of Rwanda). *Recensement general de la population et de l'habitat au 15 aout 1991—Analyse des resultats definitifs.* Vol. 1. Kigali: Commision Nationale de Recensement, 1994.

Gould, Chandre, and Verne Harris. "Memory for Justice." Nelson Mandela Foundation, 2014. Accessed February 14, 2025. https://www.nelsonmandela.org/uploads/files/MEMORY_FOR_JUSTICE_2014v2.pdf.

Gourevitch, Philip. "Letter from Rwanda: After the Genocide." *New Yorker*, December 10, 1995, 78–95.

Gourevitch, Philip. *We Wish to Inform You That Tomorrow We Will Be Killed with Our Families.* New York: Picador, 1998.

Graybill, Lyn, and Kimberly Lanegran. "Truth, Justice, and Reconciliation in Africa: Issues and Cases." *African Studies Quarterly* 8, no. 1 (2004): 1–18.

Grzyb, Amanda F. "Unsettled Memory: Genocide Memorial Sites in Rwanda." *Brown Journal of World Affairs* 25, no. 11 (2019): 185–98.

Guichaoua, André. *From War to Genocide: Criminal Politics in Rwanda, 1990–1994.* Madison: University of Wisconsin Press, 2017.

Guyer, Sara. "Rwanda's Bones." *Boundary 2* 36, no. 2 (2009): 155–75.

Haglund, William D., Melissa Connor, and Douglas D. Scott. "The Archaeology of Mass Graves." *Historical Archaeology* 35, no. 1 (2001): 57–69.

Halbwachs, Maurice. *On Collective Memory.* Translated by Francis and Vida Ditter. 1925. New York: Harper and Row, 1980.

Hall, Catherine. "Doing Reparatory History: Bringing 'Race' and Slavery Home." *Race and Class* 60, no. 1 (2018): 3–21.

Hamber, Brandon, Liz Ševčenko, and Ereshnee Naidu. "Utopian Dreams or Practical Possibilities? The Challenges of Evaluating the Impact of Memorialization in Societies in Transition." *International Journal of Transitional Justice* 4, no. 3 (2010): 397–420.

Hartman, Saidiya. "Venus in Two Acts." *Small Axe* 12, no. 2 (26) (2008): 1–14.

Hatzfeld, Jean. *Into the Quick of Life.* Translated by Gerry Feehily. 2000. London: Serpent's Tail, 2005.

Hintjens, Helen. "Post-Genocide Identity Politics in Rwanda." *Ethnicities* 8, no. 1 (2008): 5–41.

Hinton, Alexander, ed. *Transitional Justice: Global Mechanisms and Local Realities After Genocide and Mass Violence.* New Brunswick, NJ: Rutgers University Press, 2010.

Hobsbawm, Eric. "Introduction: Inventing Traditions." In *The Invention of Tradition*, edited by Eric Hobsbawm and Terence Ranger, 1–14. Cambridge: Cambridge University Press, 1983.

Howland, Todd. "Mirage, Magic, or Mixed Bag: The United Nations High Commissioner for Human Rights' Field Operation in Rwanda." *Human Rights Quarterly* 21, no. 1 (1999): 1–55.

Huband, Mark. "A Holocaust We Chose Not to See." *Observer*, April 2, 1995.

Huband, Mark. "Churchyard Slaughter Beyond Comprehension." *Guardian*, May 31, 1994.

Human Rights Watch. "Rwanda: Repression Across Borders." January 28, 2014. https://www.hrw.org/news/2014/01/28/rwanda-repression-across-borders.

Human Rights Watch. *Rwanda: The Search for Security and Human Rights Abuses*. April 2000. https://www.hrw.org/reports/2000/rwanda/index.htm.

Huyssen, Andreas. "International Human Rights and the Politics of Memory: Limits and Challenges." *Criticism* 53, no. 4 (2011): 607–24.

Huyssen, Andreas. "Present Pasts: Media, Politics, Amnesia." *Public Culture* 12, no. 1 (2000): 21–38.

Huyssen, Andreas. *Present Pasts: Urban Palimpsests and the Politics of Memory*. Stanford, CA: Stanford University Press, 2003.

Ibarra, Mario. "Apuntes para una cronología de los pueblos indígenas en el derecho internacional." In *La Festa degli Indios: Il quinto centenario visto dagli Indigeni dell'America Latina*, edited by Gerardo Bamonte and Giulia Della Marina, 23–52. Rome: Bulzoni, 1992.

Ibarra, Mario. *I Mapuche: La resistenza degli Indios contro la dittatura Cilena*. Rome: Edizioni Associate, 1989.

Ibarra, Mario. *Notas sobre algunos instrumentos, documentos y actividades internacionales para una discusión e implementación del derecho de libre determinación de los pueblos Indígenas*. Guatemala City, Guatemala: Sotz'il, 2007.

Ibreck, Rachel. "International Constructions of National Memories: The Aims and Effects of Foreign Donors' Support for Genocide Remembrance in Rwanda." *Journal of Intervention and Statebuilding* 7, no. 2 (2013): 149–69.

Ibreck, Rachel. "The Politics of Mourning: Survivor Contributions to Memorials in Post-Genocide Rwanda." *Memory Studies* 3, no. 4 (2010): 330–43.

Ibreck, Rachel. "A Time of Mourning: The Politics of Commemorating the Tutsi Genocide in Rwanda." In *Public Memory, Public Media, and the Politics of Justice*, edited by Philip Lee and Pradip Thomas, 98–121. London: Palgrave Macmillan, 2012.

Ingelaere, Bert. "Do We Understand Life After Genocide? Center and Periphery in the Construction of Knowledge in Postgenocide Rwanda." *African Studies Review* 53, no. 1 (2010): 41–59.

Ingelaere, Bert. *Inside Rwanda's Gacaca Courts: Seeking Justice After Genocide*. Madison: University of Wisconsin Press, 2016.

Ingelaere, Bert. "Learning 'to Be' Kinyarwanda in Postgenocide Rwanda: Immersion, Iteration, and Reflexivity in Times of Transition." *Canadian Journal of Law and Society* 30, no. 2 (2015): 277–92.

Ingelaere, Bert. "Living the Transition: Inside Rwanda's Conflict Cycle at the Grassroots." *Journal of Eastern African Studies* 3, no. 3 (2009): 438–63.

Jackson, Steven J. "Rethinking Repair." In *Media Technologies: Essays on Communication, Materiality, and Society*, edited by Tarleton Gillespie, Pablo J. Boczkowski, and Kirsten A. Foot, 221–40. Cambridge, MA: MIT Press, 2014.

Jacobs, Jane. *The Death and Life of Great American Cities*. New York: Vintage Books, 1961.

Jelin, Elizabeth. "The Politics of Memory: The Human Rights Movements and the Construction of Democracy in Argentina." *Latin American Perspectives* 21, no. 2 (1994): 38–58.

Jelin, Elizabeth. *State Repression and the Labors of Memory.* Translated by Judy Rein and Marcial Godoy-Anativia. Minneapolis: University of Minnesota Press, 2003.

Jelin, Elizabeth. *Los trabajos de la memoria.* Madrid: Siglo XXI de España Editores, 2002.

Jessee, Erin. "The Limits of Oral History: Ethics and Methodology amid Highly Politicized Research Settings." *Oral History Review* 38, no. 2 (2011): 287–307.

Jessee, Erin. "The Micro-Politics of Remembering 'the 1994 Genocide Against the Tutsi' in Rwanda." In *Localising Memory in Transitional Justice*, edited by Mina Rauschenbach, Julia Viebach, and Stephan Parmentier, 83–106. New York: Routledge, 2022.

Jessee, Erin. *Negotiating Genocide in Rwanda: The Politics of History.* New York: Palgrave Macmillan, 2017.

Jessee, Erin. "Promoting Reconciliation Through Exhuming and Identifying Victims in the 1994 Rwandan Genocide." Africa Initiative Discussion Paper 4. Waterloo, Canada: Africa Initiative, Centre for International Governance Innovation, 2012.

Jessee, Erin, and David Mwambari. "Memory Law and the Duty to Remember the '1994 Genocide Against the Tutsi' in Rwanda." In *Memory Laws and Historical Justice*, edited by Elazar Barkan and Ariella Lang, 291–319. New York: Palgrave Macmillan, 2022.

Johnson, Walter. "On Agency." *Journal of Social History* 37, no. 1 (2003): 113–24.

Kaban, Elif. "Rwanda Remembers Genocide Two Years On as Killers Walk Free Abroad." *The Herald* (Glasgow), April 8, 1996.

Kagame, Alexis. *Les organisations socio-familiales de l'ancien Rwanda.* Brussels: Académie des Sciences Coloniales, 1954.

Kanamugire, Louis. "Témoignages recueillis et reflexions personnelles de l'ancien responsable de la Commission pour le Memorial du Genocide et des Massacres au Rwanda, 1995–2003." Translated by Delia Wendel. Unpublished memoir, 2013.

Karnik, Niranjan S. "Rwanda and the Media: Imagery, War, Refuge." *Review of African Political Economy* 25, no. 78 (1998): 611–23.

Keane, Fergal. "Journey into Darkness." BBC Panorama News Special, BBC2, August 30, 1994.

Keane, Fergal. *Season of Blood: A Rwandan Journey.* London: Viking, 1995.

Kelley, Robin D. G. *Freedom Dreams: The Black Radical Imagination.* Boston: Beacon, 2002.

Khalidi, Walid. *All That Remains: The Palestinian Villages Occupied and Depopulated by Israel in 1948.* Beirut: Institute for Palestine Studies, 1992.

King, Elisabeth. "Memory Controversies in Post-Genocide Rwanda: Implications for Peacebuilding." *Genocide Studies and Prevention* 5, no. 3 (2010): 293–309.

Koff, Clea. *The Bone Woman: A Forensic Anthropologist's Search for Truth in Rwanda, Bosnia, Croatia, and Kosovo.* New York: Random House, 2004.

Korman, Rémi. "Bury or Display? The Politics of Exhumation in Post-Genocide Rwanda." In *Human Remains and Identification: Mass Violence, Genocide, and the "Forensic Turn,"* edited by Élisabeth Anstett and Jean-Marc Dreyfus, 203–20. Manchester: Manchester University Press, 2015.

Korman, Rémi. "L'état rwandais et la mémoire du génocide: Commémorer sur les ruines (1994–1996)." *Vingtième Siècle: Revue d'Histoire*, no. 122 (2014): 987–98.

Korman, Rémi. "Mobilising the Dead? The Place of Bones and Corpses in the Commemoration of the Tutsi Genocide in Rwanda." *Human Remains and Violence* 1, no. 2 (2015): 56–70.

Korman, Rémi. "La politique de mémoire du génocide des Tutsi au Rwanda: Enjeux et évolutions." *Droit et Culture*, no. 66 (2013): 87–101.

Korman, Rémi. "Les universitaires et intellectuels rwandais à l'épreuve du génocide des Tutsi: Première mémoire, première histoire." *Les Cahiers de Framespa*, no. 41 (2022). https://doi.org/10.4000/framespa.13693.

Krauss, Rosalind. "Sculpture in the Expanded Field." *October* 8 (1979): 30–44.

LaCapra, Dominick. *Writing History, Writing Trauma*. Ithaca, NY: Cornell University Press, 2001.

Lakin, Samantha. "Memory and Victimhood in Post-Genocide Rwanda: Legal, Political, and Social Realities." In *Narratives of Mass Atrocity: Victims and Perpetrators in the Aftermath*, edited by Sarah Federman and Ronald Niezen, 201–21. Cambridge: Cambridge University Press, 2022.

Lame, Danielle de. *A Hill Among a Thousand: Transformations and Ruptures in Rural Rwanda*. Translated by H. Arnold. Madison: University of Wisconsin Press, 2005.

Landsberg, Alison. *Prosthetic Memory: The Transformation of American Remembrance in the Age of Mass Culture*. New York: Columbia University Press, 2004.

Lasso, Jose Ayala. "Defining the Mandate." *Harvard International Review* 17, no. 1 (1994/95): 38–41, 78.

Leebaw, Bronwyn Anne. "The Irreconcilable Goals of Transitional Justice." *Human Rights Quarterly* 30, no. 1 (2008): 95–118.

Lemarchand, René. "The Politics of Memory in Post-Genocide Rwanda." In *After Genocide: Transitional Justice, Post-Conflict Reconstruction, and Reconciliation in Rwanda and Beyond*, edited by Phil Clark and Zachary D. Kaufman, 65–76. London: Hurst, 2008.

Levi, Primo. *The Drowned and the Saved*. New York: Simon and Schuster, 1986.

Levy, Daniel, and Natan Sznaider. *Holocaust and Memory in the Global Age*. Translated by Assenka Oksiloff. Philadelphia: Temple University Press, 2005.

Levy, Daniel, and Natan Sznaider. *Human Rights and Memory*. State College, PA: Penn State University Press, 2010.

Levy, Daniel, and Natan Sznaider. "Memory Unbound: The Holocaust and the Formation of Cosmopolitan Memory." *European Journal of Social Theory* 5, no. 1 (2002): 87–106.

Lipsitz, George. *Time Passages: Collective Memory and American Popular Culture*. Minneapolis: University of Minnesota Press, 1990.

Lischer, Sarah Kenyon. "Narrating Atrocity: Genocide Memorials, Dark Tourism, and the Politics of Memory." *Review of International Studies* 45, no. 5 (2019): 805–27.

Longman, Timothy. "An Assessment of Rwanda's Gacaca Courts." *Peace Review* 21, no. 3 (2009): 304–12.

Longman, Timothy. *Christianity and Genocide in Rwanda*. New York: Cambridge University Press, 2010.

Longman, Timothy. *Memory and Justice in Post-Genocide Rwanda*. New York: Cambridge University Press, 2017.

Longman, Timothy, and Théonèste Rutagengwa. "Memory, Identity, and Community in Rwanda." In *My Neighbor, My Enemy: Justice and Community in the Aftermath of Mass Atrocity*, edited by Eric Stover and Harvey M. Weinstein, 162–82. Cambridge: Cambridge University Press, 2004.

Longman, Timothy, and Théonèste Rutagengwa. "Religion, Memory, and Violence in Rwanda." In *Religion, Violence, Memory, and Place*, edited by Oren Baruch Stier and J. Shawn Landres, 32–149. Bloomington: Indiana University Press, 2006.

Longoni, Ana. "Photographs and Silhouettes: Visual Politics in the Human Rights Movement of Argentina." *Afterall: A Journal of Art, Context and Enquiry* 25 (2010): 5–17.

Lorch, Donatella. "Rwanda Jails: No Space, No Food, No Justice." *New York Times*, April 15, 1995. https://www.nytimes.com/1995/04/15/world/rwanda-jails-no-space-no-food-no-justice.html.

Lundy, Patricia, and Mark McGovern. "Whose Justice? Rethinking Transitional Justice from the Bottom Up." *Journal of Law and Society* 35, no. 2 (2008): 265–92.

Lykes, M. Brinton, Martin Terre Blanche, and Brandon Hamber. "Narrating Survival and Change in Guatemala and South Africa: The Politics of Representation and a Liberatory Community Psychology." *American Journal of Community Psychology* 31, no. 1/2 (2003): 79–90.

Lynch, Kevin. *A Theory of Good City Form*. Cambridge, MA: MIT Press, 1981.

Mahler, Anne Garland. *From the Tricontinental to the Global South: Race, Radicalism, and Solidarity*. Durham, NC: Duke University Press, 2018.

Major, Laura. "Unearthing, Untangling and Re-Articulating Genocide Corpses in Rwanda." *Critical African Studies* 7, no. 2 (2015): 164–81.

Malkki, Liisa. *Purity and Exile: Violence, Memory, and National Cosmology Among Hutu Refugees in Tanzania*. Chicago: University of Chicago Press, 1995.

Marcuse, Harold. "Holocaust Memorials: The Emergence of a Genre." *American Historical Review* 115, no. 1 (2010): 53–89.

Martin, Ian. "A New Frontier: The Early Experience and Future of International Human Rights Operations." *Netherlands Quarterly of Human Rights* 16, no. 2 (1998): 121–39.

Mason, Randall. "Conserving Rwandan Genocide Memorials." *APT Bulletin: The Journal of Preservation Technology* 50, no. 2/3 (2019): 17–26.

Mbembe, Achille. "Necropolitics." *Public Culture* 15, no. 1 (2003): 11–40.

McKinley, James C. "From a Grave in Rwanda, Hundreds of Dead Tell Their Tale." *New York Times*, February 16, 1996. https://www.nytimes.com/1996/02/16/world/from-a-grave-in-rwanda-hundreds-of-dead-tell-their-tale.html.

McKinley, James C. "76,000 Still in Jail in Rwanda Awaiting Trial in '94 Slayings." *New York Times*, June 24, 1996. https://www.nytimes.com/1996/06/24/world/76000-still-in-jail-in-rwanda-awaiting-trial-in-94-slayings.html.

McNeil, Donald G. "Ntarama Journal; At Church, Testament to Horror." *New York Times*, August 4, 1995. https://www.nytimes.com/1995/08/04/world/ntarama-journal-at-church-testament-to-horror.html.

Meierhenrich, Jens. "Topographies of Remembering and Forgetting: The Transformation of Lieux de Mémoire in Rwanda." In *Remaking Rwanda: State Building and Hu-*

*man Rights After Mass Violence*, edited by Scott Straus and Lars Waldorf, 283–96. Madison: University of Wisconsin Press, 2011.
Meierhenrich, Jens, and Martha Lagace. "Photo Essay: Tropes of Memory." *Humanity: An International Journal of Human Rights, Humanitarianism, and Development* 4, no. 2 (2013): 289–312.
Minde, Henry. "The Destination and the Journey: Indigenous Peoples and the United Nations from the 1960s Through 1985." In *Indigenous Peoples: Self-Determination, Knowledge, Indigeneity*, edited by Henry Minde, Harald Gaski, Svein Jentoft, and Georges Midré, 49–86. Delft, Netherlands: Eburon, 2008.
Miriri, Duncan, and Katharine Houreld. "Moi's Kenyan Torture Victims Mourn a Reckoning That Never Came." *Reuters*, February 4, 2020. https://www.reuters.com/article/idUSKBN1ZY1XV/.
Misago, Célestin Kanimba. "Commission Nationale de Lutte contre le Génocide: Contexte et perspectives." *Revue d'Histoire de la Shoah*, no. 190 (2009): 437–50.
Misago, Célestin Kanimba. "Les instruments de la mémoire génocide et traumatisme au Rwanda." *Gradhiva*, no. 5 (2007): 2–14.
Misago, Célestin Kanimba. "Préservation de la mémoire du génocide: Rôles, actions, et stratégies." *Études Rwandaises: L'Informateur* 9 (2005): 128–47.
Moore, Jina. "Rwanda's Keeper of the Dead." *Buzzfeed News*, April 7, 2014. https://www.buzzfeednews.com/article/jinamoore/rwandas-keeper-of-the-dead.
Morrison, Toni. "The Site of Memory." In *Inventing the Truth: The Art and Craft of Memoir*, edited by William Zinsser, 183–200. Boston: Houghton Mifflin, 1998.
Mullings, Beverley. "Insider or Outsider, Both or Neither: Some Dilemmas of Interviewing in a Cross-Cultural Setting." *Geoforum* 30, no. 4 (1990): 337–50.
Mwambari, David. "*Agaciro*, Vernacular Memory, and the Politics of Memory in Post-Genocide Rwanda." *African Affairs* 120, no. 481 (2021): 611–28.
Mwambari, David. "Music and the Politics of the Past: Kizito Mihigo and Music in the Commemoration of the Genocide Against the Tutsi in Rwanda." *Memory Studies* 13, no. 6 (2020): 1321–36.
Mwambari, David. *Navigating Cultural Memory: Commemoration and Narrative in Post-Genocide Rwanda*. New York: Oxford University Press, 2023.
National Commission for the Protection of Human Subjects of Biomedical and Behavioral Research. *The Belmont Report: Ethical Principles and Guidelines for the Protection of Human Subjects of Research*. Washington, DC: US Department of Health and Human Services, 1979.
Newbury, Catherine. *The Cohesion of Oppression: Clientship and Ethnicity in Rwanda, 1860–1960*. New York: Columbia University Press, 1988.
Newbury, Catherine. "Ethnicity and the Politics of History in Rwanda." *Africa Today* 45, no. 1 (1998): 7–24.
Nora, Pierre. "Between Memory and History: Les Lieux de Mémoire." *Representations*, no. 26 (1989): 7–24.
Norridge, Zoë. "Photography, Film, and Visibly Wounded Genocide Survivors in Rwanda." *Journal of Genocide Research* 21, no. 1 (2019): 47–70.
Norridge, Zoë. "Writing Against Genocide: Genres of Opposition in Narratives from

and About Rwanda." In *Postcolonial Poetics: Genre and Form*, edited by Patrick Crowley and Jane Hiddleston, 240–61. Liverpool: Liverpool University Press, 2011.
Nsabimana, Natacha. "Genocide-Time: Political Violence Reckoning in Rwanda." *American Anthropologist* 125, no. 4 (2023): 741–914.
Ntakirutimana, Évariste. "Génocide: Un mot du droit pour un crime sans nom." *Les Cahiers de la Justice* 1, no. 1 (2017): 95–104.
Ntirenganya, Emmanuel. "Muyumbu, Home to Rwanda's First Genocide Memorial." *New Times*, April 20, 2017. https://www.newtimes.co.rw/article/139897/News/muyumbu-home-to-rwandaas-first-genocide-memorial.
Nyirubugara, Olivier. *Complexities and Dangers of Remembering and Forgetting in Rwanda*. Leiden, Netherlands: Sidestone, 2013.
Olick, Jeffrey K. *The Politics of Regret: On Collective Memory and Historical Responsibility*. New York: Routledge, 2007.
Page, Max, ed. *Memories of Buenos Aires: Signs of State Terrorism in Argentina*. Translated by Karen Robert and Jonathan Soria. Boston: University of Massachusetts Press, 2013.
Peress, Gilles. *The Silence: Rwanda*. New York: Scalo, 1995.
Petrie, Jon. "The Secular Word 'Holocaust': Scholarly Myths, History, and 20th Century Meanings." *Journal of Genocide Research* 2, no. 1 (2000): 31–63.
Physicians for Human Rights (PHR). *Investigations in Eastern Congo and Western Rwanda*. Report to the U.S. House International Relations Committee, June 16, 1997.
Pickard, Terry. *Combat Medic: An Australian's Eyewitness Account of the Kibeho Massacre*. Newport, NSW: Big Sky, 2008.
Portelli, Alessandro. *The Death of Luigi Trastulli and Other Stories: Form and Meaning in Oral History*. Albany: State University of New York Press, 1991.
Pottier, Johan. *Re-Imagining Rwanda: Conflict, Survival and Disinformation in the Late Twentieth Century*. Cambridge: Cambridge University Press, 2002.
Prescod, Colin. "Archives, Race, Class, and Rage." *Race and Class* 58, no. 4 (2017): 76–84.
Prescod, Colin. "Gaming the System: Imagining Justice4Grenfell." *Funambulist*, no. 30 (2020): 52–55.
Prunier, Gerard. *Africa's World War: Congo, the Rwandan Genocide, and the Making of a Continental Catastrophe*. Oxford: Oxford University Press, 2009.
Prunier, Gerard. "Opération Turquoise: A Humanitarian Escape from a Political Dead End." In *The Path of a Genocide: The Rwanda Crisis from Uganda to Zaire*, edited by Howard Adelman and Astri Suhrke, 281–306. New Brunswick, NJ: Transaction, 1999.
Purdeková, Andrea. *Making Ubumwe: Power, State, and Camps in Rwanda's Unity-Building Project*. New York: Berghahn Books, 2015.
Rajagopal, Balakrishnan. "Opinion—Domicide: The Mass Destruction of Homes Should Be a Crime Against Humanity." Photos by Yaqeen Baker. *New York Times*, January 29, 2024. https://www.nytimes.com/interactive/2024/01/29/opinion/destruction-of-homes-crime-domicide.html.
Réra, Nathan. "Rwanda, de l'espace médiatique au dispositif artistique: Les métamorphoses de la photographie." In *L'image d'archives: Une image en devein*, edited by Julie Maeck and Matthias Steinle, 99–115. Rennes: Presses universitaires de Rennes, 2016.

Reyntjens, Filip. *Political Governance in Post-Genocide Rwanda*. Cambridge: Cambridge University Press, 2013.

Reyntjens, Filip. "The Struggle over Truth: Rwanda and the BBC." *African Affairs* 114, no. 457 (2015): 637–48.

Reyntjens, Filip. "Talking or Fighting? Political Evolution in Rwanda and Burundi, 1998–1999." *Current African Issues* 21. Uppsala: Nordiska Afrikainstitutet, 1999.

Ricoeur, Paul. *Memory, History, Forgetting*. Chicago: University of Chicago Press, 2004.

Rittner, Carol, John K. Roth, and Wendy Whitworth, eds. *Genocide in Rwanda: Complicity of the Churches?* St. Paul, MN: Paragon House, 2004.

Robben, Antonius C. G. M. "How Traumatized Societies Remember: The Aftermath of Argentina's Dirty War." *Cultural Critique*, no. 59 (2005): 120–64.

Ross, Fiona C. "Speech and Silence: Women's Testimony in the First Five Weeks of Public Hearings of the South African Truth and Reconciliation Commission." In *Remaking a World: Violence, Social Suffering, and Recovery*, edited by Veena Das, Arthur Kleinman, Margaret M. Lock, Mamphela Ramphele, and Pamela Reynolds, 250–73. Berkeley: University of California Press, 2001.

Rossi, Aldo. *Architecture of the City*. Cambridge, MA: MIT Press, 1982.

Rothberg, Michael. "Between Memory and Memory: From Lieux de Mémoire to Noeuds de Mémoire." In "Noeuds de Mémoire: Multidirectional Memory in Postwar French and Francophone Culture," edited by Michael Rothberg, Debarati Sanyal, and Max Silverman. *Yale French Studies*, no. 118/119 (2010): 3–12.

Rothberg, Michael. *Multidirectional Memory: Remembering the Holocaust in the Age of Decolonization*. Stanford, CA: Stanford University Press, 2009.

Rothberg, Michael, and Yasmin Yildiz. "Memory Citizenship: Migrant Archives of Holocaust Remembrance in Contemporary Germany." *Parallax* 17, no. 4 (2011): 32–48.

Rutayisire, Paul. "Approche locale du génocide: La region de Nyarubuye." *Vingtième Siècle: Revue d'Histoire*, no. 122 (2014): 37–49.

Rutayisire, Paul, Mulinda Charles Kabwete, Gakwenzire Philibert, and Piton Florent. "Kwandika amateka ya jenoside yakorewe Abatutsi mu Rwanda hashingiwe ku bimenyetso ndangamateka byo mu gihugu." *Materials and Fieldwork in African Studies*, no. 5 (2022): 277–302.

Rutazibwa, Privat, and Paul Rutayisire. *Génocide à Nyarubuye: Monographie sur l'un des principaux sites du gènocide des Tutsi de 1994 au Rwanda*. Kigali: Editions Rwandaises, 2007.

Sa'di, Ahmad H., and Lila Abu-Lughod, eds. *Nakba: Palestine, 1948, and the Claims of Memory*. New York: Columbia University Press, 2007.

Sadruddin, Aalyia. "Death in an Ordinary Time: Reflections from Rwanda." *Medical Anthropology Quarterly* 36, no. 2 (2022): 198–216.

Sanford, Victoria. *Buried Secrets: Truth and Human Rights in Guatemala*. New York: Palgrave Macmillan, 2004.

Sanford, Victoria. "'What Is Written in Our Hearts': Memory, Justice, and the Healing of Fragmented Communities." In *Political Transition: Politics and Cultures*, edited by Paul Gready, 70–89. London: Pluto, 2003.

Scarry, Elaine. *The Body in Pain: The Making and Unmaking of the World*. New York: Oxford University Press, 1985.

Schindel, Estela, and Pamela Colombo, eds. *Space and the Memories of Violence*. New York: Palgrave Macmillan, 2014.

Schotsmans, Martien. *A l'écoute des rescapés: Recherche sur la perception par les rescapés de leur situation actuelle*. Kigali: Deutsche Gesellschaft für Technische Zusammenarbeit (GTZ), 2000.

Schuessler, Jennifer. "Ranking History's Atrocities by Counting the Corpses." *New York Times*, November 9, 2011. https://www.nytimes.com/2011/11/09/books/the-great-big-book-of-horrible-things-by-matthew-white.html?_r=1.

Scott, David. "Preface: A Reparatory History of the Present." *Small Axe* 21, no. 1 (52) (2017): vii–x.

Scott, James C. *Domination and the Arts of Resistance: Hidden Transcripts*. New Haven, CT: Yale University Press, 1990.

Selimovic, Johanna M. "Gender, Narrative, Affect: Top-Down Politics of Commemoration in Post-Genocide Rwanda." *Memory Studies* 13, no. 2 (2020): 131–45.

Selimovic, Johanna M. "Making Peace, Making Memory: Peacebuilding and the Politics of Remembrance at Memorials of Mass Atrocities." *Peacebuilding* 1, no. 3 (2013): 334–48.

Sharpe, Christina. "And to Survive." *Small Axe* 22, no. 3 (57) (2018): 177–80.

Shaw, Rosalind, Lars Waldorf, and Pierre Hazan. *Localizing Transitional Justice: Interventions and Priorities After Mass Violence*. Stanford, CA: Stanford University Press, 2010.

Shenker, Noah. "Through the Lens of the Shoah: The Holocaust as a Paradigm for Documenting Genocide Testimonies." *History and Memory* 28, no. 1 (2016): 141–75.

Sheridan, Sean. *Testimony:Africa*. Colorado Springs, CO: 4:Minute.Media, 2010.

Smith, Laurajane. *Uses of Heritage*. London: Routledge, 2006.

Smith, Laurajane, and Natsuko Akagawa, eds. *Intangible Heritage*. New York: Routledge, 2009.

Sodaro, Amy. *Exhibiting Atrocity: Memorial Museums and the Politics of Past Violence*. New Brunswick, NJ: Rutgers University Press, 2018.

Soyinka, Wole. *The Burden of Memory, the Muse of Forgiveness*. Oxford: Oxford University Press, 1999.

Stoler, Ann. "Colonial Archives and the Arts of Governance." *Archival Science* 2, no. 1–2 (2002): 87–109.

Straus, Scott. *The Order of Genocide: Race, Power, and War in Rwanda*. Ithaca, NY: Cornell University Press, 2006.

Sumartojo, Shanti. "Memorials and State-Sponsored History." In *The Palgrave Handbook of State-Sponsored History After 1945*, edited by Berber Bevernage and Nico Wouters, 449–76. London: Palgrave Macmillan, 2018.

Susman, Tina. "New Horror in Cool Hills in Rwanda." *Washington Post*, June 1, 1994. https://www.washingtonpost.com/archive/politics/1994/06/01/new-horror-in-cool-hills-of-rwanda/ee389a52-7f4d-488f-b374-16ecb00dd84d/.

Taylor, Christopher C. *Milk, Honey, and Money: Changing Concepts in Rwandan Healing*. Washington, DC: Smithsonian Institution Press, 1992.

Teitel, Ruti G. "Transitional Justice Genealogy." *Harvard Human Rights Journal* 16 (2003): 69–94.
Terdiman, Richard. *Present Past: Modernity and the Memory Crisis.* Ithaca, NY: Cornell University Press, 1993.
Theidon, Kimberly. "The Milk of Sorrow: A Theory on the Violence of Memory." *Canadian Woman Studies* 27, no. 1 (2009): 8–16.
Thompson, Allan, ed. *The Media and the Rwanda Genocide.* London: Pluto, 2007.
Thomson, Susan. "Getting Close to Rwandans Since the Genocide: Studying Everyday Life in Highly Politicized Research Settings." *African Studies Review* 53, no. 3 (2010): 19–34.
Thomson, Susan. *Whispering Truth to Power: Everyday Resistance to Reconciliation in Postgenocide Rwanda.* Madison: University of Wisconsin Press, 2013.
Thomson, Susan, An Ansoms, and Jude Murison, eds. *Emotional and Ethical Challenges for Field Research in Africa: The Story Behind the Findings.* London: Palgrave Macmillan, 2013.
Thorin, Valérie. "Au pays des milles souffrances." *Jeune Afrique L'Intelligent* 40, no. 2066–67 (August 15–28, 2000): 168–71.
Till, Karen. "Artistic and Activist Memory-Work: Approaching Place-Based Practice." *Memory Studies* 1, no. 1 (2008): 99–113.
Tillet, Salamishah. *Sites of Slavery: Citizenship and Racial Democracy in the Post–Civil Rights Imagination.* Durham, NC: Duke University Press, 2012.
Till-Mobley, Mamie, and Christopher Benson. *Death of Innocence: The Story of the Hate Crime That Changed America.* New York: Random House, 2003.
Totten, Samuel, and Rafiki Ubaldo, eds. *We Cannot Forget: Interviews with Survivors of the 1994 Genocide in Rwanda.* New Brunswick, NJ: Rutgers University Press, 2011.
Tuan, Yuan F. *Space and Place: The Perspective of Experience.* Minneapolis: University of Minnesota Press, 1977.
Ulbrich, Jeffrey. "Death of Peacekeeper Halts UN Operations in Rwandan Capital." Associated Press, May 31, 1994.
Umutesi, Marie Béatrice. *Surviving the Slaughter: The Ordeal of a Rwandan Refugee in Zaire.* Translated by Julia Emerson. (Originally published in French by L'Harmattan, 2000.) Madison: University of Wisconsin Press, 2004.
U.S. Department of State. *Rwanda 2022 Human Rights Report.* Washington, DC: Bureau of Democracy, Human Rights and Labor, 2022. https://www.state.gov/reports/2022-country-reports-on-human-rights-practices/rwanda/.
van't Spijker, Gerard. *Les usages funéraires et la mission de l'Eglise: Une étude anthropologique et théologique des rites funéraires au Rwanda.* Kampen, Netherlands: Kok, 1990.
Verwimp, Philip. "Machetes and Firearms: The Organization of Massacres in Rwanda." *Journal of Peace Research* 43, no. 1 (2006): 5–22.
Vidal, Claudine. "La commémoration du génocide au Rwanda: Violence symbolique, mémorisation forcée et histoire officielle." *Cahiers d'Études Africaines,* no. 175 (2004): 575–92.

Vidal, Claudine. "Les commémorations du génocide au Rwanda." *Les Temps Modernes* no. 613 (2001): 1–46.

Vidal, Claudine. "Les humanitaires, témoins pour l'histoire." *Les Temps Modernes*, no. 627 (2004): 92–107.

Viebach, Julia. "Aletheia and the Making of the World: Inner and Outer Dimensions of Memorials in Rwanda." In *Memorials in Times of Transition*, edited by Susanne Buckley-Zistel and Stefanie Schäfer, 69–94. Cambridge, UK: Intersentia, 2014.

Viebach, Julia. "Mediating 'Absence-Presence' at Rwanda's Genocide Memorials: Of Caretaking, Memory and Proximity to the Dead." *Critical African Studies* 12, no. 2 (2020): 237–69.

Viebach, Julia. "Of Other Times: Temporality, Memory, and Trauma in Post-Genocide Rwanda." *International Review of Victimology* 25, no. 3 (2019): 277–301.

Viebach, Julia. "*Transitional Archives*: Towards a Conceptualisation of Archives in Transitional Justice." *International Journal of Human Rights* 24, no. 3 (2021): 403–39.

Vielle, Stephanie. "Transitional Justice: A Colonizing Field?" *Amsterdam Law Forum* 4, no. 3 (2012): 58–68.

Waldorf, Lars. "Censorship and Propaganda in Post-Genocide Rwanda." In *The Media and the Rwanda Genocide*, edited by Allan Thompson, 404–16. London: Pluto, 2007.

Walker, Margaret Urban. "Making Reparations Possible: Theorizing Reparative Justice." In *Theorizing Transitional Justice*, edited by Claudio Corradetti, Nir Eisikovits, and Jack Volpe Rotondi, 211–22. London: Ashgate, 2015.

Waltz, Susan. "Reclaiming and Rebuilding the History of the Universal Declaration of Human Rights." *Third World Quarterly* 23, no. 3 (2002): 437–48.

Webber-Heffernan, Shalon. "Remembering Differently: Activating Legacies of Violence in the Southern US Through Soil." *Performance Research* 28, no. 8 (2024): 14–23.

Wendel, Delia D. B. "*Duture Neza, Duture Heza*: Planning and Building a 'Liberal Peace.'" In *Wiley Blackwell Companion to Cultural and Social Geography*, edited by Jamie Winders and Ishan Ashutosh, 23–36. New York: Wiley Blackwell, 2025.

Wendel, Delia D. B. "The Ethics of Stability: Rebuilding Rwanda After the 1994 Genocide." PhD diss., Harvard University, 2016.

Wendel, Delia D. B. "Roof Politics: The Materiality of Interpellation." *Journal of Architecture* 28, no. 2 (2023): 284–309.

Wendel, Delia D. B. "Umudugudu w'Ingunguru: An 'Ordinary' Model Village." Keynote lecture at Through Local Eyes Conference, Addis Ababa, Ethiopia, October 31, 2018.

White, Matthew. *Atrocities: The 100 Deadliest Episodes in Human History*. New York: W. W. Norton, 2012.

Wiesel, Elie. "The Holocaust as Literary Inspiration." In *Dimensions of the Holocaust: Lectures at Northwestern University*. 2nd ed. Edited by Elie Wiesel, Lucy Dawidowicz, Dorothy Rabinowitz, and Robert McAfee Brown, 5–20. Evanston: Northwestern University Press, 1990.

Wiesel, Elie. "Hope, Despair, and Memory." Nobel Peace Prize speech, December 11, 1986. https://www.nobelprize.org/prizes/peace/1986/wiesel/lecture/.

Wieviorka, Annette. *The Era of the Witness*. Translated by Jared Stark. (French edition published in Paris by Plon, 1998.) Ithaca, NY: Cornell University Press, 2006.

Williams, Paul. *Memorial Museums: The Global Rush to Commemorate Atrocities*. London: Bloomsbury, 2007.

Wosińska, Małgorzata. "Murambi Is Not Auschwitz: The Holocaust in Representations of the Rwandan Genocide." In *Replicating Atonement: Foreign Models in the Commemoration of Atrocities*, edited by Mischa Gabowitsch, 187–208. New York: Palgrave Macmillan, 2017.

Wrong, Michela. *Do Not Disturb: The Story of a Political Murder and an African Regime Gone Bad*. New York: Harper Collins, 2021.

Young, James E. *The Texture of Memory: Holocaust Memorials and Meaning*. New Haven, CT: Yale University Press, 1993.

Zelizer, Barbie. *Visual Culture and the Holocaust*. New Brunswick, NJ: Rutgers University Press, 2001.

# INDEX

*Note:* Page references in *italics* indicate photographs and figures.